BIBLICAL FIGURES
OUTSIDE THE BIBLE

BIBLICAL FIGURES
OUTSIDE THE BIBLE

Edited by
Michael E. Stone
and
Theodore A. Bergren

TRINITY PRESS INTERNATIONAL
Harrisburg, Pennsylvania

Trinity Press International, P.O. Box 1321, Harrisburg, PA 17105
Trinity Press International is a division of the Morehouse Group

Library of Congress Cataloging-in-Publication Data

Biblical figures outside the Bible / edited by Michael E. Stone and
   Theodore A. Bergren.
      p.   cm.
   Includes bibliographical references and index.
   ISBN 1-56338-247-4 (alk. paper)
    1. Bible. O.T. – Biography. 2. Christian literature, Early –
History and criticism. 3. Rabbinical literature – History and
criticism. 4. Apocryphal books (Old Testament) – Criticism,
interpretation, etc. I. Stone, Michael E., 1938- . II. Bergren,
Theodore A.
   BS571.B53 1998
   220.9′2 – dc21   98-39935

Printed in the United States of America

98   99   00   01   02   10 9 8 7 6 5 4 3 2 1

CONTENTS

CONTRIBUTORS
AND EDITORS

Philip S. Alexander is Professor of Postbiblical Jewish Literature at the University of Manchester. (Enoch)

Gary A. Anderson is Professor of Old Testament at the Harvard Divinity School. (Adam and Eve)

Theodore A. Bergren is Associate Professor of Religion at the University of Richmond. (Coeditor; Ezra and Nehemiah)

Devorah Dimant is George and Florence Wise Professor of Judaism in the Ancient World at the University of Haifa. (Noah)

Steven D. Fraade is Mark Taper Professor of the History of Judaism at Yale University. (Enosh)

Harm W. Hollander is Lecturer in New Testament at the Rijksuniversiteit Leiden. (Joseph)

Marinus de Jonge is Professor Emeritus of New Testament and Early Christian Literature at the Rijksuniversiteit Leiden. (Levi, coauthor)

George W. E. Nickelsburg is Professor of Religion at the University of Iowa. (Abraham)

Birger A. Pearson is Professor Emeritus of Religious Studies at the University of California, Santa Barbara. (Melchizedek)

Aviva Schussman is Senior Lecturer in Arabic and Islam at the David Yellin Teachers College of Jerusalem. (Ezekiel)

Michael E. Stone is Gail Levin de Nur Professor of Religion and Professor of Armenian Studies at the Hebrew University of Jerusalem. (Coeditor)

Johannes Tromp is Lecturer in Early Judaism at the Rijksuniversiteit Leiden. (Levi, coauthor)

John D. Turner is Cotner Professor of Religious Studies and Professor of Classics and History at the University of Nebraska–Lincoln. (Seth)

Benjamin G. Wright is Associate Professor of Religion Studies at Lehigh University. (Ezekiel)

J. Edward Wright is Assistant Professor of Near Eastern and Judaic Studies at the University of Arizona. (Baruch)

ABBREVIATIONS

AB	Anchor Bible
ABD	D. N. Freedman, ed., *Anchor Bible Dictionary*
AbrN	*Abr-Nahrain*
AGJU	Arbeiten zur Geschichte des antiken Judentums und des Urchristentums
ALGHJ	Arbeiten zur Literatur und Geschichte des hellenistischen Judentums
AnBib	Analecta biblica
ANET	J. B. Pritchard, ed., *Ancient Near Eastern Texts*
ANF	The Ante-Nicene Fathers
ANRW	W. Haase and H. Temporini, eds., *Aufstieg und Niedergang der römischen Welt* (Berlin/New York: de Gruyter, 1972–)
AOAT	Alter Orient und Altes Testament
APOT	R. H. Charles, ed., *Apocrypha and Pseudepigrapha of the Old Testament*
BAGD	W. Bauer, W. F. Arndt, F. W. Gingrich, and F. W. Danker, *Greek-English Lexicon of the New Testament* (Chicago: University of Chicago Press, 1979)
BCNH	Bibliothèque copte de Nag Hammadi
BETL	Bibliotheca ephemeridum theologicarum lovaniensium
BG	(Papyrus) Berolinensis Gnosticus (8502)
BHT	Beiträge zur historischen Theologie
Bib	*Biblica*
BibOr	Biblica et orientalia
BIOSCS	*Bulletin of the International Organization for Septuagint and Cognate Studies*
BJS	Brown Judaic Studies
BTB	*Biblical Theology Bulletin*
BZ	*Biblische Zeitschrift*
BZAW	Beihefte zur *ZAW*

CBC	Cambridge Bible Commentary
CBQ	*Catholic Biblical Quarterly*
CBQMS	Catholic Biblical Quarterly Monograph Series
CG	(Codex) Cairensis Gnosticus
ConBOT	Coniectanea biblica, Old Testament
CRINT	Compendia rerum iudaicarum ad novum testamentum
CSCO	Corpus scriptorum christianorum orientalium
CTM	*Concordia Theological Monthly*
DJD	Discoveries in the Judaean Desert
Ebib	Etudes bibliques
EI¹	*Encyclopaedia of Islam,* 1st ed. (1927)
EI²	*Encyclopaedia of Islam,* new ed. (1971)
EncJud	*Encyclopaedia Judaica* (1971)
EvT	*Evangelische Theologie*
ExpTim	*Expository Times*
FB	Forschung zur Bibel
GCS	Griechischen christlichen Schriftsteller
HALAT	W. Baumgartner et al., *Hebräisches und aramäisches Lexicon zum Alten Testament*
HAT	Handbuch zum Alten Testament
HBC	J. L. Mays et al., eds., *Harper's Bible Commentary*
HSM	Harvard Semitic Monographs
HTR	*Harvard Theological Review*
HTS	Harvard Theological Studies
HUCA	*Hebrew Union College Annual*
HUCM	Monographs of the Hebrew Union College
IBS	*Irish Biblical Studies*
ICC	International Critical Commentary
IDB	G. A. Buttrick, ed., *Interpreter's Dictionary of the Bible* 2
IDBSup	Supplementary volume to G. A. Buttrick, ed., *Interpreter's Dictionary of the Bible*
IEJ	*Israel Exploration Journal*
Int	*Interpretation*
JBL	*Journal of Biblical Literature*
JCS	*Journal of Cuneiform Studies*
JJS	*Journal of Jewish Studies*
JNES	*Journal of Near Eastern Studies*

JQR	*Jewish Quarterly Review*
JSHRZ	Jüdische Schriften aus hellenistisch-römischer Zeit
JSJ	*Journal for the Study of Judaism in the Persian, Hellenistic, and Roman Period*
JSNTSup	Journal for the Study of the New Testament Supplement Series
JSOT	*Journal for the Study of the Old Testament*
JSOTSup	Journal for the Study of the Old Testament Supplement Series
JSP	*Journal for the Study of the Pseudepigrapha*
JSPSup	Journal for the Study of the Pseudepigrapha Supplement Series
JSS	*Journal of Semitic Studies*
JTS	*Journal of Theological Studies*
LCL	Loeb Classical Library
LSJ	Liddell-Scott-Jones, *Greek-English Lexicon, with Supplement* (Oxford: Clarendon, 1983)
MGWJ	*Monatsschrift für Geschichte und Wissenschaft des Judentums*
MTZ	*Münchener theologische Zeitschrift*
Mus	*Muséon*
NedThT	*Nederlands theologisch tijdschrift*
NHC	Nag Hammadi Codex
NHMS	Nag Hammadi and Manichaean Studies
NHS	Nag Hammadi Studies
NIGTC	The New International Greek Testament Commentary
NovT	*Novum Testamentum*
NovTSup	Novum Testamentum, Supplements
OBO	Orbis biblicus et orientalis
OLP	*Orientalia Lovaniensia periodica*
OTL	Old Testament Library
OTP	J. H. Charlesworth, ed., *The Old Testament Pseudepigrapha*, 2 vols.
OTS	*Oudtestamentische Studiën*
PAAJR	*Proceedings of the American Academy of Jewish Research*
PG	J. Migne, *Patrologia graeca*
PGM	K. Preisendanz, ed., *Papyri graecae magicae*
PL	J. Migne, *Patrologia latina*
PVTG	Pseudepigrapha Veteris Testamenti graece
RAC	T. Klausner et al., eds., *Reallexicon für Antike und Christentum: Sachwörterbuch zur Auseinandersetzung des Urchristentums mit der antiken Welt* (Stuttgart: A. Hiersemann, 1950–)

RB	*Revue biblique*
RBén	*Revue bénédictine*
RechBib	Recherches bibliques
REJ	*Revue des études juives*
RevQ	*Revue de Qumran*
RHR	*Revue de l'histoire des religions*
RSPT	*Revue des sciences philosophiques et théologiques*
RSR	*Recherches de science religieuse*
SAC	Studies in Antiquity and Christianity
SBL	Society of Biblical Literature
SBLDS	SBL Dissertation Series
SBLEJL	SBL Early Judaism and Its Literature
SBLMS	SBL Monograph Series
SBLSBS	SBL Sources for Biblical Study
SBLSCS	SBL Septuagint and Cognate Studies
SBLSP	SBL Seminar Papers
SBLTT	SBL Texts and Translations
SBT	Studies in Biblical Theology
SC	Sources chrétiennes
SD	Studies and Documents
Sem	*Semitica*
SJ	Studia judaica
SNT	Studien zum Neuen Testament
SNTSMS	Society for New Testament Studies Monograph Series
SPB	Studia postbiblica
SR	*Studies in Religion*
SSN	Studia semitica neerlandica
STDJ	Studies on the Texts of the Desert of Judah
Str-B	[H. Strack and] P. Billerbeck, *Kommentar zum Neuen Testament*
SVTP	Studia in Veteris Testamenti pseudepigrapha
TDNT	G. Kittel and G. Friedrich, eds., *Theological Dictionary of the New Testament*
TextsS	Texts and Studies
TRE	G. Krause and G. Müller, eds., *Theologisches Realenzyklopädie* (Berlin: de Gruyter, 1977–)
TSAJ	Texte und Studien zum antiken Judentum
TSK	*Theologische Studien und Kritiken*

TU	Texte und Untersuchungen zur Geschichte der altchristlichen Literatur
VC	*Vigiliae christianae*
VT	*Vetus Testamentum*
VTSup	Vetus Testamentum Supplements
WBC	Word Biblical Commentary
WMANT	Wissenschaftliche Monographien zum Alten und Neuen Testament
WUNT	Wissenschaftliche Untersuchungen zum Neuen Testament
ZAW	*Zeitschrift für die alttestamentliche Wissenschaft*
ZRGG	*Zeitschrift für Religions- und Geistesgeschichte*

INTRODUCTION

Michael E. Stone and
Theodore A. Bergren

In recent years, it has been increasingly recognized that the extrabiblical traditions are critically important for understanding early Judaism and Christianity. This is a new and exciting development in the study of these religious movements. It reflects the interplay of two factors, and it is not always easy to see which has been the cause and which the result. On the one hand, access to material about ancient Judaism has become easier. There have been publications of collections of apocryphal and pseudepigraphical literature, of major introductions to this material, and of numerous specialized studies. On the other hand, the last decades have witnessed the discovery and publication of the Dead Sea Scrolls and the Nag Hammadi Gnostic writings. As we write, the publication of the Dead Sea Scrolls proceeds apace and new texts become available almost on a monthly basis. These factors have in turn contributed to the renewed interest in the wider extrabiblical literature.

First and foremost, this resurgence of interest — especially since the 1970s — was the result of intellectual developments. The Dead Sea Scrolls and Nag Hammadi codices served to stimulate and forward study, but it was the renewed interest in the context of Christian origins that formed the seedbed in which research sprouted. On the one hand, Christian scholars interested in the emergence of the Christian tradition, provided since the 1920s with sophisticated tools for the study of the early Christian literature (especially the Gospels) proper, became increasingly aware that material surviving within the Christian context could

1

carry them only so far, and that proper understanding of even the "Christian" material depended on knowledge of the Jewish and Greco-Roman cultural milieus. The period since 1970 also witnessed a tendency for scholars of early Christianity to set aside theological concerns and to embrace more purely "historical" methods and perspectives; such approaches naturally led to a greater interest in Greco-Roman Judaism.

On the other hand, influenced by some of the same factors, Jewish scholars began to feel freed from traditional biases against "variant" forms of Judaism in the Second Temple and subsequent periods and to display more interest in the widely diverse forms of Judaism that flourished in these eras. In particular, the impact of the discovery of the Dead Sea Scrolls in Hebrew and Aramaic was significant. The varied Judaism of the Second Temple period is starting to be appreciated in its own right. Archaeological discoveries relating to the Jewish diaspora, such as the great synagogue at Sardis, and the study of many Jewish Hellenistic inscriptions were another stimulating factor in this new approach. In today's research related to the Dead Sea Scrolls more and more aspects of the richly variegated Judaism of this age are being excitingly illuminated.

In this period of vigorous interest in the extrabiblical literature, one major source for the recovery of surviving ancient works and traditions has been largely ignored. This is the wealth of later Jewish and Christian (and to some extent Islamic) texts, citations, and traditions relating to biblical figures. One reason for the relative neglect of this material is that it is difficult of access, demanding a range of knowledge extending beyond the biblical material, through patristics and into medieval studies. Yet it is absolutely clear that the continuing traditions of Judaism and Christianity, in particular, have preserved ancient materials, at times reworking and adapting them. This is the case, for example, for a previously unknown Jewish work from Qumran, the so-called 4QTestNaph or Hebrew Testament of Naphtali. It has been shown that it, or a text very much like it, was the direct source of material on Naphtali in the medieval Jewish midrash *Bereshit Rabbati*, written by R. Moses the Preacher in Narbonne (eleventh century). The transmission of ancient Jewish materials in patristic citation, for example the quotations from "Ezekiel" discussed in Benjamin Wright's contribution to this volume, has been well-known since the work of Fabricius in the eighteenth century and that of M. R. James and A.-M. Denis in the present century.

Only in recent years have the later apocrypha devoted to figures from the Hebrew Bible been brought into the picture. They have been shown sometimes to preserve embedded ancient texts; on other occasions they maintain, as it were, the imprint of the shape of a tradition. There is much to be learned from these later apocrypha as well as from later hagiographical compositions devoted to various Old Testament figures. At the same time, earlier pseudepigrapha and other contemporary literatures must continue to be explored for their contributions to our understanding of the development of historical and hagiographic traditions.

In dealing with these extrabiblical materials, there are a number of possible avenues of approach. We have based the studies in this volume on traditions associated with individual biblical figures. The figures represented here have been selected on consideration of the value and wealth of the traditions associated with them. They are all biblical in origin and have had a significant postbiblical development in Jewish, Christian, and other tradition. Contributors were invited on the basis of their known expertise in traditions associated with the various figures. Since each essay focuses on the ways in which a particular biblical figure has been perceived and represented over time, the common attribution of traditional material to the figure lends uniformity to the data and allows it to be organized and understood in a coherent fashion. Ideally, as a result of these studies, readers will emerge with a sense of connectedness among a variety of periods and literatures that they did not necessarily hold before, simply because of the common thread — namely, the biblical figure — that holds together the material.

The thirteen studies in this volume deliberately demonstrate a wide range of approaches toward the figures treated. The angle taken depends partly on the area of expertise of the author, and partly on how he or she decided to deal with the data. Most of our authors have adopted a wide, synthetic approach, trying to encompass as much historical and literary material as feasible within a given time frame. This is the approach taken, for example, in Philip Alexander's essay on Enoch, Birger Pearson's essay on Melchizedek, Marinus de Jonge and Johannes Tromp's essay on Levi, Harm Hollander's essay on Joseph, Edward Wright's essay on Baruch, and Benjamin Wright's essay on Ezekiel. All of these authors begin with extrabiblical Jewish tradition as early as it can be traced, but each has a slightly different plan of attack and *terminus ad quem*. Each of these studies includes treatment of early Christian materials, insofar as these exist.

Steven Fraade, in his study of Enosh, also takes a chronologically oriented, synthetic approach, but finds that his analysis naturally divides itself into contrasting attitudes expressed in Christian patristic and Jewish rabbinic sources. Devorah Dimant's essay on Noah restricts itself to Jewish literature through the period of Qumran. John Turner's essay on Seth, while broadly based, largely amounts to a study of this figure within Gnosticism, simply because this is where the bulk of the evidence lies. Aviva Schussman's essay on Ezekiel deals only with evidence for this figure in Islamic contexts.

Several authors, by contrast, have chosen to focus on particular themes or pieces of literature within the tradition. Gary Anderson's essay on Adam and Eve elucidates certain aspects of how these characters are portrayed in the "Life of Adam and Eve." George Nickelsburg attempts to show connections between the treatment of Abraham in early Jewish literature and the treatment by Paul. Theodore Bergren's essay on Ezra and Nehemiah comprises two parts, a synthetic survey and a study of these figures in four particular apocrypha.

Besides elucidating traditions associated with these particular figures, this volume is intended to serve additional purposes of research and pedagogy. These purposes are accomplished largely by the annotated bibliography appended to each study. This bibliography serves first as a resource for further study. Thus, all of the most important research sources for each figure are listed here, together with a brief description, even if the source in question does not figure prominently in the essay itself. In this way the bibliographies facilitate further research on the figure in question, making this a work of general reference value.

Second, the bibliographies, and indeed the essays themselves, serve a pedagogical function in that they can point the student in directions that might not otherwise have been considered. The bibliography of Turner's essay on Seth, for example, contains works that could also be consulted for *other* biblical figures within Gnosticism. The bibliography of Fraade's piece on Enosh is a model of methodology for researching biblical figures in general in the pertinent literature, whether the literature be early Jewish, Samaritan, patristic, or rabbinic. Likewise, the bibliography of Schussman's essay, even though it concerns Ezekiel (*Hizqīl*) in particular, will also be relevant to those interested in other biblical figures in an Islamic context. This also enhances the reference value of the book.

A word is in order concerning the bibliographical plan of the book. The basic resource for checking references is the cumulative bibliography at the end of the volume. This contains all the sources found in the notes and bibliography of each essay. The notes of each essay give only short references. The annotated bibliography at the end of each essay is intended to be a research resource for that particular figure; it does *not* necessarily contain all of the sources referred to in the notes of that essay.

The editors are indebted to a number of individuals, mostly in the Department of Religion at the University of Richmond, who have assisted in the editing and computer formatting of the essays. We especially thank Shirley Ann Fisk, Cara Griggs, JoEllyn Moore, and Diana Bourdier. The indexes were typed by Karen Carroll of the National Humanities Center.

ADAM AND EVE IN
THE "LIFE OF ADAM AND EVE"

Gary A. Anderson

The story of Adam and Eve is one of the most commented-upon texts in the entire Bible. The rabbis and the church fathers spent many a page on the exposition of this terse narrative. As though this early period of scriptural exposition was not adequate, medieval commentators in both traditions returned to the narrative with renewed vigor. In recent times the exegetical labors of these early Jewish and Christian commentators have been the subject of numerous studies. Curiously, one set of sources is often ignored when the exegetical legacy of Genesis 1–3 is surveyed: the apocryphal legends about our first human couple. The world of late antiquity was witness to numerous such narratives, all purporting to fill in for the reader, in humble narrative form, the important details left absent or ambiguous by the biblical author. Among the myriad of apocryphal tales that took root around these biblical chapters, pride of place must go to the "Life of Adam and Eve" (hereafter *Vita*).[1] Indeed, of all biblical apocrypha written

---

1. We use the term "Vita" to simplify matters. Since each version has its own unique name, to refer constantly to all of them by their unique names would be chaos. The commonly cited edition for the Latin is Meyer, "Vita Adae et Evae," 185–250. A more recent discussion of the Latin material can be found in Halford, "Apocryphal *Vita Adae et Evae*," 417–27. For the Greek most scholars have consulted Tischendorf, *Apocalypses Apocryphae.* One should compare the more recent text of M. Nagel in Denis, *Concordance grecque.* Nagel's text is very odd; he selects from numerous manuscripts across different families for reasons that are not always clear. For a full discussion of the Greek see Nagel, *Vie grecque.* For the Slavonic one should consult Jagic, "Slavische Beiträge," 1–104. For the Armenian see Stone, *Penitence of Adam,* and for the Georgian see Mahé, "Livre d'Adam géorgien," 227–60. The Coptic fragments await publication. For an excel-

and transmitted in late antiquity, this particular narrative had the largest influence on later Western literature and even art. Evidence of the tale's influence can be found as far afield as early Renaissance literature, including such works as Spenser's *Fairie Queene*[2] and Milton's *Paradise Lost.*[3]

No doubt part of the explanation is due to the fact that the tale became associated with the legend about the origins of the wood of the cross.[4] Because the cross was thought to redeem humankind from the legacy of primal sin, it is not surprising that an apocryphal writer would attempt to connect the origins of this cross with the lives of the very first human couple. And this is, in fact, exactly what happened. When Adam falls ill, at the end of the *Vita,* he sends Seth forth to see if he can procure some of the oil of mercy from the garden in order to alleviate his bodily pain. In the most primitive form of the *Vita,* Seth presents himself at the gate of the garden and makes an impassioned appeal for the oil. The archangel Michael appears and tells Seth that this oil cannot be given to any human being until the Son of God comes.[5] Seth returns and reports this news to Adam, who reacts unhappily and dies almost immediately. But in some manuscripts of the *Vita* one finds a very different ending. In these obviously later, but quite significant Latin manuscripts, Michael gives Seth a branch broken off from the tree of knowledge and tells him to take it back

---

lent discussion of the text-critical problems that attend the entire range of the various versions of the *Vita,* see the treatment of Stone in *History of the Literature of Adam and Eve.*

2. See Nohrnberg's observations about the role of the quest of Seth in Spenser's *Fairie Queene.* In bk. 1, canto 11, Spenser's hero, the Red Cross Knight, engages the Dragon-monster in fierce combat. In a sequence that mimes the conflict between Christ and Satan during Christ's *descensus,* the hero absorbs numerous fearsome blows and twice appears to collapse with mortal injury. The first time he is revived by the Well of Life. On the second occasion he falls underneath the Tree of Life. While he sleeps beneath an olive tree, the unguents of that tree slowly come forth and fall on his head: "From that first tree forth flowed, as from a well — A trickling stream of balm, most sovereign" (stanza 48). The next day, having been anointed with this healing unguent, he comes back to life poised to defeat the Dragon. The combination of being healed by water and oil recalls the pairing of the submersion in water and chrismatic anointing that constitutes the baptismal rite. Both these means of salvation were prophesied in the *Vita* and function prominently therein. On the interaction of these themes in the *Vita* see Stone, "Fall of Satan," 148–53.

3. Evans, *Paradise Lost.*

4. The classic study is that of Meyer, "Geschichte des Kreuzholzes," 187–250. See the comparative treatment of Quinn, *Quest of Seth.*

5. *Vita* 44:1–3.

to Adam.[6] When Adam sees the branch — which is to become the tree used for the wood of the cross — he rejoices in spite of his pain, for now he knows that his sin will be undone.

A careful reading of the tale discloses that the addition of this motif of the branch not only serves to connect this tale with a burgeoning literature about the origins of the wood of the cross, but also alters substantially the manner in which this portion of the tale concludes. In the early version of the narrative, in spite of the christological promise of Michael, Adam dies unhappily and in pain. Yet those tales that have Adam receive the branch portray Adam's reaction quite differently. His bodily pain, to be sure, remains unabated, but now Adam's spirit is comforted, for he knows that his sin will be forgiven. By almost every reader of the *Vita* in the modern period this late addition has been either ignored or said to be of no consequence for understanding the primitive form of the narrative. At one level, such a perspective can hardly be challenged. There is no question that the manuscripts which contain this material are late and secondary. Yet a close examination of the Latin text will disclose that this late editorial addition is quite in keeping with the way in which the entire narrative was being shaped and redacted in the medieval period. The motif of the Holy Rood is no doubt new, but its harmonious fit with the preexisting narrative is too exact to be considered an "intrusion." Indeed, careful attention to the way this motif becomes part of the *Vita* may tell us something very significant about the way the entire tale functioned in medieval Christianity.

But we have run ahead of ourselves. We will return at the end of this essay to consider this scene and its relation to the *Vita* as a whole. First, we must consider the origins of the work and its extensive reach in late antiquity.

---

6. This story can be found in the family III manuscripts edited by Meyer. He did not include this material in his critical edition of the *Vita*. Since he believed it to be quite late and secondary, he chose to print these texts in his later study of the legends of the Holy Rood (see n. 4). Meyer claims they could not be earlier than the twelfth century, when we first have evidence of the branch tradition in western Europe (Johannes Beleth's *Rationale divinorum officiorum*, ca. 1170). But against this argument one should note the presence of the motif in Slavonic and Armenian tradition (see n. 36), evidence that may argue for an earlier date or at least for a far more complicated pattern of transmission. In the manuscripts edited by Mozley ("Vitae Adae," 121–49) a similar addition can be found, only here Michael gives Seth seeds instead of a branch. But the end is the same: from those seeds, planted in Adam's mouth, comes the wood of the cross.

Versional Evidence

The tale itself has long been known to Western European readers in Latin. For some time the study of the text meant a
study of its Latin textual form. This changed in the late nineteenth century when Tischendorf published an edition of the tale
in Greek.[7] Shortly thereafter a Slavonic version appeared.[8] For
some time scholars worked diligently on the problem of how
the Greek, Latin, and, to a lesser degree, Slavonic texts were
to be understood. This is evident from the way in which the
text was rendered in the collection of the apocrypha and pseudepigrapha edited by R. H. Charles.[9] There the text was presented
in two columns, one each for the Greek and Latin, though a third
column was added for the Slavonic version of the penitence cycle. The more recent edition of Charlesworth has also printed a
columnar version of the tale, though only the Greek and Latin
are represented.[10]

For the last hundred years or so, scholars have tried to understand the relationship of the Greek and Latin forms of the text
(see table 1). This has not been an easy task, for the Latin has several literary units that are absent in the Greek, the most important
being the rather long narrative at the beginning concerning Adam
and Eve's penitence. The Greek also has a long independent narrative in the middle of its text. In this portion of the text Eve
recounts the entire history of how the transgression took place
and was punished, an apparent doublet of a similar but far briefer
account given by Adam in an earlier portion of the narrative. Because of a general scholarly tendency to consider Greek materials
as prior to Latin ones, a consensus gradually emerged that the
Latin additions were secondary.

The entire picture changed, however, in 1981 when M. Stone
published the Armenian, and J.-P. Mahé the Georgian version of
the tale.[11] Each of these Oriental versions contained the major

---

7. Tischendorf, *Apocalypses Apocryphae.*
8. Jagic, "Slavische Beiträge."
9. L. S. A. Wells, trans., in *APOT* 2.130–54.
10. M. Johnson, trans., in *OTP* 2.249–95.
11. Stone, *Penitence of Adam;* Mahé, "Livre d'Adam géorgien."

Table 1

Narrative Unit	Greek	Latin
Penitence	absent	1–22
Cain and Abel	1–4	23–24[12]
Adam's Story of the Fall/Quest of Seth	5–14	30–44
Eve's Story of the Fall	15–30	absent
Death and Burial of Adam and Eve	31–42	45–48

additions that were unique to the Latin and Greek. Though one could argue that these Oriental versions were later conflations of the shorter, and more pristine, Greek and Latin texts, there were sufficient grounds for suspecting just the opposite. It appears more and more likely that the Greek and Latin versions derived from an original that looked closer to the present form of the Georgian and Armenian.[13] Both Stone and Mahé have shown that these Oriental versions were translations of earlier Greek *Vorlagen*. G. Anderson and M. Stone have maintained in a series of publications that for a number of individual literary units, the form of the tale found in either the Armenian or the Georgian is more primitive.[14] Thus it appears quite likely that a Greek version of the *Vita* must have circulated in antiquity in a form that differed radically from the Greek that we now possess, and that this form of the Greek has strongest claim to be the most primitive form of the document.

A striking confirmation of this proposal may be close at hand. In 1922, St. John Seymour, while working on a tenth-century poem in Old Irish, the *Saltair na Rann,* concluded that the lengthy section of the work devoted to Adam and Eve had made extensive and systematic use of both the Latin and Greek versions of the *Vita.*[15] This was because the *Saltair* included the penance material

---

12. We have left out the Latin narrative of Adam's vision (chaps. 25–29). Though it is important in its own right, a discussion of it in this context would prove a needless complication. On this vision and other problems involving the Latin and Greek versions see Nickelsburg, "Some Related Traditions," 2.515–39.

13. This argument was made already by Stone in *Penitence of Adam.*

14. Anderson, "Penitence Narrative," 1–38; Stone, "Fall of Satan."

15. Seymour, "Book of Adam and Eve," 121–33.

(unique to the Latin) and Eve's recapitulation of the fall (unique to the Greek). This assessment was subsequently confirmed and deepened by Brian Murdoch in 1976 in a commentary on the relevant portions of the text.[16] Murdoch, like Seymour, was at a loss as to how this peculiar phenomenon was to be accounted for. Either the composer of the poem had access to both the Latin and Greek versions of the *Vita* or he had a copy of the Greek version in a Latin translation — a translation, we might add, that is unattested anywhere else. A far simpler solution was suggested recently by M. Stone.[17] Rather than presume that both of these independent versions were spliced together by a resourceful editor, why not suppose that the composer of this text had access to the very Greek textual family that had spawned the Armenian and the Georgian versions? Proof of this hypothesis would involve a careful study of each literary unit in the *Saltair* where we have material found only in the Greek, Armenian, and Georgian versions. If the *Saltair* used a text form that conforms more closely to the Armenian or Georgian than to our present Greek, then we would have strong reason to believe that the composers of the *Saltair* had access to a form of the Greek text that underlay those Oriental versions.

Henceforth no serious study of the *Vita* can ignore the important textual witness of the Georgian and Armenian versions. The commonly consulted editions of Charles and Charlesworth are no longer adequate for the study of this text. The recent publication by G. Anderson and M. Stone of a synoptic edition of the story across all five versions is an important step forward in the study of this text.[18] The study of any given unit of the tale must be done in view of the complete range of versional evidence.

A Jewish "Book of Adam"?

For most of the past century scholars have presumed that the *Vita* goes back to a now lost Hebrew or Aramaic original. Because the

---

16. Murdoch, "Early Irish Adam and Eve," 146–77.
17. Stone, "Jewish Tradition," 438–41.
18. Anderson and Stone, *Synopsis*.

tale has so few overt references to anything christological, it is assumed that those few references are secondary, editorial additions to an ancient, pristine Jewish document.

Perhaps the most brilliant expositor of this viewpoint was L. Ginzberg.[19] In his article on the "Book of Adam" (= *Vita*) he asserted that this book must have been of Jewish origin and then proceeded to outline its most archaic (yet nowhere attested) form. He summarized the penitence section of the tale as follows:

> Banished from the garden... Adam and Eve settled in the neighborhood of Eden in the East (*Gen. Rab.* 21:9). They were no sooner out of their blissful abode than a paralyzing terror befell them. Unaccustomed to the earthly life and unfamiliar with the changes of the day and of the weather — in paradise an eternal light had surrounded them (*Gen. Rab.* 11:2) — they were terrified when the darkness of night began to fall upon the earth (*b. 'Abod. Zar.* 8a), and the intercession of God's word (*memra'*) was necessary to explain to them the new order of things. From this moment the sufferings of life began; for Adam and Eve were afraid to partake of earthly food, and fasted for the first seven days after their expulsion from paradise, as is prescribed in Talmudic law before an imminent famine (*m. Ta'an.* 1:6).
>
> Humiliated and weakened by hunger and suffering, Adam became conscious of the gravity of his sin, for which he was now prepared to atone (*b. 'Erub.* 18b; *Gen. Rab.* 22:13). He, therefore, like Moses, Elijah, and Abraham (*Apoc. Abraham* 12) fasted for forty days, during which he stood up to his neck in the waters of the river Gihon (*gîhôn*), the name of which is etymologically connected by the writer with the roots *g-h-n* "to stoop" and *g-h-y* "to pray aloud" (*Pirqe R. El.* 20). According to the *Vita Adae et Evae*, Adam stood in the Jordan — a version which may be ascribed to the Christian copyists who, for obvious reasons, wished to represent Adam as having had his baptism in the Jordan, forgetting that since Eve, as they themselves stated, bathed in the Tigris, Adam would have selected another of the rivers of paradise for that purpose.

It is striking that the summary presented here represents no extant literary work. Ginzberg has taken the basic story line of the *Vita* and filled it out with references to comparable material in rabbinic sources or other apocrypha. Thus each and every narrative detail that has a Jewish parallel is glossed accordingly. If the Jewish parallel shows any significant variation from the *Vita* narrative itself, then Ginzberg concludes that the Jewish source must

---

19. Ginzberg, "Adam, Book of," 1.179–80.

be primary. Hence he describes Adam's penance in the Gihon in conformity to the tradition found in *Pirqe R. El.* 20, but in contrast to the *Vita* itself. This example is particularly revealing, for its influence can be seen as late as the 1985 edition of the *Vita* printed in Charlesworth.[20] There the editor of the text cites the very reference to *Pirqe R. El.* 20 found in Ginzberg.

A close inspection of the penitence narrative will disclose that the development of that narrative is far more complicated than Ginzberg's summary would allow. Equally complicated, we might add, is the question of the tale's Jewish or Christian origin. To illustrate this point let us consider the story's structure:

> Adam and Eve leave the Garden of Eden and find themselves bereft of their paradaisical food. Having begun to search for comestibles, they soon discover that none are to be had. Several unsuccessful searches and pleaful petitions later, they decide to embark on a formidable penance: to fast in separate rivers for forty days (thirty-four for Eve)[21] in hopes of procuring better food. A little more than halfway through the cycle, Satan appears to Eve in the guise of an angel and tempts her to leave the river and rejoin Adam as their prayers have been heard and their food now awaits them. Adam, upon seeing Eve, immediately bemoans her decision to disobey their penitential vow. Eve, having recognized her fault, begs leave of Adam to go to the west, where she will die. Adam meanwhile remains in the Jordan.
>
> At the end of Adam's period of penance in the Jordan, Eve suddenly feels the sharp pains of childbirth — evidently she became pregnant prior to their expulsion from the Garden — and cries out to Adam from halfway across the world. Adam, hearing this plea, steps out of the river to go assist Eve. However, since this is also the exact moment when the penance cycle concludes, Adam first must receive the fruits of his penitential labor — the food or "seeds" he had so earnestly appealed for. Having received this boon, Adam hastens off to assist Eve, who then gives birth to Cain.

The Latin, Georgian, and Armenian versions are in basic agreement through most of this narrative until the very end. At this point we find a significant variation. In the Georgian and Armenian versions the response of Adam to Eve and the reception of seeds are closely coordinated events; not so for the Latin:

---

20. M. Johnson, trans., in *OTP* 2.260.
21. The number of days can vary in the different versions. In general, Adam remains six or seven days longer than Eve.

Latin	Armenian	Georgian
20:1 In that very hour Adam said: "The lament of Eve has come to me.	20:1a Then Adam, in the river Jordan, heard Eve's cry and her weeping.	20:1a Then Adam, in the river Jordan, heard her tearful crying and misfortunes.
	20:1b When God hearkened to the sound of Adam's penitence, he taught him sowing and reaping and that which was to come upon him and his seed.	20:1b Then God hearkened to Adam's prayer and sent him the angel Michael, who brought him seeds, sealed with the divine seal, destined to be brought to Adam. Then he taught him sowing and the work related to it, so that thus they might be saved, (they) and all their descendants.
Perhaps the serpent has fought with her again."	20:1c Then Adam heard the sound of Eve's entreaty in the west, and Adam said to himself, "That voice and weeping are of my flesh. Let me arise and go to her and see why she is crying out. Perhaps the beast is fighting with her once more!"	20:1c And when Adam (had) heard the prayer of Eve and the wailing of her tears from the west, Adam recognized her voice and said in his heart, "This is the voice of my rib, the voice of my lamb; I will arise and I will see why she cries. Perhaps the serpent is attacking her once more?"

In the Latin version there is no mention of any seeds. This scene was moved to a different place in the narrative altogether. Only after Eve has delivered Cain, and Adam and Eve have ventured further to the east, does the Latin tale tell us of the delivery of seeds.

Latin	Armenian	Georgian
22:1 Adam took Eve and the boy and led them to the east.	22(1):2 Thenceforth Adam took Eve and the child and brought them to the eastern region, and he was there with her, and then eighteen years and two months were completed.	22(1):2 As for Adam, he took Eve and the child and he brought them into the eastern parts and he stayed there. And when the eighth year and the second month were completed [. . .]
22:2 The Lord God sent various seeds by Michael the angel, who gave them to Adam and showed them how to work and tend the ground, in order to have fruit, from which they and all their generations might live.		

Latin	Armenian	Georgian
22:3 Afterwards, Eve conceived and bore a son, whose name was Abel, and Cain and Abel remained together as one.	22(1):3 She became pregnant and bore a son, Ap'at', whom the midwife named and called Abel; and they dwelt together.	22(1):3 Eve became pregnant and bore another son whom the power of God called by the name Abel, and they remained there together.

It is important to note that not only has the Latin moved the delivery of the seeds to this new location, but by doing so it has effected a major change in the way the entire penitence cycle is to be viewed. For in the Latin version the delivery of the seeds is now completely divorced from the original penitential appeal of Adam. Adam, in this view, finishes his cycle of penance in the Jordan unsuccessfully. Indeed the entire penitence cycle now hangs in the air, as the Latin gives us no explicit information about its termination. To be sure, Adam does in the end get the seeds, but this gift appears to be completely unconditioned by anything Adam or Eve have done. Its appearance in the narrative is unmotivated and random.

How are we to understand the delivery scene in the Latin? Is it primary or secondary? An answer to this question will take us to the heart of the literary function of the entire narrative. Let us begin by attending to the sequence of events that is presupposed in the Georgian and Armenian. According to these versions Adam hears Eve's cry for help and quickly begins to come to her aid, only to be stopped abruptly in his tracks by the archangel Michael, who deems it time to offer Adam some instruction in the ways of agriculture. Only when Adam has been so schooled is he free to go to Eve's assistance. This interruption is, needless to say, quite awkward. The brevity of the Latin is far better suited to the tenor of this immediate situation. Yet the brevity of the Latin version comes at some cost. For now the whole penitential cycle trails off into the shadows, the reader never informed how Adam's vow of penance comes to an end. But more significantly the absence of this seed-delivery scene has interrupted what we might call *a narrativization of a piece of biblical exegesis*. To appreciate this fact, though, we must first clarify what type of biblical exegesis we are speaking about.[22]

---

22. The following section is an abbreviated version of Anderson, "Penitence Narrative."

Biblical Exegesis as Narrativization

The great medieval Jewish exegete Rashi, in commenting on Gen 3:18, was quite puzzled by one feature of the punishment of Adam: the declaration that Adam was to eat the "grass" (*'esev*) of the field.[23] This struck Rashi as odd, for just two chapters earlier in Gen 1:29 this "grass" had been given as a blessing.[24] How could a blessing in chapter 1 become a curse in chapter 3? This semantic problem had been noted nearly a thousand years earlier and "solved" rather ingeniously. Rabbinic exegetes of the Bible had noted that God makes a rather fine distinction between the type of *'esev* he is going to bestow on human beings (1:29) as opposed to the animals (1:30).[25] Humans are to receive *'esev* that propagates by seeds, whereas the animals simply receive (green) *'esev*. This distinction suggested to these ancient readers of the Bible that human *'esev* was a type of grain that could be *cultivated*, whereas the *'esev* distributed to the animals was an herbage that *grew wild*. This distinction from chapter 1 was then brought forward to chapter 3 and read into the punishment of Adam. When God first declares that Adam is to eat "the *'esev* of the field," this was understood to refer to that herbage which is normally the lot of the animals. In other words this is the food spoken of in Gen 1:30, not 1:29. Adam, on this view, is at first reduced to living the life of an animal ("you shall eat the herbage of the field"). Faced with this formidable punishment, Adam immediately breaks into tears and weeps over his fate. God, in response to this show of remorse, has pity on Adam and softens the blow by offering Adam a new form of *'esev,* that which grows by seed ("by the sweat of your brow you shall eat bread"). The process of solving the apparent contradiction between the punishment of chapter 3 and the blessing of chapter 1 has introduced a new narrative element into our story: Adam,

---

23. Gen 3:18–19a, "The earth shall produce thorns and thistles for you; *you shall eat the grass of the field;* by the sweat of your brow you shall eat bread." Emphasis added here and in subsequent citations.

24. Gen 1:29, "God said, 'I hereby give you [as a blessing] *every grass yielding seed* that is upon the face of all the earth . . . and you shall have them for food.'"

25. Gen 1:30, "And to every beast on the earth . . . I hereby give [as a blessing] *every green grass* as food."

having been reduced to the status of an animal, repents and is given a food source appropriate to his stature as a human being.

Turning to the *Vita* we can immediately see how this exegetical tradition has been "narrativized" in our tale. Here Adam, just as in the midrash, finds only animal food as he leaves the garden. Once he has repented sufficiently, God relents and provides him with seeds for grain. The Georgian is most explicit here, for it underscores the point that these seeds were set aside for Adam at the beginning of creation (Gen 1:29) but only now are disclosed. Why has the seed-delivery scene been placed so awkwardly, at the moment when Eve is to be assisted? Because the assistance Adam is going to give Eve is part of a divine plan in which the initial punishment meted out is about to be relaxed slightly. Adam's return to Eve's side and his prayerful intervention on her behalf saves Eve.[26] At the very same time, Michael's intervention and delivery of seeds saves Adam. A clever exegetical ploy, but, at the same time, a very awkward narrative sequence.

In this light we could posit a plausibly Jewish background for the penitence cycle. But notice how different it is from the reconstruction of Ginzberg. He cites the tradition of *Pirqe R. El.* 20 as primary, but this tale, though it knows of Adam's immersion in a river, has no connection with a search for food and ends with a word of general forgiveness for Adam, a theme that has no place in the *Vita*.[27] If the *Pirqe R. El.* text is related or relevant at all, it is at quite a distant remove. Indeed, one could reasonably conjecture that this tradition was a creative adaptation of the prior tradition found in the *Vita*.

But is a Jewish background for the tale absolutely necessary? We have suggested exactly this by way of the parallels we chose

---

26. Cf. Gen 3:16 LXX, "to your husband shall be your return/repentance." Evidently the rejoining of Adam and Eve and Adam's role in Eve's own penance was constructed on the basis of this verse.

27. *Pirqe R. El.* 20 reads, "On the first day of the week, Adam entered the waters of the Upper Gihon until the waters reached his neck. He did penance there for seven weeks until his body was transformed into a sieve. Adam said to the Holy One, Blessed be He: 'O Lord of the worlds, make my sin pass from me and accept my repentance. Then all generations shall learn that repentance does exist and that you accept the repentance of those who repent.' What did the Holy One, Blessed be He, do? He extended his right hand and made his sin pass from him and accepted his repentance. For it is said: 'I made known my sins and my iniquity I did not cover up. [To which God said:] "*Selah*"' (Psalm 32). [The meaning of *Selah*] is forgiveness in this world and in the world to come."

to highlight above. Yet before one rushes forward too boldly with this idea, it may be worth consulting a Christian commentator and contemporary of many a rabbi, St. Ephrem (d. 373 C.E.). St. Ephrem, like the rabbis, also considered that Adam was forced to consume the "grass of the field" like an animal when he was expelled from the garden. In his *Hymns on Paradise,* St. Ephrem compares Adam's state to that of King Nebuchadnezzar, who, having been expelled from his royal kingdom, was transformed into a grass-eating animal. This comparison is all the more fitting when one realizes that in all of the Bible, only Adam and King Nebuchadnezzar are described as having eaten the grass of the field.

> 5. David wept for Adam (Ps 49:13)
>   at how he fell
> from that royal abode
>   to that abode of wild animals.
> Because he went astray through a beast
>   he became like the beasts:
> He ate, together with them
>   as a result of the curse,
> grass and roots,
>   and he died, becoming their peer.
> Blessed is He who set him apart
>   from the wild animals again.
>
> 6. In that king
>   did God depict Adam:
> since he provoked God by his exercise of kingship,
>   God stripped him of that kingship.
> The Just One was angry and cast him out
>   into the region of wild beasts;
> he dwelt there with them
>   in the wilderness
> and only when he repented did he return
>   to his former abode and kingship.
> Blessed is He who has thus taught us to repent
>   so that we too may return to Paradise.
>   (*Hymns on Paradise* 13)

St. Ephrem's poetic comparison of Adam to King Nebuchadnezzar presumes a prior exegetical decision to treat the curse of Gen 3:18–19a as one which transforms Adam into an animal. But what of the bestowal of the grain that Adam will eat? How does St. Ephrem understand this act of divine beneficence? We saw that the rabbis presumed that this divine blessing, though spoken of in chapter 1, is not actualized until chapter 3. St. Ephrem, in his prose commentary on Genesis, also associated the gift of seeds in Gen 1:29 as a promise to be fulfilled only after the expulsion from the garden.[28]

St. Ephrem and the rabbis are in complete agreement in both their narrative portrait of Adam's expulsion and the biblical verses they use to depict it.[29] Yet one piece of the puzzle is missing in St. Ephrem's portrait — there is no explicit linking of Adam's penance with a subsequent gift of seeds. St. Ephrem does not coordinate the end of Gen 3:18, "you shall eat the *grass* of the field," with the beginning of 3:19a, "by the sweat of your brow you shall eat *bread*." Only in Jewish sources do we see these verses understood in terms of a movement away from the food of animals toward that of humans. In fact, the specific moment in time when the animals' food is replaced by human food is never addressed by St. Ephrem. And this is probably no chance event, for St. Ephrem is very concerned to underscore the fact that Adam's penance remains unfulfilled until the day he dies. King Nebuchadnezzar is an important symbolic figure for Ephrem not because his transformation to an animal mirrors Adam's, but because Nebuchadnezzar repents, *is forgiven, and is restored* to his former royal kingdom. The narrative about Nebuchadnezzar provides an important — and hitherto missing — "type" of the salvation Adam had hoped for.[30] In Ephrem's view, Nebuchadnezzar's transformation to an animal and back to an exalted royal state was a theological foreshadowing in the Old Testament of what would become a reality in the New. For in Ephrem's view, as indeed for nearly all early Christian commentators, *Adam's pen-*

---

28. See the recent translation by E. Mathews (and J. Amar), St. *Ephrem the Syrian.* The interpretation comes in the commentary on Gen 1:13–14: "The grass that would be required as food for the animals who were to be created two days later was [thus] made ready. And the new corn that would be food for Adam and his descendants, who would be thrown out of Paradise four days later, was [thus] prepared."

29. The points of agreement are the reduction of Adam to the state of a beast eating roots and tubers; the subsequent discovery/gift of seeds that serves to distinguish Adam from the animals; and the notion that the gift of these very seeds was prophesied in Gen 1:29. For St. Ephrem's view of Gen 1:29 as a prophecy of the type of food Adam would receive only when he left the garden, see n. 28.

30. On the figure of Nebuchadnezzar in early Christian sources in general see Satran, *Biblical Prophets,* 82–91.

ance cannot come to a fruitful conclusion until the arrival of the Second Adam. To have Adam achieve forgiveness and restoration would diminish if not obviate the work to be done by the Second Adam.[31]

We are now on the horns of a dilemma. Was the exegetical source of our penitence narrative Jewish or Christian? The themes we have traced are attested in both. No definitive answer can be given here, though the tendency to attribute a tale to Jewish origins simply because Jewish sources exist must be resisted.[32] The grounds for Christian composition are equally compelling, and a final arbitration of the matter would require more evidence than can be discussed here. In any event, from a Christian perspective, it must be conceded that the penitence of Adam, when construed as a rather narrow act of seeking better food, would not be an altogether laudable feature of the tale in subsequent retellings. In-

---

31. The perpetual mourning of Adam is well illustrated elsewhere in St. Ephrem's writings when he addresses the question of how Adam responded to Enoch's assumption to paradise. Note the contrast of Adam's unrelieved mourning and lamentation to that of Enoch, who also happened to be, in the thinking of St. Ephrem, a type of Christ.

> Come my brothers and let us weep here
>   so that we do not weep there;
> Come let us bear mourning and sorrow
>   that we not multiply our mourning there.
> All the just and righteous
>   by their mourning are pleasing to God;
> By weeping do they appease Him
>   and by tears they please Him.
> For nine hundred and thirty years
>   Adam wept over his fall;
> Because he was far from the glory
>   of God in Paradise.
> The beauty of his cheeks was marred
>   from the tears which had poured from his eyes,
> From the fervent heat of tears
>   arose bitter sores....
> Enoch, being pleasing, not tasting death
>   when he saw the bones of Abel,
> he bore sorrow and grief
>   for 320 years.
> When he saw the first dead man,
>   who stunk, became foul and putrefied,
> He wept and cried incessantly
>   and so was removed and did not taste death.
>   (St. Ephrem, *Sermones I*, VI, 63–85)

32. My own position on this point has evolved from my earlier arguments in "Penitence Narrative." In that article I argued much more strongly for a Jewish origin.

deed it quickly gave way, in the Latin tradition, to an entirely different set of interests.

Christian Transmission and Transformation
of the Penitence Cycle

Hitherto our discussion has been mainly "excavative" in nature.[33] We have sought exegetical parallels to a significant narrative element in the *Vita*. As in many pseudepigraphical works, a learned piece of biblical exegesis has been given narrative exposition. In general, narrativizations such as the *Vita* do not highlight in any explicit fashion the biblical text from which they derive. Rather the scholar must carefully sift the exegetical sources to see if the narrative development of the story depends, in some essential way, on a certain train of exegetical reasoning. Yet this mode of inquiry, as enlightening as it can be, can also pose problems. Because the exegetical narrativizations often have no explicit tie to the biblical text, they tend to go unrecognized by redactors and often are reworked or redeployed in rather substantial ways.[34]

A good illustration of this activity is present in the Latin recension of the *Vita*. This version, it will be recalled, does not include mention of Adam receiving seeds when he left the Jordan River to go to Eve's assistance. The immediate effect of this change is to produce a tighter and more pleasing picture of Adam's response to Eve's urgent plea for help. But other changes in the narrative also result. We mentioned one — that in the Latin, Adam's penitence in the Jordan is brought to no conclusive end. He leaves the Jordan no different than he entered; indeed his departure itself is cloaked in mystery. One may be inclined to say this change on the part of the editor is rather passive and unintentional, seeing that the elimination of the delivery of the seeds at this point of the story would necessarily leave the penitence cycle without a conclusion. But there are hints that the open-ended nature of the story that resulted was altogether intentional.

---

33. On the significance of this term in biblical exegesis, see Alter, *Art of Biblical Narrative*, 13.

34. On the tendency of later tradents of this material to "legendize" an earlier form of exegesis, see the examples given in Kugel, "Two Introductions," 131–55.

To appreciate this fact we must take into consideration the larger literary frame of the penitence cycle in the Georgian and Armenian versions. Both of these versions follow a Jewish exegetical tradition in presuming that the animals were given their "herbage" on the sixth day of creation (Gen 1:30), whereas Adam and Eve do not receive the seeds for their grain (Gen 1:29) until they have been expelled from the garden. Adam and Eve do not lament their "general sin" upon leaving the garden — indeed according to these versions Adam is not sure he has transgressed at all. Rather they rue the difficult and highly particular circumstances into which they have been cast. They have been forced to eat the food allotted to the animals. So when Adam commands the animals to join his lamentation in the Jordan he exclaims: "Let them surround me and bewail me not for their own sakes, but for me. Because God did not withhold their food from them which God appointed from the beginning, but I have been withheld from my food and from life."[35] The Latin version, on the other hand, takes great care to mute the specificity and particularity of this appeal. Instead of focusing on the food source as the event of great consequence, the Latin shifts the focus to Adam's sin considered in a most *general* fashion. Adam laments: "Let them surround me and mourn with me. Let them not lament for themselves, but for me, for they have not sinned, but I." Adam's plea concerns much more than what type of food he shall consume. His lament takes on the more general theme of his own transgression.

In certain manuscripts of the Latin version we see one more significant change that serves to tie together the several themes we have been considering. According to the Latin version there are two points in the narrative at which Adam receives seeds. The first is during Adam and Eve's journey to the East after Cain has been born. At this point Adam is given the seeds which will allow him to cultivate food (*Vita* 22:2). Though this scene originally was linked to the penitence cycle earlier in the narrative, it has been effectively cut off from that sequence in the Latin tale. The

---

35. Following the Armenian version of the *Vita*, 8:2.

second is when Adam is about to die and he sends Seth back to
the garden (*Vita* 43:2).

In order to appreciate this second scene, let us review the plot
structure of this part of the narrative:

> At the end of Adam's life he is overtaken by the severe bodily pains which
> portend death. In reaction to this Adam, calls for Seth and sends him and
> Eve back to the Garden to make an impassioned appeal for the oil of
> mercy. With this oil Adam hopes to anoint himself and relieve his pains.
> When Seth arrives at the Garden and makes the request, the archangel
> Michael appears and tells Seth that the oil cannot be given until the era of
> the Messiah.

At this point our texts read:

Latin	*Armenian*	*Georgian*
43:1 "But you, Seth, go to your father, Adam, for the time of his life is complete. Six days hence, his soul will go forth from his body, and, when it does, you will see great wonders in heaven and on earth, and in the lights of heaven."	43(13):6 "But you, go to Adam your father, for his times will be full in three days and you have to see many wonders in heavens and upon earth and in all luminaries which are in the heavens."	43(13):6 "But now, go to your father Adam, because the days of his times are completed. [In] three days his soul will go out of his body and numerous wonders will be seen in the heavens."
43:2 Saying this, Michael at once withdrew from Seth.	43(14):1a When the angel had spoken this, he disappeared behind a tree of the Garden.	43(14):1a When the angel had told that to him, [immediately] he was hidden underneath the plant of the Garden.
43:3 *Seth and Eve went home, carrying with them spices — nard, crocus, calaminth, and cinnamon.*		

Up to this point the Latin, Georgian, and Armenian versions
are in basic agreement. Afterward the Latin version adds a crucial
new piece of information. We are told that Seth and Eve leave
with a set of aromatic spices, whose purpose is most likely cultic
or sacrificial (cf. *Jub.* 3:27).

It is very difficult to dissociate this statement from the former
scene about the agricultural seeds. Both scenes come at the end
of penitential activity, and Michael is the agent in both cases.
The seeds that Michael provides, though important, are somewhat pedestrian in nature in that they provide for mortal life. The

gift of the aromatic spices, on the other hand, points to a larger horizon: the beginning of cultic activity and the saving of human souls. The transition to a larger plane of salvation becomes subject to another dramatic development in numerous manuscripts of the Latin *Vita,* which is the addition to the story of the Holy Rood material.

In the critical text of the Latin which Meyer published, the text in question reads: "Seth and Eve went home, carrying with them spices — nard, crocus, calaminth, and cinnamon." Yet in the medieval manuscripts from family III (no earlier than 1170)[36] there is a very significant addition: "They took with them *the branch* and the spices: nard, crocus, calaminth, and cinnamon." Here we see a major innovation in the development of the tradition. For this (small) branch is no ordinary branch; it is nothing other than a piece from the tree of knowledge which will evolve into the very wood of the cross.

In E. Quinn's major study of the motif she makes a strong case that the story of the origins of this branch which grew into the wood of the cross did not include the figures of Adam or Seth.[37] The earliest exemplars trace the wood back to the rod of Moses. Yet the desire for an even more ancient protology led the tradents of this material eventually to tie the origins to the story of Adam and Eve. The most frequent point of correlation was that of Seth's quest. Yet as good as Quinn's study is, her interest in the way the motif functioned in a myriad of medieval texts has blinded her from attending to the specific way in which this branch tradition has been "grafted" into the *Vita.* For this innovative redactional addition, as pathbreaking as it may seem, was well prepared for in the evolution of the Latin manuscript tradition. The correlation of the initial penitential request of Adam with the later one has

---

36. See n. 6. This date is based on Meyer's assessment on the basis of the comparable Latin material that he knew at that time (1878). This problem should be reexamined in light of the Slavonic and Armenian evidence. For the Slavonic see, for now, the treatment of Jagic, "Slavische Beiträge"; much remains to be done in this field. For the Armenian, see "Adam Fragment 1" in Stone, *Armenian Apocrypha Relating to the Patriarchs,* and "Adam Fragment 1" in Stone, *Armenian Apocrypha Relating to Adam and Eve.*

37. Quinn, *Quest of Seth,* 48–84. She argues that the earliest versions began with the story of Moses' rod, and then gradually over time this motif was pushed back further and further, at first to the branches brought to Noah (from paradise, according to the legend) and then to the branch Seth is given just before Adam's death.

prepared the reader to see a progression in the type of answers Adam will receive.

But there is more. We noted that Adam's first penitential vow ends on an unhappy note. Adam hears no answer to his pleas for general forgiveness; he leaves the Jordan in silence, his entreaties unattended to. This correlation (plea for forgiveness, denial of such) is, of course, altogether expected in a Christian text, as we noted earlier. The introduction of the wood of the cross alerts the reader that Adam's sin will, in the future, be forgiven. Though the reader is well-prepared to draw all the proper deductions about the nature and role of this branch, how could one expect that *Adam himself* could do such? A good writer will need to protect the innocence of Adam about the precise christological importance of this branch, but at the same time allow Adam, within the literary confines of the story, to perceive its potential redemptive significance. And this is exactly what our writer does. We witness such a literary move in what Meyer referred to as the family III set of Latin manuscripts. Let us consider its particular version of the story:

Latin	*Latin–family III*
43:3 Seth and Eve went home, carrying with them spices — nard, crocus, calaminth, and cinnamon.	43:3a They took with them *the branch* and the spices: nard, crocus, calaminth, and cinnamon.
	43:3b *When Eve and Seth crossed the Jordan, lo, the branch which the angel gave him fell into the middle of the river.*
44:1 When Seth and his mother reached Adam, they said to him that the beast, the serpent, had bitten Seth.	44:1 When Seth and his mother reached Adam, they said to him all that had happened.
44:2 Adam said to Eve: "What have you done? You have brought on us a great affliction, fault and sin unto all our generations. What you have done will be passed on to your children after my death,	44:2 Adam said to Eve: "What have you done? You have brought on us a great affliction, fault and sin unto all our generations. What you have done will be passed on to your children after my death,
44:3 for those who arise from us will not have all they need from their labors, but will be lacking. They will curse us, saying:	44:3 for those who arise from us will not have all they need from their labors, but will be lacking. They will curse us, saying:
44:4 'Our parents, who were from the beginning, brought all these evils on us.' "	44:4 'Our parents, who were from the beginning, brought all these evils on us.' "

Latin	Latin-family III
44:5 Hearing this, Eve began to weep and moan.	44:5 Hearing this, Eve began to weep and moan. *And Adam said to Seth his son, "Didn't the angel send me anything?" Seth, being very confused and frightened, because he could not find what the angel gave him, said to his father: "The angel gave me a branch from paradise which I dropped into the flowing waters of the Jordan." His father replied: "Go my son and in the very place where it fell find it and bring it to me so that I can see it before I die and bless you." Seth went back to the flowing river and found the branch in the middle of the flowing stream, it not having budged an inch. Seth brought it back with joy to his father. When Adam received it, he was glad and said with great joy: "Behold my death and resurrection." He asked his son to plant it at the head of his tomb.*

There are two crucial insertions in the family III manuscripts. The first concerns the branch which Seth receives as he is about to depart from the garden. As Seth heads home with the branch he accidentally drops it in the Jordan. When he returns to Adam, evidently embarrassed over his foolish mistake and quite ignorant of the significance of the branch and the river into which it fell, he decides not to disclose this detail (43:3b). Later, however, when Adam is lying heartbroken on his deathbed, Seth is asked once more about his journey to the garden.

"Didn't the angel send me anything?" Adam inquires. Seth, confused and frightened because he could not find what the angel gave him, says to his father: "The angel gave me a branch from paradise which I dropped into the flowing waters of the *Jordan*." Evidently Adam, at this point ignorant of what the branch signifies, nevertheless knows that it is from the garden and that it has fallen into the Jordan River, the spot of his failed attempt to make atonement for his sins. "Go my son," Adam implores, "and in *the very place where it fell* find it and bring it to me so that I can see it before I die and bless you." Seth then returns to the flowing waters of the Jordan and finds the branch in the middle of the turbulent stream; quite miraculously, it had not budged an inch. Seth brings it back with joy to his father. When Adam receives it, he is glad and says with great joy: "Behold my death and resurrection." He then asks Seth to plant it at the head of his tomb.[38]

One could follow the lead of E. Quinn and suggest that Seth's dropping of the twig is a symbolic representation of his own fall.[39] Or one could say that it represents a common motif in folklore of delaying the deliverance of the hero by a last-minute calamity. This ratcheting up of the tension in the story makes the recounting of the deliverance all the more fabulous. Though both of these explanations carry with them an element of truth, there is more. Our redactor is quite conscious of the fact that not only is the branch itself significant, but also *the spot* where the branch will be found. By framing the story in this way our writer has made a brilliant connection to Adam's initial penitential appeal in the Jordan, an appeal that necessarily ended without success. We might add that the explanation that the waters of the Jordan were in full flow is certainly an allusion to Joshua 3, which includes the miracle of the Jordan's waters reversing their flow prior to the Israelites crossing into the promised land. It cannot be accidental that this very text was also used typologically in early Christian catechesis as an Old Testament illustration of the redemptive power of baptism.[40]

It is also no accident that the Jordan is at full force when Seth drops the branch into its waters. For as we have seen, our author has a real narratological problem here: how will Adam know what this branch signifies? One option would be to sacrifice the integrity of Adam as a literary character and simply announce the unvarnished truth about the branch — it portends the advent of

---

38. Latin, *Vita* 44:4
39. Quinn, *Quest of Seth*, 98.
40. In the NT the Israelites' crossing of the Red Sea was the more favored text (cf. 1 Cor 10:1–5). But this text was problematic for catechetical usage, for though it used the passage through water as an illustration of salvation, it provided no linkage with the practice of penitence. Since most catechumens in the early church had just undergone the rigors of the forty-day Lenten fast, the association of crossing the Jordan (Joshua 3–5) after the forty-year period of wandering in the wilderness seemed a much closer match. One should also add that the very next event in the Book of Joshua is the entrance into Eretz Israel, the "land flowing with milk and honey," a type, Christians were wont to argue, of the return to paradise or entry into the church. Thus the Book of Joshua, in early Christian eyes, nicely juxtaposed the ritual cycle of penitence, baptism, and entry into the church.

Christ. The versions of the *Vita* found in England, published by Mozley, do exactly this.[41] But if the literary integrity of Adam is to be retained, then another strategy must be employed, a strategy that allows Adam to see the salvific significance of the branch without its specific christological trappings. And indeed this is exactly what has happened. For the branch falls into the turbulent waters of the Jordan, the very waters that Adam left in an unsuccessful attempt at penance many years earlier, and then is retrieved miraculously by Seth as Adam lies on his deathbed. The presence of his branch, maintaining its stationary position in the midst of a strong current, is a sufficient sign for Adam.[42] His penance has now come full circle. The river that many years before had provided no sign of forgiveness, now, at the end of his life, "reverses itself" and in so doing provides assurance for Adam of his (coming) redemption.

This motif is sufficiently christological for any contemporary medieval reader to see the clear connections to the sacrament of baptism. Yet the enactment of this motif in its present literary setting is sufficiently subtle that we need not require of Adam the same type of "eschatological" knowledge. The branch's salvific role is made clear by its miraculous presence in the river; the specific details about its future function, though, are left deliberately unstated. Adam's literary integrity is preserved. He perceives the token of redemption offered to him, but not in the same manner as the medieval readers will understand it. This deft touch by our

---

41. See Mozley, "Vitae Adae." In certain manuscripts, Seth does not return with a branch but with a vision and/or seeds.

> Seth said to his father Adam, "Lord father, I saw a wondrous sign in Paradise." Adam said, "Tell me, Seth, my son, what did you see there? Perhaps I will know how to interpret that wonder." Seth answered, saying to his father Adam, "My father, as I looked into Paradise I saw a virgin sitting at the top of a tree and a boy holding a cross in his hands."

This rather baroque vision of redemption serves as proof for Adam of his future redemption:

> But Adam, looking to heaven on bent knees, raised up his hands to God and said, "Blessed are you, Lord, Father, for all things, most omnipotent and most merciful God, because now I truly know that a virgin will conceive a son who will die on a cross, and from this we will all be saved."

42. One should also note that the waters of the Jordan which the Israelites cross (Josh 3:15) were also at the peak of their seasonal turbulence, hence heightening the effect of the miracle.

author serves a much larger purpose than merely heightening the tension of the drama.

•

The "Life of Adam and Eve" is a colorful story with a rich legacy in medieval literature and art. The work has been said to represent an ancient Jewish pseudepigraph, perhaps one that dates back to the Second Temple period. So confident of this approach was L. Ginzberg that he, with considerable ingenuity and genius — not to mention aplomb — reconstructed this prototype on the basis of parallel Jewish literature. Many themes of the *Vita* do indeed have Jewish parallels. We treated one such example, that of the bequest of seeds to Adam after his expulsion and penance. In so doing we showed that the Jewish exegetical tradition that lay behind that motif was far more complicated than Ginzberg had imagined. There are numerous other motifs within the work that would be amenable to this type of analysis, including the story of Satan's fall, the imputation of all blame to Eve, Seth's taming of the wild beast, and the slaying of Abel by Cain. A close examination of each of these themes would have to be attentive not only to possible sources within early Jewish exegetical traditions but also to the ways in which the motifs came into early Christian sources. The long and creative history of the transmission of this text allowed for considerable rewriting and reshaping, oftentimes demonstrating obvious signs of Christian influence. In our study we have seen how an uneasiness with the limited nature of Adam's penance (for better food) and its success would have troubled Christian tradents. The transformations we observed in the later Latin versions allowed for Adam's penance to encompass his general state of sin and estrangement from God and at the same time made his appeal for forgiveness unsuccessful. It is no accident that exactly this perspective emerged in classic Christian thinking regarding the legacy of original sin.

Bibliography

Alexander, P. S. "The Fall into Knowledge: The Garden of Eden/Paradise in Gnostic Literature." In *A Walk in the Garden: Biblical, Iconographical and Literary Images of Eden.* Ed. P. Morris and D. Sawyer. Sheffield: JSOT Press, 1992. Pp. 91–103. A lengthy discussion and exegesis of a passage in the *Hypostasis of the Archons* about the Garden of Eden. Gnostic treatments of the garden were numerous and extremely important for understanding the rise of Christian exegesis. Alexander gives a masterful commentary on this text and provides references to other Gnostic material.

Alexandre, M. *Le Commencement du Livre Genèse I–V: La version grecque de la Septante et sa réception.* Paris: Beauchesne, 1988. An invaluable commentary on the Septuagint translation of the Bible. Compares this translation to the Hebrew original and provides a useful synopsis of how the Greek Bible was interpreted by Philo and the Greek patristic tradition.

Anderson, G. A. "Celibacy or Consummation in the Garden: Reflections on Early Jewish and Christian Interpretations of the Garden of Eden." *HTR* 82 (1989) 121–48. A treatment of how various early interpreters understood the sexuality of Adam and Eve in view of their conception of Eden's sacral nature. Special emphasis is given to the book of *Jubilees* and the relationship between early rabbinic and Syriac traditions.

———. "The Penitence Narrative in the *Life of Adam and Eve.*" *HUCA* 63 (1993) 1–38. A description of how the penitence narrative was constructed from biblical exegesis found in early Jewish sources.

Anderson, G. A., and M. E. Stone, eds. *A Synopsis of the Books of Adam and Eve.* SBLEJL 5. Atlanta: Scholars Press, 1994. Lays out the five principal versions of the "Life of Adam and Eve" in parallel columns so that the texts can be easily compared.

Barr, J. *The Garden of Eden and the Hope of Immortality.* Minneapolis: Fortress, 1993. A recent attempt to understand the story of Adam and Eve in a modern vein. Argues that the story of Adam and Eve was not a "fall" in its original form. Adam and Eve had a chance at immortality in the garden but lost it.

Evans, J. M. *Paradise Lost and the Genesis Traditions.* Oxford: Clarendon, 1968. A learned guide to a wide variety of patristic and medieval exegesis of Genesis 1–3 as well as a thorough review of the material in medieval narrative settings. Concludes with a consideration of how this material came to bear on the writing of *Paradise Lost.*

Kronholm, T. *Motifs from Genesis 1–11 in the Genuine Hymns of Ephrem the Syrian with Particular Reference to the Influence of Jewish Exegetical Tradition.* ConBOT 11. Lund: Gleerup, 1978. A detailed analysis of Ephrem's hymns with the aim of articulating how Ephrem interpreted the primeval cycle of Genesis 1–11. Frequent comparisons are drawn with parallel Jewish ideas.

Levison, J. *Portraits of Adam in Early Judaism: From Sirach to 2 Baruch.* JSOTSup 1. Sheffield: JSOT Press, 1988. A concise and reliable treatment of the various apocryphal and pseudepigraphical treatments of Adam, including a fine section on Philo. The treatment of the "Life of Adam and Eve" relies solely on the Greek and Latin versions and, hence, is dated.

Lipscomb, W. L. *The Armenian Apocryphal Adam Literature.* University of Pennsylvania Armenian Texts and Studies 8. Atlanta: Scholars Press, 1990. A useful collection of Armenian traditions about Adam, many of which show close connections to themes in the "Life of Adam and Eve."

Pagels, E. *Adam, Eve, and the Serpent.* New York: Random Books, 1988. A popular book on the treatment of Genesis 1–3 in early Christian and Gnostic sources. Tends to emphasize the political nature of these developments over against the exegetical.

Quinn, E. C. *The Quest of Seth for the Oil of Life.* Chicago: University of Chicago Press, 1962. A masterful treatment of perhaps the most famous section of the "Life of Adam and Eve." Quinn follows this motif from its origins in the biblical story up to its flowering in the Middle Ages.

Schäfer, P. "Adam in jüdischen Überlieferung." In *Vom alten zum neuen Adam: Urzeitmythos und Heilsgeschichte.* Ed. W. Strolz. Freiburg: Herder, 1986. Pp. 69–93. A short description of the treatment of Adam in classical rabbinic texts and early kabbalistic literature.

Stone, M. E. *Armenian Apocrypha Relating to the Patriarchs and Prophets.* Jerusalem, Israel Academy of Sciences and Humanities, 1982. Translation and discussion of numerous Armenian traditions about Adam and Eve.

———. "The Fall of Satan and Adam's Penance: Three Notes on the Books of Adam and Eve." *JTS* 44 (1993) 142–56. This article has two principal parts: (1) a consideration of the fall of Satan story in the "Life of Adam and Eve" and its relationship to a similar tradition in 2 (Slavonic) Enoch; and (2) an argument that the fuller form of the text (including both the penitence narrative and Eve's account of the fall) found in the Armenian and Georgian versions is the most primitive form of the story.

———. *A History of the Literature of Adam and Eve.* SBLEJL 3. Atlanta: Scholars Press, 1992. The most complete discussion available of the current state of the Adam literature. Includes a full bibliography of the principal versions, a discussion of its relationship to the secondary Adam literature, and directions for future research.

Tennant, F. R. *The Sources of the Doctrines of the Fall and Original Sin.* Cambridge: Cambridge University Press, 1903. Reprint, New York: Schocken, 1968. A classic, frequently cited summary of how early Christian writers came to define the concepts of "fall" and "original sin."

Williams, N. P. *The Ideas of the Fall and of Original Sin.* London: Longmans, Green and Co., 1927. This work is similar to Tennant's treatment, but is far more comprehensive. It also has a decided theological focus: it wishes to discern what the central Christian teaching about this doctrine is.

THE GNOSTIC SETH

John D. Turner

The Biblical Seth

The origins of the Gnostic Seth are to be found in the privileged position that Seth seems to have occupied in the theological reflections and speculations of postexilic Jews living in both Palestine and the diaspora. Their reflections were directed toward the basic source of information about Seth, the primeval history of the Book of Genesis. In particular, the Gnostic picture of Seth is founded upon two key passages in Genesis:

> And Adam knew his wife again, and she bore a son and called his name Seth, for she said: "God has appointed for me another seed instead of Abel, for Cain slew him." (Gen 4:25 RSV)

> When Adam had lived a hundred and thirty years, he became the father of a son in his own likeness, after his image, and named him Seth. (Gen 5:3 RSV)

It is clear from many sources that ancient interpreters, Gnostic and otherwise, had noticed and explored solutions to a number of discrepancies and contrasts in the text of the Genesis protology and anthropogony.[1] As part of its own way of resolving apparent discrepancies in the Genesis accounts, modern biblical criticism has assigned these two passages to separate literary sources.[2] The

---

1. The sources on Seth have been collected by Klijn, *Seth;* Pearson, "Figure of Seth," 2.472–504; and Stroumsa, *Another Seed,* 49–53, 73–80. For the biblical and postbiblical Jewish evidence, see especially Klijn, *Seth,* 4–32. Both Klijn (*Seth,* 112) and Pearson ("Figure of Seth," 496, 503) conclude that the Gnostics derived all their ideas about Seth from Jewish sources.

2. Klijn, *Seth,* 1–2.

sections of the Book of Genesis in which Seth is mentioned (4:25–26; 5:3–4, 6–8), according to modern criticism, come from two sources: the Priestly (P) and Yahwist (J) sources. P contains Gen 1:1–2:4a, which deals with the creation of heaven and earth in six days; Gen 5:1–32, which presents the lineage of Seth from Adam, who fathered a son in his image and likeness after 130 years, and traces Seth's progeny (Enosh, Kenan, Mahalalel, Jared, Enoch, Methuselah, Lamech) to Noah and the birth of Shem, Ham, and Japheth; and, finally, Gen 6:9–22, which tells the story of the righteous Noah. P mentions neither the Fall of Adam and Eve nor the story of Cain and Abel, but speaks instead of Seth as the only son of Adam, whose descendants, ending with Noah and his sons, all lived righteously.

Initially, J includes chapters 2:4b–4:26; this is the story of Adam's life in paradise, the origin of Eve, the Fall, the expulsion from paradise, the birth of Cain and Abel, and the death of Abel. Gen 4:25 adds that God then gave Adam another (new) seed with the birth of Seth. Of Seth's progeny, only Enosh is mentioned; he was the first to call upon the name of Yahweh (4:26). J goes on in Gen 6:1–8 to relate the intercourse between the sons of God and the daughters of men resulting in the birth of the gigantic Nephilim, prompting God's decision to destroy by flood all humankind apart from Noah. Thus, both Pentateuchal sources seem to attribute an important position to Seth. Likewise, the ancients, who knew nothing of modern biblical criticism, were quick to grasp this importance, as well as to notice certain discrepancies in the biblical account.

Extrabiblical Jewish Traditions about Seth

A number of ancient biblical translations are aware of the difference between the two Genesis genealogies, one beginning with Cain (Gen 4:17–24) and the other beginning with Seth (Gen 5:3–32), and tend to regard the Sethite genealogy as the only legitimate one.[3] Although reporting the birth of Cain at 4:1 and rendering the Hebrew text of Gen 4:25 literally with σπέρμα

---

3. Klijn, *Seth*, 4–5.

ἕτερον ("another seed"), the Septuagint (Old Greek) translation of Genesis omits the word "again" (עוד) found in the Hebrew text of 4:25, perhaps implying that Adam and Eve had no intercourse before the birth of Seth. *Targum Pseudo-Jonathan* 5:1–3 seems to regard the genealogy of Seth as the only true one, since it considers Cain to be a son, not of Adam, but of Samael, the angel of death:

> And Adam was aware that his wife had conceived from Samael the angel, and she became pregnant and bore Cain, and he was like those on high, not like those below; and she said, "I have acquired a man, the angel of the Lord." And she went on to bear from Adam, her husband, the twin sister and Abel. And Abel was a keeper of sheep, but Cain was a man working in the earth.[4]

Again, according to certain passages of *Midrash Genesis Rabbah*, Cain and Abel were really sons of the devil, and Seth was the only true son of Adam.[5] In the *Pirqe de Rabbi Eliezer* it is further maintained that Samael was joined to Eve, who then conceived Cain, the father of a wicked race.[6] Rabbi Simeon says that "from Seth were born and descended all the generations of the just; from Cain were born and descended all the generations of the wicked."[7] Cain's progeny are the licentious "daughters of men"

---

4. Translated by Bowker, *Targums and Rabbinic Literature*, 132. Cf. Klijn, *Seth*, 3–4. For other testimonies to this tradition of the origin of Cain, see *2 Enoch* 31:6; *b. Yebam.* 103b; *b. 'Abod. Zar.* 22b; *b. Šabb.* 146a; *Zohar* 3.76b; John 8:44; and 1 John 3:12. Cf. Pearson, "Figure of Norea," 143–52, esp. pp. 149, 151; and idem, "Figure of Seth," 478–79. On Samael in Jewish tradition and Gnosticism see, e.g., Pearson, "Jewish Haggadic Traditions," 467.

5. *Gen. Rab.* 24.6: "Rabbi Simon said: 'In the 130 years since Eve separated from Adam, male spirits became passionate for her, and she generated from them; female spirits became passionate for Adam, and generated from him.'"

6. In *Pirqe R. El.* 21–22 it is stated explicitly, with reference to Gen 5:3, that Cain is not the seed of Adam, neither in his likeness nor in his image. It is therefore not surprising that the generation of Cain has been identified by some (see Klijn, *Seth*, 9, about Rabbi Meir, *Pirqe R. El.* 22) with an immoral generation or by others with the "daughters of men" of Gen 6:2, who had (sexual) relations with the "sons of God" of Gen 6:1; see Alexander, "Targumim," 60–71. As for Samael (the etymology of which is disputed; see Klijn, *Seth*, 3, n. 6), he appears in various Jewish, Christian, and Gnostic apocrypha (see Bullard, *Hypostasis of the Archons*, 52–54). This figure, who, according to *Ps.-Jon.* Gen 3:6, was the angel of death and, according to *Gen. Rab.* 10.110, was the leader of all the devils, was to become from the third century C.E. "the main figure in Jewish demonology, both Rabbinic and Cabalistic, who embodies all previous demonological traditions" (Barc, "Samaël," 136). Extensive citation of traditions stemming from Gen 6:1–2 drawn from *1 Enoch*, Zosimos, and Berossos is offered by George Syncellus, *Chronographia*, in Dindorf, ed., *Georgius Syncellus et Nicephorus*, 16–28.

7. *Pirqe R. El.* 22; see Klijn, *Seth*, 8.

of Gen 6:2 who mixed sexually with the angelic "sons of God,"
elsewhere called the Watchers (ἐγρήγοροι). Seth is the progenitor,
not only of righteous humanity, but even of the Messiah.[8] A similar conception seems to underlie *1 Enoch* 85–90, the so-called
Animal Apocalypse. This text describes a vision in which Enoch
sees the entire sweep of history from the time of creation to the
coming of the Messiah. In symbolism typical of the apocalyptic
genre, animals represent humans. In the antediluvian period, Seth
is described as a white bull and the people of Israel as a nation
of white bulls, and the Messiah too is a white bull. But the rest
of humanity is symbolically represented as a collection of black
oxen,[9] suggesting that Seth is the father of the chosen race and,
ultimately, of the Messiah.[10] All this puts Seth and his progeny in
a privileged position.

Elsewhere Seth is considered to have had special knowledge of
the events preceding the expulsion of Adam from paradise. This
is what the pseudepigraphical *Books of Adam and Eve* tell us,
although, according to these texts, this knowledge was not immediately transmitted to Seth's generation, but was preserved for
his later posterity.[11] Seth functions here only as a secondary recipient and transmitter of revelations originally received by Adam
(and Eve).[12] Seth had been primordially enlightened through the
receipt of secrets concerning the future course of history revealed
to Adam after Adam had eaten of the tree of knowledge. According to the *Apocalypse of Moses,* the Greek version of the *Books
of Adam and Eve,* Eve had also related to Seth her vision of the
throne or chariot of God drawn by four radiant eagles.[13] This
vision is based upon Ezekiel's (chap. 1) vision of the four living

---

8. *Midrash Gen. Rab.* XII, 5; cf. the Sethian genealogy of Jesus in Luke 3:23–38.

9. *1 Enoch* 85:8–10: "After that, she bore two snow-white cows, and, after it, she
bore many more cows as well as dark heifers. I also saw in my sleep that snow-white
bull, and he grew big likewise and became a great snow-white bull, and there proceeded
forth from him many white cows which resembled him. Then they began to give birth to
many snow-white cows which resembled them, each one following many others" (trans.
E. Isaac, *OTP* 1.63).

10. Pearson, "Figure of Seth," 491.

11. *Vita Adam et Evae* (the Latin version of the *Books of Adam and Eve*) 49–51, esp.
51:3. Cf. Klijn, *Seth,* 16–18; see also Stone, "Report on Seth Traditions," 2.468–69.

12. Nickelsburg, "Some Related Traditions," 2.539.

13. *Apocalypse of Moses* 33. Perhaps these four radiant beings were the inspiration of
the Sethian doctrine of the four Luminaries.

creatures and certain wheels that bore up a crystalline firmament, above which was enthroned a being in the form of a human, at which point Ezekiel is addressed by the divine voice.[14] In the Latin *Vita Adam et Evae,* chaps. 49–51, after the death of Adam, Eve prophesies a coming judgment by water and fire, and Seth (with his siblings) is instructed to preserve for posterity the details of her and Adam's life on tablets made of stone (safe from the flood) and brick (safe from the conflagration). A similar tradition is related by Josephus, according to which the progeny of Seth, having lived righteously for seven generations after which they fell into a life of depravity, inscribed their astronomical and cosmological discoveries on two steles, one of brick to survive destruction by fire, and the other of stone to survive destruction by flood (*Ant.* 1.67–71). Josephus then reports that the stone stele still survives "in the land of Seiris" (κατὰ γῆν τὴν Σειρίδα).[15] Also in connection with Seth as a transmitter of secret knowledge to his posterity, one notes that recently published materials from Qumran Cave 4 contain fragments of a "Vision of the Haguy" (or Hagoy, חזון ההגוי), a "Book of Memory" (ספר זכרון) consisting of certain "mysteries of what we shall be" (רז נהיה). As in Gnostic sources, Seth functions as recipient and transmitter of revelations reserved for an elite:[16]

> For the law (מחוקק) is etched by God for all [. . .] sons of Seth. And the Book of Memory (זכרון) is inscribed before him (God) for those who observe his word. And it is the vision of the meditation (ההגוי), as a Book of Memory. And he [Seth?] bequeathed it to Enosh with the people of the spirit [or: bequeathed his spirit to the weak of the people] because he created it as a sacred blueprint (תבנית). But meditation (הגוי) had not as yet been entrusted to the spirit of flesh since it had as yet not known the distinction between good and evil. (4Q417 2 i 15–18)[17]

---

14. Perhaps this was the basis for the divine revelation, "Man exists and the Son of Man," uttered by a voice on high to the chief archon in several Sethian texts; see *Ap. John* NHC II,*1:* 14,13–18; BG 47,14–20; *Gos. Eg.* NHC III,*2:* 59,1–3.

15. See Pearson's discussion in "Figure of Seth," 493; the "land of Seiris" is probably Egypt, but other testimonies refer to Mount Sir (the Ararat of Gen 8:4; the Mount Nisir of the Babylonian Gilgamesh epic [*ANET* 2, 94, tab. XI, 140]). Cf. esp. *Hyp. Arch.* 92, 14.

16. See section below on "Seth as Recipient and Transmitter of Divine Revelation."

17. Wacholder and Abegg, eds., *Preliminary Edition,* xiii. The *Damascus Document* (10.6; 13.2) specifies that every judge must be expert in the Book of Hago; elsewhere, it is required study for every youth (1QSa 1:7), to be studied during a third of the evening throughout the year (1QS 6:7).

Echoes of these traditions recur in the realm of Hellenistic Judaism. Commenting on Gen 4:17–25 in *On the Posterity and Exile of Cain,* Philo of Alexandria touches upon the nature of Seth and the generation that follows him. From Cain only the wicked could have descended. Therefore all Seth's descendants are the seed (σπέρμα) of virtue.[18] Philo allegorizes Seth's name as the "watering," ποτισμός (a play on Heb. שת, "Seth," and a derivative of שתה, "to drink"), of the soul by the sweet stream of wisdom (σοφία);[19] although no baptismal or other ritual reference is detectable here, this reference may point to a tradition in which Seth was identified as the bearer of a divine wisdom portrayed with aquatic metaphors.[20] He is the "seed of human virtue," sown by God.[21] Thus the descendants of Seth are not confined only to the antediluvian period, but in fact are to be found among the whole of humanity. This interpretation seems in some way to anticipate, even if on a purely ethical level, the Gnostic proclivity to assign a higher spiritual status to those human beings who belong to the progeny or "seed" of Seth. Such an interpretation of the "other seed" of Gen 4:25 occurs only in Jewish and Gnostic sources.

The Gnostic Appropriation of Seth

Why did the Gnostics settle on Seth, of all the biblical heroes, as the symbol of their identity and lineage, their link to the past, their source of enlightenment, and the ground of their hope? Why not Adam or Enoch, Noah or Moses, all of whom captured the imagination of later Judaism, and, unlike Seth, received extensive treatment in postbiblical didactic and revelatory literature? Adam was the original parent of humankind, formed in the image of God. Enoch, placed in Eden (from which all humankind since Adam and Eve were expelled, and which escaped the flood in

---

18. *Post. Caini* 42.

19. *Post. Caini* 125–26 (cf. 10; 170).

20. Wisdom is a fountain, spring, or river (cf. Sir 15:3; 24:30; Philo, *Fuga* 97, 195; Philo, *Somn.* 2.242), and is equated with the living water of which God is the source (compare Prov 14:27; 16:22; Cant 4:15; and Bar 3:12 with Jer 2:13; 17:13 [LXX]; John 4:10; 7:38; and *Odes Sol.* 11:5–9; 30:1–6).

21. *Post. Caini* 173; see Kraft, "Philo on Seth," 2.457–58.

order that Enoch might testify against human wickedness), was reputed to be the first to learn writing, knowledge, and wisdom, and to record and systematize astronomy (*Jub.* 4:16–25). The righteous Noah obediently preserved a remnant of the human stock from the same world catastrophe. Moses was the quintessential prophet, who led Israel from servitude and mediated to her the wisdom of God's greatest gift, the Torah.

Despite the high status enjoyed by all of these figures in early Judaism, we find Gnostic sources rejecting the Mosaic teaching ("Not as Moses said"; *Ap. John* II,1: 13,19–20; 22,22; 23,3; 26,6), and the name of Enoch is hardly mentioned in them. On the other hand, the figure of Adam occurs repeatedly in Gnostic sources as the heavenly prototypical human being (Adamas), in whose image the earthly Adam is produced. The heavenly Adam functions as a subordinate being in the protological stage of the great Gnostic cosmologies, where he does little else than request a son to be the father of the incorruptible race. The earthly Adam, however, is the central focus of the Gnostic anthropogony. Yet he is portrayed as a haplessly automated lump of clay in the hands of a half-witted and jealous demiurge who botches his attempt to construct an earthly copy of the heavenly Adam. The earthly Adam's only distinction is that he responds positively to certain saving initiatives from the divine world, usually mediated to him by his enlightened wife Eve, in order that he and Eve might bring into the world the true father of the Gnostic race, Seth. Perhaps most significant, while Seth is the father of a unique segment of righteous humanity, Adam could be viewed as the father of all humanity, both righteous and wicked.

One might hypothesize that in Gnostic eyes, what distinguished most traditional biblical heroes from Seth was their apparent servitude to the creator God of traditional Judaism, whom many Gnostics viewed as the bungling, if not malevolent, source of a defective human condition. Perhaps Gnostics would have viewed figures like Enoch, whom Genesis connected with the building of a city (4:17) and with walking closely with God (5:21–24; cf. Sir 44:16), and whom Jewish tradition also associated with the advent of the arts and sciences (see, e.g., the astronomical treatise of *1 Enoch* 72–82), as encouraging the corrupt ease and luxury of a lazy, indulgent, even wicked and materialistic human race.[22] The fact that not Seth, but Enosh, Seth's son, was among the first to call upon the name of Yahweh (Gen 4:26),[23] implied that the same might be true also for the rest of Seth's antediluvian progeny; although they did not mix with the immoral race of Cain, their common invocation of the creator God, considered by Gnostics as a being less than the supreme deity, would be a blemish on their claim to authentic divine sonship. Seth, however, stands as a solitary figure between, and untouched by, the murderous materialism of Cain and the homicidal giants who became dominant at the time of the flood.

It will be seen that almost the entirety of the Gnostic picture of Seth is based on Jewish interpretations of biblical traditions about him. It seems that Seth, who plays a rather minor role in surviving Jewish literature, offered Gnostics a fresh and distinctive figure illustrative of ideal humanity, a figure free from associations with the biblical creator God. Born in the true image of God, Seth could qualify as a figure to whom no one could impute any direct responsibility for the behavior of a promiscuous and materialistic human mainstream from which the Gnostics wished to separate themselves.

Sources Treating the Gnostic Seth

During the period 175–475 C.E., several early Christian authors produced antiheretical writings in which they refer to Gnostic groups that they call "Sethian": Irenaeus of Lyons (*Haer.* 1.30); Hippolytus of Rome (preserved in Pseudo-Tertullian, *Haer.* 2); Filastrius of Brescia (*Haer.* 3); Theodoret of Cyrrhus (*Haer.* 1.14); and Epiphanius of Salamis (*Haer.* 26; 39–40). Apart from these references, we have no record of any group, Gnostic or otherwise, who called themselves "Sethians." On the other hand, when one consults the large collection of original Gnostic sources contained

---

22. See the interpretation of Gen 6:1–4 in the *Apocryphon of John* (NHC II,1: 29,16–30,11).

23. In nearly all rabbinic exegesis of Gen 4:26, "it was begun [from חלל] to call upon the name" is rendered "the name was profaned [also from חלל]," and the name Enosh (or "human"; אנוש) was often equated with imperfection (אנש, "weak"), suggesting that decline and idolatry began after Seth. See the essay on Enosh in this volume.

in the Coptic Gnostic library from Nag Hammadi, dating from about 350 C.E., one finds many treatises that refer to a special segment of humanity called "the great generation," "strangers," "the immovable, incorruptible race," "the seed of Seth," "the living and unshakable race," "the children of Seth," "the holy seed of Seth," and "those who are worthy." It happens that the terms "generation," "race," "seed," and "strangers" are all plays on the tradition of Seth's birth as "another seed" (σπέρμα ἕτερον) in Gen 4:25. Hans-Martin Schenke was the first to delineate those works that current scholarship considers to be representative of "Sethian" Gnosticism:[24]

1. the report on the "Sethoitae" by Pseudo-Tertullian, *Haer.* 2 (based on Hippolytus's lost *Syntagma*);

2. the "Barbeloite" report of Irenaeus (*Haer.* 1.29); perhaps also a digest of certain "others" (*alii*) in *Haer.* 1.30 (identified as Sethians/Ophites by Theodoret, *Haer.* 1.14);

3. the reports on the Sethians and Archontics by Epiphanius (*Haer.* 26; 39–40), Pseudo-Tertullian (*Haer.* 2), and Filastrius (*Haer.* 3);

4. the untitled text from the Bruce Codex (Bruce, *Untitled*); and

5. fourteen treatises from the Nag Hammadi Codices (NHC) and Berlin Gnostic Codex (BG 8502):[25]

> *The Apocryphon of John* (*Ap. John*, four copies in two versions: short [BG 8502,2; NHC III,1]; long [NHC II,1; NHC IV,1]);
>
> *The Hypostasis of the Archons* (*Hyp. Arch.*: NHC II,4);
>
> *The Gospel of the Egyptians* (*Gos. Eg.*: NHC III,2; NHC IV,2);
>
> *The Apocalypse of Adam* (*Apoc. Adam*: NHC V,5);
>
> *The Three Steles of Seth* (*Steles Seth*: NHC VII,5);
>
> *Zostrianos* (*Zost.*: NHC VIII,1);
>
> *Marsanes* (*Marsanes*: NHC X,1);
>
> *Melchizedek* (*Melch.*: NHC IX,1);

---

24. Schenke, "Sethianische System," 165–73; idem, "Phenomenon and Significance," 2.588–616.

25. See the English translations of these texts in *The Nag Hammadi Library in English* (ed. Robinson and Meyer). For critical editions of the Coptic texts, see the volumes of *The Coptic Gnostic Library: Edited with English Translation, Introduction, and Notes* (Robinson, ed.; NHS 4, 11, 13, 15, 21, and 28; cited in the bibliography). Photographic reproductions of the papyrus pages of all the codices appear in *The Facsimile Edition of the Nag Hammadi Codices.*

The Thought of Norea (Norea: NHC IX,2);

Allogenes (*Allogenes:* NHC XI,3); and

The Trimorphic Protennoia (*Trim. Prot.:* NHC XIII,1)

Within the original Gnostic texts listed under headings 4 and 5, there is no direct mention of Seth in the *Thought of Norea,* the *Trimorphic Protennoia, Allogenes, Marsanes,* or Bruce, *Untitled* (which, like *Zostrianos,* contains the name "Setheus"), and but a single mention of the "children of Seth" in *Melchizedek.* Although the name Seth occurs in the titles of two Nag Hammadi treatises, the *Second Treatise of the Great Seth* and the *Three Steles of Seth,* Seth is mentioned in the body of the latter only. This leaves the *Apocalypse of Adam,* the *Hypostasis of the Archons,* the *Gospel of the Egyptians,* the *Apocryphon of John,* the *Three Steles of Seth,* and *Zostrianos* as the most important of the original "Sethian" works that actually deal with the figure of Seth.

Seth in Patristic Sources

Among the patristic testimonies[26] to groups honoring Seth, Pseudo-Tertullian, though omitting mention of Adam and Eve, reports that the "Sethoitae" believed that Cain and Abel were the offspring of two different groups of angels; that after the death of Abel, the "Mother" wanted Seth to be conceived and born; and finally that Christ was virtually identical with Seth.

In *Haer.* 1.29, Irenaeus describes the theology of the "Barbeloites," almost all of which reappears in the Coptic Sethian treatises. Then, as if dealing with a distinct group, he continues in *Haer.* 1.30 with certain "other" Gnostics, identified by Theodoret of Cyrrhus as "Sethians whom some call Ophites or Ophians" (*Haer.* 1.14). They held Seth to have been born from the providence of Prunikos and his sister Norea; Norea and Seth subsequently became the parents of the rest of humanity.

---

26. The earliest important patristic testimonies are Irenaeus's *Adversus Haereses* (ca. 175 c.e.) and the lost *Syntagma* of Hippolytus (ca. 210), on both of which are based the writings of Pseudo-Tertullian (225–50), Filastrius of Brescia (380/90), and Theodoret of Cyrrhus (ca. 453).

Epiphanius's report on the Sethians seems based on Pseudo-Tertullian, although he thought he had personally encountered them in Egypt. He refers to seven of their books under the name of Seth, others under those of Abraham and Moses, and still others called *Allogeneis* (*Haer.* 39.1.3). As for their doctrine, Epiphanius says that the Sethians, who are found everywhere, claim descent from Seth, whom they hold to be identical with Christ, or at least to be the one from whom Christ descended "by seed and lineage" (*Haer.* 39.3.5). After the death of Abel, the birth of Seth at the behest of the "Mother" on high put an end to the struggle that broke out among the wicked angels at the birth of Cain and Abel; she implanted in Seth a seed from the power above, which ensured the rise of a righteous and chosen race through which the angels and other humans could be purified. So too Seth's wife Horaia (= Norea/Na'amah) was produced as a spiritual power in her own right.[27] Then the Mother destroyed the wicked race of Cain through the flood, and even though the angels ensured the promulgation of the antediluvian wickedness of the Cainites by sneaking Ham aboard the ark, she saw to the preservation of the righteous race of Seth. Epiphanius also describes, besides the Sethians, two other obviously related groups: (1) the Archontics, who also possessed books in the name of Seth and his seven sons, the "Allogeneis" (*Haer.* 40); and (2) certain licentious "Gnostics" (*Haer.* 26).[28] Of Palestinian provenance, the Archontics count Cain and Abel as the offspring of Eve and the devil; Adam and Eve's only true son is Seth, called Allogenes, who was taken above and returned to earth endowed with spiritual power, making him invisible and thus invulnerable to the hostile world-creator.

Seth in the Coptic Gnostic Treatises from Nag Hammadi

When we turn to the original Coptic Gnostic sources mentioned above, it becomes clear that we are dealing with essentially the

---

27. On Norea (the biblical Na'amah; cf. Gen 4:22), see Pearson, "Figure of Norea"; and idem, "Revisiting Norea," 265–75.

28. Tardieu, "Livres," 206, argues, probably correctly, that these three movements described by Epiphanius in *Haer.* 26, 39, and 40 are one and the same.

same cluster of traditions about Seth as found in the testimonies of the early church writers. Gnostic literature distinguishes two aspects of Seth: (1) the heavenly Seth, an ideal or transcendental prototype of the earthly figure; and (2) Seth as manifested on the earth. In dealing with the earthly Seth, we will follow the approach of Birger Pearson,[29] who presents a picture of Seth that arises from the four most important facts about his life discussed in the sources. These are the birth of Seth, and his three most important roles: (1) father of the elite race of Gnostics; (2) recipient and transmitter of a divine revelation reserved for this elite; and (3) savior of this progeny and perhaps of humankind in general.

The Heavenly Seth

An essential aspect of Gnostic reflection on Seth has to do with spelling out the ramifications of Seth's status as the likeness and image (Gen 5:3) of his father Adam, who was the image and likeness of God (Gen 1:26). In the Gnostic view, as in that of a Hellenistic Jew like Philo of Alexandria, the protology of Genesis occurs on two planes, the heavenly (the creation according to Gen 1:1–2:3) and the earthly (the creation according to Gen 2:4ff.). The first creation story tells of the creation of an intelligible world whose contents form the prototypes for the creation of its perceptible counterpart in the second account. Thus, for the Gnostics, there are two creative divinities, the supreme deity as ultimate source of the transcendent heavenly world (the equivalent of the Platonic realm of the ideal archetypes), and his lowly counterpart, the archon who creates the lower phenomenal world (consisting of its psychic, or animated/emotional, and its material or inanimate dimensions) as a copy of the heavenly world. Likewise, there are two "wisdom" figures, the Mother on high, consort of the supreme deity, and the lower mother, usually called Sophia, who mistakenly gives birth to the lower creator Yaldabaoth. So also there is the heavenly Adam, called Adamas or Pigeradamas, and his earthly copy Adam, shaped by the archon; a heavenly Eve, called Zoe or the Epinoia of light, and the earthly Eve produced from Adam's side by the archon; and a heavenly

---

29. "Figure of Seth," 478–500.

Seth ("the great Seth"), whose earthly image was produced by
the earthly Adam and Eve once they had been enlightened by
the Mother on high. Thus Gen 1:26 ("Let us create man/Adam
in our image, according to our likeness") could be construed to
mean that the high deity must be the absolute Human ("Man");
his offspring, the heavenly Adamas, would be the Son of Man;
and Adamas's son would be "the son of the Son of Man," or the
like. While the Sethian treatises refer to the supreme deity and
Adamas, his son, as "Man and the Son of Man" (*Ap. John* NHC
II,*1:* 14,14–15), the term "son of the Son of Man" occurs only in
a treatise not usually reckoned among the Gnostic Sethian works,
Eugnostos the Blessed (NHC III,*3:* 85,9–14), where it is probably
a designation for Seth.[30]

Compare the following passage from the *Gospel of the Egyptians* (NHC III,*2:* 51,5–22):

> The incorruptible man Adamas asked from them a son out of himself, in
> order that he [the son] may become father of the immovable, incorruptible
> race, so that, through it [the race], the silence and the voice may appear,
> and, through it, the dead aeon may raise itself, so that it may dissolve. And
> thus there came forth, from above, the power of the great light Prophania.
> She gave birth to the four great Luminaries; Harmozel, Oroiael, Davithe,
> Eleleth, and the great incorruptible Seth, the son of the incorruptible man
> Adamas.

Subsequently, Adamas is installed in the first Luminary Harmozel,
Seth in the second Luminary Oroiael, Seth's seed (Enosh through
Lamech?) in the third Luminary Davithe, and such of subsequent humankind as makes common cause with the righteous
progeny of Seth, in the fourth Luminary Eleleth. These spiritual
denizens of the four Luminaries are the heavenly counterparts of
the earthly offspring of Seth and their associates.

As the son of Adamas (*Zostrianos,* NHC VIII,*1:* 6,25–26;
30,9–10; 51,14; in the *Three Steles of Seth* VII,*5:* 118,25–27
Seth calls Pigeradamas his father), it is this heavenly Seth who
is referred to by names like Emmacha Seth (the *Three Steles
of Seth,* NHC VII,*5:* 118,27), Seth Emmacha Seth (*Zostrianos,*
NHC VIII,*1:* 6,25; 51,14–15), and "the thrice male Child, Telmael Telmael (H)eli (H)eli Machar Machar Seth" (the *Gospel of*

---

30. See Parrott, "Religious Syncretism," 175–80; and idem, "Introduction," in *Nag
Hammadi Codices III,3–4 and V,1*, 11–12.

the Egyptians, NHC III,2: 62,2–4; cf. 65,8–9; IV,2: 77,2–4; and 59,16–21, where he also seems to be identified with "the great Christ"). In accord with the testimony of Epiphanius that Seth and his seven sons could be called *Allogene[i]s* ("stranger[s]"), the treatise *Allogenes,* dictated to Allogenes and deposited on a mountain as "the seal of all the books of Allogenes" (NHC XI,3: 69,16–20), might also be understood as a revelation to Seth, which he recounts to his "son" Messos.[31]

The Earthly Seth

The Birth of Seth. The Gnostic accounts of the birth of the earthly Seth are restatements of biblical traditions about the origins of Eve's children in Genesis 4 and 5, exegetically similar to those of the Jewish interpreters cited above. The *Hypostasis of the Archons* (NHC II,4: 91,11–14) mentions the birth of Cain to Eve and the archons (Cain is "their" son by the rape of Eve [89,18–20]) and of Abel to Adam and Eve. By Adam, Eve conceives Seth as "[another] man ... in place [of Abel]" (91,30–33, a pastiche of Gen 4:1 and 25). Here, the biblical σπέρμα ἕτερον of Gen 4:25 is not taken to imply the rise of a special race descended from Seth; instead, as Pearson points out, it is Norea, Seth's sister, who is appointed as a virginal (in contrast to the defiled Eve) "helper" (βοήθεια, Gen 2:18) for the salvation of future humanity.

The longer version of the *Apocryphon of John* (NHC II,1: 24,18–26) relates the birth of Cain and Abel as the result of Eve's seduction by the chief archon, the creator Yaldabaoth. Not the true children of Adam and Eve, it is through them that future humanity is cursed with sexual procreation and promiscuity. Whereas they are born from the mere material likeness of Eve, the true heavenly Eve (the Epinoia of light sent below by the Mother on high) bears Seth to the earthly Adam as the likeness (cf. εἰκών in Gen 5:3) of the Son of Man, that is, of the heavenly Adam (Pigeradamas), after whom the earthly Adam was copied by the archons. Upon the birth of Seth, the Mother again sends him her

---

31. Schenke ("Bemerkungen," 417–24) identifies this Messos ("mediator") with Moses, the postdiluvian recipient of Allogenes' (= Seth's) antediluvian visions of the transcendental world, on analogy with Philo's interpretation of Moses' ascent of Mount Sinai as his contemplative vision of the world of the Platonic forms. Cf. Exod 25:9, 40; 2 *Apoc. Bar.* 4:5; Heb 8:5.

spirit by which she will prepare and install Seth in a special heavenly dwelling, perhaps the four Luminaries, for the preservation of him and his seed (NHC II,*1*: 24,24–25,16). Thus, as in the patristic sources, the birth of Seth is caused by the Mother on high, usually depicted as the consort of the supreme deity, while that of Cain and Abel is caused by mere lust, whether that of the earthly Adam and Eve, or that of the jealous archon, creator of the material world and of the earthly Adam.

The *Gospel of the Egyptians,* which describes the production only of the heavenly Seth, associates his earthly appearance not with his birth from Adam and Eve, but with the heavenly Seth's manifestation in the form of a "logos-begotten body prepared for himself secretly through the virgin." This body seems to be that of Jesus, whom he "puts on." He then defeats ("nails") the powers of the thirteen aeons and confers upon his seed a baptism, the Five Seals, as the means of their ultimate salvific enlightenment (*Gos. Eg.* III,*2*: 62,24–64,9).[32]

Seth as the Father of the Gnostic Race. G. W. MacRae claimed that the doctrine of Seth as the father of the Gnostic race is "the fixed point of what may be called Sethian Gnosticism."[33] In a passage quoted above (*Gos. Eg.* III,*2*: 51,5–22), the heavenly Adamas requests a son, in order that the son might become father of the immovable, incorruptible race, whereupon Seth and his seed appear and are placed in the second and third Luminaries. Seth's seed is then sown into the created aeons (III,*2*: 60,9–11):

> Then the great Seth came and brought his seed. And it was sown in the aeons which had been brought forth, their number being the amount of Sodom. Some say that Sodom is the place of pasture of the great Seth, which is Gomorrah. But others [say] that the great Seth took his plant out of Gomorrah and planted it in the second place to which he gave the name Sodom.[34] This is the race which came forth through Edokla. For she

---

32. One notes here what may be allusions to Christ's virgin birth, his baptism in the Jordan, and his nailing to the cross. Cf. *Trim. Prot.* XIII,*1*: 50,12–20, where Protennoia "puts on Jesus." As Pearson notes ("Figure of Seth," 497, n. 88), the role of Seth has been bypassed, since it is the heavenly Mother herself who puts on Jesus without manifesting herself as Seth.

33. MacRae, "Seth," 21–22.

34. The word "plant" (Coptic *toce*) may be a Hebrew pun on the name of Seth (שֵׁת) in Gen 4:25, where שָׁת־לִי ("[God] has appointed for me") is related to the word שָׁתִיל, "plant," "shoot," or "branch" (so Klijn, *Seth,* 34, referring to the Syriac *Book of the Bee* XVII and XXX). To judge from *Gos. Eg.* NHC III,*2*: 56,4–12; 60,9–18 and NHC

gave birth through the word to Truth and Justice, the origin of the seed of the eternal life which is with those who will persevere because of the knowledge of their emanation. This is the great, incorruptible race which has come forth through three worlds to the world. And the flood came as an example for the consummation of the aeon. But it will be sent into the world because of this race. A conflagration will come upon the earth. And grace will be with those who belong to the race through the prophets and the guardians who guard the life of the race. Because of this race famines will occur and plagues. But these things will happen because of the great, incorruptible race. Because of this race temptations will come, a falsehood of false prophets.

A similar account of the transcendent origin of Seth and his seed (which, however, is instead called "the immovable race") is present in the *Apocryphon of John,* where they are installed respectively in the second and third Luminaries (NHC II,*1:* 9,11–24). In the *Three Steles of Seth,* Seth is the "Father of the living and unshakable race" (VII,*5:* 118,12–13; cf. 120,8–10). *Zostrianos* also mentions "the sons of Seth" (7,8–9), the "living seed," and "holy seed of Seth" (30,10–14; 130,16–17).

As in the *Gospel of the Egyptians,* in the *Apocalypse of Adam* Adam reveals the future to his son Seth: "I myself have called you by the name [i.e., Seth] of that man who is the seed [cf. σπέρμα ἕτερον of Gen 4:25] of the great generation," that is, the Gnostics. The *Apocalypse of Adam* goes on to reveal a history of the race of Seth from its origins through its survival of flood and fire until the final coming of the Illuminator, no doubt in the form of Seth himself.[35] A somewhat similar salvational history is found in Epiphanius's description of the Sethians cited above; these should be compared with the passage in *1 Enoch* 85:8–10 cited above (n. 9).

Seth as Recipient and Transmitter of Divine Revelation to the Gnostic Race. The *Apocalypse of Adam* is a good example of how Gnostic reflections on Seth are based on traditions like those of so much Jewish apocryphal literature, in which Seth appears as

---

IV,2: 71,18–30, Gomorrah seems to refer to the heavenly place and source of Seth's seed (perhaps in the Light Daveithai) born from Plesithea, and Sodom to the earthly place of Seth's seed created by the angel Hormos through mortal virgins.

35. The *Apocalypse of Adam* has the same testamentary genre as the *Books of Adam and Eve* and the *Apocalypse of Moses.* See Perkins, "Apocalyptic Schematization," 591–95; Nickelsburg, "Some Related Traditions," 2.539; and Stone, "Report on Seth Traditions," 2.459–71.

the repository (but not yet the revealer) of esoteric knowledge. Like the *Books of Adam and Eve* and the *Testament of Adam,* the *Apocalypse of Adam* is a testamentary speech of Adam, just before his death, to his son Seth. As in the *Books of Adam and Eve,* Adam tells of his and Eve's experience in paradise, as well as of a vision he had received of the future of the chosen race, the impending destructions by flood and fire, and the coming of the Illuminator. Seth is said to have taught his seed these reve-lations of Adam, written by angels and left on a high mountain; they constitute a holy baptism (*Apoc. Adam* V,5: 85,10–31).

The *Gospel of the Egyptians* claims itself to have been written by the divine Seth himself (NHC III,2: 68,10–69,5):

> The great Seth wrote this book with letters in one hundred and thirty years. He placed it in the mountain that is called Charaxio,[36] in order that, at the end of the times and eras, by the will of the divine Autogenes and the whole pleroma, through the gift of the untraceable, unthinkable, fatherly love, it may come forth and reveal this incorruptible holy race of the great savior, and those who dwell with them in love, and the great invisible eternal Spirit and his only begotten Son, and the eternal light and his great, incorruptible consort, and the incorruptible Sophia and the Barbelon and the whole pleroma in eternity. Amen.

Likewise, in *Allogenes,* Allogenes writes down the contents of the things he has learned and seen "for the sake of those who will be worthy," deposits the book on a mountain guarded by a "dreadful" guardian, and teaches them to his "son" Messos, who is to proclaim them as the "seal of all the books of Allogenes" (*Allogenes* XI,3: 68,6–69,19).[37] In the *Three Steles of Seth,* the heavenly Seth is claimed as the author of the three steles inscribed with the series of praises that he offered up to the ultimate divine triad of Father (the preexistent supreme deity), Mother (Barbelo), and Son (Autogenes); and Dositheus[38] claims to have read and transmitted the content of these steles to "the elect."[39] At the end of *Zostrianos,* Zostrianos says that he "wrote three wooden

---

36. Perhaps "Mount of the Worthy" (Hebrew הר plus Greek ἄξιοι; cf. Pearson, "Figure of Seth," 495, n. 79).

37. Cf. the testimony of Epiphanius concerning the Sethian (*Haer.* 39.5.1) books of "Allogenes" and the archontic (*Haer.* 40.2.2) books of "Allogeneis." "Seal" (σφραγίς) may here mean something like "authentification" or "final and summary."

38. See Beltz, "Samaritanertum und Gnosis," 89–95.

39. Cf. the traditions of the stone and brick steles recorded by Josephus and the *Vita Adam et Evae,* referred to above.

tablets, and left them as knowledge for those who come after me, the living elect" (*Zost.* VIII,*1:* 130,3–4; cf. *Gos. Eg.* III,*2:* 68,10–23). Pearson[40] surmises that both Allogenes and Zostrianos, as well as the figures of Melchizedek (in the treatise bearing his name) and the Christ of the *Second Treatise of the Great Seth* (in which Seth is not mentioned), are all forms or guises which Seth adopted for his earthly manifestations.

Seth as Savior of the Gnostic Race. Besides transmitting an antediluvian saving revelation to his progeny, Seth also appears at the end of time in various guises for both the judgment of the powers that afflict his seed, and for his seed's immediate enlightenment. Certainly for Gnostics, any figure who reveals saving knowledge is in effect a savior. The Gnostic Sethian treatises divide the history of Seth's salvific activity into four distinct epochs, demarcated by the flood, the conflagration, and the judgment of the powers.

In the *Gospel of the Egyptians,* Seth is clearly identified with the Savior. The place occupied by Seth in the pleromatic hierarchy of this text is not unlike that assigned to him in the *Apocryphon of John,* but the *Gospel of the Egyptians* emphasizes his salvific role to a greater degree. After the initial triad of the Father, Mother/Barbelo, and Son (each of whom has an ogdoad of powers, all of them surrounded by Domedon Doxomedon, an aeon that envelops the world of light) comes the great Christ, the thrice-male child; then come the male virgin Youel and the child of the child Esephech. Then the Logos, the son of the great Christ, appears and generates Mirothoe, who produces the heavenly Adamas of Light. One suspects that the identification of the thrice-male child with Christ may be an instance of secondary Christianization. Both the *Apocryphon of John* and the *Trimorphic Protennoia* include "thrice-male" among the attributes of Barbelo; one wonders whether the thrice-male child and the child of the child might not originally have been a designation of the heavenly Adam and his child Seth. Finally, at Adam's behest, Prophania appears and generates the four Luminaries (Harmozel,

---

40. "Figure of Seth," 495.

Oroiael, Davithe, and Eleleth) and the "great incorruptible Seth, the son of Adamas, the incorruptible man."[41]

Among the events that will mark stages of the Sethian Gnostics' history of salvation, this text specifies those events that pose a threat to the seed of Seth: flood, conflagration, temptations, and false prophets.[42] The great Seth, aware of these dangers to his seed, calls upon the higher powers to give him guardians to protect the ancestry of the elect. Four hundred angels are sent, with the great Seth himself at their head. He endures three *parousiai,* or advents (flood, conflagration, and judgment of the archons), "to save her [the race] who went astray, through the reconciliation [or: "killing"] of the world and the baptism through a Logos-begotten body which the great Seth prepared for himself, secretly through the virgin."[43] Apparently, by the crucifixion of Jesus, Seth defeats the archontic powers of the thirteen aeons and equips his followers with an invincible Gnosis. What is striking is that this Gnosis is conveyed by means of a baptismal rite known as the Five Seals, which Seth, at the behest of the Mother on high, confers upon the Gnostics for their salvation.[44]

The baptism of the Five Seals is a recurrent motif in the Sethian treatises, where it is a form of final enlightenment ultimately provided by the supreme Mother (Barbelo). Of the treatises that identify the one who confers the sacred baptism, only the *Gospel of the Egyptians* actually identifies Seth as the one who confers this rite upon his earthly seed; the *Apocryphon of John* attributes it directly to the Mother appearing in the form of the divine Providence (whom the dialogical frame narrative identifies with Christ!), whereas the *Trimorphic Protennoia,* in which Seth is

---

41. NHC III,2: 51,20ff. = NHC IV,2: 63,15ff., quoted above.

42. NHC III,2: 61,3ff. = NHC IV,2: 72,11ff., quoted above.

43. NHC III,2: 63,8ff. = NHC IV,2: 74,22ff.

44. The term "the Five Seals," usually referring to some kind of baptism, occurs in *Ap. John* II,1: 31,24; IV,1: 49,4; *Gos. Eg.* IV,2: 56,25; 58,6; 58,27–28; 59,27–28; 66,25–26; 74,16; 78,4–5; III,2: 55,12; 63,3; 66,3; the Bruce *Untitled* treatise 32,10 (Schmidt-MacDermot); and *Trim. Prot.* XIII,1: 48,31; 49,27–28; 47,29; 50,9–10. While the Five Seals may originally have referred to a quintuple immersion in "living water," in *Trim. Prot.* (NHC XIII,1: 48,15–35) the Five Seals are interpreted as a five-stage ritual of psychic ascent: the investiture with light of the stripped Spirit; its enthronement; its baptism by Micheus, Michar, and Mnesinous in the spring of Living Water; its glorification with the Fatherhood; and its rapture into the light (perhaps the Four Lights) by the servants of the Four Lights (Kamaliel, [. . .]anen, and Samblo).

never named, attributes it to the Mother appearing in the form
of the Logos. Furthermore, in both the *Trimorphic Protennoia*
and the *Gospel of the Egyptians,* the one who confers the baptism, respectively the Logos and Seth, "puts on" Jesus either to
rescue him from the archons or to use him to defeat the archons.
Whence the association among Seth, Jesus, and the baptism of
the Five Seals?

The solution seems to lie in the recognition that the Sethianism
of the Nag Hammadi treatises is apparently a product of two distinct but not unrelated speculative movements within or on the
fringe of Hellenistic Judaism: (1) that segment of the wisdom tradition that was in conversation with contemporary Platonism,[45]
which seems to be the originating milieu of the "Barbeloite" (as
in Irenaeus, *Haer.* 1.29) speculation on the divine triad (Father,
Mother, Son) and the Sophia responsible for the creation of the
world through her defective, demiurgical son, the archon; and
(2) the more apocalyptically oriented form of speculation on the
traditions concerning the primordial figures of Adam and Seth
that gave rise to the sacred history of the seed of Seth. The first
movement imagined the receipt of revelation as a kind of baptism
in wisdom, conceived as a light or knowledge, and conferred by
the Logos, Voice, or First Thought of the high deity. The second
group, which I might call "Sethites" (in distinction from *Gnostic*
Sethians), conceived of revelation as deriving from certain ancient
records containing the sacred history of the enlightenment of their
primordial ancestors, records which had been brought to light by
a recent reappearance of Seth, the original and chief recipient of
this revelation.

It seems that the link between Seth and baptism stems from
neither Sethite nor Barbeloite mythology, but from the encounter

---

45. Schmidt, *Plotins Stellung;* Boyancé, "Dieu cosmique"; Crahay, "Elements"; Krämer,
Ursprung; Elsas, *Gnostische Weltablehnung;* Sieber, "Introduction to the Tractate Zostri-
anos," 233–40; idem, "Introduction" to *Zostrianos* (NHC VIII,1), *Nag Hammadi Codex
VIII,* 19–25; Tardieu, "Trois stèles de Seth"; Robinson, "*Three Steles of Seth*"; Arm-
strong, "Gnosis and Greek Philosophy"; Pearson, "Tractate Marsanes (NHC X) and the
Platonic Tradition"; idem, "Gnosticism as Platonism"; idem, "Introduction" to *Marsanes*
(NHC X), *Nag Hammadi Codices IX and X,* 244–50; Turner, "Gnostic Threefold Path";
idem, "Sethian Gnosticism"; idem, "Gnosticism and Platonism"; Turner and Wintermute,
"Text, Translation, and Notes"; and Wire, "Introduction" to *Allogenes, Nag Hammadi
Codices XI, XII, and XIII;* and an unpublished paper by Wallis, "Plotinus and the
Gnostics."

of both with Christian speculation. The Barbeloite precursors of the Gnostic Sethians seem to have sustained their initial encounter with Christianity as fellow practitioners of an initiatory baptism, wherein the initiate acquired a new identity. The baptismal rite provided a natural point of contact between these Barbeloites and Christians who likewise viewed their own baptism as a rebirth into a higher mode of existence, and saw the baptism of Jesus as the liminal occasion through which the preexistent savior had inaugurated his revelatory mission in the world, if not the point at which the Son of God had appeared in the world and entered into Jesus (cf. the baptism of Jesus in Mark 1:9–11 par.). Such an encounter seems to have caused the Barbeloites to identify the third member of their Father-Mother-Son triad with the preexistent Christ, and to identify the Mother's final appearance in the world with the descent of the Logos who raised Jesus from the cross, as in the *Trimorphic Protennoia*. Under the influence of the Christian identification of Christ with the Logos, the figure bearing the Five Seals became conceived in the form of Christ. Given this identification, a further encounter between such Christianized Barbeloites and Sethite groups who claimed to be the beneficiaries of revelations received through a recent manifestation of the primordial Seth might have suggested for these Sethites an identification between Seth and the Logos, or even between Seth and the Christ who had descended upon Jesus at his baptism. By an analogy between Christ and Seth as manifestations of the divine image, this figure became naturally conceived also in the form of Seth himself or of Seth in the guise of Christ. This mythology and the rite interpreted by it were only gradually connected with the figure of Seth and the sacred history relating to him. Thus Seth is savior, not only because he is the bearer of a saving revelation, but also by virtue of a special baptism making possible the recipient's visionary ascent into the aeons of the four Luminaries. It is perhaps ironic that, while aspects of Christian baptismal theology may have been a catalyst in the formation of Sethian Gnosticism, the resultant amalgam could proclaim Seth to be the savior, not only of his seed, but of Jesus as well.[46]

---

46. Jesus himself was one of the seed of Seth, according to Luke 3:23–38.

Bibliography

English Translation of the Treatises in the Nag Hammadi Library

Robinson, J. M., and M. W. Meyer, eds. *The Nag Hammadi Library in English.* San Francisco: Harper and Row, 1981.

Critical Editions of the Sethian Gnostic Treatises

Bullard, R. A. *The Hypostasis of the Archons.* Patristische Texte und Studien 10. Berlin: de Gruyter, 1970.

Böhlig, A., and F. Wisse, eds. and trans. *Nag Hammadi Codices III,2 and IV,2: The Gospel of the Egyptians.* NHS 4. Leiden: Brill, 1975.

Krause, M., and P. Labib, eds. and trans. *Die drei Versionen des Apocryphon des Johannes im koptischen Museum zu Alt-Kairo.* Abhandlungen des deutschen archäologischen Instituts Kairo, koptische Reihe 1. Wiesbaden: O. Harrassowitz, 1962.

Layton, B., trans. "The Hypostasis of the Archons." In *Nag Hammadi Codex II,2–7, together with XIII, 2*, Brit. Lib. Or. 4926(1) and P. Oxy. 1, 654, 655.* Vol. 1: *Gospel according to Thomas, Gospel according to Philip, Hypostasis of the Archons, and Indexes.* Ed. B. Layton. NHS 21. Leiden: Brill, 1989.

MacRae, G. W., trans. "The Apocalypse of Adam." In *Nag Hammadi Codices V,2–5 and VI with Papyrus Berolinensis 8502,1 and 4.* Ed. D. M. Parrott. NHS 11. Leiden: Brill, 1979.

Pearson, B. A. "Introduction." In *Nag Hammadi Codices IX and X.* Ed. B. A. Pearson. NHS 15. Leiden: Brill, 1981.

———, trans. "Marsanes." In *Nag Hammadi Codices IX and X.* Ed. B. A. Pearson. NHS 15. Leiden: Brill, 1981.

Pearson, B. A., and S. Giverson, trans. "Melchizedek" and "The Thought of Norea." In *Nag Hammadi Codices IX and X.* Ed. B. A. Pearson. NHS 15. Leiden: Brill, 1981.

Schmidt, C., ed. *The Books of Jeu and the Untitled Text in the Bruce Codex.* Trans. V. MacDermot. NHS 13. Leiden: Brill, 1978.

Turner, J. D., trans. "Trimorphic Protennoia." In *Nag Hammadi Codices XI, XII, and XIII.* Ed. C. W. Hedrick. NHS 28. Leiden: Brill, 1990.

Turner, J. D. "Text, Translation, and Notes." In *Nag Hammadi Codices XI, XII, and XIII.* Ed. C. W. Hedrick. NHS 28. Leiden: Brill, 1990.

Turner, J. D., and O. Wintermute, trans. "Allogenes." In *Nag Hammadi Codices XI, XII, and XIII.* Ed. C. W. Hedrick. NHS 28. Leiden: Brill, 1990.

Wisse, F., and M. Waldstein, eds. *The Apocryphon of John: Synopsis of Nag Hammadi Codices II, 1; III, 1 and IV, 1, with BG 8502, 2.* NHMS 33. Leiden: Brill, 1995.

Patristic Heresiological Commentary on the Sethians

Coxe, A. C., trans. *The Apostolic Fathers with Justin Martyr and Irenaeus: American Edition Chronologically Arranged, with Brief Notes and Preface, Vol. 1.* London: T. & T. Clark, 1885. Reprint, Grand Rapids, Mich.: Eerdmans, 1989. English translation of Irenaeus.

Harvey, W. W., ed. *Irenaeus, Libros quinque adversus haereses.* Cambridge: Academy, 1857. Reprint, Ridgewood, N.J.: Gregg, 1965. Greek text.

Williams, F., trans. *The Panarion of Epiphanius of Salamis, Book 1 (Secs. 1–46).* NHS 35. Leiden: Brill, 1987. English translation.

Books and Articles on the Gnostic Sethian Literature

Barc, B. "Samaël — Saklas — Yaldabaôth. Recherche sur l'origine d'un mythe gnostique." In *Colloque International sur les Textes de Nag Hammadi, Québec, 22–25 Août 1978.* Ed. B. Barc. Bibliothèque Copte de Nag Hammadi, Etudes 1. Quebec: Université Laval; Louvain: Peeters, 1981. Pp. 123–50. Argues that the figure of the ignorant creator Samael originates from the image (Heb. סמל) of jealousy seated at the northern entrance of the heavenly temple in the vision of Ezek 8:3–6.

Layton, B., ed. *The Rediscovery of Gnosticism: Proceedings of the International Conference on Gnosticism at Yale, March 28–31, 1978.* Vol. 2: *Sethian Gnosticism.* Supplements to Numen 41. Leiden: Brill, 1981. An important collection of essays.

Perkins, P. "Apocalyptic Schematization in the Apocalypse of Adam and the Gospel of the Egyptians." In *SBLSP 1972.* Missoula, Mont.: Scholars Press, 1972. Pp. 591–95. Shows that the *Gospel of the Egyptians* and the *Apocalypse of Adam* share a tripartite periodization of revelation similar to that found in the *Books of Adam and Eve* and Josephus, *Ant.* 1.68–70.

Schenke, H.-M. "Bemerkungen zur Apocalypse des Allogenes (NHC XI,3)." In *Coptic Studies: Acts of the Third International Congress of Coptic Studies, Warsaw, 20–25 August 1984.* Ed. W. Godlewski. Centre d'Archaeologie Mediterranéenne de l'Academie Polonaise des Sciences. Warsaw: PWN, 1990. Pp. 417–24. Speculates that *Allogenes* was a revelation granted by Adam to Seth for delivery to Moses; i.e., the phrase "my [Seth's] son Messos" refers to Moses.

———. "The Phenomenon and Significance of Gnostic Sethianism." In Layton, ed., *Rediscovery.* 2.588–616. A complete restatement of the criteria by which certain Gnostic treatises are to be identified.

———. "Das sethianische System nach Nag-hammadi-Handschriften." In *Studia Coptica.* Ed. P. Nagel. Berliner Byzantinische Arbeiten 45. Berlin: Akademie, 1974. Pp. 165–73. Lays out the groundbreaking argument that certain Nag Hammadi treatises belong to a single group of Gnostic sources that contain a common "Sethian system" of mythologoumena.

Stroumsa, G. A. G. *Another Seed: Studies in Gnostic Mythology.* NHS 24. Leiden: Brill, 1984. An excellent thesis on the origins of Sethian mythology as speculation on Judaic traditions in the light of a radical concern with the origin of evil.

Tardieu, M. "Les livres mis sous le nom de Seth et les Séthiens de l'hérésiologie." In *Gnosis and Gnosticism: Papers Read at the Seventh International Conference of Patristic Studies, Oxford, September 8–13, 1975.* Ed. M. Krause. NHS 8. Leiden: Brill, 1977. Pp. 204–10. Argues that the various books of Seth mentioned in Epiphanius's descriptions of the Sethians and Archontics were probably a single work, and disputes H.-M. Schenke's thesis of an entity that can be called Sethian Gnosticism.

Turner, J. D. "The Gnostic Threefold Path to Enlightenment: The Ascent of Mind and the Descent of Wisdom." *NovT* 22 (1980) 324–51. A study of the thematic relationships among various Sethian Gnostic treatises from Nag Hammadi.

———. "Sethian Gnosticism: A Literary History." In *Nag Hammadi, Gnosticism, and Early Christianity.* Ed. C. W. Hedrick and R. Hodgson. Peabody, Mass.: Hendrickson, 1986. Pp. 55–86. A study of literary and historical relationships among various Sethian Gnostic treatises from Nag Hammadi.

Books and Articles on the Gnostic Seth

Klijn, A. F. J. *Seth in Jewish, Christian, and Gnostic Literature.* NovTSup 46. Leiden: Brill, 1977. A nearly exhaustive survey of Jewish, Christian, Gnostic, and Manichaean use of the figure of and traditions relating to Seth.

MacRae, G. W. "Seth in Gnostic Texts and Traditions." In *SBLSP 1977.* Ed. P. K. Achtemeier. Missoula, Mont.: Scholars Press, 1977. Pp. 17–24. A perceptive and pioneering analysis of the Gnostic appropriation of Seth in the Nag Hammadi treatises.

Pearson, B. A. "The Figure of Seth in Gnostic Literature." In Layton, ed., *Rediscovery.* 2.472–504. A magisterial and comprehensive survey of all the instances of the Gnostic literary appropriation of Seth, and the basic model for the present treatment.

Articles on Seth's Wife/Sister Norea

Pearson, B. A. "The Figure of Norea in Gnostic Literature." In *Proceedings of the International Colloquium on Gnosticism, Stockholm, August 20–25, 1973.* Ed. G. Widengren. Kungl. Vitterhets Historie och Antikvitets Akademiens Handlingar, Filologisk-filosofiska serien 17. Stockholm: Almqvist & Wiksell, 1977. Pp. 143–52. A study of the Judaic identity and background of the figure of Na'amah/Norea/Orea/Oraia, the wife/sister of Seth.

———. "Revisiting Norea." In *Images of the Feminine in Gnosticism.* Ed. K. L. King. Studies in Christianity and Antiquity. Philadelphia: Fortress, 1988. Pp. 265–75. An update of Pearson's previous study of the Judaic identity and background of the figure of Na'amah/Norea/Orea/Oraia, the wife/sister of Seth.

Books and Articles Relevant to the Study of Sethian Gnosticism

Beltz, W. "Samaritanertum und Gnosis." In *Gnosis und Neues Testament: Studien aus Religionswissenschaft und Theologie*. Ed. K.-W. Tröger. Berlin: Evangelische Verlagsanstalt, 1973. Pp. 89–95. An investigation into the possibility of Samaria as a setting for the development of Gnostic teachings, with special reference to Simon Magus and the *Three Steles of Seth*.

Parrott, D. M. "Evidence for Religious Syncretism in Gnostic Texts from Nag Hammadi." In *Religious Syncretism: Essays in Conversation with Geo Widengren*. Ed. B. A. Pearson. Missoula, Mont.: Scholars Press, 1975. Pp. 175–80. An examination of the combination of elements from Judaism and Greek philosophy in Gnosticism, with special reference to *Eugnostos the Blessed*.

———. Introduction to and translation of "Eugnostos the Blessed" in *Nag Hammadi Codices III,3–4 and V,1 with Papyrus Berolinensis 8502,3 and Oxyrhynchus Papyrus 1081: Eugnostos and the Sophia of Jesus Christ*. Ed. D. M. Parrott. NHS 27. Leiden: Brill, 1991. Coptic text, English translation, introduction, and notes to *Eugnostos the Blessed*, a Nag Hammadi treatise containing traditions about the heavenly Adam and Seth.

Works Relating to the Interpretation of the Genesis Primordial History

Alexander, P. S. "The Targumim and Early Exegesis of 'Sons of God' in Genesis 6." *JJS* 23 (1972) 60–71. Seeks to show that from the second century on, among Palestinian rabbis, the "Sons of God" of Genesis 6 were identified not as angels, but as certain righteous human beings (though not Sethites).

Bezold, C., ed. and trans. *Die Schatzhöhle*. Leipzig: J. C. Hinrichs, 1883. German translation of the Syriac fifth- to sixth-century *Cave of Treasures* (traditionally ascribed to Mar Ephrem), a legendary history of the primordial Sethite generations.

Bowker, J. *The Targums and Rabbinic Literature: An Introduction to Jewish Interpretations of Scripture*. Cambridge: Cambridge University Press, 1969. English translation and analysis of *Targum Pseudo-Jonathan*, the Aramaic paraphrase of Genesis.

Charlesworth, J. H., ed. *The Old Testament Pseudepigrapha*. 2 vols. Garden City, N.Y.: Doubleday, 1983–85. English translations of pseudepigraphical works relating to the traditions of the Hebrew Bible.

Dindorf, W., ed. *Georgius Syncellus et Nicephorus*. Corpus Scriptorum Historiae Byzantinae 6. Bonn: Weber, 1828. An early-ninth-century chronography offering a wealth of information on Seth drawn from sources antedating the Nag Hammadi Library.

Friedländer, G., trans. *Pirkê de Rabbi Eliezer*. Reprint, New York: Hermon, 1965. German translation of the sayings of Rabbi Eliezer.

Kraft, R. A. "Philo on Seth." In Layton, ed., *Rediscovery*. 2.457–58. Summary of Philo Judaeus's interpretation of the figure of Seth.

Neusner, J., trans. *Genesis Rabbah: The Judaic Commentary on the Book of Genesis, a New American Translation.* 3 vols. BJS 101. Atlanta: Scholars Press, 1985.

Nickelsburg, G. W. E. "Some Related Traditions in the *Apocalypse of Adam, the Books of Adam and Eve,* and *1 Enoch.*" In Layton, ed., *Rediscovery.* 2.514–39. A survey and comparative analysis of the relationships between apocryphal and Gnostic traditions relating to Adam, Eve, and Seth.

Pearson, B. A. "Jewish Haggadic Traditions in the *Testimony of Truth* from Nag Hammadi (CG IX,3)." In *Ex Orbe Religionum: Studia Geo Widengren.* Ed. J. Bergman et al. Supplements to Numen 21. Leiden: Brill, 1972. A study of the Gnostic use of Judaic exegetical techniques as applied to the Genesis protology.

Stone, M. E. "Report on Seth Traditions in the Armenian Adam Books." In Layton, ed., *Rediscovery.* 2.459–71. Information from Armenian sources containing traditions relating to Adam, Eve, and Seth.

Wacholder, B. Z., and M. G. Abegg, eds. *A Preliminary Edition of the Unpublished Dead Sea Scrolls: The Hebrew and Aramaic Texts from Cave Four, Fascicle Two.* Washington, D.C.: Biblical Archaeology Society, 1992. Contains the Hebrew text of fragmentary remains of sapiential revelations transmitted to the sons of Seth, recorded in the "Book of Haguy."

ENOSH AND HIS
GENERATION REVISITED

Steven D. Fraade

Introduction

In recent years there has been a burgeoning of interest in the study
of the interpretive practices of ancient Judaism and Christianity,
particularly those relating to biblical personalities. This expansion
of interest is due in part to the continued publication and study of
the Dead Sea Scrolls, which reveal the prominent place of such biblical personalities (e.g., Enoch, Noah, Melchizedek, and Daniel)
not only in the traditions of the Dead Sea community itself, but
also in the writings of other Jewish groups which are collected
among the Dead Sea Scrolls. Similarly, the continued publication,
translation, and study of the Nag Hammadi codices has height-
ened awareness of the interpretive place of biblical figures in the
varieties of early Christianity.[1] Thus, we now have a significantly

---

1. So far as I can tell, having looked at recent concordances and scriptural indices,
there are still no explicit references to Enosh the individual or to Gen 4:26 in the extant
Dead Sea Scrolls. Note, however, that a recently published fragment (4Q369 1 i 1–7) is
named by its editors (Attridge and Strugnell) "Prayer of Enosh" (*Qumran Cave 4. VIII*,
353–56), since it appears in a broken genealogy before a restored notice of Kenan (Enosh's
son), presumably after what would have been a notice of Enosh. Unfortunately Enosh's
name is not preserved, nor does the language directly derive from or allude to Gen 4:26.
The broken text appears to be an address, presumably to God, concerning the judgment of
some guilty party. The editors suggest that this is a prayer uttered by Enosh, intended as an
elaboration of Gen 4:26b, taken to refer to Enosh having "called on the name of the Lord"
(as in *Jub.* 4:12, on which see below). Similarly, notwithstanding the prominence of Seth
and his descendants in some of the Nag Hammadi texts, Enosh does not appear therein.
One of my reviewers, George Brooke (*JSS* 31, p. 260), points to a couple of textual gaps
in Nag Hammadi codices where Enosh's name *might* have been included, but admits that

expanded corpus of texts, translations, and studies from which
to consider the exegetical practices, particularly as they relate to
biblical figures, of the early varieties of Judaism and Christianity.[2]
More broadly, the study of the formative periods of Judaism (Second Temple and rabbinic) and Christianity (New Testament and
patristic) has benefited from increased cross-fertilization between
the two fields, as well as greater methodological sophistication
under the influences of such academic disciplines as literary and
historical criticism and the social sciences.

In 1980 I completed my dissertation on "Enosh and His Generation," subsequently revised and published as a monograph of the
same title.[3] The main focus of this monograph was on interpretive practices in Second Temple and rabbinic Judaism and in early
Christianity. Because of the focus of this work, and due to the developments sketched above, it is fitting, in light of the fruits of the
subsequent years of scholarship, to revisit "Enosh and His Generation." My approach in reconsidering my earlier evaluations will
be both to extend their implications and to problematize some of
the presuppositions upon which they rest.[4]

Much recent comparative study of the varieties of ancient Jewish and Christian scriptural interpretation has accentuated the
shared body of exegetical traditions upon which they drew and
the overall similarities in their hermeneutical approaches to scripture.[5] In studying the variety of portrayals of Enosh and his times,
all deriving from the single verse of Gen 4:26, I was struck by the

---

this is speculative. As Brooke points out, Gen 4:26 might be alluded to in the *Three Steles
of Seth,* NHC VII,5: 119,20–21: "I [Seth] shall utter thy name."

2. This is not the place to give a bibliography of such work, but as an example, two
recent publications on the traditions of Adam and Eve may be cited: Anderson and Stone,
eds., *Synopsis;* and Stone, *History.* I know of no new studies of Enosh or of Gen 4:26
since my book was published. The only "new" text of which I am aware is the Armenian
"History of the Forefathers: Adam and His Sons and Grandsons" (in Stone, ed., *Armenian
Apocrypha Relating to Adam and Eve*), where Enosh is treated in secs. 33–45, referred
to below. I thank Professor Stone for making this text available to me in advance of its
publication.

3. "Enosh and His Generation: Scriptural Translation and Interpretation in Late Antiquity" (Ph.D. diss., University of Pennsylvania, 1980); *Enosh and His Generation:
Pre-Israelite Hero and History in Post-biblical Interpretation,* SBLMS 30 (Chico, Calif.:
Scholars Press, 1984).

4. I have gained several insights from the reviews of my book, *Enosh and His
Generation,* some of which are referred to below.

5. To *Enosh and His Generation,* 2, n. 2, add in particular Kugel, *Potiphar's House,*
esp. pp. 266–68.

varieties of interpretation, stemming, subtly at first, from the earliest known usages of that verse, but becoming more pronounced with time. These differences can be traced in the first instance to a syntactical ambiguity in the Hebrew text's notice, immediately following its announcement of Enosh's birth as the son of Seth, that "Then it was begun (אז הוחל) to call on/by the name of the Lord" (4:26b). Who so began: Enosh himself (the immediate antecedent in the verse), the people of his time in general (suggested by the indefinite passive verb), or the descendants of Seth (immediately following in Genesis 5), as opposed to those of Cain (previously narrated in 4:17–24)?

Prerabbinic Jewish Interpretations

Our earliest extrabiblical Hebrew reflection on Enosh is found in Ben Sira (Hebrew: 49:14–16), who includes Enosh in a selective list of antediluvian heroes (chaps. 44, 49), but says nothing specific about him.[6] All we can surmise is that Enosh's inclusion reflects a positive understanding of Gen 4:26b as referring to Enosh the individual. Ben Sira's praise of Enosh, along with his praise of Enoch, Joseph, Shem, Seth, and Adam, does not come, as might be expected, in chronological sequence near the beginning of Sira's "Praise of the Ancestors." Rather, it comes penultimately, after his praise of the last biblical ancestor, Nehemiah, but before his concluding praise of his contemporary, the high priest Simon (ca. 200 B.C.E.). By this placement, the earliest righteous heroes immediately anticipate the latest, with Simon being directly preceded by Adam and Enosh, primeval, idealized "men," as their names denote in subsequent traditions. I stress this now since we can already see, albeit subtly, a pattern which will be repeated in later Jewish, Christian, and Samaritan exegeses: the earliest righteous humans, standing at the beginning of sacred history, foreshadow its consummation. Etiologies are traced from the vantage of teleological hindsight, for Ben Sira that

---

6. For a fuller treatment, see Fraade, *Enosh and His Generation*, 12–16.

being defined by the preeminence of Simon, the high priest of his time ("greatest among his kindred, the glory of his people").[7]

The book of *Jubilees* (19:23–25) similarly includes Enosh in a selective chain of seven righteous pre-Israelite men, listed in reverse chronological order from Shem to Adam.[8] But unlike Ben Sira, *Jubilees* gives us the reason for Enosh's inclusion: "He began to call on the name of the Lord on the Earth" (4:12).[9]

The early Jewish rendering of Gen 4:26 which was to have the greatest impact on the subsequent history of that verse's interpretation, via Philo and the early church fathers, was that of the Septuagint. Like *Jubilees,* the Jewish Greek version takes the subject of Gen 4:26b to be Enosh the individual, but renders the verse's verb very differently: "This one *hoped* to call (οὖτος ἤλπισεν ἐπικαλεῖσθαι) upon the name of the Lord God." This could reflect either the Greek translator's understanding of a Hebrew consonantal *Vorlage* identical to the MT (אז הוחל) or his literal rendering of a variant Hebrew *Vorlage* (זה הוחיל), which might in turn have originated as an "internal translation" of אז הוחל.[10] Be that as it may, the Septuagint in solving one set of ambiguities has created another: What is the nature of Enosh's hope, and might the middle form ἐπικαλεῖσθαι ("to call") be construed as passive ("to be called")?[11]

The idea of Enosh as "hoper" is exploited especially by Philo

---

7. Sir 50:1, trans. Skehan and Di Lella, *Wisdom of Ben Sira,* 547. Thus, the heroic ancestral chain is bracketed by the originary "glory of Adam" (49:16) and the contemporary "glory of his people."

8. In *2 Enoch* 33:10–11, Enosh is similarly included in a list of Enoch's six ancestors, beginning with Adam, who have transmitted to Enoch esoteric writings. In a fragment usually appended to *2 Enoch,* Enosh is included among the priestly antecedents to Melchizedek. See Fraade, *Enosh and His Generation,* 18–19.

9. Compare 4Q 369 (discussed in n. 1), understood by its editors as a prayer of Enosh. For fuller discussion of the *Jubilees* passage, see Fraade, *Enosh and His Generation,* 16–18.

10. Reviewers (especially Brooke, review of *Enosh and His Generation,* 257) who criticized me for not having given serious enough consideration to the existence of a variant Hebrew *Vorlage* failed to recognize that even had such a variant existed, it might itself have been the product of an interpretive transmission of a Hebrew original identical to the MT. The question then becomes whether such an interpretation originated with the Greek translator or in an antecedent stage of Hebrew textual transmission. I claim simply that all of the variations reflected in ancient witnesses *could* have derived from the syntactical ambiguity in what would become the MT, אז הוחל, which is both a *hapax legomenon* and the *lectio difficilior.*

11. For a fuller discussion of the LXX version, see Fraade, *Enosh and His Generation,* 5–11.

of Alexandria, who provides the earliest extensive discussion of Enosh.[12] Philo sets Enosh as the first of a triad, followed by Enoch and Noah, of virtuous ancestors.[13] They, in turn, are followed by the triad Abraham, Isaac, and Jacob, all of whom prepare for Moses, the apex of human virtue. Enosh is an exemplar of the virtue of hope, in particular "the hope and expectation in receiving good things from the one bountiful God."[14] Philo is the first to link his interpretation of Gen 4:26b to Enosh's name, meaning "man" in Hebrew and Aramaic, but taken by Philo to denote ideal man: the true man sets his hope in God.[15] Although Philo lauds Enosh as the "true man," a model of virtue, standing at the head of a chain of virtuous biblical models, he also qualifies his praise: compared to the successive stages in the progression of human perfection, Enosh is "defective inasmuch as though he always desired the excellent, he has not yet been able to attain it, but resembles sailors eager to put into port, who yet remain at sea unable to reach their haven."[16] Enosh hoped to call on the name of God, but did not fully attain his goal. Enosh, like the other pre-Israelite righteous individuals, represents an important virtue, but compared to his Israelite successors and especially to Moses, the apogee of human spirituality, his is only a preliminary stage in the pursuit of virtue.

While Josephus does not say anything substantive about Enosh per se, he provides an understanding of Seth's descendants in general that will be important for the subsequent history of interpretation.[17] According to Josephus, the progeny of Seth were initially like him in virtue, in contrast to the descendants of Cain, who were violent and insolent.[18] But after seven generations, the

---

12. For a fuller treatment, see Fraade, *Enosh and His Generation*, 19–25.

13. *Abr.* 7–15.

14. *Quod det. pot.* 138 (trans. Colson, LCL 2.295).

15. *Quod det. pot.* 138–40; *Abr.* 9–11; *Quaest. in Gen.* 1.80.

16. *Abr.* 47 (trans. Colson, LCL 6.29). Philo plays on Enosh the hoper (ὁ ἐλπίζων) who is defective (ἐλλιπής). For a similarly mixed view of Enosh, based on word plays on his name and the verb ἤπισεν, see Eusebius, *Praep. evang.* 11.6, who may be dependent on Philo.

17. For a fuller treatment, see Fraade, *Enosh and His Generation*, 25–27.

18. While Josephus does not draw this contrast explicitly, his positioning of his praise of Seth and his descendants (*Ant.* 1.68–71), immediately following his negative presentation of the Cainites (*Ant.* 1.60–66), makes the contrast unmistakable. Josephus never suggests, as is the case in later Christian exegesis, that the flood resulted from the mixing of the

Sethites "abandoned the customs of their fathers for a life of depravity.... They no longer rendered to God God's due honors ... but displayed by their actions a zeal for vice twofold greater than they had formerly shown for virtue, and drew upon themselves the enmity of God."[19] Josephus continues his retelling of the biblical narrative with the story of the "angels of God" who consort with the "daughters of men" to produce the "giants," bringing on the flood. Thus, in paraphrasing biblical history, Josephus does not include Enosh in a chain of righteous people preparing for and foreshadowing some later righteous figure, as do other prerabbinic Jewish sources. Rather, he subsumes Seth's immediate descendants under a scheme that describes their initial collective virtue followed by progressive depravity leading up to the flood.[20]

Although the evidence for prerabbinic Jewish interpretation of Enosh is not as substantial as that for other antediluvians, several exegetical patterns can be discerned that will develop more clearly and fully, but very differently, in the subsequent literatures of Samaritanism, rabbinic Judaism, and early Christianity. (1) Enosh is a link in the chain of righteous biblical ancestors which continues through, or culminates in, such biblical figures as Abraham and Moses. (2) Enosh's inclusion in such a chain, and his significance within it, derives from interpretation of his name and from the notice of his birth in Gen 4:26, he being the first, or "hoping" (following the LXX), "to call on the name of the Lord." (3) Although such interpretations lay the groundwork for an idealization of the antediluvian Enosh (as the ideal "man"), they also plant the seeds of a more qualified, if not negative, view of Enosh and/or his contemporaries, whether in contrast to later, more righteous figures, or in the shadow of subsequent human degradation leading to the flood.

We shall see how each of these lines of interpretation is de-

---

descendants of Seth (the "sons of God" of Gen 6:2, 4) with those of Cain (the "daughters of men," 6:2, 4).

19. *Ant.* 1.72 (trans. Thackeray, LCL 4.35).

20. Josephus's account is also significant for its positive attribution of astrological discoveries to the Sethites (rather than to Enoch in particular, as in *Jub.* 4:17–19 and *1 Enoch* 72–82), and their recording of these discoveries on two pillars (later referred to as the "Stelae of Seth") so as to survive destruction by fire or water. See *Ant.* 1.69–70.

veloped, usually with significant adaptation, by Samaritan, early Christian, and rabbinic interpreters. However, determining the lines of connection between the Jewish traditions of Second Temple times and those subsequent traditions is difficult. It cannot simply be assumed that along with a shared biblical text (albeit in different versions), a common pool of tradition, retrievable from the extant sources, lies at the heart of the variety of subsequent traditions. My methodological caution rests on several considerations, primary among which are these:

1. We have in each case a gap of at least two centuries between our latest Second Temple sources and our earliest Samaritan, rabbinic, and Christian sources. While these latter sources undoubtedly contain traditions that significantly antedate their present authorial or editorial settings, isolating such earlier traditions is, if not an impossible task, at least a hermeneutically circular one.

2. Although we know increasingly more about Judaism in Second Temple times, thanks largely to the discovery of the Dead Sea Scrolls and related texts, our extant sources for that period remain highly selective, and therefore possibly unrepresentative of the whole. In the case of the Dead Sea Scrolls, it is not always clear which texts are the products of the Dead Sea community, and thus are sectarian in character, and which derive from other varieties of Judaism, being reflective of traditions and practices more widely shared. Thus, in our particular case, how should we construe the fact that neither Enosh nor Gen 4:26 appears in the scrolls made public thus far? Did he hold no particular significance for this community? On the other hand, we might surmise that the importance attached to Enosh in some of the Second Temple sources surveyed above (especially Philo, but also *Jubilees* and Ben Sira) is exceptional, specific to the authors or communities responsible for them.

Furthermore, those Second Temple literary sources not preserved among the Dead Sea Scrolls are extant mainly because of their transmission by later Christian churches, their selection for preservation reflecting the ideological and interpretive proclivities of those communities. This is not to say that such texts were necessarily Christianized in overt ways (as some were), but rather that, had a different "mix" of texts been preserved, the complexion of Second Temple Jewish ideologies and practices that we construct from them might look very different.[21]

We will see that our earliest rabbinic texts already *assume* interpretations of Gen 4:26 that are nowhere evidenced in extant Second Temple sources. Either (*a*) these interpretations developed in the intervening years as responses to changed religious, political, or social circumstances attendant upon the destruction of the Temple in 70 C.E., or (*b*) they were already in circulation in Second Temple times, but are not preserved among the texts that the Dead Sea community chose to hide or that early Christian churches preserved and transmitted. To hope, as one reviewer did, that we might identify a shared "Jewish-Christian" tradition from which all the subsequent exegetical developments derive, may, given the nature of our extant sources, be wishful thinking.[22]

Samaritan Interpretations

The Samaritan Pentateuch preserves Gen 4:26b as אז החל, presumably with a third-person singular subject ("Then he began").[23] Therefore the Samaritan interpretive tradition, here represented by the *Samaritan Targum* and the fourth-century *Memar Marqah* (*Tibat Marqe*), identifies the subject of the phrase as Enosh.[24] Marqah frequently includes Enosh in select lists of righteous biblical ancestors, culminating sometimes, as we might expect, with Moses, but in other cases with Phinehas, Joshua, or Caleb. Enosh is distinguished for having called upon the name

---

21. This applies not simply to which texts were preserved, but also to which parts of which texts were preserved. For example, *1 Enoch* as we know it from the Ethiopic version and as we have it in the Aramaic fragments found among the Dead Sea Scrolls has different complexions depending on what parts of the Enochic cycle are preserved in each case. On the larger question of Christian transmission of the pseudepigrapha, see Kraft, "Pseudepigrapha in Christianity," 55–86.

22. See Brooke, review of *Enosh and His Generation*, 259.

23. For fuller treatment of the Samaritan traditions, see Fraade, *Enosh and His Generation*, 29–38. For present purposes, we need not dwell on the Mandaean figure of Anush, treated in *Enosh and His Generation*, 38–45.

24. One version of the *Samaritan Targum* renders the verb "to call" passively: "Then he began/was the first to be called by the name of the Lord." See Fraade, *Enosh and His Generation*, 34, 37.

of the Lord. He is credited with being the founder of mankind, a play on his name Enosh ("man"). Of particular note are formulations in which Enosh foreshadows later biblical figures and events. For example, אז in Gen 4:26 is linked to the same word in Exod 15:1, suggesting that Moses' Song at the Sea was a fulfillment of Enosh's calling upon God's name.[25] Similarly, Enosh and Abraham are said to foreshadow Moses by their calling upon the name of God, which had not been revealed to the unbelievers.[26] Since in Samaritan tradition, as we saw in Philo, Moses epitomizes the highest level of human piety, earlier biblical figures such as Enosh prepare for Moses, who in turn anticipates a future redeemer figure.

Christian Interpretations

Although Enosh is not mentioned in the NT, there is a wealth of interpretive materials about him and Gen 4:26 in the writings of Christian authors beginning in the early fourth century. Initially, this interpretation seems to follow patterns familiar from traditions we have already surveyed: Enosh is a link in the chain of righteous biblical ancestors, his particular merit, where specified, deriving from his name, or "hoping" (following the LXX), or his "calling upon the name of the Lord." At first, these interpretations have little explicitly Christian content, except that their righteous chains now extend to and culminate in Jesus. With time, however, the interpretation of Enosh and his contemporaries takes on a distinctly Christian character, even as it continues to develop lines of interpretation familiar to us from earlier Jewish tradition.

Because of the chronological gap between the latest Second Temple sources and the earliest Christian writings that treat Enosh, it is difficult to determine whether these "Christian" traditions extend back to the origins of Christianity, presumably

---

25. *Memar Marqah* (ed. Macdonald) 2.6 / *Tibat Marqe* (ed. Ben-Hayyim) 70a. On Enosh as the founder of humankind, see *Memar Marqah* (ed. Macdonald) 1.9; 6.2 / *Tibat Marqe* (ed. Ben-Hayyim) 40b, 274a. For discussion, see Fraade, *Enosh and His Generation*, 32–33, n. 16.

26. *Memar Marqah* 2.12 / *Tibat Marqe* 105a.

inherited from its Second Temple Jewish milieu, or whether they are of more recent vintage, having developed either independently within Christianity or through contact with post-Temple varieties of Judaism that have left no independent record. After we have surveyed contemporary rabbinic interpretations of Gen 4:26, which are strikingly different from their Christian counterparts, we will need to ask whether the two are responding to one another, or represent independent exegetical trajectories.

Let us begin with three of the earliest Christian commentators (third to fourth centuries) for whom Enosh has special significance. Although these commentators are reminiscent in some regards of Philo's interpretation of Enosh, they evidence the first traces of a distinctly Christian understanding.[27]

Origen, like Philo, offers inconsistent and qualified praise of Enosh. In commenting on Rom 10:12, Origen places Enosh alongside Moses, Aaron, and Samuel as "mighty and outstanding ones" for having called upon the Lord *Jesus,* thereby foreshadowing the later Christian faithful.[28] Elsewhere, however, he says that Enosh, living in the shadow of Adam's sin, only hoped to call upon the Lord, feigning and delaying to do so.[29] Thus, on the one hand, Enosh, along with other righteous biblical figures, foreshadows later Christian faithful. On the other hand, he cannot be their equal since, having lived before both Moses and Jesus, he can only look forward to salvation. While Philo idealizes Enosh allegorically, Origen does so typologically. While Philo views Enosh as preparatory to the later patriarchs and Moses, Origen views all righteous figures of the Hebrew Bible as preparatory to Jesus and the Christian faithful.

By contrast, Eusebius Pamphili of Caesarea and Ambrose of Milan offer unqualified praise of Enosh, but still in ways that are reminiscent of Philo.[30] For Eusebius, Enosh is the first and most

---

27. Prior to these commentators, Enosh is included in Christian lists of righteous biblical ancestors, but without anything specific being said about him. See Fraade, *Enosh and His Generation,* 49–52.

28. *Commentary to Romans,* Book 8.3, with reference to Joel 2:32 (3:5); Ps 98 (99):6; Rom 10:14; 1 Cor 1:2.

29. *Commentary to Romans,* Book 5.1, commenting on Rom 5:12–14. For a fuller treatment of Origen, see Fraade, *Enosh and His Generation,* 52–56.

30. For fuller treatments of these two, see Fraade, *Enosh and His Generation,* 56–63.

important in the line of righteous ancestors, ten in all, culminating in Moses, his particular merit being in the virtuous hope (now wholly positive) with which he called upon God.[31] Like Philo, Eusebius emphasizes the meaning of Enosh's name as denoting true (or ideal) man (ἀληθὴς ἄνθρωπος), so designated for his attainment of knowledge of God and his piety, in distinction from the animals and from common man, who is represented by Adam. Thus, Enosh's "calling" and "hoping" are combined positively, as they were not in Philo and Origen: by calling upon God, Enosh attains knowledge of God, whereas in hoping in God, he attains piety. In both regards, Enosh is a model to be emulated. According to Eusebius, Enosh is not only the first to call upon God in hope, but the "first of the beloved of God" (πρῶτος θεοφίλων). Eusebius's ideal allegorization of Enosh is not qualified by his preliminary place in the chain of righteous biblical figures, since for him the OT as a whole is preparatory to Jesus and the church. Enosh stands in the shadow neither of Adam's sin, nor of Abraham's or Moses' subsequent attainments, but on his own as a model of faith and piety.

Ambrose, like Eusebius, gives unqualified praise to Enosh among a select group of antediluvian righteous figures, interpreting his "hoping" in a wholly positive manner. Like Philo and Eusebius, he stresses Enosh's name as denoting ideal man. But he goes one step further in linking ideal man with the "image of God," an idea that will be developed by other Christian commentators: not all humans share equally in the divine image, only the righteous elite.[32] Ambrose also goes further than his predecessors in interpreting Enosh's hope in and calling upon God's names in ascetic terms: as true man he withdrew himself from the "plea-

---

31. *Praep. evang.* 7.8.

32. *De Paradiso* 1.3.19–23. See also my treatment of Didymus the Blind in *Enosh and His Generation*, 68–70. This same connection between the ideal man and the image of God is drawn in the Armenian "History of the Forefathers" (see above, n. 2), sec. 34: "Enosh demonstrated the renewal of the corrupted image of humans in many ways. First, by his name, for Enosh means 'man' in the likeness of the archetype" (trans. M. E. Stone). Thus, the divine image implanted in Adam was corrupted by his sin, only to be restored with Enosh. Other Christian commentators associate the renewal of the divine image with Seth, which seems more natural based on Gen 4:25; 5:3. As we shall see, early rabbinic texts suggest that humans fully embodied the divine image from Adam through Enosh, in whose time it began to diminish.

sures of flesh," lifting his soul from his body and from the earth in longing for reunion with God.[33]

We see, therefore, in these early Christian commentators an increasing tendency to spiritualize Enosh. By hoping in and calling upon the name of God, Enosh, as ideal man, becomes himself more godlike.

This tendency to stress the godlike qualities of Enosh receives a major boost when, beginning in the fourth century, Christian commentators understand the verb ἐπικαλεῖσθαι of LXX Gen 4:26b as passive in voice, thereby announcing that Enosh "hoped *to be called* by the name of the Lord God." Such an interpretation is first evidenced in a fragment of a commentary attributed to Eusebius of Emesa, who understands this verse to mean that Enosh hoped to be called "God" or "son of God." In recognition of their godlike righteousness, the descendants of Seth (through Enosh) were so called, this being the explanation of the term "sons of God" in Gen 6:2: they were not angels but righteous humans.[34] Gen 6:2–4, according to this reading, describes the first intermingling of the righteous descendants of Seth with the wicked descendants of Cain, reminiscent of Josephus's description of the degeneration of the Sethites in conjunction with this episode, resulting in the flood.[35] Enosh's role in all of this is unclear. Was he, in fact, called "God" or "son of God," or did he only hope to be so called? While Seth stands at the head of this righteous line, it would appear to be Enosh who is first associated with the attribution of divine epithets to righteous (godlike) humans. Subsequent Christian commentators will work out these

---

33. *De Isaac et Anima* 1.2.

34. This tradition and its attribution are found in a note to Origen's Hexapla. Early Christian exegetes certainly knew of interpretations of Gen 6:2 which regarded the "sons of God" as fallen angels; see Fraade, *Enosh and His Generation*, 65, n. 53. By understanding this phrase as referring to humans, exegetes could "demythologize" or "naturalize" the evil that led to the flood. For fuller treatment, see *Enosh and His Generation*, 63–68.

35. Although Josephus does not explicitly connect the degeneration of the Sethites with their sexual mingling with the Cainite women, it is easy to see how such an inference could be drawn. Our earliest source interpreting the "sons of God" of Gen 6:2 as referring to the descendants of Seth is a fragment attributed to the *Chronicles* of Julius Africanus (ca. 160–240 C.E.). However, Africanus makes no connection between this interpretation and Gen 4:26 or Enosh. He simply claims that the whole Sethite line, down to Jesus, can be referred to as "sons of God."

wrinkles in a variety of ways, but the basic terms of interpretation have now been set in place.

Some, like Didymus the Blind, follow the line, begun with Philo, of stressing Enosh's virtue and ideal character, while qualifying this approbation: Enosh only hoped to be called by the name of God.[36] But others, like John Chrysostom, stress Enosh's preeminence among the early biblical righteous figures, he being the first to be considered a godlike human and to be called by God's name. The association of these qualities of Enosh with Jesus and the Christian faithful, at the other end of sacred history, is particularly stressed by Augustine and Cyril of Alexandria, in whose writings the Christianization of Enosh achieves its fullest expression.[37]

For Augustine, Enosh, in his hope to call on the name of the Lord God, prophetically foreshadows Christian faith in the resurrection of Jesus. Of all the antediluvian righteous, Enosh best typifies the Sethite line, from which the messiah descends, as representing the City of God on earth (the Earthly City being represented by the Cainites). Bearing the name "man," Enosh is nameless, meaning otherworldly and asexual, placing his faith in God's name, which he in turn bears as a "son of God" and "son of the resurrection" (cf. Luke 20:35–36). He thereby foreshadows Jesus and the Christian faithful who would similarly call and be called, inhabiting the City of God.[38]

For Cyril of Alexandria, as for others before him, Enosh is called "God" by his contemporaries (reflecting a passive understanding of ἐπικαλεῖσθαι) in recognition of his righteousness and piety. However, for Cyril, this designation is a consequence not simply of human approbation, but of divine grace: by recognizing (calling upon, or hoping in) Jesus as *the* Son of God, pious humans can attain to the same level as Enosh. Enosh was, therefore, the first and paradigmatic "adopted Son (υἱοθεσία) of God," a status he shares with Jesus and later Christians. The "sons of God" of Gen 6:2 are so called not because of their own righteous-

---

36. *On Genesis*, at Gen 4:26. See Fraade, *Enosh and His Generation*, 68–70.

37. *Homilies in Genesis* 20.4; 22.2–3; *Expositio in Psalmum* 49:1. See Fraade, *Enosh and His Generation*, 70–75.

38. *De Civitate Dei* 15.17–18. See Fraade, *Enosh and His Generation*, 75–80.

ness, but because of their genealogical descent from the godlike Enosh.[39]

In the later Byzantine chronicles, Seth reemerges as the righteous paradigm of the Sethite line, while Enosh's role diminishes. The "sons of God" of Gen 6:2 earn this designation by virtue of the qualities they inherit from the godlike Seth. Enosh is venerated as one link in this chain of righteous Sethites, but it is through Seth's deeds, including his discovery of arts and the tools of civilization, that they derive their special status.[40] Gen 4:26b is now understood with Seth as its subject.[41] In one Byzantine chronographer, however, we find a new interpretation of Enosh's name: Enosh as "man" prefigures Jesus as "son of (true) man."[42]

A similar tendency, to focus less on Enosh and more on the righteous Sethites, in contrast to the evil Cainites, can be seen in Syriac Christian commentaries. Ephraem, for example, links Gen 4:26b to the Sethites as a group, who are called by the name of God and await their redemption through the resurrection of the NT Son of God.[43] The ninth-century Ishodad of Merv, in his commentary on Gen 4:26, collects a number of interpretations of Enosh's name and his "calling on the name of the Lord" which show the influence of earlier Greek interpretation, but are modified to fit the Peshitta version (which does not allow a passive understanding of the verb "to call"). Here Enosh's role is again more central. Because Enosh placed his hope and faith in God, he merited being called "of God," or a "son of God," meaning an "intimate of God," as did his righteous descendants.[44]

While we have seen significant diversity in early Christian interpretations of Enosh and of Gen 4:26, several patterns emerge

---

39. *Glaphyra*, Book 2; *Contra Julianum*, Book 9. See Fraade, *Enosh and His Generation*, 80–85, where a possible development in Cyril's interpretation is sketched.

40. Echoes of Josephus (see above, n. 20), whether direct or indirect, are strongest in these sources.

41. See *Paschal Chronicle*; George Syncellus, *Chronographia*; John Malalas, *Chronographia*. For discussion and parallels in other Byzantine chronographers, see Fraade, *Enosh and His Generation*, 85–90.

42. George Syncellus, *Chronographia*, citing Africanus's *Natural History*. See Fraade, *Enosh and His Generation*, 86–88. On the Byzantine chronicles' interpretation of early biblical history, see Adler, *Time Immemorial*.

43. *Commentary to Genesis*, at Gen 4:26; *De Nativitate* 1.48. See Fraade, *Enosh and His Generation*, 92–97.

44. See Fraade, *Enosh and His Generation*, 97–104.

that mark the increasingly pronounced Christian nature of these interpretations over time. Although Christian interpretations initially follow patterns evidenced in Second Temple Jewish sources, as well as in early Samaritan interpretations, by the fourth century they begin to assume a distinctive form and content. If their antecedents viewed Enosh at or near the beginning of a chain of righteous biblical persons culminating in a later figure such as Moses, Christian interpreters increasingly viewed the whole chain of OT heroes as preparing for Jesus, and eventually the Christian church. But unlike the Jewish model, the Christian paradigm views Jesus not simply as the most recent in a progression of increasingly pious humans, but as the end to which all the others point, standing opposite to, while succeeding, the OT chain as a whole. Enosh, in many cases appearing first in the OT chain by virtue of his being the first to call upon or place his hope in the Lord, stands directly opposite Jesus as the object of that calling or hope. Enosh's primacy, in some traditions, is certainly aided by his name, which already with Philo was understood to denote "true" or "ideal man," a replacement, in some sense, for Adam. As ideal man, Enosh is barely mortal, having been called by God's name in recognition of his superiority to common man. In this status he foreshadows and prepares for Jesus and the Christian faithful, even as his status as ideal or godlike man derives from his recognition of Jesus. As an adopted son of God, he stands outside of time as brother to Jesus and his followers.

We see here a significant development within Christian exegesis that distinguishes it from its Jewish and Samaritan antecedents: Enosh is not simply a link in the chain of righteous figures, but defines a group, the righteous Sethites, in opposition to the wicked Cainites, thereby prefiguring the Christians. Thus, as Christian commentators looked to antediluvian times for the etiology of both human piety and sinfulness, they did so with an eye to finding mirrored therein the culminating climax of and conflict between the two in their own times. As ideal "man" of otherworldly hope and expectation, Enosh stands allegorically outside of history. But, standing historically between God's failed creation of Adam and God's retributive triumph over evil through the flood, Enosh typologically points forward in history to the Christian salvation. Allegorical (inherited from Judaism) and typological (distinctively Christian) interpretations of Enosh coalesce.

Rabbinic Interpretations

In contrast to the prerabbinic Jewish, Samaritan, and Christian traditions we have surveyed, Enosh plays only a minor role in the rabbinic interpretation of Gen 4:26 and its scriptural context. That verse is interpreted in two ways strikingly different from what we have seen elsewhere. First, rather than taking Gen 4:26b to refer to the deeds and character of Enosh, rabbinic interpreters universally understand it to refer to his contemporaries, what comes to be termed the "Generation of Enosh" (דור אנוש). Second, rather than understanding the verse positively to allude to the beginnings of divine worship or faith, rabbinic commentators take it to refer to the beginnings of idolatrous worship and its disastrous consequences. As noted earlier, both of these lines of interpretation are not only evidenced, but *presumed* in our earliest rabbinic texts of interpretation (mid–third century C.E. in their redacted forms). Thus, it is difficult to know their origins, especially whether they might go back to Second Temple times, and therefore have coexisted with Second Temple period interpretations of the verse as referring positively to Enosh, or whether they came into being only after 70 C.E., possibly in some relation to the emergence of Christianity in the decades thereafter.

The rabbinic targumim, with the exception of *Targum Onqelos,* translate Gen 4:26b as follows, with slight variations: "Then men began[45] to make idols for themselves,[46] calling them by the name of the Memra of the Lord"[47] (*Tg. Neofiti*). Thus, the indefinite passive construction הוחל ("was begun") is actively understood, with its subject being the people of Enosh's time. The direct object of the verb "to call" is now assumed to be

---

45. *Fragmentary Tg.:* "In his [Enosh's] days, then, men began..." *Tg. Pseudo-Jonathan:* "That was the generation in whose days they began..."

46. *Fragmentary Tg.* and *Tg. Neofiti* margin: "worshiping foreign cults..." *Tg. Pseudo-Jonathan:* "to go astray, making idols for themselves..."

47. *Tg. Pseudo-Jonathan:* "calling their idols by the name of the Memra of the Lord."

not "the name of the Lord," but elliptical "idols," to whom are applied God's name in false worship. In this way, the verse is interpreted to refer to a double sin: the worship of false gods and the application of the true God's name in that worship. It is this twofold activity that defines "idolatry" in classical Jewish thought.[48] Thus, in its barest form, Gen 4:26 is translated with a slight expansion so as to denote the behavior of Enosh's contemporaries: "Then was begun [by men] the calling upon [false gods] by the name of the Lord."[49] *Targum Onqelos* reflects a somewhat similar, but converse translation of the verse: "Then, in his days, men refrained from praying in the name of the Lord." In keeping with its "literal" character, this translation renders the obscure Hebrew indefinite passive verb הוחל with the active Aramaic verb חליו, thereby staying closer to the Hebrew original than do the so-called Palestinian targumim.[50] From a rabbinic perspective, of course, ceasing to pray to God is equivalent to turning to the worship of false gods.[51]

This understanding of Gen 4:26b, as marking the origins of idolatrous worship by Enosh's contemporaries, is precisely the interpretation of that verse which is *presumed* in our earliest rabbinic midrashic sources which employ it: the *Mekilta of R. Ishmael* and the *Sipre to Deuteronomy*.[52] As in several Christian sources that we surveyed, the interpretation of Gen 4:26 is occasioned by the question of why scripture refers to nondeities by divine epithets, now in relation to the "other gods" in the second commandment of the decalogue (Exod 20:3; Deut 5:7). We are told that such nongods were first called by God's name in the days of Enosh, according to Gen 4:26b (as targumically

---

48. See Faur, "Idea of Idolatry," 1–15; Faur and Rabinowitz, "Idolatry," 8.1227–37.

49. See Fraade, *Enosh and His Generation*, 112–16.

50. For this sense of *Tg. Onqelos*'s literalness, see Fraade, *Enosh and His Generation*, 119.

51. See Fraade, *Enosh and His Generation*, 116–19.

52. This need not presume that the targumic texts in their extant forms are chronologically anterior to our extant midrashic texts, or vice versa, but simply that the understanding of Gen 4:26b that the Palestinian targumim express was presumed by the creators of the midrashic traditions and their audience. For the midrashic texts, see *Mek. Bahodesh* 6; *Sipre Deut*. 43. These texts were probably edited in the mid–third century, but contain earlier traditions, in our case attributed to Palestinian sages of the second century c.e. For fuller presentation of these texts, see Fraade, *Enosh and His Generation*, 119–31.

understood). The midrashim then describe the divine response to
this idolatrous worship: God causes the ocean to flood one-third
of the world. God's response fits humanity's deeds "measure for
measure:" just as they do something *new* (emphasizing הוחל) in
changing their relationship with God, so God does something
new in altering the order of nature; just as they *call upon* false
gods, God *calls upon* the waters to overflow their God-set boundaries to flood the earth as punishment. Human "might" is no
match for God's. Thus the practice of idolatry, a cardinal sin, is
traced back to the time of Enosh.

Just as the midrash presumes familiarity with Gen 4:26 as an
announcement of the origins of idolatry, it appears to presume familiarity with the tradition of a flood in Enosh's time; no attempt
is made here to derive this tradition from Gen 4:26. Rather, the
emphasis is on demonstrating the appropriateness of the punishment to the sin: each element of the people's sin is mirrored in
God's response. The flood in Enosh's time may be viewed as a
prelude to the more total flooding in Noah's time, just as the sin
of Enosh's contemporaries prepares for that of Noah's.[53]

The Amoraic midrashim build upon their predecessors in several significant ways.[54] First, Enosh's contemporaries are now
regularly referred to as the "Generation of Enosh" (דור אנוש),
taking their place as the first of a series of pre-Israelite rebellious generations, followed by the "Generation of the Flood,"
the "Generation of the Separation" (the Tower of Babel), and
the "People of Sodom." Each generation rebels against God by
introducing some cardinal vice and each is accordingly pun-

---

53. As noted earlier, it is difficult to know how much to make of the fact that the tradition of a flood in Enosh's time, presumed in our earliest rabbinic texts, is not attested
in prerabbinic sources. One could argue that this tradition was the creation of early rabbinic exegesis, but was well enough known, at least in rabbinic circles, by the time of the
editing of the *Sipre* and *Mekilta,* not to require demonstration. But it is also possible that
this tradition, together with the negative interpretation of Gen 4:26, did indeed circulate
in Second Temple times, but simply was not preserved within extant sources from that
period. For possible pagan, Greco-Roman analogues to a series of primeval floods, see
Fraade, *Enosh and His Generation,* 215–16.

54. For treatment of the individual Amoraic texts, only a few of which are referred to
here, see Fraade, *Enosh and His Generation,* 131–56. These collections, in their edited
forms, span the third through fifth centuries, while the sages to whom traditions concerning Enosh and the Generation of Enosh are attributed lived in the third and fourth
centuries in Palestine.

ished by God, with none learning from its predecessor.[55] This sequence, what I call the "degeneration of the generations," appears irreversible, until Abraham appears to arrest and reverse the universal downward spiral and to initiate an Israelite, upward spiral, culminating in the revelation of the Torah at Mount Sinai.[56]

One way this pattern of decline and its reversal is expressed is through the idea of the "removal of the Shekinah." Beginning with Adam's sin, the Shekinah (divine indwelling) progressively removes itself from humanity's midst (seven stages in all), until with Abraham the process is reversed, and finally with Moses (the seventh patriarch) the Shekinah is restored among Israel at Mount Sinai.[57] Thus, God's establishment of a covenant with, and revelation to, one people is set against the backdrop of the failure of humankind as a whole, both before and after the flood in Noah's time, to refrain from such cardinal vices as idolatry, bloodshed, and sexual immorality as the minimal requirements for constituting a covenantal partner to God. Interestingly, this pattern is traced less to the individual sins of Adam or Cain than to the collective behavior of the Generation of Enosh, which, in its turning from divine to idolatrous worship, prepares for the other forms of depravity.

Our earliest Amoraic texts continue another pattern as well. Rather than concentrating on the nature of the sin of Enosh's contemporaries, they focus in greater detail on its consequences. The partial flood in Enosh's time is understood as having established the boundaries of the Mediterranean Sea.[58] Elsewhere, it is said that these flooding waters are the primeval waters contained by God at creation, in anticipation of such human rebellion.[59] Just as this topographical change is permanent, so are the accompa-

---

55. For the failure of each generation to learn from its predecessors, see *Gen. Rab.* 26.7; 38.2; *Pesiq. R.* supp. 1.

56. For this pattern, see *Gen. Rab.* 2.3; *Lev. Rab.* 23.3. In later sources, see *Pesiq. R.* 40, 42; *Tanhuma Wayyera'* 18; *Exod. Rab.* 15.7.

57. See *Gen. Rab.* 19.7, and discussion in Fraade, *Enosh and His Generation*, 148–49. But one later source (discussed below) describes the removal of the Shekinah as having occurred at once in response to the idolatry of Enosh's contemporaries. See *3 Enoch* (*Sepher Hekalot*) 5.3–13, with discussion in Fraade, *Enosh and His Generation*, 163–66.

58. *Gen. Rab.* 23.7, discussed in Fraade, *Enosh and His Generation*, 143–47.

59. See *Gen. Rab.* 5.1; *Lev. Rab.* 11.7.

nying anthropological changes. Humans, having previously been formed in the divine image, now become more beastlike (like centaurs), in both physique and behavior. The animals, over whom they initially were given dominion (Gen 1:26, 28; 9:2), now become their predators; the animals become punishing agents of God in response to humanity's turn to idolatry. By turning from the worship of God to the worship of God's creations, humanity loses its privileged, godlike position in the order of creation.[60] Whereas Philo and some Christian interpreters regarded Enosh, the ideal man, as marking the beginning of a chain of righteous, godlike humans, the midrashic tradition views him as marking an initial stage in humanity's decline from godlike to beastlike characters.

Post-Amoraic midrashic sources continue, for the most part, the lines of interpretation we have surveyed in earlier rabbinic literature. However, as we move into early medieval times, a few new tendencies emerge. For example, the rebellious nature of the idolatry of Enosh's generation is portrayed in more provocative terms: they sought to arouse God's anger by violating God's commandment to them, presumably to worship only God.[61] Unlike their antecedents, later rabbinic texts describe in greater, even exaggerated detail the nature of the idolatrous worship initiated by the Generation of Enosh. One source, *3 Enoch* (*Sepher Hekalot*) 5:3–13, depicts how these people, having lived in the protective radiance of the Shekinah, gathered precious materials from all over the world from which to fashion idols of enormous size, which they spread throughout the world. They then caused the celestial bodies to descend to earth to attend before the idols as they had previously attended before God. These people accomplished these acts through magical arts learned from the fallen angels Uzza and Azza'el.[62] As in Christian sources, we find here

---

60. *Gen. Rab.* 23.6 and parallels, discussed in Fraade, *Enosh and His Generation*, 131–43. As noted there, these changes, presently associated with the Generation of Enosh and subsequent rebellious generations, are in other rabbinic sources connected to Adam and Eve's expulsion from the Garden of Eden.

61. *Pesiq. R.* 42, and supp. 1; *Yal. Shim'oni Bereshit* 47; *Ber. Rabbati* (ed. Albeck), p. 41. See Fraade, *Enosh and His Generation*, 159–63.

62. For text and fuller discussion, see Fraade, *Enosh and His Generation*, 163–66. For a similar description of the idolatrous behavior of the Generation of Enosh, see *Ber. Rab-*

a linking of Gen 4:26 with Gen 6:2–4. In Christian interpretations, however, it is Enosh and his descendants (the Sethite line) who are *positively* associated with the godlike yet human "sons of God" of Gen 6:2–4, whereas here it is the Generation of Enosh who are *negatively* associated with the corruption of humankind by the fallen angelic "sons of God" of the same verses.

Finally, in later midrashim we see a tendency to link exegetically the inherited tradition of the Generation of Enosh to the actual words of Gen 4:26, especially by wordplays. According to *3 Enoch*, the ministering angels question God's favoring of humankind with God's presence, in view of the behavior of the Generation of Enosh. Citing Ps 8:5, they exclaim: "What is man (אנוש) that you are mindful of him," taking the verse to refer to Enosh, "the head of the idol worshipers." In response, God removes the Shekinah from humankind's midst entirely.[63] Other medieval midrashic collections similarly link a negative interpretation of Enosh's name as an expression of weakness, sickness, or calamity to the degeneration and punishment of humankind in his days.[64] In two passages, Enosh's name, signifying weakness, is linked to a play on the verb הוחל as denoting the profanation (חלול) of God's name or worship.[65] Once again, this may be compared with Philo and Christian interpreters, for whom interpretation of Enosh's name is similarly linked to their construal of Gen 4:26b. They, however, interpret Enosh's name positively ("true man"), as they do Gen 4:26b, whereas the rabbinic commentaries view both negatively.

The tradition of tracing the origins of idolatry to Enosh's generation finds poetic, liturgical expression in several *piyyutim*. They set this tradition in the context of retelling Israelite sacred history,

---

bati (ed. Albeck), p. 41. For fuller treatment of that text, see Fraade, *Enosh and His Generation*, 167–68.

63. Contrast this to the tradition mentioned earlier of the removal of the Shekinah in seven steps, beginning with Adam and continuing until Abraham. Here, as in *Gen. Rab.* 23.6, the idyllic state associated with the Garden of Eden continues until the Generation of Enosh, whereupon God's relation to humanity, and humanity's relation to nature, is radically transformed as a result of humankind's idolatry. In the Christian sources that we have examined, the relation between God and humans, corrupted by Adam and Eve, is at least partially repaired through Enosh, as a prelude to its total reparation through Jesus.

64. See *Ber. Rabbati* (ed. Albeck), pp. 31, 56.

65. *Midr. Haggadol*, at Gen 4:26; *Midr. 'Aggadah*, at Gen 4:26.

which serves as the backdrop to the atonement ritual performed by the high priest on the Day of Atonement. While the exegetical motifs — the people's sin of worshiping false gods by applying to them God's name, and God's response of calling upon the sea to overflow its boundaries — are not new, their narrative contextualization is. The rejection of God's dominion and commandments by the pre-Israelite generations sets the stage for God's establishing a covenant with Abraham, the maintenance of which is the work of Aaron's descendants, the priests, and the ultimate expression of which is the high priest's atonement rite in the Holy of Holies on the Day of Atonement. We may contrast this with Ben Sira's poetic paean to the high priest Simon, who culminates a chain of righteous ancestors going back to the antediluvians Adam, Seth, Enosh, and Enoch. These *piyyutim* also see the high priest as the culmination of Israelite sacred history, but one that stands now in sharp *contrast* to the progressive degeneration of the pre-Israelite generations.[66]

Comparisons and Conclusions

Although early rabbinic and Christian exegetes share the scriptural text of Genesis (notwithstanding important differences between the versions from which they work),[67] inherit a common body of Second Temple Jewish tradition,[68] rely on similar methods of scriptural interpretation,[69] and see themselves as descendants of the same righteous biblical figures, they have arrived at

---

66. For the *piyyut* texts and fuller discussion, see Fraade, *Enosh and His Generation*, 171–73.

67. The overall differences between rabbinic and early Christian interpretations of Enosh and Gen 4:26 cannot simply be traced to the differences between their respective scriptural versions, since those Christian interpreters who worked from the Old Latin and Syriac versions express interpretations similar to those who worked from the LXX, and these in turn take a different tack from Jewish interpreters, such as Philo, who worked from the LXX.

68. Note my earlier cautionary comments: it is impossible to know to what extent existing Second Temple texts are representative of what would have been available to either early rabbinic or early Christian exegetes.

69. For example, several exegetes have sought meaning in the abrupt juxtaposition of Gen 4:26 and 5:1, several have interpreted Gen 4:26b as an explanation of Enosh's naming in 4:26a, and many have interpreted Enosh's (or his generation's) actions through plays on his name and/or another word in the verse.

strikingly dissimilar interpretations of Gen 4:26 and the figure of Enosh.[70] Whereas Christian interpreters focus on Enosh as a paradigm of faith and piety, and eventually as a prototype of Jesus and his followers, rabbinic commentators show little interest in Enosh as an individual. Rather, their emphasis is on the moral and physical decline of his contemporaries, it being unclear whether, or to what extent, Enosh participated in that decline.[71] Early Christian sources locate Enosh as a link, often the initial link, in a chain of righteous individuals who foreshadow and culminate in Jesus and the Christian faithful. By contrast, early rabbinic sources identify the Generation of Enosh as the first step in the progressive corruption of humankind until it is reversed, at least partially, by Abraham and his patriarchal and Israelite successors.

For Christian commentators, Enosh, as true and godlike man, effects a partial remedy to the primal sin of Adam and Eve. He typifies the line of Seth as "sons of God," who are contrasted with the wicked line of Cain and whose intermixing with Cain's line (Gen 6:2–4) necessitated the flood in Noah's time. The flood is, in turn, a prefiguration of the final apocalyptic redemption of the faithful followers of Jesus. Thus, Jesus and his followers represent not only the extension of the Sethite line, but its fulfillment and ultimate triumph.

For the rabbis, the Generation of Enosh, like the successive pre-Israelite generations, corrupt the divine image through their actions, resulting in their alienation from God and nature. Humanity's decline is contrasted with, and reversed by, the upward trend initiated by Abraham and his Israelite descendants, with whom the divine-human covenant is finally established with the revelation of the Torah at Mount Sinai. Through study and observance of the Torah, Israel, and ultimately all of humanity, can

---

70. This is not to claim that either rabbinic or Christian interpretations are monolithic or mutually exclusive on specific points, but that the overall thrusts of the two bodies of interpretation point in decidedly different directions.

71. Only one rabbinic text of the Amoraic period identifies Enosh himself as an idolater: *b. Shabb.* 118b according to the Munich manuscript, but not the printed editions. See Fraade, *Enosh and His Generation*, 153–54. *Gen. Rab.* 23:6 suggests that Enosh himself was still in the divine image, and that this ceased, or at least was compromised, only after his birth. See *Enosh and His Generation*, 133–34. See also *3 Enoch (Sepher Hekalot)* 5:3–13, treated above, where Enosh is said to have been the "head of the idol worshipers."

be restored to its full potential as creations in the divine image, thereby bringing about the redemption of creation.

Thus, whereas in later Christian piety Enosh serves as a *paradigm,* in the rabbinic view the Generation of Enosh functions as a *foil* to the emergence of an Israelite covenantal history in which the rabbis view themselves as the latest link. The differences between these interpretive strategies cannot be explained exclusively either by a process of "reverse engineering," whereby one retraces the internal hermeneutical steps by which interpreters move from scriptural text to interpretation,[72] or by seeking external, intercommunal polemics as the root cause of these diverging interpretive paths.[73] Likewise, as much as broader Greco-Roman cultural influences might have left their mark on the shape of the Jewish and Christian interpretations, these alone cannot explain the differences between the two, since rabbis and church fathers both were susceptible to the same forces.[74]

Rather, as each interpretive community focused its etiological attention on early biblical heroes and generations, it did so from the vantage point of its particular sense of teleology. As

---

72. For the application of this term to ancient scriptural interpretation see Kugel, *Potiphar's House,* 251–53. The extant traditions of interpretation are the products not solely of direct exegetical encounter with scriptural textual irritants but also of the continuing assessment and reformulation of received *traditions* of interpretation. In our case, we simply lack evidence for many of these intermediary stages of tradition transmission and transformation.

73. Consider the suggestion of Brooke, review of *Enosh and His Generation,* 260–61, that the rabbinic interpretations of Enosh and his generation can best be seen as an attempt to purge Judaism of Gnostic elements. Unfortunately, he is unable to adduce any texts to support this tantalizing explanation. See above, n. 1. For a broader discussion of scholarly tendencies to overplay either hermeneuticist or historicist explanations of scriptural interpretation, see my book, *From Tradition to Commentary,* 14–15. In the absence of interpretations that explicitly evidence intercommunal polemics, it is difficult to know when such polemics lie behind the interpretations of each community, especially since it is often unclear what the level of contact or familiarity might have been between interpretive communities. For example, in the case at hand I find no interpretations that necessitate rabbinic anti-Christian polemic or vice versa. The thrust of rabbinic interpretation is not to belittle Enosh or Seth, who are venerated in Christian tradition. Neither is the thrust of Christian exegesis to elevate Enosh's contemporaries overall. Notwithstanding common points of departure and shared methods of interpretation, the two traditions have entirely different preoccupations. This is not to deny the possibility of some degree of cross-influence. However, since each community's exegesis can be understood in relation to that community's broader interpretive praxis, not just the possibility but the probability of such polemic as a primary, generative motivation has to be established.

74. See in particular my explication of rabbinic exegesis in terms of widespread currents of chronological, cultural primitivism in Greco-Roman thought and literature: *Enosh and His Generation,* 208–11, 218–23.

much as each tradition of interpretation has to be understood in terms of its close reading of Gen 4:26, and the cultural context within which it operates, it also needs to be seen within a broader practice of scriptural reading and explication as an expression of each community's theological self-understanding within the sacred metanarrative of beginnings and endings. Early Christian and rabbinic traditions both trace, in one case positively and in the other negatively, the origins of their respective redemptive expectations to the universal, antediluvian period of biblical history, with Gen 4:26's notice about Enosh or the Generation of Enosh receiving close attention. For both traditions, the culmination of that redemptive process would be played out again on the canvas of universal history, but by very different redemptive media: for the one through Jesus; for the other through Torah.

Bibliography

An extensive bibliography relating to Enosh and his generation, as well as associated exegetical motifs, can be found in Fraade, *Enosh and His Generation*, 248–62.

Previous studies specific to Enosh and the interpretation of Gen 4:26, exclusive of standard biblical commentaries, have been few and limited in scope:

Horst, F. "Die Notiz vom Anfang des Jahwehkultes in Genesis 4,26." In *Libertas Christiana: Friedrich Delekat zum 65. Geburtstag.* Ed. E. Wolf and W. Matthias. Munich: C. Kaiser, 1957. Pp. 68–74.

Sandmel, S. "Genesis 4:26b." *HUCA* 32 (1961) 19–29.

Schäfer, P. "Der Götzendienst des Enosch: Zur Bildung und Entwicklung aggadischer Traditionen im nachbiblischen Judentum." In *Studien zur Geschichte und Theologie des rabbinischen Judentums.* AGJU 15. Leiden: Brill, 1978. Pp. 134–52.

von Mutius, H.-G. "Gen. 4,26, Philo von Byblos und die jüdische Haggada." *Biblische Notizen* 13 (1980) 46–48.

No ancient text or major section of a text is devoted solely to Enosh or attributed to him. A possible exception is a fragment from the Dead Sea Scrolls (4Q369 1 i 1–7) that has been named by its editors (H. Attridge and J. Strugnell) "Prayer of Enosh," even though Enosh's name does not appear therein (see above, n. 1):

VanderKam, J. C., and J. T. Milik, eds. *Qumran Cave 4. VIII: Parabiblical Texts, Part 1*. DJD 13. Oxford: Clarendon, 1994. Pp. 353–56.

For the most part, Enosh and Gen 4:26 are interpreted either in the context of running translation and commentary to the Book of Genesis, or in the context of treatment of related biblical passages or themes.

In order to locate such scattered treatments of a minor biblical figure such as Enosh, indexes to ancient literature, whether by names or scriptural verses, are particularly helpful. For Josephus and Philo, see the general index for the former and the scriptural and name indexes for the latter in the final volume of each in the LCL editions. For Western Christian literature see the indexes to *PL* and *PG*. Other indexes include:

Biblia Patristica. Vols. 1–6. Paris: Editions du Centre National de la Recherche Scientifique, 1975–95. *Biblia Patristica Supplément*. Paris, 1982. For Philo.

Ginzberg, L. *The Legends of the Jews*. 7 vols. Philadelphia: Jewish Publication Society of America, 1909–38. Vol. 7 contains a detailed subject index.

Hyman, H. *Toledot tanna'im we'amora'im*. Rev. ed. 3 vols. Tel Aviv: Dvir, 1979. Rabbinic literature according to verse citations.

Ulrich, E. "An Index of the Passages in the Biblical Manuscripts from the Judean Desert." *Dead Sea Discoveries* 1 (1994) 113–29; 2 (1995) 86–107.

To the extent that the ancient primary texts are now electronically readable and searchable, locating references to a figure such as Enosh is faster and more thorough.

For above-mentioned sources in which interpretations of Enosh, Gen 4:26, and/or their scriptural context occur most prominently, the following editions and translations may be consulted:

Second Temple Jewish Writings

The Book of Ben Sira: Text, Concordance, and an Analysis of the Vocabulary. The Historical Dictionary of the Hebrew Language. Jerusalem: The Academy of the Hebrew Language and the Shrine of the Book, 1973.

Josephus. *Complete Works*. Ed. and trans. H. St. J. Thackeray, R. Marcus, A. Wikgren, and L. H. Feldman. 9 vols. LCL. London: Heinemann; Cambridge: Harvard University Press, 1926–65.

Philo. *Complete Works*. Ed. and trans. F. H. Colson, R. Marcus, and C. H. Whitaker. 10 vols. and 2 supp. vols. LCL. London: Heinemann; Cambridge: Harvard University Press, 1929–62.

Sapientia Jesu Filii Sirach. Ed. J. Ziegler. Vol. 12, pt. 2. Septuaginta: Vetus Testamentum Graecum. Göttingen: Vandenhoeck & Ruprecht, 1965.

Septuaginta: Vetus Testamentum Graece iuxta LXX interpretes. Ed. A. Rahlfs. 2 vols. Stuttgart: Württembergische Bibelanstalt, 1935.

Aramaic Targums

The Bible in Aramaic. Ed. A. Sperber. 4 vols. Leiden: Brill, 1959–73.

The Fragment-Targums of the Pentateuch according to Their Extant Sources. Ed. M. L. Klein. 2 vols. Rome: Biblical Institute Press, 1980.

Neophyti I. Ed. A. Diez Macho. 6 vols. Madrid and Barcelona: Consejo Superior de Investigaciones Científicas, 1968–79.

The Palestinian Targum to the Pentateuch: Codex Vatican [*Tg. Neofiti*]. Facsimile ed. Jerusalem: Makor, 1970.

"Targum Pseudo-Jonathan" of the Pentateuch: Text and Concordance. Ed. E. G. Clarke et al. Hoboken, N.J.: Ktav, 1984.

Rabbinic Literature

Mekilta de-Rabbi Ishmael. Ed. and trans. J. Lauterbach. 3 vols. Philadelphia: Jewish Publication Society, 1933–35.

Midrasch Tanchuma: Ein agadischer Kommentar zum Pentateuch von Rabbi Tanchuma ben Rabbi Abba. Ed. S. Buber. Vilna: Romm, 1885.

Midrash Bereshit Rabba: Critical Edition with Notes and Commentary. Ed. J. Theodor and C. Albeck. 3 vols. Berlin, 1903–36. Reprinted with corrections, Jerusalem: Wahrmann, 1965.

Midrash Bereshit Rabbati ex Libro R. Mosis Haddarsan. Ed. C. Albeck. Jerusalem: Mekize Nirdamim, 1940. Reprint, Jerusalem: Mossad Harav Kook, 1967.

Midrash rabba ʿal hamishsha hummeshe tora wehamesh megillot. 2 vols. Vilna: Romm, 1884–87.

Midrash tanhuma ʿal hamishsha hummeshe tora. Jerusalem: Lewin-Epstein, 1973–74.

Midrash Wayyikra Rabbah. Ed. M. Margulies. 5 vols. Jerusalem, 1953–60. Reprint, five volumes in three, Jerusalem: Wahrmann, 1972.

Pesikta Rabbati: Midrasch für den Fest-cyclus und die ausgezeichneten Sabbathe. Ed. M. Friedmann. Vienna, 1880.

3 Enoch; or the Hebrew Book of Enoch. Ed. and trans. H. Odeberg. Cambridge: Cambridge University Press, 1928. Reprinted with prolegomenon by J. C. Greenfield, New York: Ktav, 1973.

Samaritan Writings

Der Hebräische Pentateuch der Samaritaner. Ed. A. von Gall. Giessen: Töpelmann, 1914–18.

The Samaritan Targum of the Pentateuch: A Critical Edition. Ed. A. Tal. 3 vols. Tel-Aviv: University of Tel-Aviv Press, 1980–83.

Tibat Marqe: A Collection of Samaritan Midrashim. Ed. and trans. Z. Ben-Hayyim. Jerusalem: Israel Academy of Sciences and Humanities, 1988.

Early Christian Writings

The Book of the Cave of Treasures. Trans. E. A. Wallis Budge. London: Religious Tract Society, 1927.

Cyril of Alexandria. *In sancti patris nostri Cyrilli archiepiscopi Alexandrini in d. Joannis evangelium.* Ed. P. E. Pusey. 3 vols. Oxford, 1892. Reprint, Brussels: Impression Anastaltique Culture et Civilisation, 1965.

Didyme L'Aveugle. *Sur la Genèse.* Ed. and trans. P. Nautin. 2 vols. SC 233, 244. Paris: Cerf, 1976–78.

Ephraem Syrus. *Des heiligen Ephraem des Syrers Hymnen de Nativitate (Epiphania).* Ed. E. Beck. 2 vols. CSCO 186–87. Louvain: Peeters, 1959.

———. *Sancti Ephraem Syri in Genesim et in Exodum commentarii.* Ed. R.-M. Tonneau. 2 vols. CSCO 152–53. Louvain: Peeters, 1957.

Eusebius Pamphili. *Evangelicae praeparationis.* Ed. and trans. E. H. Gifford. Four volumes in five. Oxford: E Typographeo Academico, 1903.

———. *Die praeparatio evangelica.* Ed. K. Mras. 2 vols. GCS 43. Berlin: Akademie, 1954–56.

Vetus Testamentum Syriace: Iuxta simplicem syrorus versionem. The Peshitta Institute, Leiden. Pt. 1, fascicle 1. Leiden: Brill, 1977.

FROM SON OF ADAM
TO SECOND GOD

Transformations of the Biblical Enoch

PHILIP S. ALEXANDER

───────────

Enoch is a most unlikely biblical hero. Though the Bible itself devotes only six verses to his life, largely in the form of a prosaic genealogy,[1] certain Jewish intellectuals in the Second Temple period came to regard him as a major figure of sacred history. They attributed to him an important body of revealed doctrine and elevated him to a position which equaled, and indeed rivaled, that of Moses, the lawgiver of Israel. They started a tradition which continued evolving with surprising vitality down to the Middle Ages and which constantly challenged the dominant Mosaic paradigm of Judaism. They created a figure who, transcending Judaism, was assimilated into Christianity, Gnosticism, and Islam, and became one of the universal religious teachers of late antiquity. Despite his obscure origins Enoch enjoyed one of the most illustrious careers in myth and legend of all the biblical patriarchs.

The earliest and fullest evidence of intense interest in Enoch is to be found in the so-called *First Book of Enoch*. This is now available in more or less its entirety only in a classical Ethiopic (Geʿez) version probably made in the sixth century C.E. The Ethiopic was translated from a Greek text, partially extant in manuscript fragments and patristic quotations, composed in the first century C.E. The Greek in turn was derived from an Ara-

───────────

1. Gen 5:18–19, 21–24.

maic original, remnants of which, along with related materials not attested in the Greek and Ethiopic forms, have been discovered among the Dead Sea Scrolls. The original Aramaic *1 Enoch* probably dates from the first century B.C.E., but is manifestly a composite work — a loose collection of originally independent Enochic texts imperfectly patched together, some of which may be as early as the fourth century B.C.E.[2]

1 Enoch depicts Enoch as a great sage, the possessor of special knowledge — secrets not available on earth which came to him by divine revelation, sometimes in visions and dreams, sometimes through ascents to heaven where he was able to consult the heavenly tablets and records, sometimes in journeys through the cosmos in the company of angelic guides.

Enoch's wisdom covers a number of distinct subjects. He knew the mysteries of God's heavenly dwelling and of the throne of God itself. *1 Enoch* 14:8–25 gives an impressively detailed description of God's celestial palace.[3] *1 Enoch* is also full of angelological lore. Enoch frequents the company of the angels, talks with them and knows their names, many of which are transparently related to their roles. They belong to different orders (Watchers, Holy Ones, Cherubim, and "Presences" — the four archangels, Michael, Raphael, Gabriel, and Phanuel, who minister directly before the Throne of God),[4] and they seem to be marshaled into hierarchies. They perform various tasks, and in short are the agents through whom God rules the world. Central to the angelology of *1 Enoch* is the myth of the fallen Watchers — a band of angels that descended from heaven, had sexual intercourse with human women, and sired through them a race of Giants who oppressed mankind. These fallen angels corrupted mankind by revealing to them forbidden knowledge and by teaching them dark arts.[5]

---

2. Texts: Ethiopic: Knibb, *Book of Enoch;* Greek: Black, *Apocalypsis Henochi Graece;* Aramaic fragments from Qumran: Milik, *Books of Enoch.* Translations and notes: Charles, *Book of Enoch;* Isaac, OTP 1.5–89; Black, *Book of Enoch.* For general surveys of the Enochic traditions see especially VanderKam, *Enoch and the Growth;* Berger, "Henoch," 14.473–545; and Milik, *Books of Enoch,* 4–135.

3. A second detailed account of God's palace and throne occurs at *1 Enoch* 71:5–10.

4. *1 Enoch* 40:2–10.

5. See esp. *1 Enoch* 6–16.

Enoch's wisdom also extended to the workings of the cosmos. Time and again Enoch claims that his angelic mentors disclosed to him the mysteries of the natural world. They took him on a tour of the habitable earth and showed him its wonders. They revealed to him how the sun, moon, and stars function and determine the times and the seasons. While the cosmographical descriptions are impressionistic and full of fabulous elements, the account of the motions of the heavenly bodies is detailed and precise. The Ethiopic version appears to be severely abridged. The Qumran fragments point to the existence of a longer text which circulated as an independent treatise, though still under the name of Enoch. Behind this astronomical treatise may lie a polemical purpose, namely to promote a solar calendar of 364 days as according to the will of God and the natural order of the universe.

Finally, Enoch's wisdom embraces the future. Enoch is shown by the angels the history of the world from his own day down to the end of time and the creation of a new heaven and a new earth. Though visions of the future are scattered throughout *1 Enoch,* they are most comprehensively and systematically encoded in the cryptic *Apocalypse of Weeks* (93:3–10; 91:11–17) and the *Zoomorphic History of the World* (chaps. 85–90). This vision of the future is dominated by the theme of divine judgment: God will in the end punish the wicked and vindicate the righteous. The motif of imminent divine judgment is all-pervasive in *1 Enoch* and unifies its very diverse elements. The note of the ultimate triumph of the righteous and the destruction of the wicked, struck in the opening chapter, forms the key signature of the entire composition. *1 Enoch* casts Enoch in the role of a classic prophet: in God's name, as the recipient of divine revelation, he utters woes against the wicked, warns them of the coming day of the Lord, and comforts the righteous remnant with assurances of their final vindication and deliverance.

All this wisdom Enoch was supposed to have committed to writing. *1 Enoch* speaks throughout in the first person in Enoch's own voice. In terms of its content *1 Enoch* is an apocalypse — a revelation of secrets and mysteries — but this revelation has been cast, following a well-known literary pattern of ancient wisdom, as Enoch's moral last will and testament to his son Methuselah

(81:5). Enoch instructs his son at the angels' express command. His teaching is meant for future generations. Chapters 92–105, which go under the title of the *Epistle of Enoch,* are addressed not only to "all my children," but also "to later generations, to all dwellers on earth who observe uprightness and peace" (92:1). Noah played a key role in the transmission of Enoch's teaching: *1 Enoch* 65:1 states that he consulted Enoch about the future judgment, and in 68:1 the archangel Michael explains to him "all the things that are secret" in the book of his great-grandfather Enoch. *1 Enoch* claims the status of inspired scripture: it is based on divine revelation and was transcribed directly from the heavenly tablets. Modern source criticism of *1 Enoch* has demonstrated that it draws on a number of originally independent Enochic texts. By the first century B.C.E. at least five substantial works attributed to Enoch were in circulation. It may have been originally by virtue of all this supposed literary activity that Enoch was accorded the title of "skilled scribe."[6]

The Enoch who emerges from the pages of *1 Enoch* at first sight bears little resemblance to his biblical namesake. On closer inspection, however, numerous links begin to appear. The authors of *1 Enoch* clearly knew Genesis 5–6, apparently in the form in which we now have it: they quote from it more or less verbatim at a number of points. Almost everything said about Enoch in the Bible is enigmatic and can be interpreted in a number of highly suggestive ways. It seems to allude to a much fuller body of Enochic legends. Since Gen 5:18–25 belongs to a strand of the Pentateuch which may not have been finally redacted until postexilic times,[7] and since there is a stratum of *1 Enoch,* the *Book of the Heavenly Luminaries* (chaps. 72–82), probably going back to the Persian period (fourth century B.C.E.), it is tempting to suppose that *1 Enoch* drew not only on Genesis 5 but on the sources that stand behind Genesis 5. The theory is attractive, but detailed analysis rather rules it out. The relationship of *1 Enoch* to the biblical text seems to be predominantly exegetical. There is no need to postulate that the authors of *1 Enoch* had before them

---

6. *1 Enoch* 92:1.
7. In terms of the classic Documentary Hypothesis it belongs to the so-called P source.

any other account of the antediluvian sage than that contained in Genesis. They treated that account as authoritative scripture and applied to it procedures well attested in early Jewish Bible exegesis. By exploiting its ambiguities and its narrative lacunae they were able to attach to scripture ideas which were not found there, to confer validity on those ideas, and to incorporate them into the traditions of Israel.[8]

Gen 5:18–25 runs as follows:

> And Jared lived a hundred and sixty-two years and begat Enoch: and Jared lived after he begat Enoch eight hundred years, and begat sons and daughters: and all the days of Jared were nine hundred and sixty and two years and he died. And Enoch lived sixty and five years and begat Methuselah. And Enoch walked with God after he begat Methuselah three hundred years, and begat sons and daughters: and all the days of Enoch were three hundred and sixty-five years: and Enoch walked with God: and he was not; for God took him. And Methuselah lived a hundred and eighty and seven years, and begat Lamech.

A number of phrases here immediately catch the attention. Enoch "walked with God" (ויתהלך חנוך את האלהים; vv. 22, 24). At first this suggests the idea of close communion with God — a life of outstanding piety and devotion. It should come as no surprise, therefore, to find Enoch depicted in *1 Enoch* as an outstandingly righteous man. This view could be reinforced by the fact that he belonged to the godly line of Seth. He is a foil to Lamech, his counterpart in the ungodly line of Cain. Lamech, a morally dubious character, is explicitly associated in the Bible with violence (Gen 4:23–24). Enoch is the seventh in line from Adam, and this, following an almost universal folk numerology, points to him as an "elect one," chosen by God for a special destiny. Contextual considerations can be brought into play. Enoch's piety would have set him apart from his generation. He lived in the period just before the flood, when wickedness and corruption were rampant on the earth. This suggests for him a prophetic role — standing against the spirit of the age, rebuking his contemporaries, and warning them of impending divine judgment.

---

8. This is not to deny that there are sources behind the biblical text (for a brief discussion see Hess, "Enoch," 2.508), but significantly, insofar as we can reconstruct those sources, they do not show any striking correlation with the distinctive traditions of *1 Enoch*.

1 Enoch, as stated earlier, gives a distinctive explanation for the wickedness of the antediluvian generations: they were corrupted by fallen angels. This idea is derived from Gen 6:1, where the "sons of God" are taken as angels — *1 Enoch,* as we noted, calls them "Watchers" — who were seduced by the beauty of human women, descended to the earth, and had sexual intercourse with them. These Watchers imparted knowledge to men which corrupted them. They taught them metalworking. Here *1 Enoch* once again converges with the biblical narrative, which associates metalworking first with Tubal-Cain, the son of Lamech, Enoch's contemporary.[9] *1 Enoch,* following a widespread mythological idea classically expressed by the myth of Prometheus, cannot envisage such an enormous technological advance occurring without extraterrestrial help. The art of metallurgy was used for baleful ends — to make weapons of war: hence, doubtless, the "violence" which characterized the period before the flood.[10] *1 Enoch* relates this "violence" also to the behavior of the monstrous offspring of the angels and the women — a race of giants which oppressed mankind.[11] The Bible itself is rather vague as to when the "sons of God" descended to the earth. *1 Enoch* dates the event to the lifetime of Enoch's father Jared, an obvious piece of exegesis which sees in his name an allusion to the descent (ירידה) of the angels. This ploy allows the stories of Enoch and of the Watchers to be intertwined. All these elements, then, in *1 Enoch* can be derived directly from the biblical text.

But the phrase "and Enoch walked with God" has further possibilities and can be interpreted in another less obvious way: אלהים may be taken in the sense of "gods," i.e., angels. Enoch then becomes someone who had a special relationship with the angels. This opens up the possibility that he ascended to heaven and learned secrets from the angels, or acted as an intermedi-

---

9. Gen 4:22. See further Sawyer, "Cain and Hephaestus," 155–66. This antitechnological attitude is very revealing for the mentality of the group that stands behind *1 Enoch.* It is not Luddite, since the Enochic literature is redolent not of the crafts and labor but of the academic cloister. It reflects a deep intellectual conservatism that is frightened by technological change. Interestingly — but consistently — it seems to be coupled with an ingrained puritanism and a negative view of women. *1 Enoch* was probably edited at a time of considerable social upheaval.

10. Gen 6:11–13.

11. *1 Enoch* 15:8–16:3.

ary or intercessor between earth and heaven. Enoch's journey through the cosmos, so graphically described in *1 Enoch,* may be an expansion of this element of the biblical narrative: Enoch went through the length and breadth of the cosmos[12] in the company of angels who revealed to him the mysteries of creation.

Equally suggestive is the statement "and he was not, for God took him." In Enoch's case the Bible pointedly avoids saying that he died: rather he was "taken" by God. This could be interpreted as meaning that he was removed from earth, or from human society, in some unusual way. Thus he becomes the first person in the biblical history to escape death. This understanding of the text is reinforced by the parallelism with Elijah, who was also "taken" by God, translated physically to heaven in a fiery chariot (2 Kgs 2:11). When the text is read in this way a host of narrative lacunae clamor to be filled. Why did God remove Enoch? Enoch's life span of 365 years is notably shorter than those of the other figures in the Sethite genealogy. This might point to abrupt, premature removal. But why? To where was Enoch taken — to heaven, to paradise, or to some other place? If he was removed without dying, then presumably he is still alive in this other place. What is he doing there, and what function does his preservation play in the divine scheme of things? How was he removed — in a chariot like Elijah, or in a whirlwind, or by some other means? Was physical translation involved and if so was his physical body transformed, or was his removal nothing more than a trance or dream ascent to heaven? Was the translation permanent? Did he, or will he in the future, return to earth to fulfill some God-given mission? The words "and he was not" are wonderfully vivid and evocative: they conjure up the picture of Enoch mysteriously vanishing and leaving his contemporaries baffled as to where he has gone.

So then it is possible to derive the salient features of Enoch in *1 Enoch* from the present text of Genesis. But it is unlikely that the potential of the biblical narrative would have been so richly realized without some strong external stimuli. These impressive developments can only have taken place because Enoch "spoke"

---

12. Note the force of the *hitpa'el.*

to a group of people and served their agenda. *1 Enoch,* in fact, fuses two quite distinct images of Enoch which served different purposes and may have had different origins. In the first image Enoch plays the role of a prophet who preaches righteousness and warns of divine judgment. In the second image he is a great sage who brings back to earth heavenly wisdom, notably a knowledge of astronomy and of the workings of the true calendar.

Enoch the preacher of righteousness seems to have been created in late Second Temple times by Jewish circles marked by a strongly eschatological worldview. They believed that they were living at the end of history and that catastrophic divine judgment was imminent. Their mentality was deeply sectarian: they were a righteous and persecuted minority standing out against an ungodly generation. They sensed a close parallelism between their own times and the period before the flood, when a similarly evil world order had been brought to an end by divine judgment, with only a righteous remnant being spared. For these circles Enoch, and to a lesser degree Noah, served as icons. Enoch had walked with God and rebuked the impiety of his contemporaries, warning them of impending disaster. He had left words of consolation which assured the righteous that the good would be rewarded and the wicked punished, and that they would with the help of God and his angels triumph over their enemies. Enoch's judgment of the fallen Watchers was an earnest that those in their own days who continued to follow the Watchers' corrupt ways would meet a similar fate. Indeed, Enoch himself, who had been physically removed from the world without seeing death, would return at the end of history to take part in the great final judgment.

Enoch the sage played a rather different role. His function was to authenticate a body of scientific doctrine relating to the heavenly bodies, the winds, and the structure of the world. It is probably no accident that this doctrine is concentrated in what is generally regarded as the oldest stratum of *1 Enoch,* the *Book of the Heavenly Luminaries* (chaps. 72–82), which may date to the fourth century B.C.E. Broadly speaking this is a wisdom text, though the wisdom circles in which it originated may have had a large priestly component, since the priests were probably responsible for the calendar in ancient Israel, and the doctrine had obvious calendric implications. In Judah of the fourth century B.C.E. this was alien wisdom. Where it came from is unclear: Babylonia is the most likely source, though its astronomical ideas are primitive and would have fallen short of the best in contemporary Babylonian science. One thing is reasonably certain: it is unlikely that anything resembling the *Book of the Heavenly Luminaries* had been seen before in Israel. Wisdom circles had, indeed, shown a keen interest in the marvels of nature, but that interest was expressed largely in poetry: nature was seen as evidence of God's glory and majesty, and there was a feeling, powerfully articulated in God's speech at the end of Job,[13] that its ways were inscrutable to the human intellect. In *1 Enoch* the emphasis has dramatically shifted: it is now considered proper to give a scientific description of the workings of nature, even of those most mysterious and inaccessible natural phenomena — the heavenly bodies. The sense of wonder is still there (as is the response of praise to God), but instead of stifling rational inquiry it spurred it on: the scientific description is a disclosure of the mind and purposes of God.

These wisdom circles chose Enoch as the "patron saint" of the new science, and he served their purposes well. Tradition clearly represented him as a righteous man, and seemed to hint that he had ascended to heaven and conversed with the angels. They could claim that it was in heaven that he learned the teaching and brought it back from there to earth. Perhaps they saw in his life span an allusion to the length of the solar year, which forms a core element of the doctrine. It was also an advantage that Enoch belonged to the early period of biblical history, before the flood, since antiquity conveyed prestige and authority. These were not newfangled ideas, but coeval with the dawn of time. And in attributing the new astronomy to Enoch they were, as we noted earlier, subscribing to the widespread notion that all great advances in human knowledge were the result of the disclosure of heavenly wisdom, imparted to the human race by culture-bringers — human figures who ascended to heaven, or

---

13. See Job 28 and 38–42. Job may have been composed in the late sixth or early fifth century B.C.E., no more than two hundred years before the *Book of the Heavenly Luminaries*.

quasi-divine figures who descended to earth. By attaching these ideas to Enoch the wisdom circles were able to validate them and to domesticate them within the traditions of Israel.

The image of Enoch as a sage belongs to the earliest recoverable strata of *1 Enoch*. Whether it predates the image of Enoch as a prophet is hard to say. It is equally uncertain whether the image of Enoch the prophet emerged in exactly the same circles as created the image of Enoch the sage. There are grounds for thinking that it did not, and that the image of Enoch the prophet was overlaid upon the image of Enoch the sage. This probably occurred, as we shall see presently, later than the appearance of the *Book of Jubilees* in ca. 150 B.C.E. There is a curious tension between the two images in our present *Book of Enoch*. In the *Book of the Watchers* (*1 Enoch* 1–36), the Watchers function, just as much as Enoch, as culture-bringers. There is no attempt to deny that the arts they brought involve heavenly wisdom, and yet that knowledge is viewed in a negative light: it should not have been disclosed and the result of its disclosure was to corrupt mankind and bring the flood. This reveals a deep uneasiness toward cultural innovation and change, which sits awkwardly with the espousal of Enoch the sage. Nowhere is it adequately explained why Enoch's wisdom was good and the Watchers' wisdom was bad. Enoch the prophet was probably the creation of a rather different circle, which took over and adapted the figure of Enoch the sage, reshaping in the process some of the traditions relating to the latter. We cannot be sure. One thing, however, is certain: in *1 Enoch*, as we now have it, the two images have been tightly intertwined into a single, richly composite figure.

In the Second Temple period an extensive literature circulated purporting to have been written by Enoch the great sage who lived before the flood. This literature claimed for itself high authority: it supposedly embodied revelations received directly from God and his angels, and had relevance for all time. That some took this claim very seriously is well illustrated by the *Book of Jubilees,* a retelling of Genesis which dates to around 150 B.C.E.[14]

---

14. Like *1 Enoch, Jubilees* has survived intact only in Ethiopic. Edition: VanderKam, *Book of Jubilees*. Commentary: Charles, *Book of Jubilees*.

The author of *Jubilees* evidently knew much of the material now contained in *1 Enoch* and he summarizes it very fairly.[15] He refers explicitly to a Book of the Signs of the Heavens (4:17), which may be the *Book of the Heavenly Luminaries* (*1 Enoch* 72–82), and to a testimony which Enoch left for future generations (4:18–19), perhaps an allusion to the *Epistle of Enoch* (*1 Enoch* 92–105) or some other hortatory part of *1 Enoch*. But there are intriguing differences in detail between *Jubilees* and *1 Enoch*. These may be explained in a number of ways. The author of *Jubilees* may have utilized the traditions in a different, probably earlier, form than that in which we now find them in *1 Enoch*,[16] or he may have had access to texts which are no longer extant. It is also possible that differences have arisen through exegesis. The author of *Jubilees* may have treated the Enochic literature as scripture, to be read and interpreted with the same care and attention as any other sacred text. As we have seen, *1 Enoch* bears a closer, more exegetical relationship to Genesis than might at first sight be supposed. Broadly speaking, exegesis is the dynamic which drives the tradition forward, but it is not always exegesis directly of Genesis. It may be exegesis of other forms of the tradition which have, in effect, acquired the status of scripture. The result of this secondary exegesis is ultimately to carry the tradition further and further away from the Genesis narrative.

The following are some of the more noteworthy differences between *Jubilees* and *1 Enoch*:

1. *Jub.* 4:15 implies that the Watchers' descent to the earth was initially for good reasons — "in order to teach the sons of men and to perform judgment and uprightness upon the earth." Only later did they begin "to mingle with the daughters of men so that they might be polluted" (4:22). According to this account the Watchers were originally beneficent bringers of culture, just

---

15. See especially *Jub.* 4:15–26.

16. It should be borne in mind that only two sections of *1 Enoch* can be dated with any certainty earlier than 150 B.C.E., the probable date of *Jubilees*, namely, the *Book of the Heavenly Luminaries* (*1 Enoch* 72–82) and the *Book of the Watchers* (*1 Enoch* 1–36), and even they may have been reworked later. This is certainly true for the *Book of the Heavenly Luminaries*. The relationship between *Jubilees* and *1 Enoch* is complex. However, *Jubilees* only makes sense if it is summarizing an extensive body of authoritative Enochic tradition, much of which is accurately reflected in our current *1 Enoch*.

like Enoch himself. In stark contrast, *1 Enoch,* as we have already seen, regards the Watchers as wicked from the start: their descent to earth was a fall from grace and the knowledge which they brought was in itself corrupting. It is almost certain that this represents a later reworking of the story. It reflects a more conservative and reactionary attitude toward cultural change, and may be a concomitant of the process of overlaying the image of Enoch the sage with that of Enoch the prophet.

2. *Jub.* 4:17 states that Enoch was "the first who learned writing." This seems to imply that he *invented* writing, or introduced it to mankind as part of the wisdom which he brought down to earth. This is nowhere explicitly asserted in *1 Enoch.* It is true that one of Enoch's titles in *1 Enoch* is "scribe,"[17] but this can be interpreted in a number of ways. "Scribe" may simply be a synonym for "sage" or "scholar," or it may be descriptive of Enoch's role as the recorder of humans' deeds, or as the author of a revealed text or texts. *Jubilees* may be exegeting the term "scribe." It would have been tempting, given Enoch's very early date in the biblical history and the frequent references to him in the tradition as writing, to conclude that he invented writing. Early mythmakers and historians saw the invention of writing as one of the great advances of civilization, and they speculated on when and by whom it was introduced.

3. The fixed solar calendar described in *1 Enoch* was almost certainly an innovation when it was promulgated in the fourth century B.C.E., and it diverged from the lunisolar calendar current in Judaism at that time. Yet *1 Enoch*'s account of the calendar is remarkably cool and scientific, and nowhere are its radical implications for religious observance explicitly drawn out. *Jubilees,* in contrast, is much more polemical in tone: the solar calendar was revealed to Enoch "so that the sons of man might know the [appointed] times of the years according to their order, with respect to each of their months" (4:17). In other words, Enoch's calendar is the true calendar which should be followed in observing festivals. Instead of the academic calm of *1 Enoch* we find in *Jubilees* the crusading spirit of religious reform. The divisive nature

---

17. See n. 6 above.

of *Jubilees'* claim can hardly be overestimated. The adoption of the Enochic calendar may have been one of the most important factors in defining the Qumran community as a sect within Israel and in setting it in radical opposition to the Jerusalem authorities and to the majority of Jews.

4. The author of *Jubilees* provides certain family details not found in *1 Enoch*. Thus we learn that Enoch's wife was Edni (or Edna) the daughter of Dan'el (4:20), and that his mother was Baraka the daughter of Rasuyal (4:15). *Jubilees* is here probably reflecting a lost source. There were circles in Second Temple Judaism interested in such genealogical minutiae. Their speculations feature prominently in Pseudo-Philo's *Biblical Antiquities,* which adds a plethora of names to the biblical genealogies, including five sons and three daughters of Enoch who were unknown to the author of Genesis.[18] The origins of these names are usually completely obscure. Some of those associated with Enoch in *Jubilees* are, however, reasonably transparent: Edna seems to echo Eden = paradise, to which Enoch was translated; and the etymology of Dan'el ("God has judged") is clearly appropriate in the context of Enoch's role in divine judgment.

5. *Jubilees* states emphatically that when Enoch was removed from the earth he was taken to the Garden of Eden, where he records the deeds of men. These records will be used by God in passing sentence in the great assize at the end of human history.[19] All this is implicit in *1 Enoch,* though it is nowhere expressed with such simplicity and force. *Jubilees,* however, adds a few touches of its own. First, it claims that because of Enoch "none of the waters of the flood came upon the whole land of Eden" (4:24). Evidently in the geography of *Jubilees,* as in the geography of *1 Enoch,* Eden is located on the same landmass as the habitable earth. The flood was a judgment on sinners, so it is logical that it should not have affected Eden where righteous Enoch dwelled. There is a hint here of an important theological idea, namely that the merit of the righteous can save the world, just as surely as the sins of the ungodly can destroy it. Second, *Jubilees* assigns to

---

18. Pseudo-Philo, *Bib. Ant.* 1:15–17.
19. *Jub.* 4:23–24; 10:17.

Enoch another role besides that of recording scribe. He officiates as a priest, burning incense at evening in a sanctuary on Mount Qater in the East of the world (4:25). This priestly role for Enoch is absent in *1 Enoch,* but was taken up strongly in later tradition.

6. Finally, Enoch is cited twice in *Jubilees* as an authority on religious law — once regarding aspects of sacrificial procedure (21:10), and once regarding firstfruits (7:38–39). This is totally unexpected, since, if we exclude the calendar, Enoch is nowhere represented in *1 Enoch* as a revealer of *halakhah.* Both sacrifices and firstfruits are covered in the Mosaic legislation. To invoke a pre-Sinai figure as authoritative in such matters is potentially significant, since it could suggest a diminution of the importance of the Sinai revelation and of its mediator Moses. We shall return to this point later.

Enochic literature appears to have been widely disseminated in late Second Temple Judaism and, as a result, Enoch was regarded as a figure of authority by very different sects and parties. The numerous fragments of Enochic literature preserved among the Dead Sea Scrolls testify to the esteem in which it was held at Qumran. It is a moot point whether or not it was regarded as scripture, but it was accorded sufficient status for the community to feel obliged to follow the solar calendar which it advocated.

Some Enochic traditions reached the Samaritans. This emerges from the fragments of Pseudo-Eupolemus preserved by Eusebius in his *Praeparatio Evangelica* 9.17.1–9 and 9.19.2. From internal evidence the author of these fragments was a Samaritan who lived in the mid–second century B.C.E.[20] He claims that Abraham taught the Egyptian priests at Heliopolis "astrology and the other sciences . . . saying that the Babylonians had obtained this knowledge. However, he attributed the discovery of them to Enoch. Enoch first discovered astrology, not the Egyptians." He goes on to assert that "the Greeks say that Atlas discovered astrology. However, Atlas is the same as Enoch." He concludes: "The son of Enoch was Methuselah. He learned everything through the angels of God, and so knowledge came to us."

---

20. Text, translation, commentary: Holladay, "Pseudo-Eupolemus (Anonymous)," 157–87. For other references to Enoch in Samaritan sources see *Memar Markah* 2:10 and 4:9, and the *Samaritan Targum* to Gen 5:24.

The standing of Enoch and Enochic literature seems to have been high also in early Christianity. Jude 14–15 regards Enoch, "the seventh from Adam," as a prophet and quotes *1 Enoch* 1:9. This quotation is all the more significant because the New Testament writers normally cite directly only the books of the standard synagogue canon. 2 Pet 2:4 may echo *1 Enoch* 10:4–6, and Christ's descent and proclamation to the imprisoned spirits in 2 Pet 3:19–20 has often been compared with Enoch's visit and proclamation to the fallen Watchers in the underworld in *1 Enoch* 12–13. Enoch figures in the great catalog of the exemplars of faith in Hebrews 11: "By faith Enoch was translated that he should not see death; and he was not found because God translated him: for before his translation he had witness borne to him that he had been well-pleasing to God" (Heb 11:5). There are grounds for believing that Enoch the prophet and sage was revered across the whole religious spectrum of Second Temple Judaism: he belonged to catholic Israel in much the same way as did Moses and David.

The continuing vitality of the Enochic tradition at the end of the Second Temple period is well illustrated by the so-called *Second Book of Enoch*. This enigmatic work survives now only in Slavonic in a bewildering variety of recensions and versions which attest its popularity in the Russian Orthodox church. Its tradition history has never been properly clarified and may be beyond recovery. Nor has any consensus been reached as to when and where it was written. However, there is evidence to suggest that behind the extant texts, which have been worked over by Christian scribes, stands a Jewish work composed in Greek in Alexandria in the first century of the current era.[21]

2 Enoch repeats many of the themes and motifs of *1 Enoch,* but it also has distinctive features which give it a character all its own. The story line is clear and strong, and fills out imaginatively the skeletal biblical narrative. Enoch, speaking in the first person, tells how in his 365th year he was taken up to heaven by two angels (identified in 33:6 as Samoila and Raguila). These angelic guardians escort him upward through six heavens, explaining the

---

21. Slavonic text: Vaillant, *Livre des Secrets d'Hénoch.* Translation and commentary: Andersen, "2 Enoch," *OTP* 1.92–221.

sights to be seen in each. At the edge of the seventh heaven they leave him, and Gabriel, or, according to an alternative tradition, Michael, carries him up and sets him before the face of the Lord. The Lord bids the archangel Vrevoil to bring out the books from the heavenly storehouses and to read them to Enoch, who, armed with a "pen for speed-writing," fills at the angel's dictation 366 books. The Lord then instructs Enoch to return to earth and tell his sons "all that I have told you and everything that you have seen, from the lowest heavens up to my throne... and give them the books in your handwriting" (33:6, 8). He descends again to his house, summons his sons, and for thirty days disburdens himself of all the heavenly wisdom which he has received. At the end of this period he announces his final departure. He addresses parting admonitions to a crowd who gather to pay their last respects, and "when Enoch had spoken to his people the Lord sent the gloom onto the earth, and it became dark and covered the men who were standing and talking with Enoch. And the angels hurried and grasped Enoch and carried him up to highest heaven, where the Lord received him and made him stand in front of his face for eternity" (67:1–3).

The Enoch of 2 *Enoch* is broadly the same as the Enoch of the earlier writings: again he is depicted as a great sage to whom the mysterious workings of nature were revealed on a heavenly journey; as a prophet who admonishes his contemporaries to walk in righteousness and warns them of judgment if they do not; and as a heavenly scribe who records humans' deeds pending the last judgment (though the theme of judgment is less prominent in 2 *Enoch* than in 1 *Enoch*). On one point, however, 2 *Enoch* marks a radical new departure: it claims unequivocally that Enoch ascended *bodily* and that this ascent resulted in his physical transformation into an angel. The assertion that a human could bodily enter the upper world was profoundly problematic within the worldview of early Judaism. How could the human body endure such a journey? On what would it live? How was it conceivable that Enoch could perform the exalted role of heavenly scribe while still encumbered by the gross limitations of flesh and blood? The problem was more than practical: it was deeply theological. Heaven was the realm of God and God's angels;

earth belonged to humankind. It was not easy to admit that the boundary between these two worlds could be crossed, since this implied some form of ontological transformation which blurred the distinction between human and divine: descent from heaven involved "incarnation," ascent from earth "deification."

The care with which the authors of *1 Enoch* skirt around these problems shows how sensitive it was to them. Enoch's ascent to heaven, *1 Enoch* seems to say, was in a dream during sleep. The implication is that his body remained on earth and only his "soul" ascended to heaven. And when he finally departed from the world he was taken, not to heaven, but to paradise, which is located on the eastern rim of the habitable earth and consequently enjoys the same physical environment as the rest of the world. Enoch's cosmic journeys, borne bodily along by a whirlwind, take him to many strange places, but all appear to be strictly within the confines of the habitable earth. At only one point in the complex traditions of *1 Enoch* do we get a hint of the possible transformation of Enoch into an angelic being. This is in 71:14 where Enoch is apparently identified with the heavenly Son of Man. The Son of Man is the chief protagonist of the so-called *Parables of Enoch* (*1 Enoch* 37–71). He is a transcendent, angelic being who functions as the celestial champion of the righteous on earth and the judge of their wicked enemies. As Daniel 7 shows, he originated outside the Enochic tradition, and he is depicted in the *Parables* as quite distinct from Enoch (Enoch is *shown* the Son of Man). Only at the end, in an unexpected twist, is it asserted that Enoch *is* the Son of Man, and that what he has been observing is his own history: "And that angel came to me and greeted me with his voice, and said to me, You are the Son of Man who was born to righteousness, and righteousness remains over you, and the righteousness of the Head of Days will not leave you."[22] The fusion of the two figures is not without its logic, given Enoch's role as the representative of the righteous and as an agent of divine judgment. The date of the *Parables of Enoch* has been much debated, but there is now a consensus that it represents some of the latest material in our cur-

---

22. *1 Enoch* 71:14.

rent text of *1 Enoch*. It may even be post-Christian. Chapter 71, where Enoch is identified as the Son of Man, is almost certainly a late addition to the *Parables*. It is, therefore, possibly later in date than the original version of *2 Enoch*. It may even have emerged from the same circles that produced that work.

2 Enoch asserts with a boldness and clarity nowhere matched in *1 Enoch* that Enoch ascended *bodily* to heaven and was transformed into an angel. It is true that the story of his ascent begins when he is asleep, but it is expressly stated that his guardian angels woke him up, and that he rose and went out from his house, closing the door behind him. Such an ascent cannot be achieved without a physical transformation, so when he reaches God's presence, God tells Michael, "Go, and extract Enoch from his earthly clothing. And anoint him with my delightful oil, and put him into the clothes of my glory. And so Michael did, just as the Lord had said to him. And the appearance of that oil is greater than the greatest light, and its ointment is like sweet dew, and its fragrance myrrh, and it is like the rays of the glittering sun." Transformed Enoch, looking at himself, observes that he has "become like one of the Lord's glorious ones and there was no observable difference" (*2 Enoch* 22:8–10). Since Enoch has become an angel, his reverse journey back to earth now becomes a problem. How could mortals endure the advent of such a glorious one? This problem is addressed in *2 Enoch* 37, where Enoch's face is said to have been "chilled," because otherwise no human being would have been able to look at it. Back on earth, Methusalam offers to prepare Enoch a meal, but Enoch replies: "Since the time the Lord anointed me with the ointment of his glory, food has not come into me, and earthly pleasure my soul does not remember; nor do I desire anything earthly" (*2 Enoch* 56:2). And when Enoch finally returns to heaven it is to stand forever before the Lord as one of the angels of the presence (*2 Enoch 67:2*).

The theme of the physical transformation of Enoch was to open the way to astonishingly daring speculations about his heavenly role. Some of our earliest evidence for this speculation is to be found in the *Third Book of Enoch,* a late Hebrew apocalypse (probably in its present form dating to the sixth/seventh century C.E.) which has been transmitted as part of the corpus of early Jewish mystical writings known as the Heikhalot literature.[23] *3 Enoch* tells how Rabbi Ishmael ascended to heaven and met the archangel Metatron, who revealed to him a range of secrets, about the angelic hierarchies and their liturgy, about the workings of the cosmos, and about the future redemption, rather similar to those we find in *1* and *2 Enoch*. However, the real focus of interest in *3 Enoch* is the figure of Metatron himself. He belongs to the very highest order of archangels, the Princes of the Presence (שׂרי הפנים), who alone are allowed to see God's face. He is the prince of the world; the heavenly high priest who officiates in the celestial sanctuary, the tabernacle of Metatron; the prince of Torah who mediated the Torah to Moses on Sinai; Israel's representative and advocate in the celestial law court; the angel in whom in a special way God has put God's Name.[24] The insignia of Metatron's high office — his throne, crown, and robe — are described in detail, and they match the insignia of God.[25] In short, Metatron is God's vice-regent: God has placed him over all the other angels, committed to him the governance of the world, and designated him "the Lesser YHWH" [יהוה הקטון].[26] "I made honor, majesty, and glory his garment," says God, "beauty, pride, and strength, his outer robe, and a kingly crown, five hundred times five hundred parasangs, his diadem. I bestowed on him some of my majesty, some of my magnificence, some of the splendor of my glory, which is on the throne of glory, and I called him by my name, 'The Lesser YHWH, Prince of the Divine Presence, knower of secrets.' Every secret I have revealed to him in love, every mystery I have made known to him in uprightness. I have fixed his throne at the door of my palace, on the outside, so that

---

23. Hebrew text: Odeberg, *3 Enoch*; Schäfer, *Synopse*. Translations and commentaries: Alexander, *OTP* 1.223–315; Mopsik, *Livre hébreu*; Schäfer and Hermann, *Übersetzung*. The references follow the edition of Odeberg. In his introduction Schäfer gives a table correlating this system with that employed in the *Synopse*.

24. For Enoch as prince of the world see *3 Enoch* 48C:9–10; as heavenly high priest, *3 Enoch* 15B; as prince of Torah, *3 Enoch* 48C:12; 48D:6–10; as Israel's representative in the heavenly law court, see Alexander, *OTP* 1.243; as the angel in whom God has put God's Name, *3 Enoch* 3:2; 12:5; 48D:1.

25. *3 Enoch* 10 and 12.

26. *3 Enoch* 12:5.

he might sit and execute judgment over all my household in the height."[27]

It comes as something of a shock to learn that this exalted being, second only to God in the cosmic hierarchy, is none other than the patriarch Enoch, the son of Jared, who, having been taken up to heaven as a witness to God's justice in bringing the flood,[28] was transformed into an angel. Like *2 Enoch, 3 Enoch* clearly envisages *bodily* ascent and so postulates the physical metamorphosis of Enoch: "When the Holy One, blessed be He, took me to serve the throne of glory, the wheels of the chariot and all the needs of the Shekhinah, at once my flesh turned to flame, my sinews to blazing fire, my bones to juniper coals, my eyelashes to lightning flashes, my eyeballs to fiery torches, the hairs of my head to hot flames, all my limbs to wings of burning fire, and the substance of my body to blazing fire."[29] So Enoch becomes, like the other angels, physically composed of fire. Another part of his transformation involved the enlargement of his body until it equaled the dimensions of the world: "I was enlarged and increased in size until I matched the world in its length and breadth. He made to grow on me seventy-two wings, thirty-six on one side and thirty-six on the other, and each single wing covered an entire world. He fixed in me 365,000 eyes and each eye was like the Great Light. There was no sort of splendor, brilliance, brightness, or beauty in the luminaries of the world that he failed to fix in me."[30] We shall return later to the possible significance of this bizarre tradition.

Metatron and Enoch, like Enoch and the heavenly Son of Man, were originally distinct figures. The similarities of their roles led to convergence and finally to identification. The result of the identification of Metatron and Enoch is clear: Enoch, a man with an earthly existence and genealogy, has been deified. Moreover there is a hint in *3 Enoch* that this process of deification will be replicated in the case of other men. *3 Enoch* presents a significant

---

27. *3 Enoch* 48C:7–8. This is part of the Alphabet of Aqiva traditions appended to the main text of *3 Enoch*.

28. *3 Enoch* 4 and 48C. *3 Enoch* makes considerable play of the idea that Enoch was taken up as a witness.

29. *3 Enoch* 15.

30. *3 Enoch* 9.

parallelism between the ascension of Ishmael and the ascension of Enoch. It seems to imply that Enoch's transformation prefigures that of every adept: he is the "forerunner" who has charted the way that others can follow.[31]

We have traced the figure of Enoch through Jewish literature from Second Temple times down to the early Middle Ages. Let us pause for a moment and take stock. The analysis so far suggests two important general observations. First, we seem to be faced with a genuine, ongoing *tradition*. The persistence of certain motifs is astonishing. For example, Enoch in *Jubilees* in the second century B.C.E. is a high priest. Almost a thousand years later he retains that role in the Heikhalot texts, though in a rather different setting. The figure, indeed, changes and evolves, but in a coherent way, so that the later phases of development can be seen as growing out of the earlier. Already in *1 Enoch* Enoch has a heavenly role. This looms larger and larger in the tradition and becomes ever more exalted. And yet the figure of Enoch in *3 Enoch* retains a recognizable family resemblance to his predecessor in the Second Temple period. Though we are clearly dealing with some form of intertextuality, direct literary dependence seems to be ruled out, since there is no evidence that the author of *2 Enoch* had *1 Enoch* in front of him, still less that *3 Enoch* knew *1* or *2 Enoch* directly. Such continuity is hard to explain other than in terms of apocalyptic circles that speculated about Enoch and passed on Enochic lore through the ages from one to the other. These circles may be shadowy and ill-defined, but their existence seems to be a necessary postulate of the literary remains.

The second general observation is that a powerful subtext can

---

31. There has been endless speculation on the origin of the name Metatron, but it is possible that it means something like "the forerunner." One very plausible etymology derives it from the Latin *metator*, which occurs in Greek as a loanword under the form *mitator*. The *metator* was the officer in the Roman army who went ahead of the column on the march to mark out the campsite where the troops would bivouac for the night. Hence, figuratively, "forerunner." There can be little doubt that the Latin *metator* was known to the rabbis and that as a loanword they spelled it *metatron/mitatron*. The appellation may first have been given to the angel of the Lord who led the Israelites through the wilderness: that angel acted like a Roman army *metator*, guiding the Israelites on their way. The name could then have been extended to express the idea that Enoch was a *metator* for the other adepts, showing them how they could escape from the wilderness of this world into the promised land of heaven. See further, Alexander, *OTP* 1.228.

be detected in the Enochic tradition, implying a contrast between Enoch and Moses. Moses, the lawgiver of Israel, was the founder of the Jewish polity. The circles which looked to Enoch as their patron were, at least to some extent, challenging Moses's primacy. We noted earlier the polemical potential of the fact that Enoch lived long before Moses and the Sinai revelation. It has been plausibly argued that late in the Second Temple period the Enochic writings were canonized into five books — a Pentateuch to rival the Five Books of Moses.[32] We found Enoch cited occasionally as a legal authority who pronounced on halakhic matters explicitly covered in the Torah of Moses. Nor should we miss the subversive potential of the claim in *3 Enoch* that it was Enoch-Metatron who, as prince of Torah, dispensed the Law to Moses on Sinai. This clarifies the relationship between Enoch and Moses in no uncertain terms. Moreover, if the adepts have direct access to the prince of Torah who instructed Moses, they are surely on a similar footing to Moses, and have less need to depend on him.

This implicit challenge to the primacy of Moses was recognized and countered in two main ways. First an attempt was made to cut off the Enochic development from its exegetical roots: Enoch, it was argued, was not such a righteous man, nor did he ascend to heaven, nor was he translated so that he did not see death. We find elements of this counterattack already in Philo's *De Abrahamo*, where Enoch is seen as an example of repentance, and a contrast is drawn between him as a "penitent" (μετατεθειμένος) who devoted the earlier part of his life to vice but the latter to virtue, and the "perfect man" (τέλειος) who was virtuous from the first.[33] Philo's attitude is all the more significant when it is recalled that *2 Enoch* was probably written in Alexandria in the first century C.E., and that Philo attributes to *Moses* many of the exalted characteristics of Enoch.[34] It is, however, in rabbinic literature — not surprisingly — that the exegetical counterattack to the exaltation of Enoch is most obvious. There is generally a marked silence about Enoch in rabbinic aggadah. Such observa-

---

32. Milik, *Books of Enoch*, 54–55 and *passim*.
33. *Abr.* 47. Philo takes a rather different, more favorable line in the *Quaest. in Gen.* 1.86.
34. See further below.

tions as exist are pointedly negative. The *locus classicus* is *Genesis Rabbah* 25:1:[35]

> "And Enoch walked with God, and he was not, for God took him" (Gen 5:24). Rabbi Hama the son of Rabbi Hosha'ya said: ["And he was not" means] that he was not inscribed in the scroll of the righteous but in the scroll of the wicked. Rabbi Aivu said: Enoch was a hypocrite acting sometimes as a righteous, sometimes as a wicked man. Therefore the Holy One, blessed be he, said: "While he is righteous I will remove him." Rabbi Aivu also said: He judged him on New Year, when he judges all the inhabitants of world. Heretics asked Rabbi Abbahu: "We do not find that death is mentioned in the case of Enoch?" "How so?" he inquired. They said: " 'Taking' is mentioned here and also in connection with Elijah: 'Do you know that today the Lord is taking your master away from you?' " (2 Kgs 2:5). "If you stress the word 'taking,' " he answered, "then 'taking' is mentioned here, while in Ezekiel it is said, 'Behold, I take away from you the desire of your eyes [with a plague]' " (Ezek 24:16). Rabbi Tanhuma observed: "He answered them well." A matron asked Rabbi Jose: "We do not find death stated of Enoch." Said he to her: "If it had said, 'And Enoch walked with God,' and no more, I would agree with you. Since, however, it says, 'And he was not, for God took him,' it means that he was no more in the world, 'for God took him [in death].' "

A second line of counterattack was to build up the figure of Moses and to attribute to him the same transcendent qualities as Enoch. Thus some claimed that *Moses* had ascended into heaven, had received heavenly wisdom, now played a cosmic role as a heavenly being, and had been, in some sense, "deified." Elements of this process of exalting Moses may be found as early as the *Exagoge* of Ezekiel the Tragedian (second century B.C.E.). Philo, as we have already hinted, accords to Moses divine status, which clearly parallels that assigned elsewhere to Enoch, while at the same time he rather denigrates Enoch.[36] 2 *Apoc. Bar.* 59:5–12 is an instructive case: there God shows to Moses "the measures

---

35. Note also *Targum Onqelos*'s translation of Gen 5:24: "And Enoch walked in the fear of the Lord; and he was not for the Lord caused him to die" (the variant "for the Lord did *not* cause him to die" is almost certainly secondary). Contrast this with *Targum Pseudo-Jonathan*: "And Enoch served before the Lord in uprightness, and, behold, he was not with the dwellers on earth, for he was withdrawn and went up to the firmament by the word before the Lord, and his name was called Metatron the great scribe." William Tyndale's understanding of Gen 5:24, "Enos walked with God and was no more seen: that is, he lived godly and died," reflects classic rabbinic interpretation (it is notably close to *Targum Onqelos* and to Rashi), but where he got it is hard to say: see Hammond, *English Bible*, 35–36.

36. For a useful and careful survey of the evidence see Hurtado, *One God, One Lord*, 51–70.

of fire, the depths of the abyss, the weight of the winds" and so forth, cosmological doctrines closely associated in earlier tradition with Enoch. A similar transference of Enochic roles to Ezra — as Moses redivivus — is implied in 4 Ezra 14:50.

Chronology suggests that the Enochic traditions have the primacy. It is the supporters of Moses who are trying to steal Enoch's clothes. That the transference went the other way, from Moses to Enoch, is much less likely. However we view it, we should recognize that there is a hidden agenda here: the same system can hardly accommodate two such figures. Moses and Enoch are being set up in some sense as rivals, as representing competing paradigms of Judaism. The circles that looked primarily to *Moshe rabbenu* had a different outlook from those that looked primarily to *Hanokh rabbenu*. Historically speaking, the Mosaic paradigm predominated (it was the one embraced by the Pharisaic-rabbinic tradition), but the Enochic paradigm showed remarkable vitality and fed a number of sectarian movements within Judaism — notably the Dead Sea sect and early Christianity. It was also an important source of inspiration for later Gnostic systems, Manichaeism, and the medieval kabbala.

3 Enoch can be taken as a turning point in the history of the Enochic traditions; it marks the close of a development which began in the third century B.C.E., and the beginning of new departures which gave a new lease of life to the biblical patriarch. Within Judaism three strands can be distinguished in the Enoch traditions after *3 Enoch*. First, we have the direct continuation of the *3 Enoch* line of Enoch as an exalted, heavenly being. Second there was the reaffirmation of the denigrating rabbinic tradition, classically expressed in *Genesis Rabbah*. Third, we find a mediating position in which Enoch is regarded in a positive light as a righteous person and a folk hero, who is invoked in contexts of moral exhortation as a model of piety. It may be claimed that he had ascended to heaven, but little or no attention is paid to his heavenly existence.

Enoch's continuing cosmic and celestial life is bound up with the figure of Metatron. Metatron was of great interest to both the medieval Hasidei Ashkenaz and the kabbalists of Spain. He is identified sometimes as a high archangel distinct from God, and sometimes as a manifestation of God or as an entity or potency within the godhead (in the kabbala often as the Sefirah *Malkhut*).[37] It is unclear to what extent we should regard the history of Metatron in the Middle Ages as automatically part of the history of Enoch. As we noted earlier Metatron was originally an independent figure, so it cannot be assumed that his identification with Enoch is everywhere presupposed. However, the link with Enoch was widely known and is mentioned on many occasions. The *Zohar* illustrates some of these developments. Its author clearly knew a version of the fall of the Watchers (called by him 'Uzza and 'Aza'el), whom he identifies with the *Nefilim* of Gen 6:4. He was also aware of the tradition of Enoch's entry into paradise:[38]

> When [Enoch] was born he found himself near the Garden. The light [i.e., the supernal radiance] began to shine within him. He was beautified with the beauty of holiness and the sparkling light rested upon him. He entered the Garden of Eden and found the Tree of Life there, the boughs and the fruit of the tree.

Elsewhere the "supernal radiance" is identified with the heavenly soul of Adam which had quitted him when he sinned but had returned to be reincarnated in Enoch.[39]

Behind these passages is a concept of Metatron as a divine entity first incarnate in Adam and then reincarnate in Enoch. Enoch, having perfected himself, in contrast to Adam who sinned and fell, reascends to his heavenly home and takes his rightful place in the heights of the universe, above the highest angels. And there is a clear implication that what Enoch has done others may do as well. The heavenly *gnosis* through which Enoch perfected himself in the Garden of Eden is still available to the adepts and can be used by them to perfect themselves and to ascend like him. What is involved is little short of the deification of man. Enoch thus becomes a redeemer figure — a second Adam through whom humanity is restored.[40] There were hints of these ideas earlier in the tradition. *3 Enoch,* as we noted, spoke of Enoch's physical

---

37. See Abrams, "Boundaries of Divine Ontology," 291–321.

38. *Zohar Hadash, Terumah* 42d. The translation is based on Tishby, *Wisdom of the Zohar,* 2.627. See further *Zohar* I, 37b, 55b.

39. Cf. *Zohar Hadash* to Song of Songs, 69a–b.

40. Tishby's eloquent exposition of the idea deserves to be quoted in full:

transformation as involving an increase in the size of his body until it matched the dimensions of the world. In certain rabbinic traditions, primordial Adam's body, like that of the Gnostic *protanthropos,* corresponded to the world in size, but was diminished to the present limited dimensions of the human body as a result of the fall. *3 Enoch* may be expressing in mythological language the idea that Enoch reversed the fall of Adam. Moreover, we noted that in *3 Enoch* Enoch-Metatron was in some sense represented as a "forerunner," blazing a trail that could ultimately be followed by every adept. But these ideas are put nowhere with the clarity and force with which we find them expressed in the kabbala.[41]

The classic rabbinic view of Enoch as found in *Genesis Rabbah* is repeated in the Middle Ages, particularly by biblical commentators. The *Yalqut Shim'oni* simply reproduces *Genesis Rabbah* as its comment on Gen 4:25. Rashi takes a softer line, reflecting specifically the view of Rabbi Aivu, that Enoch was removed by God while righteous to prevent him from falling back into sin.

An interesting representative of the mediating position is the eleventh-century paraphrase of Genesis known as *Sefer ha-Yashar.* This takes the view that Enoch was a righteous man who was translated to heaven, but it draws a veil over his heavenly life.

The Enoch-Metatron legend, especially when supplemented by kabbalistic ideas, expresses in a very striking way the awesome nature of man at the peak of perfection. The kabbalistic doctrine of man, based on earlier Jewish ideas, teaches that he is the crown of Creation and the most choice of all God's creatures, higher even than the angels in his real essence. The soul, which is alone the essence of man according to the Zohar, is extracted from the pure radiance of the divine emanation. It is a divine spark that has been inserted into the physical body. The soul descends and assumes a physical form only in order to acquire a special perfection in the terrestrial world (the world of "making"). At root, therefore, in his eternal, spiritual essence, man is very near indeed to the divine realm, and his folly and contamination by sin are no more than manifestations of corruption and degeneration occasioned by his temporal, physical existence. The unique man, Enoch, who was able to achieve the ideal, supernal perfection that was indeed destined for the whole of mankind, but taken from them because of Adam's sin, purified himself of the material defects inherent in corporeal existence, and ascended to the highest levels of the angelic hierarchy. Enoch-Metatron symbolizes the culmination of the ascent for which man is destined to strive, and in this refined image perfect man is superior to the angels. (*Wisdom of the Zohar* 2.630–31)

41. The idea that the body of primordial Adam matched the world in size is found in *Gen. Rab.* 8.1; *b. Hag.* 12a; and, possibly, in *Pesiq. Rab. Kah.* 1.1. For a discussion see Idel, "Enoch Is Metatron," 151–70. On Enoch-Metatron as the "forerunner," see n. 31 above.

As far as *Sefer ha-Yashar* is concerned his disappearance from the earth is the end of the story. *Sefer ha-Yashar* is full of embellishments not found elsewhere. Enoch is represented as a philosopher-king who ruled over the whole world and taught mankind morality and "the ways of the Lord." There is no hint of the antediluvian violence and disorder that is stressed elsewhere in the tradition.[42]

Enoch is a Jewish figure, and the Jewish sources, so full, clear, and coherent, form the key tradition in his evolution. But we should not forget that he had a life outside of Judaism as well. The picture would be incomplete without some concluding remarks — however brief — on developments in Christianity, in the Hermetic and Gnostic traditions, and in Islam.

Direct quotations and allusions show, as we have already noted, that at least some New Testament writers knew the Enochic literature. These references doubtless helped to commend the Enochic writings to the early Christians. Two of our major surviving Enochic texts, *1* and *2 Enoch,* though Jewish in origin, were preserved for posterity not within the synagogue but within the church. Interest in Enoch was widespread in the Christian world, but it seems to have been particularly strong in two areas — Egypt and the Balkans. *1 Enoch,* though of Palestinian origin, circulated in Egypt, from where it may have passed southward to Ethiopia. It was translated into Ge'ez and was highly regarded by the Ethiopian church.[43] From the Balkans *2 Enoch,* which originated in Egypt, seems to have been carried northeastward into Russia, where it was studied, copied, and reworked again and again by Russian Orthodox scholars.

---

42. Hebrew text: Goldschmidt, *Sefer hajaschar,* 8–14; Eisenstein, *Ozar Midrashim,* 1.182–83 (under the title "The Life of Enoch"). *Sefer ha-Yashar* was probably written in southern Spain at the end of the eleventh century. Its picture of Enoch as a philosopher-king may be influenced by Islamic sources. Herr, *EncJud* 16.1517, shrewdly observes that the structure of *Sefer ha-Yashar* is reminiscent of Pseudo-Philo's *Book of Biblical Antiquities.* It should be noted that the opening sections of Petrus Alphonsi's *Disciplina Clericalis* were translated into Hebrew and circulated under the title of *Sefer Hanokh.* Editions: Pichard, *Livre d'Hénoch;* Amzalak, *Da Amizade.* Apart from the opening sentence, "Enoch the philosopher, who is called Idris in Arabic, said to his son, 'Let the fear of God be your business, and profit shall come to you without pain,' " the text has nothing to do with the patriarch Enoch.

43. On the complex question of the canonic status of Enoch in Ethiopia, see Beckwith, *Old Testament Canon,* 478–505. It is uncertain whether *1 Enoch* came to Ethiopia from Egypt or from Syria.

The influence of the Jewish Enochic traditions on Christian thought, though potentially great, is not easy to document. Whether or not the appellation "Son of Man" in the Gospels was ever intended to link Jesus with the heavenly figure of Daniel 7 and *1 Enoch* 37–71 is a fiercely debated question. A case can certainly be made that the Gospel of Matthew's account of the Last Judgment (Matt 25:31–46) owes something to the judgment scene in *1 Enoch* 62–63, with Jesus being implicitly identified as the heavenly "Son of Man." There can be no denying that Enoch and Christ are remarkably similar in Jewish and Christian sources. The ascent and celestial role of Enoch in *2* and *3 Enoch* can easily be paralleled in christological texts. If we add Enoch's functions as a redeemer, as a second Adam, as a "forerunner," and as an earthly incarnation of the preexistent divine being Metatron, then the convergence is too exact to be accidental. The parallelism has, of course, been noticed by scholars in the twentieth century,[44] but they were by no means the first to do so. Earlier it had also struck Christian missionaries and apologists and Christian kabbalists, who exploited it for polemical purposes to argue that Judaism in fact knew of divine redeemers similar to Christ, and that the Jews could not, therefore, simply dismiss the orthodox Christian doctrine of Christ as a heretical aberration patently at odds with Jewish monotheism.[45] There may even be in the synagogue liturgy a concealed allusion to Jesus as Metatron.[46] What is not clear, however, is whether the figure of Enoch in early Judaism influenced the *origins* of Christology. Did the Jewish Enoch provide the first Christians with a serviceable model for interpreting the person and work of Christ? Or did the influence operate in the other direction: was Enoch-Metatron based on, and was he, perhaps, a polemical reaction to, the Christian claims about Christ? Both positions may, in principle, be correct: we should probably see here an intense dialectic between the two traditions.[47]

---

44. E.g., Bietenhard, *Himmlische Welt;* Murtonen, "Figure of Metatron," 409–11.

45. Abrams, "Boundaries of Divine Ontology," 317–21, draws particular attention to the early-eighteenth-century writers Johannan Kemper and Caspar Calvor.

46. See Liebes, "Angels of the Shofar," 171–96.

47. Enoch provided a paradigm, but at the same time he also posed a threat, since by definition he possessed many of the powers and functions of Christ. He was, therefore, a

One development seems to be characteristically Christian. There was a widespread Christian belief that Enoch and Elijah would return at the end of history to challenge the Antichrist. They would be killed by him but would be raised from the dead and ascend to heaven. This tradition is rooted in the reference to the two unnamed witnesses in Rev 11:3–13.[48] Thus Enoch was assigned a secure place in Christian apocalyptic literature, and by far the commonest representations of him in Christian art show him as one of the two eschatological witnesses.[49] Jewish sources, of course, also saw a similarity between Enoch and Elijah (both were "taken" up to heaven by God), but apart from the hints in *1 Enoch* of Enoch's role in the last judgment, the motif of a future return of Enoch at the end of history is not prominent in Jewish apocalyptic.[50]

Enoch was also adopted by the Hermetic tradition. There are obvious similarities between Hermes-Thoth — the inventor of writing, the revealer of secrets, the guide of souls after death[51] — and the Enoch of postbiblical Judaism, so obvious, indeed, that it is surprising more was not made of them. It has long been accepted that the early Hermetic writers drew on Jewish sources, and some have plausibly argued that they knew specifically the Enochic literature (there are possible echoes of *1 Enoch*'s account

---

potential rival to Christ, just as he was to Moses in Jewish tradition. The early Christians were aware of the problem: the story of the transfiguration (Mark 9:2–8 and parallels) is an attempt to assert Christ's priority over two such potential rivals who had also ascended to heaven and been transfigured and glorified. Those two rivals are Moses and Elijah, but they could equally have been Moses and Enoch.

48. Further: Bauckham, "Martyrdom of Enoch," 447–58.

49. Emmerson, *Antichrist,* 139–41. For earlier references to the two witnesses, see the classic study by Bousset, *Antichrist Legend,* 203–5.

50. For example, he plays no part in the late Hebrew apocalypse known as *Sefer Zerub-babel,* though one should note that in the scenario of the end-time presented in this work, Armilos (Antichrist) is opposed by two messianic figures, one of whom is martyred by him, and his body left ignominiously outside the gates of Jerusalem for forty-one days. It should also be noted that the vision is revealed by Metatron, though he is identified with the archangel Michael, not with Enoch. See Lévi, "L'apocalypse de Zorobabel," 129–60.

51. The tradition that Metatron teaches Torah to the souls of unborn infants suggests that he performs some of the functions of a psychopomp: see *3 Enoch* 48C:12, "Moreover, Metatron sits for three hours every day in the heavens above, and assembles all the souls of the dead that have died in their mothers' wombs, and the babes that have died at their mothers' breasts, and of the schoolchildren that have died while studying the five books of the Torah. He brings them beneath the throne of glory, and sits them around him in classes, in companies, and in groups, and teaches them Torah, and wisdom, and haggadah, and tradition, and he completes for them their study of the scroll of the Law."

of the fall of the angels in the Asclepius),[52] but it is uncertain whether they identified Hermes with Enoch in the way in which they identified Hermes with Thoth. However, the Sabians of Harran in northern Mesopotamia in the early Middle Ages explicitly made the connection. They went on to equate Hermes with Idris in the Qur'an, thereby, incidentally, identifying Enoch and Idris.[53] There was also some interest in Enoch among the scholars who rediscovered the Hermetic corpus in Renaissance and post-Renaissance Europe, though once again the possibilities were not exploited as much as they might have been to legitimate Hermetic doctrine.[54]

Enoch played a role in various forms of Gnosticism. Enochic literature was known to the Gnostics in Egypt: *2 Enoch,* as we have already noted, was composed in Egypt, and *1 Enoch* circulated there. Two fragmentary Enoch apocrypha (otherwise unattested) have survived in Coptic, and in the Egyptian Gnostic work, the *Pistis Sophia,* Jesus tells his disciples of the mysteries contained in the two Books of Jeou which Enoch wrote in paradise.[55] Manichaeism also embraced the figure of Enoch. Mani in his youth seems to have read Jewish apocalyptic litera-

---

52. Nag Hammadi Codex 6.73.5–6; Latin Asclepius 25. See Philonenko, "Allusion de l'Asclépius," 2.161–63. Cf. also the myth of the fall of the souls in *Stobaei Hermetica* 23 (Kore Kosmou). Comparison has also been made, though less convincingly, between the apocalyptic schema of *Corpus Hermeticum* I (the *Poimandres*) and that of *2 Enoch*.

53. The texts are conveniently assembled in the monumental study by Chwolson, *Ssabier und der Ssabismus,* 2.398, 409, 417, 419, 425, 439, 502, 511, 534, 608, 621, with the discussion in 1.637–38 and 787–89. See further below on Enoch in Islamic tradition. On the Sabians: Green, *City of the Moon God,* esp. p. 170; Gündüz, *Knowledge of Life;* Massignon, "Littérature hermétique," 1.384–400, esp. p. 385. The identification of Enoch with Hermes probably came first, when Christianity was the dominant religion of the region. The identification of Enoch with Idris would have been made after the Islamic conquest. Hermes and Enoch appear to be already equated in the incantation bowls from pre-Islamic Babylonia: see Milik, *Books of Enoch,* 338. Milik rightly insists that the magical bowls attest the circulation of Enochic literature in Babylonia in the Sasanian period.

54. Both Ludovico Lazarelli and Heinrich Cornelius Agrippa identified Hermes as a grandson of Enoch. John Dee invoked the precedent of Enoch, from whom he may have claimed to have received revelations through his medium Edward Kelley. The best introduction to Hermeticism at the time of the Renaissance is still Yates, *Giordano Bruno.* For John Dee, see French, *John Dee,* esp. p. 110. Although *1* and *2 Enoch* were not known in the West at this time, the failure to exploit the figure of Enoch cannot be totally explained by a lack of knowledge of Jewish texts. The Christian kabbalists certainly knew some kabbalistic traditions about Enoch. Moreover, a great deal could have been gleaned from the available patristic and apocryphal sources, as may be seen from Drusius, *Henoch,* and Fabricius, *Codex pseudepigraphicus.*

55. See further Pearson, "Pierpont Morgan Fragments," 227–84, esp. p. 228.

ture. The Cologne Mani Codex mentions apocalypses of Adam, Seth, Enosh, Shem, and Enoch, and Enoch was revered by the Manichaeans as one of the great prophets of history, along with Seth, Enosh, Shem, the Buddha, Zoroaster, and Paul. The canonical Manichaean *Book of Giants* has been shown to be based on an Enochic text, fragments of which have been preserved in Aramaic among the Dead Sea Scrolls and in a Hebrew epitome in the medieval *Midrash of Shemhazai and 'Aza'el.*[56] *2 Enoch* influenced Bogomil-Cathar mythology in the Balkans, and was given by the Bogomils a thoroughly Gnostic reinterpretation.[57]

It is not hard to see why Enoch caught the Gnostics' attention. His postbiblical Jewish profile has features which would have interested them greatly. His role as "lesser YHWH" and as "prince of the world" could have suggested analogies with the Demiurge. Moreover, as a revealer of heavenly *gnosis* and as a "forerunner" who has escaped from the material world and returned to the celestial regions from which he had come, he can be seen as a redeemer who has charted the way for others to follow. But it would be an oversimplification always to assume that it was the Gnostics who borrowed from Jewish sources. Within Judaism Enoch-Metatron was a central figure both in the Heikhalot mysticism of late antiquity and in the kabbala of the Middle Ages. Both these systems are arguably *Jewish* forms of Gnosticism.[58] It is possible, therefore, that Enoch was, at least in part, shaped within Judaism under the influence of Gnostic ideas. The problem is similar to that of the relationship between Christ and Enoch-Metatron: rather than supposing one-way traffic in either direction, we should probably postulate a multisided interchange of ideas between traditions in continuous dialectic and conflict.

Finally, we note that the enigmatic figure of Idris mentioned

---

56. See Milik, *Books of Enoch*, 298–339; further, Lieu, *Manichaeism*, 33.

57. Unpublished paper by Stoyanov on "The Enochic Traditions in the *Secret Supper.*" See further his study *Hidden Tradition*, esp. p. 212.

58. The classification of Heikhalot mysticism as "Gnosticism" is controversial. It was strongly argued by Scholem in *Jewish Gnosticism*. I and others have raised objections: see my essay, "Comparing Merkavah Mysticism," 1–18. However, since writing that article I have modified my stance. I would now hold that if one takes a broad view there is considerable merit in seeing Heikhalot mysticism as a form of Jewish Gnosticism. See further Dan, *Gershom Scholem*, 41–43. The Gnostic character of the medieval kabbala seems hardly in doubt.

twice in the Qur'an[59] was commonly identified by Muslim scholars with the biblical Enoch, and that this identification opened the way for importing into Islam a substantial body of postbiblical Jewish legend about the character and exploits of the antediluvian patriarch. The Qur'anic references, though brief, are suggestive. In both Idris is said to have been a righteous man; and in one he is called a prophet whom "we raised...to a high place." There are no grounds for believing that the identification of Idris as Enoch is correct. It is more likely that the name Idris is derived from the biblical Ezra, via its Greek spelling Esdras. The identification of Enoch with Idris may have been taken over by Muslim scholars from the Sabians of Harran. We have already noted that the Harranians linked Hermes Trismegistus both with Enoch in the Bible and with Idris in the Qur'an. They probably did so in order to locate their prophet and teacher within both Christian and Islamic tradition and thereby to try to give their heterodoxy legitimacy in the eyes of the two great world religions of their day. The inevitable outcome was to equate Enoch and Idris.

However the identification was first made, it enabled Muslim scholars to draw on Jewish sources about Enoch in order to throw light on a dark corner of the Qur'an. Much of the Islamic material on Enoch-Idris is recognizably Jewish. Enoch-Idris is said to have lived between the times of Adam and Noah. He was a culture-bringer who was credited with numerous discoveries, including the invention of writing. He left behind books containing revelations about various arts and sciences. He entered paradise alive, where the Prophet met him during his ascent to heaven. And he also made a journey through hell. However, the Muslim traditions are much less concerned than the Jewish texts with Enoch's exalted, heavenly life, and they do not see him as fulfilling a cosmic function. He is a prophet and nothing more. To have accorded him greater status or honor would doubtless have been problematic, and brought him into conflict with the figure

---

59. Sura 19:57–58; 21:85, with the commentaries of Beidawi and Tabari *ad loca.* For Muslim accounts of Enoch see Tabari, *History,* ed. Leiden, I, 166–79 (trans. Rosenthal, *History of al-Tabari,* 1.336–48); and Mas'udi, *Meadows of Gold,* ed. Meynard-Courteille, I, 73. The articles on "Idris" in *EI*[1] (A. J. Wensinck) and *EI*[2] (G. Vajda) provide a useful introduction to the Islamic material.

of Muhammad, thus replicating within Islam the rivalry within Judaism between Enoch and Moses.

Bibliography

General Treatments

Though they are by no means complete, the three most comprehensive surveys of the Enochic tradition are:

Berger, K. "Henoch." *RAC* 14.473–545. Good for its coverage of the patristic evidence.

Milik, J. T. *The Books of Enoch: Aramaic Fragments of Qumran Cave 4.* Oxford: Clarendon, 1976. Publishes the important Qumran fragments and sets them in the context of a wide-ranging history of the Enochic traditions.

VanderKam, J. C. *Enoch: A Man for all Generations.* Studies on Personalities of the Old Testament. Columbia: University of South Carolina Press, 1996.

Bible and Near Eastern Background

Hess, R. S. "Enoch." *ABD* 2.508. A useful, short survey.

Kvanvig, H. S. *Roots of Apocalyptic: The Mesopotamian Background of the Enoch Figure and of the Son of Man.* WMANT 61. Neukirchen-Vluyn: Neukirchener Verlag, 1988.

Lambert, W. G. "Enmeduranki and Related Matters." *JCS* 21 (1967) 126–38.

Early Jewish Apocalyptic and Qumran

Andersen, F. I. "2 Enoch." *OTP* 1.92–221. An accessible introduction, translation, and commentary to the Slavonic Enoch.

Black, M. *The Book of Enoch or 1 Enoch.* SVTP 7. Leiden: Brill, 1985. Translation of the Ethiopic Enoch, with detailed commentary.

Charles, R. H. *The Book of Enoch.* 2d ed. Oxford: Clarendon, 1912. The notes remain valuable because of Charles's vast knowledge of the cognate texts.

Grelot, P. "La légende d'Henoch dans les apocryphes et dans la Bible: origine et signification." *RSR* 46 (1958) 5–26, 181–210.

Jansen, H. L. *Die Henochgestalt: Eine vergleichende religionsgeschictliche Untersuchung.* Skrifter utgitt av det Norske Videnskaps-Akademi i Oslo, II, Historisk-Filosofisk Klasse, 1939.1. Oslo: I Kommisjon Hos Jacob Dybwad, 1939.

Mach, M. *Entwicklungstudien des jüdischen Engelglaubens in vorrabbinischer Zeit.* Texte und Studien zum antiken Judentum 34. Tübingen: Mohr-Siebeck, 1992.

VanderKam, J. C. *Enoch and the Growth of an Apocalyptic Tradition.* CBQMS 16. Washington, D.C.: Catholic Biblical Association of America, 1984.

The most comprehensive study of the impact of the Enochic traditions on Second Temple apocalyptic.

Later Jewish Tradition and the Kabbala

Abrams, D. "The Boundaries of Divine Ontology: The Inclusion and Exclusion of Metatron from the Godhead." *HTR* 87 (1994) 291–321. A wide-ranging survey of the development of Metatron-Enoch as a divine figure.

Alexander, P. S. "The Historical Setting of the Hebrew Book of Enoch." *JJS* 28 (1977) 156–80. Discusses the evolution of the figure of Metatron.

———. "3 Enoch." *OTP* 1.223–315. Contains introduction, translation, and a brief commentary.

Ginzberg, L. *The Legends of the Jews.* 7 vols. Philadelphia: Jewish Publication Society of America, 1909–38. See index under "Enoch." Important for its analysis of the rabbinic traditions.

Idel, M. "Enoch Is Metatron." In *Proceedings of the First International Conference on the History of Jewish Mysticism: Early Jewish Mysticism.* Jerusalem Studies in Jewish Thought 6.1–2. Jerusalem: Hebrew University of Jerusalem, 1987. Pp. 151–70. In Hebrew. A French translation may found in Mopsik, *Le livre hébreu d'Hénoch,* 381–406. Speculative but important.

Mopsik, C. *Le livre hébreu d'Hénoch.* Paris: Verdier, 1989. A very full commentary on *3 Enoch,* though it tends to overinterpret the text.

Murtonen, A. "The Figure of Metatron." *VT* 3 (1953) 409–11. A pioneering discussion of possible christological influences on the development of the figure of Enoch-Metatron.

Odeberg, H., ed. and trans. *3 Enoch; or the Hebrew Book of Enoch.* Cambridge: Cambridge University Press, 1928. Reprinted with prolegomenon by J. C. Greenfield, New York: Ktav, 1973. The introduction still contains the fullest listing of references to Metatron in later Jewish literature.

Schäfer, P., and K. Hermann. *Übersetzung der Hekhalot-Literatur I.* Tübingen: Mohr-Siebeck, 1995. An important new German translation of *3 Enoch.*

Scholem, G. "Metatron." *EncJud* 11.1443–46. A masterly survey of the Metatron traditions in Merkavah mysticism and the kabbala.

Tishby, I. *The Wisdom of the Zohar.* 3 vols. Littman Library of Jewish Civilization. Oxford: Oxford University Press, 1989. 2.625–32, 643–45. A clear and authoritative analysis of the Enoch-Metatron traditions in the Zohar.

Christian

Barker, M. *The Lost Prophet: The Book of Enoch and Its Influence on Christianity.* London: SPCK, 1988. Full of interesting ideas, but at times too daring and undisciplined in its speculation.

Davis, P. G. "Divine Agents, Mediators, and New Testament Christology." *JTS* 45 (1994) 480–503.

———. "The Mythic Enoch: New Light on New Testament Christology." *SR* 13 (1984) 335–41.

Hurtado, L. W. *One God, One Lord: Early Christian Devotion and Ancient Jewish Monotheism.* Philadelphia: Fortress, 1988. Especially pp. 51–56. A good summary of the possible influence of the Enoch traditions on New Testament Christology.

Lindars, B. "Enoch and Christology." *ExpTim* 92 (1980–81) 295–99. Sets out the issues very clearly.

Morray-Jones, C. "Transformational Mysticism in the Apocalyptic-Merkabah Tradition." *JJS* 43 (1992) 1–31. A profound discussion of the theme of transformation during ascent to heaven.

Rowland, C. C. *The Open Heaven: A Study of Apocalyptic in Judaism and Early Christianity.* London: SPCK, 1982. Studies the Enoch traditions throughout, and sets them within the framework of early apocalypticism.

Gnosticism and Hermeticism

Chwolson, D. *Die Ssabier und der Ssabismus.* 2 vols. St. Petersburg, 1856. Dated, but still contains an indispensable collection of traditions relating to the Sabian identification of Enoch with Idris and with Hermes Trismegistus.

Copenhaver, B. P. *Hermetica: The Greek Corpus Hermeticum and the Latin Asclepius in a New English Translation, with Notes and Introduction.* Cambridge: Cambridge University Press, 1992. Introduction, esp. p. xlvi on the Sabian identification of Hermes with Enoch.

Fossum, J. E. *The Name of God and the Angel of the Lord: Samaritan and Jewish Concepts of Intermediation and the Origin of Gnosticism.* WUNT 36. Tübingen: Mohr-Siebeck, 1985. A detailed study of how Jewish ideas of angelic figures such as Enoch-Metatron may have been taken up into Gnosticism.

Pearson, B. A. "The Pierpont Morgan Fragments of a Coptic Enoch Apocryphon." In *Studies in the Testament of Abraham.* Ed. G. W. E. Nickelsburg. SBLSCS 6. Missoula, Mont.: Scholars Press, 1976. Pp. 227–84.

Philonenko, M. "Une allusion de l'Asclépius au livre d'Henoch." In *Christianity, Judaism, and Other Greco-Roman Cults.* Ed. J. Neusner. 4 vols. Leiden: Brill, 1975. 2.161–63.

Islam

Alexander, P. S. "Enoch-Idris in early Islamic Tradition." In *Studies in Muslim-Jewish Relations.* Vol. 3. Harwood Academic Publishers/Oxford Centre for Hebrew and Jewish Studies. Forthcoming. Argues that Idris in the Qur'an was not originally meant to be Enoch; the identification was invented by the Sabians.

Schwarzbaum, H. *Biblical and Extra-biblical Legends in Islamic Folk-Literature.* Beiträge zur Sprach- und Kulturgeschichte des Orients 30. Waldorf-Hessen: Orientalkunde Dr. H. Vorndran, 1982. Throughout and esp. pp. 8, 13, 53, 119–20, 127–28, 146–47. Takes a folklore approach to the material.

Speyer, H. *Die biblischen Erzählungen im Qoran.* 2d ed. Hildesheim: Olms, 1961. A fundamental study of the use of Jewish traditions in Islam, though it does not deal specifically with Enoch-Idris.

Two important surveys by masters of both Jewish and Islamic tradition are:

Vajda, G. "Idris." *EI.* New ed. Leiden: Brill, 1971. 3.1030–31.

Wensinck, A. J. "Idris." *EI.* 1st ed. Leiden: Brill, 1927. 3.449–50.

NOAH IN EARLY JEWISH LITERATURE

DEVORAH DIMANT

The story of the flood and its righteous survivor has ancient roots, which go back as far as Sumerian and Babylonian legends.[1] The author of Genesis undoubtedly knew these stories and drew on them,[2] as may have the prophet Ezekiel, who mentions Noah with Daniel and Job as three exemplary models of righteousness (Ezek 14:14, 20).[3]

In its biblical garb the story of the flood and its righteous hero has a special place in the primeval history of mankind. The prominence of Noah's career is well reflected by the amount of space devoted to it: five out of the eleven chapters in Genesis dealing with primordial history concern Noah.[4] Tenth of the first ten generations, Noah completes Adam's genealogy, and thus stands in a chiastic relationship to Adam at the head of the list. He is the direct descendant of the Sethian line and, as such, an heir to the image of God (Gen 5:1). Noah is analogous to Adam in other respects as well. Both were founders of new races: Adam fathered mankind, Noah the postdiluvian race. But Noah was privileged in a way that Adam was not. For he was righteous and blameless amid generations of wickedness (Gen 6:8–9), thus righteous

---

1. Cf. Heidel, *Gilgamesh Epic*; Lambert and Millard, *Atra-hasis*.
2. Cf. Heidel, *Gilgamesh Epic*; Kikawada, "Noah."
3. Cf. Zimmerli, *Ezekiel 1*, 314. In Isa 54:9 the flood is labeled as "the waters of Noah."
4. A similar prominence is observed in *Jubilees*, which devotes five chapters to Noah, and in the Qumran Aramaic midrash the *Genesis Apocryphon*, which devotes more than twelve columns to him (1QapGen 1–12).

by choice, whereas Adam was created blameless but sinned. That Noah "found favor in the eyes of God" (Gen 6:8–9) was a recognition of his virtue, rewarded by his surviving the flood. He was also the first human partner to a divine covenant, later to be echoed by God's covenant with the people of Israel. In this way Noah was not only the father of mankind and the ancestor of the Semite genealogy, but also the prototype of the patriarchs and people of Israel.

Rich in detail and pregnant with meaning, Noah's story captured the imagination of many generations. It was subjected to numerous and diverse interpretations.[5] Of special interest, however, are the earliest Jewish interpretations. Some of these may have been authored not much later than the final redaction of the biblical story itself. As it happens, the most prominent and elaborate treatments of Noah's career are also among the most ancient nonbiblical sources for this story. It is noteworthy that they all belong to a well-defined circle of writings, to the circle of Qumran manuscripts and related works, spanning the years 300 B.C.E. to 100 C.E. It is, therefore, appropriate to devote a literary survey of the figure of Noah mainly to the writings of this Qumranic circle. Scattered remarks found in other contemporary sources illuminate and underline various strands of these Noachic traditions.

Noah's biography as treated in these sources falls into three distinct periods: (*a*) the period including Noah's naming, birth, and activity before the flood; (*b*) the period of the ark and the flood; and (*c*) the aftermath of the flood, including Noah's sacrifice, covenant, and drunkenness, and tales of Noah's sons.

Noah's Naming, Birth, and Activity before the Flood

The biblical story underscores Noah's key role by adducing a paronomastic explanation of his name, announcing his future destiny, a qualification not provided to any other member of Noah's lineage. This etymology is put into the mouth of Noah's father, Lamech: "This one will bring us relief" (or: "comfort")

---

5. See the surveys of Lewis, *Study*; Feldman, "Josephus' Portrait of Noah," *PAAJR* 55.

(Gen 5:29). As it stands in the Hebrew MT the pun is made on the Hebrew root נחם[6] rather than on the more obvious root נוח, which is identical with the name of Noah (נח). The discrepancy did not escape the eyes of ancient exegetes.[7] Already the old Bible versions were divided over the solution to the difficulty. Some reproduce the sense of the MT, "to comfort."[8] In the LXX, however, the name is derived from the root נוח in the sense "to rest, repose."[9] Yet a third variant derives the name Noah from another sense of the same root נוח, "to remain, to be left,"[10] an etymology that reflects Noah's career. This last-mentioned etymology is prominent in the short notice on Noah included by Ben Sira in his "Praise of Israel's Ancestors," a section which concludes his sapiential work. The "Praise" itself opens with Enoch and Noah, thus implying that these two are the true ancestors of Abraham and Israel:[11]

> Noah was found perfect and righteous, in the time of destruction
>   he became a substitution.[12]
> Because of him a remnant was left, and with his covenant the flood
>   stopped.

---

6. Playing upon another usage of נחם in the flood story, in the sense of "to regret." See Gen 6:6–7: "And God regretted that He had made man ... for I regret that I made them." See VanderKam, "Birth of Noah," 220–22.

7. As expressed in the words of R. Yohanan: "The name is not the midrash and the midrash is not the name. Either let him be called Noah, then it ought to be read 'he shall set us at rest,' or Nahman (ינחמן), 'he shall comfort us' " (*Gen. Rab.* 28.2).

8. Thus the Greek translation attributed to Aquila, the Aramaic Targums (*Onqelos, Neofiti, Pseudo-Jonathan, Samaritan Targum*), the Syriac, and the Vulgate. The same etymology is present in *Jub.* 4:28. For the Hebrew see *HALAT* 3.650; Jastrow, *Dictionary*, 2.895. Note the play on the roots נחם/נוח in Ezek 5:13 and perhaps in Esth 9:16. For an exegetical play on both see *Exod. Rab.* 20 on Exod 13:7. See the survey of sources on Noah's name by Ginzberg, *Legends*, 5.168.

9. In both *qal* (e.g., Isa 14:7; Neh 9:28; Sir 34:4) and *hif'il* (e.g., Deut 3:20; Prov 29:17; note esp. 1 Chr 22:9); in both biblical and mishnaic Hebrew. See *HALAT* 3.642; Jastrow, *Dictionary*, 2.886. The LXX is followed by the Old Latin and Ethiopic translations of Genesis, Philo (e.g., *Leg. All.* 3.77; *Quaest. in Gen.* 1.87), and many of the church fathers. The same etymology is reflected in *1 Enoch* 106:17–18 and *Gen. Rab.* 25.2; 30.4. For Christian exegesis in this sense see the references listed by Alexandre, *Commencement*, 394, and the notice of Harl, *Bible d'Alexandrie*, 128–29.

10. In the *hif'il* (e.g., Gen 42:33; 2 Sam 16:21). Cf. *HALAT* 3.642; Jastrow, *Dictionary*, 2.885. Besides Ben Sira and the Enochic literature, this etymology may also underlie Wis 10:4 and *2 Enoch* 35:1.

11. The same view underlies Tob 4:12 (MSS BA); *Jub.* 19:24; 21:10; and *T. Benj.* 10:6; in the latter, Noah is listed as one of the patriarchs.

12. "Substitution" renders the Hebrew תחליף, which also occurs in 46:12; 48:8. The LXX ἀντάλλαγμα reflects the same word.

> With eternal sign (a covenant) was made with him, that never should all
> flesh be destroyed. (Sir 44:17–18)[13]

In this short notice Ben Sira presents the essential ingredients
of the biblical story. But Ben Sira ascribes to the motif of Noah as
remnant an importance not found in the Genesis account.[14] The
same motif is underscored in the Qumranic literature, probably
because in this literature Noah as righteous remnant was seen as
a prototype of the righteous at the End of Days, a concept central
to the thinking of the Qumran community and apocalyptic works
related to it.

The same concept predominates in *1 Enoch* and the *Book of
Jubilees*.[15] Taking the biblical account as a point of departure,
both writings develop, supplement, and elaborate various details
of the original flood story. The main features of the biblical account serve as a framework: the iniquity before the flood and
the corruption of creation, the righteousness of Noah, the flood
as punishment, and Noah as the founder of a new world. Since
the nature of antediluvian iniquity remains unspecified in the biblical account, the gap is filled by identifying the sinners as the
sons of God, namely angels,[16] and by ascribing to them serious
transgressions.

---

13. Translating the Masada Ben Sira scroll and the Geniza Hebrew manuscript B, published in *Book of Ben Sira*, 54. The Greek version presents a slightly different form: "Noah
was found a perfectly righteous one; in the time of wrath he was taken in exchange. Therefore a remnant was left when the flood came. Everlasting covenants were made with him
that all flesh should not be annihilated by a flood." For an edition of the Greek text, see
Ziegler, *Sapientia Iesu filii Sirach*. Translations of the apocrypha, unless otherwise noted,
are drawn from the *New Oxford Annotated Apocrypha*. Cf. also Skehan and Di Lella,
Wisdom of Ben Sira, 30.

14. In the Geniza version this motif is expressed by the Hebrew שארית ("remnant"),
rendered by the Greek κατάλειμμα. Cf. n. 37.

15. The precise dating of these two writings is still a matter of conjecture. *1 Enoch* as a
collection of sources of distinct character, some of which are composite, seems to contain
traditions about Noah that are more ancient than those in *Jubilees* (contra VanderKam,
"Righteousness of Noah," 15; 28, n. 16). *Jubilees* is usually assigned to the first half of
the second century B.C.E.

16. In accordance with biblical parlance (cf. Ps 29:1; Job 1:6; 38:7). The identification
of the sinners as angels is adopted by all the Qumranic documents (CD 2:18; 4Q180 1 7–
10; 1QapGen 2:2, 16; generally in *1 Enoch*, esp. chaps. 6–16; 86–88; 106–7; *Jub.* 4:22;
5:1; 7:21). See also Josephus, *Ant.* 1.73. Such an interpretation was vigorously contested
by later Jewish as well as Christian exegetes, who variously interpreted the term בני אלהים
("sons of God") as the sons of the judges or the magnates (cf. Exod 21:6; 22:8 – *Gen.
Rab.* 26.5; *Sipre Num.* 11.3; Aramaic targums to Gen 6:1). In later works the sons of God
are presented as Cainites, the descendants of Cain (e.g., *Test. Adam* 3:5). See the surveys
of Alexander, "Targumim," 60–71; and Fraade, *Enosh*, 65–66.

Drawing on a variety of sources and traditions, *1 Enoch* and *Jubilees* offer, nonetheless, more than one explanation for the corruption before the flood. One tale attributes it to the sins of the angels, the so-called Watchers,[17] who, together with their leader Shemyehzeh,[18] lusted after human women, descended from heaven, took mortal wives, and begat giant offspring. In doing so, in the words of Enoch to his son Methuselah, the angels

> transgressed the word of the Lord, departing from the covenant of heaven.[19] And behold, they sin and transgress the custom and have to do with women and sin with them, and they have married wives from among them; and they bear children not like spirits but of flesh. (*1 Enoch* 106:13–14, 17)[20]

Another passage in the *Book of the Watchers* spells out the angels' sins more explicitly. Being eternal, holy and pure, by leaving their holy heavenly abode to unite with mortal women, defiled by menstrual blood,[21] they infringed the fundamental laws of creation. Of no less gravity was their desire to procreate. For procreation was intended for mortals alone (*1 Enoch* 15:1–8). The unlawful mixture of fundamentally opposed natures, angelic and human, is graphically represented in the symbolic vision of the *Animal Apocalypse*. With angels represented as humans and men as domesticated animals, their mixture produces aberrant offspring, unnaturally big and wild animals: elephants, camels,

---

17. The name Watchers renders the Aramaic עירין (sing. עיר) (cf. Dan 4:10, 14, 20) and the Hebrew form עירים (Greek ἐγρήγοροι), "those who do not sleep." They were considered a class of angels (e.g., *1 Enoch* 12:2, 3; 39:12–13), some of whom committed the transgression (cf. CD 2:18; 1QapGen 2:1, 12; *1 Enoch* 6–16; 106–7; *Jub.* 4:15, 22; 7:21; 8:3; 10:5; *2 Enoch* 18:1–2; *Test. Reub.* 5:6–7; *Test. Naph.* 3:5). In *Sib. Or.* 1:95–100 the Watchers are a class of humans, but their characters and actions are similar to those of the sinful angelic Watchers.

18. This is the form in the Aramaic Qumran fragments: שמיחזה. Cf. Milik, *Books of Enoch*, Aramaic glossary.

19. The editor of the text had not recognized the underlying phrase from Isa 24:5, "...they transgressed teachings [or: statutes], violated laws..." (עברו תורת חלפו חק). Compare the formulation of *Jub.* 7:21: "[T]he Watchers deviated from the ordinance which ruled them..." (following the French translation of Caquot, "Jubilés," 670).

20. Following the Greek rendering of chaps. 97–107, preserved in a fourth-century papyrus codex. For edition and translation see Bonner and Youtie, *Last Chapters of Enoch*, 95–96.

21. Cf. *1 Enoch* 15:4 (Greek version); perhaps also alluded to in *1 Enoch* 7:1. See Dimant, "'The Fallen Angels,'" 42–44. For the Greek see Black, *Apocalypsis Henochi Graece*, 29.

and asses, symbolic of three different races of giants.[22] The perversity of this unnatural progeny was further revealed by their cruel violence and insatiability. They engaged in murder, violence, and robbery,[23] were in constant wars, ate flesh and works of mankind, drank their blood, and finally devoured each other. Since antediluvian charter decreed a vegetarian diet for humans (Gen 1:29), the giants' eating practices and cannibalism constituted another serious infringement of fundamental ordinances. Other sources speak of the giants' arrogance, folly, and stupidity. They were thus a paradigm of sin.[24]

While the main legend variant presents mankind as suffering from the sins of the angels and their offspring, a secondary version sees the roots of evil in the arts taught by the angels to mankind: sorcery, magic,[25] and other forbidden and corrupting sciences, such as the use of roots and plants, and astronomy (*1 Enoch* 7:1; 65:6).[26]

Traces of an altogether different version, with yet another explanation for the antediluvian corruption, are embedded in the *Book of the Watchers* (*1 Enoch* 8:1–2) and the *Animal Apocalypse* (chap. 88). Here the antagonist is a single angel named

---

22. *1 Enoch* 86:4–5. This tradition is also attested by the Greek version of Syncellus to *1 Enoch* 7:1–2 and by *Jub.* 7:21–25. It reflects the understanding that the three names given in Gen 6:4 to the offspring of the union with the women — the Nephilim, the Gibborim, and the Men of Renown — were three separate races of giants. Later authors were reluctant to admit an actual communion between the angels and the women, and presented the story as if the women conceived by lusting and imagining the angels. See *T. Reub.* 5:6–7. In other texts, such as *Gen. Rab.* 26.2, 28.8–9, and *2 Enoch* 34:1, the unlawful mixture consists of sodomy and bestiality.

23. Similarly Josephus, *Ant.* 1.73–74 and *Gen. Rab.* 31.3–7 of the generation of the flood.

24. They are included in catalogs of sinners mentioned in Sir 16:7 (Greek); Bar 3:26–28; Wis 14:6; 3 Macc 2:4; *3 Baruch* 3:26–28; *b. Sanh.* 108a; and *Gen. Rab.* 30.10. In Jdt 16:6 they are characterized by their strength and power. Cf. n. 46. Thus, together with their angelic progenitors, the giants exemplify sin and punishment, rather than accounting for the presence of evil in the world. This is rightly emphasized by Molenberg, "Shemihaza and Asael," 145.

25. For the association of the angels with medicine and sorcery see *1 Enoch* 7:2; 8:3; 65:6; 69:12; and *Bib. Ant.* 34:4. *1 Enoch* 65:11 speaks only of "secrets" taught to mankind by the angels.

26. Cf. *1 Enoch* 8:3; *Jub.* 8:3. The connection of the Watchers to astronomy is suggested by certain of their names, such as Anan'el, Sims'el, and Sahr'el. See Black, *Book of Enoch*, 122–23. These were probably the angels responsible for these astronomical bodies (cf. *Jub.* 2:2). In *1 Enoch* 72:1, 80:1, it is the angel Uriel who teaches Enoch the true astronomy. Josephus, *Ant.* 1.69, attributes such knowledge to the human Sethians.

Asael or Azazel,[27] and his sin consists of teaching men several maleficent crafts: making arms, working precious metals,[28] and the arts of cosmetics and fine clothing.

With all their differences, the various legends reflect the same basic transgressions committed by the antediluvians,[29] later epitomized in the sins prohibited, according to the rabbis, to all mankind: murder, idolatry or blasphemy, and fornication.[30] This underlying identity may be due to certain common elements in all the stories. In fact, at an early stage, already attested in the present form of *1 Enoch* 6–11, the distinct stories about Shemyehzeh and Asael/Azazel were conflated.[31] In this section Asael already appears as one of the angels under the authority of Shemyehzeh. Additionally, traces of the conflation can still be detected in other documents, such as the Enochic *Book of Parables* (*1 Enoch* 54:8) and the Qumranic *Pesher on the Periods* (*4Q180*), which places Azazel at the head of the sinful angels.[32]

27. Cf. the variants in the Aramaic fragments of *1 Enoch*: עשאל/עסאל (occur in 4Q201 [= 4QEnᵃ] iii 9; 4Q202 [= 4QEnᵇ] 1 ii 26; 4Q204 [= 4QEnᶜ] 1 ii 26). In a copy of the *Book of Giants* found at Qumran, the form עזא[ ]ל is found (4Q203 [= EnGiantsᵃ] 7 i 6), which Milik, *Books of Enoch*, 313 reconstructs as עזא[ז]ל. The variant עזזאל as the name of the angels' leader appears in the *Pesher on the Periods*, 4Q180 1 8, published by Allegro, *Qumrân Cave 4*, 78. See my edition and discussion in "The Pesher on the Periods," 77–102.

28. In *1 Enoch* 65:6–7 teaching the working of gold and silver is attributed to the sinful angels and is explicitly connected with making idols and idolatry. In *Jub.* 11:4 idolatry is said to have been started by the sons of Noah after his death, with the encouragement of the impure spirits from the dead giants (similarly *2 Enoch* 34:1).

29. Cf. *Jub.* 7:23–24; *2 Enoch* 34:1–2; *Sib. Or.* 1:175–80; *Gen. Rab.* 31.6.

30. For traditions on the three fundamental prohibitions binding the sons of Noah — namely, idolatry, adultery, and murder — see *b. Sanh.* 74a; compare the antediluvian sins enumerated in *Gen. Rab.* 31.1–6. Variant but similar lists appear in *Jub.* 7:20 and CD 4:18–15. The longer list of seven such prohibitions also includes a ban on eating blood and raw flesh. Cf. *b. Sanh.* 56a; *t. 'Abod. Zar.* 8.4–8; *Gen. Rab.* 16.16; 31.1–7. For patristic evidence see the survey of Lewis, *Study*, 16, n. 2. Cf. my discussion in " 'The Fallen Angels,' " 50–51. The argument was partly summarized in my "*1 Enoch* 6–11," 323–39. On the commandments of the sons of Noah, see Finkelstein, "Maccabean Halakha," 21–25. See also the survey of Novak, *Image of the Non-Jew*, 3–51.

31. See the discussion in Dimant, " 'The Fallen Angels,' " 53–72. Compare the similar analysis of Nickelsburg, "Apocalyptic and Myth," 383–405.

32. Cf. 4Q180 1 7. See my edition and discussion in "Pesher on the Periods." Such a version may also underlie the description in the *Animal Apocalypse* (*1 Enoch* 85–90), where only one angel is alluded to, distinct from the sinful angels as a group. On the similarity of *1 Enoch* 54 to *1 Enoch* 6–11, see my discussion in " 'The Fallen Angels,' " 87–90; and Suter, *Tradition and Composition*, 59. In later rabbinic traditions the complex of these motifs is compressed into a picture of only a pair of angels, Uzza and Azael, whose sins have brought them down from heaven. Cf. *b. Yoma* 67b; *b. Nid.* 61a; Rashi ad loc.; *Deut. Rab.*, end of chap. 11; et al. The two appear as demons in medieval magical writings. In " 'The Fallen Angels,' " I show that even in this schematic form the two

Against this backdrop of antediluvian iniquity Noah's righteousness and covenant acquire their full significance. In contrast
with the sinfulness of his contemporaries Noah was, in the words
of *Jub.* 5:19, the only human being who "did not transgress from
anything that has been ordained for him."[33] He thus merited not
only being rescued from the flood, but also being the designated
lawgiver of future humanity.

In the Qumranic literature Noah's singular piety is underlined
by the legend about his miraculous birth. Attested in several versions at Qumran, this story emphasizes Noah's divine nature,
piety, and wisdom, apparent from the moment of his birth. One
version of the story, preserved in *1 Enoch* 106-7, tells how
Noah's father, Lamech, was frightened by the angelic appearance of the infant: by his radiant face, white hair, and rosy skin,
and that he sprang from the midwife's arms and praised God.
A Hebrew fragment of a similar description was found at Qumran.[34] Apprehensive of the possibility that the infant might be
an offspring of the Watchers,[35] Lamech suspects his wife of being untrue, a suspicion vigorously denied by Lamech's wife in a
third version of the legend, preserved in the *Genesis Apocryphon*
(1QapGen) 2.[36] Both *1 Enoch* and the *Genesis Apocryphon* relate how Lamech seeks the advice of his father Methuselah, and
how Methuselah himself turns to consult his own father Enoch.
Enoch assures Methuselah that Noah is the true son of Lamech,

---

reflect respectively different characters, which must go back to the older, more elaborate
traditions (see pp. 175–82). Some of these materials were also discussed by Milik, *Books
of Enoch*, 317–39.

33. Philo underscores the idea that survival from the flood was a reward for Noah's
piety and righteousness: cf. *Praem. poen.* 22–23.

34. 1Q19 3. Other fragments from this scroll, 1Q19 1 and 1Q19 bis, contain passages
corresponding to *1 Enoch* 7:5–6; 8:10–11. Cf Milik, *Qumran Cave I*, 84–85, 152. See
also below, the appendix on the *Book of Noah*.

35. According to the chronologies of *1 Enoch* 106:13 and *Jub.* 4:16 the angels descended to earth in the days of Enoch's father Yered, an obvious pun on the name ירד,
"descend." According to *Jub.* 4:16, 5:6, they were first sent down in order to teach
mankind justice, but a few centuries later were seduced by the beauty of the women
(*Jub.* 5:1).

36. For editions see Fitzmyer, *Genesis Apocryphon*, 50–52; Beyer, *Aramäischen Texte*,
168–69. In preparing this article I was able to consult a considerably improved text of
1QapGen, esp. cols. 1–20, to be published in *Abr Nahrain* by E. Qimron, M. Morgen-
stern, and D. Sivan. I thank my colleague Elisha Qimron for placing this manuscript at my
disposal. For a more detailed analysis of the birth story, cf. recently VanderKam, "Birth of
Noah," 213–31.

and informs him of the approaching flood and of the destiny awaiting Noah:

> And this child that is born shall be left, and his three sons shall be saved when they who are on earth are dead; and he shall bring rest upon the earth from the corruption that is upon it. And now tell Lamech that he is his son in truth and holiness, [and] call his name [Noah]; for he shall be a remnant[37] of you whereby you shall have rest, and his sons, from the corruption of the earth and from all the sinners and from all the wickedness [on the earth]. (*1 Enoch* 106:16–18)[38]

Here, all three etymologies of Noah's name are used to describe his activities. However, the foreknowledge of Noah's destiny is pronounced not by his father, but by his great-grandfather Enoch, a famous sage, well-versed in the future of mankind.[39]

A curious parallel to Noah's miraculous birth, appended to *2 Enoch* (chaps. 69–70),[40] puts in relief the significance of Noah's own story. Most of *2 Enoch* relates Enoch's ascension through the seven heavens to see the Great Glory. At the end, however, a narrative about an unknown brother of Noah, Nir, is appended. The story tells about Nir's miraculous birth, and his delivery from the flood by being transported into paradise for seven years. Nir is invested with priesthood by his grandfather Methuselah, is renamed Melchizedek (Gen 14:18; Ps 110:4), and after the flood fathers a high-priestly genealogy. The emphasis on Nir's righteousness, wisdom, and priesthood renders this story a parallel version to that of Noah.

Noah's life matched his birth. His exemplary piety was evident throughout his life. In sharp contrast to the adulterous angels and women, he married into his own family, and like his descendants, the Israelite patriarchs, took his cousin for a wife.[41] In addition to

---

37. The Greek here has κατάλειμμα ("remnant"), as in Sir 44:17. Cf. n. 14.

38. Translating the Greek version of Papyrus Bonner (fourth century). Cf. Bonner and Youtie, *Last Chapters of Enoch*.

39. Enoch drew his knowledge from the heavenly tablets, on which all human history is engraved. See *1 Enoch* 93:2; 106:19. Rabbinic tradition attributes the gift of prophecy to both Lamech and Noah. For Noah as a prophet, see Tob 4:19; *Jub.* 8:18; Philo, *Leg. all.* 3.77; *S. 'Olam* 21. For Noah's prophecies concerning the coming flood, see *Sib. Or.* 1:180–89. Josephus, *Ant.* 1.70–71, attributes such a prophecy to Adam. The coming flood was disclosed to Noah through an intermediary, variously identified as coming through an angel (*1 Enoch* 10:1–2; 65–66), through his great-grandfather Enoch (*1 Enoch* 65:10), or in a vision (1QapGen 6).

40. Cf. the translation by Anderson, "2 Enoch," *OTP* 1.91–221.

41. See *Jub.* 4:33; Tob 4:12. Cf. n. 11.

his own personal piety he addressed to his contemporaries a call for repentance.[42] In terms of biblical legal concepts, such a call constituted a reproof, required also by Qumranic and rabbinic legal systems in order to establish intentionality and the degree of criminal responsibility.[43] Their refusal to heed the call defines the degree of the criminal responsibility of antediluvian sinners, and, consequently, the justice of their punishment. Other sources link the reproof motif with curtailing man's span of life to 120 years (Gen 6:3), and see it as a delay given to those generations so that they could repent. In refusing to do so the sinners became liable to the punishment of the flood.[44]

The flood was, however, not the only punishment. The various traditions list others, corresponding to different categories of sinners. The sinful angels were punished by being bound and thrown into a dark place of punishment, there to await their final judgment on the Day of Judgment.[45] According to the main version of the story, their giant offspring were annihilated by their own strife and internecine battles.[46] Another variant states that the gi-

---

42. Philo, *Quaest. in Gen.* 2.13; Josephus, *Ant.* 1.74; *Sib. Or.* 1:175, 150–95; 2 Pet 2:5; *b. Sanh.* 108a; *Gen. Rab.* 30.7; *Tanhuma*, Noah 5. For this theme in Josephus, see the discussions of Fraxman, *Genesis and the "Jewish Antiquities,"* 81–82; Feldman, "Josephus' Portrait of Noah," 4–42. In Heb 11:7 the piety of Noah consists in his faith in things to come. Underscoring this piety is the rabbinic tradition according to which Noah was born circumcised, a characteristic he shared with Moses. Cf. *Tanhuma*, Genesis 11. On the whole, the rabbis both praised and criticized Noah. Cf. the survey in Fraade, *Enosh*, 212–13. The absence of the repentance motif in *1 Enoch* and *Jubilees* led VanderKam ("Righteousness of Noah," 16) to conclude that it is a "later tradition." But this is not necessarily the case. The motif might have been dropped from both *1 Enoch* and *Jubilees*, because in this literature Enoch assumed the role of preacher to his generation.

43. This corresponds to the reproof in the Qumranic legal system and the warning in the rabbinic one. Cf. Schiffman, *Sectarian Law*, 89–109. For rabbinic sources, see Fraade, *Enosh*, 214, n. 116.

44. Cf., e.g., Philo, *Quaest. in Gen.* 1.94; 2.9; the Aramaic targums (*Onqelos, Pseudo-Jonathan, Neofiti*), and rabbinic sources (*Mek., beshalah* on Exodus 15; *b. Sanh.* 108a; *Gen. Rab.* 28.6; 30.7). See my discussion in " 'The Fallen Angels,' " 68–71, 96. This view may also be implied by the *Pesher on Genesis*, 4Q252 1 i 1–3. This *pesher* is a collection of various, slightly reworked passages from Genesis, occasionally amplified by small midrashic additions. See the edition of Brooke; Brooke, "Thematic Content," 33–59 (text on 33–35). See the discussions of Lim, "Chronology," 288–98; and Bernstein, "4Q252," 1–17. More generally see Brooke, "Genre of 4Q252," 161–79.

45. See *1 Enoch* 10:12–13; 19:1; 21:3; 67:6–7; 88:3; *Jub.* 5:10–11. Apparently this is the same place of punishment for the Sons of Darkness that is referred to in 1QS 4:12–13.

46. *1 Enoch* 10:9–10; 88:2; *Jub.* 5:9; 7:22–23. Compare CD 2:19–20 and Sir 15:7 (Greek version), where the giants head a listing of sinners and their respective punishments. In *T. Naph.* 3:5, the Watchers are the sinners.

ants perished in the flood.[47] Several formulations of this variant consider the curtailing of man's life to 120 years (Gen 6:3) as referring to the span of time left for the giants to live until the flood,[48] a view expressed, perhaps, by the Qumranic *Pesher on Genesis* (4Q252),[49] and by the rabbinic tradition according to which the giant Og (Deut 3:11) survived the flood by riding on the ark.[50] According to *Jub.* 5:7–9 it was the span of time until the giants were annihilated by the sword.[51] But the versions are unanimous in considering the flood as cleansing and purifying the earth from evil,[52] a view already implying the idea of the flood as a cosmic baptismal purification.[53]

Though the traditions in *1 Enoch* and *Jubilees* speak of the flood as effacing previous evils, one tradition views the evils as still lingering in the postdiluvian world. This story states that the spirits which came out of the dead giants became demons, who continued to plague and mislead humankind even after the flood (*1 Enoch* 15:8–16:1; *Jub.* 7:27; 10:1–14). Thus, the aberrant effects of the angelic sins could not be entirely eradicated from the earth. A partial remedy to such evil was, according to *Jubilees,* provided by God in answer to Noah's prayer. By God's command the Angels of Presence imprison nine-tenths of the demons beneath the earth, leaving only one-tenth active. As protection,

---

47. See CD 2:19–20; Wis 14:6–7; 3 Macc 2:4; *3 Apoc. Bar.* 3:10. Bar 3:26–28 speaks in a general way of their perishing.

48. This version of the legend is apparently based on the variant ידור ("will dwell") instead of ידין ("will judge") in the MT of Gen 6:3, a variant attested in 4Q252 and often discussed. See most recently Bernstein, "4Q252," 5–6. Such a variant underlies the versions of the LXX, Old Latin, Vulgate, and Syriac. The fortunes of the giants before the flood is the subject of an Aramaic work discovered at Qumran, the so-called *Book of Giants.* Cf. Milik, *Books of Enoch,* 298–317. Milik has shown that this Aramaic work is identical to the one incorporated in the Manichean scriptures; Persian fragments of it were found in Turfan. Cf. Milik, "Turfan et Qumran," 117–27. For a recent treatment of the subject and its ramifications in Manichean literature, see Reeves, *Jewish Lore in Manichaean Cosmogony.* See now the edition of the Aramaic work by Stuckenbruck, *The Book of Giants.*

49. 4Q252 1 i 1–3.

50. Cf. *b. Nid.* 61a; *Gen. Rab.* 42.8; *Tg. Ps.-J.* Gen 14:13.

51. I have analyzed in detail the various narrative strands of these legends in " 'The Fallen Angels.' " For a similar analysis, cf. Nickelsburg, "Apocalyptic and Myth."

52. Cf. *1 Enoch* 10:4–7; 107:17; *Jub.* 7:24, 33.

53. This analogy was later given a Christian interpretation, and in 1 Pet 3:21 the flood is explicitly compared to Christian baptism. See Schlosser, "Jours de Noé," 13–36. Cf. n. 62.

Noah was also given by the Angels of Presence medicines to combat the demonic diseases, medicines which he compiled in a book and bequeathed to his son Shem (*Jub.* 10:14).[54]

Noah, the Ark, and the Flood

Between antediluvian transgression of primeval law, and post-diluvian reinstatement of the correct order, the flood is a chaotic reversal. The return of chaos is signified in the biblical account by the return of the waters, an element prominent in the pre-creation chaotic state. It is accomplished by reopening the upper and lower sources of water (Gen 6:11; 8:2), a detail taken up in both *Jubilees* (5:24–25) and the Enochic *Animal Apocalypse* (*1 Enoch* 89:2–3).[55] The mightiness of the upheaval highlights the fragility of the ark, the miraculous character of the deliverance, and the enormity of the task of rebuilding a new world.[56] Indeed, the Enochic *Book of Parables* (*1 Enoch* 37–71) relates that the building of the ark was a job done by the angels (*1 Enoch* 67:2). In the *Animal Apocalypse* (*1 Enoch* 85–90) Noah himself became angel-like in order to build the ark (*1 Enoch* 89:1).[57] According to *Jub.*

---

54. The tradition that Noah (variant tradition: Adam) received a "book of secrets" from the angel Raziel is recorded in various Greco-Roman, Byzantine, and medieval Jewish Hebrew writings. In its introduction, a variant of this tradition identifies as such the *Sepher ha-Razim* (see Margalioth, *Sepher ha-Razim*), a third- or fourth-century magical collection. Also identified as Noah's book of medicines is a collection of medicines, *The Book of Asaf the Physician* (cf. Muntner, *Introduction,* 147–49), apparently roughly contemporary with *Sepher ha-Razim.* However, the version in *The Book of Asaf the Physician* is strikingly reminiscent of *Jubilees* 10, as observed by Rönsch, *Buch der Jubiläen,* 385–88. A third version is that published in the introduction of the late kabbalistic and magical collection known as *The Book of the Angel Raziel* (Amsterdam, 1804). All three notices were assembled and published under the title *The Book of Noah* by Jellinek, *Bet Ha-Midrasch,* 3.155–60. I have reproduced the texts in "'The Fallen Angels,'" 183–92.

55. Both works speak of seven heavenly floodgates which were opened for this purpose, a number not mentioned in the biblical story.

56. Emphasized by Wis 10:4; Philo, *Vita Mosis* 1.112; and *Sib. Or.* 1:130–35, 225. See Winston, *Wisdom of Solomon,* 214; Larcher, *Le Livre de la Sagesse,* 2.618.

57. The reference is found in the *Animal Apocalypse* (*1 Enoch* 85–90), which relates human history symbolically, as angels are represented as humans and humans as animals. Noah is born as an animal but is turned into a human in order to build the ark. The same transformation happens to Moses before he builds the tabernacle (*1 Enoch* 89:36). Note, however, that for Noah this statement is attested by the Ethiopic, and not the Aramaic fragments. Black, *The Book of Enoch,* 262, believes that the Ethiopic is not necessarily secondary, but could represent "a longer recension of the Aramaic."

6:23 it was the Angels of Presence who brought the animals into the ark, and God who sealed it.[58]

Although chaotic in nature, the flood was nevertheless precisely orchestrated. Its various stages took place in a strict yearly sequence.[59] In *Jubilees* 7 and the *Pesher on Genesis* (4Q252 1 i–ii) this chronology becomes a major issue. It is reworked to match the 364-day solar calendar espoused by the Qumran community.[60] The *pesher* even supplies the dates with the corresponding week days. It seems that the Qumran community saw in the flood chronology a biblical proof-text for its solar calendar, thus investing that calendar with cosmic significance and divine intention.

The catastrophic nature of the flood, and its function as a punishment for wickedness, made it an ideal prototype for the last generation and the cataclysmic punishment at the End of Days. In the schematic history of the Enochic *Apocalypse of Weeks* (*1 Enoch* 93:3–10; 91:11–17), the flood is termed the "first end," analogous to the "last end" (*1 Enoch* 93:4). In this context Noah, the righteous survivor, becomes the prototype of the small group of righteous that is active amidst wickedness at the dawn of the eschatological era, a group that will survive and build the new and just world to come.[61] This is expressed by the epithet "Plant of Righteousness," applied to both Noah and the righteous in the final age. The analogy between the flood and the End of Days, and between Noah and the group of righteous, is also reflected in the practice, common in contemporary apocalyptic writings, of

---

58. The flood as a divine plan is emphasized in *Sib. Or.* 1:200–280.

59. A year and ten days according to the MT; exactly one year according to the LXX. Josephus, *Ant.* 1.80–88, also uses the story of the flood to discuss calendrical matters. See the comments of Fraxman, *Genesis and the "Jewish Antiquities,"* 86–87. For surveys of various flood chronologies, cf. Lewis, *Study,* 190–92; Feldman, "Josephus' Portrait of Noah."

60. The passage relevant to Noah appears in 4Q252 1 i–ii. Cf. Lim, "Chronology"; Bernstein, "4Q252"; Eisenman and Wise, *Dead Sea Scrolls Uncovered,* 78–79, 104. A detailed analysis and general discussion of the calendrical problems in this text is offered by Glessmer, "Antike und moderne Auslegungen," 3–79.

61. On Noah see *1 Enoch* 10:16; 84:6. On the righteous see *1 Enoch* 93:10. The concept is central to the Qumran community writings, and is expressed in the term מטעת עולם ("eternal plant"), e.g., 1QS 8:5; 11:8; 1QH 6:15; 8:6. See Licht, "Plant Eternal," 49–75. The analogy between the first and the last judgments is emphasized by structural parallelism. Cf. VanderKam, "Studies in the Apocalypse of Weeks," 519.

juxtaposing apocalyptic forecasts with descriptions of the flood.[62] Such an analogy appealed to the Qumran community in particular, as it corresponds to the community's self-image as a small group living on the verge of the final age.[63] This may account for the Qumranites' interest in Noah's fortunes. A similar interest motivated the early Christians.[64]

The Aftermath of the Flood: Noah's Sacrifice, Covenant, and Drunkenness, and Noah's Sons

The fragments concerning Noah which survive in the Enochic literature do not elaborate on events which took place after the flood. This may be due to the fact that the Noachic materials there were drawn from a more comprehensive source, now lost, where these events were also treated. The focus of the Enochic literature being the prediluvian career of Enoch, Noah was introduced only insofar as he was relevant to his ancestor's circumstances.

Jubilees, by contrast, systematically reworking the primeval and patriarchal biblical history, had no such constraints. It turns Noah into a paradigm of the correct morality of the renewed world.[65] In line with its ideology, *Jubilees* brings into the foreground particular aspects of this new order. From the biblical story are taken the reestablishment of natural order, epitomized in the covenant God made with Noah, and in God's promises never again to bring a flood on the earth. The rainbow is given as a sign for reestablishing the normal rhythm of yearly seasons (Gen

---

62. Cf., e.g., *1 Enoch* 10–11, 83–84, paralleling 85–90; 107:1; *Jub.* 6:32–38; 7:21–27; *2 Enoch* 34–35; *Bib. Ant.* 3:10. This is also expressed by the fact that the Watchers are to be punished only at the End of Days (cf. *1 Enoch* 10:12; 16:1; 90:24). This combination is also found in the NT: cf. nn. 42, 53, and 64. Another aspect of the similarity between the flood and the final purification is the analogy between the flood of water in Noah's days and the flood of fire at the end of days. See Josephus, *Ant.* 1.70–71; *Adam and Eve* 49:3; *Mek.,* Amalek 3.14; compare *Sib. Or.* 3:689–90. Connected with this theme is the paradigmatic analogy between the punishment of the flood in water and the punishment of the Sodomites in fire. The two events are often linked in lists of sinners. Cf. Lührmann, "Noah und Lot," 75–83; Schlosser, "Jours de Noé."

63. Cf., e.g., CD 4:10–18; 1QpHab 7:10–14; 1QH 8:4–14.

64. Cf. Matt 24:37–39; Luke 17:26. The analogy is also made in *b. Sanh.* 99a.

65. 4 Ezra 3:11 makes Noah the father of a genealogy of righteous, an idea already implied in the *Apocalypse of Weeks* (*1 Enoch* 91:11–17; 93:3–10).

8:22; 9:8–17). *Jub.* 6:4 summarizes this part in a few words. The author of *Jubilees* is more interested in the cultic significance of the covenant. Noah's building of the altar and the sacrifices upon emerging from the ark are turned into a sacrificial ceremony as prescribed by the Torah. Acting as a priest, Noah brings sacrifices "to atone for the land" (*Jub.* 6:1–3).[66] The Noachide covenant is transformed into a paradigm of the covenant with Israel on Mount Sinai. The analogy is made explicit between Noah's prohibition of shedding and eating blood, and similar Torah injunctions, as well as with the prescription to sprinkle blood on the altar (Exod 24:8; Lev 17:10; *Jub.* 6:6–14). By placing Noah's covenant in the third month (*Jub.* 6:1), *Jubilees* takes the analogy further and identifies the celebration of Noah's covenant with the festival of *shavuot*, implying the well-known view that *shavuot* celebrates the giving of the Torah. In this way not only is Noah's covenant turned into a prototype of the Sinai covenant, but Noah himself becomes a figure analogous to Moses. Characteristically, *Jubilees* attaches to the celebration a future forecast prophesying that the sons of Noah and the Israelites will forget this injunction and eat blood (*Jubilees* 18–19).[67] This festival acquires a particular divine and cosmic character by the attribution of its practice to the angels from creation until the time of Noah (*Jub.* 6:18).

The agricultural aspect of the *shavuot* festival is linked by *Jubilees* to calendrical matters, for the calendar regulates man's relationship with nature, and his capacity to harvest produce and sustain himself. Therefore, adopting a correct calendar implies for *Jubilees* the ability to practice husbandry, as well as a correct cultic rhythm.[68] Aware of this significance, and of linking

---

66. The same description is also found in 1QapGen 10:13: לכול ארעא כולהא כפרת ("I atoned for all the land"). See Fitzmyer, *Genesis Apocryphon*, 56–57. Note the similarity to the Qumran community's own aim "to atone for the land" ...(לכפר בעד הארץ), stated in 1QS 8:6. The building of the altar is omitted by the *Pesher on Genesis*, 4Q252 1 ii 4–5. Note that Noah's priestly functions are indicated also by the fact that, together with Enoch, he transmits books with instructions for the correct way to sacrifice, books which Abraham used (*Jub.* 21:10). For Noah as a priest, cf. *Apostolic Constitutions* 8:5. On the priestly character of Noah's activities, see Albeck, *Buch der Jubiläen,* 21, 33; VanderKam, "Righteousness of Noah," 20. Cf. n. 76.

67. This tradition is also recorded in CD 3:6. The theme of Noachide laws as prefigurations of the Mosaic Torah is also developed by Philo, *Abr.* 34.

68. The connection between normal agriculture and the establishment of a proper sequence of seasons is already linked with Noah in the biblical story (Gen 5:29; 9:20).

the calendar to the renewed world, *Jubilees* uses the occasion of
the flood story to lay out in detail the solar calendar. Also here
a polemical prophecy is appended, forecasting that the Israelites
will forget this calendar (*Jub.* 6:22–38).

The same calendrical and priestly considerations underlie *Jubilees*' version of Noah's vineyard and drunkenness. According to
Jubilees Noah planted vines on Mount Lubar, where the ark came
to rest. He gathered the vines' produce on the seventh month
of the fourth year, made wine of it, and stored the wine until
the end of that year. At the beginning of the fifth year, on the
first day of the first month, he celebrated the festival,[69] brought
atonement sacrifices according to the prescriptions in Num 29:1–
6, sprinkled wine on them, and then drank some of it together
with his sons (*Jub.* 7:1–6).[70] In doing so Noah was, in fact,
practicing the Torah law of fourth-year produce,[71] namely, the
prohibition against eating fruits of newly planted trees for the
first three years, and the obligation to consecrate the produce of
the fourth year "to God" (Lev 19:23–25). It appears that during Second Temple times the manner in which this law should be
practiced was disputed. According to the Pharisees the produce
had to be consumed by its owners in Jerusalem, or redeemed and
the equivalent spent on pilgrimage to Jerusalem.[72] The Qumranic
halakhah, however, mandated that the produce be consumed by
the priests in the Temple.[73] As Noah was the owner of the wine

Rabbinic midrash describes Noah's husbandry both before and after the flood. Cf. *Gen.
Rab.* 25.2–3, where the "rest" with which Noah is connected constitutes the reestablishing
of productive agriculture. Similarly Philo, *Quaest. in Gen.* 2.66.

69. According to *Jub.* 6:23 this was the first of the four Days of Remembrance. The
same festival is mentioned in 1QapGen 10:13. Kister, "Some Aspects," 2.584, suggests
that both *Jubilees* and the *Genesis Apocryphon* considered the festival as *Sukkot*, but
"used a different system to designate the beginning of the year." However, *Jub.* 7:1 specifies that the ingathering of the vine's fruits was separated from the festival. The ingathering
indeed took place on the seventh month, namely at *Sukkot*, the biblical ingathering festival. But Noah's celebration took place on the first day of the first month of the following,
fifth year, which should be the month of Nisan, if we follow the biblical festival calendar. It is, however, noteworthy that the sacrifices brought by Noah are those prescribed
by the Torah for the first of the seventh month (Tishrei), considered to be the first of the
agricultural calendar.

70. Cf. Lev 19:23–25. See Albeck, *Buch der Jubiläen.* The view that Noah's sacrifices
followed the Torah prescriptions is expressed also in *Gen. Rab.* 34.9.

71. נטע רבעי in rabbinic terminology.

72. Cf. *y. Pe'a* 7.6. See also Josephus, *Ant.* 4.227. For discussion, see Baumgarten,
"Laws of Orlah," 195–202; Kister, "Some Aspects," 2.576–78.

73. Cf. 11QTemple 60:3–4; *Miqṣat Maʿaśei ha-Torah* (4QMMT) 62–63 (=4Q396 1–2

he drank, it has recently been suggested that his practice reflects the Pharisaic mode of interpretation.[74] But such an understanding contradicts Noah's own commandment to his sons to give this produce to the priests (*Jub.* 7:36–37).[75] If, however, Noah is seen as the first priest, as is indicated by his practice and ceremonial functions, he conforms with the *halakhah* as taught in the Qumranic works.[76] Moreover, in turning the drinking of the wine into a religious ceremony, *Jubilees* alleviates any misgivings that may be provoked by the episode of Noah's drunkenness. In this light, Ham's offense constitutes an act of disrespect not only to his father, but also to the festival ordinances.[77]

In *Jubilees* Noah's career concludes with three episodes: his commandments and exhortations to his sons (*Jub.* 7:39); the division of the land among Shem, Ham, and Japheth (*Jubilees* 8–9); and the dealings with the demons (*Jub.* 10:8–11). In all three Noah is revealed as a leader, ruler, and lawgiver.[78] In his teaching, commandments, and exhortations, he expresses his major concerns, which coincide with the main interests of *Jubilees:* warning

---

iii 2–3). See Qimron and Strugnell, *Qumran Cave 4. V.*, 19, 52; *Jub.* 7:35–36. Cf. Albeck, *Buch der Jubiläen*, 32–33; Baumgarten, "Laws of Orlah"; Kister, "Some Aspects." Kister also raises the question why Noah would practice on Mount Lubar, obviously outside the land of Israel (in Ararat, located in Armenia according to *Jub.* 8:21. Thus also Josephus, *Ant.* 1.90; *Sib. Or.* 1:260; and the tradition of some Greek translations of the Bible). *Jub.* 8:21, however, places Mount Lubar within the section assigned to Shem, as is the land of Israel. Mount Lubar, therefore, may have been understood by *Jubilees* as part of the pre-Sinaitic "holy land."

74. Thus Kister, "Some Aspects," 2.585–86.

75. Kister, "Some Aspects," 2.586–87, suggests that the discrepancies between Noah's exhortation and the story of the wine reflect originally different sources. He rejects other explanations by Albeck (*Buch der Jubiläen*) and Baumgarten ("The Laws of Orlah") as "rather forced" (2.585), whereas, in fact, his own explanation is much more so.

76. Thus Albeck, *Buch der Jubiläen*, 32–33; Baumgarten, "The Laws of Orlah," 198. Baumgarten suggests this as only one possible explanation. *Jubilees*, however, makes it particularly clear that Noah and his sons drank only *some* of the wine (*Jub.* 7:6), immediately after the sacrifice and as part of the festival, which indicates that they performed it as a priestly act. The chronology of the planting, gathering the fruits, and drinking the wine shows that according to *Jubilees*, fourth-year fruits had to be gathered but could not be eaten, and that consuming them was permitted in the fifth year, but only after the priests had offered some on the altar, and taken their own share. Cf. Baumgarten, "Laws of Orlah," 196–98.

77. Interestingly, the *Pesher on Genesis* (4Q252) omits the planting of the vineyard, but explains that Canaan instead of Ham was cursed, because Ham had already been blessed by God (Gen 9:1). The same explanation is given in *Tanhuma*, Genesis 16. See the comments of Bernstein, "4Q252," 10–12. On Josephus's treatment of this episode and the curse of Canaan, see Fraxman, *Genesis and the "Jewish Antiquities,"* 112–13. On other aspects of Noah's drunkenness, see H. H. Cohen, *Drunkenness of Noah*, 14–21.

78. This is emphasized by Josephus, *Ant.* 1.80.

against the Watchers' promiscuity; interdiction of bloodshed and the eating of blood; and the obligation to give tithes to the priests (*Jub.* 7:2–39). His Moses-like nature is underscored by his allotting the land to his sons sometime before his death, an act which corresponds to Moses' role in allotting Canaan to the Israelite tribes (Numbers 32–36; Deuteronomy 29–34; *Jub.* 8:11).

It is perhaps fitting that the author of *Jubilees* finishes Noah's biography with a section on demons, a major concern of *Jubilees*. Thus, Noah's legacy consists not only of a new order, a set of commandments, and moral instructions, but also of the means to combat demons, and thus their ruler, the archdemon Mastema (*Jub.* 10:8–11). This episode also indicates Noah's literary legacy. According to *Jub.* 21:10, Noah left not only a book of medicines, but also books of instructions concerning proper sacrifices.[79] In this literature, then, Noah stands for righteousness and wisdom,[80] not only "in his own generation," but also as a paradigm of piety and transmitter of wisdom for future generations.

Conclusion

A witness to the disappearance of the prediluvian universe, and situated on the threshold of a new world, Noah stands out as paradigmatic and unique. As the virtuous survivor of the flood he is the prototype of the righteous person living amidst corruption, calling for repentance, and saved by God from catastrophic punishment. At the opposite pole stand the paradigmatic wicked — the Watchers, their gigantic offspring, and sinful humanity — who transgress the laws of creation and are consigned to punishment. Noah's righteousness makes him an example to follow — the founder, leader, and lawgiver of a new humanity. The covenant between him and God lays down the cosmological and behavioral principles of the new order. The division of the inhabited

---

79. A book by Noah is also mentioned in an *Aramaic Levi Document* (*ALD*) related to the *Testament of Levi*, which survives in Aramaic fragments from Qumran and the Geniza, as well as in fragments of a Greek translation. The reference to Noah's book is found in Bodelian manuscript D, l. 57. For a translation see Greenfield and Stone, "Aramaic and Greek Fragments of a Levi Document," 465.

80. On Noah as an exemplary wise person, see Wis 10:4; Philo, *Abr.* 27.31; *Gen. Rab.* 33.2; *Exod. Rab.* 50.2.

world among his descendants seals Noah's place as organizer of the postdiluvian universe.

Already embedded in the biblical narrative, these elements must have had a special appeal to the circles which produced the Qumranic and related literature, such as *1 Enoch* and *Jubilees*. Most extant adaptations of Noachic traditions come from precisely these circles. Apparently, the single righteous one saved from wickedness and punishment was perceived as a prototype of the Qumranic community and of the times and circumstances of various apocryphal authors. This principle is particularly applicable to the Qumran community, whose members considered themselves the small group of righteous living in a world of wickedness at the threshold of the eschaton, a group destined to found an eschatological world (see 1QH 8:26; compare *1 Enoch* 91:14; 93:10). Significantly, Noah's typology had a similar appeal for another, contemporary eschatological community, namely, the first Christians (see Matt 24:37–39; Luke 17:26–27).

The significant role played by prediluvian heroes and events in Qumranite and related circles becomes fully apparent within the framework of historical periodization, a concept espoused by these circles. In the context of a sequence of periods which compose the historical process, the flood is situated at the beginning of the present historical sequence, while the eschaton concludes this sequence. Thus, the flood and the eschatological end are opposing counterparts of the same symmetry between the primordial and final judgments (see *1 Enoch* 93:4, 9–10; 91:12–13).

The emblematic analogy between the flood and the eschaton was not confined to theoretical speculations. It had immediate practical implications for the Qumranites. For the analogical relationships were perceived as expressions of a divine, premeditated law which governs history, and thus as providing indications for the nature of the eschaton, and the correct behavior to be practiced at its eve. Such an interest may well account for the presence of the Noachic and Enochic literature at Qumran.

Once Noah was selected as emblematic for the Qumran community, his biography served as a vehicle for the community's distinctive ideology in several ways. This was done by supplementing the biblical narrative with themes characteristic of the community's thought. Four additions stand out: Noah's miraculous birth; Noah as a tradent of esoteric knowledge; Noah as a priest; and Noah as combating demons. These themes are not as unrelated as they may appear at first glance. Noah's priesthood concords with his righteousness and concern to follow the commandments. As such, he is the only person fit to transmit the divine, esoteric knowledge revealed to his forefather Enoch. This he does by transmitting Enoch's writings to his favorite son Shem (*Jub.* 10:14; 12:27; 21:10). According to *Jub.* 4:18, Enoch received calendrical and chronological reckoning, but it was Noah who actually applied this reckoning to the flood. He thus inaugurated the correct calculation of time according to the solar calendar, which was to be maintained in the new order. Possessing knowledge of the correct calendar implied ability to calculate the dates of the yearly festivals. Noah was, then, the one best qualified for celebrating festivals, namely, for functioning as a priest. According to *Jub.* 6:17–18 he was, in fact, the first to celebrate *shavuot*. Noah's proficiency in offering sacrifices is confirmed not only by his actual practice, but also by the fact that he transmitted to his descendants books with information on how to offer sacrifices (*Jub.* 21:10). In addition, Noah received particular knowledge relevant to his contemporary situation, namely recipes for preparing medicines to combat the demons. Interestingly, *Jubilees* does not mention the demons and their leader Mastema before the flood. They have no place in the plan of creation. The demons came into being only as the aberrant issues of the perverse and unlawful union between the angels and the human women. Thus, Noah is depicted in *Jubilees* as the righteous counterpart to Mastema and the demons. Noah was, in fact, the first human to encounter demons and their ruler Mastema (*Jubilees* 11). It was therefore fitting that he receive the medicines against them. Favored and excelling in such ways, Noah was considered to have been endowed with supernatural qualities, a view expressed by stories about his miraculous birth.

The choice of prediluvian heroes as models seems also to have been influenced by the general worldview of the Qumranic and apocalyptic literature. Clearly expressed in *Jubilees,* this view regards the Mosaic Torah as expressing the cosmic principles of the created world, the true, cosmic law obeyed by both angels and humans. The transmission of divine knowledge regarding calendar and festivals by angels to Enoch and Noah constituted revelation of cosmic principles to the human race. This material was passed from Enoch and Noah to Shem and Abraham, and then to the people of Israel. The Qumranic claim to be the heirs of the Noachic science implied that they possessed the only true and authoritative teaching, which was ancient and of divine origin.

In this light, it is interesting to note that precisely these traditions of prediluvian generations, and of Noah and the flood, have ancient roots in Mesopotamian culture. Already biblical authors were consciously reworking older, Babylonian traditions, and this practice continued in the works found at Qumran, especially the Aramaic ones, like *1 Enoch* and the so-called *Book of Giants*. Noah himself probably derives from early Mesopotamian traditions about the hero of the flood. One may well ask whether the Qumranites and apocalyptic authors, fully aware of the ancient roots of the Noachic traditions, were not adapting these legends precisely to anchor their own innovative teachings in pre-Israelite tradition. The Qumranites could have appropriated old Babylonian traditions in an attempt to affirm the antiquity of their own ideas and to create a link with the universally known ancient heroes of Mesopotamia.

Be that as it may, it is worth noting that some of the later rabbis attempted to play down Noah's unique righteousness (see *Gen. Rab.* 30.9). Perhaps this was done to counter the prominence he indisputably acquired in circles related to the Qumran community and early Christianity — an example of the ongoing polemic among various strands of early Judaism.

The prominence in the Noachic materials of apocalyptic ideas, priestly elements, demonic powers, and the solar calendar indicates that the authors of these materials belonged to circles closely linked to the Qumran community. The concern for purity is especially evident in the legends about the Watchers. In *1 Enoch* 15:3–4 the Watchers are explicitly accused of breaching the heavenly law and their holy status by defiling themselves through sexual intercourse with mortal women and through menstrual blood. This is intriguingly reminiscent of the accusations leveled by the Qumranites against the contemporary Jerusalem priesthood (see CD 5:6–7). Noah was apparently viewed by the community as the prototype of its own priestly ideals, whereas the Watchers stood for the contemporary priestly transgressors. The Qumranites' belief that they were the earthly counterparts of the heavenly angel-priests suggests that they considered themselves as opposite to the Watchers. Other priestly concerns in the Noachic legends, such as sacrifices and covenantal law, also show that their authors belonged to priestly ranks. Who these priestly authors were, how they were related to the Qumran community, and how and why they drew on Mesopotamian traditions are questions that will occupy Qumran research in the decades to come.

Appendix: The So-Called *Book of Noah*

One of the most popular theories in current research postulates the past existence of an ancient Jewish pseudepigraphon ascribed to Noah, lost very early in its transmission. Despite the absence of any reference to such a book in the patristic lists of pseudepigrapha,[81] the existence of such a book has been postulated from the mention of Noachic books in *Jub.* 10:21; 21:10; and *T. Levi* 2:3 (Greek). Traces of this supposed lost *Book of Noah* were allegedly recognized in various passages in *1 Enoch,* which dealt with Noah rather than Enoch, and appeared to be out of context and of distinct form and content (*1 Enoch* 6–11; 54:1–55:2; 60; 65:1–69:25; 106–7).[82] To these was added *Jub.* 10:20–39, which relates Noah's commandments to his sons, and includes his interactions with the demons.[83] The existence of late Hebrew midrashic fragments about Noah and his book of medicines was seen as another "proof" for the existence of a lost *Book*

---

81. See Denis, *Introduction,* xiv–xv.
82. This is the list given by Charles, *Book of Enoch,* xlvii. It has remained the most influential version of the theory.
83. Cf. Charles, *Book of Jubilees,* 61.

of Noah.[84] This theory gained such wide support[85] that when Hebrew fragments relating to Noah and the flood were discovered at Qumran, they were immediately assigned to the supposedly lost *Book of Noah,* and even published under that title.[86]

Nonetheless, this whole theory rests on shaky grounds. First, the assertion that a *Book of Noah* once existed, made on the basis of references to Noachic books in ancient works such as *Jubilees* and the *Testament of Levi,* cannot withstand criticism. For fictional postulations of such works in pseudepigraphic and legendary writings cannot be taken as historical evidence, unless there exists reliable, independent confirmation. Second, as has been pointed out,[87] in spite of a general resemblance in themes, the Qumranic "Noachic" fragments diverge in form and detail. It is difficult to see how they could have belonged together with the Noachic passages to one and the same work. Also, other passages typically assigned to the *Book of Noah* are of diverse character. Thus, for example, *1 Enoch* 6–11 is a fragment of a narrative account, devoted to the angels' sins, of which only three verses (10:1–3) actually concern Noah. *1 Enoch* 106–7 is another narrative section which, by telling the story of Noah's miraculous birth, emphasizes the role of Enoch in the episode. By contrast, the main "Noachic" passage in the Enochic *Book of Parables, 1 Enoch* 65:1–69:2, is not a narrative, but a discourse by Noah about what he has seen before the flood. Other passages often assigned to the *Book of Noah, 1 Enoch* 54–55 and 60, fit better with Enoch's career than with Noah's.[88] Thus, the very diversity

---

84. These midrashim were assembled by Jellinek, *Bet ha-Midrasch,* 3.xxx–xxxiii, 155–60. I have discussed and republished them from improved editions in " 'The Fallen Angels,' " 183–90. Already Margalioth, *Sepher ha-Razim,* 60, notes that the three passages published by Jellinek come from different books and that there are no grounds to assign them to a *Book of Noah.*

85. See, for instance, the influential book of Russell, *Method and Message,* 66. A few dissenting voices were raised: e.g., Torrey, *Apocryphal Literature,* 112; Frost, *Old Testament Apocalyptic,* 166; Lewis, *Study,* 13–14.

86. Fragments 1Q19 and 1Q19bis (cf. n. 34). Drawing on such a supposed lost work was initially advanced as an explanation for the presence of similar materials in 1QapGen.

87. Cf. Lewis, *Study,* 14–15; Dimant, " 'The Fallen Angels,' " 122–40.

88. Scholars assigned chap. 60 to Noah because 60:1, 8 apparently refer to Noah rather than to Enoch. However, the materials in the chapter, the type of journeys, and the angelic instructions are similar to what is elsewhere shown and explained to Enoch. In any case, these passages in themselves do not constitute proof of the existence of a *Book of Noah,* as observed by Torrey, *Apocryphal Literature,* 112. For literary and structural reasons to

of the fragments assigned to the alleged *Book of Noah* discredits the entire theory.[89] The general affinity of themes and motifs may be better explained as stemming from shared underlying traditions rather than from a distinct written document. In conclusion, there is no evidence for the existence of a *Book of Noah*.

Notwithstanding, a case can be made for the existence of a more comprehensive Hebrew narrative midrash, written perhaps in a style similar to the Aramaic *Genesis Apocryphon,* which would have included at least some of the materials dealing with Noah, such as the story of his miraculous birth. Such a midrash could have covered most of the Genesis primeval and patriarchal history. All the extant "Noachic" narrative sections could be fitted into such an overall narrative framework, as is, indeed, the case for many passages in *Jubilees* and in Pseudo-Philo's *Biblical Antiquities.*[90] As a matter of fact, recent improved deciphering of the first columns in the *Genesis Apocryphon* shows that it constituted such a midrash. It interlaces discourses of Enoch, Methuselah, Lamech, and Noah. The *Genesis Apocryphon* probably covered the entire Genesis narrative sequence, or a good part of it.[91]

---

view the Noah passages as an integral part of the third parable of the Enochic *Book of Parables* (1 *Enoch* 36–71), see Suter, *Tradition and Composition,* 133–35.

89. Similarly Suter, *Tradition and Composition,* 32–33, 102, 154. Another unlikely candidate for the *Book of Noah* is an Aramaic fragment, the so-called 4QMess Ar (= 4Q534), which describes a divinely inspired figure. This was originally thought to be a messianic figure; later it was suggested that the text refers to Noah (cf. Fitzmyer, "The Aramaic 'Elect of God' Text," 158–60). A number of scholars subscribed to this view: cf., e.g., Milik, *Books of Enoch,* 56; Grelot, "Hénoch et ses écritures," 481–500; Kvanvig, *Roots of Apocalyptic,* 90; and most recently García Martínez, *Qumran and Apocalyptic,* 1–24. However, in the absence of textual evidence, such a suggestion remains unconvincing and must be rejected.

90. The outline of the supposed *Book of Noah,* as drawn up by García Martínez, *Qumran and Apocalyptic,* 39, would fit as well with such a midrash.

91. The improved text of 1QapGen I–XII serves to discard recent arguments in favor of the existence of a *Book of Noah,* a thesis advanced by Steiner, "Heading of the *Book of the Words of Noah,*" 66–71.

Bibliography

Critical Editions, Translations, and Commentaries for Primary Sources

1 Enoch

Qumran Aramaic fragments: K. Beyer, *Die aramäischen Texte vom Toten Meer* (Göttingen: Vandenhoeck & Ruprecht, 1984); J. T. Milik, *The Books of Enoch: Aramaic Fragments of Qumran Cave 4* (Oxford: Clarendon, 1976).

Greek fragments: M. Black, *Apocalypsis Henochi Graece* (PVTG 3; Leiden: Brill, 1970).

Ethiopic version: M. A. Knibb, *The Ethiopic Book of Enoch* (2 vols.; Oxford: Clarendon, 1978) vol. 1.

Latin fragment: M. R. James, ed., *Apocrypha Anecdota* (Texts 2, 3; Cambridge: Cambridge University Press, 1893) 136–50.

Translations: M. Black, *The Book of Enoch or 1 Enoch* (SVTP 7; Leiden: Brill, 1985); M. A. Knibb, *The Ethiopic Book of Enoch* (2 vols.; Oxford: Clarendon, 1978) vol. 2.

Commentaries: M. Black, *The Book of Enoch or 1 Enoch* (SVTP 7; Leiden: Brill, 1985); R. H. Charles, *The Book of Enoch* (2d ed.; Oxford: Clarendon, 1912).

Jubilees

Qumran *Jubilees* Hebrew fragments and other related fragments: see the edition with introduction and notes by J. C. VanderKam and J. T. Milik in *Qumran Cave 4. VIII: Parabiblical Texts, Part 1* (DJD 13; Oxford: Clarendon, 1994) 1–185.

Ethiopic version: J. C. VanderKam, *The Book of Jubilees* (CSCO 510; Louvain: Peeters, 1989).

Translation of the Ethiopic: J. C. VanderKam, *The Book of Jubilees* (CSCO 511; Louvain: Peeters, 1989).

Commentaries: K. Berger, *Das Buch der Jubiläen* (JSHRZ 2, 3; Gütersloh: Mohn, 1981); R. H. Charles, *The Book of Jubilees or the Little Genesis* (London: A. & C. Black, 1902).

Qumran Fragments

1Q Genesis Apocryphon: K. Beyer, *Die aramäischen Texte vom Toten Meer* (Göttingen: Vandenhoeck & Ruprecht, 1984) 165–88 (edition, with some improvements on Fitzmyer's below, and translation); J. A. Fitzmyer, *The Genesis Apocryphon of Qumran Cave 1* (2d ed.; BibOr 18a; Rome: Biblical Institute Press, 1971) (edition, translation, and commentary); J. C. Greenfield and E. Qimron, "The Genesis Apocryphon, Col. XII," in *Studies in Qumran Aramaic* (ed. T. Muraoka; Louvain: Peeters, 1992) 70–77.

1Q19: J. T. Milik in *Qumran Cave I* (DJD 1; Oxford: Clarendon, 1955) 84–85, 152.

4Q180: J. Allegro, *Qumrân Cave 4* (DJD 5; Oxford: Clarendon, 1968) 78; D. Dimant, "The Pesher on the Periods (4Q180) and 4Q181," *Israel Oriental Studies* 9 (1979) 77–102.

4Q252: Edited by G. J. Brooke in *Qumran Cave 4.XVII: Parabiblical Texts, pt. 3* (DJD 22; Oxford: Clarendon, 1996). G. J. Brooke, "The Thematic Content of 4Q252," *JQR* 85 (1994) 33–59.

The Damascus Document: M. Broshi, ed., *The Damascus Document Reconsidered* (Jerusalem: Israel Exploration Society, 1992) 9–49 (new edition of the Geniza manuscripts by E. Qimron; on Qumran Cave 4 copies see the texts published by J. M. Baumgarten and J. T. Milik, *Qumran Cave 4.XIII: The Damascus Document* (4Q266–273) (DJD 18; Oxford: Clarendon, 1996).

Major Qumranic works, such as the Rule of the Community (1QS) and Hodayot (1QH), as well as others, may be found in English translation with introductions in G. Vermes, ed., *The Dead Sea Scrolls in English* (4th rev. ed.; London: Penguin, 1995).

Apocryphal Books

Judith, Tobit, Ben Sira, Wisdom of Solomon, and Baruch. Greek texts are edited in the series Septuaginta: Vetus Testamentum Graecum (Göttingen: Vandenhoeck & Ruprecht). Translations are available in Catholic and scholarly versions of the Bible. For scholarly translations and commentaries see the Anchor Bible series (New York: Doubleday).

Pseudepigraphical Writings

1 Enoch, 2 Enoch, Jubilees, 3 Baruch, 3 Maccabees, 4 Ezra, *Sibylline Oracles, Biblical Antiquities* (Pseudo-Philo), the *Testaments of the Twelve Patriarchs,* and the *Testament of Adam:* short introductions with translations and brief notes on each of these may be found in J. H. Charlesworth, ed., *Old Testament Pseudepigrapha* (2 vols.; Garden City, N.Y.: Doubleday, 1983–85). For most of these writings translations are also available in H. F. D. Sparks, ed., *The Apocryphal Old Testament* (Oxford: Clarendon, 1984).

Jewish Hellenistic Authors

Josephus, *Jewish Antiquities,* books 1–4, edition and translation by H. St. J. Thackeray in the Loeb Classical Library (Cambridge: Harvard University Press, 1967).

Philo of Alexandria: see the respective volumes in the Loeb Classical Library (Cambridge: Harvard University Press).

Rabbinic Works

Rabbinic sources are cited from Hebrew editions, mostly current traditional ones. Whenever available, a critical edition is cited. For *Genesis Rabbah* the following editions are used: *The Geniza Fragments of Bereshit Rabba,* ed. M. Sokoloff (Jerusalem: Israel Academy for Sciences and Humanities,

1982) (in Hebrew); *Midrash Bereshit Rabba,* ed. J. Theodor and C. Albeck (Jerusalem: Wahrmann, 1965) vol. 1 (in Hebrew).

Studies

Alexander, P. S. "The Targumim and Early Exegesis of 'Sons of God' in Genesis 6." *JJS* 23 (1972) 60–71. A survey and analysis of interpretations of Gen 6:3 in Aramaic targums and related Jewish documents. Should now be supplemented with the Qumranic 4Q252.

Cohen, H. H. *The Drunkenness of Noah.* Tuscaloosa: University of Alabama Press, 1974.

Dimant, D. " 'The Fallen Angels' in the Dead Sea Scrolls and in the Apocryphal and Pseudepigraphic Books Related to Them" (Ph.D. diss.; Jerusalem: Hebrew University, 1974) (in Hebrew). An analysis of the ancient Jewish texts and traditions related to the legend of the fallen angels, including observations on the survival of such traditions in medieval midrashim. Especially important for identifying the various strands of the legend about the Watchers and the Giants.

———. "1 Enoch 6–11: A Methodological Perspective." *SBLSP 1978* (Missoula, Mont.: Scholars Press, 1978) 323–39. A summary of some sections of the above work, mainly those dealing with the versions of the legends about the Watchers in *1 Enoch* and *Jubilees.*

———. "The Pesher on the Periods (4Q180) and 4Q181." *Israel Oriental Studies* 9 (1979) 77–102. A new edition of these two fragments, with special emphasis on 4Q*180* as an interpretation of the sequence of historical periods. The *pesher* includes a pericope on the fallen angels.

Feldman, L. H. "Josephus' Portrait of Noah and Its Parallels in Philo, Pseudo-Philo's *Biblical Antiquities,* and Rabbinic Midrashim." *PAAJR* 55 (1988) 4–57. Analyzes thematic connections between Josephus and a number of other works.

Fraade, S. D. *Enosh and His Generation: Pre-Israelite Hero and History in Post-biblical Interpretation.* SBLMS 30. Chico, Calif.: Scholars Press, 1984. An analysis of the figure of Enosh and his generation, interesting as a counterpart and analogy to Noah and his generation.

Fraxman, T. W. *Genesis and the "Jewish Antiquities" of Flavius Josephus.* BibOr 35. Rome: Biblical Institute Press, 1979. Pp. 77–116. Discusses the interpretation of Genesis in Josephus's work.

Ginzberg, L. *Die Haggada bei den Kirchenvätern und in der apokryphischen Literatur.* Berlin: S. Calvary, 1900. Pp. 73–89. A still useful survey of legendary traditions shared by the apocryphal literature and the church fathers.

Lewis, J. P. *A Study of the Interpretation of Noah and the Flood in Jewish and Christian Literature.* Leiden: Brill, 1968. A rich collection of materials on Noah; still the most thorough analysis of the subject.

Nickelsburg, G. W. E. "Apocalyptic and Myth in *1 Enoch* 6–11." *JBL* 96 (1977) 383–405. An analysis of the double tradition on the Watchers at-

tested in *1 Enoch* 6–11. The results are very similar to those arrived at in
D. Dimant's dissertation.

Schlosser, J. "Les Jours de Noé et de Lot." *RB* 80 (1973) 13–36. Makes interesting observations on the typology of the flood and the punishment of
Sodom and Gomorrah.

Suter, D. W. *Tradition and Composition in the Parables of Enoch.* SBLDS 47.
Missoula, Mont.: Scholars Press, 1977. Important for understanding the
structure and contents of this work, and the place of the so-called Noah
passages within it.

Tiller, P. A. *A Commentary on the Animal Apocalypse of 1 Enoch.* SBLEJL 4.
Atlanta: Scholars Press, 1993. A detailed commentary on *1 Enoch* 84–90.

VanderKam, J. C. "The Birth of Noah." In *Intertestamental Essays in Honour of
Jósef Tadeusz Milik.* Ed. Z. J. Kapera. Qumranica Mogilanensia 6. Krakow:
Enigma, 1992. Pp. 213–31. Discusses traditions about the birth of Noah in
early sources.

———. "The Righteousness of Noah." In *Ideal Figures in Ancient Judaism.* Ed.
J. J. Collins and G. W. E. Nickelsburg. Chico, Calif.: Scholars Press, 1980.
Pp. 13–32. Treats various aspects of the figure of Noah in early sources.

ABRAHAM THE CONVERT

A Jewish Tradition and Its Use by the Apostle Paul

George W. E. Nickelsburg

The figure of Abraham looms large in the lore of the Hebrew Bible and the Jewish and Christian traditions derived from the biblical sources.[1] Two elements in these sources tend to dominate the Jewish and Christian *Nachgeschichte*. For Jews, in particular, Abraham is seen as the patriarch par excellence, the father or, more properly, the great-grandfather of the nation and the one

---

This paper has seen three previous incarnations: at a symposium on Abraham at Concordia Seminary, St. Louis, in 1968; at the Annual Meeting of the Society of Biblical Literature in Los Angeles in 1972; and at the biennial meeting of the Taskforce on Apocalyptic of the Wissenschaftliche Gesellschaft für Theologie in Bethel, Germany, in 1991. I profited from the discussion on all of these occasions. My long hesitation in publishing the piece was overcome when Theodore Bergren offered to help with the footnotes. By rights he should be listed as coauthor, because they are as extensive as the text. Since he has declined this recognition, I note for the record that while the ideas and arguments are my own, credit for the thorough, knowledgeable, and well-balanced documentation and referencing belongs to him, as do my thanks.

1. See Genesis 11–26; 49:30–31; Luke 16:19–31; John 8:33–59; Acts 7:1–17; Romans 4; Gal 3:6–29; Heb 6:13–7:10; Jas 2:21–24; Sir 44:19–21; 1 Macc 12:19–23; 4 Maccabees 13–20; the *Apocalypse of Abraham;* the *Testament of Abraham; Jubilees* 11–23; Pseudo-Eupolemus; Artapanus; *2 Baruch* 57; *Apocalypse of Zephaniah* 9, 11; *1 Enoch* 93:5; *3 Enoch* 44; *Sib. Or.* 2:246; Philo the Epic Poet; the sources used by Alexander Polyhistor; *Prayer of Jacob* 5; *Bib. Ant.* 6–8; 23:4–8; 32:1–4; the *Testament of Isaac; Testament of Levi* 12; *T. Jud.* 25:1; *T. Benj.* 10:4–6; Philo, *De Abrahamo, De migratione Abrahami;* Josephus, *Ant.* 1.148–256; 1QapGen cols. 18–22; CD 3:2; a lost astrological treatise attributed to Abraham; *b. B. Bat.* 16b; and *Apocalypse of Paul* 47.

For pagan references, see Berossos, in the writings of Josephus, *Ant.* 1.158; Apollonius Molon, in the writings of Eusebius, *Praep. evang.* 9.19.1–3; Nicolaus of Damascus, in the writings of Josephus, *Ant.* 1.159–60; Pompeius Trogus, from the epitome by Justinus, *Historiae Philippicae* 36.2.1; Alexander Polyhistor, in the writings of Eusebius, *Praep. evang.* 9.18.2; Vettius Valens, *Anthologiae* 2.28–29; and Firmicus Maternus, *Mathesis* 4.5.

who first staked out the territory of Eretz Israel.[2] For Christians, Abraham is also a kind of patriarch, but his foundational status lies in the paradigmatic quality of his faith.[3] In the words of Paul, "You are children of Abraham" by faith and thus "heirs according to the promise" that Abraham apprehended by faith (Gal 3:29). In the language of Gen 15:6 — which was celebrated and developed by Paul — when one believes, one is considered, or reckoned, to be righteous.[4]

The purpose of this paper is not to focus on Abraham the patriarch as such, or on his justifying faith as this was evident in his acceptance of God's promise in Gen 15:6. Rather, it will consider traditions about the events that led to his *becoming* the patriarch. These events in Mesopotamia, which are only sketched in Gen 11:20–12:5, are recounted at some length in the book of *Jubilees* and in later Jewish sources from the first century C.E. The discussion of these texts will focus on two questions: (1) Is there evidence that the author of *Jubilees* is transmitting older traditions? and (2) How did these traditions continue to be used by later Jews and their Christian contemporaries? With respect to the latter question it will be proposed that the apostle Paul used these traditions in his missionary preaching among the Gentiles.

Jubilees 11–12

The book of *Jubilees,* which dates from the mid–second century B.C.E., is an extensive elaboration of the biblical account in Genesis 1 through Exodus 12.[5] Written in Hebrew and translated into Greek, it survives in full only in a tertiary Ethiopic version. The

---

2. See, e.g., *1 Enoch* 93:5; *Apocalypse of Abraham* 20; 4 Ezra 3:15; *Bib. Ant.* 7:4; 8:1–3; Rom 11:1; 2 Cor 11:22. On Abraham's staking out the land, see 1QapGen 21:15–19.

3. See especially Romans 4; Gal 3:6–18, 29; 4:22–23; Heb 11:17; Jas 2:21–23. For Jewish references, see Sir 44:20; 1 Macc 2:52; Jdt 8:24–27; *Jub.* 17:17–18.

4. See Rom 4:3, 22; Gal 3:6; Jas 2:23.

5. Major studies of *Jubilees* include Charles, *Book of Jubilees;* VanderKam, *Textual and Historical Studies;* and Nickelsburg, "The Bible Rewritten," 97–104. For full publication of the Qumran Hebrew fragments of *Jubilees,* see VanderKam and Milik, eds., *Qumran Cave 4. VIII.,* 1–185.

Jubilees reflects the events immediately preceding the Maccabean revolt, and is usually dated in the period 170–140 B.C.E. For alternative datings within this period, see Nickelsburg, "The Bible Rewritten," 101–3.

material on Abraham in *Jub.* 11:1–13:1 recasts Gen 11:20–12:5 with special attention to Abraham's rejection of his pagan environment. *Jub.* 11:1–8 sets the scene. The children of Noah begin to make war, shed blood, and take captives (11:2). In the city of Ur, the people begin to make molten images (*sebkawāt*), and each worships the idol (*ṭaʿot*) he has made as his molten image. In addition, they make statues, images, and unclean things (11:4). All this is done at the instigation of the prince of Mastema, the chief of the evil spirits who are the progeny of the rebellious Watchers.[6] These same spirits initiate bloodshed and every sort of violence and sin (11:5). Serug, Abraham's great-grandfather, grew up in this environment, worshiped idols, and taught his son, Nahor, about the astrological research of the Chaldeans, their divination and auguring by the signs of heaven (11:7–8). Thus astrology is added to the idolatrous religion of the Chaldeans. Although the source of this astrological information is not identified here, according to 8:3 it was introduced by the Watchers.[7]

With the birth of Terah (11:9–10), the author introduces a new narrative thread. The prince of Mastema sends birds to devour the seed that is being sown, so that humans are deprived of the fruits of their labor; the birds also eat the fruit on the trees (11:11–13).[8] Thus, the flood notwithstanding, the world is again plagued with all the ills first brought to the earth by the Watchers and their progeny, the giants: violence and bloodshed; the use

---

6. The title "prince of *(the) mastema*" (prince of animosity) is the chief designation for the archdemon in *Jubilees*, appearing both in its full form and by the shorthand "mastema" (10:8; 11:5, 11; 17:16; 18:9, 12; 19:28; 48:2, 9, 12, 15). The Hebrew word משטמה ("animosity") occurs in Hos 9:7–8, and is an attribute of the archdemon Belial in 1QM 13:4, 11; 13:9. The root of the noun may be related to the root שטן. For the term "Satan" (Eth. *saytan* in *Jubilees*), see 10:11; 23:29. *Jubilees* does not explicitly describe the origins of Mastema, although 10:1–9 identifies him as the chief of those spirits who proceeded from the giants who were killed at the time of the flood (cf. 5:1–10; 7:20–27).

7. According to this verse, Arpachshad taught writing to his son Cainan. Cainan in his travels then found and transcribed a "writing" which the "ancestors" had engraved on stone, which contained the astrological teachings of the Watchers. The valuation is negative: Cainan "sinned because of what was in it [the inscription]" (*Jub.* 8:3). Negative evaluations of the introduction of astrology also appear in *1 Enoch* 8:3 and *Bib. Ant.* 4:16. Cf. *Jub.* 11:8; 12:16–20; *Bib. Ant.* 19:10. See also nn. 13, 21.

8. According to several Syriac accounts, it is God rather than the prince of Mastema who sends the birds. S. P. Brock has attempted to demonstrate that these accounts represent a tradition that is independent of *Jubilees* ("Abraham and the Ravens," 135–52, cited in *OTP* 2.79, n. i). Note that *Jubilees* attributes to the prince of Mastema several actions that are carried out by God in the biblical account: cf. 17:15–18:13; 48:2–3, 12 (cf. Nickelsburg, *Resurrection,* 12–13).

of metallurgy (here to make idols); astrology; and devastation of crops.[9]

The author now drops the story about the prince of Mastema and the birds and returns to the scene that had been previously set. Abram is born in pagan Ur and quickly comes to understand the error (*seḥtat*) of the land that is evidenced in its idolatrous statues and uncleanness, and he begins to pray to the Creator that he might be saved from their error and uncleanness (11:14–17).

Once again, the author proceeds to interweave his narratives (11:18–24). Abram the fourteen-year-old *Wunderkind*, perhaps enlightened by his prayer, drives away the birds by talking to them,[10] and invents a farm implement that sows the seed and immediately plows it under. The land is rescued from the prince of Mastema's birds.

In the next segment of the story, the author returns to the motif of idolatry. We hear Abram in conversation with his father (12:1–8). Abram, now twenty-eight years old, preaches against the folly of idolatry. Idols, the fabrications of human hands, are dead and useless, and are not worthy of the worship that is appropriate only to the God of heaven, the Creator and Preserver of the earth.[11] Terah agrees that Abram is right, but reveals that because of his fear of his fellow citizens, he continues to "serve" as an idolatrous priest (*'etla'ak qedmēhomu*, v. 6). He warns Abram to keep silent, lest the idolatrous Chaldeans kill him.

Abram, however, takes matters into his own hands. He slips

---

9. *Jub.* 5:1–11; 7:21–24 mention only the violent activity of the giants as the result of the rebellion of the Watchers, while 4:15 interprets their instruction of humanity in a different way. However, see *1 Enoch* 8:1–3 for the Watchers' revelation of the secrets of metallurgy and celestial prognostication.

10. In the Syriac accounts cited in n. 8, Abram is able to drive away the ravens only by appealing to God for help.

11. The motif of idolatry and its folly is a major one in Second Temple Jewish literature, presumably because many Jews were living in environments in which the worship of idols was commonplace. Polemic against idolatry does, of course, have biblical roots: cf. Pss 115:3–8; 135:15–18; Isa 40:18–20; 41:6–7; 44:9–20; 45:20; 46:1–7; Jer 10:2–16; Hab 2:18–19. In the Second Temple period, see especially the Epistle of Jeremiah; Bel and the Dragon; Wisdom of Solomon 13–15; 2 Macc 2:1–3; *1 Enoch* 99:6–9, 14; *2 Enoch* 10:6; 34:1–3; 66:1–5; *Apocalypse of Abraham* 1–8; *Testament of Job* 2–5; the *Letter of Aristeas passim*; *Jannes and Jambres*; *Bib. Ant.* 2:9; 4:16; chaps. 6–7; 9:2; chap. 12; 19:7; chap. 25; 30:1; chap. 34; 44:6–10; *Jos. As. passim*; *Sibylline Oracle* 3; *3 Bar.* 13:4; and *Ladd. Jac.* 7:22–25.

out at night and sets the idolatrous temple on fire (12:12). The Chaldeans, of course, want to rescue their gods from the flames, and Abram's brother, Haran, is burnt to death in the attempt (12:13–14). This is an interesting haggadic turn on Gen 11:28: "Haran died...in Ur of the Chaldeans."[12]

Having dealt with the idols, Abram, now living in Haran, must contend with the second major religious aberration (12:16–21). As he sits up at night observing the stars for signs that forecast the amount of rain expected in the coming year, a word enters his heart, and he realizes that all the heavenly phenomena are under the control of God, who sends or does not send rain as God wishes.[13] Astrological prognostication is a demonic science and constitutes error, just as idolatry does.

At this point, with Abram's recognition of the total sovereignty of the God of heaven, this God commands him to leave Mesopotamia for a new land (12:22–24 = Gen 12:1–3). God then instructs the angel of the presence to teach Abram Hebrew, the language of creation and, incidentally, the original language of the book of *Jubilees*.[14] Having then become versed in "the books of

---

12. The point, of course, is that the Hebrew word for "Ur" (אור) is identical to that for "flame." On this interpretation see Nickelsburg, *Jewish Literature*, 295; Kister, "Observations," 1–34, esp. pp. 6–7.

The idea that Haran died in "fire" is commonplace in the pseudepigrapha and rabbinic literature, and is accounted for in various ways. *Apocalypse of Abraham* 8 states that Terah and his household were burned by fire from heaven in punishment for their persistence in idolatry. Rabbinic sources say that Haran was burned because he refused to worship fire, and that it was a Chaldean custom to immerse their children in fire. See Ginzberg, *Legends,* 1.202; 5.214–15 (n. 40).

13. Abraham was, in many sources (both Jewish and pagan), regarded as an adept in astrology. See the discussion below in this paper; Bowley, "Compositions," 215–38; idem, *Traditions of Abraham;* Siker, "Abraham in Greco-Roman Paganism," 188–208; idem, *Disinheriting the Jews.*

This notion was known even in rabbinic literature (*Gen. Rab.* 11:28; *b. B. Bat.* 16b) and may derive ultimately from Gen 15:5. Cf. *Apocalypse of Abraham* 1–7. *Bib. Ant.* 4:16, on the other hand, refutes the notion that Abraham or anyone else in his family practiced astrology.

For the idea that Abraham came to know God through his own reasoning about the physical universe, as described here in *Jubilees,* see *Num. Rab.* 14:2; *Pesiq. R.* 33.150; *Gen. Rab.* 38:13; *b. B. Bat.* 10a; *Yashar Noah* 20a–b; and *Midr. Hagadol Gen.* 1.189. See also nn. 7, 21.

14. For Hebrew as the language of creation and the original language of humanity, which was then lost to most at the Tower of Babel, see *Gen. Rab.* 18.4; 31.8; 42.8; *Pirqe R. El.* 24.26; *Tg. Yer.* Gen 11:1, 8; *Midr. Tan. B* 1.56; *Jub.* 12:25–26; cf. Ps.-Clem. *Recognitiones* 1.30; Origen, *Contr. Cels.* 5.30; and *Zohar* 1.75. See Ginzberg, *Legends,* 5.94 (n. 58), 5.205–6; and Charles, *Book of Jubilees,* 95–96 (notes to 12:25–26).

his father" (12:27),[15] Abram leaves Haran, after receiving Terah's blessing, and sets out for Canaan (12:28–13:1 = Gen 12:4–5).

Jub. 11:1–13:1 constitutes a highly elaborated form of the Genesis story about Abram in Mesopotamia.[16] The content of the expansions is noteworthy. The land of the Chaldeans is marked by religious error in the form of idolatry and astrology. In Abram's family, these traditions go back three generations. Serug worshiped idols and taught his son Nahor astrology (11:7–8). Terah was an idolatrous priest (12:6), and Haran has sufficient investment in the cult to die in an attempt to rescue his gods (12:14). In contrast to this, Abram comes to a knowledge of the Creator, the God of heaven, and rejects both idolatry and astrology. On the basis of this conversion to the true God, this God chooses Abram to be the recipient of the blessing and the promise.[17]

Jubilees 11–12 as Tradition

A comparison of these Abraham stories with other passages on Abraham in *Jubilees* indicates that the author of the book has a substantial investment in the criticism of idolatry.[18] Abraham's testamentary speeches to his descendants in general (20:7–9), to Isaac (21:3–5, 21–23), and to Jacob (22:16–22) all echo the anti-

---

15. There is a long tradition in Jewish literature of wise individuals studying and learning from the writings of their ancestors. See, for example, Exod 17:14; 24:7; Deut 31:9–19; 32:46; *1 Enoch* 68:1; 81.6; 82:1–3; 83:10; 92:1; 93:1–3; 100:6; 104:10–13; 108:1, 10; Dan 12:4, 9–10; Tobit 12:20; *2 Enoch* 19:5; 23:3–6; 33:3–12; 35:2–36:4; chap. 40; 47:1–2; 48:6–9; 54:1; etc.; *Life of Adam and Eve* 50:1–2; *As. Mos.* 1:16; 11:1; 4 Ezra 12:36–38; 14:22, 26, 45–46; *2 Baruch* 77:12, 17; 84:9; 1QapGen 19.25; *Par. Jer.* 6:19; the *Testament of Kohath*; the *Testament of Amram*; Rev 22:10; and the introduction to *Sefer ha-Razim*. This is also a consistent theme in *Jubilees*: see 1:5–6; 4:17–23; 7:38–39; 10:13–14; 21:10; 39:6–7; and 45:16.

16. This type of exegesis of and elaboration on the biblical story is common in Second Temple Jewish literature: besides *Jubilees*, see the *Genesis Apocryphon*, Ps.-Philo's *Biblical Antiquities*, *1* and *2 Enoch*, the *Books of Adam and Eve*, *Joseph and Aseneth*, the *Martyrdom of Isaiah*, and Josephus, *Jewish Antiquities*. See Nickelsburg, "The Bible Rewritten."

17. In Gen 12:1–3, no rationale is given for God's sudden choice and blessing of Abraham. It seems reasonable to suppose that one motive for the elaborate story in *Jub.* 12:1–21 was to provide such a rationale (cf. 12:22–24).

18. The motif of anti-idolatry in *Jubilees* is usually understood with reference to the apparent background of the book in the period of the Maccabean revolt (see n. 5). For anti-idolatry in the Second Temple period, see n. 11.

idol polemics in the earlier stories, and they are a constitutive part of the author's admonition that Israel maintain its identity by avoiding the ways of the Gentiles.

Nonetheless, several features in *Jubilees* 11–12 suggest that this text preserves a traditional elaboration of Genesis 11–12, elements of which preceded the writing of *Jubilees*.[19] The first feature is a certain unevenness in the narrative. Certain nonbiblical elements that are present in the story are taken for granted. On the one hand, the story features a conversation between Abram and Terah (12:1–7) that does not appear in Genesis. On the other hand, this conversation takes a good deal for granted. (*a*) It merely alludes to Terah being a priest (12:6). (*b*) It *suggests* that there are tensions between the father and the Chaldeans (12:7). (*c*) The story touches briefly on the motif of Abram's negative interaction with his brothers and suggests a kind of boldness and lack of fear that fits well with the faith that is characteristic of Abram (12:8). (*d*) It describes the story of the temple fire in very brief form (12:12–14). All of this suggests that *Jubilees* presents a written epitome of a longer, perhaps oral, retelling of the Genesis story. This suggestion may also be supported by the interweaving of the two distinct narratives, one about Chaldean religion (11:1–8, 14–17; 12:1–31), the other about the birds' devastation of the land (11:9–13, 18–24).[20]

The motif of Abram's origin in an idolatrous land is an old one. While the Genesis story may imply the motif of astrology by setting the story in Chaldea (Gen 11:24–32),[21] the motif of idolatry appears explicitly in the Deuteronomic retelling of the story in Joshua 24, where the rejection of idolatry is the governing mo-

---

19. For a discussion of possible traditional material in *Jubilees*, cf. Charles, *Book of Jubilees*, xliv–xlvii. Charles cites the ten trials of Abraham as a case in point, but does not note that *Jubilees* mentions the number ten, but only enumerates eight instances (17:17–19:10).

20. See above, n. 8.

21. For early, extrabiblical attestation of the idea of the Jews' rejection of astrology despite their origins in the "homeland" of this science, see *Sib. Or.* 3:218–33. See also *1 Enoch* 80:7; *Sib. Or.* 13:69–73; *Bib. Ant.* 4:16; 19:10; *Ladder of Jacob* 2:12, 14; Philo, *Migr. Abr.* 176–86; idem, *Abr.* 66–88; and Josephus, *J.W.* 5.212–14; 6.228–92.

Many rabbinic sources stress that God commanded Abraham not to rely on astrology: see *Gen. Rab.* 44.8–12; *Midr. Pss.* 2.10; 21.179; *2 'Abot R. Nat.* 43.122; *'Ag. Shir* 1.5; *b. Shab.* 150a, 156a; *b. Ned.* 32a; *Tanhuma Shofetim* 11; *Pesiq. R.* 43.179a; etc. (cf. Ginzberg, *Legends* 5.227, n. 108). See also nn. 7, 13.

tif.[22] Joshua's speech to the people is punctuated by references to the motif and by repeated use of the verbs "to serve" (עבד) and "to set aside" (סור). The fathers served other gods beyond the River (24:2, 14, 15), and Israel did the same in Egypt (24:14). Now the people, too, are to set aside these gods (24:15–16) and serve Yahweh. With perhaps an inverted allusion to the story of Abraham's election, the people are challenged to choose (24:15). Both the fictional and the real settings of this speech provide good reason for the emphasis. In the narrative world of the text, Israel stands on the verge of occupying the land of Canaan, and its promise to abandon other gods stands as a negative witness to the repeated idolatry that will characterize the narrative in the Book of Judges. In the real world of the text, the motif is integral to the events of the Josianic reform with which the Deuteronomic history is associated.

In light of this emphasis in the Deuteronomic version of the Abram story, and given all the anti-idolatry material in the later strata of the Hebrew Bible, it seems highly unlikely that the narratives in *Jubilees* 11–12 were *de novo* creations by the author of that book. In fact, a number of references preserved in fragments of works from the third and second centuries B.C.E. indicate that there was a developed lore about Abraham the astronomer.

The so-called Orphic fragment, a Jewish hymn attributed to Orpheus that Eusebius claims to have found in a work by the Jewish philosopher Aristobulus (fl. 155–145 B.C.E.), speaks of

> a certain unique man, an offshoot from far back of the race of the Chaldeans. For he was knowledgeable about the path of the star, and how the movement of the sphere goes around the earth.[23]

---

22. Joshua 24 narrates the covenant between God and the Israelites made at Shechem after the conquest of the land of Canaan. As often, the covenant ceremony is preceded by a historical review in which the leader summarizes the mighty acts of God on behalf of the people, providing a basis for the people's pledging their allegiance to God. See also, e.g., Neh 9:6–37.

23. The long version of the fragment, in which alone this citation occurs, is preserved in two sources: Eusebius's *Praeparatio evangelica* (13.12.5) (early fourth century) and a fifth-century self-styled "Theosophical" text. The translation given here is by M. Lafargue, *OTP* 2.799, ll. 26–28. The larger context of Eusebius's quotation of Aristobulus is provided in *OTP* 2.840. Lafargue, who accepts Eusebius's claim about his source for the fragment, first notes that the work is clearly Jewish (*OTP* 2.795). On the identity of the mysterious figure, he notes that "possibly Abraham is meant here. But Philo (*Vita Mosis* 1.5) thinks also of Moses as a Chaldean schooled in astronomy" (*OTP* 2.799). (Cf.

A fragment of Eupolemus, a Jewish historian who also wrote probably in the mid–second century B.C.E., says that

> Abraham excelled all in nobility and wisdom; he sought and obtained the knowledge of astrology and the Chaldean craft, and pleased God because he eagerly sought to be reverent.... [He taught] the Phoenicians the cycles of the sun and moon.... He explained astrology and the other sciences to [the Egyptian priests], saying that the Babylonians and he himself had obtained this knowledge.[24]

Josephus attributes a similar statement to Berossos, the third-century B.C.E. Babylonian priest:

> Berossos mentions our father Abram without naming him, when he says thus: "In the tenth generation after the flood there lived among the Chaldeans a man just and great, and versed in celestial lore." (*Ant.* 1.158)[25]

This fragmentary evidence associates Abraham in Mesopotamia with astrological knowledge, a notion, of course, that could

---

Bib. Ant. 19:10.) Lafargue concludes that it is difficult to determine whether Abraham or Moses is meant here. See further Lafargue, "Jewish Orpheus," 2.137–44.

Abraham seems the more likely candidate, since Philo states not that Moses was a Chaldean, but that the Egyptians and the inhabitants of the neighboring countries taught him the Chaldean sciences of astronomy and astrology.

24. Despite Eusebius's attribution of this fragment to Eupolemus (*Praep. evang.* 9.17.2–9), the fragment has traditionally been ascribed to "Pseudo-Eupolemus." Doran, in *OTP* 2.873–82, argues that the fragment is genuine. The fragment is translated by Doran in *OTP* 2.880–81.

According to this fragment, Abraham was personally responsible for spreading the knowledge of astrology from Babylonia to Phoenicia to Egypt. Abraham, however, according to Eupolemus, attributed the discovery of this science to Enoch: "Enoch first discovered astrology, not the Egyptians" (*OTP* 2.881). This statement relates to accounts found in *1 Enoch*, *Jubilees*, and elsewhere about the origins of writing, astronomy, and knowledge of the arts and sciences. See esp. *1 Enoch* 12:1–6; chaps. 14–36; 37:2–4; chaps. 72–82; *Jub.* 4:17–26; 1QapGen 2:21; and *2 Enoch passim*.

Eupolemus states that Abraham "was born in the tenth generation in the Babylonian city Camarina" (*OTP* 2.880).

A second fragment traditionally ascribed to Pseudo-Eupolemus also cites the tradition of Abraham's learning astrology and spreading it to Phoenicia and Egypt; cf. *OTP* 2.882. Doran holds that this material was compiled by Alexander Polyhistor out of statements made in the fragment discussed above (*OTP* 2.878). See also n. 26.

25. Berossos, around 290 B.C.E., wrote in Greek the *Babyloniaca*, an apologetic history of Babylon. He is said to have been versed in astrology. Josephus's claim that Berossos was referring to Abraham is controversial. For a survey of scholars who argue both for and against this possibility, see Bowley, "Compositions," 234, n. 23.

The reference to the "tenth generation" is noteworthy in connection with a similar statement made by Eupolemus; see n. 24.

Note that Artapanus, a Jewish writer of the third or second century B.C.E., states that Abraham "came to Egypt... to the Egyptian king Pharethothes, and taught him astrology, [and] remained there twenty years" (trans. J. J. Collins, *OTP* 2.897; frag. 1; Eusebius, *Praep. evang.* 9.18.1).

have been triggered by the reference in Gen 15:5. Nonetheless, these texts, along with *Jubilees, explicitly* associate Abraham with astrological lore. The similarity in very different, yet roughly contemporary, texts suggests that this notion was not the invention of the author of *Jubilees,* and that the stories in *Jubilees* 11–12 have older roots, going back at least to the third or fourth century B.C.E.[26]

Jewish Texts from the First Two Centuries of the Common Era

Several Jewish texts from the first or early second century C.E. display striking parallels with the stories in *Jubilees* 11–12 and indicate that the older stories have an ongoing life in the Jewish tradition.

Josephus, Jewish Antiquities *1.154–57*

The first of these is Josephus's *Jewish Antiquities,* written in 93–94 C.E.[27] The passage in question immediately precedes the one just cited as the source of the quotation from Berossos. The biblical locus is Gen 11:31–12:8. According to Josephus, Abram

> was a man of ready intelligence on all matters, persuasive to his hearers, and not mistaken in his inferences. Hence he began to have more lofty conceptions of virtue than the rest of mankind, and determined to reform and change the ideas universally current concerning God. He was thus the first boldly to declare that God, the creator of the universe, is one, and that, if any other being contributed anything to man's welfare, each did so by his [God's] command and not in virtue of its own inherent power. This he inferred from the irregular phenomena to which land and sea are subject, as well as those that happen to the sun and moon, and all the

---

26. There are other ancient documents that associate Abraham with astrology. Alexander Polyhistor, in *On the Jews,* cites several anonymous sources to this effect (cf. Eusebius, *Praep. evang.* 9.18.2). Vettius Valens of Antioch (second century C.E.) mentions Abraham as an expert in the ninth horoscopic position and claims to know an astrological treatise by him (*Anthologiae* 2.28–29). Firmicus Maternus (fourth century C.E.) also claims to have known and used an astrological work by Abraham (*Mathesis* 4.5). On the latter two authors, see Bowley, "Compositions," 228–33.

27. For Josephus in general, see Attridge, "Josephus and His Works," 185–232; Cohen, *Josephus in Galilee and Rome.* For the *Antiquities,* see esp. Attridge, *Interpretation;* Schalit, *Yosef ben Mattatyahu.*

heavenly bodies; for, he argued, were these bodies endowed with power, they would have provided for their own regularity, but since they lacked this last, it was manifest that even those virtues in which they cooperate for our greater benefit they render not in virtue of their own author-ity, but through the might of their commanding sovereign.... It was, in fact, owing to these opinions that the Chaldeans and the other peoples in Mesopotamia rose against him, and he, thinking fit to emigrate, at the will and with the aid of God, settled in the land of Canaan. (*Ant.* 1.154–57)[28]

Although Josephus's typically Hellenistic cast is readily discern-ible in this passage,[29] a number of elements in it parallel the *Jubilees* story. Abraham is a pioneer in proclaiming the oneness of God the Creator. God's creative power is evident in the di-vine control over the universe and its elements. Abraham is driven out of Babylon, a notion that is consonant with the story of his burning of the idolatrous temple. While we cannot exclude the possibility that Josephus knew the book of *Jubilees*,[30] it seems much more likely that he is drawing on a haggadic tradition that derived from a common source.[31] Abraham comes to a knowl-edge of the true God that conflicts with the ideas of Chaldean idolatry and astrology; his proclamation of this (mirrored in the conversations with his brothers alluded to in *Jub.* 12:8) results in his flight or forcible expulsion from Ur.[32]

Philo, De Migratione Abrahami *(On the Migration of Abraham) 176–86; and* De Abrahamo *(On Abraham) 66–88*

In his exegetical comments on Gen 11:31–12:4, Philo of Alexan-dria, writing in the first half of the first century c.e., appears also to be aware of the tradition that associates Abraham with the

---

28. Quoted according to the translation by H. St. J. Thackeray in LCL, Josephus, vol. 4 (adapted).

29. One example of this is the "proof" of the sole sovereignty of the one God.

30. See, e.g., Attridge, *Interpretation,* 33 and n. 1, 147 and n. 1; Bilde, *Flavius Josephus,* 150.

31. For Josephus's use of sources in the first part of the *Antiquities,* see Attridge, "Jose-phus and His Works," 211–16; idem, *Interpretation,* 29–38; S. J. D. Cohen, *Josephus in Galilee and Rome,* 24–66; Feldman, "Sources of Josephus' Antiquities," 320–33; and idem, "Josephus," *ABD* 3.981–98, esp. pp. 985–91.

32. *Ant.* 1:167–68 is also relevant in that it shows Abram teaching arithmetic and as-trology to the Egyptians when he arrives there. Compare (Ps.-)Eupolemus and Artapanus, cited above.

rejection of astrology. Although his treatments are typically allegorical, Philo ties Abraham's migration from Ur to Haran with
the observation that the Chaldeans were well-known for their
astronomical and astrological calculations (*Migr. Abr.* 178–79,
184; *Abr.* 69–71, 77, 82). He cites texts in which he believes
that Moses is rejecting an astrological worldview,[33] and takes
Gen 11:31–12:4 as an admonition to leave behind meddling
with heavenly concerns (symbolized by Ur) and to focus on
self-knowledge (symbolized by Haran).[34] *De Abrahamo* explicitly identifies Abraham during his time in Chaldea not only as
engaging in astrological speculation (secs. 70, 77), but indeed as
"tak[ing] care of the Chaldean tenets as a father would of his children" (sec. 82).[35] Thus the pattern in Philo's interpretation can
clearly be overlaid with the narrative pattern in the older story
about Abraham in *Jubilees* 11–12.[36]

Pseudo-Philo, Liber Antiquitatum Biblicarum *4:16–7:5*

A third relevant text, situated chronologically between Philo and
Josephus's *Jewish Antiquities,* is the *Book of Biblical Antiquities* of so-called Pseudo-Philo. Written around 70 c.e., this book
retells biblical history from Adam to the death of Saul.[37] *Bib. Ant.*
4:16, in a section that parallels Genesis 11, states:

> Then those who inhabited the earth began to observe the stars and started
> to reckon by them and to make predictions and to have their sons and
> daughters pass through the fire. But Serug and his sons did not act as
> these did.

Present here are the familiar twin motifs of astrology and idolatry.[38] As in *Jubilees* 11, Serug is explicitly mentioned, but in direct

---

33. E.g., Gen 12:7; 17:5; Exod 17:6; Deut 4:39.

34. See esp. *Migr. Abr.* 187 and *Abr.* 70–72. According to Philo, Haran, which he interprets as "hole," represents the openings in the body used for sense perception. Knowledge
of sense perception, or self-knowledge, in turn, is an appropriate halfway point between a
concern for astrology (Ur) and an apprehension of higher spiritual realities (Canaan).

35. This latter observation is based on an etymological interpretation of the name
"Abram" (*Abr.* 82).

36. See also Philo, *Quaest. in Gen.* 3.1; *Somn.* 1.41–60; *Quis heres* 96–99.

37. On Pseudo-Philo, see Murphy, *Pseudo-Philo;* Perrot and Bogaert, eds., *Pseudo-
Philon.*

38. On the cultic practice of passing one's child through the fire (child sacrifice), see
Gray, *I & II Kings,* 631–32.

contrast to that book (cf. *Jub.* 11:7–8) he is said to have rejected these errors.

The first major story about Abram himself in *Liber Antiquitatum Biblicarum* (chap. 6) associates him with the building of the Tower of Babel. The tale is a variant on the Danielic story of the three young men in the fiery furnace (Daniel 3). Twelve leaders in Babylon refuse to bake bricks in the furnace for the tower, because they consider the building of the tower idolatry that conflicts with their worship of the One God (6:2–4). Given the chance, eleven of the twelve flee for their lives (6:6–10). Only Abram refuses to leave, and is thrown into the furnace (6:11–16). The idolaters are consumed by the flames leaping out of the furnace, but Abram emerges unscathed (6:17). The section that immediately follows (chap. 7) recapitulates the biblical text, contrasting the builders of the tower, who will be scattered, with Abram, whom God chooses to bring out of Mesopotamia into the land of Canaan.[39]

Several elements in this story parallel *Jubilees* 11–12. At the risk of his life, Abram rejects the idolatry of his compatriots. A great fire (this one not of his own making) is associated with the Babylonian idolatry. As a result of his rejection of idolatry, Abram is chosen by God and sent forth from Mesopotamia to the land of Canaan. Perhaps one should not make too much of the major elements in this story, since most of them are also present in Daniel 3. However, the attachment of the story of the fiery furnace to Abraham could very well indicate that the author of *Liber Antiquitatum Biblicarum* knew a tradition about Abraham that associated him with a conflagration that was, in turn, related to his rejection of idolatry.[40]

The traditional character of at least one element in *Biblical Antiquities* 6–7 appears to be attested in the Wisdom of Solomon, a text from around the turn of the era.[41] According to Wis 10:5,

---

39. See also *Bib. Ant.* 32:1. Note the appropriateness of the conflation of these stories: at the same time that other peoples are "scattered" throughout the earth, Abram is "scattered" into Canaan.

40. On the story of Abraham and the fiery furnace, see Murphy, *Pseudo-Philo*, 41–48. Murphy summarizes the theme of idolatry in Ps.-Philo on pp. 252–54.

41. On the Wisdom of Solomon, see Winston, *Wisdom of Solomon*; Clarke, *Wisdom of Solomon*.

> When the nations were confounded because of
>   [their] wicked agreement, [Wisdom] recognized
> the righteous one and
>   preserved him blameless before God. . . .

This text appears to refer to Abraham, and to imply that Abraham was present at the time of the building of the Tower of Babel.[42] With the help of Wisdom, he declined to participate, and thus remained righteous and blameless before God.[43]

Apocalypse of Abraham *1–8*

One further text from the late first century c.e. deals with the theme of Abraham's rejection of idolatry. Chapters 1–8 of the *Apocalypse of Abraham* recount a series of events in which Abraham moves from the idolatry of his father to the worship of the true God.[44] A number of features in it parallel the stories in *Jubilees*. Terah, although he is not explicitly called a priest, is an idol maker (1:7–2:1 and *passim*), and Abraham takes part in idolatrous sacrifices (1:1–3). In the various episodes, Abraham works through a mental process of searching for "the God of gods," in which he gradually concludes that idols are not true deities. Another narrative feature is several conversations with Terah about the folly of idolatry (chaps. 4, 6–7). The interaction is stronger and more argumentative than in *Jubilees* 12, but both narratives feature a difference of opinion between the son and father (cf. *Apoc. Abr.* 26:3–5). The *Apocalypse of Abraham,* like *Jubilees,* also develops a connection between idolatry and astrology (*Apoc. Abr.* 7:7–9; cf. *Jub.* 12:16–17). In both texts, Abraham concludes that God has ultimate control over all cosmic and earthly phenomena (*Apoc. Abr.* 7:10–12; *Jub.* 12:18–21). Again, in both

---

42. See Winston, *Wisdom of Solomon,* 211–14; Clarke, *Wisdom of Solomon,* 69–70. Cf. *Gen. Rab.* 38.6; *S. 'Olam Rab.* 1; and *Biblical Antiquities* 6, all of which depict Abraham as living at the time of the Tower of Babel.

43. This passage is part of the wisdom hymn in Wisdom of Solomon 10 that describes Wisdom's saving power in the careers of seven biblical heroes. Note that Wisdom of Solomon also has a strong anti-idolatry focus (11:15–16; 12:23–27; 13:1–15:19).

44. The *Apocalypse of Abraham* seems to have been written in response to the Roman destruction of Jerusalem in 70 c.e.; cf. Nickelsburg, *Jewish Literature,* 294–99. The book's condemnation of idolatry in chaps. 1–8 probably reflects the view that incorrect cultic activity in the Temple, construed here as idolatry, led to that destruction.

texts it is this realization that leads to Abraham's call by God (*Apocalypse of Abraham* 8; *Jub.* 12:22–24).

Another parallel element between the two texts is fire. In the episode in *Apocalypse of Abraham* 5, one of Terah's idols falls into the fire and burns. In chapter 7, Abraham tells his father that fire is in fact more powerful than the idols (cf. *Jub.* 12:12–14). At the end of the narrative (chap. 8), Abraham literally leaves his father's house, which is struck by lightning and consumed by divine fire, which also destroys everything in it, the idols included. The narrative line of the story is that Abraham rejects the idolatry of his father and as a consequence is called and sent forth by God. The next episode is the sacrifice described in Genesis 15 (*Apocalypse of Abraham* 9–15). Abraham then ascends to heaven to God's throne and is commissioned as patriarch (chaps. 15–32).

Testament of Job 2–5

Before leaving the Jewish texts about Abraham, I shall discuss one non-Abrahamic text which, however, is clearly related to the story in *Jubilees* 11–12, namely, *Testament of Job* 2–5.[45] Although this text was preserved and copied in Christian circles, it is most likely Jewish in origin.[46] It was probably composed in the first century B.C.E. or C.E.

The relevant portion is as follows:

> When I was called Jobab, I used to dwell quite near a venerated idol. And as I continually saw whole burnt offerings being offered up to it, I debated within myself, saying, "Can this be the God who made heaven and earth and the sea and our very selves? How then shall I know?"
>
> And in the night as I was sleeping, a loud voice came to me, a voice in a great light, saying, "Jobab, Jobab!"
>
> And I said, "Behold it is I."
>
> And he said, "Arise, and I shall tell you who this is whom you wish to know. This one to whom they bring whole burnt offerings and to whom

---

45. The *Testament of Job* creatively retells the biblical story of Job using the classic testament genre. It was probably written in Greek, perhaps in Egypt. See Spittler, "Testament of Job," *OTP* 1.829–68; Brock, *Testamentum Iobi.*

46. Few modern scholars defend a Christian origin for the work. Spittler, for example, notes that "although Christian editing is possible, the work is essentially Jewish in character" (*OTP* 1.833). Some have seen it as reflecting the Hellenistic Jewish mission, or as originating among the Therapeutae.

they pour out libations is not God, but this is the power of the devil by which human nature is deceived."

And when I heard, I fell on my bed worshiping and saying, "My Lord, who came for the salvation of my soul, I beg you, if this is indeed the place of Satan in which men are deceived, grant me authority to go and purge his place so that we no longer make libation to him. And who is there who prevents me, since I rule this region?" (2:2–3:7)

Job receives permission from God and destroys the temple (chaps. 4–5).

The points of similarity with the Jewish stories of Abraham, and with *Jubilees* in particular, are obvious. Job is seeking the true God and carrying on an internal conversation with himself about this. In particular, he is concerned about a local idol temple, which he eventually demolishes. God appears to him at night. One curious element in the story lies in Job's words, "And who is there who prevents me, since I rule this region?" (3:7; καὶ τίς ἐστιν ὁ κωλύων με βασιλεύοντα ταύτης τῆς χώρας;). The formula τί κωλύει is remarkable for its frequency in New Testament baptismal contexts.[47] Its occurrence here in a "conversion" setting may indicate knowledge of a technical usage, either in a Christian baptismal setting or in some analogous Jewish *Sitz im Leben*. The precise relationship of this story to the Abraham stories in *Jubilees* 11–12 is uncertain. However, it should be noted that the *Jubilees* version of the *Akedah*, the story of Abraham's intended sacrifice of his son Isaac (*Jubilees* 18; Genesis 22), is prefaced with a prologue in a heavenly setting, in which the prince of Mastema and the Angels of the Presence debate the reasons for Abraham's righteousness (*Jub.* 17:15–18).[48] This narrative setting indicates that the author of *Jubilees* read the Abrahamic story in light of the opening two chapters of Job.[49] *Testament of Job*

---

47. See, e.g., Acts 8:36; 10:47; 11:17; cf. Mark 10:14 par.; Matt 3:14; *Gos. Eb.* in the writings of Epiphanius, *Pan.* 30.13; and Ps.-Clem. *Hom.* 13.5.1; 11.2.

Cullmann's proposal that τί κωλύει in Acts, etc., comes from a primitive baptismal ritual (*Baptism*, 71–80) has garnered a mixed reception. See, e.g., Beasley-Murray, *Baptism*, 322–25; Jeremias, *Kindertaufe*, 66–67. Argyle, "Cullmann's Theory," 17, is especially skeptical.

48. See Nickelsburg, *Jewish Literature*, 75–76, and nn. 6 and 8 of this essay. For the *Akedah* in general, see Agus, *Binding*; Davies and Chilton, "Aqedah," 514–46; Feldman, "Josephus as a Biblical Interpreter," 212–52; Ginzberg, *Legends*, 1.279–86, 5.250–55; Milgrom, *Binding of Isaac*; and Charles, *Book of Jubilees*, 120–24.

49. For discussion of the relationship between *Testament of Job* 2–5 and the *Jubilees Akedah*, see Haas, "Job's Perseverance," 117–54, esp. pp. 148–50.

2–5 conversely reshapes an Abrahamic story into a Joban story. Both describe the conversion of a searching Gentile to the one, true God.

In summary, several first-century C.E. Jewish texts show significant parallels to the stories in *Jubilees* 11–12. In these texts Abraham rejects idolatry and astrology and turns to the worship of the one, true God. It is difficult to ascertain the precise relationship between this set of stories and the *Jubilees* text that antedates them by three centuries. Clearly the narratives in the *Apocalypse of Abraham* that were surveyed above reflect traditional motifs present in such texts as Deutero-Isaiah and Bel and the Dragon, to name two.[50] It remains uncertain whether the authors of the various first-century C.E. texts knew *Jubilees* or drew on a common tradition; direct dependence on *Jubilees* is far from being proven.[51] The texts, especially *Jubilees* and the *Apocalypse of Abraham*, require a closer comparative analysis before the relationships between them can be evaluated with confidence.

Elements of the Abraham Story in the Epistles of Paul

This final section will consider some elements of the Abraham materials as they are presented in the Pauline Epistles, mainly the Epistle to the Galatians.

A striking aspect of this text is the manner in which Paul introduces the figure of Abraham without explanation (3:6) and then moves into a detailed and complex exegesis of the Genesis texts (Gal 3:6–4:11). How would these groups of Gentiles in the heartland of Asia Minor have heard about this hero of the Israelite scriptures?[52] How would they have been sufficiently familiar with the Abraham stories that Paul could launch into a

---

50. See esp. Isa 40:18–20; 41:6–7; 44:9–20; 45:20; 46:1–7; Bel *passim,* esp. vv. 4–7.

51. The earliest attested reference to *Jubilees* is in the Qumran Damascus Document, usually dated to 100–75 B.C.E., which cites *Jubilees* (CD 16:3–4). Eleven fragmentary Hebrew manuscripts of *Jubilees* have also been found at Qumran, the earliest dating from around 100 B.C.E.; see VanderKam and Milik, eds., *Qumran Cave 4. VIII.,* 2.

Interestingly, *Jubilees* is not attested definitely again until the fourth century C.E., when it is cited by Epiphanius (*Haer.* 39.6.1–7; *De mens. et pond.* 22) and Jerome (*Ep.* 78).

52. For the Gentileness of Paul's audience, see Betz, *Galatians,* 1–5, esp. p. 4 and n. 17; Bruce, *Galatians,* 31–32; Lührmann, *Galatians,* 3, 83.

detailed exegesis with no explanation or introduction? It is possible that the figure of Abraham was introduced to the Galatians by Paul's opponents as a basis for their arguments about circumcision.[53] The considerations that follow suggest that it is just as likely that when the Apostle established his churches in Galatia, he employed the Abraham stories as a central feature in his instruction.

It would have been natural that, in his preaching to the Gentiles, Paul should have recounted stories about Abraham, the enlightened prototypical gentile convert, who turned from the errors of idolatry and astrology to the worship of the one true God. Common elements in the narrative worlds of these stories would have offered familiar points of contact with the real world of the Gentiles to whom Paul preached. A pagan reflects on the folly of false religion and finds his way to knowledge of the God of heaven, the creator of the elements. Tension arises in the interaction between the convert and his family, and between the convert and his compatriots. The convert's decision, however, is vindicated as the newly revealed God chooses the convert and institutes a covenantal relationship with him.

That Paul in Galatians drew heavily upon the biblical texts about Abraham is clear enough. Quotations from Genesis 15 are explicit. Indeed the section on Abraham begins with a quotation of Gen 15:6 (Gal 3:6; cf. Rom 4:3), and then moves on to cite an earlier passage in Gen 12:3, when God calls Abraham out of Haran, promising him that "In you all the nations will be blessed" (Gal 3:8; cf. Gen 22:18). Of course this passage is a natural one to quote in discussion with Gentiles. But what of the extrabiblical stories about Abraham's conversion?

The use of these stories would have been a natural way to address the Galatians' situation described in 4:8–10:

> But then, when you did not know God, you were enslaved to those who by nature were not gods. Now, however, when you know God, or rather, you are known by God, how is it that you turn back again to the weak

---

53. The issue of the sudden introduction of this theme is often missed by commentators. An exception is Burton (*Galatians,* 153–54), who argues that this issue is precisely one that had been raised by Paul's opponents. This idea is adopted by Lührmann (*Galatians,* 56), who proposes that Paul might have been "forced" to advance his own interpretation of Gen 15:6 due to the propaganda of his opponents.

and beggarly elements, to which again you wish to be enslaved? You observe days and months and times and years.

This passage reflects on the Galatians' former situation as worshippers of idols.[54] Instead of the natural word for religious service (λατρεύειν), which appears, for example, in the Old Greek version of Joshua 24,[55] Paul employs δουλεύειν, which interprets their service as slavery.[56] Although he does not speak explicitly about their conversion to the worship of the true God, he alludes to it by referring specifically to their reconversion to their former slavery: "you turn back again" (4:9; ἐπιστρέφετε πάλιν).

In another of Paul's Epistles, 1 Thessalonians, we find the use of these same verbs with reference to these Gentiles' conversion from idolatry: " ... you turned (ἐπεστρέψατε) to God from idols, to serve (δουλεύειν) the living and true God" (1:9).[57]

Now, what the Galatians turn back to (ἐπιστρέφειν) are the "weak and beggarly" στοιχεῖα.[58] Paul evidently equates these with the spirit beings that stand behind the idols, those things

---

54. Cf. Betz, *Galatians*, 213–19; Bruce, *Galatians*, 201–07; Lührmann, *Galatians*, 83–85; Burton, *Galatians*, 227–34.

55. *Passim*; fifteen occurrences, mostly concentrated in vv. 14–24. The word is also used in this sense about forty times in the Old Greek Pentateuch.

Λατρεύειν is used for religious (cultic) service often in early Christian literature. In the Pauline corpus, it denotes serving God in Rom 1:9 and Phil 3:3. It occurs in early Christian literature twice in the negative sense of "serving" things other than God (Acts 7:42; Rom 1:25).

56. The use of δουλεύειν to signify "service" to God is frequent in the LXX and in early Jewish and Christian literature. As service to foreign gods, see Exod 23:33. In the sense of "serving" elemental spirits, it occurs only here in Gal 4:8–9; compare, however, *PGM* 13.72: "Lord, I serve your angel under your cosmos." In Gal 4:3, Paul uses δουλοῦν for service to the στοιχεῖα; compare *Diogn.* 2:10 and *Barn.* 16:9.

57. This passage is sometimes supposed to represent a pre-Pauline formula used in missionary preaching to Gentiles. For a summary, see Wanamaker, *Thessalonians*, 84–86. For these verbs, see also Gal 2:14; 4:9; Acts 9:35; 11:24; 14:15; 15:19; and 26:20. Cf. Betz, *Galatians*, 216, n. 31; Burton, *Galatians*, 232.

58. The basic meaning of στοιχεῖα is "fundamental principles" or "fundamental elements." In our period, the word can be used in the sense of "elemental substances"; of basic elements of which the world is composed (cf. Wis 7:17; 19:18; 4 Macc 12:13); of the four elements; and even of heavenly bodies (for the latter, see n. 63).

The phrase τὰ στοιχεῖα τοῦ κόσμου occurs in Gal 4:3 (and by implication 4:9); and Col 2:8, 20 (cf. *Sib. Or.* 2.206; 3.80–81; 8.337; 2 Pet 3:10–12; *Cologne Mani Codex* 16:1–16). It could be interpreted here as referring to deities associated with or identical to the "fundamental elements" of the universe described above (see, e.g., Philo, *Vita contempl.* 3; *Decal.* 53). It could also imply the widespread notion that the heavenly bodies (planets, stars, etc.) are divine beings.

For στοιχεῖα, see the standard lexica; also *Exegetical Dictionary of the New Testament*, 3 vols. (Grand Rapids, Mich.: Eerdmans, 1990–1993) 3.277–78; *TDNT* 7.670–87; *ABD* 2.444–45; Betz, *Galatians*, 204–5 (esp. n. 30), 215–17; Burton, *Galatians*, 510–

that "by nature are not gods" (τοῖς φύσει μὴ οὖσιν θεοῖς).[59] This is traditional language found in Jewish polemics against idols.[60] What is striking is that the spirit beings behind the pagan idols are equated, if not identified, with the angelic beings that are associated with the Jewish Torah.[61] Moreover, the issue here is the observance of the Jewish calendar (4:10).[62]

Perhaps this association was facilitated by the material in the Abrahamic stories that emphasizes Abraham's espousal and then rejection of astrological speculation. We recall the story in *Jub.* 12:16–21 where Abram observes the heavens in order to gain information about the coming seasons, and finally rejects the notion that the heavenly bodies (which is one possible referent of the noun στοιχεῖα)[63] have divine status. In *Jub.* 12:20, moreover, Abram prays, "Save me from the hand of the evil spirits... O my God." Not only are the "evil spirits" (*manafest 'ekuyan*) mentioned here a possible corollary of the στοιχεῖα, but the pattern of salvation from "ruling" spirits that Abraham sets up closely corresponds to that envisioned by Paul in Gal 4:8–11. In short, while Gal 4:10 may be a simple reference to Jewish calendrical observance and need not imply an allusion to Abrahamic traditions, the reference, as well as the whole passage, links up nicely

---

18; Lohse, *Colossians and Philemon*, 96–99, 122–23; and Blinzler, "Lexikalisches," 2.427–43.

59. Cf. 1 Cor 8:4–6; 10:22; 12:2. See Betz, *Galatians*, 214–15; Burton, *Galatians*, 215–16. See also *Jos. As.* 12:9; Haas, "Job's Perseverance," 119, n. 8.

60. Cf., e.g., Wis 12:2–3. See Betz, *Galatians*, 214 and n. 14; Bruce, *Galatians*, 201; Lührmann, *Galatians*, 83.

61. For references to the Torah or Hebrew Bible being "given" by angels, see Acts 7:38, 53; Gal 3:19; Heb 2:2; cf. *Jub.* 1:27, 29; 2:1; Josephus, *Ant.* 15.136. The idea may be based on Deut 33:2–4 (esp. the LXX); Ps 68:17. Gal (3:21–)4:3 makes a connection between following the Torah and being "enslaved" (δουλοῦν) to the στοιχεῖα; this connection is strengthened by the reference to the Jewish calendar in 4:10.

For (Jewish?) angel worship, see, e.g., Col 2:18. Col 2:16–23 is remarkable in connecting observance of the Jewish calendar, kosher regulations, purity regulations, angel worship, and worship of the στοιχεῖα.

For Moses as "mediator," see, besides Gal 3:19–20, Acts 7:38; Lev 26:46; Num 36:13; and Philo, *Vita Mosis*.

See also Bandstra, *Law and the Elements;* Schweizer, "Slaves of the Elements," 455–68; *TDNT* 3.684–85; and Lührmann, *Galatians*, 84.

62. See Schweizer, "Elemente der Welt," 147–63; Betz, *Galatians*, 217–19, esp. p. 218, n. 51; Bruce, *Galatians*, 204–7; and Burton, *Galatians*, 232–34.

63. For the στοιχεῖα as heavenly bodies, see LSJ, s.v., sec. II.5; BAGD, s.v., sec. 4; *Exegetical Dictionary of the New Testament* 3.278; *TDNT* 7.680–84; and *ABD* 2.444–45. Cf. *1 Enoch* 80:6.

with a set of elements that do, in fact, recur in the stories about Abraham's conversion.[64]

It is beyond the scope of this essay to discuss Paul's broader use of the Abrahamic material.[65] However, one point is worth mentioning. In Romans 4, Paul emphasizes that because Abraham believed in God before he was circumcised, i.e., because the story in Genesis 15 chronologically precedes that in Genesis 17, therefore Abraham can be the father of both righteous Gentiles and righteous Jews, both uncircumcised and circumcised.[66] The assertion has a parallel in the Jewish traditions that we have been discussing. Abraham was a Gentile who came to faith in the true God, and as such was a prototype of all Gentiles who did the same. Thus, setting aside the circumcision issue, the Jewish texts and Paul parallel one another in their understanding of Abraham's connection to righteous Gentiles. It would be interesting to see whether Jewish thought apart from Paul used the figure of Abraham as a justification for claiming that Gentiles in their own time might be saved apart from Jewish ritual law. Apart from references to Abraham, there are Jewish texts that allow for the salvation of righteous Gentiles, those who avoid the "great sins," but who do not follow Jewish ritual observance.[67]

Conclusions

This essay has traced the development of a set of traditions about Abraham the convert, from their earliest extant form in the book of *Jubilees* into Jewish and Christian sources of the first century C.E. Further developments continue in the rabbinic sources of later centuries.[68] The *Jubilees* stories are themselves the crystallization of earlier tradition that has its roots in what we know

---

64. This possibility is hinted at by Lührmann, *Galatians*, 85.

65. For Abraham in the Pauline writings, see Berger, "Abraham in den paulinischen Hauptbriefen," 1.372–82; Hansen, *Abraham in Galatians*; Käsemann, "Faith of Abraham," 79–101; and Wilckens, "Rechtfertigung Abrahams," 111–27.

66. Rom 4:9–17; cf. Gen 17:4–6.

67. The issue as related to circumcision in particular is discussed by Collins, "Symbol of Otherness," 164–86.

68. See Ginzberg, *Legends*, 1.183–308, 5.207–69; Billerbeck, "Abrahams Leben"; and Str-B 4.1213, s.v. Abraham.

as biblical texts (namely, Gen 11:22–12:5). For the author of *Jubilees,* Abraham's rejection of idolatry has a contemporary point of reference. Other passages in *Jubilees* warn against idolatry and are part of the author's concern that readers maintain their Jewish religious identity in a gentile world.[69] Indeed, the earlier Deuteronomic retelling of the Abrahamic rejection of idolatry in Joshua 24 also has both a fictional and a real setting in the context of a threat of idolatry. Over against this "in-group" admonition, which sees Abraham as a model for *Jewish* religious behavior, stands the Pauline use of the tradition — to provide "outsiders," i.e., Gentiles, with the model of one who turned from idolatry to the living and true God. It might be useful to see where, between these poles, we might place other of the Jewish traditions that have been discussed. Is there evidence that Jewish writers apart from Paul used the story of Abraham's conversion as part of their discussion with Gentiles of their own time?

Bibliography

Comprehensive Treatments and Overviews

Klauser, T. "Abraham." *RAC* 1.18–27.
Martin-Achard, R. *Actualité d'Abraham.* Neuchâtel, Switzerland: Delachaux & Niestle, 1969. Archaeological evidence; Hebrew Bible; NT; early Judaism; and Qur'an.
Sarna, N., et al. "Abraham." *EncJud* 1.111–25.

The Hebrew Bible

van Seters, J. *Abraham in History and Tradition.* New Haven: Yale University Press, 1975. Archeological and literary (form-critical and structural) analysis of the biblical traditions, which dates the Yahwistic tradition to the Exile and the Priestly material after the Exile.

---

69. For anti-idolatry rhetoric in *Jubilees,* see esp. 20:7–9; 21:3–5; 22:16–22. For the idea of maintaining Jewish religious identity in general, see 3:31; 6:12–14, 35; 7:30; 15:33–34; chaps. 20–22; 23:16–21; chap. 25; 27:10; and chap. 30.

Early Judaism

Beer, B. *Leben Abrahams nach Auffassung der jüdischen Sage.* Leipzig: Leiner, 1859. A collection of the sources for the development and depiction of Abraham in Jewish tradition.

Billerbeck, P. "Abrahams Leben und Bedeutung nach Auffassung der älteren Haggada." *Nathanael* 15 (1899) 43–57, 118–28, 137–57, 161–79; 16 (1900) 33–57, 65–80.

Bowley, J. E. *Traditions of Abraham in Greek Historical Writings.* Ph.D. diss., Hebrew Union College-Jewish Institute of Religion, 1992.

De Menasce, P.-J. "Traditions juives sur Abraham." In *Abraham, Père des croyants.* Ed. Cardinal Tisserant. Cahiers Sioniens 5. Paris: Cerf, 1952. Pp. 96–103.

Feldman, L. H. "Abraham the Greek Philosopher in Josephus." *Transactions of the American Philological Association* 99 (1968) 143–56.

Ginzberg, L. *The Legends of the Jews.* 7 vols. Philadelphia: Jewish Publication Society of America, 1909–38. 1.185–308; 5.207–69. A compilation of Second Temple, early Christian, and rabbinic sources concerning Abraham.

Goodenough, E. *By Light, Light.* New Haven: Yale University Press, 1935. Chap. 5. Abraham in the writings of Philo.

Harrington, D. J. "Abraham Traditions in the *Testament of Abraham* and in the 'Rewritten Bible' of the Intertestamental Period." In *Studies on the Testament of Abraham.* Ed. G. W. E. Nickelsburg. SBLSCS 6. Missoula, Mont.: Scholars Press, 1976. Pp. 165–72.

James, M. R. *The Lost Apocrypha of the Old Testament: Their Titles and Fragments.* London: SPCK, 1920. Survey of references to writings ascribed to or about Abraham.

Knox, W. L. "Abraham and the Quest for God." *HTR* 28 (1935) 55–60. Traces this motif in Hellenistic Jewish writings.

Mayer, G. "Aspekte des Abrahambildes in der hellenistisch-jüdischen Literatur." *EvT* 32 (1972) 118–27. Organizes the material under four themes: universal fatherhood; culture-bringer; philosopher; and ideal ruler.

Nickelsburg, G. W. E., ed. *Studies on the Testament of Abraham.* SBLSCS 6. Missoula, Mont.: Scholars Press, 1976. A collection of essays on various aspects of *T. Abraham.*

Sandmel, S. *Philo's Place in Judaism: A Study of Conceptions of Abraham in Jewish Literature.* Cincinnati: Hebrew Union College Press, 1956. Reprint, New York: Ktav, 1971. See esp. pp. 30–95. Studies the depiction of Abraham in a wide variety of Jewish sources.

Vermes, G. *Scripture and Tradition in Judaism.* 2d ed. Leiden: Brill, 1973. Pp. 66–126. Development of biblical material in Jewish haggadah.

Wacholder, B. Z. *Eupolemus.* Cincinnati: Hebrew Union College–Jewish Institute of Religion, 1974. P. 76.

———. "Pseudo-Eupolemus' Two Greek Fragments on the Life of Abraham." *HUCA* 34 (1963) 83–113.

The New Testament

Baird, W. "Abraham in the New Testament: Tradition and the New Identity." *Int* 42 (1988) 367–79.

Berger, K. "Abraham in den paulinischen Hauptbriefen." *TRE* 1.372–82 (also *MTZ* 17 [1966] 47–89).

Démann, P. "La signification d'Abraham dans la perspective du Nouveau Testament." In *Abraham, Père des croyants*. Ed. Cardinal Tisserant. Cahiers Sioniens 5. Paris: Cerf, 1952. Pp. 44–67.

Soards, M. L. "The Early Christian Interpretation of Abraham and the Place of James within That Context." *IBS* 9 (1987) 18–26.

Ward, R. B. "The Works of Abraham: James 2:14–26." *HTR* 61 (1968) 283–90.

Wieser, F. E. *Die Abrahamvorstellungen im Neuen Testament*. Bern: Lang, 1987. Covers the whole range of NT texts.

Early Christianity

Daniélou, J. "Abraham dans la tradition chrétienne." In *Abraham, Père des croyants*. Ed. Cardinal Tisserant. Cahiers Sioniens 5. Paris: Cerf, 1952. Pp. 68–87.

Siker, J. S. *Disinheriting the Jews: Abraham in Early Christian Controversy*. Louisville: Westminster, 1991. Wide-ranging study of NT and second-century Christian interpretations of Abraham which argues that they moved from a gentile inclusion in God's promises to a Jewish exclusion.

———. "From Gentile Inclusion to Jewish Exclusion: Abraham in Early Christian Controversy with Jews." *BTB* 19 (1989) 30–36. Based on the concluding chapter of Siker's *Disinheriting the Jews*.

Ward, R. B. "Abraham Traditions in Early Christianity." In *Septuagint and Cognate Studies 2*. Ed. R. A. Kraft. Missoula, Mont.: Scholars Press, 1972. Pp. 165–79. (Also in *Studies on the Testament of Abraham*. Ed. G. W. E. Nickelsburg. SBLSCS 6. Missoula, Mont.: Scholars Press, 1976. Pp. 173–84.) Survey of material about Abraham in the NT and apostolic fathers.

Wilken, R. "The Christianizing of Abraham: The Interpretation of Abraham in Early Christianity." *CTM* 43 (1972) 723–31.

Jewish and Christian Sources

Bogaert, P.-M., ed. *Abraham dans la Bible et dans la tradition juive*. Brussels: Institutum Iudaicum, 1977. Essays on Genesis 12, 18, and 22; Pseudo-Philo; and Paul.

Bowley, J. E. "The Compositions of Abraham." In *Tracing the Threads: Studies in the Vitality of Jewish Pseudepigrapha*. Ed. J. C. Reeves. SBLEJL 6. Atlanta: Scholars Press, 1994. Pp. 215–38. Surveys various books in antiquity purporting to have been written by Abraham. The portraits of Abraham conform to one of two models: the righteous and faithful patriarch, or the expert astrologer.

Schmitz, O. "Abraham im Spätjudentum und Urchristentum." In *Aus Schrift und Geschichte: Theologische Abhandlungen A. Schlatter dargebracht.* Ed. K. Bornhäuser. Stuttgart: Calwer, 1922. Pp. 99–123.

Tisserant, Cardinal, ed. *Abraham, Père des croyants.* Cahiers Sioniens 5. Paris: Cerf, 1952.

Völker, W. "Das Abraham-Bild bei Philo, Origenes, und Ambrosius." *TSK* 103 (1931) 199–207.

Non-Judeo-Christian Sources

Siker, J. S. "Abraham in Graeco-Roman Paganism." *JSJ* 18 (1987) 188–208. Pagan sources have a relatively positive view of Abraham and a vague notion of his relationship to the Jews. They emphasize his association with magic and astrology.

SEVEN

MELCHIZEDEK IN EARLY JUDAISM, CHRISTIANITY, AND GNOSTICISM

BIRGER A. PEARSON

Introduction

Melchizedek is one of the more enigmatic of the biblical figures treated in this book, about whom a great range of speculation developed in early Jewish, Christian, and Gnostic groups. It might be said that the interpretive imagination devoted to Melchizedek in extrabiblical sources stands in inverse proportion to the sparsity of data found in the Bible about him. In the Hebrew Bible he is mentioned only twice, and in the New Testament he appears only in a single book, the Epistle to the Hebrews.

Melchizedek in the Hebrew Bible

Melchizedek appears first in Gen 14:18–20, a passage that seems to be a secondary interpolation into the text of Genesis 14. The context has Abram returning victorious from a battle with Chedorlaomer and allied kings, and meeting up with the king of Sodom in the Valley of Shaveh (14:17).[1] At that point Melchizedek, "king of Salem" and "priest of El Elyon," brings out bread

---

1. According to the traditional identification of this valley ("the King's Valley," 14:17; cf. 2 Sam 18:18), it is either a part of, or equatable with, the Kidron Valley, to the east of Jerusalem. This accords with the traditional identification of "Salem" with Jerusalem.

and wine and pronounces the blessing of El Elyon ("God Most High") on Abram, who responds by giving Melchizedek a tithe of his booty.

The other passage in the Hebrew Bible that mentions Melchizedek is Ps 110:4: "The LORD has sworn and will not change his mind, 'You are a priest forever according to the order of Melchizedek.'"[2] This is to be read as an oracle addressed to a king, giving him eternal priestly prerogatives. The priesthood in question is that of Melchizedek, not of Aaron and the tribe of Levi. The passage presumes that Melchizedek is a known figure from the past. Does this mean that the psalmist knew and alluded to Gen 14:18–20? Or are the two passages independent attestations of an earlier tradition?

The question of the relationship between Gen 14:18–20 and Ps 110:4 has been answered very differently by different scholars, as has the question of the dating and historical contexts of these passages (estimates ranging from the time of David in the tenth century B.C.E. to the time of the Maccabean Simon in the mid-second).[3] These questions need not detain us here, for we are interested in what happens to the figure of Melchizedek in extrabiblical interpretation.

Melchizedek in the New Testament

As for Melchizedek's appearance in the Epistle to the Hebrews, we note, first, that both Gen 14:18–20 and Ps 110:4 are quoted and interpreted. For the author of Hebrews they are obviously canonical texts, part of "scripture." But, second, we shall also see in Hebrews' depiction of Melchizedek evidence of influence from Jewish sources outside the Bible, as well as the "spin" that the author himself places on the traditions that he uses.

The treatment of Melchizedek in Hebrews begins in 5:5–6:

---

2. Unless otherwise noted, biblical quotations are from the NRSV.

3. For discussion of these and other issues, see, e.g., Horton, *Melchizedek Tradition*, 12–53; Gianotto, *Melchisedek*, 11–43; and scholarly commentaries on Genesis and the Psalms. An older scholarly opinion that situates Psalm 110 and other "royal" psalms in the Maccabean period has recently been defended by M. Astour in "Melchizedek," 684.

So also Christ did not glorify himself in becoming a high priest,[4] but was appointed by the one who said to him, "You are my Son, today I have begotten you" [Ps 2:7]; as he says also in another place, "You are a priest forever, according to the order of Melchizedek [Ps 110:4]."

The designation of Jesus as "high priest according to the order of Melchizedek" is reiterated in 5:10, but the development of the argument is postponed until chapter 7, with the theme enunciated in 5:10 being reiterated at the end of chapter 6 (6:20). Chapter 7, which in its entirety can be called a Melchizedek midrash, constitutes the "solid food" promised by the author in 5:14, but interrupted by parenesis.[5] The midrash, then, is presented as special teaching for the "mature" (τέλειοι, 5:14).

The midrash itself does not begin with Ps 110:4, which had already been cited several times. Rather, it commences with selected quotations from Gen 14:17–20:

This "King Melchizedek of Salem," "priest of the Most High God" [14:18], "met [Abraham] as he was returning from defeating the kings" [14:17] and "blessed him" [14:19], and to him Abraham apportioned "one-tenth of everything" [14:20].[6]

The rest of the midrash comments on this text. Melchizedek's name is interpreted to mean "king of righteousness," "king of Salem" to mean "king of peace" (Heb 7:2). Next comes an argument from silence: lack of any other information about Melchizedek in scripture prompts the author to claim that he is "without father, without mother, without genealogy (ἀπάτωρ, ἀμήτωρ, ἀγενεαλόγητος), having neither beginning of days nor end of life, but resembling the Son of God (ἀφωμοιωμένος δὲ τῷ υἱῷ τοῦ θεοῦ), he remains a priest forever (μένει ἱερεὺς εἰς τὸ διηνεκές)" (7:3). This last detail picks up Ps 110:4, though with different wording.[7]

The midrash goes on to interpret the payment of tithes to Melchizedek (Gen 14:20) as a sign of Melchizedek's superiority to

---

4. Christ has already been referred to as "high priest" in 2:17; 3:1; and 4:14–15; in 5:1–4 the proper function of a "high priest" and the requisite divine calling are set forth.

5. On Hebrews 7 see especially Attridge, *Hebrews*, 186–215.

6. I have rearranged the quotation marks in the NRSV translation, and have added the references plus "Abraham." Note that the actual blessing in Gen 14:19–20 is omitted, as well as the offering of bread and wine mentioned in Gen 14:18.

7. Ps 110 (109):4 reads (in the LXX) ἱερεὺς εἰς τὸν αἰῶνα.

Abraham and, by implication, to the levitical priesthood (Heb 7:4–10). The need for another priest, "according to the order of Melchizedek" (Ps 110:4), from a nonlevitical tribe, is then underscored and seen to be fulfilled in "our Lord," a descendant of Judah (Heb 7:11–14). It is he who has arisen as the one resembling Melchizedek (κατὰ τὴν ὁμοιότητα Μελχισέδεκ, 7:15), who fulfills the testimony of Ps 110:4 (7:16–17). With Jesus as a "better hope," access to God has been introduced, which implies the "abrogation of an earlier commandment" (7:18–19), and the introduction of a "better covenant" (7:20–22). In contrast to the levitical priests, Jesus is an eternal priest (7:23–25). He is the sinless "high priest" (7:26), whose offering of himself "once for all" involves his appointment by divine oath (cf. Ps 110:4a) as "a Son who has been made perfect forever" (7:27–28).

This midrash, of course, has principally to do with the role and dignity of Jesus Christ, and it is clear from 7:3 that the author of Hebrews sees Jesus Christ, "the Son of God" (type), as superior to Melchizedek (antitype).[8] But what this midrash says about Melchizedek is our main concern here. And we note several things in the midrash that go beyond the information supplied in the two biblical passages on which it is based. These include the etymologies, "king of righteousness" and "king of peace" (7:2), Melchizedek's timelessness and lack of human parentage and genealogy, his resemblance to the "Son of God" (7:3), and his immortality (7:3, 8). Thus, Melchizedek appears virtually as a divine or semidivine being. Christ's role as "high priest according to the order of Melchizedek" (5:10; 6:20; cf. 7:26–28) may also indicate that Melchizedek himself was understood by the author of Hebrews as a "high priest." Is all of this due to this author's inventiveness as an interpreter of scripture? Or, rather, does Hebrews reflect the existence of nonbiblical Jewish interpretive traditions on which its author draws, if only to subordinate Melchizedek to Christ?

In what follows we shall see that the latter question is the relevant one, and that an affirmative answer can be given.

---

8. This interpretation of Heb 7:3 is convincingly argued by Horton (*Melchizedek Tradition*, 152–65). The one who arises as "resembling Melchizedek" (7:15) is, therefore, Jesus, the Son incarnate.

Melchizedek in Extra-Biblical Judaism

In this section we shall first explore the relevant sources in Jewish literature for evidence of those features of the figure of Melchizedek that we encountered in Hebrews. Then we shall discuss briefly other aspects of Melchizedek interpretation in Jewish literature.

Philo of Alexandria

We turn first to the extensive treatment of Melchizedek given by Philo in book 3 of his *Allegorical Interpretation of Genesis* (*Leg. all.* 3.79–82).[9] Here we find both of the etymologies encountered in Hebrews: "righteous king" and "king of peace" (3.79). Melchizedek's offering of bread and wine, a detail missing from Hebrews, is interpreted allegorically as food for the soul (3.81), the wine signifying the soul's "divine intoxication, more sober than sobriety itself" (3.82). Melchizedek himself as "priest of the Most High" is interpreted as the divine Logos. Philo also refers to Melchizedek as the one whom God has made as his own priest, a detail which may reflect Ps 110:4.[10] Philo does not use the term "high priest" here, but in his treatise *On Abraham* he refers to Melchizedek[11] as ὁ μέγας ἱερεύς, "the great priest" (*Abr.* 2.35), which may be taken as an equivalent of ἀρχιερεύς and translated as "high priest."[12] Melchizedek offers sacrifices of thanksgiving for the victory that God had bestowed upon Abraham (*Abr.* 2.35). Note that nothing is said here, or in the previous passage, about Abraham's payment of tithes (Gen 14:20). Abraham's payment of tithes is interpreted in another of Philo's works, *On the Preliminary Studies*, as a justification of tithing, but the implication of that passage (*Congr.* 99) is that the tithe was offered not to Melchizedek but to God, whose priest he is. Indeed, Melchizedek's priesthood here is said to be "self-taught" (αὐτομαθῆ

---

9. I cite the LCL edition.
10. So Horton, *Melchizedek Tradition,* 56.
11. Melchizedek is not actually named in the text, but the context makes it clear who is meant.
12. It is so rendered by Colson in the LCL edition.

καὶ αὐτοδίδακτόν), which probably reflects a tradition found in Josephus that Melchizedek was the first priest to God.[13]

It is not always easy in Philo's works to tell where he is interpreting scripture ad hoc and where he is picking up current traditions in his own interpretive work, the main purpose of which is to read scripture in terms of the quest of the human soul for wisdom, virtue, and the vision of God. It appears, however, that much of Philo's interpretation of Melchizedek that parallels what we found in Hebrews is traditional, if only because it can be found in other Jewish sources. This is certainly the case with his etymology of Melchizedek's name, "righteous king,"[14] and probably also with the etymology of Salem as "peace."[15] This is the case, too, with Melchizedek's dignity as a "high priest."[16] But what about his status as a divine or semidivine being?

On this point we can only speculate. Philo does refer to Melchizedek as the Logos (*Leg. all.* 3.82). What he says of the divine Logos elsewhere may, however, provide a clue: the Logos is the "image of God" (*Conf.* 146) and embodies the names and powers of God (*Vit. Mos.* 2.99–199); it is the first-begotten Son of the Uncreated Father (*Conf.* 146; *Somn.* 1.215), an "archangel" (*Quis heres* 205), high priest of the universe (*Fuga* 108; *Somn.* 1.215), and "second" to God (*Leg. all.* 2.86).[17] So Philo's interpretation of Melchizedek as the Logos may imply his knowledge of a Jewish tradition ascribing divine or semidivine status to Melchizedek. This cannot, of course, be established with certainty, given the way in which Philo interprets scripture. That such a tradition did exist in certain Jewish circles before Philo can nevertheless be affirmed, thanks to the manuscript discoveries in the Judean desert, i.e., the Dead Sea Scrolls.

---

13. Josephus, *J. W.* 6.438.

14. See Josephus, *J. W.* 6.438; idem, *Ant.* 1.180; *Tg. Ps.-J.* ("king of righteousness").

15. R. Williamson (*Philo*) has shown conclusively that the author of Hebrews did not use any of Philo's writings. Thus Philo and Hebrews evidently share a common tradition.

16. This is also found in one of the Hellenistic Jewish synagogue prayers embedded in the *Apostolic Constitutions* at 8.12.13 (for which see *OTP* 2.693) and in some targums. On these texts see Le Déaut, "Le titre de *summus sacerdos*." The idea is also implied in 11QMelch, on which see below.

17. For a brief but useful discussion of the Logos in Hellenistic Jewish tradition, including Philo, see Tobin, "Logos," 4.348–56, esp. pp. 350–51.

Melchizedek in the Qumran Scrolls

Melchizedek appears in two fragmentary texts from Qumran, and may also have been mentioned in a third, in material now lost. In the *Genesis Apocryphon,* usually dated to the second century B.C.E., Gen 14:18–20 is paraphrased (1QapGen xxii 13–17), with minor and insignificant additions to the text. In the *Testament of Amram,* also dated to the second century B.C.E., Melchizedek may have been one of the three names of the chief angel of light, lost in a lacuna (4QAmram 3 1–2). This is probable because one of the three names of the chief angel of darkness is Melchiresha' ("king of evil," 4QAmram 2 3), which correlates with Melchizedek ("king of righteousness").[18]

The most important text from Qumran on Melchizedek is clearly 11QMelch. This text, usually assigned to the mid- or late first century B.C.E.,[19] leaves no doubt as to the angelic, semidivine status of Melchizedek, presented as a heavenly warrior and high priest virtually identical with the archangel Michael. He appears in the tenth and final jubilee of world history (ii 7) to rescue his "children" (ii 5) from Belial and Belial's fellow wicked spirits (ii 13, 25) and to "judge the holy ones of God" (ii 9). The end of the tenth jubilee is said to be the Day of Atonement (ii 7), "when all the Sons of [Light] and the men of the Lot of Mel[chi]zedek will be atoned for" (ii 8). This implies a high-priestly role for Melchizedek as well.[20] He is even referred to in this text as "God" (אלהים, ii 25).

Thus we see that, by the first century B.C.E., speculation on the figure of Melchizedek among some Jews had reached a very advanced stage. The ancient "priest of God Most High" had become a heavenly, semidivine being. I find it probable that such speculation on Melchizedek was known to Philo and the author of Hebrews, and contributed to their respective interpretations of him.

---

18. See especially Kobelski, *Melchizedek,* 24–36.

19. On this text see especially Kobelski, *Melchizedek,* 3–23. I cite the translation by Vermes, *Dead Sea Scrolls in English,* 360–62.

20. On this aspect of *Melchizedek* and its background in Jewish angelology, see especially Gianotto, *Melchisedek,* 82–86.

Melchizedek in Other Jewish Sources

Before we turn to the Christian and Gnostic material, some brief remarks on other aspects of the interpretation of Melchizedek in Jewish sources are in order. We begin with a text that is usually taken to be the product of a Samaritan author and dated to the second century B.C.E., "Pseudo-Eupolemus."[21] This text is known only from excerpts quoted by the Christian author Eusebius, who attributes them to the Jewish historian Eupolemus. One of these excerpts has the following statement about Melchizedek:

> Abraham was treated as a guest by the city in the temple Argarizim, which means "mountain of the Most High." He received gifts from Melchizedek, its ruler and priest of God. (Eusebius, *Praep. evang.* 9.17.5–6)

Here we note that "Salem" in Gen 14:18 is equated with the Samaritan Mount Gerizim, and that Abraham was the recipient rather than the giver of gifts. Melchizedek's priesthood is also related to the temple on Mount Gerizim, presupposing a Samaritan legend of that temple's foundation.[22]

We have already alluded to Josephus's treatment of Melchizedek. He has no doubt as to the location of "Salem." In his *Jewish Antiquities* (1.180),[23] he says that Abraham "was received by the king of Solyma, Melchizedek; this name means 'righteous king.' ... Solyma was in fact that place afterwards called Hierosolyma (Ἱεροσόλυμα)." In his *Jewish War* (6.438) Josephus says of Jerusalem that "its original founder was a Canaanite chief (χαναναίων δυναστής), called in the native tongue 'Righteous King.' " Here, too, Josephus refers to Melchizedek as the first priest, the first to build a temple, and the one responsible for renaming the city previously called Solyma "Jerusalem" (6.438). Josephus's view that Melchizedek was originally a Canaanite is an interesting precursor to the modern scholarly opinion that the story in Genesis reflects pre-Israelite, i.e., Jebusite, lore.[24]

---

21. For a translation see *OTP* 2.873–82. The translator, R. Doran, argues that "Pseudo-Eupolemus" is not of Samaritan origin and should not be distinguished from the Jewish historian Eupolemus. I find his arguments unconvincing.

22. For discussion see especially Gianotto, *Melchisedek*, 51–58.

23. Josephus is quoted from Thackeray's translation in the LCL edition.

24. See, e.g., Rowley, "Melchizedek and Zadok," 461–72; Schmid, "Melchisedek und Abraham," 148–51; Delcor, "Melchizedek from Genesis," 115–20.

The eschatological role of Melchizedek, which was so notable in 11QMelch, is given a different twist in another Jewish writing, *2 Enoch,* arguably datable to the first century C.E.[25] Preserved only in Old Church Slavonic, *2 Enoch* was originally written in Greek, probably in Alexandria. While this text deals mainly with the heavenly ascent and revelations of Enoch, it also contains at the end a remarkable passage about Melchizedek (*2 Enoch* 71–72).[26] Noah's brother Nir, a priest, has an aged and barren wife who miraculously conceives, dies, and bears posthumously a son. The boy has a glorious appearance and is marked with the badge of priesthood on his chest (71:19). He is given the name "Melchizedek" (71:21). Nir then receives a night vision in which God tells him of the impending flood; he is informed that the archangel Michael will bring Melchizedek to paradise for protection until after the flood, when Melchizedek will be the first of twelve priests (71:27–34). After forty days Michael is instructed by God to take Melchizedek to paradise for protection from the flood (72:1). Michael then goes to Nir to take the child to paradise (72:2–5). In one recension (J) Michael tells Nir about two other Melchizedeks, one of whom will be priest and king in Salim (72:6), and the other of whom will function at the end-time in a messianic capacity (72:7). (This material is absent from the A recension.)

Despite the presence of Christian additions elsewhere in *2 Enoch,* there do not seem to be any obviously Christian features in this passage about Melchizedek. It appears to stem from early Jewish circles interested in the figure of Melchizedek.[27] Indeed, Melchizedek can be seen here as an analogue to Enoch himself: like Enoch, Melchizedek is born before the flood and is destined to play a messianic (in this case priestly) role at the end-time (cf. *1 Enoch* 48–71).

---

25. Milik dates this writing in the Byzantine period (*Books of Enoch,* 114–15), but his view is not widely shared. See especially Andersen's introduction and translation in *OTP* 1.91–221. Andersen dates *2 Enoch* to around the turn of the era (pp. 96–97), which is probably correct.

26. This passage is not treated by Horton or Gianotto.

27. So Delcor, "Melchizedek from Genesis," 127–30; Gruenwald, "Messianic Image," 90–92.

All of the texts treated thus far were written before the end of the first century C.E. But speculation on the figure of Melchizedek continued in Jewish circles, as can be seen from rabbinic sources. Some of the rabbinic interpretation of Melchizedek may have developed as a reaction to Christian views. We cannot take up the rabbinic material in anything more than a cursory fashion,[28] with reference to two interpretive traditions.

The first has to do with Melchizedek's identity. Melchizedek is none other than Shem, son of Noah. This is a widespread tradition, found in the targums (e.g., *Tg. Ps.–J., Frg. Tg., Tg. Neof.* on Gen 14:18), midrashim (e.g., *'Abot R. Nat.* 2; *Gen. Rab.* 43.1; 44.7), and Talmud (e.g., *b. Ned.* 32b). In identifying Melchizedek with Shem (on the basis of calculations of Shem's longevity after the flood), any possibility of a Canaanite origin for Melchizedek is removed. One interpretive development of this identification redounds to Melchizedek-Shem's disadvantage: The Holy One, blessed be He, wanted to derive the (levitical) priesthood from Shem, but because Shem, in his blessing (Gen 14:19–20), named Abraham before God, the priesthood was derived instead from Abraham (and his descendant Levi), and Shem's (other) descendants were not priests (*b. Ned.* 32b). This may be taken as an implicit polemic against Christian claims to the Melchizedek priesthood, with its concomitant denigration of the levitical priesthood.[29]

The second interpretive tradition in rabbinic literature concerns an eschatological role for Melchizedek. The "four blacksmiths" of Zech 1:20 (= 2:3 in the MT) are interpreted in one text as Messiah ben David, Messiah ben Joseph, Elijah, and Kohen Ṣedeq (*b. Sukk.* 52b), and in another as Elijah, King Messiah, Melchizedek, and the Anointed for War (*Cant. Rab.* 2.13.4). "Kohen Ṣedeq" ("priest of righteousness") is evidently equivalent to Melchizedek, as can be seen from another passage (*'Abot R. Nat.* 34) in which Ps 110:4 is quoted, but in which it is then said that

---

28. For more extensive treatments, see especially Aptowitzer, "Malkizedek"; Horton, *Melchizedek Tradition,* 114–30; Gianotto, *Melchisedek,* 171–85.

29. So Delcor, "Melchizedek from Genesis," 132; Simon, "Melchisédech," 107–8. On the other hand, Petuchowski ("Controversial Figure," *passim*) sees in this text a reflection of Pharisaic anti-Maccabean polemic.

"King Messiah is more beloved than a righteous priest (*kohen ṣedeq*)." Although Melchizedek is given an eschatological role, he is subordinated to the royal Messiah.

Thus, while Melchizedek's eschatological function, already traditional in Second Temple Judaism, is retained in the rabbinic discussions, it tends to be downplayed. There is no trace at all in rabbinic sources that Melchizedek is a heavenly, semidivine being, such as we saw in the case of 11QMelch.

Melchizedek in Early Christianity

The starting point for virtually all Christian interpretation of Melchizedek is the Melchizedek midrash in Hebrews 7, discussed above.[30] To be sure, there are some passing references to Melchizedek among several second-century church fathers where influence from Hebrews is not demonstrable, beginning with Justin Martyr. Our survey will treat the relevant Christian material through the fourth century.

Early Patristic Interpretations

Justin Martyr, in his *Dialogue with Trypho,* disputes the necessity for circumcision by pointing out all of the ancient worthies in scripture, including "Melchizedek, the priest of the Most High," who were not circumcised (*Dial.* 19). Later (*Dial.* 33) Justin argues that Psalm 110 refers not to Hezekiah but to "our Jesus." Ps 110:4 is quoted to show that Jesus is "high priest after the order of Melchizedek" and priest to the uncircumcised (gentile Christians). This interpretation was probably traditional by Justin's day, i.e., it was not based directly on a reading of Hebrews (which Justin never cites).[31]

Tertullian, in his polemic against the Mosaic Law, refers to Melchizedek, who was chosen to the priesthood even though he

---

30. This point has been established by Horton (*Melchizedek Tradition,* 87–113, 152–65). Exceptions do occur in later Gnostic literature, on which see below.

31. Melchizedek was later counted in rabbinic tradition (*'Abot R. Nat.* 1.12) as one of the ancients who had been born circumcised. This may have developed in response to the Christian claim enunciated here by Justin.

was uncircumcised and did not observe the sabbath (*Adv. Iud.* 2). In his treatise *Against Marcion,* Tertullian, like Justin before him, argues that Ps 110:4 refers not to Hezekiah, as Marcion and the Jews think, but to Christ, the high priest of God (*Adv. Marc.* 5.9). Both Justin and Tertullian pick up aspects of a developing Christian anti-Judaic polemic.

Theophilus of Antioch, on the other hand, uses Jewish tradition to make a point about the reliability of the scriptures. He cites "a righteous king called Melchizedek in the city of Salem, which now is Jerusalem ('Ιεροσόλυμα)." He was "the first priest of the Most High God, and from him the above-named city Hierosolyma ('Ιεροσόλυμα) was called Jerusalem ('Ιεροσαλήμ)" (*Ad Autol.* 2.31).[32] All of this we have seen in Josephus,[33] except what appears to be an attempt at etymology: 'Ιεροσαλήμ derives from ἱερεύς plus Σαλήμ.

New interpretations of Melchizedek appear among several third-century church fathers. Hippolytus, in a fragment of a lost commentary on Genesis,[34] introduces a typology according to which Melchizedek is a type of John the Baptist. This is based on the supposition that Melchizedek was really the unnamed person who circumcised Abraham (cf. Gen 17:23–27)! As Melchizedek circumcised Abraham, John the Baptist baptized Jesus.

With Clement of Alexandria (*Strom.* 4.161.3) and Cyprian of Carthage (*Ep.* 63.4), the eucharistic interpretation of the bread and wine in Gen 14:18 (absent in Hebrews 7) begins.

Origen picks up the christological interpretation of Ps 110:4, and states that whereas humans can be priests according to the order of Aaron, only Christ can be a priest "according to the order of Melchizedek" (*In Ioh.* 1.11; cf. 19.19). Another doctrine attributed to Origen and his pupil Didymus ("the Blind") by Jerome (*Ep.* 73.1), that Melchizedek is an angel, is found nowhere in the great Alexandrian's extant works. Generally, it was only among more extreme "heretics" that the doctrine of Mel-

---

32. I quote the translation in ANF vol. 2.
33. See the discussion above of *J.W.* 6.438 and *Ant.* 1.180.
34. The fragment is preserved in an Arabic catena containing excerpts from Hippolytus's commentaries on the Pentateuch. For an Italian translation with commentary, see Gianotto, *Melchisedek,* 160–62.

chizedek's angelic or heavenly status was held among Christians.
To these we now turn.

The *"Melchizedekian Heresy"*

Epiphanius of Salamis devotes a lengthy section in his *Panarion*
to a group of sectarians who, he says, "call themselves Melchizedekians" (*Pan.* 55).

> They honor the Melchizedek who is mentioned in the scriptures and re-
> gard him as a sort of great power (μεγάλην τινὰ δύναμιν). He is on high
> in places which cannot be named, and in [fact] is not just a power; in-
> deed, they claim in their error that he is greater than Christ.... Christ has
> merely come and been given the order of Melchizedek. Christ is younger
> than Melchizedek, they say. (*Pan.* 55.1.1–3)[35]

Epiphanius goes on to say that the heretics quote Heb 7:3
("without father, without mother, without genealogy") to underscore Melchizedek's greatness. They also fabricate spurious books
(55.1.4–5). After extensive refutation (55.1.6–7.3), Epiphanius
elaborates further on the Melchizedekian sect:

> This sect makes its offerings in Melchizedek's name, and says that it is
> he who gives access to God, and that we must offer to God through him
> because he is the archon of righteousness (ἄρχων δικαιοσύνης) ordained
> in heaven by God for this very purpose, a spiritual being and appointed
> to God's priesthood. And we must make offerings to him, they say, so
> that they may be offered through him on our behalf, and we may attain
> salvation through him. (55.8.1–2)

Epiphanius accuses these heretics of denying Christ by asserting
that he came into existence only with his birth from Mary. Christ
was purely human, in their view, and not the divine eternal Logos.

Epiphanius's lengthy refutation underscores Melchizedek's
purely human status — he even provides the names of Melchizedek's parents, Heracles and Astarth/Astoriane (55.2.1).[36] He
also introduces and refutes other views about Melchizedek: the
Samaritan belief that Melchizedek is Noah's son Shem (55.6.1);
the Jewish belief that Melchizedek, though himself righteous, was

---

35. I cite the translation by Williams, *Panarion*, vol. 2.
36. These are construed as human beings, not as gods or heroes. For another tradition regarding Melchizedek's parents, Melchi and Salem, see Ps.-Athanasius, *Historia de
Melchisedek*, PG 28:525.

the son of a harlot with an unknown father (55.7.1);[37] and other Christian heresies based on a misinterpretation of Heb 7:3. These other heresies include that of the Egyptian heresiarch Hierakas, that Melchizedek is the Holy Spirit (55.5.2);[38] the belief of "some who are members of the church...that he is the actual Son of God" (55.7.3);[39] and the belief of yet others that "this same Melchizedek is the Father of our Lord Jesus Christ" (55.9.11).

In this lengthy discussion Epiphanius actually tells us little about the "Melchizedekian" sect itself. Indeed, it is likely that such a sect is really his own invention.[40] We can trace something of the origin of this invention from what he says at the beginning of his discussion: "[T]hey may be an offshoot of the group who are known as Theodotians" (5.1.1). These "Theodotians" should probably be understood as the followers of one Theodotus "the banker," himself a former follower of another Theodotus "from Byzantium."[41] Both of these Theodoti were active in Rome in the second century. According to Hippolytus (*Ref.* 7.35), Theodotus of Byzantium taught that Jesus was a mere man upon whom "the Christ" came down at his baptism. Eusebius, citing an early anonymous report (*Hist. eccl.* 5.28.6), refers to this Theodotus as "the cobbler," who was excommunicated in Rome by bishop Victor (fl. 189–99 C.E.). Theodotus the banker, in turn, introduced the doctrine that Melchizedek is the "great power," in whose likeness is the Christ who came down into Jesus (*Ref.* 7.36). Here, apparently, we have the origins of the supposed Melchizedekian heresy. Additional information is supplied by Pseudo-Tertullian, *Against All Heresies*,[42] according to which Melchizedek acts as

---

37. The "Samaritan" belief is the rabbinic view, discussed above. As to the "Jewish" one, V. Aptowitzer ("Malkizedek," 108–11) suggests that this story must have applied to another Melchizedek, not the biblical one, and refers to the Melchizedek material in *2 Enoch*. But there is no trace of such a belief in Jewish literature, not even in *2 Enoch*.

38. Epiphanius devotes a whole section to Hierakas and his followers (*Pan.* 67), on which see below.

39. On this belief, popular in certain monastic communities, see below; see also NHC IX,1: *Melchizedek*, discussed below.

40. So Bardy, "Melchisédech," 505; he is followed by Horton, *Melchizedek Tradition*, 98.

41. Epiphanius, however, fails to distinguish between the two Theodoti. He devotes the previous section of his *Panarion* to Theodotus the cobbler from Byzantium and to his followers, the "Theodotians" (*Pan.* 54). Nothing is said of Melchizedek in that section.

42. This work is often equated with Hippolytus's lost *Syntagma*.

a heavenly advocate for the angels as Christ acts as an advocate for humans (*Haer.* 8). Melchizedek is superior to Christ in that he lacks genealogy (Heb 7:3).

This is the information that Epiphanius seems to have at his disposal in his invention of a "Melchizedekian" sect. Even the detail about the sect's offerings in Melchizedek's name (55.8.1, cited above) can be construed as a misunderstanding of what is said in Pseudo-Tertullian about the intercessory role of Melchizedek — unless, perchance, Epiphanius reflects here some vague information about Gnostic cultic activity in Egypt involving Melchizedek.[43] There is, of course, nothing specifically "Gnostic" about the Melchizedekian heresy described by Epiphanius.[44]

Hierakas the Egyptian

Hierakas (fl. ca. 300) is described by Epiphanius as a man highly educated in both Greek and Coptic, able to recite the Old and New Testaments from memory (*Pan.* 67.1.1–4). Hierakas rejected the doctrine of the resurrection of the flesh (67.1.7) and insisted on celibacy, rejecting matrimony for Christians (67.1.7). Epiphanius finds no fault with Hierakas's Christology ("the Son is really begotten of the Father," 67.3.1); what is wrong is that he equates the Holy Spirit with Melchizedek. Hierakas's "proof" for this doctrine is given by juxtaposing Paul's statement about the (priestly) intercession of the Holy Spirit (Rom 8:26) with what is said of Melchizedek in Heb 7:3: a "priest forever." Melchizedek's divine status is also indicated by his lack of genealogy (Heb 7:3). As a final "proof," Hierakas cites Isaiah's vision in the *Ascension of Isaiah* of "the Beloved" (= Christ) at the right hand of God, and the Holy Spirit, resembling the Beloved, at the left (*Asc. Isa.* 9.33–36).[45] Hierakas interprets the Holy Spirit's resemblance to

---

43. So Gianotto, *Melchisedek*, 250, referring to NHC IX,1: *Melchizedek* and *2 Jeu*. On these texts see below.

44. That the Melchizedekians were "Gnostics" is an older view, represented, e.g., by Friedländer ("La secte de Melchisédec") and Wuttke (*Melchisedech*, 29–32).

45. Schneemelcher and Wilson, eds., *New Testament Apocrypha*, 2.616; English translation of the Ethiopic version. The Greek quotation in Epiphanius differs somewhat from the Ethiopic (most of the original Greek of the *Ascension of Isaiah* is lost). In Epiphanius's version Isaiah is told, "This is the Holy Spirit..."; cf. the Ethiopic: "This is the angel of the Holy Spirit."

the Beloved with reference to Heb 7:3 ("resembling the Son of God").

Hierakas's interpretation of Melchizedek seems quite independent of the "Melchizedekian" heresy discussed above. It evidently reflects Hierakas's own independent interpretation of Hebrews 7 and other scriptures.

The doctrine that Melchizedek is the Holy Spirit is also found in a late-fourth-century Latin work traditionally ascribed to Augustine, *Quaestiones Veteris et Novi Testamenti CXXVII*, question number 109. This may represent a revival of Hierakas's theory, and elicited a reply by Jerome (*Ep.* 73), in which he stresses the human nature of Melchizedek and cites the Jewish identification of Melchizedek with Shem, son of Noah.[46]

Other "Heretical" Views

Epiphanius refers to people in the church who equate Melchizedek with the Son of God (*Pan.* 5.7.3, cited above). This seems to have been a view especially prominent in certain monastic communities. According to the ninth-century Syriac writer Thomas of Marga,

> When the heresy of the Melchizedekians broke out at Scete in the land of Egypt through the contemptible monks who said that Melchizedek was the Son of God, although there were doctors and famous bishops in those days, yet Theophilus, Bishop of Alexandria, allowed the Blessed Macarius, a monk, to make refutation of this error; and that holy man actually did so, and made manifest the foolishness of their opinions.[47]

In the *Apophthegmata Patrum* there is a story about an old visionary who believed Melchizedek to be the Son of God. This monk was corrected by Archbishop Cyril of Alexandria (*PG* 65:160). Mark the Hermit (early fifth century) wrote a treatise *On Melchizedek* in which he castigated opponents who claimed that Melchizedek was the Logos, the Son of God, and even "God" (θεός) before the incarnation (*PG* 65:1120). The divine status of Melchizedek (as "God") could lead an Epiphanius to

---

46. For discussion, see Horton, *Melchizedek Tradition*, 109–11.
47. Budge, ed., *Book of Governors*, 2.94–95, quoted and discussed in Evelyn-White, *Monasteries*, 2.116.

think that these heretics were equating Melchizedek with God the Father (*Pan.* 55.9.11, cited above).[48]

It should be noted, in concluding this section, that all of the Christian heresies that view Melchizedek as a heavenly being are ultimately grounded on an interpretation of Hebrews 7. This will be seen to be the case also with some (though not all) of the Gnostic material, to which we now turn.

Melchizedek in Gnosticism[49]

Melchizedek figures in a number of Coptic Gnostic texts, all stemming from Christian Gnostic circles in Egypt.[50] We shall take these up in a plausible chronological order.

The Bala'izah Fragment

A parchment leaf and fragments of two others, found at the ruins of the Monastery of Apa Apollo at Deir al-Bala'izah, contain portions of a Gnostic dialogue between Jesus and his disciple John.[51] After discussion of paradise and its five trees, Cain and Abel, and Noah and his ark, John says to the Savior,

> Moreover, [I wish] to [ask that you] explain [to me] about Mel[chizedek]. Is it not said [about him], "he is [without father, without] mother," his generation not being [mentioned], not having a beginning of days, nor end of life, resembling the Son [of] God, being "a priest forever"? Moreover it is said about him, that ...[52]

Unfortunately the text breaks off, leaving us to guess what the rest of John's question was, and how the Savior responded.

---

48. See especially Horton, *Melchizedek Tradition*, 105–11.

49. My discussion here is an abbreviated version of the fuller treatment in my "Figure of Melchizedek." See also Gianotto, *Melchisedek*, 187–235; and Horton, *Melchizedek Tradition*, 131–51. Horton omits NHC IX,1: *Melchizedek*.

50. Not all ancient Gnostics were Christians. The Mandaeans are a case in point, and the Nag Hammadi corpus contains non-Christian Gnostic works. On my understanding of Gnosticism as a "religion" in its own right, originally independent of Christianity, see my introduction to Pearson, *Gnosticism, Judaism, and Egyptian Christianity*, 7–9; and now also Pearson, "Is Gnosticism a Religion?" 105–14.

51. See especially Kahle, *Bala'izah*, 1.473–77 (text no. 52).

52. Lines 78–90, my translation.

Whether or not the placement of this passage directly after the interpretation of Noah and the ark reflects knowledge of the Jewish tradition identifying Melchizedek with Shem,[53] the important feature in the extant material is its use of Heb 7:3 as the key text for interpreting the figure of Melchizedek. That the Gnostic author of this dialogue regarded Melchizedek as a heavenly being can be taken as likely, given the other "heretical" cases already discussed. But further speculation is baseless.

NHC IX,1: Melchizedek

This fragmentary text is an apocalypse attributed to the ancient Melchizedek, "priest of God Most High" (12,10–11).[54] In it revelations are given by heavenly emissaries to Melchizedek for transmission to the elect of a later generation. The core of the revealed material has to do with the future career of the Savior, Jesus Christ, and the ultimate identification of Jesus Christ with the recipient of the revelation, Melchizedek himself.[55] This identification, as is the case with other examples already treated, is based on an interpretation of Heb 7:3: Jesus Christ is regarded as the heavenly, high-priestly alter ego of the earthly priest, Melchizedek, his "image" (15,12). It is Melchizedek who becomes reincarnated as the crucified and risen Jesus Christ (25,1–26,14).

While Heb 7:3 is a key text in *Melchizedek*, other influences in the latter bear upon its presentation of the figure of Melchizedek. Melchizedek is depicted as a heavenly holy warrior, a "high priest" who does battle with demonic forces and is congratulated upon his victory over his enemies (26,1–9). This depiction of Melchizedek resembles that in 11QMelch, discussed above.

The presence of typically "Sethian Gnostic"[56] features in *Melchizedek* allows us to identify it as a "Gnostic" text. One of these

---

53. So Horton, *Melchizedek Tradition,* 134.

54. For the *editio princeps,* with introduction, translation, and notes, see Pearson, *Nag Hammadi Codices IX and X,* 19–85.

55. See my discussion in *Nag Hammadi Codices IX and X,* 28–31.

56. On Sethian Gnosticism see especially Schenke, "Phenomenon and Significance of Gnostic Sethianism," 2.588–616.

features is the invocation of divine beings of the heavenly world, including Barbelo, the four "Luminaries" (Harmozel, Oroiael, Daveithe, Eleleth), and others (5,24–6,14; 16,16–18,7).[57] The occurrence of the phrase, "the congregation of [the children] of Seth" (5,19–20), is another indication of its "Sethian" stamp. Indeed, one might conclude from the juxtaposition of Melchizedek with Seth that the final redactor of *Melchizedek* regarded Melchizedek as an incarnation or "avatar" of the heavenly Seth.[58] Certain liturgical features of the text are also noteworthy: a prayer offered by Melchizedek to the Father of All (14,15–16,6); an oblation in which Melchizedek offers himself and his own (= the Gnostic elect) to God (16,7–11); and a baptism that also includes the pronunciation of his name (16,11–16) and the invocational hymn addressed to the heavenly beings (16,16–18,7). In these cultic sections it appears that Melchizedek (= Seth, = Jesus Christ), as "high priest," also functions as the paradigm for Gnostic initiates in their reception of the sacrament of baptism.[59]

How can we account for this mixture of Christian, Jewish, and Gnostic traditions? Hans-Martin Schenke regards *Melchizedek* as an example of a full-blown "Christianized Sethian Gnosis."[60] However, since the Gnostic features tend to be concentrated in certain sections of the text, I prefer to take these as secondary additions to a Christian apocalypse strongly infused with pre-Christian Jewish traditions about Melchizedek, such as those exemplified in 11QMelch. What sort of community would have produced such a text is hard to say, but there are intriguing points of contact with the "Melchizedekian heresy" discussed above. *Melchizedek* may have arisen originally in an Egyptian community which had been influenced by followers of the aforementioned Theodotus, the banker.[61]

---

57. On these passages, which reflect a cultic context, see Sevrin, *Le dossier baptismal,* 221–46.
58. Pearson, "Figure of Seth," 78.
59. Beltz, "Melchisedek."
60. Schenke, "Jüdische Melchisedek-Gestalt," 123–25.
61. For additional discussion see Pearson, *Nag Hammadi Codices IX and X,* 38–40.

The Second Book of Jeu

Melchizedek appears in two passages in *2 Jeu*.[62] Here, Melchizedek is a heavenly being involved in baptismal ritual. In this latter respect we are reminded of *Melchizedek*, and it is possible that the author of *2 Jeu* knew the Nag Hammadi tractate. In *2 Jeu* Melchizedek has a double name, "Zorokothora Melchizedek," one which reflects Egyptian magical traditions.[63] In the context, Jesus is revealing to his disciples the mysteries of the Treasury of Light, and invites them to receive three baptisms, of fire, water, and the Spirit. In a cultic scene Jesus offers a prayer and calls upon the Father to send fifteen helpers and Zorokothora to come and administer the baptism: "May Zorokothora come and bring forth the water of the baptism of life in one of these pitchers of wine" (*2 Jeu* 45). The wine in one of the pitchers at the altar changes into water, and Jesus then baptizes his disciples, offers them the "offering" (προσφορά), i.e., bread and wine, and seals them with a special seal.

A similar ritual is depicted in connection with the baptism of fire, as Jesus prays to the Father,

> Cause Zorokothora Melchizedek to come in secret and bring the water of the baptism of fire of the Virgin of Light,[64] the judge....Cause Zorokothora to come and bring the water of the baptism of fire of the Virgin of Light, that I may baptize my disciples in it. (*2 Jeu* 46)

Melchizedek plays no further role in *2 Jeu*. Here he is a heavenly being whose "bringing forth" of the water of baptism is crucial to the performance of the ritual; he is thus construed as a heavenly priest. Since the Epistle to the Hebrews is notably absent from *2 Jeu*, Melchizedek's role as a heavenly priest must derive from another source (NHC IX,1: *Melchizedek?*). It is possible that the "bread and wine" of Gen 14:18 that Melchizedek "brings out" (absent from Hebrews) is alluded to in the passages featuring Melchizedek, especially *2 Jeu* 45 (cited above),

---

62. For text and translation see Schmidt, ed., *Books of Jeu*, 98–141. In quotations from this work I use but modify MacDermot's translation.

63. See *PGM* XIII.958, and the translation in Betz, ed., *Greek Magical Papyri*, 193.

64. The "Virgin of Light" is a prominent figure in Manichaean mythology, and Manichaean influence may be reflected here. On the "Virgin of Light" in Manichaeism, see, e.g., my discussion in "The Figure of Norea," 87.

wherein Melchizedek is to "bring forth" the wine that becomes baptismal water.

Pistis Sophia, *Book 4*

Pistis Sophia is the collective name given to the disparate Gnostic materials found in the Askew Codex (a fifth-century Coptic manuscript).[65] These materials are organized in four books; book 4 is usually regarded as the oldest. Here Zorokothora Melchizedek is identified in a revelation given by Jesus to Mary as "the envoy (πρεσβευτής) of all the lights which are purified in the archons, as he takes them into the Treasury of Light" (chap. 139). As a heavenly light being, Melchizedek divests the cosmic archons of the light (human souls) and brings the light particles into the Treasury of Light (what in other Gnostic systems is called the "Pleroma"). Zorokothora Melchizedek plays an analogous role in another passage (chap. 140), where he destroys "all of the places of Hekate" and carries off the souls that are held by her for punishment back into the world, where they can be reborn and given another chance at reaching the Treasury of Light. Melchizedek is, therefore, a heavenly savior figure.

The author of *Pistis Sophia,* book 4, was probably familiar with *2 Jeu,* but Melchizedek's baptismal role is here replaced by loftier duties as a heavenly psychopomp. There is no trace left in this material of the biblical texts from which the figure of Melchizedek derives.

Pistis Sophia, *Books 1–3*

The role played by Melchizedek becomes even loftier in books 1–3, now without his other name, Zorokothora. Melchizedek is here referred to as "the Receiver of the Light," who comes to the archons, disarms them, and takes away the purified particles of light and carries them to the Treasury of Light (1, chap. 25). As "the great Receiver of Light,"[66] Melchizedek also has sub-

---

65. For a text and translation of *Pistis Sophia,* see Schmidt, ed., *Pistis Sophia.*

66. In addition to 1.25, see also 1.26 and 86; 3.112 and 131. The Greek words παραλήμπτωρ and παραλήμπτης are used interchangeably.

ordinates to assist him, "the receivers of Melchizedek,"[67] who actually descend into the cosmos for their work of transferring the light to the Treasury.

We noted that Melchizedek is referred to as an "envoy" in *2 Jeu,* wherein other (unnamed) "receivers" perform the task of bringing souls into the light. In *Pistis Sophia* Melchizedek himself has assumed that role.[68]

In book 3 Melchizedek appears in a cultic context in an interesting passage (chap. 112) in which Jesus reveals to Mary the fate of a good soul who has not listened to the "counterfeit spirit."[69] The receivers take it to the Virgin of Light,[70] who, with seven other virgins of light, examines the soul. After the Virgin of Light seals the soul, the receivers of the light baptize it and give it spiritual chrism. After several sealings by other heavenly beings, Melchizedek seals the soul as well, and his receivers take it to the Treasury of Light. What precisely is involved in these "sealings" is not clear, but we see that Melchizedek plays a crucial role in the salvation of souls.

In *Pistis Sophia* as a whole, the role of Melchizedek is a highly developed one, building upon several layers of Christian tradition that are rather unsystematically thrown together. But all traces of the biblical texts from which the figure of Melchizedek derives are gone. In that respect *Pistis Sophia* stands far outside the mainstrain of Christian tradition, "heretical" or "orthodox," in its interpretation of Melchizedek.

However, there may be a reflection of noncanonical Jewish traditions concerning Melchizedek in *Pistis Sophia*'s presentation of the role played by Melchizedek in the transfer of light-particles (souls) to the Treasury of Light. Here we recall what is said of the heavenly Melchizedek in 11QMelch: he is a savior who does battle with the demonic forces of Belial and restores the "sons of light" to the company of the "sons of heaven," from which

---

67. 1.25; 3.112, 128, and 129.

68. For other Gnostic examples of the use of the term "receiver" for beings who transfer saved souls to life, see, e.g., *Ap. John* BG 8502,2: 66,1–7; *Gos. Eg.* NHC III,2: 64,22–65,1.

69. Cf. *Ap. John* BG 8502,2: 71,4–75,10.

70. Cf. *2 Jeu* 46 and n. 64, above.

they have been cut off during the "dominion of Belial."[71] *Pistis Sophia*'s treatment of Melchizedek could easily be seen as a Gnostic reinterpretation of what is found in 11QMelch.

Summary and Conclusions

In this survey of interpretation of the figure of Melchizedek in Jewish, Christian, and Gnostic sources,[72] we have noted two very different trends. In one trend Melchizedek is interpreted strictly as a human being; in the other he is depicted as a heavenly, semidivine being. A variant of each trend is to view him as an eschatological figure.

Thus, one line of interpretation expands on the biblical sources by providing additional information about Melchizedek the human priest: Josephus, Pseudo-Eupolemus, and the rabbis are important examples. Josephus views Melchizedek as a Canaanite chief and "righteous king" who founded the city of Jerusalem. He was also the first priest, and builder of the first Temple. The rabbis continue this trend, but implicitly deny Melchizedek's Canaanite origins by equating him with Shem, the son of Noah. They also diminish Melchizedek-Shem's priestly role by tracing the levitical priesthood to Abraham rather than to any other descendant of Shem (e.g., Judah). The Samaritan author Pseudo-Eupolemus refers to Melchizedek as ruler and priest of Mount Gerizim (= Salem), and associates his priesthood with the Samaritan temple.

This trend, begun among Jewish interpreters, is continued on the Christian side by the "orthodox" opponents of those heretics who impute a divine or heavenly status to Melchizedek; Epiphanius and Jerome are the most important examples of this "orthodox" view. Thus, Epiphanius underscores Melchizedek's human status by providing the names of his parents. Jerome, too, stresses Melchizedek's human nature in his polemic against the

---

71. See especially 11QMelch ii 4–13, and the discussion above.
72. Melchizedek does not appear in the Qur'an or other early Islamic sources. For his appearance in later Islamic sectarian sources, see Vajda, "Melchisédec."

view that Melchizedek is the Holy Spirit. He is also aware of the Jewish identification of Melchizedek with Shem.

The eschatological variant of this trend is represented only by Jewish interpreters, such as *2 Enoch* and the rabbis. *2 Enoch* posits a Melchizedek redivivus functioning as a priest in the end-time. A rabbinic view has Melchizedek playing a messianic role in the end-time, but subordinate to "King Messiah." This eschatological variant is eschewed by Christian interpreters except in the case of NHC IX,*1: Melchizedek,* wherein the earthly priest Melchizedek is given an eschatological role by equating him with Jesus Christ.

The other trend, in which Melchizedek is treated as a heavenly, semidivine being, emerges surprisingly early in pre-Christian Judaism. Its first attestation is 11QMelch (mid- or late first century B.C.E.), and it was arguably known to Philo and the author of Hebrews. 11QMelch presents Melchizedek as a heavenly warrior-high priest functioning in the end-time to redeem the elect of God. Philo does not expressly refer to Melchizedek as a heavenly being, but in interpreting Melchizedek allegorically as the Logos he may reflect knowledge of such a view. The argumentation of the author of the Melchizedek midrash in Hebrews 7 implies knowledge of a Jewish tradition in which Melchizedek is given a heavenly status.

Hebrews provides grist for the continuation of this interpretation in Christianity, mainly among "heretics." This trend ends abruptly in post–Second Temple Judaism, however, and is fiercely resisted on the Christian side by the "orthodox," who now pose counterinterpretations of Hebrews 7 to combat the "heretical" view that Melchizedek is a heavenly being. The various "Melchizedekian heresies" posit that Melchizedek is either superior to, or somehow identifiable with, Jesus Christ. One variant, represented by Hierakas, equates Melchizedek with the Holy Spirit.

The eschatological variant of this trend appears already in 11QMelch, but is absent from the Christian sources, except for NHC IX,*1: Melchizedek,* wherein Melchizedek's eschatological role is merged with that of Jesus Christ.

The Gnostic interpretations offer some interesting variations on the second trend. Hebrews 7 plays a central role in the

Bala'izah fragment and in *Melchizedek,* but none at all in *2 Jeu* and *Pistis Sophia.* In the case of *Melchizedek,* we probably are dealing with an originally non-Gnostic writing that interpreted Hebrews 7 to mean that the heavenly Christ is the divine alter ego of the earthly Melchizedek. However, the Gnostic redactor presumably would have thought of Melchizedek as a heavenly being, though this is not certain. *2 Jeu* and *Pistis Sophia* certainly impute a heavenly status to Melchizedek, but without any identifiably Christian influence at this point.

Finally, we saw that *Pistis Sophia*'s presentation in books 1–3, i.e., in its latest stratum, bears some striking formal resemblances to 11QMelch, such that one could easily see in *Pistis Sophia* a Gnostic reinterpretation of the ancient Jewish apocalypse that contains the earliest evidence for a heavenly, eschatological Melchizedek. If this is true, we can see in *Pistis Sophia* the final point of a trajectory of interpretation that runs from pre-Christian Judaism to the "decadent" Gnosticism of third- or fourth-century Egypt, with the midpoint of that trajectory being totally submerged. This latter is a Gnosticism whose Christian character is but a thin veneer; in its Melchizedek lore, even the veneer is lacking.

Bibliography

General Treatments

Astour, M. "Melchizedek." *ABD* 4.684–86. A brief discussion of the biblical and Jewish sources.

Delcor, M. "Melchizedek from Genesis to the Qumran Texts and the Epistle to the Hebrews." *JSJ* 2 (1971) 115–33. A discussion of the biblical and Jewish sources.

Gianotto, C. *Melchisedek e la sua tipologia.* Supplementi alla Rivista Biblica 12. Brescia: Paideia Editrice, 1984. An extensive treatment of the biblical, Jewish, Christian, and Gnostic sources through the fourth century.

Horton, F. L., Jr. *The Melchizedek Tradition: A Critical Examination of the Sources to the Fifth Century A.D. and in the Epistle to the Hebrews.* SNTSMS 30. Cambridge: Cambridge University Press, 1976. An extensive treatment of the biblical, early Jewish, early Christian, rabbinic, and Gnostic sources (except NHC IX,*1*), leading to an interpretation of Melchizedek in Hebrews.

Simon, M. "Melchisédek dans la polémique entre juifs et chrétiens et dans la légende." In *Recherches d'histoire judéo-chrétienne*. Etudes juives 6. Paris: Mouton, 1962. Pp. 101–26. A discussion of the Jewish and Christian sources, including late Oriental Christian writings.

Wuttke, G. *Melchisedech der Priesterkönig von Salem: Eine Studie zur Geschichte der Exegese*. Giessen: Töpelmann, 1927. A history of Jewish and Christian exegesis of the biblical Melchizedek, beginning with Hebrews, and carried into the medieval and modern periods. Somewhat out of date.

Jewish Sources

Aptowitzer, V. "Malkizedek: Zu den Sagen der Agada." *MGWJ* 70 (1926) 93–113. A treatment of the rabbinic sources, with attention also to patristic uses of Jewish traditions.

Fitzmyer, J. A. "Further Light on Melchizedek from Qumran Cave 11." *JBL* 86 (1967) 25–41. A discussion of 11QMelch.

Ginzberg, L. *The Legends of the Jews*. 7 vols. Philadelphia: Jewish Publication Society of America, 1909–38. The classic treatment of Jewish interpretations of biblical events and personages, including some material on Melchizedek (for which see the index volume).

Gruenwald, I. "The Messianic Image of Melchizedek." *Mahanaim* 124 (1970) 88–98 [in Hebrew]. A discussion of the eschatological role of Melchizedek according to early Jewish and rabbinic sources.

Kobelski, P. J. *Melchizedek and Melchiresaʿ*. CBQMS 10. Washington, D.C.: Catholic Biblical Association of America, 1981. A detailed study, with texts and translations, of the Qumran sources, with a chapter on 11QMelch and the New Testament.

Le Déaut, R. "Le titre de *summus sacerdos* donné a Melchisédech est-il d'origine juive?" *RSR* 50 (1962) 222–29. A discussion of the early Jewish sources in which Melchizedek is referred to as a high priest.

Petuchowski, J. J. "The Controversial Figure of Melchizedek." *HUCA* 28 (1957) 127–36. A discussion of *b. Ned.* 32b, arguing that it reflects Pharisaic anti-Maccabean polemic.

van der Woude, A. S. "Melchisedek als himmlische Erlösergestalt in den neugefundenen eschatologischen Midraschim aus Qumran Höhle XI." *OTS* 14 (1965) 354–73. The *editio princeps* of 11QMelch, with extensive commentary.

Early Christian Sources

Attridge, H. W. *The Epistle to the Hebrews*. Hermeneia. Philadelphia: Fortress, 1989. The best available commentary on Hebrews, with an excursus on Melchizedek (pp. 192–95).

Bardy, G. "Melchisédech dans la tradition patristique." *RB* 35 (1926) 496–509; 36 (1927) 25–45. An extensive discussion of the patristic sources.

Friedländer, M. "La secte de Melchisédec et l'epître aux Hébreux." *REJ* 5 (1882) 1–26, 188–98; 6 (1883) 187–99. A detailed discussion of Epiphanius's treatment of the Melchizedekian heresy, tracing it back through Hebrews to a pre-Christian Alexandrian Jewish Gnosticism.

Stork, H. *Die sogenannten Melchisedekianer, mit Untersuchung ihrer Quellen auf Gedankengehalt und dogmengeschichtliche Entwicklung.* Forschungen zur Geschichte des neutestamentliche Kanons und der altkirchlichen Literatur 8:2. Leipzig: A. Deichertsche Verlagsbuchhandlung D. Werner Scholl, 1928. A study of the Melchizedekian heresies, their background, and their development.

Gnostic Sources

Beltz, W. "Melchisedek — Eine gnostische Initiationsliturgie." *ZRGG* 33 (1981) 155–58. A brief discussion of the liturgical context of NHC IX,*1: Melchizedek.*

Pearson, B. A. "The Figure of Melchizedek in Gnostic Literature." In Pearson, *Gnosticism, Judaism, and Egyptian Christianity.* SAC 5. Minneapolis: Fortress, 1990. Pp. 108–23. A discussion of the Coptic Gnostic sources relating to Melchizedek.

———. "The Figure of Norea in Gnostic Literature." In Pearson, *Gnosticism, Judaism, and Egyptian Christianity.* Pp. 84–94. A discussion of the Coptic Gnostic sources relating to Norea.

———. "The Figure of Seth in Gnostic Literature." In Pearson, *Gnosticism, Judaism, and Egyptian Christianity.* Pp. 52–83. A discussion of the Coptic Gnostic sources relating to Seth.

———. *Nag Hammadi Codices IX and X.* NHS 15. Leiden: Brill, 1981. Contains the *editio princeps,* with introduction, translation, and notes, of NHC IX,*1* (pp. 19–85).

Schenke, H.-M. "Die jüdische Melchisedek-Gestalt als Thema der Gnosis." In *Altes Testament-Frühjudentum-Gnosis: Neue Studien zu "Gnosis und Bibel."* Ed. K.-W. Tröger. Berlin: Evangelische Verlagsanstalt, 1980. Pp. 111–36. Contains a German translation, with discussion, of NHC IX,*1: Melchizedek.*

Sevrin, J.-M. *Le dossier baptismal séthien: Etudes sur la sacramentaire gnostique.* BCNH, "Etudes" 2. Québec: Université Laval, 1986. Contains a chapter on NHC IX,*1* (pp. 222–46), with a treatment of its cultic passages.

Islamic Sources

Vajda, G. "Melchisédec dans la mythologie ismaélienne." *Journal Asiatique* 234 (1943–45) 173–83. A discussion of some late medieval Ismaili texts in Arabic in which Melchizedek appears, presumably reflecting knowledge of a Syriac version of the Bible.

JACOB'S SON LEVI IN THE OLD TESTAMENT PSEUDEPIGRAPHA AND RELATED LITERATURE

Marinus de Jonge and Johannes Tromp

Introduction

The Literary Sources

Among the so-called Old Testament pseudepigrapha there are three that devote considerable attention to Jacob's son Levi: *Jubilees*, the *Testament of Levi* in the *Testaments of the Twelve Patriarchs*, and *Joseph and Aseneth*. An analysis of the picture of Levi in these documents constitutes the major part of this essay. A number of points held in common between *Jubilees* and the *Testament of Levi* require special investigation.

In *Jubilees* Levi and his descendants are chosen for the priesthood, and other services in the Temple, after Simeon's and Levi's punishment of Shechem (*Jubilees* 30; cf. Genesis 34). Levi (with his brother Judah) is blessed by his grandfather Isaac (31:13–17) and is then invested and ordained by his father Jacob (32:1–9). The *Testament of Levi* treats the same events, but adds an interesting feature: both before and after Levi's exploits at Shechem it describes at some length a vision connected with Levi's call to the priesthood (*Testament of Levi* 2–5, 8). Levi and Judah are mentioned together in other parts of the *Testaments of the Twelve Patriarchs* as well, in connection with the future salvation of Israel and humanity.

In connection with these aspects of *Jubilees* and the *Testaments of the Twelve Patriarchs,* it will also be necessary to examine the *Aramaic Levi Document* (extant in the form of fragments of diverse provenance). This, in turn, is connected with documents ascribed to Levi's son Kohath and grandson Amram (Moses' father); fragments of these writings were found at Qumran. This sequence of writings, again, leads to a brief analysis of the parting words of Moses, known (incompletely) in Latin as the *Assumption of Moses.*

Joseph and Aseneth, like *Jubilees* and the *Testament of Levi,* refers to the events recorded in Genesis 34, but focuses its attention on the actions of Simeon and Levi in defending Aseneth against the evil intentions of Pharaoh's son.

The story of Levi in Genesis 34 has also attracted the attention of other ancient authors. We will survey extracts from the historian Demetrius and the epic poet Theodotus preserved in Eusebius's *Praeparatio evangelica* (9.21.1–19 and 9.22.1–11 respectively). In a brief final section some other Jewish sources are mentioned.

Levi in the Hebrew Bible

The pseudepigraphical sources presuppose the biblical account of Levi. The Hebrew Bible says little about Levi himself, but much about his sons. These are often divided into two classes: the priests and the Levites. Material about these figures must also be taken into consideration, insofar as views on the tasks of these figures seem to be reflected in the picture of Levi presented in our sources.

The Book of Genesis states that Levi was the third son of Jacob and Leah, and connects his name with the Hebrew root לוה ("to join"). Leah says: "Now my husband will be joined to me" (Gen 29:34). With Simeon, Levi is active in the expedition against Shechem in Genesis 34 (see especially vv. 25–31), and according to the LXX also in the negotiations with Hamor and Shechem (34:14). The pseudepigraphical sources pay much attention to this biblical story, often trying to explain or gloss over its more problematic aspects. In Jacob's farewell discourse (Genesis 49)

Simeon and Levi are fiercely condemned (vv. 5–7). Levi is mentioned elsewhere in Genesis only in the lists of Jacob's children in 35:23 and 46:11. In the latter, Jacob's grandchildren are also mentioned; Levi's children are Gershon, Kohath, and Merari.

Jacob's unfavorable verdict on (Simeon and) Levi is outweighed by the favorable mention of Levi in the Blessing of Moses in Deut 33:8–11. Here the patriarch represents his tribe and is praised for his loyalty to the covenant of God, which he regarded as more important than family ties (see Exod 32:26–28). Levi is to teach the ordinances of the Lord, place incense before God, and bring burnt offerings to the altar. Important for a right understanding of some of the texts to be discussed below is the praise bestowed in Numbers 25 on Phinehas, son of Eleazar, son of Aaron, for manifesting zeal on behalf of the Lord in punishing those who had relations with foreign women and worshiped the Baal of Peor. God grants him a covenant of peace (v. 12). "It shall be for him and for his descendants after him a covenant of eternal priesthood, because he was zealous for his God and made atonement for the Israelites" (v. 13). This theme returns in Ps 106:30–31; Wis 18:20–25; Sir 45:23–24; and Philo, *Spec. leg.* 1.56–57. In this context, Malachi's reference to God's covenant of life and peace with Levi in 2:4–9 (cf. 3:3) should also be mentioned. Levi is here called a man of instruction, walking in integrity and uprightness.

The Presentation of the Literary Sources in This Essay

The documents reviewed in this essay present (or presuppose) views of Levi, constructed on the basis of the few biblical texts about Levi and the many texts about his descendants. We should also bear in mind that difficulties in the texts themselves and discrepancies between different texts have left their mark in the retelling and expansion of the biblical stories.[1] The pictures that are given may be supposed to reflect the historical situations in which the documents were written and the particular ideas current in the groups in which they originated. There is clearly an

---

1. This point has been made cogently by Kugel in his recent articles, "Story of Dinah," 1–34; and "Levi's Elevation," 1–64.

interplay between the biblical texts and the ideas. It is difficult to
assess exactly the various factors operative in the genesis of any
particular picture of Levi (or any other biblical figure), and it is
equally challenging to trace developments. Our first task will be
to give a clear analysis of the characteristics of the presentations
in the individual writings under discussion.

We discuss the relevant documents in the following order: *Jubilees;* the *Aramaic Levi Document* (with an excursus on writings
connected with Kohath, Amram, and Moses); the *Testament of
Levi; Joseph and Aseneth;* fragments of Demetrius; fragments
of Theodotus; and references in other Jewish authors. Decisions
on this sequence are especially difficult with regard to the first
three documents. *Jubilees,* the *Aramaic Levi Document,* and the
Testament of Levi are clearly related. Do these relations indicate literary dependence in some direction? It will become clear
that the *Testament of Levi,* as part of the *Testaments of the
Twelve Patriarchs,* which are Christian in their present form, is
dependent on a document very much like the *Aramaic Levi Document.* Furthermore, it is likely that *Jubilees,* with its distinctive
retelling of the biblical story, utilized already-existing traditions
about Levi. It seems unlikely that the *Aramaic Levi Document,* a
document specifically devoted to Levi, borrowed traditions from
Jubilees, omitting its special framework and adding material from
other sources. It is difficult to prove, however, that *Jubilees* used
the *Aramaic Levi Document* in the form in which we know it.
First, the *Aramaic Levi Document* is difficult to date, and second, it is very fragmentary.[2] For these reasons it seemed unwise to
begin our survey with the *Aramaic Levi Document* fragments; it
seemed more logical to start with *Jubilees,* which gives a coherent
story.[3]

---

2. Both Grelot, "Livre des Jubilés," 109–33, and Stone, "Enoch, Aramaic Levi, and
Sectarian Origins," 159–70, now in idem, *Selected Studies,* 247–58, assume that *Jubilees*
used the *Aramaic Levi Document.* In his recent article "Levi's Elevation," J. Kugel tries to
distinguish various stages in the development of the Second Temple traditions concerning
Levi's appointment to the priesthood. Much of this is speculative, as he himself admits.
According to him, both *Jubilees* and the *Aramaic Levi Document* use older documents;
the *Aramaic Levi Document* in its present form reflects the account of Levi's elevation
found in *Jubilees.* The *Aramaic Levi Document* takes over passages found in *Jubilees,*
while omitting exegetical details essential for the picture given in this writing.

3. In his recent study *From Patriarch to Priest,* which appeared after this essay was

Levi in the Pseudepigraphical Sources

Jubilees

The book of *Jubilees* is a retelling of biblical history from the creation to the giving of the law to Moses on Mount Sinai. The extra revelation, purportedly of the contents of secret "heavenly tablets," mainly concerns the division of history into periods of forty-nine years ("jubilees") and laws about priesthood, cult, and purity other than the laws contained in the Pentateuch. The heavenly tablets also serve as the source from which the patriarchs who lived before Moses allegedly received their knowledge of the law. Haggadic material, sometimes extensive, is added, often in order to provide an occasion for the insertion of halakha.

It is uncertain when *Jubilees* was written, but arguments based on literary and tradition-historical considerations recommend the first half of the second century B.C.E.[4] The book was composed in Hebrew, probably in Palestine, but not much more can be said about its milieu of origin. When one considers the extremely favorable depiction of Levi in *Jubilees,* one is inclined to theorize that the book derives from priestly circles. "Priestly circles" is, however, a vague label. Literacy was still not common in Palestine in the early Hellenistic period, and priests are likely candidates for having written almost any Jewish book from this time. The figure of Levi is, in any case, not central to the author.

Jubilees contains three main passages about Levi in chapters 30–32.[5] These passages are all grouped around a paraphrase of Genesis 34 and 35, the Shechem and Bethel episodes. The Shechem episode (*Jub.* 30:1–4) is strongly abbreviated and leads

---

written, R. A. Kugler has attempted to reconstruct "Aramaic Levi" and to illustrate the dependence of the *Testament of Levi* on it. He also reconstructs an intermediate stage, a pre-Christian "Original Testament of Levi." In our opinion this intermediate stage is highly hypothetical. According to Kugler, "Aramaic Levi" — tentatively dated to the (late) third century B.C.E. — and *Jubilees* depend on a lost Levi apocryphon as a common source.

4. The earliest manuscript evidence (4QJub[a] or 4Q216) is dated to the middle to late second century B.C.E.; see VanderKam and Milik, "First Jubilees Manuscript from Qumran Cave 4," 243–46, esp. p. 246. That this manuscript was found at Qumran does not mean that *Jubilees* originated in Qumran circles. It is likely that *Jubilees* was read by a larger audience, including members of the Qumran community.

5. Other references to Levi are found in *Jub.* 28:14; 33:22; 34:20; 38:6; and 44:14, but they consist mainly of genealogical information and are not significant for our discussion. On *Jub.* 45:16, see below.

to a large section on the prohibition of intermarriage (*Jub.* 30:5–23).[6] The Bethel episode, on the other hand, is expanded by nonbiblical traditions which lead to the commandment to give tithes of everything to the priests (*Jubilees* 32). In between, *Jubilees* recounts Isaac's blessing of two of Jacob's sons, Levi and Judah (*Jubilees* 31). The contents of the blessings are traditional (to Levi and his descendants the eternal priesthood is promised, to Judah and his descendants the eternal kingship); also, that Levi was blessed by his grandfather appears to be a fixed element in the Levi traditions (see below). The narrative framework of the blessings, however, seems to be an invention of the author of *Jubilees.*

In *Jubilees,* the rape of Dinah (cf. Gen 34:1–5) is briefly paraphrased. The negotiations about the terms for Dinah's marriage, which take the most space in the biblical account (Gen 34:6–24), are summarized in one sentence in *Jubilees:* Jacob's sons "spoke deceptively with them [the Shechemites], acted in a crafty way toward them, and deceived them" (*Jub.* 30:3b). The slaughter of the Shechemites is also briefly paraphrased (*Jub.* 30:4; cf. Gen 34:25–29).

The reasons why Jacob's sons deceived the Shechemites are not given at this stage, nor does the author indicate how they beguiled their adversaries. Apparently the author supposed the story to have been known to his readers, because later (in *Jub.* 30:12), when he comments on this episode, he quotes Gen 34:14, the phrase with which Jacob's sons initially refuse to give Dinah to Shechem: "We cannot give our sister to one who is uncircumcised." Moreover, it is clear why the treacherous negotiations are largely disregarded: the circumcision of the Shechemites, before they were killed, would have complicated the author's halakhic discourse, which prohibits the intercourse and marriage of Israelite "daughters" with uncircumcised men.[7]

In the halakhic conclusions drawn from this story (*Jub.* 30:5–23), the defilement of Dinah is interpreted as a defilement of the Lord's Temple.[8] Thus, the author links the Shechem episode to the

---

6. Compare Berger, *Das Buch der Jubiläen,* 469.
7. See Endres, *Biblical Interpretation,* 129.
8. See Berger, *Das Buch der Jubiläen,* 473; Endres, *Biblical Interpretation,* 140–41.

priesthood: Levi's zeal for righteousness and his vengeance against the enemies of Israel is said to be rewarded with the eternal priesthood for him and his descendants (*Jub.* 30:18). In 30:19–20 much attention is paid to Levi's righteousness, which is said to be written on the heavenly tablets. Also, Levi is called a "friend," presumably of God (see below, *Aramaic Levi Document* 83).

In *Jubilees* 31–32, a paraphrase of Genesis 35, the author reorganizes the Genesis account so as to make it more coherent, and fills it in with much new material, to a large extent concerning Levi.

Jub. 31:1–2 narrates the purification of Jacob's household. Then, in 31:3, *Jubilees* has Jacob travel to Bethel. There he erects a pillar of stone and invites his father Isaac to come and sacrifice. Instead, Jacob is asked to go to his father (31:4–5) because Isaac is too weak to travel. Here the author inserts a new episode on Jacob's visit to Isaac, during which Levi and Judah are blessed (31:6–30; see below). After Jacob's visit to his father, he travels to Bethel (31:30–32), where Levi dreams that he and his offspring will be appointed to the priesthood forever (32:1). On the next morning Jacob tithes all his possessions (32:2). He then casts the Lord's lot among his sons,[9] and when the lot falls on Levi, he is ordained as a priest by Jacob, and another tithe of everything is entrusted to him (32:4–8). "Levi...served as priest in Bethel before his father Jacob. There he was priest, and Jacob gave what he had vowed. In this way he again gave a tithe to the Lord" (32:9). This story leads to a section on the law on the "heavenly tablets," which are said to prescribe a second tithe to the priests of the Lord (32:10–15).

Jub. 31:4–32 consists entirely of material not found in Genesis 34–35. After having made preparations to depart for Bethel (*Jub.* 31:1–3; cf. Gen 35:1–4), Jacob, together with his sons Levi and Judah, visits Isaac. Isaac blesses his grandsons and prophesies that they and their offspring will be priests and kings forever.

---

9. In 32:3 the author remarks that Rachel became pregnant with Benjamin. Apparently this is told here in order to include Benjamin when the lot is cast. See Berger, *Das Buch der Jubiläen,* 481. Kugel, "Levi's Elevation," 13–17, points out that Jacob counts his sons from Benjamin onward, so that the lot falls on Levi (Jacob's third son). This traditional motif is introduced as an occasion to insert the halakha on the priestly privilege of the second tithes (32:10–15).

Although the tradition of Isaac's blessing of Levi may well have existed before *Jubilees* was written, the form it takes in this book is probably the work of the author, who presumably wished to replace Jacob's blessing of Levi in Gen 49:5–7. Jacob's blessing of Simeon and Levi in the biblical version is actually a curse, and is therefore unwelcome to the author of *Jubilees,* who holds Levi in high regard. The solution that he adopted is illustrative of the author's remarkably free treatment of the biblical material. In his paraphrase of Genesis, the author of *Jubilees* leaves out almost the whole of Genesis 49. Just as drastic is the author's decision to omit the story in Genesis 48. That story, according to which Jacob blessed Joseph's sons Ephraim and Manasseh, was used as a prototype for Isaac's blessing of Levi and Judah in *Jubilees* 31. Thus, the biblical narrative of Jacob's blessing of Joseph's two sons is brought forward in history one generation, and is transformed into Isaac's blessing of Jacob's two sons.[10]

Isaac's blessing of Levi (*Jub.* 31:13–17) describes the eponymous priest as the ideal officer of the temple service. This blessing is, in fact, a collection of traditional images of the priest. Some of its details can be traced back directly to biblical passages. Thus the etymology of Levi's name in *Jub.* 31:16a–c is the one already offered in Gen 29:34, although the interpretations differ (in the biblical account Levi "joins" Leah to Jacob). *Jub.* 31:15b–c, 17 derives from Moses' blessing of Levi in Deut 33:10–11.

A number of elements in the blessing of Levi also occur in several statements about particular priests or the priesthood in general. The honor and holiness of Levi's priesthood (*Jub.* 31:14a, d–e) are stressed also in Sirach's praise of the priests Aaron (Sir 45:6–8), Phinehas (Sir 45:23), and Simon (Sir 50:5–11). The election of Levi and his descendants alone as priests (*Jub.* 31:14b) is paralleled by the exclusive election of Aaron and

---

10. On other occasions, too, the author of *Jubilees* introduces blessings of grandsons by their grandfathers; see *Jub.* 7:20–39 (Noah's farewell speech to his grandsons, alluding to Enoch's instructions to his son and grandsons in 7:39); 19:15–31; and 22:10–30 (Abraham's blessings for Jacob). According to Kugel, "Levi's Elevation," 17–24, Isaac is introduced as blessing Levi because the author of *Jubilees* did not regard Jacob as a priest, in contradistinction to all the other patriarchs from Adam to Levi. Thus, Isaac's blessing of Levi would serve to ensure the *successio pontificalis.* However, the author of *Jubilees* does not appear to regard the sacrifices brought by the patriarchs as signals of their priesthood. If he had considered them priests, he surely would have said so.

his descendants in Sir 45:13, 16, 18, 25; cf. 50:13. The eternity of the priesthood (*Jub.* 31:13, 14e; compare 30:18; 32:1) is also mentioned in Exod 40:15 (cf. Sir 45:7, 15) and Num 25:13 (cf. Ps 106:30–31; Sir 45:24; 1 Macc 2:54); see further 1QSb iii 24. *Jub.* 31:14c notes that the ministry of the priests runs parallel to the angelic priesthood in heaven (cf. *Jub.* 30:18); this concept was current in Hellenistic Jewish thought (e.g., Wis 9:8; *As. Mos.* 10:2; 1QSb iii 6; 1QM xii 1).[11]

In *Jubilees* Levi's tasks as a priest include teaching the law, acting as judge, and blessing the people (*Jub.* 31:15). To this one may compare Mal 2:4–9, where precisely these functions constitute God's covenant with Levi. In connection with particular priests or the priesthood in general, instruction in the law is also mentioned in Deut 33:10; Sir 45:17; 1QSb iii 22–23; and *Aramaic Levi Document* 88–90.[12] The priests' judicial function occurs, e.g., in Deut 17:8–13; 1 Chr 23:4; 2 Chr 19:8–10; and 1QSa i 24. The function of blessing is mentioned in Num 6:22–26 and Sir 50:20–21.

Jubilees also states that Levi is to be ruler of his people (31:15a);[13] compare Sir 45:24; 50:1; 1QSa i 24; 1QSb iii 5; 1QLevi 1; *Aramaic Levi Document* 67. The concept of priests being kings may be compared to Exod 19:6, which states that Israel must be a "kingdom of priests."[14] Finally, *Jub.* 31:16e–h speaks of Levi's privileges in offering the sacrifices to God from which the priests derived their livelihood (compare again the halakha

---

11. Compare Schäfer, *Rivalität zwischen Engeln und Menschen*, 36–40, on the "liturgical communion" of humans and angels at Qumran.

12. Note also that in *Jub.* 45:16 Jacob is said to entrust "all his books and the books of his fathers to his son Levi, so that he could preserve them and renew them for his sons until today." This is a reference to the tradition of the knowledge that the patriarchs had of the heavenly law before Moses' law was published (see further the section on Kohath and Amram below). The preservation of the books of the law is entrusted to the Levites in Deut 31:25–26.

13. VanderKam, "Jubilees and the Priestly Messiah," 362, notes as a further parallel the title "messenger" (*Jub.* 31:15; compare Mal 2:7). In his edition, VanderKam reads *malā'ᵉkt* ("messengers"), but translates the variant reading "leaders" (*'amāl'ᵉkt*), obviously because of the context. For a Levite as "messenger," see *As. Mos.* 11:17 (Moses, *magnus nuntius*).

14. It may be that in *Jubilees*, the figure of Levi attracted some of Judah's functions (see Stone, "Ideal Figures," 575–86, esp. p. 580; also in idem, *Selected Studies*, 259–70, p. 264). There is no reason, however, to interpret the description of Levi as messianic.

on the second tithe for the priests in *Jub.* 32:8–15).[15] Similar privileges are mentioned in Sir 45:21.

This selection of statements on priests and priesthood from a wide range of sources shows that the image of Levi in Isaac's blessing is largely a projection of the figure of the ideal priest onto Levi.[16] It may be added that in *Jub.* 30:18 the priesthood is given to Levi and his sons because of his "zeal." The connection between zeal for the Lord and Phinehas's priesthood was made in Num 25:11–13 (see also Sir 45:23–24; 1 Macc 2:54; cf. Wis 18:20–25; Philo, *Spec. leg.* 1.57), but again it was probably understood to concern the tribe of Levi in general before the author of *Jubilees* applied it to the tribe's patriarch in this passage.

It is important to note that making atonement for the people, one of the priests' most important functions elsewhere (e.g., Sir 45:16), is absent from *Jubilees.* It seems that the author of *Jubilees* is primarily concerned with priestly *rights,* and is less interested in describing the benefits of priests' actions for others. This stress on priests' rights might also explain the author's effort to project all priestly claims onto the most ancient of priests, Levi himself. The author thus suggests that already to Levi the priesthood was promised, together with all its advantages, as laid down from eternity in the heavenly tablets.

The image of Levi in *Jubilees,* then, is that of a man rightfully angered by the defilement of his sister. The revenge that he and his brother Simeon exacted was a deed of zeal and righteousness, for which Levi and his descendants were rewarded with the priesthood forever. Isaac's blessing of Levi is a picture of the ideal priest, whose tasks include ruling Israel, dispensing justice, teaching the Lord's will, and blessing the people. Sacrifice is mentioned

---

15. Cf. Davenport, *Eschatology,* 63. For the postexilic and Qumranic use of the term "table," see Jaubert, *Notion d'alliance,* 204–5.

16. It has been argued that the author of *Jubilees* himself gathered various bits of biblical information to shape his image of the eponymous hero of the priestly tribe; see VanderKam, "Jubilees and the Priestly Messiah," 361–62, esp. p. 361: "The author of *Jubilees* found warrant in Malachi... for speaking of a priestly contract with Levi. Thus, as he associated Genesis 34 and Numbers 25, he had prophetic sanction for assigning a covenant of priesthood to Levi — a covenant termed a 'covenant of peace.' " See also the characteristic reconstruction by Kugel, "Levi's Elevation," 31–33. However, it is probable that an image such as that given in *Jubilees* was traditional before the book's composition.

only to justify the priests' share in the offerings; atonement is not mentioned at all.

If *Jubilees* does derive from priestly circles, this blessing of Levi clearly accords with the interests of that class. The image of Levi in Isaac's blessing is essentially a laudatory description of actual functions of priests in the Hellenistic period, when Jerusalem priests were in fact the rulers, teachers, and judges. In *Jubilees,* these functions are ascribed to the first priest, Levi himself, assuring their antiquity. They are even said to have been written down in the heavenly tablets, and thus ordained by God from eternity. At the time of the writing of *Jubilees,* the priests were probably the effective local rulers of Jerusalem, and, apart from having to legitimize the nonbiblical priestly dues (the "second tithes"), they had no need for stronger ideological claims.[17] In this relatively comfortable position, they could even afford to grant Judah a place next to Levi, on the left side of Isaac. The sequel to Isaac's blessing (*Jub.* 32:1-9), however, clearly shows the relative predominance of Levi.

The Aramaic Levi Document (ALD)

The *Aramaic Levi Document* is known to us only through Aramaic fragments found in the Cairo Genizah and at Qumran, supplemented by two large Greek fragments found as additions to *T. Levi* 2:3 and 18:2 in the Greek manuscript Athos Koutloumous 39 (eleventh century).

This document is difficult to date. The oldest textual witnesses are the Qumran fragments, one of which is thought to date to the end of the second century B.C.E. M. E. Stone places the *Aramaic Levi Document* in the third century, but this is not certain; a date in the second century cannot be excluded.[18] The document seems

---

17. The case was somewhat different for the Hasmoneans' need to justify their office of high priest, for which reason John Hyrcanus had 1 Maccabees written (see Lebram, *Legitimiteit en charisma*). But this special case does not invalidate these remarks on the priestly class in general.

18. See Stone, "Enoch, Aramaic Levi, and Sectarian Origins," esp. p. 159, n. 2, and pp. 168-69. He regards the composition of *Jubilees* as the *terminus ante quem,* but in our opinion it is difficult to prove that *Jubilees* used the present *Aramaic Levi Document* (see n. 2). He also points to the use of the calendar known from *Jubilees* and the oldest (third century) parts of *1 Enoch* — but clearly the use of this calendar does not prove that the

to belong to the body of literature copied at Qumran, but not composed there.

It is best to speak of the "Aramaic Levi Document" rather than the "Aramaic Testament of Levi." Since the beginning and end are missing we cannot be sure that this writing was actually called a testament. There are, however, links with 4QQahat and 4QAmram, fragments of which were found at Qumran, which purport to give these persons' final instructions to their sons (see below). There was clearly an interest in bridging the gap between Levi and Moses/Aaron (see also *ALD* 66–80 and Demetrius) and in handing down the wise counsel of Levi and his sons.

The *Aramaic Levi Document* must be studied in connection with the *Testament of Levi* in the *Testaments of the Twelve Patriarchs*. The *Testament of Levi*, in many respects different from the other testaments, was acquainted with material found in the *Aramaic Levi Document*, and probably even with a document similar to the *Aramaic Levi Document*; the *Testament of Levi* may be used, with caution, to help determine the contents of the *Aramaic Levi Document* and the correct order of the preserved fragments.

The *Aramaic Levi Document* contained a prayer of Levi, followed by a vision of heaven (of which only the introduction is preserved).[19] After this prayer and vision (comparable to *Testament of Levi* 2–5) followed a report, poorly preserved, on the expedition against Shechem (cf. *Testament of Levi* 5–7). Next we have a few lines of the conclusion of a (second?) vision (corresponding to *Testament of Levi* 8), followed by elaborate priestly instructions given by Isaac (cf. *Testament of Levi* 9). The *Aramaic Levi Document* has no parallel to *Testament of Levi* 10, but does contain a counterpart of the biographical account of Levi, his children, and grandchildren found in *Testament of Levi* 11–12. A number of overlapping fragments from the Genizah and

---

Aramaic Levi Document must be as old as that part of *1 Enoch*. He finds in the *Aramaic Levi Document* the expectation of a priestly messiah with royal functions, whereas at Qumran priest and king appear alongside one another. The passages at issue do not quite warrant this conclusion (see n. 21).

19. It is possible that the words added in MS Koutloumous 39 at *T. Levi* 5:2, "To you will be given the priesthood and to your seed in order to serve the Most High in the midst of the earth and to make atonement for the sins of ignorance of the earth," derive from the (Greek) *Aramaic Levi Document*.

Qumran witness to a text extolling wisdom and the wise person, which may be compared to *Testament of Levi* 13. After this the situation is uncertain. There is a very small fragment of what may have been an invective against priests, comparable to *T. Levi* 14:3–4.[20]

What picture emerges from this fragmentary material? In the prayer of Levi and its introduction, all the emphasis is placed on purification (vv. 1–2, 14). Levi prays that he may be far from the unrighteous spirit, evil thought, fornication, and pride (v. 7). He asks to be shown the holy spirit, counsel, and wisdom, and to be granted strength (v. 8). His desire is to be God's servant (δοῦλος), and to be close to God as God's servant (παῖς). The prayer ends, "Make [me] a participant in your words.... And do not remove the son of your servant from your countenance all the days of the world" (vv. 18–19).

Of the few words left of the second vision, v. 6 is especially important. Here we read, as the parting words of seven angels, "Now see how we elevated you above all and how we give you the greatness [anointing? — Aramaic רבות] of eternal peace." This is reminiscent of Exod 40:15 and Num 25:12–13 (see also Sir 45:15; Mal 2:5; 1QM xii 3). In vv. 4–6, "the kingdom of the sword" is mentioned alongside "the greatness of eternal peace." It is not clear whether the "kingdom of the sword" is opposed to or compared with the priesthood.[21] It is possible that this expression

---

20. The present *T. Levi* 17:2–11 is clearly an extract from a source giving an account of seven jubilees. Further, E. Puech ("Fragments d'un apocryphe") has identified a parallel between *T. Levi* 17:8–10 and 4QAhA bis, fragment 1, and suggested that this scroll be renamed 4QTestLevi^c. The same author has also found a parallel between 4QAhA 9 i 3–5, called by him 4QTestLevi^d, and *T. Levi* 18:2–4. While the first parallel is uncertain, the second is very interesting. Yet the overall evidence, in these fragments and in others from the same scrolls, is so slight that it is difficult to prove that we have here witnesses for the *Aramaic Levi Document*. Hence we do not consider this material in the present context. Also, Kugler, in *From Patriarch to Priest*, does not assign the fragments with supposed parallels to *Testament of Levi* 17–18 to "Aramaic Levi."

21. In 1QLevi, frag. 1, we encounter the expression "the kingdom of the priesthood." It is compared with another kingdom, whose nature is unknown because the fragment breaks off at this point. See now also frag. A4, col. 2 of Eisenman and Wise, line 16, "your [pl.] kingdom." In this connection we note that in the remark about Kohath in vv. 66–67 (probably alluding to a passage in Gen 49:10, belonging to the blessing of Judah), Levi is said to have seen that this son "would have an assembly of all [the people and that] he would have the high priesthood [for all Is]rael." The Greek parallel here adds "He and his seed will be the beginning [or: the rule; Gr. ἀρχή] of kings, a priesthood for Israel." There seems, therefore, to be a tendency to ascribe royal functions to Levi and his descendants.

refers to Levi's exploits at Shechem, probably recounted immediately before. What remains of the *Aramaic Levi Document* does not allow us to establish this connection with certainty, but it seems likely, in view of the fact that *Jubilees* also connects Levi's priesthood with his zeal in the Shechem episode. In *ALD* 78–79, Levi's action at Shechem is mentioned before his appointment to the priesthood.[22]

The account of the vision ends with the statement that Levi kept this vision, like the former one, secret. A visit to Isaac is mentioned only briefly: "And we went to my father Isaac and he thus blessed me" (v. 8). Compared with *Jubilees*, the *Aramaic Levi Document* plays down the significance of Isaac's blessing after Levi's visions (in place of which *Jubilees* mentions only a dream in Bethel [32:1]). Immediately after this, Jacob appoints Levi to be priest and consecrates him, and Levi receives tithes and offers sacrifices (vv. 8–10).

From Bethel, all return to Isaac, who instructs Levi at length. "When he learned that I was priest of the Most High God, the Lord of heaven, he began to teach me the law of the priesthood" (v. 13).[23] These instructions (vv. 14–61) are extensive, and not without repetition. They concern many aspects of the offering of different sacrifices, and seem intended for a priestly community that is expected to put them into practice. Significantly, they begin with commands to remain pure: "You are near to God and near to all his holy ones. Now be pure in your flesh from every impurity of mankind" (v. 18; cf. *Jub.* 21:16; 30:18). The theme of holiness returns in vv. 48–50 and 58–61, where the eternal nature of the priesthood is emphasized. The connections with the prayer of Levi are obvious.

It is going too far to suspect behind this the expectation of a priestly messiah with royal functions (see nn. 14 and 18).

22. If, on the other hand, the addition to *T. Levi* 5:2 mentioned in n. 19 belongs to the *Aramaic Levi Document,* it will have formed the end of the first vision, including an appointment to the priesthood (as in the *Testament of Levi*). It will have to be explained as a reference to sacrifices of atonement (note the strong verbal similarity to 3:5–6) rather than being connected with Phinehas's "atonement for the Israelites" mentioned in Num 25:10–12.

23. The equivalents in *Jubilees* are Abraham's instructions to Jacob in chap. 21. In the *Aramaic Levi Document,* Isaac refers to instructions by Abraham in vv. 22, 50, and 57. Note also the reference to the Book of Noah in v. 57.

The emphasis on insight, wisdom, and true judgment in the prayer of Levi ("God's beloved one," v. 83) — an important aspect of the priesthood since Deut 33:10, as we saw in our discussion of *Jub.* 31:15 and 17[24] — returns in *ALD* 81, where Levi's instructions to his sons in his 118th year are recorded: "May truth be the essence of your acts and may justice always be with you" (v. 85). The duty of his sons is to "teach reading and writing [and] the teaching of wisdom to your children" (v. 88).

In view of the contents of the *Aramaic Levi Document,* it seems most likely that it was written by priests in order to extol the role of the tribe of Levi in Israel. They emphasized the necessity of purity and holiness in carrying out the priestly duties in sacrifices, and at the same time they portrayed Levi and his sons as wise men, teachers, and leaders. In view of the fragmentary condition of the text, as well as its uncertain date, it is difficult to draw further conclusions about its provenance or origin.

Excursus on Kohath, Amram, and Moses

A few words are in order here about Levi's son and grandson, Kohath and Amram. Among the discoveries at Qumran were portions of farewell discourses by these patriarchs. In the Bible, no attention is paid to these figures aside from their genealogical role, Amram being the father of Moses (e.g., Exod 6:19; Num 26:59). It seems likely that the "testaments" of Kohath and Amram are not reflections of established traditions about these individuals, but constructions of an author who wished to fill the genealogical gap between Levi and Moses.[25] An examination of the contents of the extant fragments verifies this impression.

The fragments of the *Testament of Kohath* (probably dating from the last quarter of the second century B.C.E., but of uncertain provenance)[26] begin with Kohath's blessing of his sons. In

---

24. On this aspect of the *Aramaic Levi Document* see especially Stone, "Ideal Figures." On this section of the *Aramaic Levi Document* in comparison with *Testament of Levi* 13, see also Hollander, *Joseph as an Ethical Model*, 57–62.

25. So also Puech, "Le Testament de Qahat," 52.

26. Puech, "Le Testament de Qahat," 51–53.

terms traditionally connected with law and wisdom, Kohath assures them that God will make God's light shine on them forever (4QTQah i 1–3; see below on *T. Levi* 4:2–3).[27] Further on, attention shifts to the instructions Kohath's sons are to transmit to their sons (4QTQah i 4–5). These instructions are those ordained by Jacob, Abraham, Levi, and Kohath himself (4QTQah i 7–8; cf. *ALD* 57; *Jub.* 7:38–39; 45:16). Kohath's sons are to stay holy and pure, and are to keep the inheritance they received so as to give joy and glory to their ancestors (4QTQah i 8–12). This inheritance is defined as "truth, justice, righteousness, perfection, purity, holiness, and priesthood" (4QTQah i 12–13). Note that the priesthood is mentioned last and only in passing.[28] Kohath's priesthood is also mentioned in *ALD* 67, but in Levi's farewell discourse in *ALD* 82–95, the main issues are truth and wisdom.

The inheritance of the patriarchs is entrusted to Kohath's son Amram in particular. "[All the books] they gave to Levi, my father; and Levi, my father, g[ave] them to me" (4QTQah ii 9–11); Kohath then gives to Amram "all these books as a witness" (4QTQah ii 11–13). Clearly Kohath is depicted as transmitting laws already known to Abraham. It may be assumed that a farewell discourse was constructed for Kohath to ensure an unbroken chain of transmission from Levi to Moses and Aaron. This is evident from the fact that Amram in particular, and not his brothers, receives the books in order to pass them on to his sons, at least to Moses.

A farewell discourse was also ascribed to Amram (4QAmram, of approximately the same date as 4QTQah).[29] One fragment found at Qumran contains the opening lines: "A copy of the book about the visions of Amram, the son of Kohath, the son of Levi, al[l that] he told his sons, and (all the things) which he gave them as instructions on the day of his de[ath]" (4QAmram[c] 1–2). 4QAmram[b] (to be read in connection with 4QAmram[a]) contains

---

27. For the well-known metaphor of the teaching of the law as a shining light, see Jaubert, *Notion d'alliance*, 177.

28. Cf. the comments by Stone, "Ideal Figures," 263–65.

29. See, again, Puech, "Le Testament de Qahat," 51–53.

Amram's account of a vision he had of two angels disputing over him. The angels ask Amram which of the two he will choose. One of the angels is later identified as Melkireshaʿ, "King of Evil," while the other presents himself as the ruler of light.[30] Although the sequel to this narrative is lost,[31] Amram presumably chooses the angel of light.

These two "testaments" indicate that certain authors were concerned to construct a chain of transmission from Abraham to Moses, evidently to ensure that the Jewish patriarchs already had a knowledge of the law prior to the public revelation to Moses on Mount Sinai. This tradition of esoteric revelation, handed down from generation to generation, also included as a recipient Moses himself, not only in *Jubilees,* but also in another farewell discourse, the *Assumption of Moses.* Thus, the idea arose that there was a tradition of knowledge of divine things not only before the revelation of the law on Sinai, but also parallel to it. This esoteric secret knowledge complements the exoteric law of Moses in that it concerns higher and more significant matters.

The *Assumption of Moses,* written in Palestine in the early first century c.e.,[32] claims to contain a book given by Moses to his successor Joshua. The book is a prophecy of the future of the Jewish people from their entrance into the land of Israel until the coming of God's kingdom. The *Assumption of Moses* is mentioned here because one of its chief figures, bearing the enigmatic name "Taxo," is said to come "from the tribe of Levi" (*As. Mos.* 9:1). When a ruthless tyrant threatens to destroy Judaism, Taxo prefers to die rather than "transgress the commandments of the Lord of Lords" (*As. Mos.* 9:6). Again, a person from the tribe of Levi is associated with zeal for the Law. Although the text is not altogether clear, it is probable that this Levite, too, is rewarded with an eternal priesthood, namely the priesthood in heaven (*As. Mos.* 10:2).[33]

---

30. Visions about angels also occur in *ALD* 4–7 and *Testament of Levi* 2–6, 8. Mention of a vision of Levi is made in *Jub.* 32:1.

31. See, however, Milik, "4Q Visions de ʿAmram," 90.

32. Tromp, *Assumption of Moses,* 116–17.

33. For this interpretation, see Tromp, "Taxo," 200–209; and idem, *Assumption of Moses,* 229–31.

The Testament of Levi *in the* Testaments of the Twelve Patriarchs

In composing the *Testament of Levi,* the author(s) of the *Testaments of the Twelve Patriarchs* had available much special material, as is shown by the *Aramaic Levi Document.* We can safely assume that the author(s) of the *Testament of Levi* made use of a document similar to the *Aramaic Levi Document.* Hence, the *Testament of Levi* is in many ways different from the other testaments in the *Testaments of the Twelve Patriarchs.* We can also assume that the *Testaments of the Twelve Patriarchs* in their present form cannot be traced back earlier than the end of the second century C.E., and that it is impossible to reconstruct a pre-Christian, Hellenistic-Jewish original.[34] This also becomes evident when we study the figure of Levi in the *Testaments of the Twelve Patriarchs.* Levi is mentioned in many of the testaments besides his own, often together with his brother Judah; they represent the priesthood and kingship, respectively, and in *T. Judah* 21:1–6a the former is considered the more important. Also, the future coming of an "agent of divine deliverance" (in the *Testaments of the Twelve Patriarchs,* clearly Jesus Christ) is connected with the two tribes, or with Judah in particular.[35]

In the *Testament of Levi* Levi's two visions (2:5–5:6 and chap. 8) receive a prominent place; the introductory and concluding passages of the second (8:1, 18–19) make it clear that it is intended to corroborate the first. The visions are too complex to discuss in detail, but it is worth noting what they tell us about Levi's priesthood.

The visions are situated near Shechem. The first begins when Levi perceives lawlessness dominating on the earth. After praying that he may be saved (2:3–4; cf. the Prayer of Levi in the *Aramaic Levi Document*), he falls asleep, and in a vision takes a journey through the heavens. In 2:10–12 an angel promises Levi that he

---

34. On this see Hollander and de Jonge, *Testaments,* and other publications by de Jonge, beginning with *Testaments.* Kugler's (*From Patriarch to Priest*) attempt (the latest in a long series) to reconstruct a pre-Christian testament of Levi is ingenious but speculative; moreover it remains sketchy. Note that Kugler does not discuss the Levi priestly tradition in the Christian testament as we have it.

35. See de Jonge, "Two Messiahs," 191–203.

will stand near God, be God's minister, and declare God's mysteries to humans.[36] At the end of the vision, Levi beholds God on a throne and receives the blessing of the priesthood (5:1–2). After his return to earth, God's angel gives him a sword and commands him to execute vengeance on Shechem. Throughout, Levi acts as a zealous fighter for God's cause (6:3), like his descendant Phinehas (Numbers 25).[37]

The vision in chap. 8 recounts Levi's investiture as priest by seven men in white clothing (i.e., angels). Here stands a full and complex description (vv. 1–10) of what is presupposed in what is left of this vision in the *Aramaic Levi Document*.[38] In the remainder of the vision, angels announce that Levi's seed will be divided into three offices (v. 11); in v. 17 "high priests and judges and scribes" are mentioned. Thus, as in *Jubilees* and the *Aramaic Levi Document*, the tasks of the levitical priests are not restricted to temple service.

Regarding what happens after the visions, the *Testament of Levi* remains close to the *Aramaic Levi Document*. Levi visits Isaac (with Judah!) and receives a blessing "according to all the words of the vision which I had seen" (9:1–2). After receiving a vision that Levi should be a priest, Jacob gives tithes to God through Levi. No investiture of Levi by Jacob is mentioned. As in the *Aramaic Levi Document*, Jacob and his family return to Isaac, who teaches Levi "the law of the priesthood" (9:7). *T. Levi* 9:6–14 gives, however, only a short extract of the elaborate instructions found in the *Aramaic Levi Document*. The author of the *Testaments of the Twelve Patriarchs* still clearly believed that Levi and his descendants had a task in the Temple, but was no longer interested in its details.

---

36. This in itself is a perfect answer to the prayer of Levi in 2:4. The angel continues, however, "and will proclaim him who will redeem Israel." This is explained in 2:11 with the statement "and by you and Judah, the Lord will appear among men, saving through them the whole race of men," a clearly Christian statement.

37. Note that, contrary to what is stated in *Jubilees*, Levi receives the blessing of the priesthood before acting at Shechem on divine command; this connection may also have been present in the *Aramaic Levi Document* (see n. 22).

38. Note that *T. Levi* 12:5, following *ALD* 78–79, puts Levi's vengeance on Shechem before his appointment as priest. The investiture recorded in *Testament of Levi* 8 may have been regarded as the actual beginning of Levi's priestly service.

Throughout the *Testament of Levi,* it is clear that Levi is called to be a priest, and that he is the patriarch of the priestly tribe. As in the *Aramaic Levi Document* and *Jubilees,* he receives insight, knowledge, and true judgment (2:10–11; 8:2, 4). This is especially clear in 4:2–3, verses that presuppose Levi's prayer in the *Aramaic Levi Document:* "The Most High, therefore, has heard your prayer to separate you from unrighteousness and that you should become to him a son and a servant and a minister of his presence. You will light up a bright light of knowledge in Jacob." Levi's seed will share in his blessing (v. 4a), but here there is a significant difference from the *Aramaic Levi Document.* Levi's priesthood lasts only until the coming of Jesus Christ, who will suffer at the hands of Levi's sons (v. 4b). As God says to Levi in 5:2, "I have given you the blessings of the priesthood until I come and sojourn in the midst of Israel" (cf. 4:4–5).

The theme of the sins of Levi's sons, as well as that of their enmity against Jesus Christ, returns in chapters 10, 14–15, and 16. Isaac warns Levi about the spirit of impurity, which will "defile the holy things by your seed" (9:9). The close of the testament describes a continual deterioration of the priesthood (chap. 17), followed by the arrival of a new priest (chap. 18). This priest will execute a judgment of truth; he will light up the light of knowledge and shine like the sun (vv. 3–4). The echo of 4:3 is obvious,[39] but it is not stated that this new priest will be a descendant of Levi; *Testament of Judah* 24, on the other hand, hails the new future king as a descendant of Judah. In fact, *T. Levi* 18:3 states that the priest's "star will arise in heaven, as a king."[40] In both cases Jesus Christ is in view, as is clear from *T. Levi* 18:7–8 and *T. Judah* 25:2.

Notwithstanding the Christian framework, the *Testament of Levi* gives in chapter 13 an exhortatory discourse that closely resembles the parallel passage in *ALD* 81–95; it speaks in general terms about fear of the Lord, wisdom, and righteousness. Noth-

---

39. See now the parallel in 4QAhA 9 i 3–4: "His word is as a word from heaven and his teaching in accordance with God's will. His eternal sun will shine, and his fire will burn in all corners of the earth.... "

40. Also during his investiture Levi receives some royal attributes (8:4, 7, 9).

ing is said about specifically priestly functions of the sons of Levi; thus, it was also suitable for a Christian audience. Remarkably, *Testament of Levi* 13 stresses the importance of the Law (vv. 2–4; cf. 19:1), whereas *ALD* 81–95 focuses on wisdom.

The Shechem episode is treated at length.[41] As already noted, *T. Levi* 5:1–6:2 describes Levi's action as vengeance for Dinah (5:3), vengeance carried out on God's command and with the help of an angel. Levi's role is lauded, since he acted out of zeal for God (6:4; cf. Jdt 9:4; *Jub.* 30:18; Numbers 25). As in *Jubilees,* his appointment to the priesthood is directly connected with his exploits at Shechem.

The question of circumcision for the Shechemites is raised, remarkably enough, by Levi, who advises that it be done.[42] The progress of the negotiations is not described, but clearly the Shechemites were circumcised. The conflict between Jacob and his sons on this matter (Gen 34:30–31) is not concealed (6:6); there is even a veiled reference to Jacob's censure in Gen 49:5–7 (6:6; cf. *T. Sim.* 5:6). Levi admits to having erred in acting against his father's will, but claims that he reminded his father of God's promise(s) to give the land to him and his descendants and to destroy the Canaanites (7:1).

It is interesting that in the present form of the *Testaments of the Twelve Patriarchs,* which bears such a clearly Christian stamp, Levi remains so important, in his own right as well as together with Judah. In the NT, Levi is mentioned only in Hebrews 7, which argues that Jesus, a descendant of Judah (7:4), is a priest forever, according to the order of Melchizedek (7:20; cf. Ps 110:4), and is therefore superior to Abraham, Levi, and the priestly descendants of Levi (cf. Gen 14:18–20; Heb 7:4–10).[43]

---

41. For recent treatments of this topic see Kugel, "The Story of Dinah," and Baarda, "The Shechem Episode," 11–73.

42. Kugel ("The Story of Dinah") and Baarda ("The Shechem Episode"), following the reading of a single manuscript, try to explain why Levi advised that the sons of Hamor *not* be circumcised. From a text-critical point of view, this reading must be regarded as secondary. *ALD* 1–2 is too fragmentary to allow any conclusion as to a possible *Vorlage* of the story in the *Testament of Levi*. Here also Jacob and Reuben are mentioned together, and it is clear that the Shechemites were asked to circumcise themselves; it is, however, unclear who asked them. The subject of the introductory phrase "we said to them" is uncertain, but there is no reason to exclude Levi.

43. Compare *T. Levi* 8:14 and *T. Reub.* 6:8b.

Indeed, there is little evidence for a positive interest in Levi in early Christianity.[44]

Given the nature of their work, the author(s) of the *Testaments of the Twelve Patriarchs* had to include Levi. They used traditional material about Levi known to us from the *Aramaic Levi Document,* probably in the form of a document very much like the *Aramaic Levi Document.* Apparently they followed it rather closely, abbreviating at times, correcting inconsistencies, and adding references to the coming of Jesus Christ where it seemed appropriate. In doing so, however, they honored the position of Levi and his tribe in Israel between the time of the sons of Jacob and the coming of Jesus Christ.

We note that in the last chapter of the *Testament of Levi,* the patriarch's final exhortation is followed by the words, "And we answered our father saying: 'Before the Lord we will walk, according to his law'" (19:2). This "we" is not found in the other testaments and indicates that the author(s) regarded himself as a "son" of Levi. The phrase would have been at home in the *Aramaic Levi Document* (where, unfortunately, it is not preserved). Yet Christians kept (if not coined) it. Perhaps we may point to Justin Martyr's description of the Christians as "the true high priestly race" (*Dial.* 116:3).[45]

Joseph and Aseneth

With *Joseph and Aseneth,* a romance written for Greek-speaking Jews and Jewish sympathizers in Egypt, we enter an entirely different world. Most scholars date this writing between 100 B.C.E. and 100 C.E.

The first part of the work (chaps. 1–21) describes the encounter between Joseph, a pious man of God, and Aseneth, who converts to the God of Israel. She meets Joseph when he visits the house of her father Pentephres, and subsequently falls in love with him. Joseph's obedience to God and his chastity make Aseneth realize that she will be worthy of Joseph only when she gives up

---

44. See Hollander and de Jonge, *Testaments,* 76–79; and de Jonge, "Hippolytus' 'Benedictions.'"

45. See further de Jonge, "The Testament of Levi and 'Aramaic Levi,'" 383–85.

idol worship and serves the Jewish God. Chapters 10–19 recount Aseneth's repentance and conversion; she is the ideal proselyte and a patroness of all proselytes. In the second part of the story (chaps. 22–29), Joseph's brothers come to the fore. Most of them remain loyal to the Pharaoh and successfully protect Aseneth from the attacks of Pharaoh's son.

The first two brothers to be mentioned in this second part are Simeon and Levi, the sons of Leah (22:11–13). Later, Pharaoh's son, who has heard about their exploits at Shechem, seeks their help in a plot to kill Joseph and to take Aseneth as his wife; they refuse (22:1–17). The prince then turns to Dan, Gad, Naphtali, and Asher, the sons of the maidservants, already introduced as being envious and hostile toward Joseph (22:11). Through a subterfuge, he tricks them into becoming his partners in crime (chap. 24).[46] The plot, however, ends in disaster; Levi perceives the situation and mobilizes the sons of Leah, who kill two thousand men (26:6; 27:6). The lives of the four hostile brothers are spared only because Aseneth intercedes for them (chap. 28). Due to Levi's generosity, Pharaoh's son is brought back to his father, only to die a few days later. Pharaoh himself then falls ill, dies, and is succeeded by Joseph (chap. 29).

Let us look more closely at the portrait of Levi. At his introduction in the story (22:13), he is called "one who attached himself to the Lord" (cf. *Jub.* 31:16), "a prudent man" (συνίων). In a sense he is the Israelite counterpart of the proselytes represented by Aseneth, which may be why these two are so closely linked in this part of the story. We note that in Deut 4:5–8, Israel, in its observance of God's commandments, is called "a wise and discerning people" (v. 6; LXX λαὸς σοφὸς καὶ ἐπιστήμων) by the nations. By this standard, too, Levi is a good Israelite. The emphasis on his prudence and wisdom reminds us of the wisdom elements in the *Aramaic Levi Document* and the *Testament of Levi* (and elsewhere in the *Testaments of the Twelve Patriarchs*).

---

46. See, for Dan's anger against Joseph, *T. Dan* 1:4–8 (cf. *T. Zeb.* 4:7–13), and, for Gad's hatred, *T. Gad* 1:4–2:4. The reason given is that Joseph told his father that the sons of Zilpah and Bilhah, against the judgment of Judah and Reuben, were slaying the best of the flock (*T. Gad* 1:6; cf. Gen 37:2). On this see also G. Delling, "Einwirkungen der Sprache," 29–56, esp. pp. 49–51.

Levi is then characterized in 22:13 as "a prophet of the Most High...and sharp-sighted with his eyes"; "he used to see letters (γράμματα) written in heaven by the finger of God, and he knew the unspeakable mysteries of the Most High God and revealed them to Aseneth in secret." Again we are reminded of Levi's visions in the *Aramaic Levi Document* and the *Testament of Levi;* one should note, in particular, that in *T. Levi* 8:2 Levi receives "the ephod of prophecy" and that, according to 2:10, "he will declare his [God's] mysteries to men." Interestingly, however, *Joseph and Aseneth* nowhere mentions Levi's priesthood. The "letters written in heaven" may refer to the "Book of the Living" mentioned on the occasion of Aseneth's conversion in 15:4, 12b. In 15:12b, "all names in the book are unspeakable (ἄρρητα)." To this compare 16:14, where "the ineffable (ἀπόρρητα) mysteries of the Most High" are revealed to Aseneth. This interpretation receives support from 22:13b, where Levi is said to "see her [Aseneth's] place of rest in the highest."[47] Delling and Burchard[48] refer to the mention of "heavenly tablets" in *Jub.* 32:21; *T. Levi* 6:8; *1 Enoch* 103:2; 106:19; etc.[49]

Levi is also called a prophet in 23:8; he is said to be "sharp-sighted with (both) his mind and his eyes," for "he used to read what is written in the heart of men." In fact, he knows "the intention of [Simeon's] heart" and is able to prevent his attack on Pharaoh's son.[50] In 26:6 Levi "perceives in his spirit as a prophet" the attack planned on Aseneth and acts accordingly.[51] This recalls the mention of Simeon and Levi's battle around Shechem in chapter 23. Pharaoh's son praises them for it. The brothers, however, characterize their action as having been conducted on behalf of God and with God's help (v. 14; cf. Jdt 9:2; *T. Levi* 5:3; 6:1).

The brothers call themselves "men who worship God" (θεοσεβεῖς); thus they are not allowed to "injure anyone in any way"

---

47. On this expression see Delling, "Einwirkungen der Sprache," 49–50.

48. See Delling, "Einwirkungen der Sprache," 49; and Burchard, "Joseph and Aseneth," *OTP* 2.139, note on 22:13.

49. For further examples see Hollander and de Jonge, *Testaments,* commentary on *T. Ash.* 2:10.

50. Burchard, "Joseph and Aseneth," *OTP* 2.240, in his note on 23:8 rightly points to Luke 7:39; Mark 2:8 par.; and John 2:25.

51. A similar idea may be expressed in 28:15–17. Levi knows that his brothers are nearby in a thicket of reeds, but in order to prevent their punishment does not tell anyone.

(23:12). As Levi tells Simeon, "[I]t does not befit us to repay evil for evil."[52] This theme recurs in chap. 28, where the sons of Bilhah and Zilpah ask Aseneth for forgiveness (see esp. 28:5). Aseneth, in her endeavor to save the hostile brothers, appeals to the principle of not repaying evil with evil in her words to the brothers in general (v. 10) and to Simeon in particular (v. 14). It is Levi again who prevents Benjamin from killing Pharaoh's son (29:3).

The rule formulated in these sections is one of the foremost ethical commands in the second part of *Joseph and Aseneth.* Burchard points out that the closest parallels are found in Rom 12:17; 1 Thess 5:15; and 1 Pet 3:9.[53] In chapter 29 Levi's attitude resembles love of one's enemy as prescribed in Matt 5:43–48 (cf. Luke 6:27–28, 32–36) and as illustrated in the parable of the good Samaritan (Luke 10:29–37).[54] On the other hand, Levi acts as one who exhibits clemency to the enemy he has defeated; the situation is thus different from that depicted in the Christian scriptures. Still, the attitude advocated and practiced by Levi and Aseneth goes beyond the forgiveness and magnanimity displayed by Joseph toward his brothers in Gen 50:15–22 (cf. *T. Sim.* 4:4–6; *T. Zeb.* 8:4–5; *T. Jos.* 17:4–7).

In conclusion, the picture of Levi in *Joseph and Aseneth* shows points of agreement with that found in *Jubilees,* the *Aramaic Levi Document,* and the *Testaments of the Twelve Patriarchs. Joseph and Aseneth* 23 contains an explicit reference to the Shechem story, and it is clear that the author is acquainted with retellings of the story like the ones analyzed above. The author may even have deliberately portrayed Pharaoh's son as a counterpart to Shechem, and Aseneth as a new Dinah, with Levi and Simeon as her protectors.[55] In any case, in this romance Levi, who plays a more central role than Simeon or any of the other brothers

---

52. For the expression οὐ προσήκει ἀνδρὶ θεοσεβεῖ in connection with Joseph, see also 8:5–7; 21:1.

53. This is in his notes on 23:9 and 29:5, "Joseph and Aseneth," *OTP* 2.240 and 2.247.

54. The possibility of Christian additions and embellishments here cannot be excluded. See also Levi's statement to Benjamin in 29:4, "put your sword back in its place," a nearly exact verbal parallel to Matt 26:52 (cf. John 18:11). Certainly passages like these provided an additional reason for reading and copying *Joseph and Aseneth* in Christian circles.

55. See Aptowitzer, "Asenath," 239–306. Aptowitzer also points to Jewish sources identifying Aseneth as the daughter of Dinah and Shechem.

except Joseph, is no longer important as a priest; he is rather the prototype of the ideal Israelite (like Joseph), and one "who has attached himself to the Lord" (like Aseneth). He is prudent, wise, and possesses prophetic insight. He is ready to protect God's servants on earth, yet is also compassionate toward their adversaries.

Demetrius and Theodotus

This section treats briefly some fragments from the Jewish exegete-historian Demetrius (fl. 220–200 B.C.E., probably in Egypt) and the Jewish epic poet Theodotus (probably late second century B.C.E.).[56] Demetrius, who writes to show the Greeks the antiquity of Moses and the Jewish people, stays very close to the biblical text. Theodotus is more interesting for our purposes, because in his poem about Shechem he incorporates nonbiblical traditions about Simeon and Levi's exploits that are also attested elsewhere.

Demetrius is most interested in the historical chronology of the (Greek) Bible. The dates that he gives concerning Levi are located in a long fragment about Jacob and his offspring (Eusebius, *Praep. evang.* 9.21.1–19). After seven years with Laban, Jacob married his two daughters; within seven more years, twelve children were born to him, with Levi coming in the sixth month of the tenth year (secs. 3–5; cf. Gen 29:21–30:24). Jacob arrives at Shechem (sec. 8), where, after ten years of peaceful coexistence, the events narrated in Genesis 34 take place. These are briefly summarized in section 9, where again the chronological element prevails.

Demetrius next mentions that Levi was forty-three when he went to Egypt (sec. 17; cf. Gen 46:11). The fragment ends with a long passage (sec. 19) in which Levi, Kohath, Amram, Aaron, and Moses are mentioned (cf. Exod 6:16–20).[57]

---

56. These fragments are preserved in the *Praeparatio evangelica* of Eusebius, who, in turn, took them from *On the Jews,* compiled by Alexander Polyhistor (mid–first century B.C.E.).

57. N. Walter, reconstructing the text by adding two passages presumably omitted by Polyhistor, points out that Demetrius's purpose is to explain the figure of 430 years given

Demetrius's chronological interests may be compared to those of *Jubilees;* both are concerned to develop more precise and systematic presentations of biblical chronology. Demetrius, however, shows no concern to explicate or expand the biblical account of Levi.

The fragment of Theodotus quoted by Eusebius (*Praep. evang.* 9.22.1–11, immediately after the citation of Demetrius) is quite different. Theodotus describes the city of Shechem and Jacob's arrival there. As in Genesis 34, the rape of Dinah leads to negotiations over a proper marriage.[58] Jacob, the sole negotiator (secs. 5–7), insists on circumcision, since "Hebrews" may not intermarry with foreigners. Theodotus emphasizes that circumcision is an "unshaken" command of God to Abraham. Simeon, however, refuses to accept what has been done to his sister and vows revenge. He asks Levi to join him, appealing to a divine oracle (secs. 8–9). God influenced Levi and Simeon to think in this way, Theodotus says, because the people of Shechem were impious and required punishment. The two brothers then attack Shechem (secs. 10–11); only later do the other brothers appear on the scene.

Theodotus's retelling of the Shechem event reflects, at several points, traditions found in other nonbiblical sources. There is, first, an emphasis on avoiding intermarriage (cf. *Jubilees* 30). Remarkably, Jacob is here the chief negotiator; Simeon and Levi appear only later, and the other brothers only at the end.

We have already seen that in *Jubilees* and the *Testaments of the Twelve Patriarchs,* the two brothers are portrayed as carrying out a divine command. Theodotus, however, explicitly refers to a divine oracle, probably Gen 15:18–21. His description of the evil deeds of the Shechemites is similar to *T. Levi* 6:8–10. The detail that Simeon killed Hamor and Levi killed Shechem is also found in *T. Levi* 6:4. For Theodotus, Simeon is the principal figure in gaining revenge, just as in Jdt 9:2. Levi is only his assistant, and in no way functions in a priestly role.

---

in Exod 12:40 LXX for the time spent by the Israelites in Canaan and Egypt. See Walter's notes on sec. 19 in *Fragmente jüdisch-hellenistischer Exegeten,* 289–90.

58. Dinah visited Shechem on the occasion of a festival, a detail also mentioned by Josephus, *Ant.* 1.337–41.

Theodotus is not interested in Simeon and Levi as individuals; he mentions them only because Genesis 34 portrays them as leaders on this occasion. The principal conflict is between the inhabitants of Shechem and the sons of Jacob. This may reflect Jewish-Samaritan hostility, perhaps at the time of John Hyrcanus, who destroyed the Samaritan temple in 129/8 and the city of Samaria in 109 B.C.E.

Other Jewish Sources

Levi appears also in other extrabiblical sources that echo the biblical narrative. Pseudo-Philo, *Bib. Ant.* 8:7, cites Gen 34:25–26 in an abbreviated form, while Josephus, *Ant.* 1.337–41, gives a version of the Shechem story in which the awkward features are glossed over. Philo refers to the attack on Shechem in *Migr. Abr.* 224 and *Mut. nom.* 200. In the former, he characterizes Simeon and Levi as people who "listen to wisdom (φρόνησις) and are its pupils." Levi as priest symbolizes for him the true service of God; see, for example, *Sacrif.* 119–20 and *Somn.* 2.34. Characteristically, 4 Macc 2:19–20 censures the action taken by Simeon and Levi against Shechem (cf. Genesis 49) because they failed to control their emotions by reason.

Summary and Conclusions

In comparison with other biblical figures such as Abraham, Joseph, and Moses, Levi can hardly be said to occupy a conspicuous place in the Jewish and Christian literature of the Hellenistic and Roman periods. There are two main factors that account for his appearance in a number of writings: (1) his role in the Shechem episode of Genesis 34; and (2) the existence of a group of levitical priests who wished to extol him. It is also worth noting that in the pseudepigraphical writings in which Levi does appear, the overall image of him remains constant, if not static; there is no discernible evidence of a development in the portrayal of his character.

In the literature discussed above, Levi's role in the Shechem episode is normally evaluated positively. The negative aspects of the story, evident in both Genesis 34 and 49, are exploited only in 4 Maccabees, which advocates the control of reason over the passions, including anger. But Jacob's reproaches of Levi are ignored by Demetrius and Theodotus, as well as in Pseudo-Philo, Josephus's *Jewish Antiquities,* and Philo's remarks.

In Deuteronomy 33 and Malachi 2, Levi is first and foremost the ancestor of all priests. This fact is acknowledged by Philo, but seems unimportant to Ben Sira, in whose "Praise of the Fathers" (Sirach 44–50) Levi does not appear.

The author of *Jubilees* combines Genesis 34, the only extant biblical story about Levi, with his appointment to the priesthood. Using the pattern of Phinehas, *Jubilees* interprets Levi's pillage of Shechem as an act of zeal, and his priesthood as the reward for this deed (*Jub.* 30:18–20; cf. Num 25:11–13; Sir 45:23–24; 1 Macc 2:54). According to *Jubilees,* Levi was informed of his priestly calling in a dream. The exact contents of this vision are, however, not given. This fact suggests that a dream of Levi, important in determining his vocation, was a traditional element; otherwise, the allusion to it would be superfluous. The author of *Jubilees* may not have described the dream in order to avoid being repetitive. Before Levi's dream, the author gives a portrait of the ideal levitical priest (replacing Jacob's unwelcome blessing in Genesis 49). Isaac's blessing of Levi in *Jubilees* 31 consists of traditional material that depicts the priesthood's dignities in laudatory terms. Another traditional explanation of Levi's appointment to the priesthood (he being the tenth son of Jacob when counted backward) is connected here with the command to give a second tithe to the priests.

The author of the *Aramaic Levi Document* clearly had access to much of the same material as the author of *Jubilees.* In the *Aramaic Levi Document,* Levi probably had two visions, one preceding the expedition against Shechem and the other following it. *Jubilees* does not mention the first vision, but alludes to the second in 32:1. The *Aramaic Levi Document* mentions, but does not elaborate on, Isaac's blessing of Levi. Rather, it focuses on Isaac's lengthy instructions to Levi concerning the priesthood. Interestingly, the picture of the ideal priest in *Jubilees* barely mentions sacrifice, whereas Isaac's instructions in the *Aramaic Levi Document* are mainly concerned with offerings and their proper presentation.

Clearly these two books have traditional material, possibly even written traditions, in common. However the agreements are rarely literal, and in view of the fragmentary state of the *Aramaic Levi Document* it is impossible to define the literary relations with *Jubilees* more precisely.

The literary connection between the *Aramaic Levi Document* and the *Testament of Levi* is clearer. The Christian author of the *Testaments of the Twelve Patriarchs,* a collector of traditions, used a form of the Aramaic writing to flesh out his *Testament of Levi.* The Shechem episode is not taken up to answer a christological concern; the story is told, it seems, mainly because it is the only biblical story about Levi, while no other substantial historical traditions about Levi had developed outside the Bible. The *Aramaic Levi Document* (or a writing very similar to it) offered the author of the *Testaments of the Twelve Patriarchs* the requisite material for the "autobiographical" section of the farewell discourse. No significant changes in the image of Levi occur, besides the limitation on the time of his priesthood.

The reasons behind the composition of the *Aramaic Levi Document* remain unclear, because the extant fragments lack sufficient context to detect the writing's tendency. But in both *Jubilees* and the *Aramaic Levi Document* (as well as in the *Testament of Levi*), Levi is the son of Jacob who is rewarded with the priesthood for his zealous revenge on Shechem. The blessing of Levi by Isaac in *Jubilees* depicts the ideal priest and his rights, and both *Jubilees* and the *Aramaic Levi Document* stress the eternity of Levi's priesthood. Indeed, since it is likely that priests (experts in "teaching the law") wrote these (and other) Jewish pseudepigrapha, it is hardly surprising that Levi and his descendants are presented in a favorable light.

The figure of Levi does not, however, seem to be used as a vehicle for any special "ideological" priestly claims in the pseudepigrapha. There was, of course, an image of the ideal priest, and priestly authors did not hesitate to disseminate this image and project it back into history. However, they seem not to have made

Levi the hero of new stories beyond the bounds of credibility. The Jerusalem priests, in fact, had no need for such justification. From the Persian period until the late Hasmonean (when the offices of king and high priest were separated), they wielded all official local power.

In *Joseph and Aseneth*, Levi figures as a paragon of wisdom and piety. Elements from the traditional exegesis of the Shechem incident are adopted — one thinks especially of the sword given to Levi and Simeon. It is also obvious, however, that presenting a special honorific image of Levi was not a main priority of this author. The author of *Joseph and Aseneth* is concerned to contrast Jews, proselytes, and pagans. Because of his reputation as a zealous priest, Levi is allotted one of the more attractive roles in the story. As a virtuous character, Levi is ascribed such qualities as prudence, wisdom, and even prophecy. But the author has no special interest in Levi for his own sake, and, for this reason, this romance offers little significant independent information about the development of the figure of Levi.

Bibliography

Jubilees

The book of *Jubilees* survives in full only in Ethiopic. Substantial fragments of a Latin text were published in 1861 by A.-M. Ceriani. Smaller fragments were found in Hebrew (at Qumran), as well as in Syriac and Greek (mainly quotations in early Christian literature). The edition and translation of the Ethiopic text used here are by J. C. VanderKam, *The Book of Jubilees* (2 vols.; CSCO 510–11; Louvain: Peeters, 1989). In an appendix to his edition, Vander-Kam collects most of the extant fragments. Since then, VanderKam and J. T. Milik have published additional fragments in "The First Jubilees Manuscript from Qumran Cave 4: A Preliminary Publication," *JBL* 110 (1991) 243–70, and "A Preliminary Publication of a Jubilees Manuscript from Qumran Cave 4: 4QJub^a (4Q219)," *Bib* 73 (1992) 62–83. The Greek fragments of *Jub* 31:14, as found in A.-M. Denis, *Fragmenta pseudepigraphorum quae supersunt graeca* (PVTG 3; Leiden: Brill, 1970) 96–97, are not quotations, but a summary of the story by Syncellus the Chronographer. The German translation by K. Berger,

Das Buch der Jubiläen (JSHRZ 2, 3; Gütersloh: Mohn, 1981), deserves special mention because of its useful annotations. A detailed analysis of the principles and techniques underlying the exegesis in *Jubilees* is given by J. C. Endres, *Biblical Interpretation in the Book of Jubilees* (CBQMS 18; Washington, D.C.: Catholic Biblical Association of America, 1987).

The Aramaic Levi Document

The Genizah fragments are easily accessible in R. H. Charles, *The Greek Versions of the Testaments of the Twelve Patriarchs* (Oxford: Clarendon, 1908), appendix III. Their Greek counterparts are found in the apparatus at *T. Levi* 2:3 and 18:2 in M. de Jonge et al., eds., *The Testaments of the Twelve Patriarchs: A Critical Edition of the Greek Text* (PVTG 1, 2; Leiden: Brill, 1978); see also n. 19. Compare also J. C. Greenfield and M. E. Stone, "Remarks on the Aramaic *Testament of Levi* from the Geniza," *RB* 86 (1979) 214–30 (with a list of revised readings).

The Qumran fragments were published in D. Barthélemy and J. T. Milik, *Qumran Cave 1* (DJD 1; Oxford: Clarendon, 1955) 87–91; J. T. Milik, "Le testament de Lévi en araméen: Fragment de la grotte 4 de Qumrân," *RB* 62 (1955) 398–406; and idem, *The Books of Enoch: Aramaic Fragments of Qumran Cave 4* (Oxford: Clarendon, 1976) 23–24. All the (then) available material (together with German translations) is found in K. Beyer, *Die aramäischen Texte vom Toten Meer* (Göttingen: Vandenhoeck & Ruprecht, 1984) 188–211. See now also idem, *Die aramäischen Texte vom Toten Meer: Ergänzungsband* (Göttingen: Vandenhoeck & Ruprecht, 1994) 71–78.

In *The Dead Sea Scrolls Uncovered* (Shaftesbury: Element, 1992), R. H. Eisenman and M. Wise have published known and unknown fragments of *4Q213* and *4Q214* (pp. 136–41). A reconstruction of the *Aramaic Levi Document* on the basis of all available material has been attempted by R. A. Kugler, *From Patriarch to Priest: The Levi-Priestly Tradition from Aramaic Levi to Testament of Levi* (SBLEJL 9; Atlanta: Scholars Press, 1996).

The official edition of all the fragments was assigned to M. E. Stone and the late J. C. Greenfield. It appeared in *Qumran Cave 4.XVII: Parabiblical Texts, part 3* (DJD 22; Oxford: Clarendon, 1996).

Greenfield and Stone translated all the material published at the time in appendix 3 of H. W. Hollander and M. de Jonge, *The Testaments of the Twelve Patriarchs: A Commentary* (SVTP 8; Leiden: Brill, 1985). This translation is followed in this essay.

For an earlier assessment of the evidence see M. de Jonge, "The Testament of Levi and 'Aramaic Levi,'" *RevQ* 13 (1988) 367–85 (= M. de Jonge, *Jewish Eschatology, Early Christian Christology, and the "Testaments of the Twelve Patriarchs": Collected Essays* [ed. H. J. de Jonge; NovTSup 63; Leiden: Brill, 1991] 244–62). See also G. J. Brooke, "4QTestament of Levi[d] and the Messianic Servant High Priest," in *From Jesus to John: Essays on Jesus and New Testament Christology in Honour of Marinus de Jonge* (ed. M. C. de Boer; JSNTSup 84; Sheffield: JSOT, 1993) 83–100.

Kohath, Amram, and Moses

The texts of the farewell discourses of Kohath, Amram, and Moses were consulted in the following editions: E. Puech, "Le Testament de Qahat en araméen de la grotte 4 (*4QTQah*)," *RevQ* 16 (1991) 23–54; J. T. Milik, "4Q Visions de 'Amram et une citation d'Origène," *RB* 79 (1972) 77–97; and J. Tromp, *The Assumption of Moses: A Critical Edition with Commentary* (SVTP 10; Leiden: Brill, 1993). For 4QAmram, compare also Eisenman and Wise, *The Dead Sea Scrolls Uncovered,* 151–56.

The Testaments of the Twelve Patriarchs

We have used M. de Jonge et al., eds., *The Testaments of the Twelve Patriarchs: A Critical Edition of the Greek Text* (PVTG 1, 2; Leiden: Brill, 1978). Based on new material and a different view of the history of the text, it has superseded the earlier edition of R. H. Charles, *The Greek Versions of the Testaments of the Twelve Patriarchs* (Oxford: Clarendon, 1908). For translation and commentary see H. W. Hollander and M. de Jonge, *The Testaments of the Twelve Patriarchs: A Commentary* (SVTP 8; Leiden: Brill, 1985).

For a different assessment of Levi in the *Testaments of the Twelve Patriarchs,* see A. Hultgård, "The Ideal 'Levite,' the Davidic Messiah and the Saviour Priest in the Testaments of the Twelve Patriarchs," in *Ideal Figures in Ancient Judaism: Profiles and Paradigms* (ed. J. J. Collins and G. W. E. Nickelsburg; SBLSCS 12; Chico, Calif.: Scholars Press, 1980) 93–110. This is based on his extensive earlier work on the *Testaments of the Twelve Patriarchs,* published in *L'eschatologie des Testaments des Douze Patriarches* (2 vols.; Acta Universitatis Upsaliensis, Historia Religionum 6–7; Stockholm: Almqvist & Wiksell, 1977, 1981).

Joseph and Aseneth

We have used C. Burchard's preliminary edition of the Greek text; this can be found in the *Dielheimer Blätter zum Alten Testament* 14 (1979) 2–53, and 16 (1982) 37–39; and in A.-M. Denis, *Concordance grecque des pseudépigraphes d'Ancien Testament* (Louvain-la-Neuve: Université Catholique de Louvain, Institut Orientaliste, 1987) 851–59.

The textual history of *Joseph and Aseneth* is extremely complex: see C. Burchard, "Der jüdische Asenethroman und seine Nachwirkung: Von Egeria zu Anna Katharina Emmerick oder von Moses aus Aggel zu Karl Kerényi," *ANRW* 20, 1, 543–667. Another recent edition, that of M. Philonenko, *Joseph et Aséneth: Introduction, texte critique et notes* (SPB 13; Leiden: Brill, 1968) gives a shorter text. On the relationship between the long and short texts, see now also A. Standhartinger, *Das Frauenbild im Judentum der hellenistischen Zeit: Ein Beitrag anhand von "Joseph und Aseneth"* (AGJU 26; Leiden: Brill, 1995) 219–25.

The present authors have benefited from Burchard's insightful notes in his translations with introductions and notes in *Joseph und Aseneth* (JSHRZ 2, 4; Gütersloh: Mohn, 1983), and "Joseph and Aseneth," *OTP* 2.177–247. His *Gesammelte Studien zu Joseph und Aseneth* (SVTP 13; Leiden: Brill, 1996) appeared after the completion of this article.

Demetrius and Theodotus

The fragments of Demetrius in Eusebius, *Praep. evang.* 9, 21, 1–19, and of Theodotus in Eusebius, *Praep. evang.* 9, 22, 1–11, are easily accessible in Denis, *Fragmenta pseudepigraphorum*, 175–79 and 204–7. For introductions, translations, and notes (as well as secondary literature), see (for Demetrius) N. Walter, *Fragmente jüdisch-hellenistischer Exegeten: Aristoboulos, Demetrios, Aristeas* (JSHRZ 3, 2; Gütersloh: Mohn, 1975) 280–92; and J. Hanson, "Demetrius the Chronographer," *OTP* 2.841–54; and, for Theodotus, N. Walter, *Pseudepigraphische jüdisch-hellenistische Dichtung* (JSHRZ 4, 3; Gütersloh: Mohn, 1983) 154–63; and F. Fallon, "Theodotus," *OTP* 2.785–93.

Other Jewish Sources

On the writings discussed in this essay and other Jewish traditions on Levi, consult L. Ginzberg, *The Legends of the Jews* (7 vols.; Philadelphia: Jewish Publication Society of America, 1909–38). See in particular the sections "Jacob" (1.309–423), "Joseph" (2.1–184), and "The Sons of Jacob" (2.185–222), as well as the notes on these sections (5.270–380).

Additional Note on Christian Sources

There is as yet no treatment of the figure of Levi in Christian sources comparable to that of G. W. E. Nickelsburg on Aaron ("Aaron," *RAC Suppl.* 1.1–11). At present one may consult H. W. Hollander and M. de Jonge, *The Testaments of the Twelve Patriarchs: A Commentary* (SVTP 8; Leiden: Brill, 1985) introduction, sec. 8.4, "Jesus as (High-)Priest" (pp. 76–79); and M. de Jonge, "Hippolytus' 'Benedictions of Isaac, Jacob, and Moses' and the *Testaments of the Twelve Patriarchs*," most easily accessible in M. de Jonge, *Jewish Eschatology, Early Christian Christology, and the Testaments of the Twelve Patriarchs: Collected Essays* (ed. H. J. de Jonge; NovTSup 63; Leiden: Brill, 1991) 204–19.

THE PORTRAYAL OF JOSEPH IN HELLENISTIC JEWISH AND EARLY CHRISTIAN LITERATURE

Harm W. Hollander

Introduction

Few biblical stories have left as many traces in world literature as the Joseph narrative in Genesis 37–50. Indeed, few other biblical figures have fascinated subsequent interpreters as much as Jacob's favorite son Joseph. Jewish, Samaritan, Christian, Muslim, and other authors have employed the story of Joseph in varied cultural contexts, interpreting, paraphrasing, or adapting the biblical account. This process started with Hellenistic Jewish authors such as Artapanus, Demetrius, Philo, and Josephus, and has continued to modern times with writers like Goethe and Thomas Mann.

It would, of course, be impossible in a study of this scope to take into account all the various attempts to retell the Joseph story. This chapter rather focuses on the first recorded efforts of Jewish and Christian writers to interpret and communicate the biblical story of Joseph. These efforts were in every case generated by the specific concerns of individual authors and directed toward specific groups of readers.

The Image of Joseph in the Hebrew Bible

The story of Joseph as related in Genesis 37–50 describes how Joseph, the son of Jacob and of Jacob's favorite wife Rachel, was loved by his father but hated by his brothers; how he was almost killed by the latter and was finally sold to foreign merchants who were on their way to Egypt; how he became a successful steward in the house of Potiphar, Pharaoh's captain of the guard; how he was almost seduced by Potiphar's wife, and was falsely accused by her and sent to prison; how he interpreted Pharaoh's dreams and became governor of the land of Egypt; and how, finally, he met his brothers again and arranged for his family to move from Canaan to Egypt.

This story with its twin central themes — namely, Joseph's political career, and the tensions within Jacob's family ending in a reunion of all its members in Egypt — seems at first glance quite homogeneous. Source-critical research, however, has shown that the story, far from being a unified narrative, was composed from two or more sources, and was edited at its final stage by a priestly redactor.

Still, the overall picture of Joseph in this narrative is clear: he is a hero who, in spite of setbacks, remains faithful to God and becomes a ruler of Egypt, capable of saving his family (later to become coextensive with the Israelite people) from destruction.

Nevertheless, Joseph's traits as described in this story are not entirely positive. First, he is said to have brought to his father a "bad report" on some on his brothers who were shepherding the flocks (Gen 37:2). Moreover, he is "rebuked" by his father after having described his dreams which predicted his future dominion over his brothers and parents (Gen 37:5–11). Nevertheless, these slightly negative depictions of Joseph are insignificant when compared with the thoroughly positive general description of him presented in Genesis 37–50.

With a few exceptions, the references to Joseph elsewhere in the OT do not reflect this same positive image. The exceptions are Deut 33:13–17, Moses' blessing of Joseph, which is modeled on Jacob's blessing of Joseph in Gen 49:22–26; and Ps 105:16–22, which gives a picture of Joseph reminiscent of that found in Genesis, and which sums up, as it were, Joseph's vicissitudes as told in the Genesis story and interprets that story in terms of divine providence.

In the majority of OT references to Joseph, however, one encounters the image of Joseph as the ancestor of the tribes of Ephraim and Manasseh, which constituted the bulk of the Northern Kingdom of Israel (as opposed to the Southern Kingdom of Judah). In this regard, the name of Joseph represented a geopolitical reality, which became a symbol of religious apostasy in the eyes of certain pious Israelites and Jews. This is because after Solomon's kingship, the Northern Kingdom rejected the house of David and chose Jeroboam as its king. Several centuries later, the inhabitants of the Northern Kingdom were conquered by the Assyrians, an event considered by some to be divine punishment for their idolatry and apostasy. In the Psalms and prophets[1] we find reflections on the negative role that the Northern Kingdom, or "house of Joseph," played in the history of Israel, together with comments on the future restoration of Israel and Judah.[2] Finally, in certain places where we might expect Joseph to be mentioned, reference to him is lacking.[3]

All of this indicates that the image of Joseph in the OT is two-sided. On the one hand, he is a hero and the savior of the Israelites. On the other hand, he may, as the ancestor of the Northern Kingdom, be blamed for its idolatry and apostasy. This dual image recurs in subsequent portrayals of Joseph, though the positive view clearly dominates.

The Figure of Joseph in Selected Jewish Apocrypha and Pseudepigrapha

In early extrabiblical Jewish writings, such as those found in the apocrypha and pseudepigrapha, Joseph appears primarily as one

---

1. See, e.g., Ps 78:67; 81; Ezek 37:15–22; Amos 5:6, 15; 6:6; Zech 10:6.

2. Cf. van der Merwe, "Joseph," 221–32, esp. pp. 231–32; Korteweg, "Naphtali's Visions," 261–90, esp. pp. 282–90; E. Hilgert, "Dual Image," 5–7; Kugel, *Potiphar's House,* 14–18.

3. So, e.g., in 1 Chr 16:8–36, where, though this passage is strongly reminiscent of Psalm 105, Joseph (cf. Ps 105:16–22) is not mentioned at all.

of Israel's illustrious ancestors, and a hero of the Genesis account. Thus he is called "the leader of his brothers, the support of the people" in the Greek version of Sir 49:15.[4] Joseph is mentioned again in the wisdom hymn in Wisdom of Solomon 10, where he is placed among those of Israel's ancestors who were guided, protected, and rewarded by Wisdom. Here it is said that Joseph was sold, restrained from committing sin,[5] was accompanied by Wisdom while in prison,[6] and finally was given the scepter of kingship (10:13–14). In this passage, Joseph's encounter with Potiphar's wife is understood as the central episode of Genesis 37–50. This episode is interpreted as a time of affliction which led first to Joseph's imprisonment, but finally to his exaltation; all was due to Wisdom.[7]

1 and 4 Maccabees feature similar views of Joseph. When Mattathias exhorts his sons to "remember the deeds of the fathers," he refers among others to Joseph, who "in the time of his distress kept the commandment,[8] and became lord of Egypt" (1 Macc 2:53). Here too Joseph's political achievement is connected with, and seen as a consequence of, the steadfastness and devotion shown in his confrontation with Potiphar's wife.

---

4. ἡγούμενος ἀδελφῶν, στήριγμα λαοῦ. This phrase is not found in the Hebrew text of Ben Sira, where Joseph's funeral is referred to (cf. Gen 50:25–26; Exod 13:19; Josh 24:32). The first statement of the Greek addition, which portrays Joseph as "the leader of his brothers," is reminiscent of Gen 49:26 (LXX, ἐπὶ κορυφῆς ὧν ἡγήσατο ἀδελφῶν; cf. Deut 33:16 LXX, ἐπὶ κορυφῆς δοξασθεὶς ἐν ἀδελφοῖς; MT has in both passages נזיר אחיו). This may refer to Joseph's dominion over his brothers, as was the situation in Egypt, or more specifically to the attribution of the rights of the firstborn to Joseph (cf. 1 Chr 5:1–2). The second clause, "the support of the people," probably refers to Joseph's role as savior of the people of Israel. On this passage see also van der Merwe, "Joseph," esp. pp. 224–25; Niehoff, *Figure of Joseph*, 49–50.

5. ἐξ ἁμαρτίας ἐρρύσατο αὐτόν. The "sin" referred to probably stands for the clutches of Potiphar's wife.

6. εἰς λάκκον…ἐν δεσμοῖς. Both terms refer to Joseph's imprisonment after his refusal to sleep with Potiphar's wife. For the use of λάκκος, see also Gen 40:15; *T. Jos.* 9:2.

7. The Genesis story already contains references to Joseph's wisdom and knowledge, especially in the context of his ability to interpret dreams (Gen 41:33, 39; cf. Ps 105:22; *Jub.* 40:5; Philo, *De Jos.* 106; Josephus, *Ant.* 2.9, 87). Although the story as a whole does not belong to the category of early wisdom writing, as von Rad has tried to prove ("Josephsgeschichte," 1.272–80; "Joseph Narrative," 292–300), it cannot be denied that wisdom elements are present. It is, however, true that "the Joseph story lives in an atmosphere larger than wisdom tradition" (so Coats, "The Joseph Story," 285–97, esp. p. 296).

8. ἐφύλαξεν ἐντολήν, which is reminiscent of Gen 39:9, where Joseph rejects his master's wife with the words, "How then could I do this great wickedness, and sin against God?"

In literary contexts where Joseph's encounter with Potiphar's wife is at issue, one virtue comes to the fore: Joseph's "temperance" or "chastity" (σωφροσύνη). Thus, for example, in 4 Macc 2:1–4, in the context of a discussion of reason (λογισμός) and temperance, Joseph is praised as a prime example of these virtues: "For when he was young and in his prime for intercourse, by his reason he nullified the frenzy of the passions" (2:3).

In these texts, Joseph's stance toward Potiphar's wife, characterized by religious devotion and temperance, is interpreted as a central lesson of the Genesis story. His exaltation and appointment as king of Egypt, rewards for his pious and wise behavior, are also mentioned repeatedly.[9] He is a renowned forebear of Israel, an example for all to follow.[10]

Joseph also receives notice in two Jewish expansions of the Bible, *Jubilees* and Pseudo-Philo's *Liber antiquitatum biblicarum*. *Jubilees,* which dates to the second century B.C.E.,[11] features a detailed retelling of the story of Joseph. *Jub.* 34:10-19, chapters 39–40, and 42:1–46:8 cover almost every major aspect of the Genesis story, except for the reasons why Joseph's brothers hated him and wanted to do away with him. *Jubilees'* intention is to portray Joseph as a religious and ethical model. Thus the book focuses on Joseph's relations with his brothers and with Potiphar's wife, and above all on his behavior as a ruler in Egypt. Interestingly, *Jubilees* stresses Joseph's popularity with the Egyptian people. Far from being a harsh ruler, a trait hinted at in Genesis (see 47:16, 21), he is upright and modest:

> Joseph ruled in all the land of Egypt, and all the judges and servants of the Pharaoh and all those who did the king's work loved him because he walked uprightly and had no pompousness or arrogance or partiality, and there was no bribery because he ruled all the people of the land uprightly. And the land of Egypt was at peace before the Pharaoh on account of Joseph, because the Lord was with him. (*Jub.* 40:8–9)[12]

---

9. Cf. also the twelfth *Hellenistic Synagogal Prayer* v. 65 (found in *Apostolic Constitutions* 8.12.24): "You, O Lord, did not neglect Joseph, but gave to him to rule over Egypt — a reward of the self-control that you enable" (trans. D. R. Darnell, *OTP* 2.693).

10. Cf. 4 Macc 18:11.

11. For an analysis of the figure of Joseph in *Jubilees,* see especially Niehoff, *Figure of Joseph,* 41–46.

12. Translation by O. S. Wintermute in *OTP* 2.35–142.

Joseph brought peace not only to the people of Egypt, but also among the Israelites who lived there:

> They became a numerous people, and they were all in accord in their hearts, so that each one loved his brother and each person helped his brother, and they increased exceedingly. (46:1)

The harmony between the Egyptians and Israelites during Joseph's life is also mentioned:

> And there was no Satan or anything evil all the days of the life of Joseph which he lived after his father, Jacob, because all of the Egyptians were honoring the children of Israel all the days of the life of Joseph. (46:2)

Pseudo-Philo's *Liber antiquitatum biblicarum* (first century C.E.), which retells the history of Israel from Adam to David, dedicates only two verses to Joseph (8:9–10). The unknown author concisely summarizes the Genesis story, which he undoubtedly assumes to have been known by his readers. He mentions only the brothers' hatred toward Joseph, which caused them to sell him; Joseph's explanation of Pharaoh's dreams followed by his appointment to rule Egypt; the reunion of Joseph with his brothers and father; and Joseph's willingness to forgive his brothers.

There also existed in the Greco-Roman period at least two other Jewish expansions of the Joseph story, both known under the title *History of Joseph*.[13] One is only partially extant on some Greek papyrus fragments. The text is very fragmentary, and seems to deal with Joseph's affairs from the time he was appointed king of Egypt.[14]

A second *History of Joseph* survives in an Ethiopic version.[15] It follows the outline of the biblical story rather closely, but is much elaborated, integrating other Jewish traditions about Joseph. On the whole the story is coherent and cohesive, depicting Joseph as "pure, virginal, quiet, kind-hearted and perfectly wise." Prayers and dreams play an important role here. In contrast to the author of *Jubilees*, for example, who does not seem interested in the

---

13. There are also some fragments of a *Prayer of Joseph*, which is probably an expansion of Jacob's blessing of the sons of Joseph in Genesis 48. On this document's origin in the first century C.E., see especially J. Z. Smith in *OTP* 2.699–714.

14. For more details on this pseudepigraphon, together with a translation of the fragments, see G. T. Zervos in *OTP* 2.467–75. See also Treu, " 'Apocryphe relatif,' " 255–61.

15. See Isaac, "History of Joseph," 3–125.

dreams in the Joseph story, the unknown author of the Ethiopic *History of Joseph* stresses the divine agency of Joseph's dreams; unconsciously, the brothers cooperate in the fulfillment of these dreams. At the end of the story, when Joseph reveals himself to his brothers, he declares,

> The Lord is Most High, and blessed: he made my dreams come true. Behold, you yourselves have done obeisance to me. As for the moon [in my dreams], it is Pharaoh, the King![16] And the eleven stars are yourselves [right] here now.[17]

Joseph in the Writings of Philo and Other Egyptian Jews

It is not surprising that Hellenistic Jews living in Egypt were interested in the story of Joseph. Indeed, Joseph's administration in Egypt and the move of his family from Canaan to a new homeland are central themes in the biblical story. Egyptian Jews were deeply influenced by Hellenistic Greek culture, and integrated Greek philosophical systems with Jewish traditions. Nevertheless, they realized that they belonged to a social and religious minority within the Roman Empire. They felt the need to defend their ancestral customs and religious traditions, for example, the Torah, in a world that was sometimes not friendly toward Jews. One tactic was to claim that the best Greek ideas, for example those of Plato, were derived from the Jews, and that Moses and other famous Israelites had put their stamp on pagan culture and were responsible for many notable achievements in antiquity.

Artapanus, for example, a Jewish author who lived somewhere in Egypt (Alexandria?) in the third or second century B.C.E., attests to the idea that Egyptian culture was shaped by Abraham, Joseph, and Moses. His work, probably entitled *On the*

---

16. Joseph's mother Rachel, signified by the "moon" in Joseph's second dream (Gen 37:9–10), had died previously, on the birth of her second son Benjamin (Gen 35:16–20).

17. Translated by Isaac, *History of Joseph*, 99. J. Zandee has drawn attention to another apocryphal *History of Joseph*, written in Coptic and likewise preserved only partially. This document probably originated in Egypt, and represents "an intermediate stage on the way from Jewish apocryphal writings to Christian hagiography" ("Iosephus contra Apionem," 193–213).

Jews (Περὶ Ἰουδαίων), has been lost, but some fragments are preserved in Eusebius's *Praeparatio evangelica* 9, where the church father excerpts Alexander Polyhistor's *On the Jews;* Polyhistor had, in turn, excerpted the works of Artapanus and others. The fragments in Eusebius deal with the exploits of these three famous forefathers of the Jewish people in Egypt.[18] Artapanus, fragment 2 (*Praep. evang.* 9.23.1–4), mentions Joseph as "a descendant of Abraham and son of Jacob" who "requested the neighboring Arabs to convey him to Egypt."[19] Joseph had discerned his brothers' plot against him because he "excelled the others in understanding and wisdom." In Egypt, Joseph was "recommended to the king and became administrator of the entire land." He "was the first to divide the land and distinguish it with boundaries. He made much barren land arable. . . . " He also "discovered measurements and on account of these things he was greatly loved by the Egyptians." Joseph married Aseneth, and his father and brothers settled in Heliopolis and Saïs. The fragment ends by stating that Joseph "stored the seven year grain crop . . . and became master of Egypt."[20]

Joseph is mentioned in two other fragments from Jewish writers found in chapter 9 of the *Praeparatio evangelica;* both are again drawn from Polyhistor's *On the Jews*. The first (*Praep. evang.* 9.21.1–19) is ascribed to Demetrius the Chronographer (third century B.C.E.; fragment 2), who also lived in Egypt, presumably in Alexandria.[21] This fragment briefly treats some of the events of Joseph's career in Egypt. The author is interested mainly in the chronology of the biblical histories; he tells us, for example, how old Joseph was when he was sold (seventeen years), how many years he remained in prison (thirteen), and how many years transpired between the life of Adam and Joseph's brothers' arrival in Egypt (3,624). He also explains why Joseph, when in

---

18. On Artapanus, see Collins in *OTP* 2.889–903; and Holladay, *Fragments*, vol. 1: *Historians*, 189–243.

19. Translated by Collins in *OTP* 2.897–98.

20. Cf. also *Sib. Or.* 11:26–29, where, in a passage on the rule of Egypt, Joseph as "prisoner and judge" is told to "nurture the East and the race of Assyrian men" (trans. J. J. Collins, *OTP* 2.434).

21. On Demetrius, see Hanson in *OTP* 2.843–54 and Holladay, *Fragments*, vol. 1: *Historians*, 51–91.

Egypt, did not send for his father immediately ("because he was a shepherd, as were Joseph's brothers; and to the Egyptians it is disgraceful to be a shepherd"),[22] and why Joseph "gave Benjamin at breakfast a portion five times as much as [his brothers],"[23] and five garments instead of two.[24]

The second fragment (*Praep. evang.* 9.24.1) comes, through Polyhistor, from the work of Philo the Epic Poet, who probably lived in Alexandria around the same time as Demetrius.[25] Here Joseph is described as an "interpreter of dreams for the scepter-bearer on Egypt's throne, revolving time's secrets with the flood of fate."[26]

Another well-known Hellenistic Jewish author who also lived in Alexandria is the philosopher Philo (first century C.E.). Like his predecessors, Philo wrote on some famous Israelites of past times; this part of his work is generally intended as a political or cultural apologetic. His treatises on Isaac and Jacob are lost, but those on Abraham, Joseph, and Moses survive. A series of Philo's allegorical commentaries on several Genesis passages also refer frequently to Joseph (see below).

Strikingly, Philo, unlike the other nonbiblical authors examined thus far, presents an ambiguous portrait of Joseph. In his *De Josepho*, an encomium on Joseph's virtues, the patriarch is portrayed as an ideal statesman (πολιτικός), characterized by prudence, self-control, and piety. Philo is aware, through personal experience, of the moral dangers to which a politician is exposed, especially lust for power, and he presents Joseph as overcoming these temptations through his justice, nobility, and piety. According to Philo, Joseph's attitude toward Potiphar's wife shows his self-control not only in sexual matters, but also in political affairs, since he refuses to overturn the household order (40–53).

Idealizing the figure of Joseph, Philo in *De Josepho* omits all the negative biblical references, such as Joseph's "bad report" about his brothers (Gen 37:2). Philo emphasizes that Joseph re-

---

22. Cf. Gen 46:34. Translated by Hanson in *OTP* 2.850–51.
23. Cf. Gen 43:34.
24. Cf. Gen 45:22.
25. On the epic poet Philo, see Attridge in *OTP* 2.781–84 and Holladay, *Fragments*, vol. 2: *Poets*, 205–99.
26. Translated by Attridge in *OTP* 2.784.

counted his dreams to his brothers "in the simple innocence of his nature," without being aware of "the enmity which was lurking in his brothers' hearts" (*De Josepho* 6; cf. 171). Finally, he omits the reference in Genesis to Joseph's returning to the house "to do his work... while no one else was in the house" (Gen 39:11). This detail became a favorite theme in rabbinic discussions of Joseph's behavior: was he really blameless, or was he perhaps a willing participant in the matter?[27]

According to Philo, Joseph fulfills perfectly the three characteristics of the ideal statesman: pastoral ability (developed while Joseph was young and in charge of his father's flocks); household management (cultivated while he was steward in the house of Potiphar); and self-control (54). He was pious and God-fearing (εὐσεβής: 122, 240, 246), full of temperance (σωφροσύνη: 40, 87) and wisdom (σοφία) (e.g., 86, 106, 117, 246, 268–69), ready to forgive (ἀμνησίκακος) (e.g., 246), and displayed goodness to all people (φιλανθρωπία: 240). In sum,

> He died in a ripe old age, having lived 110 years, unsurpassed in handsomeness, wisdom and power of language. His handsomeness is attested by the furious passion which a woman conceived for him; his good sense by the equable temper he showed amid the numberless inequalities of his life, a temper which created order in disorder and concord where all was naturally discordant; his power of language by his interpretations of dreams and the fluency of his addresses and the persuasiveness which accompanied them, which secured him the obedience, not forced but voluntary, of every one of his subjects. (268–69)[28]

At three points in his panegyric, Philo interrupts the narrative flow by introducing nonliteral, allegorical interpretation of various details in the Genesis account, such as Joseph's name, his coat of many colors, the interpretation of dreams in general, and the presence of three eunuchs (the chief baker, chief butler, and chief cook) with relation to food, drink, and seasonings (28–36, 58–79, 125–56). Here Philo stresses the difficult role of the statesman and his struggle with various dangers of political life, such as the misuse of power. In these sections, he displays an ambiguous attitude toward the role of the statesman, who lives, according

---

27. See Kugel, *Potiphar's House*, 94–96; Niehoff, *Figure of Joseph*, 131–34.
28. Translated by F. H. Colson in LCL.

to him, in a world of dreams and passions.[29] This seems to be a clue to understanding Philo's ambivalent attitude toward Joseph in the whole of his work. Whereas, on a literal level, he praises Joseph as a model statesman in *De Josepho*,[30] the allegorization of Joseph elsewhere in his writings focuses on the negative potential of the statesman's life. The statesman is described as a person who is willing to compromise, who is attracted to external and worldly things, and who engages in falsehood and sophistry. This is a person who, like Joseph, suppresses the masculine rational principle — self-control — inherited from his father Jacob, and expresses the feminine principle — sense perception connected with bodily pleasure and vanity — inherited from his mother Rachel. In short, as a ruler of Egypt, which itself symbolizes the body and its passions, Joseph is "the champion of vainglory" and "the friend of vanity."[31] In this context, Philo goes so far as to praise the feelings of hatred toward Joseph on the part of his brothers, "the children of sound sense."[32] But, as Philo admits, "It is not a person that is here judged, but one of the traits or feelings that exist in every person's soul (in this case, Joseph's craving for glory and love of vanity)."[33]

Finally, Philo states that

> when [Joseph] changes his life for the better and renounces his idle visions..., when he rises from his deep slumbering to abiding wakefulness and welcomes clearness before uncertainty, truth before false supposition..., when, moved by a yearning for continence and a vast zeal for piety, he rejects bodily pleasure, the wife of the Egyptian..., when he passes step by step from betterment to betterment and...utters aloud the lesson which experience had taught him so fully, "I belong to God...," then his brethren will make with him covenants of reconciliation...and I...will not fail to praise him for his repentance. (*Somn.* 2.105–8)

In summary, Philo, in his allegories of the human soul, occasionally introduces Joseph the statesman as a warning example. Yet he is aware that the patriarch showed self-control when

---

29. Such a criticism was quite common in the Hellenistic world; see Niehoff, *Figure of Joseph*, 75, n. 88.

30. Cf. *Migr. Abr.* 16–24; *Fuga* 126–31.

31. See *Somn.* 1.77–78, 219–25; 2.1–154; *Quod det. pot.* 5–28; *Agric.* 55–59; *Migr. Abr.* 159–63, 203–04; *Mut. nom.* 89–91; *Quod deus* 111–21; *Sobr.* 12–15; *Leg. all.* 3.236–42.

32. *Somn.* 2.93–104.

33. *Somn.* 2.98. Translation by Colson and Whitaker in LCL.

tested, and was a good and prudent statesman. This is the focus of the panegyric in *De Josepho*.

Joseph in Josephus's *Jewish Antiquities*

Josephus, in the *Jewish Antiquities,* records the ancient and glorious history of the Jewish people. His goal is basically apologetic, to show the Greco-Roman world that the Jews had provided illustrious, virtuous, and wise people comparable to Solon, Socrates, and Plato. Thus he dwells extensively on figures such as Abraham, Jacob, Joseph, and Moses, since they were, in his opinion, persons of outstanding virtue.

In *Ant.* 2.9–200, Josephus retells the biblical story of Joseph. He seems to be particularly interested in this patriarch, perhaps not only because he was his namesake, but also because their lives were similar in certain respects. Both were involved in politics, and both were at some point rejected as outsiders.

Paraphrasing the biblical text, Josephus expands particularly on three episodes: Joseph's dreams and his brothers' plot to eliminate him (11–34); the confrontation with Potiphar's wife (39–59); and the final test of the brothers (111–59).

Josephus's overall picture of Joseph is clear. Joseph is an eminent leader and a person of extraordinary qualities, fulfilling the Hellenistic ideal of the philosopher-king. Josephus first mentions Joseph's good birth (εὐγένεια) and handsomeness, stereotyped features of a Greco-Roman hero. He next refers to the affection of Jacob for his son and to Joseph's dreams, both of which aroused the envy of Joseph's brothers. Like Philo, Josephus omits the reference to Joseph's "bad report" to Jacob concerning his brothers (Gen 37:2). He stresses that Joseph was ignorant of the meaning of his dreams, thus presenting him as undeserving of his brothers' enmity. Josephus states that Jacob, rather than "rebuking" his son for his dreams (Gen 37:10), was delighted with them, realizing that they forecast prosperity and honor (*Ant.* 2.9–16).

In the rest of the story, Josephus stresses Joseph's virtues of character, virtues that were widely respected in the Greco-Roman world. First there are his exceptional wisdom and speaking ability, both partly due to the education he is said to have received by order of Potiphar (39). His wisdom is seen particularly in his ability to interpret dreams, a connection made already in Genesis. Next, there is his temperance or self-control (σωφροσύνη), another traditional virtue of Joseph. The major episode in this regard is, of course, the encounter with Potiphar's wife (48, 50, 69). In the same context Josephus points to the virtue of courage or endurance (ὑπομονή): Joseph, in reacting to Potiphar's wife, states that he would "endure anything rather than submit to this request" (43).[34] Josephus remarks that

> pity could neither induce him to unchastity nor fear compel: he resisted her entreaties and yielded not to her threats, choosing to suffer unjustly and to endure even the severest penalty, rather than take advantage of the moment. (50)

> Later, when Joseph was put in prison, he sought neither to defend himself nor yet to render a strict account of what had passed, but silently underwent his bonds and confinement, confident that God, who knew the cause of his calamity and the truth, would prove stronger than those who had bound him. (60)

The last passage illustrates Joseph's piety (εὐσέβεια), another virtue.

Related to Joseph's piety and reliance on God are his justice (δικαιοσύνη), generosity (χρηστότης), and love for fellow humans (φιλανθρωπία). Josephus stresses the latter,[35] for in so doing he can counter charges of misanthropy sometimes directed against the Jews.[36] We are told that Joseph, in his generosity, had "thrown open" the corn market not only to his "fellow citizens but also to foreigners, having resolved to provide the means of subsistence to all in need" (101).[37] Josephus emphasizes the generosity that Joseph showed to his brothers in not bearing malice (162, 195), and that which he showed to the Egyptians by acting magnanimously as an administrator (193).[38] Josephus ends his paraphrase of the biblical story as follows:

---

34. Translation by H. St. J. Thackeray in LCL.

35. Philo, too, mentions Joseph's humaneness (see above).

36. Cf. also his *Contra Apionem*, which contains an apology for Judaism as a reply to common Greco-Roman feelings of anti-Semitism.

37. See also 94; and cf. 136 and 145. For the evaluation of φιλανθρωπία in Hellenistic society, see especially Berger, *Die Gesetzesauslegung Jesu*, 123–25, 143–65, 261.

38. See also 94 and 101.

Then [Joseph]...died at the age of 110 years, a man of admirable virtue, who directed all affairs by the dictates of reason and made but sparing use of his authority; to which fact he owed that great prosperity of his among the Egyptians, albeit he had come as a stranger and in such pitiful circumstances as we have previously described. (198)

Joseph in *Joseph and Aseneth*

The Jewish romance *Joseph and Aseneth,* probably written in Egypt between 100 b.c.e. and 100 c.e., falls into two parts. The second (chaps. 22–29) relates the attempts of Pharaoh's son to kidnap Aseneth, Joseph's wife, and to marry her, to kill both Joseph and the Pharaoh, and to seize power in Egypt. The plot fails, and the story ends with the death of both Pharaoh's son and Pharaoh himself. Strikingly, Joseph does not play an important part in this section of the romance.

In the first part of the romance (chaps. 1–21) Joseph does play an important role, although the principal part is assumed by Aseneth. Joseph and Aseneth meet, fall in love, and finally are married. The main theme is the conversion of Aseneth, daughter of Pentephres[39] (the latter being Pharaoh's chief counselor and priest of Heliopolis), to Judaism, a precondition to her marrying Joseph. She is a model proselyte, a "city of refuge" (15:7; 19:5) for those who follow her example. The story explains Joseph's marriage to a foreign woman, an unexpected element in the biblical story of Joseph.[40]

While touring Egypt to gather grain, Joseph meets Pentephres (cf. Gen 41:46–49). Even before Joseph's arrival, Pentephres had proposed that his daughter Aseneth marry Joseph, but she had refused: first, she "despis[es] and scorn[s] every man" (2:1),[41] and second, Joseph is "an alien,...a fugitive," who was "sold [as a

---

39. The name of Joseph's father-in-law in the MT is Potiphera (Gen 41:45, 50; 46:20); in the LXX (and Hellenistic Jewish writings dependent on the LXX) it is "Pe(n)tephres," which is also the LXX translation of Potiphar, the name of the captain of Pharaoh's guard to whom Joseph was sold (Gen 37:36; 39:1). It is not surprising that many ancient writers identified the two figures.

40. On Aseneth in Jewish sources in general and in *Joseph and Aseneth* in particular, see Aptowitzer, "Asenath," 239–306.

41. Translation by C. Burchard in *OTP* 2.177–247.

slave] ... and caught in the act of sleeping with his mistress" (4:9–
10). At first she refuses even to meet him, but when she sees him
from the window of her penthouse, she immediately falls in love.
When they finally meet, however, Joseph refuses to kiss her because "it is not fitting for a man who worships God ... to kiss a
strange woman who will bless with her mouth dead and dumb
idols" (8:5). Joseph offers a prayer for her conversion, then de-
parts and promises to return a week later (9). Chapters 10–17,
the central section, describe Aseneth's repentance and conversion
to Judaism. Finally Joseph returns and marries her.

Throughout the story, Joseph is depicted as a serene person. He
is a royal figure (5:5; 7:1), appointed by Pharaoh to be king of all
Egypt (4:7), a person to whom everyone owes strict obedience.
For giving grain to the whole land, he is their "savior."[42] Joseph
is even called "the powerful one of God" (ὁ δυνατὸς τοῦ θεοῦ;
3:4; 4:7; 18:1–2; 21:21) and "the son of God" (ὁ υἱὸς τοῦ θεοῦ;
6:3; 13:13; 21:4), expressions that emphasize his relationship to
the God of the Jews and his eminent position in Egypt.[43]

Joseph's handsomeness is mentioned together with his chastity:

All the wives and daughters of the noblemen and the satraps of the whole
land of Egypt used to molest him, (wanting) to sleep with him, and all the
wives and the daughters of the Egyptians, when they saw Joseph, suffered
badly because of his beauty. But Joseph despised them. (7:3–4)[44]

Finally, Joseph is praised for his wisdom (4:7; 13:14; 21:21).

In 4:7, the author summarizes Joseph's qualities in a few
phrases uttered by Pentephres:

Joseph is a man who worships God and is self-controlled (θεοσεβὴς καὶ
σώφρων) and a virgin..., a man powerful in wisdom and experience
(δυνατὸς ἐν σοφίᾳ καὶ ἐπιστήμῃ), and the spirit of God is upon him, and
the grace of the Lord [is] with him.

But, we emphasize, Joseph on the whole remains in the background of the story; all attention here is focused on Aseneth and
her conversion.

---

42. See 4:7: " ... saving (σῴζει) it [the land of Egypt] from the oncoming famine."
43. In 21:4, Aseneth is called "daughter of the Most High" (ἡ θυγάτηρ τοῦ ὑψίστου).
44. Cf. 6:4; 13:14; 21:21.

Summary: The Figure of Joseph
in Early Jewish Tradition

In early Judaism, Joseph was considered one of the great Israelite forefathers. His religious devotion and temperance shown in his encounter with Potiphar's wife are often adduced as models of behavior, and people are encouraged to imitate him. His exaltation in his appointment as king of Egypt, interpreted as a reward for his piety and wisdom, is a stimulus for such behavior. Joseph's exemplary role, characterized by piety, temperance, self-control, chastity, and endurance, is introduced in various life situations in which people are considered as needing moral exhortation.

The Hellenistic Jews living in the Egyptian diaspora, moreover, were particularly interested in the story of Joseph. These Jews were deeply influenced by Hellenistic Greek culture, and combined Greek philosophical systems with their Jewish traditions. They felt a need to defend their ancestral customs, and did so in part by claiming that famous Israelites of former times had put their stamp on pagan culture. Thus, they spoke and wrote with pride about their ancestor Joseph as someone who had become administrator of Egypt. Joseph had succeeded in taking measures to prevent the Egyptians from starving; furthermore, he had cultivated the country and created prosperity. In short, Joseph was repeatedly adduced as a great statesman who was renowned for his humane features, who had run the country magnanimously, who had created harmony between the Egyptians and Israelites, and who was beloved of his subjects.

This picture of Joseph is intended mainly as a political and cultural apologetic. It was advanced by Jews in Egypt (and other parts of the Greco-Roman world) who, aware that they belonged to a social and religious minority, found it appropriate and even necessary to refer to their famous ancestors in an attempt to refute their pagan opponents and to survive as a social, political, and religious entity.

Quite a different approach, however, manifesting a more critical attitude toward Joseph, occurs in rabbinic sources. In the majority of the OT references to Joseph outside Genesis, the patriarch is blamed for the idolatry and apostasy of the Northern Kingdom of Israel, since he was the ancestor of the tribes of Ephraim and Manasseh, which constituted the bulk of the Northern Kingdom. Even the Genesis story mentions some negative aspects of Joseph's behavior, and rabbinic Judaism was not blind to these aspects. The rabbis could stress Joseph's virtues on one occasion and his dubious actions on another, depending on their intentions at the time. When, for instance, they want to argue that divine punishment is a consequence of humanity's wrong actions, they put forward Joseph as an example of someone who was punished for his faults. Their picture of Joseph seems to have had nothing to do with politics or apologetics; rather they mention Joseph, his ethical behavior, and his career in an inner-Jewish context in purely theological discussions.

The Reception of the Joseph Story in Early Christian Literature: The New Testament, *1 Clement,* and the *Testaments of the Twelve Patriarchs*

Jacob's favorite son Joseph figures prominently not only in Hellenistic Jewish literature, but also in early Christian writings. In the latter, his name occurs most frequently in contexts that are either theological-historical, wherein the Joseph story is part of Israelite history, or ethical, wherein the patriarch is portrayed either as a victim of envy and hatred or as a model of virtue.

Joseph is referred to several times in NT writings. In Heb 11:22, for example, he appears in a long section on the history of Israel. The patriarchs are praised for their faith and endurance, although they did not receive the fulfillment of the promise. Joseph is introduced as one who "by faith..., at the end of his life, made mention of the exodus of the Israelites and gave instructions about his burial" (cf. Gen 50:24–25). That is, he foresaw the Israelites' return to the land of Canaan.

Another reference, again historical, occurs in Stephen's speech in Acts 7. This sketch of the history of Israel from Abraham to the time of the speaker is intended as an attack on the conduct of the people of Israel and their leaders. The passage on Joseph (7:9–16) states that the brothers, "jealous of Joseph, sold him into Egypt," but that

> God was with him, and rescued him from all his afflictions, and enabled him to win favor and to show wisdom when he stood before Pharaoh, king of Egypt, who appointed him ruler over Egypt and over all his household. (7:9–10)

After mentioning the famine in Egypt and Canaan, Acts describes the brothers' visits to Egypt to buy grain, and how Joseph "made himself known to his brothers" and "invited his father Jacob and all his relatives to come to him" (vv. 13–14). This passage thus relates a small but important part of the history of Israel, namely, the emigration of the ancestors to Egypt and the change in Joseph's circumstances from a situation of distress, caused by his brothers the patriarchs, to one of prosperity, created by God.[45]

1 Clement, an early Christian writing from the end of the first century, contains a reference to Joseph in a purely ethical context. In a passage dealing with the consequences of envy, the author provides some examples from the history of Israel. One is Joseph: "Jealousy (ζῆλος) caused Joseph to be persecuted to the death and to come into slavery" (4:9).[46]

A sterling early Christian example of Joseph's portrayal not only as a victim of envy and hatred, but above all as a model of virtue, occurs in the *Testaments of the Twelve Patriarchs.*[47] This pseudepigraphon consists of twelve "testaments," each purporting to convey the last words addressed by one of the twelve sons of Jacob to his sons and other relatives. Normally the patriarch first describes his own behavior. Next he exhorts his audience not to fall into the same sins, or, if he has been virtuous, to imitate him. Finally, he foretells what will happen to his sons and to the people of Israel (and the Gentiles) in the future.

For the author of the *Testaments of the Twelve Patriarchs,* it is

---

45. According to B. S. Rosner, there is a third, though implicit, reference to Joseph in the NT, namely 1 Cor 6:18a, where Paul exhorts the Corinthians to "flee impurity." Rosner's arguments are, however, unconvincing. See his "Possible Quotation," 123–27.

46. Translated by Kirsopp Lake in LCL.

47. Although we find in the *Testaments of the Twelve Patriarchs* many traces of Jewish traditions and sources, the writing in its present form is clearly Christian and is to be dated in the second century c.e. See especially Hollander and de Jonge, *Testaments.*

Joseph above all who represents the ideal of moral behavior. Not only is Joseph portrayed as an example to be emulated in his own "testament," but also, unlike any of the other patriarchs, he is put forth as a model in testaments other than his own. In *T. Reub.* 4:8–10, for instance, Joseph is praised as a model of virtue in a warning against fornication: despite all the attempts of Potiphar's wife to seduce him, he "purged his thoughts from all impurity" and was delivered by God "from all visible and invisible death."[48] In *T. Sim.* 4:3–7 and *T. Zeb.* 8:4–5, Joseph is portrayed as having been "compassionate and merciful (εὔσπλαγχνος καὶ ἐλεήμων)" toward his brothers in Egypt. He did not bear malice, but forgave and even "loved" his brothers.

Strikingly, the *Testaments of the Twelve Patriarchs* does not portray Joseph as a "wise" man or an interpreter of dreams.[49] Rather, he is the virtuous and good person par excellence. This becomes clear in the *Testament of Benjamin,* where the author summarizes the scattered statements concerning his ethical ideals in a discourse on "the good man" (ὁ ἀγαθὸς ἀνήρ) (chaps. 3–10). Here Joseph is adduced more than once as an example (e.g., 3:1–8; 5:5; 10:1). A "good man" fears and loves God, keeps the commandments, and loves his neighbor. He is "simple" (ἁπλοῦς) and free from hypocrisy. When oppressed, he shows mercy, holds his peace, and prays to God. Such an attitude makes sinners repent and change for the better, whereas the "good man" himself is saved, rewarded, and exalted by God.

The author of the *Testaments of the Twelve Patriarchs* also describes Joseph's moral behavior in the patriarch's own farewell discourse. This description is introduced by an individual thanksgiving (*T. Jos.* 1:4–2:6) in which Joseph thanks God for his deliverance from oppression and distress. His distress is a trial

---

48. Translation by Hollander and de Jonge, *Testaments.*

49. This is not even the case in *Testament of Levi* 13, as a comparison of this passage and some corresponding Aramaic fragments shows. In these Aramaic fragments (the so-called *Aramaic Levi Document*) of unknown date and provenance, Joseph is explicitly mentioned in connection with wisdom, as someone "who taught reading and writing and the teaching of wisdom" (vv. 83–95, esp. v. 90). It is likely that the author of the *Testaments of the Twelve Patriarchs* was familiar with a *Vorlage* of the *Aramaic Levi Document* and adapted its text to his literary needs. Cf. Philonenko, "Paradoxes Stoïciens," 99–104; Hollander, *Joseph as an Ethical Model,* 57–62. On the *Aramaic Levi Document,* see especially Hollander and de Jonge, *Testaments,* 17–20, 21–25, and 457–69 (translation by J. C. Greenfield and M. E. Stone).

from God, in which his endurance (ὑπομονή or μακροθυμία) is shown.

To illustrate Joseph's behavior in times of crisis, the author includes two nonbiblical stories about the patriarch, both probably taken over from Jewish sources and adapted to the author's own literary needs. The first (3:1–9:5) describes in ten episodes the attempts of the Egyptian woman to seduce Joseph. It contains many typically Hellenistic elements, especially material from the well-known Phaedra tradition.[50] Joseph's attitude in this encounter is that of an oppressed person who begs God for salvation: he fasts, weeps, wears sackcloth, and prays. Moreover, Joseph keeps silent and is an example of temperance (σωφροσύνη). He does not give in, despite all the woman's efforts.

The second story (11:2–16:6) narrates Joseph's adventures before he was bought by Potiphar. It describes how the Ishmaelites asked Joseph about his social standing on the way to Egypt, and then left him with a slave dealer there. In the episodes that follow, Joseph repeatedly insists that he is a slave, not revealing his true status. This leads to his imprisonment, but even then he repeats that he is a slave, out of respect and love for his brothers, in order to save their reputations. His silence indicates that he endures injustice. Thus Joseph is a righteous and pious person, a kind of martyr, who has confidence in God and knows that God is stronger than Joseph's adversaries.

Both of these stories illustrate the importance of "patience" or "endurance," as is shown by the parenetic sections that follow the stories (10:1–11:1 and 17:1–18:4):

> You see, therefore, my children, what great things patience (ἡ ὑπομονή) accomplishes. (10:1)

> You see, children, what great things I endured (ὑπέμεινα), that I should not put my brothers to shame. You also, therefore, love one another, and with patience (ἐν μακροθυμίᾳ) disregard one another's faults. (17:1–2)

Throughout the *Testaments of the Twelve Patriarchs* Joseph is the ethical model par excellence. References to him reflect a uniformly positive image. This suggests the possibility that traditions

---

50. See especially Braun, *History and Romance;* Hollander and de Jonge, *Testaments,* 372–73.

or sources that were critical of Joseph might have been remodeled by the author of the *Testaments* to make them fit his purpose. An example of this occurs in *Testament of Naphtali 5–7.*[51] These chapters describe two visions seen by Naphtali "on the Mount of Olives, on the east of Jerusalem" (5:1). The visions illustrate the coming exile of Israel and Israel's final restoration. Levi and Judah are mentioned as those who will play a positive role in Israel's future. This is entirely consistent with the author's intentions: in the eschatological sections of the *Testaments,* both of these figures receive significant attention, since the future eschatological coming of "the agent of divine deliverance" (Jesus Christ) is connected with these two tribes.[52]

Joseph is also mentioned in these two visions in *Testament of Naphtali 5–7,* but his role is obscure. In the first vision he is said to have seized a bull and ascended with it on high (5:7); in the second we read that after the brothers were shipwrecked, Joseph "fled away on a little boat" (6:6). When Naphtali tells these dreams to his father, Jacob seems to understand their significance. With regard to Joseph, the function of the dreams is to convince Jacob that his favorite son is still alive: witness Jacob's reaction, "I believe that Joseph lives, for I see always that the Lord includes him with you" (7:2).

There also exists, however, a medieval Jewish *Hebrew Testament of Naphtali* which partly runs parallel to *Testament of Naphtali 5–7,* but is much more elaborate. Research has shown that neither of these works depends on the other, but that both draw independently on another, earlier document. The *Hebrew Testament of Naphtali* seems to have preserved the original mean-

---

51. See also *T. Gad* 1:6 (cf. 1:9): "Joseph said to our father: 'The sons of Zilpah and Bilhah are slaying the best [of the flock] and eating them against the judgment of Judah and Reuben' "; this is an expansion of Gen 37:2. This accusation, which, according to Gad in the next verse, was false, is mentioned by the patriarch in order to explain his former feeling of hatred toward Joseph. Joseph's "bad report" as such, however, is presented by the author of the *Testaments of the Twelve Patriarchs* as the result of a misunderstanding: Joseph saw some of his brothers eating a lamb and assumed that they had killed it for that purpose. It is possible that the author knew a critical interpretation of Gen 37:2 and mitigated it in order to leave the (positive) image of his ethical hero Joseph untouched. On rabbinic exegesis of this "bad report," which was critical of the patriarch, see Kugel, *Potiphar's House,* 79–84.

52. See Hollander and de Jonge, *Testaments;* and especially de Jonge, "Two Messiahs," 191–203.

ing of Naphtali's visions more faithfully than the author of the *Testaments of the Twelve Patriarchs,* who edited the visions substantially.[53] Many details in the Greek version can be understood only in light of the more elaborate and consistent account in the Hebrew text. This is true of the references to Joseph in Naphtali's visions. These are unclear and obscure in the *Testament of Naphtali,* but in the *Hebrew Testament of Naphtali* Joseph's role is more consistent. Naphtali's visions seem originally to have predicted a future apostasy induced by Joseph's sons, which led to the exile. The visions warn their readers to follow Levi and Judah, but not to heed Joseph. Joseph is depicted as an evil-minded person, who quarrels with Judah and persuades his other brothers to abandon Judah (and Levi) and to follow him. The apostasy and exile are his fault, as Jacob realizes after he has heard the dreams:

> [F]or the wickedness of my son Joseph you will be sent into captivity, and you will be scattered among the nations. . . . (7:4)[54]

This negative image of Joseph is, as we have seen, fairly old.[55] Also in other later Jewish (rabbinic) literature, the figure of Joseph is not beyond reproach. In rabbinic eyes, Joseph was not an innocent victim of fate: in some way he must have deserved the divine punishment that came to him. Thus a number of later Jewish authors search for details in the Genesis story that could serve as points of departure for a more critical view of Joseph. Their interpretations of Gen 37:2 ("bad report") and Gen 39:11 (Joseph's coming into his master's house "to do his work" while "no one else was in the house"), for instance, are not favorable to the patriarch.

Obviously, the author of the *Testaments of the Twelve Patriarchs* omitted the negative references to Joseph from his Jewish source when composing *Testament of Naphtali* 5–7. He chose not to strike the name of Joseph altogether, but what remains regarding Joseph's role in Naphtali's visions is unclear and unsatisfactory. The author of the *Testaments of the Twelve Patriarchs*

---

53. So Korteweg, "Naphtali's Visions," 261–82. On the *Hebrew Testament of Naphtali,* see also Hollander and de Jonge, *Testaments,* 25–26, 296–97; 446–50 (translation).

54. Translated by R. H. Charles and A. van der Heide in Hollander and de Jonge, *Testaments,* 449.

55. See above, "The Image of Joseph in the Hebrew Bible."

preferred to give a less than coherent account of Naphtali's visions than to undermine the positive image of Joseph in the *Testaments* as a whole.

In later Christian literature, the positive image of Joseph remains intact. He continues to be a hero, a virtuous, chaste, and pious man who in times of distress is confident in God's help. He is an example to imitate, as, for instance, in Ephrem's *Commentary on Genesis*[56] and in his sermons on Joseph.[57] In Christian circles, Joseph was even regarded as a type or prefiguration of Jesus Christ: both had to suffer unjustly, and both were rescued, rewarded, and exalted by God. A fine example of this interpretive scheme is found in Ambrosius's *De Joseph Patriarcha*.[58]

Summary: The Figure of Joseph in Early Christian Tradition

Early Christian writers often refer to Jacob's favorite son Joseph. The first Christians considered themselves the new people of God and regarded the Hebrew Bible as their holy scripture (later as a part of their scriptures). In theological discussion and in their polemics against Jews, they often refer to the history of Israel, including the story of Joseph. For example, they attack the conduct of the people of Israel and their leaders, and the Jewish refusal to believe in Jesus, by referring to the crimes of the Israelite forefathers, including the brothers of Joseph.

Normally, however, Joseph is mentioned by Christians in an ethical context. Here the early Christians were influenced by the Jewish Hellenistic tradition of Joseph as a model of faith, endurance, chastity, temperance, and self-control. Joseph is considered a hero, a chaste and pious man, who in times of distress remains confident in God's help. In various situations where moral exhortation is required, including religious services, the example of Joseph is frequently adduced.

Finally, many Christians regarded Joseph as a "type" of Jesus.

---

56. Tonneau, ed., *Sancti Ephraem Syri.*
57. Lamy, ed., *Sancti Ephraem Syri*, vols. 3 and 4.
58. *PL* 14:673–704.

They read the OT from a christological perspective and interpreted many passages allegorically or typologically to refer to the activities of Jesus or the early church. In this context, they understood Joseph as a prefiguration of Jesus insofar as both had suffered unjustly at the hands of their adversaries. The Genesis story of Joseph was read not for its own sake, but as a key to understanding typologically what had befallen Jesus. Approaching the Joseph story in this way, Christians could be comforted by the realization that many of the sufferings endured by Jesus were prefigured, or predicted, in the story of the innocent and righteous Joseph.

Conclusion

Both Jews and Christians have displayed a deep and longstanding interest in the figure of Joseph. Emphasis has been placed above all on his moral virtues: Joseph was regarded as a paradigm of righteousness and piety. His name is mentioned in many Jewish and Christian exhortatory writings which instruct their readers how to live and behave properly. The Joseph story was, furthermore, also used in apologetic and polemical situations. Diaspora Jews living in Egypt, for example, wishing to defend their ancestral customs and religious traditions, took pride in their ancestor Joseph as the famous administrator of Egypt in ancient times. They did this in an attempt to survive as a social, political, and religious minority in a Greco-Roman world that was to some degree hostile to Judaism. Early Christians, for their part, adduced the Joseph story in their polemics against the Jews, emphasizing the underhanded deeds of Joseph's brothers, the Jewish patriarchs.

Bibliography

The OT Narrative of Joseph (Genesis 37–50)

For a survey of books and articles on the biblical story of Joseph, see M. Niehoff, *The Figure of Joseph in Post-biblical Jewish Literature* (AGJU 16; Leiden-New York: Brill, 1992) 16, nn. 6–8, and the "Select Bibliography" on pp. 165–73. See further R. N. Whybray, "The Joseph Story and Pentateuchal Criticism," *VT* 18 (1968) 522–28; E. I. Lowenthal, *The Joseph Narrative in Genesis* (New York: Ktav, 1973); A. Meinhold, "Die Gattung der Josephgeschichte und des Estherbuches: Diasporanovelle," *ZAW* 87 (1975) 306–24; 88 (1976) 72–93; G. W. Coats, *From Canaan to Egypt: Structural and Theological Context for the Joseph Story* (CBQMS 4; Washington, D.C.: Catholic Biblical Association of America, 1976); E. Donner, "Die literarische Gestalt der alttestamentlichen Josephgeschichte," in *Sitzungsberichte der Heidelberger Akademie der Wissenschaften, Phil.-Hist. Klasse* 1976, 2 (Heidelberg: Winter-Universitätsverlag, 1976); J. R. King, "The Joseph Story and Divine Politics: A Comparative Study of a Biographic Formula from the Ancient Near East," *JBL* 106 (1987) 577–94; L. Ruppert, "Zur neueren Diskussion um die Josefsgeschichte der Genesis," *BZ* 33 (1989) 92–97; and H. Ringgren, "Die Versuchung Josefs (Gen 39)," in *Die Väter Israels: Beiträge zur Theologie der Patriarchenüberlieferungen im Alten Testament* (ed. M. Görg and A. R. Müller; Stuttgart: Katholisches Bibelwerk, 1989) 267–70.

Joseph in Jewish, Samaritan, Early Christian, and Islamic Sources

For comparative studies on the figure of Joseph in Hellenistic Jewish, rabbinic, early Christian, and Islamic literature, see B. Marmorstein, "Die Gestalt Josefs in der Agada und die Evangeliengeschichte," *ΑΓΓΕΛΟΣ: Archiv für neutestamentliche Zeitgeschichte und Kulturkunde* 4 (1932) 51–55; M. Braun, *History and Romance in Graeco-Oriental Literature* (Oxford: Blackwell, 1938); H. A. Brongers, *De Jozefsgeschiedenis bij Joden, Christenen en Mohammedanen* (Wageningen: Veenman, 1962); D. J. Harrington, "Joseph in the Testament of Joseph, Pseudo-Philo, and Philo," in *Studies on the Testament of Joseph* (ed. G. W. E. Nickelsburg; SBLSCS 5; Missoula, Mont.: Scholars Press, 1975) 127–31; E. W. Smith, Jr., "Joseph Material in Joseph and Asenath and Josephus Relating to the Testament of Joseph," in *Studies on the Testament of Joseph* (ed. G. W. E. Nickelsburg; SBLSCS 5; Missoula, Mont.: Scholars Press, 1975) 133–37; E. Hilgert, "The Dual Image of Joseph in Hebrew and Early Jewish Literature," *Papers of the Chicago Society of Biblical Research* 30 (1985) 5–21; J. L. Kugel, *In Potiphar's House: The Interpretive Life of Biblical Texts* (San Francisco: Harper, 1990) pt. 1 (pp. 13–155); G. Teugels, "De kuise Jozef: De receptie van een bijbels model," *NedThT* 45 (1991) 193–203; and M. Niehoff, *The Figure of Joseph in Post-biblical Jewish Literature* (AGJU 16; Leiden-New York-Cologne: Brill, 1992).

On the image of Joseph in some Bible illustrations, see J. Gutmann, "Joseph Legends in the Vienna Genesis," *Proceedings of the Fifth World Congress of Jewish Studies* 4 (1973) 181–84; and I. M. Veldman and H. J. de Jonge, "The Sons of Jacob: The Twelve Patriarchs in Sixteenth-Century Netherlandish Prints and Popular Literature," *Simiolus: Netherlands Quarterly for the History of Art* 15 (1985) 176–96.

There are also studies dedicated to the figure of Joseph in some particular writing, author, or religious tradition. For Philo's portrait of Joseph, see J. M. Bassler, "Philo on Joseph: The Basic Coherence of *De Iosepho* and *De Somniis* ii," *JSJ* 16 (1985) 240–55; T. H. Tobin, "Tradition and Interpretation in Philo's Portrait of the Patriarch Joseph," *SBLSP* 25 (1986) 271–77; and D. M. Hay, "Politics and Exegesis in Philo's Treatise on Dreams," *SBLSP* 26 (1987) 429–38.

The figure of Joseph in the writings of Josephus has been studied in detail by H. Spródowsky, *Die Hellenisierung der Geschichte von Joseph in Ägypten bei Flavius Josephus* (Greifswald: Dallmeyer, 1937); and L. H. Feldman, "Josephus' Portrait of Joseph," *RB* 99 (1992) 379–417, 504–28.

The role of Joseph in some midrashim has been analyzed by B. Geller, "Joseph in the Tannaitic Midrashim," in *Studies on the Testament of Joseph* (ed. G. W. E. Nickelsburg; SBLSCS 5; Missoula, Mont.: Scholars Press, 1975) 139–46.

On the role of Joseph in the *Testaments of the Twelve Patriarchs,* see G. W. E. Nickelsburg, ed., *Studies on the Testament of Joseph* (SBLSCS 5; Missoula, Mont.: Scholars Press, 1975); H. W. Hollander, "El 'hombre bueno' en los pasajes éticos del Testamento de Benjamín," *Estudios Franciscanos* 80 (1979) 209–21; and idem, *Joseph as an Ethical Model in the Testaments of the Twelve Patriarchs* (SVTP 6; Leiden: Brill, 1981).

For Joseph's part in other early Christian literature, including the NT, and in patristic literature, see A. W. Argyle, "Joseph the Patriarch in Patristic Teaching," *ExpTim* 67 (1955–56) 199–201; H. W. Hollander, "The Influence of the Testaments of the Twelve Patriarchs in the Early Church: Joseph as Model in Prochorus' Acts of John," *OLP* 9 (1978) 75–81; and E. Richard, "The Polemical Character of the Joseph Episode in Acts 7," *JBL* 98 (1979) 255–67.

Joseph's eminent role in Samaritan sources has been studied by J. D. Purvis in "Joseph in the Samaritan Traditions," in *Studies on the Testament of Joseph* (ed. G. W. E. Nickelsburg; SBLSCS 5; Missoula, Mont.: Scholars Press, 1975) 147–53.

For the image of Joseph in the Qur'an and in Islamic tradition, see the literature mentioned in E. Isaac, "The Ethiopic History of Joseph: Translation with Introduction and Notes," *JSP* 6 (1990) 3–125, esp. p. 42. See also M. Grünbaum, "Zu 'Jussuf und Suleicha'" and "Zu Schlechta-Wssehrd's Ausgabe des 'Jussuf und Suleicha,'" in *Gesammelte Aufsätze zur Sprach- und Sagenkunde* (ed. F. Perles; Berlin: Calvary, 1901) 515–51, 552–93; J. Macdonald, "Joseph in the Qur'an and Muslim Commentary: A Comparative Study," *The Muslim World* 46 (1956) 113–31, 207–24; M. S. Stern, "Muhammad and Joseph: A Study of Koranic Narrative," *JNES* 44 (1985) 193–204; M. R. Waldman, "New Approaches to 'Biblical' Materials in the Qur'an," *The Muslim World* 75 (1985) 1–16; M. Mir, "The Qur'anic Story of Joseph: Plot, Themes, and Characters," *The Muslim World* 76 (1986) 1–15; and G. A. Rendsburg, "Literary Structures in the Qur'anic and Biblical Stories of Joseph," *The Muslim World* 78 (1988) 118–20.

Joseph in Later Christian Sources and in World Literature

There are many studies dedicated to the influence of the Joseph story on Christian and non-Christian writers through the ages. The most important are V. Grabowski, *Die Geschichte Josefs von Mar Narses nach einer syrischen Handschrift der Königl. Bibliothek in Berlin herausgegeben, übersetzt und kritisch bearbeitet* (Berlin: Itzkowski, 1889), pt. 1; H. Näf, *Syrische Josef-Gedichte: Mit Übersetzung des Gedichts von Narsai und Proben aus Balai und Jaqob von Sarug* (Zürich: Schwarzenbach, 1923); H. Priebatsch, *Die Josephgeschichte in der Weltliteratur: Eine legendgeschichtliche Studie* (Breslau: Marcus, 1937); M. Nabholz-Oberlin, *Der Josephroman in der deutschen Literatur von Grimmelshausen bis Thomas Mann* (Marburg: Bauer, 1950); L. J. Budd, "Mark Twain on Joseph the Patriarch," *American Quarterly* 16 (1964) 577–86; J. D. Yohannan, *Joseph and Potiphar's Wife in World Literature: An Anthology of the Story of the Chaste Youth and the Lustful Stepmother* (New York: New Directions, 1968); M. Derpmann, *Die Josephgeschichte: Auffassung und Darstellung im Mittelalter* (Beihefte zum "Mittellateinischen Jahrbuch" 13; Ratingen-Kastellaun-Düsseldorf: Henn, 1974); J. Lebeau, *Salvator Mundi, L''exemple' de Joseph dans le théâtre allemand au XVIe siècle* (2 vols.; Nieuwkoop: De Graaf, 1977); and K. Hamburger, *Thomas Manns biblisches Werk: Der Joseph-Roman, Die Moses-Erzählung, "Das Gesetz"* (Munich: Nymphenburger, 1981).

BARUCH

His Evolution from Scribe
to Apocalyptic Seer

J. EDWARD WRIGHT

Introduction

The sage had a prominent position in early Judaism.[1] According to Ben Sira 38–39, sages were respected for their wisdom, piety, and knowledge of Torah; because of this they became authoritative figures in their communities.[2] When a pseudepigraphic text comes to be attributed to an ancient sage, the text normally relates the new work to existing traditions about the sage. Thus, when readers encounter a new pseudepigraphon ascribed to an ancient figure, they bring to it their understanding of earlier and current traditions about that figure. The selection of an attribution for a pseudonymous text is made with reference not only to the character's biblical portrayal, but also to what the character had become in the popular imagination since or outside of the biblical material. In turn, each new text adds something new to the portraiture of the character; thus the character evolves with time.

For example, even though little is made of Enoch in the Bible, he was the focus of a wealth of traditions that circulated outside

---

1. The first part of this chapter is a revised version of Wright, "Baruch, the Ideal Sage," 193–210.
2. See Stone, "Ideal Figures," 575–86. Note also Collins, "The Sage," 343–54; and Neusner, "Sage, Priest, Messiah," 35–44.

of and in conjunction with the biblical account. Ezra and Daniel fare well both within and outside the Bible. As for Baruch ben Neriah, his persona developed from that of scribal assistant to the prophet Jeremiah to that of an ideal sage and apocalyptic seer. It is this transformation that is traced in the present essay.

Baruch in the Book of Jeremiah

The biblical Book of Jeremiah purports to record the prophetic activity of Jeremiah ben Hilkiah, a priest and prophet from the village of Anathoth (Jer 1:1). Jeremiah and his scribal assistant Baruch[3] were active during the tumultuous years surrounding the fall of Jerusalem to the Babylonians in 586 B.C.E. Baruch first appears in Jer 32:12–16 as the certifier of a land transaction between Jeremiah and his cousin Hanamel. This is a typical scribal duty.[4] Baruch appears next in Jeremiah 36, where he records Jeremiah's sermons. On account of the activities described in this passage, many think that Baruch was the editor of the Book of Jeremiah as we now have it.[5]

Baruch then figures in Jeremiah 43:1–7, where several Judaeans charge him with inciting Jeremiah to proclaim an oracle of disaster against them because they had planned to flee to Egypt to escape the Babylonian assault on their land. Finally, in Jeremiah 45, Jeremiah delivers an oracle intended personally for Baruch that warns him against his seeking "great things" and promises him personal deliverance.[6]

---

3. The name "Baruch" (ברוך) is a shortened form of ברכיהו, "Berechyahu," and means "blessed by Yahweh." The name is well attested in the late biblical and Second Temple periods. Baruch is one of the few biblical figures directly witnessed by external evidence. A clay bulla or seal impression with the inscription "Belonging to Berechyahu the son of Neriah, the scribe" (cf. Jer 36:32) was found with other bullae bearing the names and titles of royal officials of Judah. This bulla would have been attached to a document much like the one mentioned in Jeremiah 32. See Avigad, "Baruch the Scribe," 52–56.

4. On Baruch and the social standing of scribes see Lundbom, "Baruch, Seraiah, and Expanded Colophons," 107–8; and Muilenburg, "Baruch the Scribe," 232–38.

5. See Duhm, *Das Buch Jeremia,* and Mowinckel, *Komposition.* But does this passage provide a reliable model for how the Jeremianic corpus was compiled? Carroll, *Jeremiah,* 44–45, 61, and idem, "Arguing about Jeremiah," 222–35, argues that this passage cannot be used to identify who wrote any part of the biblical book.

6. Taylor, "Jeremiah 45," 79–98, proposes a contextual reading that highlights the typological significance of the text. Taylor's analysis does not, however, address the issue in the Greek version.

Baruch is not mentioned in the Bible outside the Book of Jeremiah.[7] There are, however, two distinct versions of the Book of Jeremiah — the Masoretic version found in the Hebrew Bible, and the version represented in the Old Greek (Septuagint) and attested also in Hebrew fragments discovered at Qumran. The structure of the Old Greek differs dramatically from that of the MT. The Greek text is not simply a revision of the Hebrew, but represents an entirely different literary tradition of the book.[8] The most obvious structural difference lies in the placement of the "Oracles against the Nations." In the MT these appear at the end of the book (46:1–51:58), while in the Greek version they are found in the middle (25:14–31:44). The placement of these oracles influences the location of the episodes involving Baruch. In the MT, the episodes with Baruch appear in the middle of the book, before the oracles, whereas in the Old Greek they stand at the end. Most important, in the Greek version Baruch is the last person in the book to receive a divine oracle (chap. 51 = MT chap. 45).

Although all of the passages involving Baruch in the MT and Old Greek appear in both versions, their placement specifically at the end of Greek Jeremiah indicates that the editor(s) of that version wished to stress that Baruch, too, was worthy of divine communication. Moreover, that Baruch is the last person addressed by God in the Greek Jeremiah suggests that the editor(s) envisaged Baruch as Jeremiah's prophetic successor.[9]

If the Greek Jeremiah represents a more original form of the text, the MT would constitute a rearrangement of the material

---

7. There are several traditions about the fate of Baruch. The biblical account states that he was taken unwillingly to Egypt (Jer 43:4–7). Jerome follows this tradition in his commentary on Isaiah 30:7 (*PL* 24:353), as does *S. 'Olam Rab.* 26 (ed. Ratner, p. 119). *2 Apoc. Bar.* 10:1–3; *Par. Jer.* 1:1; 4:6–7; 5:17–18; 7:36; 8:6–7; and Rashi (on Jer 44:14) report that Baruch remained in Jerusalem. The preface to the Book of Baruch (1:1–2); *y. Sanh.* 1, 19a; *b. Meg.* 16b; and *Shir HaShirim Rabba* 5 all report that Baruch lived in Babylon. Josephus, *Ant.* 10.9.5; *S. 'Olam Rab.* 26 (ed. Ratner, p. 120), and *Midr. Eser Galuyot* (ed. Jellinek, *Bet Ha-Midrasch,* 4.135) recount that although Jeremiah and Baruch went to Egypt, Nebuchadnezzar eventually conquered Egypt, and took Jeremiah, Baruch, and other Jews living there to Babylon.

8. See Tov, *Septuagint Translation;* idem, "Some Aspects," 145–67; J. G. Jansen, *Studies;* and Stulman, *Other Text,* 1–5.

9. Bogaert, "De Baruch à Jérémie," 168–73; and idem, "Le personnage de Baruch et l'histoire du livre de Jérémie: Aux origines du livre deuterocanonique de Baruch," 73–81, notes that the Greek order suggests that Baruch will witness both the proclamation and fulfillment of Jeremiah's oracles. Kessler, "Jeremiah Chapters 26–45," 81–88, similarly states that "Baruch became the next link in the Jeremiah tradition" (86).

that, for some reason, does not wish to portray Baruch as Jeremiah's successor.[10] The characterization of Baruch in the MT is simply that of a scribe performing customary scribal duties. The clear tendency in the Greek text to portray Baruch as Jeremiah's successor, on the other hand, may be at least partially responsible for the increased prominence of Baruch in later Jewish and Christian tradition.[11] The debate over whether Baruch was a prophet continued in rabbinic circles.[12] It seems clear from the evidence of Greek Jeremiah, however, that certain segments of the early Jewish community regarded Baruch as Jeremiah's prophetic successor.

The Book of Baruch

The Book of Baruch, one of the so-called apocrypha, consists of four literary units that originally circulated independently: 1:1–14, a narrative introduction; 1:15–3:8, a prayer; 3:9–4:4, a poem in praise of wisdom; and 4:5–5:9, a parenetic discourse. These components were eventually combined to form a new text. This text was appended to the end of the Greek version of Jeremiah and was not known separately as the "Book of Baruch" in the Latin church until the eighth century.[13] Some Greek fathers quote the Book of Baruch but identify their source as "Jeremiah," while others cite their locus as "Baruch."[14] This ambiguity indicates that early Christian (and Jewish?) communities were uncertain about the book's authorship. The book is anonymous apart from the narrative introduction, the only place in the work where

---

10. Bogaert, "De Baruch à Jérémie," 170–71, notes that the MT of Jer 36:26 reads "Baruch the scribe and Jeremiah the prophet," while the same passage in the Old Greek (Jer 43:26) reads "Baruch and Jeremiah." Tov and Jansen identify this as an example of "expansionistic tendencies" in the MT of Jeremiah (Tov, *Septuagint Translation*; J. G. Jansen, *Studies*). I would suggest that this "expansionistic tendency" is in this case motivated in part by the editor's wish to differentiate the roles of Baruch and Jeremiah.

11. Seitz, "Prophet Moses," 3–27, suggests that even Hebrew Jeremiah indicates that Baruch is the successor of Jeremiah (pp. 18, 23). Nevertheless, the placement of the oracle to Baruch at the end of Greek Jeremiah surely highlights this point, and that the Book of Baruch follows Jeremiah in the Greek Bible links the former to the latter and reifies Baruch's role as successor.

12. See below; cf. Bogaert, *Apocalypse de Baruch*, 1.104–8.

13. See Bogaert, "Nom de Baruch," 61–72.

14. Bogaert, "Nom de Baruch," 65–66.

Baruch is mentioned. The book as a whole was probably not associated with Baruch until the introduction was added.[15] From all of this, it appears that there was considerable fluidity in defining the limits of the Greek version of Jeremiah. Eventually, however, the "additions" were collected into an independent work and ascribed to Baruch. It should also be remembered that these "additions" appear as part of the Greek version of Jeremiah, precisely that version which suggests that Baruch was Jeremiah's prophetic successor.

The narrative introduction of the Book of Baruch (1:1–14) locates Baruch among the exiles in Babylon (1:1–2). The introduction describes the book as a writing of Baruch which was read to a gathering of Jewish exiles in Babylon (1:3–5). The author of this section portrays Baruch as a leader of the exiles by having the exiled Judean king Jehoiachin and "all the people" gather to hear Baruch's words. In response to Baruch's message, the exiles weep, fast, pray, and prepare sacrifices, activities that conform to a biblical model for repentance (cf. Judg 20:26; 2 Sam 1:2; Neh 1:4). In this role Baruch is depicted as being like Ezekiel or Jeremiah, who also had people gather around them to hear the "word of the Lord" (Jer 25:1–2; 26:7; Ezek 8:1; 33:30–32).

The second section of the book, the prayer of Baruch (1:15–3:8), portrays Baruch as a penitent who prays like Daniel. The link with Daniel is clear insofar as the text of the prayer is actually a patchwork of excerpts from Daniel 9.[16] The prayer depicts Baruch as one who has accepted the "Deuteronomistic" explanation of the fall of Jerusalem and the exile of the people: it came about because the people had failed to worship Yahweh alone. The connection with the Deuteronomistic ideology is made explicit through quotations from and allusions to Deuteronomistic

---

15. Bogaert, "Le personnage de Baruch et l'histoire du livre de Jérémie: Aux origines du livre de Baruch," 20, notes that even with the introduction, the work is better associated with Jeremiah than with Baruch because the οὗτοι οἱ λόγοι of Bar 1:1 refers back to Jeremiah, the book immediately preceding it in the Greek Bible (or perhaps the book of which it was a part).

16. For the links between the Books of Baruch and Daniel, see the notes in Tov, ed. and trans., *Book of Baruch*, 15–27. On the possible relationship between the Book of Baruch and the Theodotianic version of Daniel, see Tov, "Relations," 27–34. A different view is taken by Moore, "Toward Dating the Book of Baruch," 312–20.

materials, particularly to the Books of Daniel and Jeremiah.[17] The prayer, then, depicts Baruch as a pious person who, like Daniel, was concerned for the exiles and the condition of Jerusalem.[18] Like Daniel, Baruch accepts the exile as God's punishment for religious infidelity, seeks divine forgiveness for Israel's sins, and asks that the exiles be repatriated.

The third unit of the book (3:9–4:4), a poem in praise of wisdom,[19] exhorts its audience, in a manner reminiscent of Job 28 and 38 and Proverbs 1–9, to pursue wisdom. Wisdom is equated with obedience to the divine commandments, i.e., the Torah. This third unit, then, adds a wisdom element to the developing persona of Baruch. Baruch is becoming a paradigm of a Second Temple period sage who is devoted to wisdom, now characterized not simply as familiarity with ancient lore or as skill as a scribe, but as obedience to Torah.[20] He is, therefore, the type of leader who serves as a model of fidelity to the religious and cultural norms of the community.

The final unit of the book, 4:5–5:9, is a parenetic discourse meant to inspire the exiles to remain faithful to God despite their sufferings.[21] This section encourages the exiles to take heart (4:5, 21–30; 5:1–4), obey God's commandments (4:28), and prepare to return to Jerusalem (4:21–23, 29, 36–37; 5:5–9). Just as Jeremiah wrote to instruct and encourage the exiles, so Baruch offers them comfort and guidance. Through the ascription of this originally anonymous poem to Baruch, the portrait of Baruch as one concerned for the well-being of exiled Jews and of Jerusalem gains detail. All of this material now envisages the rather obscure biblical figure as a great leader. This reflects the community's in-

---

17. Thus the book was written after the composition of Daniel, which dates from the Maccabean period. See Schreiner, *Baruch*, 46–47. Tov, *Septuagint Translation*, 165–67, dates the Greek translation of Jeremiah and the Book of Baruch before 116 B.C.E. Bogaert, "Le personnage de Baruch et l'histoire du livre de Jérémie: Aux origines du livre de Baruch," 20, dates the Book of Baruch between 63 B.C.E. and 70 C.E.

18. Similar penitential prayers are made by Ezra in Ezra 9:5–15 and Nehemiah in Neh 1:4–11.

19. See Burke, *Poetry of Baruch*.

20. See von Rad, *Wisdom in Israel*, 240–62; Harrington, "Wisdom of the Scribe," 181–89.

21. Schreiner, *Baruch*, 47, dates this section to after 63 B.C.E. This unit has several phrases with close parallels in the *Psalms of Solomon*. It seems most likely that the two depend on another text, now lost.

terest in a leadership that promotes obedience to Torah as the way to achieve wisdom, and that heeds the desires of those living outside the land for a connection to Jerusalem. But this is only an initial stage in the transformation of Baruch from a scribe to a great sage and apocalyptic seer. The popular perception of Baruch was changing; the professional scribe was being transformed into a character of central importance to the community.

The *Paraleipomena of Jeremiah*

The *Paraleipomena of Jeremiah* purports to recount the destruction of Jerusalem by the Babylonians in 586 B.C.E., but was actually written at some time after 70 C.E.[22] The author uses the Babylonian destruction of Jerusalem as a paradigm by which to explain the Roman destruction. The text reflects the anguish that prevailed in Jewish circles after the Romans leveled the city and the Temple.

Both the *Paraleipomena of Jeremiah* and 2 (*the Syriac Apocalypse of*) *Baruch,* a work discussed in the next section, begin with parallel accounts of the fall of Jerusalem to the Babylonians. These accounts, however, depict the relationship of Baruch to Jeremiah differently. Interestingly, these deviations reflect the differing portrayals of Baruch in the two versions of the Book of Jeremiah, where Baruch was either Jeremiah's scribal assistant (MT) or his prophetic successor (Old Greek).

The parallel passages in the *Paraleipomena of Jeremiah* and *2 Baruch* have the following elements in common: (1) both state that God spoke directly to the central figure (*Par. Jer.* 1:1; *2 Apoc. Bar.* 1:1); (2) both state that the sins of the people brought about God's judgment (*Par. Jer.* 1:1; *2 Apoc. Bar.* 1:2–4); and (3) both mention the effectiveness of the prayers or actions of Jeremiah, Baruch, and their associates (*Par. Jer.* 1:2; *2 Apoc. Bar.* 2:1). These parallels indicate either that, for their introductory narratives, one of these texts depends on the other or, more likely,

---

22. On whether this is a Jewish or Christian work, see Harris, *Rest of the Words of Baruch,* 13–17; Delling, *Jüdische Lehre,* 34–36, 68–74.

that both depend on a common source.[23] Where the two texts differ, however, is in whether Jeremiah or Baruch is considered the central figure. In the *Paraleipomena of Jeremiah,* God addresses Jeremiah directly ("God spoke to Jeremiah") and instructs him to tell Baruch what to do (1:1, 8, 10; 3:14–16; 4:6–12). In *2 Baruch,* however, just the opposite occurs: God speaks directly to Baruch ("the word of the Lord came to Baruch") and commands him to instruct Jeremiah (2:1; 5:5; 10:1–5).

Clearly these texts have differing perspectives on the relationship between Jeremiah and Baruch. In the *Paraleipomena of Jeremiah,* Jeremiah remains the central figure,[24] whereas *2 Baruch* identifies Baruch as the main leader. *2 Apoc. Bar.* 5:5–7 recounts how Baruch took several leaders of the city, including Jeremiah, to the Kidron Valley to inform them what God had disclosed to him about the fall of the city. According to *2 Baruch* 6–9, Baruch alone sees angels enter the city, break down its walls, and hide the sacred vessels; in *Paraleipomena of Jeremiah* 3, however, both Baruch and Jeremiah witness these events. The *Paraleipomena of Jeremiah,* then, like the MT of Jeremiah, depicts Jeremiah as the central figure, while *2 Baruch,* which parallels the exalted depiction of Baruch in Greek Jeremiah, emphasizes the emergence of Baruch as Jeremiah's successor.[25]

Second (the Syriac Apocalypse of) Baruch

2 Baruch, introduced in the previous section, is yet another Jewish Baruch pseudepigraphon. Although the narrative setting of the text is the Babylonian destruction of the Jerusalem Temple in 586 B.C.E., the book was composed at some time after the Roman destruction of Jerusalem in 70 C.E.[26] As stated above, the unknown

---

23. See Nickelsburg, "Narrative Traditions," 60–68. Bogaert, *Apocalypse de Baruch,* 1.177–221, argues that the *Paraleipomena of Jeremiah* depends on *2 Baruch.*

24. See Riaud, "Figure de Jérémie," 373–85.

25. The *Paraleipomena of Jeremiah* may view both Baruch and Abimelech (i.e., the Ebed-melech mentioned in Jer 38:1–13; 39:15–18) as Jeremiah's successors. Whenever Jeremiah addresses Baruch in this book, he speaks to both Baruch and Abimelech, apparently viewing the two as equal. *Par. Jer.* 9:23–29 is especially important, because here Jeremiah delivers to both Baruch and Abimelech "all the mysteries which he had seen."

26. Determining the relative dates of this apocalypse and the closely related Book of

author clearly portrays Baruch as Jeremiah's prophetic successor. To connect Baruch explicitly with the biblical prophets, the author uses a standard biblical prophetic formula to introduce God's speeches to Baruch: just as "the word of the Lord came" to Jeremiah and other prophets in ancient Israel, so Baruch receives "the word of the Lord" (1:1; 10:1; 13:2). The author's use of this formula links Baruch to the line of classical prophets, thereby demonstrating that Baruch is a legitimate successor to the biblical prophets.[27]

The author of 2 Baruch also legitimates Baruch as a prophet by linking him to the greatest of all the prophets, Moses.[28] Baruch's fidelity to the Law is above reproach (2 Apoc. Bar. 38:2–4), and God has revealed to him secrets about the end of time and the measurements of the future temple, just as he had to Moses (2 Apoc. Bar. 59:4).[29] Just as Moses ascended Mount Nebo before his death and learned divine mysteries (cf. Deut 32:48–52; 34:1–8), so Baruch ascended a mountain to learn divine secrets before his departure from the world (2 Baruch 76). God also told Baruch that although he would leave this world, he would not die (2 Apoc. Bar. 43:2; 76:2) but be "taken up" into heaven (46:7); this parallels pseudepigraphic traditions about Moses.[30]

Baruch confirmed the Mosaic covenant by reiterating commandments that Moses gave to the people (2 Baruch 84). Like Moses, Baruch taught people how to live in order to merit divine favor (cf. Deuteronomy 30). In all of this material, Baruch appears as a tradent of what have become cherished, community-defining traditions. Baruch's visions and revelations are based on and confirm ancient materials. By linking the ideas in 2 Baruch with long-standing traditions, the author hopes to make this text part of a continuing chain of Jewish thought — what is new in the text is not necessarily revolutionary. The new aspects of Baruch's

---

4 Ezra is a vexing problem. For the current state of the debate, see Stone, Fourth Ezra, 9–10, 39–40.

27. The use of this technique in the Bible is elucidated by Fishbane, Biblical Interpretation, 372–79.

28. See Murphy, Structure and Meaning of Second Baruch, 117–34.

29. According to Sifre Deut. 357 (ed. Finkelstein, p. 426), God showed Moses the events of the "end of time."

30. See Loewenstamm, "Death of Moses," 185–217. Compare 2 Apoc. Bar. 84:1–11.

message are legitimated by their continuity with the old. Baruch is the prophetic successor of Jeremiah, but he is also a prophet in the tradition of Moses, after whom all legitimate prophets are patterned (cf. Deut 18:15–22).

The author of *2 Baruch* attributes to Baruch's followers speeches that indicate how highly they esteem the sage. As Baruch turns to leave the people, they lament that he is leaving them "as a father who leaves his children as orphans and goes away from them" (*2 Apoc. Bar.* 32:9). Baruch calms them by telling them that he will be away only temporarily in order to go to the Holy of Holies to receive further revelations from God (34:1). The need the community expresses for Baruch's presence indicates that they regard him as their source of life and connection to God.

Behind the pseudepigraphic veil of the text, it seems likely that this account reflects attitudes of an actual community toward its leaders.[31] The community depends on its leaders for its existence and sense of purpose. The author seems to have intended that his readers put themselves in the position of the people addressed by Baruch, and that they regard the author as a divinely inspired seer, and the text as a product of divine revelation.

Later in the book, when Baruch tells the people that he must leave them again (chaps. 44–45), their response indicates that they regard him as an inspired interpreter of Torah:

> And my son and the elders of the people said to me: "Did the Mighty One humiliate us to such an extent that he will take you away from us quickly? And shall we truly be in darkness, and will there be no light anymore for that people who are left? For where shall we again investigate the Law, or who will distinguish between death and life for us?" And I said to them: "I cannot resist the throne of the Mighty One. But Israel will not be in want of a wise man, nor the tribe of Jacob, a son of the Law. But only prepare your heart so that you obey the Law, and be subject to those who are wise and understanding with fear." (*2 Apoc. Bar.* 46:1–5)[32]

This passage depicts Baruch as an inspired, divinely authorized interpreter of Torah. He alone has the ability to "distinguish between death and life," that is, between the things that displease and please God. Baruch declares that God will provide inspired interpreters for each generation (46:4–5). As Baruch followed

---

31. See Wright, "Social Setting."
32. Quoted from Klijn, trans., "2 (Syriac Apocalypse of) Baruch," *OTP* 1.635.

Moses and Jeremiah, so there will be successors of Baruch as inspired interpreters whose teachings will preserve the life of the
community. This demonstrates the author's interest in establishing
a continuity between Baruch and his own time. In fact, it could
be argued that the author of 2 *Baruch* wishes to be regarded as a
legitimate "successor" to Baruch, continuing to instruct the community in the correct interpretation of Torah. Baruch is presented
in 77:12–16, for example, as precisely this type of divinely inspired interpreter of Torah. The people who follow his teachings
do so because they believe that these are correct understandings
of Torah that will lead to salvation.[33]

The emergence of the role of inspired interpreter of scripture
is part of a larger cultural transformation that was taking place
in Second Temple Judaism. This transition involves "making the
movement from a culture based on direct divine revelations to
one based on their study and reinterpretation."[34] Evidence of this
transition is also found at Qumran. The "Legitimate Teacher"
(or "Teacher of Righteousness") was the sect's inspired commentator on Torah, whose interpretations were regarded as divinely
inspired teachings by which the sectaries could order their lives
(1QpHab ii 1–10; viii 3–5; vii 17–viii 3).[35] By virtue of this fact,
he held a position of supreme authority. After his death the community awaited another inspired teacher (CD xix 35–xx 1; xx
14). The Legitimate Teacher apparently believed that he had been
inspired by God to interpret Torah and to reveal to his followers
the mysteries that God had given to him (cf. 1QpHab viii 1–3;
1QH ii 13–15).

The Teacher's interpretations of scripture structured the sectaries' lives and worldview. The atomistic type of biblical interpretation found in the Qumran *pesharim* presupposes that the
Hebrew Bible was an authoritative text for the community, but it
was actually only part of a group of divinely inspired documents;
together with the Bible went the Legitimate Teacher's interpre-

---

33. Nickelsburg, "*1 Enoch* and Qumran Origins," 341–60, notes that "*1 Enoch* and
the Scrolls share the common notion that the author's community possesses a revealed
interpretation of the Torah, which is necessary for salvation" (p. 351). See also idem,
"Revealed Wisdom," 73–81.

34. Fishbane, "From Scribalism to Rabbinism," 440.

35. Cf. CD 7:4–5, 20:13; 1QH 2:9–10.

tations of it. Both were authoritative.[36] Actually, many of the interpretive principles utilized by the Legitimate Teacher (and his contemporaries) had a long history in ancient Israel and were also used by later rabbinic exegetes.[37] Through the use of specific interpretive techniques, the Legitimate Teacher and others like him formulated new interpretations of biblical texts. While the hermeneutical techniques utilized by various groups may have been similar, it was the differences in the results of these techniques, i.e., in the actual interpretations of authoritative documents, that led to the development of many "sects" in early Judaism.

One of these sects, the early Christian community, originated at least in part due to a conflict over scriptural interpretation. The gospel writers depict Jesus as an inspired interpreter who provides new perspectives on the scriptures. Several times in the "sermon" in Matthew 5–7, Jesus declares, "You have heard it said...," before citing a commandment from Torah. He then continues, "but I say to you...," giving a new interpretation of it (Matt 5:21–48). Jesus' interpretations of Torah apparently led to disputes with other Jewish leaders (e.g., Mark 7:1–23 and parallels). The apostle Paul also established a following based in large measure on his personal claims to authority and his interpretations of scripture. He considered himself a divinely inspired interpreter, and often admonished his audience to obey his teachings and eschew those of his opponents (cf. Galatians *passim;* 1 Cor 11:2; 2 Corinthians 10–13). In all of these cases, each party presumably had its own interpretation of the scriptural passage(s) at issue. As a result, separate communities formed around various interpreters, based on their charisma, rhetoric, and claims to authority.

2 Baruch, then, presents Baruch as the legitimate prophetic successor of Jeremiah, one whose interpretations of Torah are authentic. His revelations derive from encounters with the divine, and he is an example of a leader whom God inspires to provide

---

36. Fishbane, "Use, Authority, and Interpretation of Mikra," 340, notes that at Qumran there were "...both Mikra and its Interpretation, as guided by the head teacher and those authorized to interpret under his guidance (or the exegetical principles laid down by him)." Compare 1QS viii 15–16.

37. See Silberman, "Unriddling the Riddle," 323–35; Feltes, *Die Gattung des Habakukkommentars.*

the correct meaning of scripture. By his interpretations he guides the community, provides answers to their problems, and reveals mysteries.

Third (the Greek Apocalypse of) Baruch

3 Baruch, a pseudepigraphical text that narrates a heavenly journey taken by Baruch, was written, probably in Greek, by an unknown Jewish or Christian author in the late first or second century C.E. The text was composed partially in response to the Roman destruction of Jerusalem in 70 C.E., and knows traditions about Baruch as a person concerned with the state of Jerusalem and the suffering of the righteous. Although the narrative setting of *3 Baruch* coincides with traditions about Baruch in the *Paraleipomena of Jeremiah* and *2 Baruch,* there is no evidence that any of these texts depended upon another; rather, they seem to rely upon common traditions.

In *3 Baruch* the depiction of Baruch takes on an additional feature: Baruch becomes an apocalyptic seer who is taken on a guided tour of the heavens. *3 Baruch*'s fictional setting is again the time of the Babylonian destruction of Jerusalem in 586 B.C.E.;[38] the actual setting, however, is some time after the Roman destruction of Jerusalem in 70 C.E., probably after the writing of *2 Baruch.* Like the writer of *2 Baruch, 3 Baruch*'s author uses the destruction of the First Temple by the Babylonians as a model by which to describe the historical circumstances and personal tragedies attending the destruction of the Second Temple by the Romans. *3 Baruch* fits, therefore, within the literary and historical contexts in which one expects to find Baruch — the fall of Jerusalem to a foreign power.

The heavenly tour recounted in *3 Baruch* comes in response to Baruch's prayers.[39] The angel Phamael leads him through five heavens, where he learns the secrets of the cosmos and of God's

---

38. For introductory matters see James, ed., *Apocrypha Anecdota II,* li–lxxi; and Gaylord, trans., "3 (Greek Apocalypse of) Baruch," *OTP* 1.653–61.
39. See Picard, "Observations," 77–103.

control over history.[40] He finds that, although this world may seem senseless and chaotic, God is in control and listens to people's prayers. The growing prominence of the ascent theme in Jewish literature of the Greco-Roman period, as evidenced in *3 Baruch,* suggests, in part, a shift among some Jews regarding the nature of, and means of claiming, religious authority.[41] It is important to note, however, that heavenly ascent functioned as a means of promoting religious status neither in the antecedent biblical materials nor in subsequent rabbinic literature.

The first possible candidate in the Bible for ascension to heaven is Enoch. Gen 5:24 states that "God took him [Enoch]." According to early Jewish interpretation of Gen 5:21–24, Enoch ascended into heaven because of his piety.[42] Likewise, Elijah at the end of his life is depicted as ascending into heaven in a whirlwind (2 Kgs 2:11). Other biblical materials, however, demonstrate that some authors did not view the idea of heavenly ascent as favorably. Deut 30:11–14, for example, stresses that God's teachings are not secreted away in heaven where one need ascend in order to learn them; rather, they are at hand in the Torah (cf. Deut 29:29). In addition, Isa 14:12–20 uses the idea of ascent to heaven derisively to ridicule the Babylonian king's hubris. From this perspective, the desire to ascend to heaven evidences wickedness, not piety. For the tradents of these materials, the claim of ascent to heaven was not welcome. Whereas these tradents did not necessarily prohibit speculation on the divine presence (see the examples cited below), they did resist the idea of a human actually entering the divine realm. Some privileged individuals may glimpse the divine presence (e.g., Moses and others in Exod 24:1–2, 9–11; Micaiah ben Imlah in 1 Kings 22; Isaiah in Isaiah 6; and Ezekiel in Ezekiel 1), but their feet never leave the ground. These are visions of the divine presence, not heavenly journeys. Ascent into heaven plays no role in the revelatory experiences recounted in the Bible.

---

40. Wright, *Cosmography,* demonstrates that the five-heaven schema of *3 Baruch* recounts a complete journey and not an abbreviated account, as many have suggested. Compare Harlow, *The Greek Apocalypse of Baruch.*

41. The ascent theme is treated by Segal, "Heavenly Ascent," 1333–94; and Himmelfarb, *Ascent to Heaven.*

42. See VanderKam, *Enoch: A Man for All Generations;* and the article on Enoch in the present volume.

The central means of revelation in the Bible is through the medium of prophecy. The authority of the Yahwistic prophet rests in the claim to have received "the word of the Lord." The common phrases "the word of the Lord was upon me" and "thus says the Lord" provide the basis for prophetic authority.[43] The revelation received is immediate and of divine origin. Once written down, however, the prophetic word becomes subject to exegesis or interpretation. Daniel 9, for example, is part of an exegetical tradition of reinterpretation of the oracle in Jeremiah 25.[44] Thus, the authority of select prophetic oracles was accepted early, and subsequent interpretation of these oracles can be found in other biblical documents. This activity started a process wherein the interpretation of authoritative documents became a basis for claiming further authority.

While the authority of prophetic speech is based on firsthand reception of the divine word, the authority of exegetical interpretation rests both on the authority of the original document and on the claim to divine inspiration by the interpreter. The claim to possess an inspired interpretation of a scriptural document was often augmented by an appeal to the authority and status of the teacher who had made the interpretation.[45] As noted above, the idea of the authority of an inspired interpreter is apparent in the attitude of the people toward Baruch in *2 Baruch,* the attitude of the Qumran sectaries toward the Legitimate Teacher, and the attitude of early Christians toward Jesus (and Paul). The citation of prominent teachers also characterizes rabbinic literature. Not only did the rabbis support their teachings by citing authoritative documents ("thus it is written . . . "), but they also appealed to authoritative teachers ("Rabbi so-and-so said . . . "). This is part of the "exegetical tradition." By claiming connection to a religiously authoritative document or person, authors can present their own ideas within the bounds of accepted tradition.

In ascent texts like *3 Baruch,* however, the appeal to authority is decidedly different. Those who have ascended to heaven have a wholly other basis for authority: they can say, "I ascended into

---

43. See Wilson, *Prophecy and Society,* 141–46, 253–63.
44. See Fishbane, *Biblical Interpretation,* 479–85.
45. On this process see Fishbane, "From Scribalism to Rabbinism," 439–56.

heaven and saw thus-and-such." This can be termed an "experiential" claim to authority. This basis for authority cannot readily be challenged since it is based on personal experience of a direct encounter with God or God's heavenly agent(s). These texts reveal the central function of the heavenly ascent as legitimating both the seer and the message.

In this regard the ascent can authorize many different things. In the *Testament of Levi* it authorizes the levitical priesthood (*T. Levi* 2:10; 4:2–6; 5:1–2). Paul uses it to authorize his claim to authority as an apostle (2 Cor 12:1–9). In the *Ascension of Isaiah* it confirms the meaning of the life and death of Jesus as recounted in the Gospels (*Ascension of Isaiah* 10–11). Generally, though, the ascent serves to validate and inculcate a set of values or religious behaviors that are revealed or encouraged during the course of the journey.

So while the rabbis and other interpreters practiced "exegetical" authorization of their teaching by citing authoritative texts and teachers, the apocalypticists valued an "experiential" authorization achieved through a mystical encounter with God or ascent to heaven. The rabbis, however, did not completely reject the "experiential" model, as later Merkabah and Hekhalot texts show. These texts, however, also conform to the "exegetical" tradition of authorization, in that, in the process of describing the ascent or descent to the divine, the visionary often cites authoritative scriptures and teachers or rabbis. In this way, the Merkabah and Hekhalot texts fall within the modes of authorization acceptable to the rabbis.

3 Baruch utilizes an "experiential" means to validate the author's message. It narrates a heavenly ascent whose purpose is to convince "Baruch" that God does attend to human prayer. Thus, the text adds the experience of a mystical heavenly ascent to the developing persona of Baruch. The author of this text obviously valued the idea of heavenly ascent as a means to demonstrate divine authority for a given set of teachings. Baruch's transformation was not, however, immediately from scribe to heavenly visitant. There was an intermediate stage wherein he had become an inspired prophet, as attested in *2 Baruch* and suggested in the Greek version of Jeremiah.

Ethiopic Baruch

Another pseudepigraphon attributed to Baruch, the *Ethiopic Apocalypse of Baruch,* circulated among the Falashas, a group of nonrabbinic, Ethiopian Jews. This work has two parts: the first recounts Baruch's ascent to heaven, where he sees places of reward and punishment, while the second records a series of apocalyptic predictions by the seer. Although the *Ethiopic Apocalypse of Baruch* was composed by Ethiopian Christians sometime after the mid–sixth century, the Falashas subsequently removed the Christian elements and transmitted it as one of their holy books.[46]

In this apocalypse Baruch's relationship to Jeremiah is not mentioned. In fact, rather than being Jeremiah's scribe, Baruch is a gatekeeper for the Temple. This suggests that the original Christian author(s) and later Falasha tradents thought that Baruch was a priest.[47] The ascent experience indicates that the communities that created and transmitted this text regarded Baruch as a holy man worthy to be ushered into the divine realm and receive information about the structure of the cosmos, the eschaton, and the fates of sinners and saints. Given the late date of the text, it is likely that its original Christian author and readers were familiar with the ideas of Baruch as apocalyptic seer (*2 Baruch*) and heavenly visitant (*3 Baruch*). The text develops both of these themes.

Additional Christian and Rabbinic Traditions about Baruch

Baruch as an Angel

In his discussions of apocryphal texts attributed to biblical figures, M. R. James mentions a book ascribed to Baruch in which

---

46. For an introduction and translation see Leslau, *Falasha Anthology,* 57–76.

47. *B. Meg.* 14b; *Sifre Num.* 78 (ed. Horovitz, p. 74); and *Sifre Zuta* 29 on Num 10:29 (ed. Horovitz, p. 263) identify Baruch as a priest. See also Bogaert, *Apocalypse de Baruch,* 1.108–10.

Baruch is an angel.[48] This book was written by Justin the Gnostic, whose teachings drew the criticism of the third-century Roman heresiologist Hippolytus.[49] Although Justin's book is entitled *Baruch,* it is apparently named not after the scribe/sage of Jewish and Christian tradition, but after the most prominent of the twelve good angels in Justin's Gnostic cosmology. This angel is named Baruch not because of any connection with Baruch ben Neriah, but because the name in Hebrew means "blessed," a fitting cognomen for an angel.

Baruch as a Prophet

As the above survey indicates, there was an ongoing debate as to whether Baruch was a prophet. This debate continues in rabbinic literature. Some texts state that certain rabbis regarded Baruch as a prophet.[50] Several Christian texts follow this Jewish tradition.[51] Although Baruch does not appear in the extant Greek version of the *Vitae prophetarum,* there is a brief vita of Baruch in an Armenian work entitled "The Names, Works, and Deaths of the Holy Prophets."[52] Baruch's name also appears in an early Christian list of seventy-two prophets and prophetesses.[53]

The *Mekhilta d'Rabbi Ishmael,* on the other hand, denies that Baruch was a prophet.[54] Here Baruch complains of not having received the prophetic spirit from his teacher Jeremiah, as Elisha had received it from Elijah and Joshua from Moses. Baruch was allegedly denied the prophetic spirit because he wanted it for selfish reasons.[55]

---

48. *Apocrypha Anecdota II,* liv; *Lost Apocrypha,* 77. See also Bogaert, *Apocalypse de Baruch,* 1.457; Denis, *Introduction,* 83.

49. Hippolytus, *Refutatio omnium haeresium* (ed. Wendland), 127–34.

50. *B. Meg.* 14b; *Sifre Num.* 78 (ed. Horovitz, p. 74); *Sifre Zuta* 29 on Num 10:29 (ed. Horovitz, p. 263); *y. Sota* 9, 24b; and *S. 'Olam Rab.* 20 (ed. Ratner, p. 87).

51. Cf. Eusebius, *Praep. evang.* 10.14.6; and Origen, *Homilies on Jeremiah* 8.5

52. Stone, *Armenian Apocrypha Relating to the Patriarchs and Prophets,* 163.

53. Schermann, ed., *Prophetarum vitae fabulosae,* 2. On Baruch in the iconography and hagiography of the medieval Eastern church, see E. Kirschbaum, et al., *Lexikon der christlichen Ikonographie,* 5.336.

54. *Mek. R. Ishmael,* Bo', 1 (ed. Horovitz-Rabin, pp. 5–6; Lauterbach, 1.13–15).

55. Baruch sought "great things" for himself (Jer 45:5). This may be what the author of the *Damascus Document* is alluding to when referring to the words Jeremiah spoke to Baruch (CD 8:20). Some Christians also denied that Baruch was a prophet. Ishodad of Merv, a ninth-century Nestorian bishop of Hedatta, claims that Baruch, upset because he

Baruch and Zoroaster

Several medieval Christian commentators identify Baruch with Zoroaster.[56] This curious connection appears in a tradition describing how Baruch/Zoroaster prophesied the birth, life, death, and resurrection of Jesus. Jacob Neusner has shown that the identification of Baruch with Zoroaster is a late Christian tradition that has no parallel in Jewish sources, and that stems from medieval debates between Christians and Zoroastrians.[57] The tradition does demonstrate, however, that some Christians regarded Baruch as a prophet who predicted the coming of Jesus as Messiah. That Christians believed or wished to prove that Baruch prophesied events in Jesus' life is apparent also in several Christian interpolations of messianic import in the Baruch pseudepigrapha.[58]

Baruch and Ebed-melech

In rabbinic tradition Baruch is occasionally identified with Ebed-melech,[59] the Ethiopian eunuch who rescued Jeremiah from the pit into which King Zedekiah's officials had placed him (Jer 38:1–13). As a reward, God promised to spare Ebed-melech from suffering during the fall of Jerusalem (Jer 39:15–18). Why would *Sifre Num.* 99 and *Pirqe R. El.* 53 identify Ebed-melech with Baruch? The answer lies in the exegetical techniques of the rabbis. Baruch and Ebed-melech both received oracles promising per-

---

had not received the gift of prophecy, left Jerusalem, became the founder of Zoroastrianism, and wrote the Avesta, the sacred books of the Zoroastrians. See Bidez and Cumont, *Les mages hellénisés*, 1.49–50; 2.131–32.

56. See Bidez and Cumont, *Les mages hellénisés*, 1.49–50; 2.129, 131, 134–35.

57. Neusner, "Note on Barukh ben Neriah," 66–69.

58. See the introductions to the various Baruch pseudepigrapha for data on Christian interpolations in these texts. The Baruch quotation in *Altercatio Simonis Judaei et Theophili Christiani*, sec. 17, in which Baruch prophesies about the birth, life, and death of Jesus, appears to be such a Christian addition to the Book of Baruch. See James, *Lost Apocrypha*, 78–79; James, ed., *Apocrypha Anecdota II*, liii–liv; and Denis, *Introduction*, 83. The passage attributed to Baruch by Cyprian (*Test.* 3.29) has affinities to *2 Baruch*, but may be an addition to one of the extant Baruch pseudepigrapha or a fragment from an otherwise unknown Baruch pseudepigraphon. See Bogaert, *Apocalypse de Baruch*, 1.259–69; James, *Lost Apocrypha*, 77–79; James, ed., *Apocrypha Anecdota II*, liv; and Denis, *Introduction*, 83–84.

59. See *Sifre Num.* 99 (ed. Horovitz, p. 99); *Pirqe R. El.* 53 (ed. Friedländer, pp. 430–31).

sonal deliverance that featured virtually identical wording (Jer 45:5 and 39:18 respectively).[60] The identification of Baruch and Ebed-melech stems from the rabbinical practice of reading verbally similar biblical passages as if they were referring to the same person.[61] Since both Baruch and Ebed-melech are given the same promise in scripture, and since one is prominent while the other is little known, the two are taken to be identical.[62] Moreover, just as some interpreters thought that Baruch escaped death (cf. *2 Apoc. Bar.* 13:3, 25:1, 46:7; 76:2), so some believed that Ebed-melech "entered the Garden of Eden alive" (*b. Der. Er. Zut.* 1).

The Location of Baruch's Tomb

Rabbi Petachia of Ratisbon traveled through the Near East and Asia in the late twelfth century.[63] While near Baghdad he learned of the tomb of Baruch ben Neriah. Baruch's tomb was outside Baghdad and was once adjacent to the tomb of the prophet Ezekiel, who, according to this text, was Baruch's teacher.[64] Once, on orders from the Islamic king, Muslims tried to open Baruch's tomb but were struck dead. The king, realizing the greatness and miraculous power of the tomb, ordered Jews to move Baruch's coffin away from the tomb of Ezekiel so that Baruch might have his own shrine. Petachia also states that a portion of Baruch's prayer shawl protruded from his coffin, leading local inhabitants to believe that his body miraculously had not decayed.

Petachia's account of the legends concerning Baruch's tomb reflects the miraculous events that are often attributed to saints' graves. Beliefs about the miraculous powers available at these sites promote both the reputation of the person commemorated and the financial success of the site. These legends depend on

---

60. See Schulte, "Baruch und Ebedmelech," 257–65; and Seitz, "The Prophet Moses," 16–23.

61. Ebed-melech and Baruch have equal status as disciples of Jeremiah in the *Paraleipomena of Jeremiah* (see above).

62. See also Bogaert, *Apocalypse de Baruch,* 1.113–18.

63. For Hebrew text and English translation see Benisch, ed. and trans., *Rabbi Petachia,* 20–23, 34–35, 50–51. Cf. Prawer, *History of the Jews,* 206–15.

64. I know of no other place where Baruch is identified as Ezekiel's student.

the tradition that Baruch resided in Babylon after the fall of Jerusalem in 586 B.C.E.[65]

Summary and Conclusions

Baruch is presented in the MT of Jeremiah as Jeremiah's scribe. Although this was a highly respected profession, the portrayal here clearly indicates that Jeremiah plays the lead role, while Baruch occupies a secondary position. The Greek version of Jeremiah, on the other hand, represents Baruch as Jeremiah's successor. The *Book of Baruch,* an addition or supplement to the Greek Jeremiah, portrays Baruch as a penitent and man of wisdom who addresses the people as one of their sages. According to the *Paraleipomena of Jeremiah,* Baruch was revered as a pious man of learning. *2 Baruch* adds other elements to the persona of Baruch: in this text he is an apocalyptic seer and inspired interpreter of Torah upon whose divinely inspired teachings the people depend for eternal life. *3 Baruch* takes the additional step of portraying Baruch as one who ascended into heaven and returned with a report of his experiences. By virtue of the heavenly ascent attributed to him in *3 Baruch,* Baruch had mysteries to teach people so that they, too, might one day gain admission into God's presence.

The evolution of the persona of Baruch as traced in the texts pseudepigraphically ascribed to him parallels a cultural shift in early Judaism. The evidence attests to an evolution from the priority of the sage/scribe who inscribed and transmitted the divine words to that of the sage/scholar who interpreted and extended them for the benefit of the community. In addition, the role of the apocalyptic seer develops during this period. The portrayals of Baruch in the "historical" apocalypse of *2 Baruch* and the "otherworldly journey" apocalypse of *3 Baruch* include this feature.[66]

According to Ben Sira (chaps. 38–39), the sage was respected

---

65. See above, n. 7.
66. For definitions and descriptions of these distinct types of apocalypse, see Collins, "Jewish Apocalypses," 34–35, 41–42.

for wisdom, piety, and knowledge of Torah. The depictions of Baruch in the texts treated in this essay include all of these elements. Baruch's persona developed from his actual historical role as a scribe to that of an ideal sage and apocalyptic seer. The stages in this metamorphosis reflect the spiritual and cultural aspirations of the communities that created and transmitted the Baruch traditions, and the larger ideological transformations that Judaism underwent during the course of the Greco-Roman period.

Bibliography

Book of Jeremiah

Bogaert, P.-M. "De Baruch à Jérémie: Les deux rédactions conservées du livre de Jérémie." In *Le livre de Jérémie: Le prophète et son milieu, les oracles et leur transmission.* Ed. P.-M. Bogaert. BETL 54. Leuven: Leuven University Press, 1981. Pp. 168–73. An examination of the Hebrew and Greek versions of Jeremiah that shows how the different tradents shaped or reshaped the text of the book.

————. "Le personnage de Baruch et l'histoire du livre de Jérémie: Aux origines du livre deutérocanonique de Baruch." In *Studia Evangelica.* Ed. E. A. Livingstone. Vol. 7. TU 126. Berlin: Akademie, 1982. Pp. 73–81. Shows that the LXX order of the Book of Jeremiah presents Baruch as the one who both recorded Jeremiah's oracles and witnessed their fulfillment.

Graupner, A. "Jeremia 45 als 'Schlusswort' des Jeremiabuches." In *Altes Testament und christliche Verkündigung: Festschrift für Antnius H. J. Gunneweg zum 65. Geburtstag.* Ed. M. Oeming and A. Graupner. Stuttgart: Kohlhammer, 1987. Pp. 287–308. Uses internal literary evidence to demonstrate that chapter 45, the oracle to Baruch, serves as the natural conclusion or summation of the Book of Jeremiah.

Jansen, J. G. *Studies in the Text of Jeremiah.* HSM 6. Cambridge: Harvard University Press, 1973. A text-critical analysis of the Hebrew and Greek versions of Jeremiah.

Lundbom, J. R. "Baruch, Seraiah, and Expanded Colophons in the Book of Jeremiah." *JSOT* 36 (1986) 89–114. Tries to identify the authorship of the Book of Jeremiah on the basis of colophons involving Baruch and his brother Seriah.

Muilenburg, J. "Baruch the Scribe." In *Proclamation and Presence.* Ed. J. I. Durham and J. R. Porter. Richmond: John Knox, 1970. Pp. 232–38. A study of the social and professional standing of Baruch.

Schulte, H. "Baruch und Ebedmelech — Persönliche Heilsorakel im Jeremiabuche." *BZ* 32:2 (1988) 257–65. A comparison and analysis of the oracles directed to Baruch and Ebed-melech in the Book of Jeremiah.

Stulman, L. *The Other Text of Jeremiah: A Reconstruction of the Hebrew Text Underlying the Greek Version of the Prose Sections of Jeremiah with English Translation.* Lanham, Md.: University Press of America, 1985. An analysis of the Greek text of Jeremiah in order to re-create its Hebrew *Vorlage.*

Tov, E. *The Septuagint Translation of Jeremiah and Baruch: A Discussion of an Early Revision of Jeremiah 29–52 and Baruch 1:1–3:8.* HSM 8. Missoula, Mont.: Scholars Press, 1976. A study of the Greek texts of the second half of the Book of Jeremiah and the first half of the Book of Baruch. Concludes that whoever revised the second half of Greek Jeremiah was also responsible for the Greek version of Baruch 1:1–3:8.

————. "Some Aspects of the Textual and Literary History of the Book of Jeremiah." In *Le livre de Jérémie: Le prophète et son milieu, les oracles et leur transmission.* Ed. P.-M. Bogaert. BETL 54. Leuven: Leuven University Press, 1981. Pp. 145–67. An examination of the Hebrew and Greek versions of Jeremiah that shows how the different tradents shaped or reshaped the book to accomplish their literary goals.

Wanke, G. *Untersuchungen zur sogenannten Baruchschrift.* BZAW 122. Berlin: de Gruyter, 1971. Attempts to identify whether and to what extent Baruch was involved in composing at least part of the Book of Jeremiah.

Book of Baruch

Burke, D. G. *The Poetry of Baruch: A Reconstruction and Analysis of Baruch 3:9–5:9.* SBLSCS 10. Chico, Calif.: Scholars Press, 1982. Reconstructs the Hebrew text underlying the Greek of Baruch 3:9–5:9.

Moore, C. A. "Toward Dating the Book of Baruch." *CBQ* 36 (1974) 312–20. Argues that Baruch 1:15–2:19 and 4:5–5:4 were composed between the fourth and second centuries B.C.E.

Schreiner, J., trans. *Baruch.* Die Neue Echter Bibel Altes Testament 14. Würzburg: Echter, 1986. Introduction and translation with copious notes.

Tov, E. "The Relations between the Greek Versions of Baruch and Daniel." In *Armenian and Biblical Studies.* Ed. M. E. Stone. Jerusalem: St. James, 1976. Pp. 27–34. Argues that the similarities between the prayers in Bar 1:15–2:19 and Dan 9:5–19 are superficial and have no bearing on identifying a dependence of either book on the other.

————, ed. and trans. *The Book of Baruch.* SBLTT 8. Missoula, Mont.: Scholars Press, 1975. Greek text and English translation of the entire book, and a reconstructed Hebrew text of 1:1–3:8 based on the Greek.

Paraleipomena of Jeremiah

Delling, G. *Jüdische Lehre und Frömmigkeit in den Paraleipomena Jeremiae.* BZAW 100. Berlin: Töpelmann, 1967. Interprets the book as the work of a Palestinian Jew, probably a Pharisee, who lived in the late first or early second century C.E.

Kraft, R. A., and A.-E. Purintun, eds. and trans. *Paraleipomena Jeremiou.* SBLTT 1, Pseudepigrapha Series 1. Missoula, Mont.: Society of Biblical Literature, 1972. A provisional critical edition of the Greek text with English translation and annotated bibliography.

Nickelsburg, G. W. E. "Narrative Traditions in the *Paraleipomena of Jeremiah* and *2 Baruch.*" *CBQ* 35 (1973) 60–68. Demonstrates that the narrative traditions in *2 Baruch* and the *Paraleipomena of Jeremiah* depend on a common source.

Riaud, J. "La figure de Jérémie dans les Paralipomena Jeremiae." In *Mélanges bibliques et orientaux en l'honneur de M. Henri Cazelles.* Ed. A. Caquot and M. Delcor. AOAT 212. Kevelaer: Butzon & Bercker; Neukirchen-Vluyn: Neukirchener Verlag, 1981. Pp. 373–85. Shows that Jeremiah is depicted as the prophet par excellence in the *Paraleipomena of Jeremiah.*

2 (the Syriac Apocalypse of) Baruch

Bogaert, P.-M. *Apocalypse de Baruch: Introduction, traduction du syriaque et commentaire.* SC 144–45. Paris: Cerf, 1969. Introduction, translation, and commentary.

———. "Le nom de Baruch dans la littérature pseudépigraphique: L'apocalypse syriaque et le livre deutérocanonique." In *La littérature juive entre Tenach et Mischna: Quelques problèmes.* Ed. W. C. Van Unnik. RechBib 9. Leiden: Brill, 1974. Pp. 61–72. *2 Baruch* was the first text pseudepigraphically attributed to Baruch (sometime after 70 C.E.). The Book of Baruch was attributed to Baruch only *after 2* and *3 Baruch* were written.

Dedering, S., ed. *Apocalypse of Baruch.* Peshitta Institute, pt. 4, fascicle 3. Leiden: Brill, 1973. Edition of the Syriac text.

Klijn, A. F. J., trans. "2 (Syriac Apocalypse of) Baruch." *OTP* 1.615–52. English translation with introduction and notes.

Murphy, F. J. *The Structure and Meaning of Second Baruch.* Atlanta: Scholars Press, 1985. Demonstrates that the purpose of the book is to move the focus of the author and reader from Temple to Torah as the center of Jewish life after 70 C.E.

Sayler, G. B. *Have the Promises Failed? A Literary Analysis of 2 Baruch.* SBLDS 72. Chico, Calif.: Scholars Press, 1984. Shows that the unifying feature of the book is a pattern of consolation by which the author attempts to transform the reader, in the wake of the destruction of Jerusalem, from grief to comfort.

3 (the Greek Apocalypse of) Baruch

Gaylord, H. E., trans. "3 (Greek Apocalypse of) Baruch." *OTP* 1.653–79. English translation with introduction and notes.

Harlow, D. C. *The Greek Apocalypse of Baruch (3 Baruch) in Hellenistic Judaism and Early Christianity.* SVTP 12. Leiden/New York/Cologne: Brill,

1996. Study of the structure and purpose of 3 *Baruch;* includes treatment of the Christian transmission context.

Picard, J.-C. "Observations sur l'Apocalypse grecque de Baruch I: Cadre historique fictif et efficacité symbolique." *Sem* 20 (1970) 77–103. Places the origin of 3 *Baruch* in the context of a shamanistic initiation seance. The goal of the seance is to "cure" the initiate of worldly concerns and to move to spiritual matters.

———, ed. *Apocalypsis Baruchi Graece.* PVTG 2. Leiden: Brill, 1967. Critical edition of the Greek text.

Wright, J. E. *The Cosmography of the Greek Apocalypse of Baruch and Its Affinities.* Ann Arbor, Mich.: University Microfilms, 1992. An analysis of the ascent to heaven recounted in 3 *Baruch* in comparison with other early Jewish and Christian ascent texts.

Ethiopic Baruch

Leslau, W. *Falasha Anthology.* Yale Judaica Series 6. New Haven/London: Yale University Press, 1951. English translations and introductory notes to several Falasha texts.

Early Jewish and Rabbinic Sources

Benisch, A., ed. and trans. *The Travels of Rabbi Petachia of Ratisbon.* London: Trubner, 1856. An account of Rabbi Petachia's travels through the Near East and Asia in the late twelfth century.

Jellinek, A., ed. *Bet Ha-Midrasch.* 3d ed. 6 vols. Jerusalem: Wahrmann, 1967. A collection of midrashic and apocryphal texts.

Wertheimer, A. *Batei Midrashot.* 2d ed. 2 vols. Jerusalem: Mosad haRav Kook, 1950–53. Reprint, Jerusalem: Ktav veSepher, 1968. A collection of midrashic and apocryphal texts.

Christian and Zoroastrian Sources

Bidez, J., and F. Cumont. *Les mages hellénisés: Zoroastre, Ostanès et Hystaspe d'après la tradition grecque.* 2 vols. Paris: "Les belles Lettres," 1973. Survey of the life, teachings, writings, and traditions of Zoroaster.

Ehrhard, A. *Überlieferung und Bestand der hagiographischen und homiletischen Literatur der grieschen Kirche: Von den Anfängen bis zum Ende des 16. Jahrhunderts.* Vol. 1. TU 50:1. Leipzig: Hinrichs, 1937. A collection of calendrical, homiletical, and narrative texts that honor biblical and early Christian notables.

Neusner, J. "Note on Barukh ben Neriah and Zoroaster." *Numen* 12:1 (1965) 66–69. Argues that the claim that Baruch and Zoroaster were the same person is a late Christian tradition with no parallel in Judaism.

Stone, M. E. *Armenian Apocrypha Relating to the Patriarchs and Prophets.* Jerusalem: Israel Academy of Sciences and Humanities, 1982. Texts and translations of Armenian apocryphal writings.

Apocalyptic and Ascent Literature in General

Halperin, D. "Heavenly Ascension in Ancient Judaism: The Nature of the Experience." *SBLSP 1987.* Ed. K. H. Richards. Atlanta: Scholars Press, 1987. Pp. 218–32. Discusses whether the ascent texts are products of personal experience or simply literary fictions.

Himmelfarb, M. *Ascent to Heaven in Jewish and Christian Apocalypses.* New York: Oxford University Press, 1993. An examination of the tradition of the ascent motif.

―――. *Tours of Hell: An Apocalyptic Form in Jewish and Christian Literature.* Philadelphia: Fortress, 1985. The origin and development of the motif of journeys to hell in early Jewish and Christian texts.

Rowland, C. C. *The Open Heaven: A Study of Apocalyptic in Judaism and Early Christianity.* London: SPCK, 1982. Surveys Jewish and Christian apocalyptic literature, motifs, and ideology.

―――. "The Visions of God in Apocalyptic Literature." *JSJ* 10 (1979) 137–54. Concludes that apocalyptic visions of heaven may be based on actual experiences of the authors.

Segal, A. F. "Heavenly Ascent in Hellenistic Judaism, Early Christianity, and Their Environment." *ANRW* II.23.2 (1980) 1333–94. Discusses the ascent motif as it appears in various ancient sources.

The Sage in the Ancient World

Collins, J. J. "The Sage in the Apocalyptic and Pseudepigraphic Literature." In *The Sage in Israel and the Ancient Near East.* Ed. J. G. Gammie and L. Perdue. Winona Lake, Ind.: Eisenbrauns, 1990. Pp. 343–54. Discusses the depiction of the sage in early Judaism.

Fishbane, M. "From Scribalism to Rabbinism: Perspectives on the Emergence of Classical Judaism." In Gammie and Perdue, *The Sage in Israel.* Pp. 439–56. Outlines religious developments in ancient Judaism by tracing the evolution of the roles of the leaders in Jewish communities.

Neusner, J. "Sage, Priest, Messiah: Three Types of Judaism in the Age of Jesus." In *Judaism in the Beginning of Christianity.* Philadelphia: Fortress, 1984. Pp. 35–44. Describes three forms of Jewish leadership in the Greco-Roman period.

Stone, M. E. "Ideal Figures and Social Context: Priest and Sage in the Early Second Temple Age." In *Ancient Israelite Religion: Essays in Honor Of Frank Moore Cross.* Ed. P. D. Miller, Jr., P. D. Hanson, and S. D. McBride. Philadelphia: Fortress, 1987. Pp. 575–86. The depictions of priests and sages in early Jewish texts indicate how these individuals served as models of piety in their communities.

ELEVEN

TALKING WITH GOD AND LOSING HIS HEAD

*Extrabiblical Traditions
about the Prophet Ezekiel*

BENJAMIN G. WRIGHT

As is the case with so many biblical personages, the biblical book that bears Ezekiel's name tells us little about the person himself, and what few details there are come in passing glimpses and short notices. He was one of the exiles who was taken to Babylon, where he prophesied to the exiled community (Ezek 1:1). He was a priest whose father's name was Buzi (Ezek 1:3). He was apparently married, and while in exile his wife died (Ezekiel 24). Nothing is told, however, of his birth or death, or much of the rest of his life. But, as with other biblical characters, the lack of detail about this often enigmatic and bizarre prophet generated subsequent traditions that attempted to fill in some of the blank spaces left by the biblical book.

Because of the importance of this prophet and his often strange visions and behavior, Judaism and Christianity possess a relatively rich set of traditions about Ezekiel. These extrabiblical Ezekiel materials consist of two basic sorts: (1) writings that circulated in his name, and (2) biographical or hagiographical information. The recent publication of several fragments from Qumran Cave 4 and analysis of several early Christian patristic citations suggest that Jews and Christians in antiquity possessed more literature in Ezekiel's name than just the biblical book. The first section of this chapter examines these apocryphal Ezekiel texts. In the hagiographical and iconographic traditions that survive, Ezekiel's death plays a prominent role. The various extant traditions, especially those treating Ezekiel's death, are the subject of the second section.

Writings in Ezekiel's Name

Of the several works that were attributed to Ezekiel, only those from the Middle Ages, primarily *Kalandologia* and *Brontologia,* survive in more than fragmentary form.[1] The apocryphal works connected with Ezekiel that stem from the first several centuries B.C.E. and C.E. come down to us only in isolated citations from Greek and Latin Christian church fathers, one Chester Beatty Greek manuscript, and several fragmentary Hebrew manuscripts from Cave 4 at Qumran. These will be my concern in what follows.

Scholars have looked to several ancient sources for testimony that in antiquity more books than the biblical one bore Ezekiel's name. The Jewish historian Josephus (*Ant.* 10.79) remarks that not only did Jeremiah predict the misfortunes that were to befall Jerusalem, but that Ezekiel did so as well, and that he wrote "two books" (δύο βίβλους) about these things, books which he "left behind."[2] The fourth-century Christian church father Epiphanius testifies more explicitly to the existence of an apocryphal Ezekiel writing. In section 64.70 of the *Panarion,* his great treatise against heresy, Epiphanius cites a parable about two men, one lame and one blind, as having come from "[Ezekiel's] own apocryphon"

---

1. These medieval works predict the character or auspiciousness of particular days, or what the occurrence of thunder means. They are attributed to several biblical personages, including Ezekiel. See James, *Lost Apocrypha,* 81; Matter, "Revelatio Esdrae."

2. Although this report appears to provide good evidence for an apocryphal Ezekiel book, several scholars have suggested that Josephus was referring to the biblical Book of Ezekiel, which he considered to be divided into two parts. See, for example, Ralph Marcus, who relies on H. St. J. Thackeray for this idea. Marcus remarks, "Josephus probably thought of the book of Ezekiel as composed of two distinct parts of 24 chapters each" (*Josephus,* 6.201, n. *e*).

(ἐν τῷ ἰδίῳ ἀποκρύφῳ). Finally, the *Stichometry of Nicephorus* lists pseudepigraphical writings attributed to Baruch, Habakkuk, Ezekiel, and Daniel.[3]

To be considered along with these ancient notices are (1) five citations found in Christian sources, all of which are attributed to Ezekiel somewhere in their transmission, although not necessarily by the earliest witnesses, and (2) several recently published fragments of a pseudepigraphical Ezekiel writing from Qumran Cave 4.[4] Several questions arise regarding these texts. How are the Greek citations linked to Ezekiel? Did they originally come from an apocryphal Ezekiel book or did they circulate in some other, more amorphous form, such as testimonia or prophetic florilegia? What is the extent of the Qumran pseudepigraphon? Were the Greek fragments and the Qumran fragments part of the same work? Can one suggest a plausible date or provenance for them? Finally, what do the ideas found in these fragments tell us about the development of the figure of Ezekiel in Second Temple Judaism and early Christianity?

The five Greek citations which have been called fragments of an *Apocryphon of Ezekiel* have been presented in detail in several publications, and I will not cite them in full here any more than is necessary to address the questions posed above.[5] The first is the above-mentioned parable cited by Epiphanius in *Pan.* 64.70.5–17. A lame man and a blind man, who were not invited to the wedding banquet of a king's son, seek revenge by destroying the king's garden. Since neither could act alone, the lame man sits upon the shoulders of the blind man, and they act in concert. The king eventually uncovers the perpetrators of the deed along with their method and punishes both men after each attempts to blame the other. Epiphanius uses this story as a lesson concerning the

---

3. On this document see Schneemelcher and Wilson, *New Testament Apocrypha*, 1.41–42.

4. On the Greek fragments see Mueller, *Five Fragments*; Mueller and Robinson, "Apocryphon of Ezekiel," *OTP* 1.487–95; and Stone, *Apocryphal Ezekiel*. For the published Qumran fragments see Strugnell and Dimant, "4Q Second Ezekiel"; idem, "The Merkabah Vision"; and Kister and Qimron, "Observations."

5. See Mueller, *Five Fragments*; Mueller and Robinson, "Apocryphon of Ezekiel"; and Stone, *Apocryphal Ezekiel*.

judgment of both the human body and soul. The parable is also told with variations in several rabbinic sources.[6]

The second fragment occurs in its fullest form in *1 Clem.* 8:3, although *1 Clement* does not provide an attribution for the quotation. Clement of Alexandria (*Paed.* 1.92.2) cites a part of what is stated in *1 Clement*, and it is he who explicitly claims that Ezekiel said it. The passage, as *1 Clement* has it, concerns the repentance of the "house of Israel" and contains verbal reminiscences of Isa 1:18. The citation in *1 Clem.* 8:3 is linked in sequence with a quotation in 8:2, which has similarities to Ezek 33:11 and which may itself have been part of the Ezekiel apocryphon.[7] A second quotation given by Clement of Alexandria (*Quis dives salvetur* 39.2–4) may also be a variant of the same "apocryphal Ezekiel" passage as is found in *1 Clem.* 8:3 and *Paed.* 1.92.2. The *Exegesis on the Soul* from Nag Hammadi may offer an independent Coptic version of this fragment.[8] As noted above, this fragment is primarily concerned with the repentance of Israel, a theme also important in the biblical Ezekiel.

A third apocryphal Ezekiel fragment survives in two variant forms. In one version it is an enigmatic saying about a heifer who gives birth but does not give birth.[9] The other simply refers to someone, indicated only by the pronoun "she," who gives birth but does not give birth.[10] Tertullian, who knows both versions, explicitly attributes the heifer form to Ezekiel (*De carne Christi* 23). Clement of Alexandria (*Strom.* 7.94) cites the second version as "scripture" (γραφή). Both of these writers use this saying as part of their arguments concerning the miraculous nature of the birth of Jesus, connecting the saying with Mary's virginal conception. Apparently some Christians, whom Tertullian calls "Academics," argued that the saying indicated that Mary did not

---

6. On the rabbinic versions and their relation to Epiphanius's work, see Bregman, "Parable."

7. For arguments in support of this conclusion, see Hagner, *Use of the Old and New Testaments*, 91; and B. G. Wright, "Fragment of Apocryphal Ezekiel."

8. For discussion of this fragment see Mueller, *Five Fragments*, 101–20; and B. G. Wright, "Fragment of Apocryphal Ezekiel."

9. This version is cited by Tertullian; Ps.-Gregory of Nyssa, *Adv. Ioud.* 3; and Epiphanius, *Pan.* 30.30.

10. This version is found in Clement of Alexandria and *Acts of Peter* 24.

really give birth to Jesus. Tertullian uses both forms of the saying to counter that claim and to assert Jesus' actual birth.

Although the transmission history of this saying is obscure, the two forms are probably variants of the same logion.[11] The passage engenders patristic interest because of the "giving birth and not giving birth" reference and because of the saying's usefulness in arguing for the virginal status of Mary. That some apparently connected even the long form of the saying to Mary, in effect calling her a "heifer," may well have caused embarrassment, even though the saying was thought to be from Ezekiel, and thus scriptural. The shorter form, with no mention of the heifer, probably developed to eliminate the embarrassing association. It has, however, no obvious parallels to any passage in the canonical form of the Book of Ezekiel. There are also no clear indications from the extant versions of this fragment what its context may have been in an Ezekiel work, or why it is connected with the biblical prophet.

A fourth fragment appears in no less than nineteen sources, in Greek, Latin, Syriac, and Armenian. In its earliest attestation, Justin Martyr's *Dialogue with Trypho* 47.5, it is reported as a saying of Jesus. It finds its attribution to Ezekiel in John Climacus, *Scala Paradisi* 7, and in Evagrius's Latin translation of the *Life of St. Anthony* 15. The meaning of the saying — "in those things in which I find you, by those I will judge [you]" — is less problematic than the variety of introductions attached to it. Besides Jesus and Ezekiel, the saying is variously attributed to "the prophets," "God through the prophets," "the divine voice," and "the Lord."

The saying probably had an introduction that referred to "the Lord." At some point the inference was made that "Lord" meant "Jesus," and the saying in Justin is therefore ascribed to Jesus; this process occurred with other sayings in early Christianity. The logion was characterized elsewhere as a saying of God mediated through the prophets, and through one in particular, Ezekiel.[12] The saying probably became attributed to Ezekiel because of its theme of judgment, and although it has no unambiguous verbal

---

11. See Mueller, *Five Fragments*, 132–37.
12. For discussion of these problems see Stone, *Apocryphal Ezekiel*; Bellinzoni, *Sayings*; and idem, "Source of the Agraphon."

parallels to any passage in the biblical book, it expresses sentiments similar to Ezek 18:30 and 33:20; 18:30 reads "Therefore I will judge you, O house of Israel, all of you according to your ways, says the Lord God."

The fifth apocryphal Ezekiel fragment constitutes the best available evidence that some kind of *Apocryphon of Ezekiel* circulated in Greek in antiquity. Clement of Alexandria (*Paed.* I.[9.]84.2–3) cites several prophetic sayings in Ezekiel's name, interspersed with his own homiletical comments. None of these sayings is found in the biblical book, but they have their closest biblical echoes in Ezekiel 34. In 1940, Campbell Bonner published Chester Beatty Papyrus 185, of which at least one fragment contains what can only be called part of a manuscript copy of an *Apocryphon of Ezekiel*.[13] This fragment, the largest preserved of the papyrus, coincides with several of the sayings found in Clement of Alexandria's work, but for two reasons they are almost certainly not dependent on Clement. First, the Chester Beatty fragment does not appear to have had room for Clement's own homiletical remarks and is thus not a direct copy of the *Paedagogus*. Second, the difficulty in the *Paedagogus* in distinguishing between the quotations from "Ezekiel" and Clement's own interpretations makes it improbable that the author of the papyrus excerpted them from a text of the *Paedagogus*.[14] One of the sayings that is shared by Clement and the Chester Beatty papyrus — "I will be nearer to them than the tunic of their skin" — is also cited by Origen (*Homilies on Jeremiah* 18.9) and the *Manichaean Psalmbook* 239. This saying probably came to these latter works as a free logion, unattached to any particular work or individual.

As Clement of Alexandria frames them, these sayings deal with God's concern to bring back those in Israel who have wandered away, just as a shepherd brings back the wayward of his flock.

---

13. Bonner, *Homily*, 183–90.

14. The other fragments of Chester Beatty Papyrus 185 do not overlap with any other apocryphal Ezekiel texts, except perhaps for fragment 1 recto, although Bonner admits that his reconstructions were inspired by the saying in *1 Clem.* 8:3. It is unclear whether they should be assigned to the *Apocryphon*. I am inclined to include them, although their fragmentary condition means that they provide little additional evidence for understanding the *Apocryphon*.

God will feed God's people as a shepherd pastures sheep and will help them cross treacherous terrain without slipping. In their context in Chester Beatty Papyrus 185, these sayings claim that God personally will shepherd the people, because some in Israel, perhaps the leaders (the verbs in the text are in the second-person plural), have not fulfilled their roles as shepherds.

Among the most recently published materials from Qumran Cave 4 are a number of manuscript fragments that have been called 4QPseudo-Ezekiel by their current editor, Devorah Dimant. In their initial publication, John Strugnell and Dimant included all the fragments numbered 4Q385–4Q390 under this rubric, but Dimant, who has now assumed responsibility for their publication, has narrowed the extent of 4QPseudo-Ezekiel to 4Q385 fragments 1–5, 12, 24 (= PsEzek[a]), all of 4Q386 (= PsEzek[b]), 4Q387 fragments 5, 7, 8 (= PsEzek[c]), and 4Q388 fragments 5, 7, 8 (= PsEzek[d]).[15] 4Q391, edited by Mark Smith, is now also recognized as containing several fragments of this work (= PsEzek[e]).[16] Thus, parts of five separate manuscripts, containing some overlapping sections, are thought to derive from this Ezekiel pseudepigraphon.

Given the fragmentary nature of the manuscript evidence, a detailed description of the Qumran Ezekiel pseudepigraphon is difficult, but several important features can be discerned. All of the fragments that have been published so far indicate that the work was written in the form of a dialogue between the prophet and God, the contents of which have both close and remote relationships with the biblical Book of Ezekiel. The texts that most closely resemble the biblical book, as one might anticipate, are Pseudo-Ezekiel's version of the Merkabah vision (4Q385 4; cf.

---

15. This work was originally called 4QSecond Ezekiel by Dimant and Strugnell. Dimant later preferred 4QPseudo-Ezekiel, the name I use in this article. See Strugnell and Dimant, "4Q Second Ezekiel"; idem, "The Merkabah Vision." In her Madrid conference paper, "New Light," Dimant reports 4Q387 and 388 as separate copies of 4QPseudo-Ezekiel, but in a later article, "Apocalyptic Interpretation," she notes 4Q387 as a copy of a Pseudo-Moses pseudepigraphon. More recently, in an oral communication, she has reconsidered some of the 4Q387 fragments and thinks they *may* belong to 4QPseudo-Ezekiel. For one 4Q387 fragment that may be from 4QPseudo-Ezekiel, see Wise, Abegg, Cook, *Dead Sea Scrolls,* 354, and B. G. Wright, "The Apocryphon of Ezekiel and 4QPseudo-Ezekiel."

16. I thank Professor Smith for his permission to examine his remarks on 4Q391 before their appearance in print. They have since appeared in M. Smith, "Pseudo-Ezekiel."

Ezekiel 1, 10), the vision of the dry bones (in at least three manuscripts, 4Q385 2, 4Q386 I, and 4Q388 8, and perhaps in 4Q391 56; cf. Ezekiel 37), and the heavenly Temple (4Q391 65; cf. Ezekiel 40–48).[17] Other fragments contain texts with a more remote relationship to the biblical book. 4Q385 24 appears to be part of an oracle mentioning כוש and מצרים that seems loosely based on the oracles against the nations in Ezekiel 30, and 4Q386 ii 5ff., by its references to Memphis, appears to be related in some way to the anti-Egypt oracle in Ezek 30:13–19.

Still other fragments among these manuscripts, even though they have no clear relationship to specific biblical passages in Ezekiel, should without doubt be included in the Ezekiel apocryphon. 4Q385 3 finds Ezekiel, here referred to by name, pleading with God to speed up the time, "in order that the children of Israel may inherit."[18] To this plea God assents. 4Q385 12 says in its first line that "all the people rose up"; subsequently God speaks in the first person to the prophet, who is here called בן אדם, the usual biblical epithet for Ezekiel. This text may be related to events following the vision of the dry bones.[19] Finally, in 4Q386 ii, "Ezekiel" is told of a wicked ruler whom God will not permit to prosper. Column iii is the beginning of an oracle concerning Babylon that has no overt connections with Ezekiel, but given its place in the manuscript, it probably comes from the same Pseudo-Ezekiel work.

Taken together, all of this evidence — the secondary testimony, the manuscript evidence, and the citations — suggests that there was at least one *Apocryphon of Ezekiel* in antiquity, perhaps more than one. Among the evidence preserved in Greek, Epiphanius's testimony and the Chester Beatty papyrus constitute the best evidence for a Greek apocryphal Ezekiel book. Into this picture one must then place Clement of Alexandria, who, although he does not provide explicit attribution for all of the texts, cites

---

17. This last fragment almost certainly has to do with Temple measurements. Thus, Dimant's claim in "Apocalyptic Interpretation" (p. 50) that none of the preserved fragments of Pseudo-Ezekiel contains any reference to Ezekiel 40–48 should perhaps be modified.

18. Brooke, "Ezekiel in Some Qumran and New Testament Texts," 327, sees Ezek 25:8 as the context for this passage. Ezek 12:21–25 might also be a remote point of contact.

19. This is Dimant's tentative interpretation of the text. See also B. G. Wright, "Qumran Pseudepigrapha."

all of the Greek fragments except the parable of the lame and the blind.

The question of whether all of the Greek fragments circulated together in one book is more difficult. When one considers the Greek patristic citations that I have dealt with, the easiest conclusion is that the transmission of these materials was very fluid. Some of the apocryphal sayings attributed to Ezekiel probably originated independently of others and, if they did eventually circulate together in one corpus, were incorporated into that corpus at different times in its history of transmission. Thematically, four of the five patristic citations, excepting the heifer saying, concern issues that can be found or interpreted to be present in the biblical Book of Ezekiel: judgment, repentance, and, at least in Epiphanius, the hope of resurrection. The parable of the lame and the blind has a different form from the other citations; it is a longer parable or story, in contrast to the oracular type of prophetic utterance characteristic of the other three (*1 Clement*'s saying on repentance, Justin's on judgment, and Chester Beatty 185 on turning back to God). That these passages have different forms or genres does not, however, mean that the four could not have belonged to the same work. Further, the form of the *Apocryphon of Ezekiel* that Clement of Alexandria knew at the end of the second century would not necessarily be identical to the one known by Epiphanius in the middle of the fourth. Material may well have been added to or removed from the work over time. And, of course, independent prophetic sayings that were never part of an apocryphal Ezekiel book may have acquired Ezekiel's name in the process of their transmission.

In conclusion, regarding the Greek nonbiblical Ezekiel citations, there is much that is unknown or uncertain. That there was a Greek *Apocryphon of Ezekiel* that was known to at least several patristic writers seems beyond doubt. Its scope and contents, however, remain unclear, especially given the lack of context for any of the citations. The most reasonable conclusions concerning the date and provenance of such a work — which would have contained at least the passages found in *1 Clem.* 8:3 and Chester Beatty Papyrus 185, and perhaps also Epiphanius's parable and the judgment saying reported by Justin — are that it dated from before the end of the first century C.E. (since *1 Clement* knew it) and that its language was Greek. If these Greek witnesses to the *Apocryphon* can in turn be shown to have derived from the same work as the Ezekiel fragments from Qumran Cave 4, it then becomes more likely that Hebrew was the original language.

The Qumran Pseudo-Ezekiel document, although very fragmentary, shows a number of clear characteristics. First, it is framed as a revelatory dialogue between the prophet and God, with the characters often speaking in the first person. As such it shows affinities with other apocalyptic works of Second Temple Judaism.[20] The scope and content of many of the extant portions of the work are based on material drawn from the biblical Book of Ezekiel, most clearly the Merkabah and dry bones visions, the oracles against the nations in Ezekiel 30–32, and the vision of the new Temple in Ezekiel 40–48. Dimant describes the Pseudo-Ezekiel document as follows:

> In a literary procedure characteristic of the pseudepigraphic literature, this work is written as if Ezekiel himself were relating the visions revealed to him. These visions reproduce through concise quotations several of the canonical visions of Ezekiel. These are amplified by explanations of God, and by additional dialogues between God and the prophet on the meaning of these visions.[21]

One question stands out at this juncture. Were the Greek patristic *Apocryphon of Ezekiel* and the Qumran Pseudo-Ezekiel document the same work, or two separate pseudepigrapha? Several considerations suggest that the Greek and Hebrew fragments could ultimately have originated in the same document. Dimant argues that a relationship between the two "seems to be excluded, as none of the quotations from this apocryphon offered by the Church Fathers are found in the surviving fragments of the Qumranic work."[22] Admittedly there is no overlap in content between the extant patristic citations and the 4QPseudo-Ezekiel fragments, but in more general terms the themes and forms of the materials could be seen to coexist well. The best examples of Greek fragments that fit nicely with the Qumran texts are *1 Clem.* 8:3 and

---

20. For this estimation of the work, see Dimant, "Apocalyptic Interpretation," 49.
21. Dimant, "Apocalyptic Interpretation," 49.
22. Dimant, "Apocalyptic Interpretation," 49.

Chester Beatty Papyrus 185. The theme of repentance expressed in *1 Clement* would not be out of place among the Qumran texts, and the desire expressed in Chester Beatty Papyrus 185 to bring back those Israelites who have wandered and to level judgment on leaders who have neglected their role is consistent also with themes found in some of the Qumran texts.[23] The vicissitudes of fragmentary transmission do not seem sufficient necessarily to discount any relation between the Greek and Hebrew texts simply because there are no textual overlaps. In fact, a possible connection between the Greek *Apocryphon* and the Qumran Pseudo-Ezekiel document is enhanced by the fact that the writing found at Qumran does not seem to have originated with the Dead Sea sect. Strugnell and Dimant argue that the vocabulary and ideas of the work are not distinctive of, and thus do not mark it as a composition of, the Qumran community, and Richard Bauckham, who believes that *Apoc. Pet.* 4:7–9 is a quotation of the same Qumran document, maintains that such a citation increases the probability that the work originated outside Qumran.[24]

To this point, I have focused on those citations in the patristic sources that are specifically attributed to Ezekiel somewhere in the tradition. The Qumran Pseudo-Ezekiel fragments have unambiguous associations with the prophet. Not only do they contain specific visions from the biblical book, but they use phrases, like "son of man" as a form of address, that are characteristic of the canonical Ezekiel. There remain, however, several unattributed citations in early Christian literature that bear enough of a resemblance to the Book of Ezekiel that some scholars have argued for their derivation from an Ezekiel apocryphon.[25] Menahem Kister and Richard Bauckham have argued in separate articles that two

---

23. On repentance, turning back to God, and God's mercy, see, for example, 1QH 4:36–37. The purification rituals practiced at Qumran were also dependent on repentance. See 4Q512 29–32 (cited in Schiffman, *Reclaiming the Dead Sea Scrolls*, 148, 299). See also CD 2:4–5. 4QMMT C21–22 says, "And this is at the end of days when they will return to Israel forever" (this is the translation of Strugnell and Qimron, *Miqsat Ma'ase Ha-Torah*, 60–61. Schiffman, *Reclaiming the Dead Sea Scrolls*, 85, translates "repent in Israel." Hebrew = שישובו בישראל). The text then cites examples of repentance, so that the addressees of the letter might "rejoice at the end of time."

24. Strugnell and Dimant, "4Q Second Ezekiel," 57–58; and Bauckham, "Quotation from *4Q Second Ezekiel*," 443.

25. For a complete list see Stone, *Apocryphal Ezekiel.*

texts in particular, *Barn.* 12:1 and *Apoc. Pet.* 4:7–9, actually quote from, or cite texts that originated in, the Pseudo-Ezekiel document from Qumran.[26] If this is the case, then the Qumran pseudepigraphon, or at least portions of it, most likely circulated in Greek translation, since *Barnabas* was written in Greek and the *Apocalypse of Peter,* while extant only in Ethiopic, was probably composed in Greek.[27] If one can find unattributed citations in early Christian literature that show close associations with the Qumran Pseudo-Ezekiel text, then it may be easier to make the case that other short or fragmentary quotations that lack attribution, but show some relationship to passages or themes from the biblical Ezekiel, may have come from an apocryphal Ezekiel work, perhaps even the Qumran pseudepigraphon.

Following the lead of Kister and Bauckham, I want to propose here that an additional text, whose author apparently knows an *Apocryphon of Ezekiel,* may also have connections with the Qumran document. *1 Clem.* 50:4 cites the following passage as scripture:

> For it has been written, "Enter into the chambers for a little while, until the time when my wrath and my anger pass away and I will remember a good day and I will raise you up out of your tombs."

1 Clement cites this passage using the phrase, "for it has been written" (γέγραπται γάρ), apparently as an authoritative text. The citation has three clauses: the first is an apocopated and variant version of Isa 26:20, the second has no apparent biblical connection, and the third appears to be a variant form of Ezek 37:12.[28] This same conjunction of biblical passages may be present in 4Q385 12, although the fragmentary nature of the appropriate sections makes it difficult to be certain.

---

26. See Kister, "Barnabas 12:1; 4:3"; and Bauckham, "Quotation from *4Q Second Ezekiel.*" Kister, "Barnabas 12:1; 4:3," 67, argues that *Barn.* 4:3 may also reflect Pseudo-Ezekiel. I find this suggestion less convincing.

27. For introductory issues on *Barnabas,* see Kraft, *Didache and Barnabas,* 39–56; and Prigent and Kraft, *Epître de Barnabé,* 9–27. On the language of the *Apocalypse of Peter* see Buchholz, *Your Eyes Will Be Opened,* 3, 16–17; and Schneemelcher and Wilson, *New Testament Apocrypha,* 2.620–25.

28. This last clause should probably be regarded as coming from Ezek 37:12 rather than Isa 26:19 ("Your dead shall live, their corpses shall rise") because it parallels closely both the MT and the LXX of Ezekiel: MT מקברותיכם עמי והבאתי אתכם; LXX καὶ ἀνάξω ὑμᾶς ἐκ τῶν μνημάτων ὑμῶν; *1 Clem.* 50:4 καὶ ἀναστήσω ὑμᾶς ἐκ τῶν θηκῶν ὑμῶν.

4Q385 12 begins with the clause "all the people rose up," perhaps indicating the events after Ezekiel prophesies to the dry bones. Then in a new section God addresses the prophet and in line 4 reveals that "they will sleep until the time when (עד אשר ישכבו)[...]." The fragment breaks off precisely at this point. The phrase "they will sleep until the time when" recalls Isa 26:20, although the verbal action is different; the MT of Isaiah has חבי כמעט־רגע ("withdraw a little while"). Before "they will sleep/rest" the letters חם are visible preceded by a stroke that is, at least, not inconsistent with a *waw*. Line 5 continues, "your (כם...) [...] and from the land." The word to which the כם is joined ends in *yod*, probably indicating a masculine plural noun. Since the context of the fragment seems to be Ezekiel 37, one might look to that chapter to provide clues for what the fragment read. One can reconstruct the beginning of line 5 as מקברותיכם ("from their graves"), a frequently occurring term in Ezek 37:12–14. In that case the same noun might also appear in the preceding line. Thus, line 4 could be reconstructed to read בקברותם ישכבו עד אשר, a close recollection of Isa 26:20. Line 5 might bring the text back to Ezekiel 37, creating a similar sequence to that found in *1 Clement*.

The change from third to second person in this fragment would reveal a shift in the text from the time of Ezekiel to the time of the author's community. Thus the text functions on two levels. The people who "rise up" in the fragment are those of Israel at the time of Ezekiel; the "you" at the end of the fragment are the contemporaries of the author, who will be raised from their graves. If this link between *1 Clement* and 4Q385 12 can be made, then another possible connection between a Greek patristic citation and the Qumran Pseudo-Ezekiel document can be added to the two mentioned above.[29]

The Ezekiel who appears in these apocryphal fragments, whether they were transmitted in a book or books or in indi-

---

29. For complete argumentation see B. G. Wright, "*1 Clement* 50:4"; idem, "Qumran Pseudepigrapha"; and idem, "The Apocryphon of Ezekiel and 4QPseudo-Ezekiel." As previously unknown pseudepigrapha from Qumran are published, a number of these previously unattributed patristic citations may be identified, and new questions may be raised about the transmission of these texts in ancient Judaism and Christianity.

vidual oracles, has much in common with the biblical Ezekiel. Even though the Qumran work does not appear to be an original composition of the community, the Qumran fragments reveal that a text attributed to Ezekiel, like those attributed to other prophets, could be understood as predicting events that would take place during the lifetime of the members of the community. Although not as explicit or as clear as the *pesharim*, the Pseudo-Ezekiel work found at Qumran deals with the problems that the community saw as critical: a rise of a wicked ruler (4Q386), the presence of oppressing nations (4Q385 24), the shortening of times (4Q385 3), resurrection (4Q385 2, 12), and the eschatological Temple (4Q391).[30] In short, this prophet reveals the events of the eschaton, a time critical to the thinking of the Qumran community.

In the Greek patristic citations, Ezekiel pronounces judgment and offers the possibility of repentance, themes present in the biblical Ezekiel. And, although the tenor of the Greek citations is not overtly eschatological, these themes mesh well with the eschatological focus of the Qumran work. The major problematic passage among the Greek citations concerns the saying about the woman/heifer who has "given birth and not given birth." It may be, however, that the context of this passage in the patristic authors, who apply the passage (without the "heifer") to Mary, is misleading. Could this saying have originated in a context in which it was a miraculous sign, perhaps associated with eschatological events? It is impossible to say, but removed from a mariological context it may not be as exceptional as it first appears.

Hagiography and Iconography

The hagiographical and iconographic traditions about Ezekiel are extremely varied. Various pieces of rabbinic and Christian literature contain isolated reports about the prophet. Several of these

---

30. The use of Ezekiel 40–48 without explicit attribution to Ezekiel is widespread at Qumran. See Dimant, "Apocalyptic Interpretation"; Brooke, "Ezekiel in Some Qumran and New Testament Texts."

traditions clearly originated in thinking about specific passages
in the biblical book. The most extensive hagiographical information about the prophet concerns his death, and I will treat that
complex of traditions in some detail.

The most substantial extracanonical text about the life and
death of Ezekiel is in the *Vitae prophetarum,* in its present form a
Christian document, which narrates the "lives" of twenty-three
biblical personages.[31] These lives give birth and death notices
and frequently include legends narrating some of the deeds of
these figures. The *Vita* of Ezekiel forms the basis for much of the
Christian hagiography on the prophet, and it is notable in that it
contains two apparently different accounts of the prophet's death.

The *Vita* reports that Ezekiel was born in the land of "Arira"
and died "in the land of the Chaldeans," where he was killed by
a leader of Israel because Ezekiel had condemned him for worshiping idols. He was buried in the "field of Maour in the tomb
of Shem and Arpachsad." The *Vita* then preserves several legends
about the prophet's activity in Babylon. Ezekiel is said to have
seen the rising and falling of the river Chebar as an omen; he
divides the water in the river in a way reminiscent of Moses to
allow the Israelites with him to escape the Chaldeans (who subsequently drown); his prayers provide a miraculous supply of fish
for the people; his miracles relieve the fear of the Israelites; and
the "omen of the bones of the dead" (cf. Ezekiel 37) gives them
hope. The *Vita* goes on to say that Ezekiel "showed the people
of Israel the things taking place in Jerusalem and in the Temple."
The prophet is subsequently transported to the holy city to "re-
buke the unfaithful." In a reference to Ezekiel 40–48, the *Vita*
reports that Ezekiel saw the plan of the Temple as did Moses.
The account of Ezekiel's life finishes with a second death notice. The prophet judged the tribes of Dan and Gad because they
were "persecuting those who were keeping the Law." He then
performed a prophetic sign in which snakes ate the children and
cattle of these people, and he foresaw that they would not return
to the land, but would remain in Media "until the completion

---

31. On the problems of the *Vitae prophetarum* see Satran, *Biblical Prophets.* The *Vitae
prophetarum* survives in a dizzying array of forms and languages. The form of Ezekiel's
Vita cited here will be that of Codex Marchalianus (Q), as translated by Satran.

of their error." The *Vita* concludes, "And the one who murdered him was from among them, for they opposed him all the days of his life."

Of all the nonbiblical traditions about the prophet, those about his death contain the most variety and engender the greatest difficulty. Outside of the *Vita* of Ezekiel one finds two other death traditions. The first is found in Origen's *Commentary on Matthew* 23:37–39, where he refers to the deaths of Isaiah, who was sawn in two, Zechariah (presumably Zechariah ben Jehoiada), who "was killed," and Ezekiel, for whom nothing more specific is supplied. This notice reminds one of the deaths of three anonymous biblical figures described in Heb 11:37; these figures are "stoned," "sawn in two," and "killed by the sword." According to 2 Chr 24:21, Zechariah ben Jehoiada was stoned, and several traditions, most notably *Asc. Isa.* 5:1–2, report that Isaiah was sawn in two. The third figure in the list in Hebrews therefore is probably Ezekiel.

The identity of the prophet stoned in Heb 11:37 is not assuredly Zechariah, however. Some traditions, such as those found in *Par. Jer.* 9:22, the *Vitae prophetarum, Apoc. Paul* 49, and the illustrations of Jeremiah's life in an eleventh-century Bible manuscript, the Roda Bible (Paris, Bibliothèque Nationale, ms. Lat. 6), attribute Jeremiah's death to stoning.[32] The *Apocalypse of Paul* positions this tradition in conjunction with the deaths of Isaiah and Ezekiel. It may be more likely, then, that the three anonymous figures in Heb 11:37 are the three "major" prophets, Isaiah, Jeremiah, and Ezekiel.

Two pictorial representations of Ezekiel's death provide further evidence that the tradition in Hebrews and that referred to by Origen are probably the same. Among the illustrated wall panels in the synagogue at Dura Europos are three treating Ezekiel. The first two depict the vision of the valley of the dry bones,

---

32. *Par. Jer.* 9:22 says, "Come then, let us not kill him by the same sort of death with which we killed Isaiah, but let us stone him with stones." For Greek and English texts see Kraft and Purintun, *Paraleipomena Jeremiou.* The *Vita* of Jeremiah says, "Jeremiah was from Anatoth, and he died in Tahpanhes (Daphne) in Egypt when he was stoned by the people" (translation from Satran, *Biblical Prophets,* 122). *Apoc. Paul* 49 reads, "I am Jeremiah, who was stoned by the children of Israel and was slain." For the Roda Bible illustration see Neuss, *Buch Ezechiel,* 215.

and the third, his death.[33] In this panel the prophet is dragged from an altar by a figure in armor and then is held by the hair by a figure who holds a sword above his head, ready to strike him.[34] The Roda Bible contains a similar illustration. The picture of Ezekiel is on one of a succession of pages that illustrate the stories of Isaiah, Jeremiah, and Ezekiel.[35] The Ezekiel material contains in succession the valley of the dry bones (Ezek 37:1–14), similar to the panels at Dura, and a depiction of the sticks representing Israel and Judah (Ezek 37:15–28). The final illustration shows a figure standing over Ezekiel with a sword raised over the prophet's head.[36]

Should the manner of Ezekiel's death depicted primarily in Heb 11:37 and in the two pictorial representations described above be understood as an explication of the nonspecific death notices reported in the *Vitae prophetarum?* E. R. Goodenough thinks so, and Gabrielle Sed-Rajna follows his lead.[37] The most that can be said for certain is that it is possible. In both of the *Vita*'s death notices, a single individual is understood to be responsible for the prophet's demise. In the first, a leader of the exiled community in Babylon killed Ezekiel; in the second, "the one who murdered him" comes either from the tribe of Dan or Gad. Goodenough argues that the figure dressed in armor in the third panel of the Ezekiel cycle at Dura, who is pulling Ezekiel away from an altar, represents the first of the two *Vita* death notices.[38] Nothing in the *Vita* passages, however, would lead one to conclude that the prophet was killed by a sword. Although it is possible that two

---

33. There has been some disagreement about whether this last panel represents the death of Ezekiel. E. R. Goodenough's conclusion that Ezekiel is the subject (*Jewish Symbols* 10.187) is accepted here. For a detailed treatment of the issues, see J. E. Wright's article on the Dura panels in Stone, *Apocryphal Ezekiel*.

34. Is the altar that of the Temple in Jerusalem? Apparently elements of other prophetic deaths are being employed here for Ezekiel. See J. E. Wright's article in Stone, *Apocryphal Ezekiel*.

35. See Sed-Rajna, *Ancient Jewish Art*, 79. The list of Isaiah, Jeremiah, and Ezekiel here may also raise the uncertainty of the identity of the figure who is stoned in Hebrews 11. The death scene of Ezekiel in this manuscript is part of a larger series of illustrations devoted to the prophet. The rest of the images follow the biblical text. For reproductions of the remainder of the Ezekiel illustrations, see Neuss, *Buch Ezechiel*, 206, 209.

36. For pictures of the Dura panel depicting Ezekiel's death and of the Roda Bible, see Sed-Rajna, *Ancient Jewish Art*, 78–79.

37. See Sed-Rajna, *Ancient Jewish Art*, 79 and 212, n. 90.

38. Goodenough, *Jewish Symbols*, 10.190.

originally separate traditions have been combined to provide a killer *and* a means of death, such a conclusion must remain little more than informed speculation.

Another, altogether different death tradition is attested first in the fourth-century Christian *Apocalypse of Paul*. Other versions appear in the Syriac *Acts of Philip* and the fifth-century Latin *Opus imperfectum in Mattheum*.[39] In the *Apocalypse of Paul*, Ezekiel follows Isaiah and Jeremiah in speaking to Paul about his death. He says, "I am Ezekiel, whom the children of Israel dragged by the feet over the stones in the mountain until they scattered my brains abroad." The version in the *Opus imperfectum* follows that in the *Apocalypse of Paul* closely, while the version in the *Acts of Philip* lacks the detail about the stones.[40]

Although this tradition in its earliest extant forms circulated independently of the *Vitae* traditions, in later medieval works the two are brought together. This happens in a number of medieval versions of the *Vitae prophetarum*, but the most illustrative case is the twelfth-century *Historia scholastica* of Peter Comester. In this work Comester reports the life of Ezekiel, which agrees in many ways with the *Vitae prophetarum* account. He reports only one death tradition, the second one found in the *Vitae*. In his version of this tradition, however, Comester, instead of identifying the murderer as an individual from the tribe of Dan or Gad, substitutes, or inherits from his source of the *Vitae*, a tradition that the people of these tribes dragged Ezekiel with horses over the rocks and dashed out his brains.[41] He follows the description of Ezekiel's death with a notice of the prophet's burial place.

Several interesting observations are possible about the two traditions that give such a specific cause of Ezekiel's death. First, both occur in contexts in which the deaths of prophets in general are recounted. Such traditions as the sawing in half of Isaiah and

---

39. For convenient texts and translations of the appropriate sections of these works, see Stone, *Apocryphal Ezekiel*.

40. Another major difference between the *Apocalypse of Paul* and *Acts of Philip* is that in the latter, Jeremiah is killed by being thrown into a "pit of mire" rather than by the more traditional stoning.

41. Although I have not been able to check it personally, there is apparently a thirteenth- to fourteenth-century Latin manuscript from Palermo (Lib. Bibl. Naz. I.F.6–F.7, Bible, II. fol. 242r) which shows Ezekiel being dragged behind horses, a detail agreeing with Comester. I owe the reference to Theodore Bergren.

the stoning of Jeremiah (or Zechariah ben Jehoiada) almost seem to call for description of a specific means of death for Ezekiel, of which, as we have seen, two eventually became available. The later, medieval *Vitae* traditions, however, incorporate only one of these, the "debraining" story. Ezekiel's death by the sword is incorporated with the death tradition found in the *Vita* of Ezekiel only iconographically, at Dura Europos, if Goodenough's conclusions are correct. I have found no evidence for the enfolding of the tradition of Ezekiel's death by sword into later literary versions of the *Vitae prophetarum*.

In connection with Ezekiel's death in the literary sources, as far back as the twelfth century travelers in the Near East have visited a site identified as the tomb of Ezekiel. The earliest notice of this place is by Rabbi Benjamin of Tudela (twelfth century). He visited the tomb, which was located on the banks of the Euphrates, about a half day's journey from Babylon. Rabbi Petachia of Regensburg also visited the site in the twelfth century. Many other travelers up to the nineteenth century have recorded visits to this tomb.[42]

The writings of the rabbinic sages, although they might not be considered strictly "hagiographical," also preserve a number of noteworthy traditions about Ezekiel.[43] The rabbis were aware, of course, that Ezekiel was part of the Israelite population that was taken to Babylon, and several traditions link him with other exilic figures, especially Daniel and the three in the furnace, Hananiah, Mishael, and Azariah. In a list in *Gen. Rab.* 5.5, the name of Ezekiel immediately follows the names of the three young Israelites and Daniel. This document also reports that God made "the heavens to open before Ezekiel," a reference to Ezek 1:1. *Song of Songs Rab.* 7.8 narrates a long encounter between Ezekiel and Hananiah, Mishael, and Azariah, who come to the prophet on the advice of Daniel to inquire whether they should bow down to the idol of Nebuchadnezzar.[44]

---

42. For a complete discussion of the tomb of Ezekiel, see Stone, *Apocryphal Ezekiel*.

43. For complete and detailed discussion of rabbinic traditions about Ezekiel and his book, see Aberbach, "Ezekiel"; Ginzberg, *Legends*.

44. Ezekiel responds to them initially with a citation of Isa 26:20 ("hide yourself a little while until my anger passes away"). This same passage may be alluded to in the Qumran Pseudo-Ezekiel work (4Q385 12, see above), and Epiphanius in his introduction to the

As might be expected, Ezekiel 1 and 37 provide grist for the mill of rabbinic interpretation. The Merkabah vision has been treated thoroughly by David Halperin, and I refer the reader to his excellent study.[45] Several rabbinic texts contain information supplemental to the events described in Ezekiel 37. *B. Sanh.* 92b reports that the miracle of the dry bones took place on the same day that the three were thrown into the furnace, and that there were six miracles on that day: "the furnace floated upward"; "its walls fell in"; "its foundation crumbled"; "the image [of Nebuchadnezzar] fell over"; "four royal suites were burned"; and "Ezekiel resurrected the dead in the valley of Dura."

The rabbinic writings preserve two different assessments of Ezekiel's answer to God's question in Ezek 37:3: "Son of Man, can these bones live?" *Gen. Rab.* 19.11, in a comment on Gen 2:12, notes that there were four people, Adam, Cain, Balaam, and Hezekiah, who were questioned by God and their answers found wanting. Ezekiel is said to be superior to these others because he answered, "O God, you know." This positive evaluation of Ezekiel's answer stands in stark contrast to that offered in *Pirqe R. El.* 33, which uses Ezekiel's answer to account for why this important prophet was buried outside of Palestine. His answer, "O God, you know," is considered to be a statement of unbelief, presumably because he hedged and did not answer "Yes." Because of this unbelief he was buried in the land of the Chaldeans.

One other tradition deserves mention in this context. *B. Hag.* 13a compares Ezekiel's visions to those of Isaiah. In the middle of a long discussion on the mishnaic injunction not to expound the Merkabah "in the presence of one," a saying is attributed to Raba. "All that Ezekiel saw, Isaiah saw. What does Ezekiel resemble? A villager who saw the king. And what does Isaiah resemble? A townsman who saw the king." The meaning apparently is that the townsman would be more familiar with seeing the king and therefore would not give such elaborate detail. The villager, who

---

quotation of "Ezekiel's own apocryphon" cites Isa 26:19. How these texts that cite Isaiah 26 relate to each other, if at all, is not clear at this juncture. *Pirqe R. El.* 3 also connects the three with Ezekiel via a citation of Ezek 37:9.

45. Halperin, *Faces of the Chariot.*

is not as used to seeing the king, would be inclined to provide more information. Thus Ezekiel and Isaiah saw the same thing, even though their reports of their visions differ.[46]

Other than their treatment of the death traditions about Ezekiel, which are not detailed in the biblical book, iconographic representations remain fairly closely focused on the scriptural record. Outside of the renderings of Ezekiel's death, I have not found any iconography concerning the prophet that contains significant nonbiblical material. By far the most frequently represented event in artistic depictions is the miracle of the valley of the dry bones (Ezekiel 37). This passage was interpreted by Christians as a foreshadowing of the resurrection of believers, and representations appear on a number of sarcophagi.[47] In pictorial images of Ezekiel 37, a fairly standard tradition of representation develops, as can be seen on a third- to fourth-century gold glass found in Cologne, on the first two panels of Ezekiel in the Dura Europos synagogue, and in the illustration from the Roda Bible mentioned above.[48] The cleft mountain that appears in the Dura panel and on the Cologne gold glass may represent a tradition, derived from Ezek 37:7, that there was an earthquake at the reassembling of the bones.[49] For the most part, however, these representations follow the biblical text closely.[50]

When one takes an overall look at the hagiographical traditions about Ezekiel, it certainly seems that those about his death and burial predominate. Few hagiographical traditions appear before the fourth or fifth century C.E., when such traditions begin to flourish in the Byzantine period.[51] This is true for both Christian and rabbinic literature. For Christians, the *Vitae prophetarum* certainly comprises the greatest treasury of nonbiblical material about Ezekiel, and it seems to constitute the basic source of hagiographical information for later Christian writers, even those

---

46. This is also the interpretation in the notes of the Soncino translation of *b. Hag.* 13a.

47. For discussion of these sarcophagi, see Neuss, *Buch Ezechiel*, 144–54.

48. For pictures of the Dura synagogue and the Roda Bible, see Sed-Rajna, *Ancient Jewish Art*, 76, 79. For the gold glass, see Neuss, *Buch Ezechiel*, 143.

49. See *Pirqe R. El.* 33.

50. For a complete discussion of the iconography of Ezekiel, see Neuss, *Buch Ezechiel*, pt. 2.

51. On the rise of interest in biographical information about biblical figures in Byzantine Palestine, see Satran, *Biblical Prophets*, 1–8.

like Peter Comester who know stories about Ezekiel's death not reported in the *Vitae*. Although some biographical information does survive in rabbinic literature, like the knowledge that Ezekiel died and was buried outside of Palestine and of his alleged connection with other exilic figures, the rabbis seem less concerned, in general, with hagiography than with explication of the biblical book.

Bibliography

Primary Texts

Bonner, C. *The Homily on the Passion by Melito Bishop of Sardis and Some Fragments of the Apocryphal Ezekiel.* SD 12. Philadelphia: University of Pennsylvania Press, 1940.

Denis, A.-M. *Fragmenta pseudepigraphorum quae supersunt graeca.* PVTG 3. Leiden: Brill, 1970. *Apocryphon of Ezekiel,* pp. 121–28.

———. *Introduction aux pseudépigraphes grecs d'Ancien Testament.* SVTP 1. Leiden: Brill, 1970. *Apocryphon of Ezekiel,* pp. 187–91.

Epstein, I., ed. *The Soncino Talmud.* 18 vols. London: Soncino, 1938.

Holl, K., ed. *Epiphanius, Ancoratus und Panarion.* 3 vols. GCS 25, 31, 37. Leipzig: Hinrichs, 1915, 1922, 1933.

Hussan, P., and P. Nautin. *Origène: Homilies sur Jérémie.* SC 238. Paris: Cerf, 1977.

Jaubert, A., ed. *Clement de Rome: Epître aux Corinthiens.* SC 167. Paris: Cerf, 1971.

Kister, M., and E. Qimron. "Observations on 4QSecond Ezekiel." *RevQ* 15 (1992) 595–602.

Klostermann, E., ed. *Origenes Werke: Zehnter Band-Origenes Matthäuserklärung: 1 Die griechische erhaltenen Tomoi.* GCS 40. Leipzig: Hinrichs, 1935.

———, ed. *Origenes Werke: Elfter Band-Origenes Matthäuserklärung: 2 Die lateinische Übersetzung der Commentariorum Series.* GCS 38. Leipzig: Hinrichs, 1933.

Kraft, R. A. *The Didache and Barnabas.* Vol. 3 of *The Apostolic Fathers.* Ed. R. M. Grant. New York: Thomas Nelson & Sons, 1965.

Mueller, J. R., and S. E. Robinson. "Apocryphon of Ezekiel." *OTP* 1.487–95.

Resch, A. *Agrapha: Aussercanonische Schriftfragmente.* 2d ed. TU 30/3–4. Leipzig: Hinrichs, 1906. See sec. 6, "Alttestamentliche Agrapha und Apokrypha 21."

Scopello, M. *L'exégèse de l'ame (Nag Hammadi, II,6): Introduction, traduction, commentaire.* NHS 25. Leiden: Brill, 1985.

Smith, M. "Pseudo-Ezekiel." In *Qumran Cave 4. XIV: Parabiblical Texts, Part 2.* Ed. M. Broshi et al. DJD 19. Oxford: Clarendon, 1995. Pp. 153–93.

Stählin, O., ed. *Clemens Alexandrinus: Protrepticus und Paedagogus.* GCS 17, 52.1. Leipzig: Hinrichs, 1909, 1972.

Strugnell, J., and D. Dimant. "4Q Second Ezekiel." *RevQ* 13 (1988) 45–58.

———. "The Merkabah Vision in Second Ezekiel (4Q385 4)." *RevQ* 14 (1990) 331–48.

Strugnell, J., and E. Qimron, eds. *Qumran Cave 4. V: Miqsat Ma'ase Ha-Torah.* DJD 10. Oxford: Clarendon, 1994.

Thackeray, H. St. J., R. Marcus, and L. H. Feldman, trans. *Josephus.* LCL. 9 vols. Cambridge, Mass.: Harvard University Press, 1926–1965.

Williams, F., trans. *The Panarion of Epiphanius of Salamis.* Bk. 1, secs. 1–46. NHS 35. Leiden: Brill, 1987.

Secondary Literature

Aberbach, M. "Ezekiel." *EncJud* 6.1095–96. A basic article on the prophet and his book.

Baker, A. "Justin's Agraphon in the *Dialogue with Trypho.*" *JBL* 87 (1968) 77–87. Concludes that the agraphon cited by Justin and others is unlikely to have come from an apocryphal Ezekiel book.

Bauckham, R. J. "A Quotation from 4Q *Second Ezekiel* in *Apocalypse of Peter.*" *RevQ* 15 (1992) 438–45. Maintains that a citation in *Apoc. Pet.* 4:7–9 originates in the dry bones vision as it appears in the Pseudo-Ezekiel work from Qumran.

Bellinzoni, A. J. *The Sayings of Jesus in the Writings of Justin Martyr.* SNT 17. Leiden: Brill, 1967. Treats all of the quotations attributed to Jesus by Justin.

———. "The Source of the Agraphon in Justin Martyr's *Dialogue with Trypho* 47:5." *VC* 17 (1963) 65–70. Attempts to establish a transmission history of this saying in order to account for its wide variety of attribution.

Bonner, C., and H. C. Youtie. *The Last Chapters of Enoch in Greek.* SD 8. London: Christophers, 1937. Contains a short discussion of the apocryphal Ezekiel material found in Chester Beatty Papyrus 185.

Bregman, M. "The Parable of the Lame and the Blind: Epiphanius' Quotation from an Apocryphon of Ezekiel." *JTS* 42 (1991) 125–38. Argues that Epiphanius's version of the parable was a Christian reworking of a rabbinic parable and probably did not come from an *Apocryphon of Ezekiel.*

Brooke, G. J. "Ezekiel in Some Qumran and New Testament Texts." In *The Madrid Qumran Congress: Proceedings of the International Congress on the Dead Sea Scrolls, Madrid, 18–21 March 1991.* Ed. J. Trebolle Barrera and L. Vegas Montaner. STDJ 11, 1. Leiden: Brill; Madrid: Editorial Complutense, 1992. Pp. 317–37. Examines the major Ezekiel materials from Qumran and juxtaposes them with NT passages that refer to Ezekiel in a like manner. Included are (1) from Qumran: biblical manuscript fragments, the Pseudo-Ezekiel document, texts with quotations of Ezekiel, and texts that allude to Ezekiel; and (2) the NT.

Dassmann, E. "Hesekiel." *RAC* 14, cols. 1132–91. A general article which includes discussion of the historical prophet, his book, and its interpretations in Judaism and Christianity, as well as some nonbiblical material.

Dehandschutter, B. "L'Apocryphe d'Ezechiel: Source de l'Exégèse sur l'ame." *OLP* 10 (1979) 227–35. Argues that, rather than being an independent witness to an *Apocryphon of Ezekiel*, *Exegesis on the Soul* 135.30–136.4 is actually dependent on the Coptic translation of *1 Clement*.

Dimant, D. "The Apocalyptic Interpretation of Ezekiel at Qumran." In *Messiah and Christos: Studies in the Jewish Origins of Christianity.* Ed. I. Gruenwald, S. Shaked, and G. G. Stroumsa. Tübingen: J. C. B. Mohr (Paul Siebeck), 1992. Pp. 31–52. Discusses how the prophet Ezekiel is used in the texts from Qumran.

———. "New Light from Qumran on the Jewish Pseudepigrapha — 4Q390." In *The Madrid Qumran Congress: Proceedings of the International Congress on the Dead Sea Scrolls, Madrid 18–21 March 1991.* Ed. J. Trebolle Barrera and L. Vegas Montaner. STDJ 11, 2. Leiden: Brill; Madrid: Editorial Complutense, 1992. Pp. 405–48. In the introduction to this article, Dimant lists those fragments that she thinks belong to 4QPseudo-Ezekiel.

Eckart, K.-G. "Die Kuh des apokryphen Ezechiel." In *Antwort aus der Geschichte.* Ed. W. Sommer and H. Ruppell. Berlin: Christlicher Zeitschriftenverlag, 1969. Pp. 44–48. Discussion of the "heifer" saying in the apocryphal Ezekiel fragments.

Ginzberg, L. *The Legends of the Jews.* 7 vols. Philadelphia: Jewish Publication Society of America, 1909–38. An exhaustive collection of rabbinic legends about the Bible and biblical figures.

Goodenough, E. R. *Jewish Symbols in the Greco-Roman Period.* 12 vols. New York: Bollingen, 1965. A foundational study of the Hellenistic influence on Judaism in the Greco-Roman period. Focuses on the archaeological evidence for Judaism.

Guillaumont, A. "Une Citation de l'Apocryphe d'Ezechiel dans l'exégèse ou sujet de l'ame." In *Essays on the Nag Hammadi Texts.* Ed. M. Krause. Leiden: Brill, 1975. Pp. 35–40. Argues that the Nag Hammadi citation paralleling *1 Clem.* 8:3 constitutes an independent witness to the saying.

Hagner, D. A. *The Use of the Old and New Testaments in Clement of Rome.* SNT 34. Leiden: Brill, 1973. Examines all the citations of other works in *1 Clement,* including 8:3, usually interpreted as a citation of the *Apocryphon of Ezekiel.*

Halperin, D. *Faces of the Chariot: Early Jewish Responses to Ezekiel's Vision.* Texte und Studien zum antiken Judentum 16. Tübingen: J. C. B. Mohr, 1988. Studies the interpretive traditions on Ezekiel chapters 1 and 10.

James, M. R. "The Apocryphal Ezekiel." *JTS* 15 (1914) 236–43. A seminal study of the apocryphal Ezekiel traditions which surveys the texts traditionally considered part of an apocryphal Ezekiel work.

Jeremias, J. *Unknown Sayings of Jesus.* 2d ed. London: SPCK, 1964. Treats the so-called agrapha, sayings that have been attributed to Jesus outside of the NT; includes the Ezekiel saying attributed to Jesus by Justin.

Kenyon, F. G. *The Chester Beatty Biblical Papyri: Descriptions and Texts of Twelve Manuscripts on Papyrus of the Greek Bible.* Fascicle 8: *Enoch and Melito.* London: Walker, 1941. Discusses the apocryphal Ezekiel passage in Chester Beatty Papyrus 185.

Kister, M. "Barnabas 12:1; 4:3 and 4Q Second Ezekiel." *RB* 97 (1990) 63–67. Argues that these two passages from the *Epistle of Barnabas* cite the Ezekiel pseudepigraphon from Qumran.

Matter, E. A. "The 'Revelatio Esdrae' in Latin and English Traditions." *RBén* 42 (1982) 376–92. Mentions several medieval works attributed to Ezekiel.

Mueller, J. R. *The Five Fragments of the Apocryphon of Ezekiel: A Critical Study.* JSPSup 5. Sheffield: Sheffield Academic Press, 1994. Discusses the five Greek fragments traditionally ascribed to a Greek *Apocryphon of Ezekiel.* Contains the most up-to-date bibliography on the *Apocryphon.*

———. "Riding Piggyback in Antiquity: The Motif of the Lame Man and the Blind Man in Ancient Literature." Paper presented at the Annual Meeting of the Society of Biblical Literature, Atlanta, November 1986. An analysis of Epiphanius's parable of the blind and the lame man.

Neuss, W. *Das Buch Ezechiel in Theologie und Kunst.* Münster: Aschendorf, 1912. Treats both the history of theology and artistic representations of the biblical Book of Ezekiel.

Ruwet, J. "Les 'agrapha' dans le oeuvres de Clement d'Alexandrie." *Bib* 30 (1949) 133–60. The last of three articles that examine in detail Clement of Alexandria's quotations from and use of nonbiblical sources.

———. "Clement d'Alexandrie, canon des escritures et apocryphe." *Bib* 29 (1948) 77–99, 240–68. The first two of the three articles referred to above.

Satran, D. *Biblical Prophets in Byzantine Palestine: Reassessing the Lives of the Prophets.* SVTP 11. Leiden: Brill, 1995. A study of the *Vitae prophetarum* that argues that its context in Byzantine Christianity needs to be taken seriously in order to understand the work.

Schiffman, L. H. *Reclaiming the Dead Sea Scrolls.* Philadelphia: Jewish Publication Society, 1994. An introduction to the current status of Qumran studies.

Scopello, M. "Les citations d'Homère dans le traité de l'Exégèse de l'ame." In *Gnosis and Gnosticism.* Ed. M. Krause. NHS 8. Leiden: Brill, 1977. Pp. 3–12. This and the following article argue that the *Exegesis on the Soul* drew the citation of the Ezekiel *Apocryphon* from a testimony book or books.

———. "Les 'Testimonia' dans le traité de 'L'exégèse de l'ame' (Nag Hammadi, II, 6)." *RHR* 191 (1977) 159–71. See above.

Sed-Rajna, G. *Ancient Jewish Art.* Paris: Flammarion, 1975. A study of Jewish art of the last two millennia; includes the synagogue art at Dura Europos.

Sevrin, J.-M. "La rédaction de l'Exégèse de l'ame (Nag Hammadi II, 6)." *Mus* 92 (1979) 237–71. Like Scopello, Sevrin argues that *Exegesis on the Soul* knew the citation of the *Apocryphon of Ezekiel* from a testimony book.

Stone, M. E., D. Satran, and B. G. Wright, eds. *The Apocryphal Ezekiel.* Forthcoming. A collection of nonbiblical traditions about Ezekiel, including the *Apocryphon of Ezekiel,* the Qumran fragments, and hagiographical traditions.

Wise, M., M. Abegg, Jr., and E. Cook. *The Dead Sea Scrolls: A New Translation.* San Francisco: HarperSanFrancisco, 1996.

Wright, B. G. "*1 Clement* 50:4 and Clement of Alexandria, *Prot.* 8.81.4: Citations of an Ezekiel Apocryphon?" Paper presented at the Annual Meeting of the Society of Biblical Literature, Chicago, November 1994. Argues that *1 Clement* probably has as its ultimate source 4Q*385* 12, and that Clement of Alexandria may reflect an apocryphal source, which however cannot be identified for certain as an Ezekiel apocryphon.

————. "The Apocryphon of Ezekiel and 4QPseudo-Ezekiel: Are They the Same Work? How Do We Know?" Paper presented at the international congress "The Dead Sea Scrolls — Fifty Years after Their Discovery." The Israel Museum, Jerusalem, July 20–25, 1997. Concludes that the Greek apocryphon and the Qumran pseudepigraphon may have belonged to the same work. The paper also contains a detailed listing of the Qumran fragments thought, thus far, to belong to Pseudo-Ezekiel.

————. "A Fragment of Apocryphal Ezekiel Contained in *First Clement.*" Paper presented at the Annual Meeting of the Society of Biblical Literature, Atlanta, November 1986. Argues that the saying in *1 Clem.* 8:3 originally belonged to an apocryphal Ezekiel text, and that the citations in Clement of Alexandria and the *Exegesis of the Soul* are independent witnesses to it.

————. "Qumran Pseudepigrapha in Early Christianity: Is *1 Clement* 50:4 a Citation of 4Q Pseudo-Ezekiel (4Q385)?" Paper presented at the Orion Center for the Study of the Dead Sea Scrolls and Associated Literature Conference, "Pseudepigraphic Perspectives," January 1997. Argues that *1 Clem.* 50:4 is probably a citation of the same Jewish Ezekiel pseudepigraphon as 4Q*385* 12.

THE PROPHET EZEKIEL IN ISLAMIC LITERATURE

Jewish Traces and Islamic Adaptations

AVIVA SCHUSSMAN

Introduction

Ezekiel (Arabic Ḥizqīl) is represented in Islamic literature as one of Muhammad's predecessors. This is indicative of the well-known Islamic theory — the grounds of which are Qur'anic — that the universal monotheistic message preached by all the prophets, beginning with Adam and ending with Muhammad, the "seal of the prophets" (Qur'an 33:40), was basically the same. Accordingly, the Qur'an is full of stories connected with biblical personalities such as Noah, Abraham, Joseph, Moses, Elijah, Jonah, David, Solomon, and Job, all of whom are considered prophets.

From a literary perspective these Qur'anic stories generally differ from their biblical counterparts by the omission of some details and the addition of others, the latter deriving either from Arabic culture or from postbiblical Judeo-Christian tradition. According to Western scholarly research, the latter phenomenon reflects the nature of Muhammad's exposure to Judaism and Christianity: he had direct contact not with Jewish or Christian scriptures, but with the "people of the scriptures" (Ahl al-Kitāb, a common Qur'anic designation for Jews and Christians), to whom he listened and with whom he conversed. This means that he became acquainted with the biblical stories orally, the result presumably being that he could neither recall their exact details nor discern between the biblical core and later homiletic adaptation. In any case, Muhammad was more interested in the morals underlying these stories than in their exact details.[1]

In this context two other Qur'anic literary features are worth noting. First, like the Qur'anic material in general, the biblical stories there are represented not consecutively and chronologically, but rather sporadically and in fragmentary fashion. Thus, in order to get the "entire" Qur'anic story of a given prophet, one must collect the relevant details from different Qur'anic passages. Second, some of these Qur'anic stories are vague and even anonymous. In such cases one must speculate even in order to identify the biblical story under consideration and the prophet involved.

This, indeed, is the situation with Ezekiel; as we shall see below, the Qur'an never mentions him by name, and the few Qur'anic passages that might be taken to refer to him consist only of vague implications. We might add that the same is true for the prophets Isaiah and Jeremiah, which means that the Qur'an almost ignores the most prominent biblical prophets, including those who prophesied around the time of the destruction of the First Temple.[2] This fact is significant with regard to the presentation of Ezekiel in post-Qur'anic sources.

In the generations following Muhammad, Muslim scholars became more directly acquainted with the Bible and with post-biblical Judeo-Christian sources, which helped them to fill in the gaps in the sometimes vague biblical stories in the Qur'an. Thus they arranged the stories in a chronological framework, added some necessary narrative details, including names and other specifications, and also embellished the stories with Islamic and folkloristic motifs.[3] They were, however, dedicated first and

---

1. From the vast scholarly literature dealing with this subject, either in general or in connection with specific biblical stories, see Firestone, *Journeys in Holy Lands;* Geiger, *Judaism;* Hayek, *Mystère d'Ismaël;* Masson, *Coran;* Moubarac, *Abraham;* T. Nagel, *Qiṣaṣ al-Anbiyā;* Obermann, "Islamic Origins," 58–119; Schwarzbaum, *Biblical and Extra-biblical Legends;* Sidersky, *Origines;* and Torrey, *Jewish Foundation.* The bibliography in Schwarzbaum, *Biblical and Extra-biblical Legends,* 178–209, is especially instructive.

2. This fact is attributed by Crone and Cook to Samaritan influence on the Qur'an, reflecting the Samaritan rejection of the extra-Pentateuchal parts of the Bible (*Hagarism,* 14–15; and compare below, n. 13). In my opinion the reason is different (see below, "Conclusion").

3. For this development in general, see the studies mentioned in n. 1. The themes of Is-

foremost to the Qur'an itself; and the more vague the Qur'anic story was, the more difficult it became for them to explicate it. This may be the reason why Ezekiel's story remains vague and confused even in post-Qur'anic sources. This is evident in the following passage, quoted from one such source, the eleventh-century Muslim commentator and *Qiṣaṣ* author Thaʿlabī's *Kitāb Qiṣaṣ al-Anbiyā*.

> When God took away Caleb [son of Yuq/fna = יפונה] and his son, He — exalted be He — sent Ḥizqīl to the children of Israel as a prophet; namely, Ḥizqīl son of Būrī [Budhī or Buzī = בוזי], whose nickname was "the son of the old lady" [*Ibn al-ʿAdjūz*]. He was given this nickname because his mother, in her old age, had asked God for a child, after growing very old and being barren. Then God — exalted be He — blessed [lit. granted] her with him, and he was the one by whom God resurrected the people…as written in the Qur'an.[4]

This account, which is typical of the Muslim post-Qur'anic treatment of Ezekiel, forms the basis for the following discussion. We will analyze it in view of the Qur'an and certain other parallels in Islamic and Jewish sources.[5] Furthermore, we will attempt to explain the specific idiosyncrasies in this and other Islamic adaptations of the Ezekiel story (such adaptations are generally referred to as *Qiṣaṣ*, "stories").

The Historical and Biographical Aspects of Ḥizqīl

Thaʿlabī's account states that Ḥizqīl was given his prophetic mission after the time of Caleb and his son. Some Muslim sources

lamization and folklorization are emphasized by Schwarzbaum, *Biblical and Extra-biblical Legends*, esp. chap. 4. See also below, "The Islamic Dimensions of the Ḥizqīl Story," and n. 30.

4. Thaʿlabī, 259 (this passage and other quotations from Islamic post-Qur'anic sources have been translated from the Arabic by the author). Compare Ṭabarī A, II, 535, 539; Fārisī, 59–61; Ṭabarsī, II, 269–71. The Qur'anic quotation referred to is discussed below, "The Prophetic Aspect of Ḥizqīl."

5. The Islamic sources represented in this article are exegetical, historiographical, geographical, and folkloristic in character (they belong to the "Qiṣaṣ al-Anbiyā," or "Tales of the Prophets" genre). They extend over a long period of time, from the ninth to the seventeenth centuries C.E. (see the bibliography to this chapter, under "Primary Islamic Sources"). Since no clear chronological development in their apprehension of Ezekiel's story has been traced (except on one issue; see below, "Dhū 'l-Kifl's Tomb"), they are discussed on equal terms. For the same reason the rabbinic parallels are also represented on equal terms, based on Ginzberg, *Legends*.

refer to Ḥizqīl's time period more specifically as the time of Eli the priest (*'Eilān al-Kāhin*).[6] With reference to standard biblical chronology, we are dealing here with the period between Joshua and the monarchy, partly parallel to the time of the judges; this is obviously different from the time of the biblical Ezekiel, who lived in the sixth century B.C.E. Indeed, some *Qiṣaṣ* sources do associate Ḥizqīl, in various and sometimes strange ways, with the period of the destruction of the First Temple (the time of the biblical Ezekiel);[7] but his assignment to the period of the judges seems to prevail in Islamic sources.

Presumably, this unusual chronology may be explained as follows. The Islamic concept of prophethood is committed to the principle of chronological continuity in the prophetic chain;[8] thus, in cases of a lack of such continuity, as in the period of the judges, this gap must be filled. Apparently Muslim adaptors found the biblical Ezekiel the most appropriate candidate to fill this gap, perhaps because they learned from Jewish sources, both biblical and rabbinic, of his priestly descent;[9] thus, he was both a priest and a prophet. Additionally, they could have learned that his later prophecies (chaps. 40–48) dealt with the priestly service in the future Temple.[10] Furthermore, they could have been aware of the

---

6. Masʿūdī, I, 103. Fārisī does not mention Eli by name, but the details of his version (below, n. 14) clearly allude to Eli's time.

7. See for instance his identification with King Hezekiah, son of Ahaz (2 Kings 18), in Yaʿqūbī, I, 69, and Djazāʾirī, 356. This confusion probably derives from the phonetic similarity between Hezekiah and Ḥizqīl (see Yaʿqūbī's note). In one case Ḥizqīl appears after Jeremiah, Ezra, Daniel, and Isaiah (Ibn Qutayba, 23), and in another he appears — as in the Bible — as one of the deportees to Babylonia (Mudjīr, I, 149). For other views see Eisenberg, "Ḥizḳīl," *EI*[2] 3.535.

8. See Schussman, *Stories*, 118–19, 154–57. The grounds of this principle are Qurʾanic (e.g., Qurʾan 10:48: "Every nation has its messenger"; 16:38: "Indeed We sent forth among every nation a messenger").

9. Ezek 1:3: יחזקאל בן בוזי הכהן, "Ezekiel the priest, son of Buzi." His family probably descended from the offspring of Zadok and his forefather Phinehas (see 1 Chr 6:2–15 [Heb 5:28–41]; see also Hartom, *Pentateuch, Prophets, Hagiographa*, "Introduction to the Book of Ezekiel," 5–7. On Phinehas, son of Eleazar, son of Aaron, see below, n. 11). Interestingly, some rabbinic legends depict Ezekiel as being descended from Joshua's and Rahab's offspring (see Ginzberg, *Legends*, 6.171, n. 12). This may also explain Ḥizqīl's representation in Islamic sources as being subsequent to Joshua and Caleb.

10. See Ezekiel 40–48. Since these prophecies partly contradict the Torah, the rabbis tried to explain away the contradictions (see Abramsky and Ta-Shemaʿ, "Ezekiel," in Klausner, *Encyclopaedia Hebraica* 19.744–45, 747–48; Aberbach, "Ezekiel," *EncJud* 6.1095–96). This means that the issue could have been known to Muslims because of its fervent discussion in rabbinic sources. In any case, there is evidence that some Muslims were acquainted with these prophecies (see below, "Conclusion," and n. 50).

special spiritual significance of the priestly duties in the period of the judges, often characterized as a time of moral decline and lack of central government, when the priests would have been those who kept the spirit of the Torah alive.[11] In other words, since Ezekiel was a prophet engaged with priesthood, it might have seemed appropriate to Muslim commentators that he fulfill his mission precisely in the time of the judges.

Admittedly, to the best of my knowledge, no Islamic source that associates Ḥizqīl's story with the time of the judges explicitly mentions his priestly lineage. Nevertheless, some versions show that Muslims did know of his priestly descent,[12] and this factor could have prompted them to insert him into the chain of prophethood at this particular point.[13]

Another aspect of Ḥizqīl's priestly connection lies in the biographical detail of his birth in his mother's old age, after she had been barren for some time. The above-mentioned connection of Ḥizqīl to the time of Eli clearly suggests the possibility of a confusion of Ḥizqīl with the biblical Samuel. Indeed, in one of the *Qiṣaṣ* sources, the story of Ḥizqīl's birth is given in detail, with almost all of the well-known features of the biblical story of Samuel's birth, including his mother's prayer and her promise to devote him to the holy service in the Temple, under the supervision of those who permanently reside there (probably an allusion to Eli and his sons).[14] Thus, Ḥizqīl is connected with the

---

11. On the issue of moral decline, see Judg 2:10–23. On the priests' functions before and during the time of the judges, see Joshua 22, which relates Phinehas's involvement in preventing the Gilead tribes from separating, and Judg 20:28, which describes his service before the ark of the covenant. The rabbis emphasized the continuity of the priesthood through Aaron's family from the time of Joshua to the judges and later, ascribing to Eleazar divine inspiration in dividing the land (see Ginzberg, *Legends*, 4.15 and 6.179, n. 47). They attributed to Phinehas successful participation in the spies' mission (Ginzberg, *Legends*, 4.5 and 6.171, n. 10), as well as longevity until the time of Elijah, with whom he is identified (Ginzberg, *Legends*, 4.53–54 and 6.214, n. 140; 4.61 and 6.220, n. 25).

12. One source implies that Ḥizqīl was given his mission between the times of Aaron and Elijah (Ibn ʿAsākir, III, 95). Could this imply a connection to Aaron's family? Another source explicitly states that Ḥizqīl was descended from Aaron (Mudjīr, I, 149).

13. According to Crone and Cook, the legitimacy of continuity in Islamic political authority (not in the prophetic chain) was influenced by the Samaritan notion of the continuity and legitimacy of the priesthood descending from Aaron's family (*Hagarism*, 26; compare n. 2).

14. Compare 1 Samuel 1 with Fārisī, 58–61, esp. pp. 58–59: "Some Muslims argue that the old woman's son was called Shemuel; God knows best." However, the story as a whole

priesthood in Islamic sources not only through his descent, but also through his association with Eli. This is somewhat similar to rabbinic legends that associate Eli with Ezekiel, although they do it in a rather different manner. Certain rabbinic sources ascribe to Eli not only devotion to the study of the Torah, but also the preparation of "crowns" for a certain copy of the Torah. This copy was allegedly preserved in the Temple for many generations until it was found by Ezekiel, who took it to Babylonia during the exile (this was also the Torah copy that was later brought back to Jerusalem by Ezra).[15] In other words, the rabbinic connection that linked Ezekiel with Eli could also have caused a confusion in Islamic sources between Samuel and Ḥizqīl.

The biographical picture of Ḥizqīl is further complicated by the fact that a few Islamic sources identify another vague Qur'anic personality — known by the nickname Dhū 'l-Kifl — with Ḥizqīl.[16] Dhū 'l-Kifl (lit. "the one endowed with *kifl*," or "responsibility") appears in the Qur'an twice (21:85–86 and 38:48), where he is depicted as an excellent and righteous man, but where no story about him is told. Muslim commentators were not unanimous as to whether he was a prophet at all; in any case, they tried to find an explanation for his nickname on the basis of Arabic etymology. Since some derivatives of the Arabic root KFL have the meanings of "self-commitment," "guarantee," "surety," or "responsibility," some commentators composed picturesque stories involving "responsibilities" that Dhū 'l-Kifl took upon himself.[17] One of these is relevant to our discussion, insofar as it may explain why Dhū 'l-Kifl was identified with Ḥizqīl. The

---

is explicitly related to Ḥizqīl, not to Samuel; but his mother's name is Bhnah (= Hannah, Samuel's mother?). Another source quotes a version in which the prophet involved is called Shamʿūn (= Shimeʿon), which may reflect a confusion with Shemuel (Ṭabarsī, II, 270).

15. For details of this legend see Ginzberg, *Legends*, 4.61 and 6.220, n. 24.

16. I have been able to find this identification explicitly in only two Islamic sources: Harawī, 76, and Ṭabarsī, II, 269. Other sources identify Dhū 'l-Kifl with other personalities (see Vajda, "Dhū 'l-Kifl," *EI*[2] 2.242, and below, "The Islamic Dimensions of the Ḥizqīl Story," and n. 41).

17. For a general description of these stories, see Goldziher, "Dhū 'l-Kifl," *EI*[1] 2.962–63. More specifically, for example: Dhū 'l-Kifl guaranteed paradise to a king who had become a true believer (Ibn Qutayba, 25); he guaranteed longevity to his people, who agreed to wage a holy war (Thaʿlabī, 169–70; is this reminiscent of Ḥizqīl's holy war?; see below, n. 28, and "Holy War"); and he committed himself to fast during the days, pray during the nights, and judge his people without anger (Djalālayn, 21:85–86; similar versions are found in Ṭabarī B, XVII, 73–76, and Rāzī, VI, 127–28).

story relates how D̲h̲ū 'l-Kifl took responsibility for the lives of seventy (or a hundred) prophets, whom he saved from death.[18] This story displays similarities to certain details that appear at the end of two Islamic versions of the above-mentioned biography of Ḥizqīl in which he is associated with Samuel: namely, that after his death the Israelites went astray, and that among other sins they killed many prophets.[19] We may thus assume that while still alive, Ḥizqīl had prevented them from killing these prophets, just as D̲h̲ū 'l-Kifl had saved the prophets. D̲h̲ū 'l-Kifl's personal responsibility, however, can be interpreted differently, namely, in connection with the biblical Ezekiel, whose mission was, among other things, to take responsibility for his people's destiny by warning them about the imminent destruction of Jerusalem (Ezek 33:1–9).[20] This leads us to conclude that, in order to establish an identification of D̲h̲ū 'l-Kifl with Ḥizqīl, Muslim sources might have borrowed some elements from the stories of either the Muslim Ḥizqīl (or Samuel) or the biblical Ezekiel. But we must bear in mind that the identification of D̲h̲ū 'l-Kifl with Ḥizqīl is rare and late (see n. 16). Its significance is treated in greater detail below.

To conclude our discussion of the historical and biographical aspects of the story of Ḥizqīl, we may say that whether or not the Muslim Ḥizqīl is identical with D̲h̲ū 'l-Kifl, his history and biography in most Islamic sources are different from what is found in the Bible. First, he is situated at the time of the judges, and second, his biography seems to be modeled after that of Samuel.

The Prophetic Aspect of Ḥizqīl

The passage from Thaʿlabī cited above, besides dealing with Ḥizqīl's history and biography, also refers to his prophetic mission, i.e., the resurrection of the dead. This seems to be related to the biblical Ezekiel's vision of the dry bones in chapter 37.

---

18. Ṭabarsī, II, 269; D̲jalālayn, 38:40.
19. Fārisī, 63; Ibn ʿAsākir, III, 95. The accusation of killing prophets is based on a general Qurʾanic concept concerning the sins of the children of Israel (e.g., Qurʾan 2:58; 3:108).
20. See Hartom, *Pentateuch, Prophets, Hagiographa,* "Introduction to the Book of Ezekiel."

The reference to resurrection is one of the few traces of Ezekiel's biblical prophecies that appear in Islamic sources. But
before discussing it, we should mention another of Ezekiel's biblical prophecies that also figures in Islamic sources: the oracle
against Gog and Magog (Ezek 38–39). This prophecy is referred
to in both the Qur'an (18:91–100; 21:96–97) and later Muslim
sources, under the title *Yādjūdj wa-Mādjūdj* (Gog and Magog).
Muslim references to this prophecy retain its eschatological character as found in the biblical version, but in their details tend to
resemble its later Christian elaborations more than its rabbinic
ones.[21] A detailed discussion of this prophecy lies beyond the
scope of this study, for the simple reason that Islamic sources did
not associate it with Ḥizqīl (or Samuel, or *Dhū* 'l-Kifl).[22] It is important, however, to mention it in order to shed light on another
aspect of Ezekiel's obscurity in Islam, namely that Islamic sources,
although preserving some traces of Ezekiel's biblical prophecies,
were not always aware of their biblical connection to him. This
phenomenon applies also to the vision of the dry bones, but only
partially, as will become evident below.

Islamic traces of Ezekiel's vision of the dry bones appear first
in the Qur'an, in two separate verses. One relates the story of an
anonymous man who, in passing by a fallen city, says:

> "How shall God give life to this now that it is dead?" So God made him
> die for a hundred years, then He raised him up, saying, "How long have
> you tarried?" He said, "I have tarried a day, or part of a day." He said,
> "No; you have tarried a hundred years. Look at your food and drink —
> it has not spoiled; and look at your donkey." "So We would make you a
> sign for the people. And look at the bones, how We shall set them up, and
> then clothe them with flesh." So, when it was made clear to him, he said,
> "I know that God is powerful over everything." (Qur'an 2:261)

Although this verse differs in many of its narrative details from
Ezekiel's biblical vision of the dry bones, two principal similarities, besides the mention of bones and their resurrection, can

---

21. This is especially the case with reference to the walls built by Alexander (= *Dhū* 'l-
Qarnayn, "the one granted with two horns") to protect humankind from the barbarian
tribes. For details, see Urbach, "God and Magog," in Klausner, *Encylopaedia Hebraica,*
10.297–99; Wensinck, "Yādjūdj wa-Mādjūdj," *EI*[1] 8.1142; Sidersky, *Origines,* 132–34.

22. I could trace only a strange allusion to such a connection, in a legend that somehow
relates Ḥizqīl's mediation in the resurrection of the bones to a "horn of iron" and a city
surrounded by a "wall" (Ṭabarī A, II, 538). Could this be Alexander's city? (see above,
n. 21).

be identified: the observer's skeptical attitude toward resurrection, and the emphasis on God's omnipotence (compare Ezek 37:3, 11–14).[23] Indeed, some Islamic commentaries, like the narrative of Ezekiel in the Bible, explained this verse as referring to the resurrection of Jerusalem (or the Holy Land) after the destruction of the Temple. Most of them, however, identified the anonymous person involved not with Ezekiel, but with Jeremiah, Isaiah, or Ezra.[24] This shows the confusion that existed in Islamic sources concerning the biblical prophets of the time around the destruction of the First Temple, including Ezekiel.

As noted above, Islamic sources did associate Ḥizqīl with a story of resurrection, but on the basis of another Qur'anic verse, also in Sura 2:

> Have you not regarded those who went forth from their habitations in their thousands fearful of death? God said to them, 'Die!' Then He gave them life. Truly God is bounteous to the people, but most of the people are not thankful. (Qur'an 2:244)

The only real connection of this verse with Ezekiel's biblical vision of the dry bones is in the underlying idea of the death and resurrection of masses of individuals.[25] The Qur'anic narrative displays no similarities to the biblical scenery of the valley, to dry bones coming to life, or to the mediation of a prophet. Yet most Islamic commentaries explicitly relate this passage to Ḥizqīl, some of them including vivid details of descriptions similar to those in the biblical vision.[26] Thus, considering in this

---

23. See Schwarzbaum, *Biblical and Extra-biblical Legends*, 78, 80.

24. Concerning Jeremiah and Ezra, see the variegated versions in Ṭabarī B, III, 28–47, and Mudjīr, I, 153–54; on Isaiah, see Hamadhānī, 98, 102. However, one version in Ibn Kathīr's commentary (fourteenth century) relates the story to "Ḥizqīl son of Bawwār" (= Buzi?) (Schwarzbaum, *Biblical and Extra-biblical Legends*, 166, n. 203). For this confusion, and especially the connection between Ezra and Jeremiah and its origins in apocalyptic literature, see Heller, "Ezra the Scribe," 216–17; Lazarus-Yafeh, *Intertwined Worlds*, 57, n. 25. I might add that the confusion with Jeremiah is reflected in tomb stories as well; one Islamic version, in discussing tombs of various saints in Iraq, refers to the tomb of "Bārūkh [the son of Neriyah?], Ḥizqīl's [!] instructor and teacher" (Harawī, 76). This confusion may have derived from legends spread among medieval Babylonian Jews that located Baruch's tomb near Ezekiel's (cf. Grintz, "Baruch ben Neriah," in Klausner, *Encyclopaedia Hebraica*, 9.502). On Ezekiel's tomb, see below, "Dhū 'l-Kifl's Tomb."

25. Schwarzbaum considers the emphasis in this verse on the masses of people to be similar to the emphasis in Ezek 37:1–2 on the mass of bones (*Biblical and Extra-biblical Legends*, 79).

26. Ṭabarī A, II, 536–40; Fārisī, 59–63; Masʿūdī, I, 103–4; Ibn Qutayba, 23; Thaʿlabī, 260–61. See also Geiger, *Judaism*, 153 and nn. 3–5.

context the Qur'anic verse examined first (2:261), we are confronted with an apparent anomaly: most of the commentaries on 2:261, which explicitly speaks of setting up bones and clothing them with flesh, relate this activity not to Ezekiel, but to Jeremiah, Isaiah, or Ezra; yet the commentaries on 2:244, which has little apparent similarity to Ezekiel's vision of the dry bones, do connect this passage with Ezekiel. Muslim exegetes must have been aware of this problem, because some of them connect the two Qur'anic verses and try to harmonize them, positing that the city mentioned in 2:261 is the same as that alluded to in 2:244.[27] Does this mean that the prophet involved was also viewed as identical? If so, who was he? Whatever answers might have been given, the exegetical confusion in this case is beyond question.

Another aspect of uncertainty here relates to the circumstances referred to at the beginning of 2:244, namely, the reason for the people's fear of death and flight from their houses. Post-Qur'anic sources suggest two possible alternatives: either a plague broke out in the city, or its king ordered the people to participate in a holy war (*Djihād*) against their enemies.[28]

At first sight, neither of these explanations seems to have biblical or rabbinic precedent. However, some similarities to the stories of both Ezekiel and Samuel in biblical and rabbinic sources can in fact be identified. Regarding the plague, some Islamic sources maintain that it broke out in Dāwardān (near or at the city of Wāsiṭ in Iraq), which reminds us of the Talmudic location of Ezekiel's vision: the valley of Dura (בקעת דורא).[29] The plague may also be reminiscent of the biblical story of God's announcement to Ezekiel concerning his wife's imminent death in a plague

---

27. See the version appearing in Ṭabarī B, III, 30, on behalf of "some other authorities"; see also Schwarzbaum, *Biblical and Extra-biblical Legends,* 79 and n. 201. On the folkloristic nature of the post-Qur'anic legends that developed around these two verses, see Schwarzbaum, *Biblical and Extra-biblical Legends,* 81–116.

28. See Ṭabarī A, II, 537–39; Fārisī, 59–63; Masʿūdī, I, 103–4; Ibn Qutayba, 23; and Djazā'irī, 355–57, all of whom refer to the plague only. On the other hand, Ṭabarī B, II, 586–90; Thaʿlabī, 259–61; and Ṭabarsī, II, 269, relate some narratives including both plague and war. Ṭabarī B, II, 30, and Ṭabarsī, II, 270, combine the two motifs, stating that the war was to take place in a plague-stricken city. For the Islamic significance of both motifs, see below, "Conduct during Plagues" and "Holy War."

29. Compare Ṭabarī A, II, 537; Thaʿlabī, 259; and Ṭabarsī, II, 270, with *b. Sanh.* 92:2.

(Heb. מגפה), as a symbolic precedent to the imminent destruction of Jerusalem (Ezek 24:15–27). Another biblical story, this one connected with Samuel, may be relevant to both plague and war. Samuel is said to have commanded the Israelites to wage a war against the Philistines that ended in a defeat: "Israel has fled before the Philistines, and there has also been a great slaughter [or: plague; Heb. מגפה] among the troops" (1 Sam 4:17). Obviously, in none of the above-mentioned cases does the *narrative setting* resemble that in the Islamic sources; rather, the similarities lie in certain of the motifs involved (location, plague, war, flight, and the involvement of a leader).

To recapitulate, not only in its historical and biographical aspects, but also in its prophetical dimensions, the mission of Ḥizqīl, as portrayed in Islamic sources, reflects a bewildering confusion of narrative elements. In each case, however, certain of these elements could have derived from the stories of Ezekiel and Samuel, as described in biblical or rabbinic sources.

The Islamic Dimensions of the Ḥizqīl Story

"Islamization" of biblical history is a well-known phenomenon in the *Qiṣaṣ* literature. Its origins go back to the Qur'an, where Abraham is explicitly represented as the first monotheist; he was neither a Jew nor a Christian, but a "Muslim" ("submitter"), who established the main Islamic sanctuary, the Ka'ba (Qur'an 2:118–25; 3:60). Qur'anic stories of other biblical personalities are also sporadically embellished with Islamic motifs. In post-Qur'anic sources this Islamization becomes a systematic method, whereby every pre-Muhammadan prophet is described as having practiced and taught Islam.[30] The aims of this method are obvious: to claim the biblical personalities as part of Islamic history, and to present Islam as an integral part of the early history of monotheism.

In the story of Ḥizqīl, four Islamic motifs are noteworthy:

---

30. For details of this method, see Schussman, *Stories*, pt. C.

Resurrection of the Dead

As argued already in rabbinic sources, the resurrection of Israel, deduced from the resurrection of the dry bones in Ezekiel, is only a proof of the resurrection of the dead in general, and an answer to those who doubt it (*b. Sanh.* 92.1–2). Similarly, the two Qur'anic verses discussed above explicitly state that death and resurrection prove God's omnipotence not only in the individual cases described in these verses, but also in a more general sense (see especially the end of each verse). Furthermore, one exegesis of 2:261 holds that the question of whether the prophet involved was Jeremiah or Ezra is insignificant, because the main aim of the verse is to demonstrate to nonbelievers God's power to give life to the dead.[31] It is therefore probable that rabbinic exegesis influenced these Qur'anic verses.

It is noteworthy, however, that the concept of resurrection is extremely important in Islam.[32] It is frequently and variously expressed in the Qur'an, including in the stories of some prophets, even when the biblical and rabbinic parallels of the stories involve no such meaning. The biblical story known as the "covenant between the pieces" (Gen 15:7–21), for example, is interpreted both in the Bible and in rabbinic sources as a promise to Abraham concerning the future of his descendants in the land of Canaan. In the Qur'an (2:262), however, it is interpreted as a proof of God's power to give life to the dead.[33] In the same way, the biblical story of the "red heifer" (Numbers 19) signifies only the purification of unclean individuals, whereas in the Qur'an (2:63–68) it shows how God resurrects the dead.[34]

When the story of Ḥizqīl is interpreted in light of these prin-

---

31. Ṭabarī B, III, 29.

32. See Tritton, "al-Baʿth," *EI*[2] 1.1092–93; Gardet, "al-Kiyāma," *EI*[2] 5.235–38.

33. Compare Gen 15:7–21 and the rabbinic versions in Ginzberg, *Legends,* 1.235–37 and 5.227–30, nn. 107–14, with Qur'an 2:262; see also Geiger, *Judaism,* 100. The only rabbinic version associating the covenant between the pieces with resurrection appears in the late Yemenite midrash *Hagadol,* which could have been influenced by the Qur'an (Schwarzbaum, *Biblical and Extra-biblical Legends,* 163–66, n. 202).

34. Compare Numbers 19 and the rabbinic version in Ginzberg, *Legends,* 3.216 and 6.79, n. 417, with Qur'an 2:63–68. Indeed, the Qur'an partially confused the "red heifer" (פרה אדומה) with the "beheaded heifer" (עגלה ערופה) (Deut 21:1–9), but even the latter, which concerns a settlement for an unknown murderer's crime, has nothing to do with resurrection.

ciples, it clearly represents a case of Islamization. Ḥizqīl is a forerunner of Islam; like Abraham (in the "covenant between the pieces") and Moses (in the "red heifer"), he too (in the "vision of the dry bones") enunciated the Islamic teaching of resurrection, which Muhammad was later to revive.

Conduct during Plagues

The Islamic story of flight from the plague — whether or not it was influenced by biblical motifs from the stories of Ezekiel and Samuel, as suggested above — was "Islamized" by associating it with certain sayings attributed to Muhammad. For example:

> If you hear of a plague in (some) city, do not venture upon [the city]; but if the plague breaks out while you are staying in [the city], do not leave in order to flee from [the plague].[35]

Islam thus prohibits its followers from imitating the conduct of Ḥizqīl's people, who fled from a plague-stricken city.

In the context of Islamic medieval history, this saying reflects the prevailing opinion among Muslims as to the recommended conduct during plagues, which indeed were troublesome in the Middle East in that period.[36] Muslim scholars in general, and Ṣūfī mystics in particular, were interested in the social morality underlying this saying, as represented, for example, in the writings of the most prominent medieval Muslim scholar and Ṣūfī, al-Ghazzālī:

> And if you ask why leaving a plague-stricken city is forbidden, ... it is because if the healthy were permitted to leave, there would have been no one left in the city but the sick, whom the plague crippled; their hearts would have been broken; they would have lost their attendants, and no one would have been left to provide them with water and food. ... The Muslims are like a building, a part of which supports the other, and the believers are like one body, that if one of its organs complains, all the others come together to its rescue.[37]

To return to the association of Ḥizqīl's story (cf. Qur'an 2:244) with the saying attributed to Muhammad, it seems that from an

---

35. Tha'labī, 260; compare this with the versions of Fārisī, 63, and Djazā'irī, 357.
36. See Dols, *Black Death,* 131–45.
37. Ghazzālī, IV, 291.

ethical point of view, Muslim authors used the story to teach believers how to behave in the case of plague. From an Islamic perspective this lesson is intended to show that Muhammad's injunction not to desert a plague-stricken city is really an early monotheistic one, or, to put it in other words, that Ḥizqīl had actually preached Islam.

Holy War (Djihād)

As noted above, the Qur'anic verse regarding flight from a city (2:244) was explained by some commentators as flight from participation in a holy war. This interpretation may derive from the fact that the subsequent verse states:

> So fight in God's way, and know that God is All-hearing, All-knowing.
> (Qur'an 2:245)

This is one of the many Qur'anic verses, appearing in various contexts, that enjoin Muslims to wage holy war (*Djihād*) against nonbelievers. Indeed the holy war, undertaken for the sake of spreading God's word (i.e., Islam) throughout the world, became an extremely important commandment, promising a high reward to participants in general, and eternal life in heaven to those who were killed in the fighting (Qur'an 2:149). Furthermore, its contribution to the political expansion of Islam is beyond doubt.[38]

Regarding the verse mentioned above (2:245), there is a difference of opinion among commentators as to whether it stands by itself as a general appeal to believers, or whether it should be associated with the previous verse of flight from a city. Those choosing the latter option explain that God hated Ḥizqīl's people because they had refused to participate in a holy war due to fear of death, and so punished them by death itself. Later, however, He resurrected them for the rest of their predetermined lives, and issued to them the commandment of *Djihād*.[39] The point here is to show that this Islamic commandment has ancient roots in the

---

38. For details, see Tyan, "Djihād," *EI*² 2:538–40; Khadduri, *War and Peace, passim,* esp. bk. 2, chaps. 4–6.

39. Ṭabarī B, II, 591–92; Thaʿlabī, 261; Ṭabarsī, II, 271.

history of monotheism, and that those who try to evade it will be punished, as were the people of Ḥizqīl's time.

Dhū 'l-Kifl's [= Ḥizqīl's] Tomb

It is well-known that since the tenth century, Babylonian Jews have been accustomed to visit a tomb, located in the village al-Kifl near the city al-Ḥilla in Iraq, which is thought to be that of the prophet Ezekiel.[40] This same tomb is also sacred to Muslims, who hold it to be that of the mysterious Dhū 'l-Kifl, identified in turn with Ḥizqīl. As noted above, however, the identification of these two figures is rare and found only in late Islamic sources. Most of the Qiṣaṣ versions identify Dhū 'l-Kifl not with Ḥizqīl, but with other ancient personalities, especially Bishr (or Bashīr), the son of Job. These sources, if they refer to Dhū 'l-Kifl's tomb at all, locate it not in Babylonia but in other places, such as at a site in Palestine near Nablus.[41] The few sources that identify Dhū 'l-Kifl with Ḥizqīl are, to my knowledge, later than the twelfth century.[42]

We may, therefore, assume that originally Ḥizqīl and Dhū 'l-Kifl were considered in Islam as two different prophets. Only later, probably in the twelfth century, after the sanctification of Ezekiel's tomb by the Jews (which occurred not later than the tenth century),[43] did Muslims seek a connection of this tomb with a Qur'anic prophet whom they could identify with Ezekiel. Dhū 'l-Kifl's obscure personality fit this purpose, and consequently the site was called al-Kifl.[44]

---

40. See Abramsky and Ta-Shema', "Ezekiel," in Klausner, *Encyclopaedia Hebraica*, 19.748; Ben Yaacob, "Ezekiel," *EncJud* 6.1096–97. For some details of the visitation (prayers, songs, etc.), see Avishur, "Judeo-Arabic Folksongs," 2.151–92; Goitein, "Ezekiel's Tomb," 1.13–18; Shiloah, "Musical Tradition," 3.122–29. See also the bibliography in Schwarzbaum, *Biblical and Extra-biblical Legends*, 163, n. 199.

41. For a general description see Goldziher, "Dhū 'l-Kifl," *EI*[1] 2.962–63; and Vajda, "Dhū 'l-Kifl," *EI*[2] 2.242. More specifically, see, e.g., Kisā'ī, 190; Thaʿlabī, 170–71; and Mudjīr, I, 73.

42. See above, n. 16. This applies to some additional Islamic sources as well, referred to by Ben-Yaʿakov, *Holy Tombs*, 45–47.

43. The tomb is first mentioned by R. Sherira Gaon (d. 986) (see *Encyclopaedia Hebraica* and *EncJud*, above, n. 40), but the notion that Ezekiel was buried in Babylonia is even earlier, appearing in *Pirqe de Rabbi Eliezer* (eighth century) (see Schwarzbaum, *Biblical and Extra-biblical Legends*, 79).

44. Goldziher ("Dhū 'l-Kifl," *EI*[1] 2.962–63) regarded this phenomenon as reflecting Muslims' general readiness to adopt holy tombs of other religions.

Thus, the sanctity of Ezekiel's (=Dhū 'l-Kifl's) tomb in Islam seems to be the result of an Islamization of a Jewish motif, the aim of which is to prove that the Muslims have their own share in the holy sites of early monotheistic tradition. In this context it is worth noting that since the twelfth century, although Muslims have sometimes tried to prevent Jews from visiting the tomb,[45] Muslim literary sources have acknowledged the tomb's Jewish sanctity, and even the precedence of the Jews in establishing this holy site; likewise, Jewish sources have acknowledged its Islamic sanctity.[46]

Conclusion

In conclusion, let us consider two main issues: first, the reason for the confused character of Ḥizqīl's story; and second, the overall characteristics of its "Islamization."

First, it is a general phenomenon in the Qiṣaṣ literature that preference is given, from a narrative point of view, to the earlier biblical personalities. Indeed, even in the Qur'an, the earlier biblical prophets — those from Adam to Moses — are treated more frequently and in greater detail than the later ones. This phenomenon is probably due to the more legendary and folkloristic character of the stories concerning earlier figures (Adam's sin, Noah's ark, etc.), which must have appealed strongly to both Muhammad and his audience, from the point of view of both the general intèrest of the stories and the lessons they teach.[47] As biblical chronology proceeds, and the narratives become gradu-

45. Goldziher, "Dhū 'l-Kifl," *EI*[1] 2.962–63; Ben-Ya'akov, *Holy Tombs*, 46; Lazarus-Yafeh, *Intertwined Worlds*, 157 and n. 48.

46. For Islamic sources, see Ben-Ya'akov, *Holy Tombs*, 45–47, and Goldziher, "Dhū 'l-Kifl," *EI*[1] 2.962–63, both of whom refer to Yaqut (d. 1229) and other Muslim authors of the fourteenth and sixteenth centuries. For Jewish sources, see Ben-Ya'akov, *Holy Tombs*, 41, and Ben Yaacob, "Ezekiel," *EncJud* 6.1096–97, which refer to travelers from the end of the twelfth century onward. Most interesting is the description of a remark in Hebrew (appearing in the margin of a fifteenth-century Jewish transcription of the Qur'an [!]) in which the copyist testifies to having seen one of the Qur'anic verses related to Dhū 'l-Kifl written on the entrance to Ezekiel's tomb (Lazarus-Yafeh, *Intertwined Worlds*, 157).

47. See, for example, the emphasis laid on these aspects at the beginning and end of the story of Joseph in the Qur'an 12:3: "We will relate to thee the fairest of stories...";
12:103–11 in general, and v. 111 in particular: "In their [the messengers'] stories is surely a lesson to men possessed of minds; it is not a tale forged, but...a guidance...").

ally more "historical" and less "legendary," the Qur'an becomes
increasingly less interested in these narratives. Indeed, the relatively few stories of later biblical personalities that do appear in
the Qur'an tend to focus mainly on legendary motifs (Solomon's
wisdom, Jonah and the whale, etc.). It is presumably for this
reason that the Qur'an almost completely ignores the later biblical prophets such as Ezekiel, adopting from his narrative only
legendary traces of the vision of the dry bones.

This situation obtains also in the post-Qur'anic *Qiṣaṣ*, but with
a slight adaptation that stems from Muslims' growing familiarity
with Jewish (and Christian) sources. The extent of this familiarity
cannot be established for certain. It is clear, however, that later
Muslim adaptations of Qur'anic stories of the earlier prophets
bear a much stronger resemblance to the relevant Jewish parallels
than do the stories of the later prophets. Apparently this reflects
the Muslims' preference for precedents already set in the Qur'an,
as mentioned above. Is this, however, the only reason for this approach? Does it in turn imply that Muslims' familiarity with the
later biblical prophets was less profound?

I would suggest the possibility that at least some Muslim authors were, in fact, familiar with the later biblical prophets, and
that their approach discussed above may actually reflect such a
familiarity. That is, these authors may have deliberately ignored
or altered certain biblical motifs of these later prophets' stories because they tended not to accord well with certain Islamic
principles or interests.

We must bear in mind that the prophecies of Isaiah, Jeremiah,
and Ezekiel reflect the most crucial event in the history of their
time, i.e., the destruction of the Jerusalem Temple. Ezekiel was
perhaps the most "nationalistic" of the three, in the sense that
his prophecies focus on this event, and culminate in the eventual
restoration of Israel. These prophecies include warning and chas-
tisement of Israel before the destruction (chaps. 1–24); oracles
against other nations that seem almost a precondition of Israel's
redemption (chaps. 25–32); consolation of Israel and prediction
of the restoration of Israel (chaps. 33–39); and finally a detailed
and picturesque description of the future Temple, its holy services,
the duties of the priests and princes, the division of the country

among the tribes of Israel, and a vision of the future Jerusalem (chaps. 40–48).

There is evidence to indicate that some Muslims were at least partially acquainted with these prophecies. We have already seen that among the various Islamic versions of Ḥizqīl's story, some evidence suggests familiarity with accounts of Ezekiel in biblical or rabbinic sources: the reference to the Temple destruction, the (admittedly confused) association with Isaiah and Jeremiah, and the location of the vision of the dry bones.[48] More significant, however, is the existence of clear evidence that some Muslims knew the biblical Book of Ezekiel directly. Part of the medieval Islamic polemic against Judaism took the form of Islamic biblical exegesis, intended to prove that the Bible had predicted the appearance of Muhammad and Islam. Such exegesis is not a systematic literary genre in itself; it appears, fragmentarily and sporadically, in the context of different genres, from the ninth century on.[49] Commentaries on two passages of the biblical Book of Ezekiel appear in an Islamic source of the ninth century, the *Kitāb al-Dīn wa-l-Dawla* (Book of religion and empire) by ʿAlī b. Rabbān. One passage treated is the parable of the vineyard (Ezek 19:10–14, a lamentation on the destruction of Israel); the other is the prophecy of the future of the Jerusalem Temple (Ezek 40–48). The *Kitāb al-Dīn wa-l-Dawla* interprets the former passage as referring to Mecca, and the latter as concerning the Meccan sanctuary.[50] This proves that Muslims were acquainted with at least these two prophecies; yet, to my knowledge, neither influenced the presentation of Ḥizqīl's story in the *Qiṣaṣ* literature.

It is possible that the authors of the *Qiṣaṣ* — despite (or perhaps because of) some knowledge of Ezekiel's actual time and

---

48. See above, n. 7 (Ibn Qutayba and Mudjīr); n. 24 (Ibn Kathīr, according to Schwarzbaum, *Biblical and Extra-biblical Legends*); and n. 29 (all the sources listed). Ibn Qutayba in fact had some knowledge of the Bible (Lazarus-Yafeh, *Intertwined Worlds*, 80 and n. 13).

49. Lazarus-Yafeh, *Intertwined Worlds*, chap. 4.

50. Lazarus-Yafeh, *Intertwined Worlds*, 87–88 and nn. 35–36. Indeed the author of these interpretations, ʿAlī b. Rabbān, was a Christian convert to Islam, which may explain his familiarity with the Bible. However, once his book had been written, other Muslims could have become familiar with it and with the biblical material it dealt with. On this author and the problem of converts in this context, see Lazarus-Yafeh, *Intertwined Worlds*, 79–83.

prophecies — preferred to picture him as prophesying in an earlier period (the time of the judges); this may have helped them
to circumvent the fervent nationalistic message of his prophecy,
and to adapt it more easily to an Islamic context. Thus, they
applied to Ḥizqīl the biography of Samuel, which is folkloristic
in nature and suits the general Qur'anic approach to the stories
of the prophets. Similarly, they ignored the original nationalistic
message of the vision of the dry bones, emphasizing only the theological notion of resurrection of the dead in this passage — again
in accordance with Qur'anic teaching.

This leads us to the second issue in our conclusion: Islamization. The Islamic motifs applied to Ḥizqīl (see above, "The
Islamic Dimensions of the Ḥizqīl Story") are in certain ways
different from those attributed to many other biblical prophets.
Muslims tended to portray the Islamic nature, especially of the
earlier prophets, through a wide range of motifs related to their
everyday lives, worship, and teaching. These prophets are described as almost exact antecedents to Muhammad: their birth,
childhood, marital life, etc., resemble Muhammad's; they are endowed with Muhammad's "light"; they practice and preach the
five "pillars" of Islam as well as other Islamic commandments;
and so on.[51] Ḥizqīl, because his history and biography were vague
and confused, apparently was presented as a Muslim not through
his everyday life and worship,[52] but through the application to
him of certain general themes in Islamic religion and civilization:
theology (the idea of resurrection), social conduct (proper activity during plagues), religio-political obedience (pursuance of holy
war), and the development of popular religion (worship of the
tombs of the saints).

In this context it is noteworthy that the Islamic biblical interpretations mentioned above, besides representing Muslim polemic
against Judaism, reflect at the same time a type of Islamization.
This type is different from that noted above in two respects. First,
the Islamization discussed above applies only to those biblical stories included in the Qur'an and the *Qiṣaṣ* literature, whereas this

---

51. See Schussman, *Stories*, 117–52.
52. This is true except for a few short references to his and his mother's religious
devotion (Islamic prayer, etc.) in one source only (Fārisī, 61, 62).

new type applies to the biblical material itself. Second, the former type looks backward, transferring the beginnings of Islamic history from Muhammad's time to that of the early history of monotheism, whereas this new type moves forward, ascribing to early biblical history predictions of future tenets of Islam. Both clearly reflect a strong sense of conviction in Muslims as to the primacy, originality, and continuity of their religion. Ezekiel, then, was an accomplished Muslim who not only preached Islam in his time, but also foresaw its future manifestation in Mecca.

Bibliography

Primary Islamic Sources

Djalālayn:
> Djalāl al-Dīn al-Maḥallī and Djalāl al-Dīn al-Suyūṭī, *Tafsīr al-Djalālayn* (Beirut: Dār al-Maʿrifa, 1969). A relatively brief Qurʾan exegesis summarizing previous exegetes (fifteenth century).

Djazāʾirī:
> Niʿmat Allāh al-Djazāʾirī, *Al-nūr al-Mubīn fī Qiṣaṣ al-Anbiyā wal-Mursalīn* (al-Nadjaf: al-Maṭbaʿa al-Ḥaydariyya, 1964). Tales of the prophets, of a sectarian (Shīʿite) nature (seventeenth century).

Fārisī:
> Abū Rifāʿa ʿUmāra b. Wathīma al-Fārisī, *Badʾ al-Khalq wa-Qiṣaṣ al-Anbiyā* (ed. R. G. Khūry; Wiesbaden: O. Harrassowitz, 1978). Tales of the prophets, of a folkloristic nature; incomplete (ninth century)

Ghazzālī:
> Abu Ḥāmid al-Ghazzālī, *Iḥyā ʿUlūm al-Dīn* (Beirut: Dār al-Maʿrifa, no date). A comprehensive religious compendium of a traditional, legal, theological, and, above all, Ṣūfī (mystical) nature (eleventh century).

Hamadhānī:
> Abu Bakr Aḥmad b. Muḥammad al-Hamadhānī, *Mukhtaṣar Kitāb al-Buldān* (ed. M. J. de Goeje; Leiden: Brill, 1885). Geography, general (ninth century).

Harawī:
> ʿAlī b. Abī Bakr al-Harawī, *Kitāb al-ʾIshārāt ila Maʿrifat al-Ziyārāt* (ed. J. Sourdel-Thomine; Damas: Institut Français, 1953). Geography, holy sites (twelfth century).

Ibn ʿAsākir:
> ʿAlī b. al-Ḥasan Ibn ʿAsākir, *Tahdhīb Taʾrīkh Dimashq al-Kabīr* (ed. ʿAbd al-Qādir Badrān; Beirut: Dār al-Maʿrifa, 1979). History of Damascus (twelfth century).

Ibn Qutayba:
'Abd Allāh b. Muslim Ibn Qutayba, *Kitāb al-Ma'ārif* (Miṣr: al-Azhar, al-Maktaba al-Ḥusayniyya al-Miṣriyya, 1934). General literary compendium, including historical remarks (ninth century).

Kisā'ī:
Muḥammad b. 'Abd Allāh al-Kisā'ī, *Qiṣaṣ al-Anbiyā* (ed. I. Eisenberg; Leiden: Brill, 1922–23). Tales of the prophets, of a folkloristic nature (ninth to eleventh centuries?).

Mas'ūdī:
'Alī b. al-Ḥusayn al-Mas'ūdī, *Kitāb Murūdj al-Dhahab wa-Ma'ādin al-Djawāhir* (ed. P. de Couteille and B. de Maynard; Paris: Société Asiatique, 1861–77). Comprehensive general and Islamic history, arranged thematically (tenth century).

Mudjīr:
'Abd al-Raḥmān Mudjīr al-Dīn al-'Ulaymī, *Al-Uns al-Djalīl bi-Ta'rīkh al-Quds wal-Khalīl* (al-Nadjaf: al-Maṭba'a al-Ḥaydariyya, 1968). History of Jerusalem and Hebron, beginning with early monotheism (sixteenth century).

Qur'an:
A. J. Arberry, *The Koran Interpreted* (London: Allen and Unwin; New York: Macmillan, 1955). English translation of the Qur'an.

Rāzī:
Fakhr al-Dīn b. 'Umar al-Rāzī, *Mafātīḥ al-Ghayb* (Beirut: Dar al-Kutub al-'Ilmiyya, 1909). Comprehensive Qur'an exegesis, of a theological nature (twelfth century).

Ṭabarī A:
Muḥammad b. Djarīr al-Ṭabarī, *Ta'rīkh al-Rusul wal-Mulūk* (ed. M. J. de Goeje; Leiden: Brill, 1879–1901). The most comprehensive general and Islamic history, arranged chronologically (ninth to tenth centuries).

Ṭabarī B:
Muḥammad b. Djarīr al-Ṭabarī, *Djāmi' al-Bayān 'an Ta'wīl al-Qur'ān* (Miṣr: Muṣṭafā al-Bābī al-Ḥalabī, 1954). The most comprehensive Qur'an exegesis in Islamic literature (ninth to tenth centuries).

Ṭabarsī:
Al-Faḍl b. al-Ḥasan al-Ṭabarsī, *Madjma' al-Bayān fī Tafsīr al-Qur'ān* (Beirut: Dār al-Fikr wa-Dār al-Kitāb al-Lubnānī, 1954–57). Qur'an exegesis, of a sectarian (Shī'ite) nature (twelfth century).

Tha'labī:
Ibn Isḥāq Aḥmad al-Tha'labī, *Kitāb Qiṣaṣ al-Anbiyā* (Miṣr: al-Maktaba al-Sa'īdiyya, no date). Tales of the prophets, of an exegetical nature (eleventh century).

Ya'qūbī:
Aḥmad b. Abī Ya'qūb al-Ya'qūbī, *Ta'rīkh al-Ya'qūbī* (ed. M. T. Houtsma; Leiden: Brill, 1883). General and Islamic history, with sectarian (Shī'ite) tendencies (ninth century).

Secondary Studies

Avishur, Y. "Judeo-Arabic Folksongs Sung by Iraqi Jewry on Pilgrimages to Saints' Graves (Ziyyara)." In *Studies on the History and Culture of Iraqi Jewry*. Ed. Y. Avishur. Vol. 2. Or-Yehuda: Institute for Research on Iraqi Jewry, 1982. Pp. 151–92. In Hebrew. Quotations, translations into Hebrew, and analysis of various pilgrimage songs, some related to Ezekiel's tomb.

Ben-Ya'akov, A. *Holy Tombs in Babylonia*. Jerusalem: Mossad Harav Kook, 1973. In Hebrew. Historical study of the emergence and development of Jewish cult around holy tombs in Babylonia (tombs of personalities from biblical, Talmudic, and Geonic times), based mainly on travelers' descriptions (Jewish, Muslim, and Christian) from the tenth century onward; with a scholarly introduction and a chapter dedicated to Ezekiel.

Crone, P., and M. Cook. *Hagarism: The Making of the Islamic World*. Cambridge: Cambridge University Press, 1977. An outstanding historical study questioning the reliability of early Islamic sources as to the emergence and development of the Islamic world and suggesting a new approach to this issue.

Dols, M. W. "The Black Death in the Middle East." Ph.D. diss., Princeton University, 1971. A sociohistorical study of this plague in the late Middle Ages.

Firestone, R. *Journeys in Holy Lands: The Evolution of the Abraham-Ishmael Legends in Islamic Exegesis*. Albany: State University of New York Press, 1990. A comprehensive study of the Abraham-Ishmael legends, stressing Islamic creativity.

Geiger, A. *Judaism and Islam*. Tel Aviv: Zohar, 1969. A prize essay, written originally in German and published in Wiesbaden in 1833, translated into English in 1898. The first profound modern scholarly study of the question, What did Muhammad borrow from Judaism?

Gibb, H. A. R., et al., eds. *The Encyclopaedia of Islam*. New ed. Leiden: Brill; London: Luzac, 1960–. The new standard compendium of Islam.

Ginzberg, L. *The Legends of the Jews*. 7 vols. Philadelphia: Jewish Publication Society of America, 1909–38. A comprehensive scholarly compendium of Jewish midrashic and other types of literature, arranged according to biblical history.

Goitein, S. D. "On the Way to Visit Ezekiel's Tomb." In *Studies on the History of Iraqi Jewry and Their Culture*. Ed. S. Moreh. Vol. 1. Or-Yehuda: Institute for Research on Iraqi Jewry, 1981. Pp. 13–18. In Hebrew. Linguistic and historical analysis of a Geniza letter in Judeo-Arabic dating from the beginning of the eleventh century. The letter describes the experiences of an Iraqi Jew on his way to visit Ezekiel's tomb.

Hartom, A. S. *Pentateuch, Prophets, Hagiographa: Bible Exegesis according to M. D. Kasuto's Method*. Tel Aviv: Yavneh, 1972. In Hebrew. A modern scholarly exegesis of the Bible, based on traditional as well as on recent historical and archaeological research. It includes introductions to each book and each weekly section.

Hayek, M. *Le Mystère d'Ismaël*. Paris: Maison Mame, 1964. Analysis of the Islamic legends dealing with Abraham and Ishmael; stresses Ishmael's personality.

Heller, D. "Ezra the Scribe in Islamic Legend." In *Zion*. Jerusalem: The Society of History and Ethnography in Eretz-Israel & Darom Publishers, 1933. Pp. 214–17. In Hebrew. Study of the character of Ezra's personality in the Qur'an and in later Islamic sources.

Houtsma, M. T., et al., eds. *The Encyclopaedia of Islam*. 1st ed. Leiden: Brill; London: Luzac, 1913–31. The classic compendium of Islam.

Khadduri, M. *War and Peace in the Law of Islam*. Baltimore: Johns Hopkins University Press, 1955. Study of the development of the Holy War notion in Islamic legal sources.

Klausner Y., et al., eds. *The Encyclopaedia Hebraica*. Jerusalem and Tel Aviv: HE — The Society of Encyclopaedias Publishing, 1949–81. In Hebrew. An encyclopedia of Jewish and Eretz Israeli history and culture.

Lazarus-Yafeh, H. *Intertwined Worlds: Medieval Islam and Bible Criticism*. Princeton, N.J.: Princeton University Press, 1992. Study of Jewish, Christian, and Hellenistic ideas reflected in medieval Muslim writings on the Bible. Considers the possibility of the influence of these writings on early Western critical studies of the Bible.

Masson, D. *Le Coran et la révélation Judéo-Chrétienne*. Paris: Adrien-Maisonneuve, 1958. A study tracing parallels between the Bible and the Qur'an.

Moubarac, Y. *Abraham dans le Coran*. Paris: J. Vrin, 1958. Analysis of the Abraham stories in the Qur'an.

Nagel, T. "Die Qiṣaṣ al-Anbiyāʾ: Ein Beitrag zur arabischen Literaturgeschichte." Thesis, Bonn, 1967. A literary analysis of the "Tales of the Prophets" genre.

Obermann, J. "Islamic Origins: A Study in Background and Foundation." In *The Arab Heritage*. Ed. N. A. Faris. Princeton, N.J.: Princeton University Press, 1944. Pp. 58–119. A study of the influence of Judaism on early Islam.

Roth, C., et al., eds. *Encyclopaedia Judaica*. Jerusalem: Keter, 1971–72. The standard modern compendium of Judaism.

Schussman, A. *Stories of the Prophets in Muslim Tradition, Mainly on the Basis of "Kiṣaṣ al-Anbiyāʾ" by Muhammad b. 'Abd Allāh al-Kisāʾī*. Jerusalem: The School for Advanced Studies Press at the Hebrew University, 1981. In Hebrew. A study of the "Tales of the Prophets" genre, focusing on al-Kisāʾī's book.

Schwarzbaum, H. *Biblical and Extra-biblical Legends in Islamic Folk-Literature*. Beiträge zur Sprach- und Kulturgeschichte des Orients 30. Waldorf-Hessen: Orientalkunde Dr. H. Vorndran, 1982. A folkloristic analysis of the legends originating in the Bible that appear in Islamic sources.

Shiloah, A. "The Musical Tradition of Iraqi Jewry." In *Studies on the History and Culture of Iraqi Jewry*. Vol. 3. Or-Yehuda: Institute for Research on Iraqi Jewry, 1983. Pp. 122–29. In Hebrew. A selection of *piyyutim* and songs in Hebrew, with musical notes, sung by Iraqi Jews on various occasions, including pilgrimages; with a scholarly introduction translated into English.

Sidersky, D. *Les origines des légendes musulmanes dans le Coran et dans les vies des Prophétes.* Paris: P. Geuthner, 1933. A study of the Jewish and Christian origins of legends appearing in the Qur'an and in the "Tales of the Prophets" genre.

Torrey, C. C. *The Jewish Foundation of Islam.* New York: Ktav, 1967. A study of the Jewish origins of biblical stories appearing in the Qur'an.

EZRA AND NEHEMIAH
SQUARE OFF IN THE APOCRYPHA
AND PSEUDEPIGRAPHA

Theodore A. Bergren

Ezra and Nehemiah, two of the most important figures in the Jewish history of the Persian period (ca. 539–330 B.C.E.), are also two of the most enigmatic.[1] This situation stems in part from the convoluted historical and textual problems concerning the biblical books associated with them, and in part from the nature of their representation in early, extrabiblical Jewish and Christian documents. The present chapter, in keeping with the character of this volume, focuses on the presentation of Ezra and Nehemiah in extrabiblical sources (especially the apocrypha and pseudepigrapha). We recognize, however, that the "canonical" and "noncanonical" groups of sources cannot be entirely dissociated, since in the case of both figures the apocryphal and pseudepigraphical documents have close ties with their canonical counterparts.

---

1. I should note that the two figures featured in this essay have already been treated in ways that go beyond the scope of a study such as this. I refer particularly to Kraft, " 'Ezra' Materials"; Stone, "Metamorphosis of Ezra"; In der Smitten, *Esra;* Schaeder, *Esra;* and Kellermann, *Nehemia.*

The observation in the text to which this note refers is based, of course, on the portrayal of Ezra and Nehemiah in the biblical documents associated with them. Some scholars, however, feel that the portrait of Ezra there is so highly idealized as to be almost incredible. In fact, Ezra's existence has even been questioned! (see Garbini, *Storia e ideologia,* and the literature cited there).

Summary Review of the Evidence
for Ezra and Nehemiah

The dates of composition of the canonical Books of Ezra and Nehemiah have not been established precisely; estimates usually range between 400 and 200 B.C.E.[2] Another controverted question is the background and origin of the apocryphal book 1 Esdras, and its relationship to the canonical materials (including 2 Chronicles). Although it is not an aim of this paper to solve this problem, some observations on it are made below. 1 Esdras is normally dated between 300 and 100 B.C.E. The book is of particular relevance for this chapter because it differs significantly from its canonical counterparts (see below).

Both the Books of Ezra and Nehemiah, which were probably written or at least finalized long after the time of Ezra himself, evince a strong tendency to idealize that figure, portraying him not only as an ideal priest and scribe, but also as a highly glorified religious leader, reformer, and hero. The Book of Nehemiah, usually assumed to contain authentic memoirs of Nehemiah (chaps. 1–7; 12:31–43; 13:4–31), also depicts Nehemiah in glowing terms, but not with the same degree of idealization that Ezra receives in the two books.

Neither Ezra nor Nehemiah is mentioned in any other canonical biblical documents.

The social and literary history of Judaism in the period between 400 and 180 B.C.E. is highly speculative. One of the chief ideological trends that seems to have characterized this age is the development of apocalyptic ideology and literature. Although Ezra does emerge as an apocalyptic hero later in time (in 4 Ezra, at the end of the first century C.E.), there is no evidence that he

---

2. On the question of dating, see esp. H. G. M. Williamson, *Ezra, Nehemiah*, xxxv–xxxvi; Myers, *Ezra, Nehemiah*, lxviii–lxx; R. W. Klein, "Ezra," "Nehemiah," 372–78, 379–86; idem, "Ezra and Nehemiah," 361–76; and Talmon, "Ezra and Nehemiah," 317–28.

Although the Books of Ezra and Nehemiah clearly contain separate and discrete source materials (esp. the "Ezra" and "Nehemiah memoirs"), they are often thought to have been compiled and redacted by the same groups of editors (see the commentaries listed above). In Jewish tradition, they are commonly linked together as one book (e.g., *b. B. Bat.* 15a; *b. Sanh.* 93b; cf. the major LXX uncials). It is possible, however, that originally they were considered separate (cf. Talmon, "Ezra and Nehemiah," 318).

was so regarded at this early stage. Other main cultural trends of this period are the beginnings of the perception of certain Jewish literature as authoritative and normative (i.e., of "canonization"), the beginnings of intensified religious intellectual reflection on this literature (i.e., scriptural exegesis or "Torah study"), and the emergence of the "scribe" as one who specializes in such reflection and teaches others in this field. One can readily see how Ezra would have been idealized during this period, or perhaps even how his very characterization in Ezra-Nehemiah could have been a product of this period. That is, he is depicted in these books as a veritable champion of the Torah, one who both carried the Law from Babylon to Judea and instructed the Judahites in its interpretation, someone associated with the Law's incipient status as authoritative, and a prototype of the ideal scribe.[3] There can be little doubt that the strongly idealized picture of Ezra in Ezra-Nehemiah is connected with these socioreligious trends in Judaism in the Persian and Greek periods.

Chronologically, the next known document in which Ezra or Nehemiah plays a part is Ben Sira, which in its "Praise of the Fathers" section (chaps. 44–50) glorifies Nehemiah (49:13) but fails to mention Ezra. This glaring omission, which has spawned considerable scholarly discussion, is again taken up in greater detail below. Ben Sira is normally dated between 200 and 175 B.C.E., in the period immediately before the Maccabean revolt. Nehemiah's presence there suggests that the Book of Nehemiah was known and considered authoritative in some circles by this time.

Like Ben Sira, many other early Jewish and Christian documents of this and later periods contain "historical reviews" in which Ezra and/or Nehemiah might be expected to play a role. One of the most renowned of these historical reviews is the

---

3. In this connection, an association of Ezra with the Law in Aramaic, or at least in Aramaic script, is often made. In Nehemiah 8, Ezra brings the "book of the law of Moses" to the central square of Jerusalem and reads from it; the Levites "helped the people to understand the law"; "they read from the book, from the law of God, clearly; and they gave the sense, so that the people understood the reading" (8:7–8). In 4 Ezra 14, Ezra, inspired by a magical potion, dictates to five scribes, to whom "the Most High gave understanding...and by turns they wrote what was dictated, in characters which they did not know" (14:42) (this is usually understood to refer to the new Aramaic script). In rabbinic sources, *b. Sanh.* 21b states that Ezra had the Bible newly written in "Assyrian" characters, while the Samaritans retained the old Hebrew script. See also Ginzberg, *Legends,* 6.443–44; Schaeder, *Esra,* 55–57.

so-called Animal Apocalypse in *1 Enoch* 85–90, the second of Enoch's two "dream visions" in this section of the book. The Animal Apocalypse seems to have been written between 165 and 160 B.C.E.[4] According to *1 Enoch* 89:72, after the metaphorical description of the Babylonian exile, "behold, two [or: three] of those sheep returned and came and entered and began building everything that had fallen of that house."[5] Unfortunately, the number of returning sheep is text-critically uncertain; "three" is the majority reading, but Tiller views "two" as preferable. If "two" is correct, these are certainly Joshua and Zerubbabel, as Tiller points out (p. 338); if it is "three," the third would be either Sheshbazzar (based on 1 Esdras 2:12; 6:20) or Nehemiah (following Ezra-Nehemiah, Sir 49:13, and 2 Macc 1:18–36; 2:13).[6] In either case, Ezra falls by the wayside. Tiller remarks significantly, "As the *Animal Apocalypse* ignores the reforms of Josiah, so it ignores the reforms of Ezra" (p. 340). One important dimension of the apparent absence of Ezra in the Animal Apocalypse is the general non-interest of this document in the Torah and matters of the Law.[7] This apparent lack of interest in the Mosaic Torah in an "Enochic" work may be indicative of the type of antithesis between Moses and Enoch posited by P. Alexander in the essay on Enoch in the present volume.

The Maccabean revolt (167–164 B.C.E.) and the subsequent Hasmonean period spawned intense feelings of national pride among the people of Israel. It seems natural that earlier figures from Jewish history, especially biblical ones, who could evoke or be connected with such nationalistic sentiments would be especially lionized during this period. Indeed, such a process seems to have occurred in the next document in which Ezra or Nehemiah figures in Jewish literature: the letter in 2 Macc. 1:10–2:18. This letter is discussed further below; suffice it to say here that it invokes Nehemiah as a model of nationalistic action in his restoration of the city and Temple of Jerusalem, and indeed seems

---

4. See Tiller, *Commentary,* 61–82.
5. Translation and subsequent comments are based on Tiller, *Commentary.*
6. See also Kellermann, *Nehemia,* 133–35.
7. Even in the Animal Apocalypse's account of the exodus, there is no reference to the giving of the Law (see Tiller, *Commentary,* 291).

to portray him in this regard as a forerunner of Judas Maccabaeus. The letter seems to have been written between 125 and 60 B.C.E.[8]

Another "historical review" in which Ezra or Nehemiah may play a role is that which occupies the bulk of the extant portion of the *Assumption of Moses,* an early-first-century C.E. Jewish apocalypse. In 4:1, at the time immediately at the end of the Babylonian exile, it is said, "Then one will enter who is above them [the people], and he will spread his hands and kneel down and pray for them." After the body of the prayer in 4:2–4, which invokes God's mercy on the exiles, the text states that God remembers the people and brings about their return from exile (4:5–6).

The identity of the unnamed intercessor in 4:1 has been a matter of much dispute, with proposed candidates ranging from an angel to Daniel, Ezra, Moses, and Nehemiah. J. Tromp, the most recent commentator on the *Assumption of Moses,* pronounces Ezra the likeliest candidate, given Ezra's chronology, his position as a leader of the people, his status as a priest, and his fame as an intercessor (including 4 Ezra! — see 8:20–36; chap. 14).[9] Although this is not the place to review the scholarly arguments, the point is that Ezra is very likely a key figure in this historical review, as one who is instrumental in instigating the return from the Babylonian exile. Interestingly, the *Assumption of Moses,* which apparently places Ezra's central intercessory role in Babylonia, is roughly contemporary with 4 Ezra, which does the same.

It is noteworthy that neither Ezra nor Nehemiah seems to appear in any other of the main "historical reviews" in early Jewish literature (e.g., *2 Baruch* 53–74) or early Christian literature (e.g., Acts 7; Hebrews 11). This suggests that in neither tradition did Ezra or Nehemiah attain the same status that was held by other, usually earlier figures who appear regularly in the historical reviews (Abraham, Moses, David, etc.). Ezra's and Nehemiah's relatively late dates may be a factor here, as may the fact that the

---

8. See Bergren, "Nehemiah in 2 Maccabees," n. 4, for a summary of opinions on this issue.

9. Tromp, *Assumption of Moses,* 174–78; 230 n. 1. According to Tromp, Reese, "Geschichte Israels," 97, identifies the intercessor as Nehemiah.

Second Temple, with which both were associated, was sometimes denigrated during this period.[10]

Neither Ezra nor Nehemiah appears in any other known Jewish (or Christian) literature of the later Second Temple period (ca. 75 B.C.E.–70 C.E.). We should, however, note three important factors about this period. First, given the extensive idealization of Ezra as a model scribe, and indeed as a second Moses, which is reflected later in 4 Ezra and rabbinic literature, one may speculate that he was looked upon highly in some Pharisaic, protorabbinic, and even apocalyptic circles during the Hasmonean and Herodian periods. Second, the earliest known fragments of a manuscript of the biblical Book of Ezra come from Qumran Cave 4 (4Q117 or 4QEzra);[11] to my knowledge, no fragment of Nehemiah has yet appeared at Qumran.[12] Third, neither Ezra nor Nehemiah is mentioned in the extant writings of Philo.[13]

The careers of Ezra and Nehemiah are, of course, both treated in detail in Josephus's *Jewish Antiquities* (ca. 95 C.E.). Josephus's account of Ezra in *Ant.* 11.120–58 is usually regarded as having utilized 1 Esdras rather than (or in addition to?) the canonical Ezra.[14] His treatment of Nehemiah (*Ant.* 11.159–83), while similar to the biblical narrative, does not adhere to it as closely as does his treatment of Ezra to 1 Esdras, leading some to speculate that Josephus might have had some other, noncanonical source for his account of Nehemiah.[15] Josephus's treatment of Ezra and Nehemiah is a complex issue that has attracted considerable scholarly attention.

The next main event in the literary histories of Ezra and Ne-

---

10. Schneemelcher maintains that Ezra's general absence in these sources, together with his lack in Philo, "could signify a certain rejection of the Ezra tradition in Hellenistic Judaism" ("Esra," 6.606).

11. The three fragments preserve Ezra 4:2–6, 9–11; and 5:17–6:5. See Ulrich, "Ezra and Qoheleth Manuscripts," 139–57.

12. It is, of course, a truism that, of the present Hebrew canon, only Esther is missing at Qumran. This reflects the point of view, mentioned above (n. 2), that Ezra and Nehemiah constitute one book.

13. Schneemelcher, "Esra," 6.606, speculates that Ezra "played no role in Egyptian Judaism." See also Katz, *Philo's Bible*, esp. p. 161.

14. See Schürer, *History*, vol. 3.2, pp. 713–14; Myers, *I and II Esdras*, 8–15; S. J. D. Cohen, *Josephus in Galilee and Rome*, 42–43; and In der Smitten, *Esra*, 77–79.

15. See Grabbe, "Josephus and the Reconstruction," 231–46, esp. pp. 232–35. For a general discussion of Nehemiah in Josephus, see Kellermann, *Nehemia*, 135–45.

hemiah is a rather dramatic one. In about 95 C.E., an unknown author writing in Israel made Ezra the hero of a sophisticated literary apocalypse, known today as 4 Ezra. The implications of the choice of Ezra, and of the fact that this ideal "scribe" and "teacher of the Law" suddenly becomes an apocalyptic seer, are discussed further below.[16] While the subsequent fate of 4 Ezra in Judaism remains obscure, the book became enormously popular in Christian circles, as evidenced by its attestation in no less than seven different language versions, all apparently transmitted mainly in Christian contexts.[17]

The end of the first century C.E. marks the limit of the main considerations of this essay. For the sake of completeness, however, some attention should also be given to the fates of Ezra and Nehemiah in subsequent Jewish and Christian tradition.

Again, proceeding chronologically, Ezra next appears in the writings of the Christian author Justin Martyr (ca. 150 C.E.), who cites in *Dialogue with Trypho* 72:1–5 a passage from "the statements that Ezra made concerning the law of the Passover" that appears in no presently known version of Ezra or any other piece of Ezra literature. Justin claims that the passage was "excised" from the Greek version of the Bible by Jewish interpreters. The validity of his contention has been variously assessed, as have the contents of the "Ezra citation," which in itself contains nothing identifiably "Christian," yet which could be, and apparently was by Justin, interpreted from a christological perspective.[18]

Justin is the first datable Christian author to refer to Ezra or Nehemiah. Ezra is also mentioned by Irenaeus, Hippolytus, Lactantius, Eusebius, Clement of Alexandria, Tertullian, Origen, Ambrose, Priscillian, and Jerome, and in the *Apostolic Constitutions*.[19] Lactantius, *Inst. div.* 4.18.22, cites the same Ezra testimonium as is found in Justin's *Dialogue with Trypho*, with-

---

16. Note that exactly this phenomenon also occurs in the case of the scribe Baruch, in 2 and 3 *Baruch*. See the essay on Baruch by J. E. Wright in this volume.

17. See Stone, *Fourth Ezra*, 1–9.

18. See Resch, *Agrapha*, 304–5; Harris, *Testimonies I*, 80–81; Kraft, "Christian Transmission," 207–26, esp. p. 209 and n. 2; idem, " 'Ezra' Materials," 126–27, 131 and n. 14; and Norelli, "Due 'testimonia,' " 231–82.

19. Many of these references are allusions to the story of Ezra renewing the Law after the Babylonian captivity: cf. Irenaeus, *Haer.* 3.21.2; Tertullian, *De cult. fem.* 1.3; Clement of Alexandria, *Strom.* 1.22.149; and Priscillian, *Tract.* 3.68. All of these authors are dis-

out, however, claiming that it was excised from Jewish scriptures. Especially intriguing is Origen's assertion that Ezra built the Second Temple.[20]

Hippolytus (fl. 200–236 C.E.), in *On the Benedictions of Isaac, Jacob, and Moses* 320, cites another saying of Ezra that is not found in any known form of the canonical Ezra or in other Ezra literature. "And Ezra, in a prophetic voice, said the same thing: 'Blessed is the Lord, who has stretched out his hands and caused Jerusalem to live again.' "[21] This saying, which has in common with Justin's citation the theme of the preservation of Jerusalem, has no apparent Christian connotation.

Perhaps the most important witness to the authority of Ezra in early Christian circles is the pseudonymous 5 Ezra (2 Esdras 1–2), usually dated between 130 and 250 C.E. This treatise invokes Ezra as a biblical-type prophet who condemns the apostasy of Israel and who predicts the advent of a "coming people" that will inherit God's patrimony (1:1–2:41). It also depicts Ezra as an apocalyptic seer (2:42–48).[22] It remains unclear why the author of 5 Ezra, which labels Ezra "the son of Chusi" (1:4), invokes Ezra as a pseudepigraphic hero in Christian guise, and what is the relationship of 5 Ezra to 4 Ezra. Another, related writing, 6 Ezra (2 Esdras 15–16), probably a Christian composition of the third century, is not properly a subject of this essay since, in its extant form, it nowhere mentions Ezra.[23]

Convenient summaries of other early Christian literature in which Ezra is mentioned are found in Robert Kraft's " 'Ezra' Ma-

---

cussed by Schneemelcher in "Esra," 6.608–10; see also the summary in Fabricius, *Codex pseudepigraphicus,* 2.1156–60.

20. *Comm. in Matt.* 16.20; *Comm. in Joh.* 6.1; 10.38 (references from Schneemelcher, "Esra," 6.609).

21. This citation is preceded in Hippolytus's work by the words "the Lord...has stretched out his hands and sanctified all those who run to him, as the hen (has done) to cover her chicks." To this compare 5 Ezra 1:30: "I [God] gathered you as a hen (gathers) her chicks under her wings" (cf. Matt 23:37; Luke 13:34). With alternate punctuation, Hippolytus could be read as attributing the "hen saying" to Ezra!

For a third Ezra agraphon, see Bergren, *Fifth Ezra,* 62–64, 131–33, 358–60; and the *Dialogue of Timothy and Aquila* 10.24, 27.

22. For commentary on 5 Ezra, see Bergren, *Fifth Ezra.*

23. 6 Ezra was given its name because, in all known Latin manuscripts of the book, it is appended to 4 Ezra, and reads as a continuation of that book. Nevertheless, 6 Ezra originated as an independent composition, and there is no way to tell who, if anyone, was originally named as author of the book's prophecies.

terials in Judaism and Christianity" and Michael Stone's "The Metamorphosis of Ezra: Jewish Apocalypse and Medieval Vision."[24] Ezra's popularity in Christian sources after about 180 is apparently due mainly to the influence of 4 Ezra, which, as noted above, was widely known and used in Christian circles. 4 Ezra seems to have inspired a number of early Christian apocalyptic writings, such as the *Greek Apocalypse of Ezra,* the *Vision of Ezra,* the *Questions of Ezra,* the *Revelation of Ezra,* and the *Apocalypse of Sedrach.*[25] As for Nehemiah in early Christian literature, there is no reference to him through the apostolic fathers; he does appear in the *Apostolic Constitutions.*

As mentioned above, Ezra is significant in rabbinic literature as the restorer of the Law after the exile and as one who, "if Moses had not anticipated him, would have received the Torah."[26] Clearly, the high status accorded Ezra in rabbinic sources is due principally to his portrayal in the canonical Book of Ezra and in later Jewish tradition as the prototypical scribe and as the postexilic restorer of the Torah in Judea. An extensive survey of Ezra's role in rabbinic and cognate literature is provided by Louis Ginzberg in *The Legends of the Jews.*[27]

Nehemiah receives rather less attention among the rabbis. Part of what is there is, interestingly, derogatory: the reason why the Books of Ezra-Nehemiah are known jointly under the name of Ezra is that Nehemiah not only was vain (Neh 5:19), but also spoke negatively about his predecessors (Neh 5:15).[28] Again,

---

24. For both articles, see n. 1. See also James, *Lost Apocrypha,* 79–81; Denis, *Introduction,* 91–96.

25. See OTP 1.561–613 (esp. Stone, "Greek Apocalypse of Ezra," 1.563–64); Denis, *Introduction,* 91–96; Himmelfarb, *Tours of Hell,* 24–26, 160–67; James, introduction to *Fourth Book,* lxxxvi–lxxxix; Schürer, *History* (rev. ed.), vol. 3.1, p. 302; Stone, *Fourth Ezra,* 43–47; and Stone, "Metamorphosis of Ezra."

26. *t. Sanh.* 4.7; see also *b. Sanh.* 21b and *y. Meg.* 1.71b; all of these explicitly compare Ezra to Moses. This theme is also found in 4 Ezra 14; Tertullian, *De cult. fem.* 1.3; and Jerome, *Adv. Helv.* 7. For Ezra as restorer of the Law, see *b. Sukk.* 20a; as the prototypical legal authority, see *Gen. Rab.* 36.

The importance of Ezra in rabbinic tradition is underlined by his traditional (but perhaps late) connection with the "men of the Great Synagogue" (cf. *b. B. Qam.* 82a; Ginzberg, *Legends,* 6.447–49). See also *m. 'Abot* 1:1.

27. Ginzberg, *Legends,* 4.353–59; 6.439–51. See also Munk, *Esra der Schriftgelehrte; Jewish Encyclopedia* 5.321–22; *EncJud* 6.1106–7; In der Smitten, *Esra,* 81–85; and Schneemelcher, "Esra," 6.607–08.

28. *b. Sanh.* 93b.

Ginzberg gives an excellent summary of Nehemiah's place in rabbinic and cognate literature.[29]

Four final points concerning the influence of Ezra in later tradition are worth noting. First, the Qur'an (9:30) offers the following provocative notice: "And the Jews say: Ezra ['Uzayr] is the son of Allah.... "[30] Second, it seems that Samaritan tradition is markedly hostile toward Ezra.[31] Third, Edgar Hennecke, in his article "Esra" in the *Reallexicon für Antike und Christentum,* summarizes the place of Ezra in early Jewish and Christian art.[32] Fourth, there is a substantial body of tradition in late antique and medieval Christianity that there were actually two Ezras: one who lived and died in Babylonia during the exile, and the other who led a return from exile about a hundred years later. This tradition is attested by Epiphanius (*Pan.* 8.8.10; *De XII gem.* 4.1.212), the *Inventiones nominum* (G 49; A 45), an Armenian canon list written by Arak'el of Siwnik', three recensions of the Armenian *Menologium,* the preface to 4 Ezra in the idiosyncratic León manuscript, and a marginal gloss in the *Onomastica Vaticana.*[33] The tradition seems to derive from a comparison of 4 Ezra ("Ezra" lives and is "taken up" in Babylonia) with the biblical Books of Ezra, Nehemiah, and 1 Esdras ("Ezra" leads a return from exile). Note, in this connection, that 5 Ezra labels Ezra the "son of Chusi" and places him under Nebuchadnezzar, and that Clement of Alexandria states that Zerubbabel "returned with Ezra to his native land" (*Strom.* 1.21.124).

Ezra and Nehemiah in Four Apocryphal Texts

As has emerged from our discussion thus far, there are four "apocryphal" writings in Jewish, extrabiblical literature of the

---

29. Ginzberg, *Legends,* 4.352; 6.437–40. See also Kellermann, *Nehemia,* 145–47; *EncJud* 12.937.

30. For the role of Ezra in Islam, see Lazarus-Yafeh, *Intertwined Worlds,* esp. chap. 3; Heller, "Ezra the Scribe"; In der Smitten, *Esra,* 85–87; Stone, *Fourth Ezra,* 47; Schaeder, *Esra,* 38 (note); and *EncJud* 6.1106–7 (with bibliography).

31. See North, "Ezra," 2.727; M. Smith, "Ezra," 141–43.

32. *RAC* 6.610–11.

33. See James, "Ego Salathiel," 167–69; idem, "Salathiel qui et Esdras," 347–49; Violet and Gressmann, *Apokalypsen des Esra,* xliv–xlvi; Klijn, ed., *Lateinische Text,* 20–22; and Stone, ed., *Armenian Version,* 35–39.

Greco-Roman period that refer to Ezra or Nehemiah directly: 1 Esdras (300–100 B.C.E.); Ben Sira (200–180 B.C.E.); the second letter affixed to the beginning of 2 Maccabees (1:10–2:18; late second century B.C.E.); and 4 Ezra (90–100 C.E.).

As is well known, in the extant versions of the biblical books that bear their names, Ezra and Nehemiah are closely linked, and the stories about them intertwined.[34] It is therefore noteworthy that in each of the four extrabiblical sources mentioned above, only *one* of our protagonists is present. 1 Esdras and 4 Ezra idealize Ezra while never mentioning Nehemiah, whereas Ben Sira and 2 Maccabees do the opposite. Thus Ezra and Nehemiah really do "square off," in a literal sense, in the extant apocryphal sources.[35]

Recent research on the history of Judaism in the Second Temple period has tended to stress in large measure, and for good reason, the actual or potential incidence of ideological conflict between "rival" Jewish factions: priests and Levites, priests and nonpriests, Zadokite priests and other kinds of priests, pro-Hasmoneans and anti-Hasmoneans, pro-Temple groups and anti- or rival-temple groups, and so on.[36] Given the unusual situation concerning Ezra and Nehemiah in the apocryphal sources, we may be justified in asking whether this also reflects some sort of intra-Jewish conflict: for example, a pro-Ezra faction versus a pro-Nehemiah faction.[37] This section of the paper seeks first to

---

34. See especially Nehemiah 8–12. This intertwining is generally understood as a secondary literary phenomenon.

35. In the period from which these apocrypha come, there is one author, Josephus, who does discuss Ezra and Nehemiah in the same context. Since Josephus is a historian, however, who is drawing upon and summarizing biblical and biblical-type sources, his work does not fall into the same category as these other "apocrypha." Moreover, even Josephus, in contradistinction to the MT, clearly separates his account of Ezra from that of Nehemiah.

36. See, for example, Hanson, *Dawn of Apocalyptic;* Talmon, "Internal Diversification," 16–43; Kampen, *Hasideans;* M. Smith, *Palestinian Parties;* Olyan, "Ben Sira's Relationship," 261–86; Tiller, *Commentary,* 45–51, 101–16; and the literature on the Dead Sea Scrolls community that discusses their relations with other, contemporary Jewish groups.

37. The clearest grounds for potential conflict between the two figures is that Ezra is allegedly a (Zadokite) priest, whereas Nehemiah is a layman. Also, Ezra is a scribe, a professional religious scholar and teacher, with few political concerns, while Nehemiah is a builder, governor, and military leader, with no credentials as a scholar or religious functionary.

On this topic see especially the work of Kellermann, *Nehemia,* who argues that Ne-

address the representations of the figures of Ezra and Nehemiah individually in each of these four writings, and then to discuss the implications of the mutual exclusivity of their treatment. I will discuss the sources in their approximate chronological order.

Each of the four writings presents its own unique problems, and 1 Esdras is no exception.[38] The controversies surrounding the origins of this work are well-known and need not be rehearsed here in detail. The first point is that, although 1 Esdras treats the same period in Jewish history as that covered in 2 Chr 35:1 through the Book of Ezra to Neh 8:13, the person of Nehemiah, who figures so prominently in Neh 1:1–7:72, has disappeared, together with the other contents of these chapters. A second point is that 1 Esdras ends suddenly, in midsentence; something seems to be missing at the end of the work. A third is that there are a number of ways in which to interpret the origin of 1 Esdras. Some argue that it is simply a secondary reworking of material already found in canonical 2 Chronicles-Ezra-Nehemiah, a reworking that begins and ends somewhat arbitrarily.[39] Others maintain that the account in 1 Esdras may be an alternative, and equally early, version of the Ezra-Nehemiah saga.[40] Another viewpoint, which does not necessarily involve an opinion on literary priority, is that 1 Esdras, far from being an arbitrary treatment or rearrangement of historical materials, is a carefully and deliberately constructed piece of historiography. Here I will attempt to defend this latter view, and to connect it with the absence of Nehemiah in the book.

It is necessary first to comment on the book's "lost ending." 1 Esdras concludes in midsentence by saying "And they [the people] came together" (9:55b); one may infer from the parallel

---

hemiah in the literature represents "Zionistic" Israel, a faction which in the postexilic state idealizes the preexilic kings and the Davidic tradition, whereas Ezra is championed by the Chronicler as the representative of "theocratic" Israel, a faction promoting the "new" tradition of government run by scribes and priests and based on the Law of Moses.

38. See especially Myers, *I and II Esdras*; Coggins and Knibb, *First and Second Books*; Pohlmann, *3. Esra-Buch*; Schürer, *History* (rev. ed.), vol. 3.2, pp. 708–18; and In der Smitten, *Esra*, 74–77.

39. For a summary of scholarly positions, see Schürer, *History* (rev. ed), vol. 3.2, p. 710, n. 312.

40. For a summary of scholarly positions, see Schürer, *History* (rev. ed), vol. 3.2, pp. 711–12 and nn. 316–22.

in Neh 8:13–18 that they "came together" to celebrate Sukkoth. Moreover, this is the last time that Ezra plays a significant role in the Masoretic version of the text of Nehemiah. This is, therefore, in the Masoretic version, the end of the Ezra story. Furthermore, Josephus, who knows and uses 1 Esdras's account of the life of Ezra, also ends the career of Ezra precisely at this point (*Ant.* 11.157–58). It seems reasonable to conclude, then, that 1 Esdras originally ended with Ezra's and the people's celebration of Sukkoth (cf. Neh 8:13–18); this is, in fact, the position taken by many commentators.[41]

In reading 1 Esdras on its own, one is immediately struck by several literary and structural features. First, the book begins and ends with celebrations of major feasts: Passover (1:1–22) and Sukkoth (see above). In each case, the feasts are presided over by major figures, one might say "ideal figures," in Jewish tradition: the first by Josiah and the second by Ezra. Furthermore, in both cases, the *uniqueness* of the feast is stressed. In Josiah's case, "no passover like it had been kept in Israel since the times of Samuel the prophet" (1 Esdr 1:20; cf. 2 Chr 35:18; 2 Kings 23:22), whereas for Ezra's Sukkoth, according to Neh 8:17, "from the days of Jeshua the son of Nun to that day the people of Israel had not done so [celebrated Sukkoth]." Josiah is, of course, king of Judah, according to the Deuteronomic history one of its most ideal kings, from the Davidic line, and a figure strongly connected with the (re)discovery of the Mosaic Law (2 Kings 22–23; 2 Chronicles 34–35). His Passover celebration is, according to the text, the greatest in the history of the monarchy. Ezra, who apparently celebrated the Sukkoth at the end of 1 Esdras, is assigned an impeccable high-priestly lineage,[42] is a highly idealized and glorified figure, and again is strongly connected with the (re)discovery of the Law of Moses, this time *after* the exile (cf. Ezra 7:10, 25–

---

41. See, for example, the comments by Myers, *I and II Esdras*, 99–100; Coggins, *First and Second Books*, 74; and Pohlmann, *3. Esra-Buch*, 421–22; see also Schürer, *History* (rev. ed), vol. 3.2, p. 713, n. 325.

42. Ezra 7:1–5; 1 Esdr 8:1–2. There is a question whether this genealogy is "authentic" or simply a fiction invented to augment Ezra's prestige. Note that a similar genealogy, beginning with Levi, is given in 1 Chr 6:1–14; in this, Jehozadak is situated in the place where Ezra stands in the Ezra genealogies. Some have argued that the Ezra genealogy was borrowed from 1 Chronicles, with Ezra's name being substituted for Jehozadak.

26; Neh 8:1–8, 13–18). His Sukkoth is the first since the entry into the land after the exodus.[43] Obviously, these two figures and festivals display pointed parallels in the text of 1 Esdras.

1 Esdras also features, in the course of its text, two additional celebrations of major festivals. Shortly after the return from exile, Jeshua, Zerubbabel, and the returned exiles rebuild the temple altar, offer sacrifices, and celebrate Sukkoth (5:47–52). Then, immediately after the completion and dedication of the temple, these same two "ideal" leaders celebrate Passover (7:10–15). Jeshua is, of course, the ideal high priest of the return from exile (cf. 5:5, 48, 56), while Zerubbabel is its ideal Davidic leader (cf. 5:5–6, 48, 56). The idealization and delineation of the functions of these two leaders are also familiar from the Books of Haggai and Zechariah.

Thus 1 Esdras describes successively, at four crucial points in the book, four major festival celebrations: Passover, Sukkoth, Passover, Sukkoth. These festivals are presided over by four ideal leaders: two ideal Davidides and two ideal priests. Furthermore, the festivals themselves serve to mark off and delineate three highly significant periods in the history of Israel: (1) the destruction of the Temple, exile, return from exile, and rebuilding of the altar; (2) the building of the Second Temple; and (3) the arrival of Ezra, purification of the returned exilic community, and *rediscovery* of the Law of Moses under Ezra.

It has by now become clear, I hope, that 1 Esdras exhibits rather striking structural features, which have both literary and ideological implications. It is for this reason that I would argue that the present form of the book, far from being a random or accidental compilation of data, represents a carefully and deliberately constructed piece of historiography. It is furthermore noteworthy that the highlighting of the ideal figures of Josiah before and Ezra after the exile, and the strong parallels drawn between these figures, apparently serve to make the theological point that the condition of the people of Israel had, after the exile, risen to the same high level as that which obtained before that

---

43. This statement does seem strange, given passages like Ezra 3:4 (cf. 1 Esdr 5:51), but it is the claim of Neh 8:17. Possibly a parallel to Neh 8:13–18 is lacking at the end of 1 Esdras because Neh 8:17 contradicts 1 Esdr 5:51.

event. That is, after a severe crisis of theodicy, the religious situation had returned to a state of normalcy, even an "ideal" state. The structuring of 1 Esdras, with Josiah at its head and Ezra at its conclusion, is again seen to exhibit a deliberate theological crafting, indicating that the latter "ideal leader" had succeeded in restoring the high religious state that had been achieved by the former, as indicated by his landmark celebration of a major feast and by his repetition of Josiah's "rediscovery" of the Mosaic law.

The question arises, then, what implications this situation has for the absence of Nehemiah from the book.[44] The MT of Nehemiah, as mentioned above, links and interweaves the two characters. It is argued by some that 1 Esdras, in separating the two accounts, preserves a more original form of the narrative, as Josephus also does.[45] Others claim that 1 Esdras, by separating Ezra from Nehemiah, is a secondary attempt to make the narrative more straightforward.[46] Whichever view is correct, however, I think that it is possible to discern a clear motive for the absence of Nehemiah from 1 Esdras. First, Nehemiah is neither an ideal Davidic figure nor an ideal priest. In fact, he does not even possess a lineage; in the biblical materials (Neh 1:1), his ancestry is traced back only to his father, Hacaliah, who is mentioned nowhere else in the Bible. Second, Nehemiah is nowhere in preserved materials connected with a feast. Third, Nehemiah is not closely associated with a restoration of the Law or with the revival of an ideal state of worship after the exile.

I would argue, then, that Nehemiah is lacking in 1 Esdras not necessarily for any substantive or polemical reason, but simply because he fails to fit into the historical, theological, and ideological *pattern* that the author of 1 Esdras seeks to promote. The author clearly wishes to construct a historical chain of events which is highly structured and paradigmatic in charac-

---

44. See Kellermann, *Nehemia*, 128–33.

45. See Myers, *I and II Esdras*, 9–10; Coggins, *First and Second Books*, 4–6. This concept would be implied by the idea, advanced by various scholars, that 1 Esdras represents an alternative, earlier, and superior account to that presently found in the MT (see Schürer, *History* [rev. ed.], vol. 3.2, pp. 711–12).

46. See Myers, *I and II Esdras*, 9–10; Coggins, *First and Second Books*, 4–6. This point of view would, of course, imply that 1 Esdras represents a secondary reworking of the material in the MT.

ter, and in which the reader can discern the working of divine order and providence. Nehemiah, as someone with no pedigree, no feast to his credit, and no significant theological accomplishment, falls victim to his confrere Ezra, who possesses all of these qualifications in a dramatic way.

Ben Sira presents a situation that is the opposite of that in 1 Esdras and that is, in some ways, even more perplexing.[47] In the so-called Praise of the Fathers section in chapters 44–50, virtually every major male figure in Jewish biblical history is represented, with a description of major deeds or attributes. Of the two individuals who are conspicuous by their absence, Saul and Ezra, Ezra is by far the more problematic.[48] In the relevant part of the list (49:11–13), Zerubbabel, Jeshua, and Nehemiah are praised in turn, but Ezra, whom one would expect to find as third in this group, is never mentioned. This situation is all the more surprising by virtue of the exalted portrayal of Ezra in the Books of Ezra and Nehemiah, by his status as a priest, scribe, and champion of the Law, and by the fact that Ben Sira is well-known for his idealization of priests, scribes, and the Law of Moses.[49]

Critics have pointed out several possible solutions to this enigma. One is that, in the changed socioeconomic conditions of Ben Sira's time, Ezra's insistence on nonintermarriage was seen as out of date, passé, and even embarrassing, and that Ezra was not mentioned for this reason.[50] Another is that the functions that Ezra exercised as a "scribe" were too narrowly conceived and legalistic for Ben Sira, who preferred a broader definition of the scribe as a sage who delved into wisdom traditions as well as legal ones.[51] Third, Ben Sira might have wanted to set up as a model for the current high priest, Onias III, not a political quietist

---

47. For Ben Sira, see Skehan and DiLella, *Wisdom of Ben Sira;* Smend, *Weisheit;* and Snaith, *Ecclesiasticus.*

48. See especially Lee, *Studies,* 208–10.

49. See, for example, Höffken, "Warum schwieg Jesus Sirach?" 184–201; Lee, *Studies,* 208–10; In der Smitten, *Esra,* 69–74.

50. See Smend, *Weisheit* 2.474; Rudolph, *Chronikbücher,* x; and Galling, *Studien zur Geschichte Israels,* 129, n. 3 (all references drawn from Lee, *Studies,* 209). This argument is called into question, however, by the fact that the biblical Nehemiah exhibits similar concerns.

51. See Herford, *Talmud and Apocrypha,* 201–2; and Box and Oesterley in *APOT* 1.506 (both references from Lee, *Studies,* 209).

like Ezra, but a bolder and more politically active figure, someone like Onias's father Simeon.[52] A fourth explanation is that Ezra exhibited levitical traits that were distasteful to the apparently antilevitical Ben Sira.[53]

While each of these suggestions has some merit, none of them strikes me as especially convincing. Rather than claiming to be able to solve the problem, however, I can only suggest two additional possible explanations for why Ezra is lacking in Ben Sira. The first takes its lead from the fact that, as Thomas Lee and others have pointed out, the "Praise of the Fathers" section is actually an extended introduction to and preparation for the encomium to Simeon ben Onias in chapter 50.[54] One notes that, although many pious men and great religious personalities are included in the list of figures before the exile, the postexilic role includes only three *builders*—the aforementioned Jeshua, Zerubbabel, and Nehemiah. Perhaps Ben Sira wanted to reserve the prime position of extreme piety and *spiritual* glory in the postexilic period for his hero Simeon, and Ezra was viewed as too potent a competitor in this area.

A second possibility centers around the oft-noted fact that the "Praise of the Fathers" section devotes its most extended attention to priestly figures who perform explicitly priestly functions, namely, Aaron (45:6–22) and Simeon ben Onias (50:1–21). One point that is clear from reading Ezra-Nehemiah, however, is that Ezra, while assigned an impeccable high-priestly genealogy in Ezra 7:1–5 (cf. 1 Esdras 8:1–2),[55] does not perform, or even seem vaguely interested in, any traditional priestly activities. It seems possible that Ben Sira omits Ezra from this section because, despite his priestly lineage, Ezra simply does not do the sorts of things that Ben Sira believes priests are supposed to do. In any case, while the situation here could in principle reflect a divergence or polemical stance between two theological positions represented by Ezra and Nehemiah, there is no reason to insist on this.

---

52. See Kellermann, *Nehemia*, 112–15 (reference from Lee, *Studies*, 210).
53. See Höffken, "Warum schwieg Jesus Sirach?"
54. See especially Lee, *Studies*, 81–245.
55. See n. 42.

The situation in 2 Maccabees is also difficult to explain.[56] Here, in the second of the two letters prefixed to the beginning of the book (1:10–2:18), the Jews of Judea, in the wake of the Maccabean revolt, write to the Jews of Egypt to encourage them to share in the forthcoming celebration of the purification of the Jerusalem Temple, and also "the festival of booths and the festival of the fire" (1:18). While the letter is almost universally regarded as a forgery — Goldstein dates it to 103 B.C.E. — the problem that concerns us lies not so much in its authenticity as in certain of its claims. Namely, the letter exhorts the Egyptian Jews to observe the aforementioned "festival of the fire given when Nehemiah, who built the Temple and the altar, offered sacrifices" (1:18), and goes on to identify Nehemiah as the one who dedicated the altar of the Second Temple (1:19–36). This is, of course, in obvious contradiction to other accounts of the origins of the Second Temple, which credit Zerubbabel and Jeshua, or Sheshbazzar, with its building and dedication.[57] Furthermore, the elaborate story of *how* Nehemiah obtained hidden sacred petroleum and initiated the cultus is unparalleled in other early sources. The question is, where did all of this material come from?

Commentators tend to gloss over this problem or simply to remark that the author of 2 Maccabees has erred. Jonathan Goldstein argues that this text is the first attestation of a later-known practice of identifying Nehemiah with Zerubbabel (see *b. Sanh.* 38a), and suggests two ways in which this identification could have taken place. The first is that Jewish exegetes, searching for a Hebrew equivalent to the Babylonian name "Zerubbabel," concluded that Nehemiah and Zerubbabel were actually the same person. The second is that the author of the letter takes a lead from remarks made in 1 Esdras 4:43–63 about Zerubbabel's

---

56. For 2 Maccabees, see Goldstein, *2 Maccabees;* Habicht, *2. Makkabäerbuch;* Doran, *Temple Propaganda;* and Kellermann, *Nehemia,* 115–24.

This section of the essay is based on an article by the present author, "Nehemiah in 2 Maccabees."

57. See Ezra 3:2–11; 5:16; 1 Esdr 5:47–6:2; 6:20–29; Hag 1:1–15; Zech 4:9; 6:12–13; and Sir 49:11–13.

rebuilding Jerusalem *and* the Temple.[58] However, neither of these explanations is, in my opinion, convincing.[59]

I would like to suggest here two possible reasons why Nehemiah is credited in 2 Macc 1:10–2:18 with the building of the Temple and the building and dedication of the altar. A first is that the author of the letter wished to defend the Second Temple against attacks on its validity. Since an account was lacking in the biblical sources of the authentification of the Second Temple by divine fire, an account such as is found for both the First Temple (2 Chr 7:1–3) and the tabernacle (Lev 9:24), this author sought to produce a *literary* account of the Second Temple's validation by divine fire, an account which appears in 2 Macc 1:18–36. It did not seem plausible to attribute such an act to Zerubbabel or Jeshua, the most logical candidates for such activity, since the biblical accounts lack such a story, and since neither of these figures was associated independently with literary records or literary activity. Nehemiah, however, was someone known to have been active in the restoration of the Second Temple state *and* to have produced written records and memoirs of his role.[60] Therefore, he was someone to whose memoirs such a miracle might creditably be attributed; and in fact, this is precisely what 2 Macc 2:13 claims!

A second explanation is that the author of the second letter, or earlier Hasmonean propagandists, deliberately sought to cultivate a connection or comparison between Judas Maccabaeus and Nehemiah. This connection is evident both implicitly in the letter, in the fact that Nehemiah furnishes the most striking *precedent* for Judas's restoration and purification of the Second Temple (see 1:18–36), and explicitly in 2 Macc 2:13–15, where the book-collecting activities of the two are compared.

Why did the author of the second letter seek to draw a connection between Judas and Nehemiah? We should first keep in mind the way in which Nehemiah is portrayed in the biblical sources: he is one of the leading figures in the restoration of the Second

---

58. See Goldstein, *2 Maccabees*, 173–76.
59. For detailed refutations of both of these arguments, see Bergren, "Nehemiah in 2 Maccabees."
60. I.e., the "Nehemiah memoir," mentioned above.

Temple state, a builder, a military hero, a political leader, and also, by his own account, an extremely pious individual. None of the other ideal figures associated with the restoration of the state possessed precisely these attributes.

Now, Judas's qualifications in the military and political spheres were clearly undisputed. It is entirely possible, however, that his religious motives and personal piety were open to question, especially among the more religiously conservative elements in the incipient Hasmonean state. An explicit comparison of him with Nehemiah, a biblical hero who appropriately furnished a paradigm of both military *and* religious virtue, would impart the message that Judas was someone not only whose military and political credentials were impeccable, but also whose personal piety was above reproach.[61]

As a function of the author's desire to extend and dramatize this comparison, Nehemiah was then credited with building and dedicating the Second Temple, actions which were depicted as parallel to, and furnishing the main precedent for, Judas's activities of restoration and purification during the Maccabean revolt. The story of Nehemiah in 2 Maccabees 1–2 could, then, be a product of pro-Judas, Hasmonean propaganda. Ezra, a political and military quietist, simply would not have been an appropriate figure to invoke in this propagandistic context, especially as a role model for Judas. Again, while a conflict between Nehemiah- and Ezra-type Jewish polity is possible, it is not demanded by the evidence.

The case of 4 Ezra does not, in my view, present the same type of interpretive problem as do the examples discussed above.[62] That is, there is really no paradox or mystery to be solved about the book. Rather, the primary question here is why the author of 4 Ezra, writing in Israel in the wake of the destruction of the Second Temple, chooses Ezra, rather than some other figure, as the book's protagonist.

---

61. For detailed argument of this point, see Bergren, "Nehemiah in 2 Maccabees." Note that the idealization of Judas as both a military *and* religious hero is precisely one of the main themes of both 1 and 2 Maccabees; thus, this letter would fall into line with these witnesses.

62. For 4 Ezra, see Stone, *Fourth Ezra;* and Myers, *I and II Esdras.*

This question can be approached from several angles. One is to ask what are the main points of 4 Ezra, and how these points might have influenced the book's attribution. One important message of the author certainly is that apocalyptic knowledge is the ultimate answer to insistent questions of theodicy. This does not, however, seem particularly relevant to the figure of Ezra in Jewish tradition, since this figure is not, as far as we know, previously connected with eschatological knowledge or with the issue of theodicy.

Another main point of 4 Ezra is that even in the wake of a dire national catastrophe such as the destruction of the Second Temple, God's people can, and will, rebound to a state of favor and salvation such as existed before the cataclysm. It is here, I think, that the traditional Ezra's status as postexilic hero finds a rationale for recapitulation in the first century C.E. Just as the biblical Ezra had promoted and embodied a renewal of the knowledge and observance of the Mosaic Law after the Babylonian destruction, so does the pseudepigraphic Ezra after the Roman destruction. It is furthermore significant that the traditional Ezra was renowned in some circles as actually being responsible for the physical restoration of the Mosaic Law after its alleged obliteration by the Babylonians, acting almost as a second Moses.[63] The author of 4 Ezra self-consciously adopts this role for the hero, not only portraying Ezra as a new Moses in chapter 14, but having him literally dictate the entire contents of the Bible, as well as seventy additional esoteric books, to his amanuenses in the same chapter. Thus the pseudepigraphic Ezra, like his biblical counterpart, embodies not only the general theme of restoration and recovery of the Jewish heritage after a devastating national catastrophe, a recovery accomplished through his extreme piety and devotion to the Law, but even more specifically the renewal of his heritage through the literary restoration of the sacred texts. This seems to be the most important point of contact between the biblical Ezra and the Ezra of 4 Ezra.

Even beyond this, however, there are several additional areas of connection. As noted above, the two Ezras have in common an

---

63. For these points, see the material presented in the first part of this essay.

extreme pitch of piety and devotion to God and the Law, manifested through fasting and other acts.[64] Both are strong leaders of the Jewish community,[65] both exercise an intercessory role between God and the community when the need arises,[66] and both address heartfelt prayers of confession to God in this capacity.[67]

A final consideration in answering the question why Ezra was chosen as the hero of 4 Ezra involves his biblical status as a scribe.[68] It may not be a coincidence that three of the great Jewish apocalypses of the late first and early second centuries C.E., 4 Ezra, *2 Baruch,* and *3 Baruch,* are attributed to individuals who appear in the Bible as "scribes." One could argue that in an era when scribal activity was becoming increasingly important and scribes increasingly visible in the context of Jewish legal observance, it would be natural for persons actually labeled as scribes in the Bible to assume a more favored and elevated status in contexts such as literary pseudepigrapha.[69] Nehemiah, of course, lacks not only Ezra's status as a scribe, but also his strong connection with the renewal of Jewish law and scripture after the exile; as in 1 Esdras, Nehemiah cannot fill the paradigmatic position so naturally occupied by Ezra.

In conclusion, let us briefly compare the roles of Ezra and Nehemiah in these four books. 1 Esdras appears to be concerned mainly with ideal Jewish heroes who have either a strong priestly or a strong Davidic lineage, who are connected with major feasts, who are associated with the restoration of either cult or law, and who fit a pattern of ideal religious status, exile, and return to ideal religious status. Ezra happens to fit all of these roles quite well, whereas Nehemiah does not. I submit that this accounts for the omission of the latter in 1 Esdras.

In Ben Sira, Nehemiah functions nicely as a precursor to and role model for Simeon II's efforts to fortify and rebuild Jerusalem. Ezra's absence, however, is incongruous and must be explained. I

---

64. Ezra 7:27–28; 8:18–31; 9:3–10:44; 4 Ezra 3:3; 4:51; 5:13–22; 6:32–36; 9:24–28; 10:39–50; 12:51; 13:53–56.

65. Ezra 7; 10:1–44; Nehemiah 8–9; 4 Ezra 5:17–18; 12:40–50; 14:23–36.

66. Ezra 9–10; 4 Ezra 7:18, 46–48; 8:15–45.

67. Ezra 9:6–15; 4 Ezra 8:19–36; 12:48.

68. Ezra 7:6, 11–12, 21; Neh 8:1, 4, 9, 13.

69. See Fishbane, "From Scribalism to Rabbinism."

have argued that either Ben Sira wished to reserve the bulk of the pietistic and spiritual glory of the postexilic period for Simeon, perhaps hinting that it was Simeon, rather than an earlier figure like Ezra, who effectively restored the postexilic state to its preexilic glory, or that Ben Sira was concerned about the lack of priestly activities on the part of Ezra, a supposed priest.

In 2 Maccabees, it is not the absence of Ezra that is problematic, but the assignment to Nehemiah of roles that are totally foreign to him in other sources. I suggest first that Nehemiah, because of his well-known literary productions, was a logical person to whom to assign an account of the authentification of the Second Temple cult by divine fire. It also seems that an incipient identification between Nehemiah and Judas Maccabaeus was promoted by Hasmonean propagandists in an effort to equate Judas and his activities with the personality and roles, especially the piety, of the earlier biblical hero. This identification in turn led to Nehemiah's being credited with various acts concerning the Temple in his day that paralleled actions with which Judas was also credited in his day.

Finally, in 4 Ezra, Ezra was chosen as the hero of the book by virtue of (*a*) his traditionally recognized role as restorer of Jewish worship, legal observance, and scripture after a threat by a foreign power (Babylon/Rome), (*b*) his extreme piety, and (*c*) his status as a scribe. Nehemiah's absence is not an enigma or an indication of rivalry; he simply did not wield Ezra's qualifications for this role.

In sum, despite the exclusivity of treatment of Ezra and Nehemiah in the four apocrypha that we have surveyed, it does not seem necessary to posit a polemic or rivalry between the two individuals or between groups associated with them. Rather, each figure, as portrayed in the Hebrew biblical writings traditionally connected with them, possessed certain attributes and an identifiable character type, and the extrabiblical writers seem to have chosen to include or exclude one or the other figure based mainly upon how this characterization accorded with their own literary and ideological needs. It is certainly possible that these literary situations mask some type of polemic between rival theological factions, but the evidence that we have surveyed does not demand or even suggest such a polemic. That in each of these apocrypha only one of the two figures was treated, seems to be a matter more of individual literary circumstance than of conscious theological design.

Bibliography

Broad Surveys of Materials Concerning Ezra or Nehemiah

Denis, A.-M. *Introduction aux pseudépigraphes grecs d'Ancien Testament.* SVTP 1. Leiden: Brill, 1970. Pp. 91–96. Discusses, in the context of a treatment of the Greek *Apocalypse of Ezra,* other Ezra-related writings of antiquity.

Ginzberg, L. *The Legends of the Jews.* 7 vols. Philadelphia: Jewish Publication Society of America, 1909–38. Vols. 4.352–59 and 6.437–51. Summary of rabbinic and cognate materials on Ezra and Nehemiah.

In der Smitten, W. T. *Esra: Quellen, Überlieferung und Geschichte.* SSN 15. Assen: Van Gorcum, 1973. General, analytical overview of traditions about Ezra, ranging from the Bible to Islam.

James, M. R. Introduction to *The Fourth Book of Ezra.* Ed. R. L. Bensly. TextsS 3, 2. Cambridge: Cambridge University Press, 1895. Pp. lxxxvi–lxxxix. A survey of Ezra writings from antiquity.

———. *The Lost Apocrypha of the Old Testament: Their Titles and Fragments.* London: SPCK, 1920. Pp. 79–81. Brief summary of Ezra writings known at the time.

Kellermann, U. *Nehemia: Quellen, Überlieferung, und Geschichte.* BZAW 102. Berlin: Töpelmann, 1967. General, analytical overview of known historical materials on Nehemiah, ranging from the Bible to rabbinic Judaism. Focuses on Nehemiah as a representative of "Zionistic" Judaism.

Kraft, R. A. " 'Ezra' Materials in Judaism and Christianity." *ANRW* II.19.1. Ed. W. Haase. Berlin: de Gruyter, 1979. Pp. 119–36. Exhaustive cataloging of Ezra literature and traditions in antiquity; attempts to group the traditions into categories.

North, R. "Ezra." *ABD* 2.726–28. A survey article.

Schaeder, H. H. *Esra der Schreiber.* BHT 5. Tübingen: Mohr, 1930. General examination of the biblical Ezra; contains some material relevant to this study.

Schneemelcher, W. "Esra." *RAC* 6.595–612. Excellent, detailed survey article.

Stone, M. E. "The Metamorphosis of Ezra: Jewish Apocalypse and Medieval Vision." *JTS,* n.s., 33 (1982) 1–18. Surveys the transition of the figure from 4 Ezra through the medieval apocalypses.

Ezra in 1 Esdras

Coggins, R. J., and M. A. Knibb. *The First and Second Books of Esdras*. CBC. Cambridge: Cambridge University Press, 1979. A commentary.

Myers, J. M. *I and II Esdras*. AB 42. Garden City, N.Y.: Doubleday, 1974. A commentary.

Pohlmann, K.-F. *3. Esra-Buch*. JSHRZ 1, 5. Gütersloh: Mohn, 1980. A translation with notes and introduction.

Ezra in 4 Ezra

Myers, J. M. *I and II Esdras*. AB 42. Garden City, N.Y.: Doubleday, 1974. A commentary.

Stone, M. E. *Fourth Ezra*. Hermeneia. Minneapolis: Fortress, 1990. A commentary.

Nehemiah in Ben Sira

Höffken, P. "Warum schwieg Jesus Sirach über Esra?" *ZAW* 87 (1975) 184–201. Argues that the antilevitical bias of Ben Sira was responsible for Ezra's omission from the "Praise of the Fathers" section.

Lee, T. R. *Studies in the Form of Sirach 44–50*. SBLDS 75. Atlanta: Scholars Press, 1986. A detailed analysis of the "Praise of the Fathers" section of Ben Sira.

Skehan, P. W., and A. A. DiLella. *The Wisdom of Ben Sira*. AB 39. New York: Doubleday, 1987. A commentary.

Smend, R. *Die Weisheit des Jesus Sirach*. Berlin: Reimer, 1906. A classic commentary.

Snaith, J. G. *Ecclesiasticus or the Wisdom of Jesus Son of Sirach*. CBC. Cambridge: Cambridge University Press, 1974. A commentary.

Nehemiah in 2 Maccabees

Bergren, T. A. "Nehemiah in 2 Maccabees 1:10–2:18." *JSJ* 28/3 (1997) 249–70. Addresses the question why Nehemiah is given such unexpected roles in this letter.

Doran, R. *Temple Propaganda: The Purpose and Character of 2 Maccabees*. CBQMS 12. Washington, D.C.: Catholic Biblical Association of America, 1981. An insightful study of the book.

Goldstein, J. A. *2 Maccabees*. AB 41A. New York: Doubleday, 1984. A commentary.

Habicht, D. *2. Makkabäerbuch*. JSHRZ 1, 3. Gütersloh: Mohn, 1976. A commentary.

Ezra and Nehemiah in the Canonical Ezra-Nehemiah

Klein, R. W. "Ezra," "Nehemiah." *HBC* 372–78, 379–86. Brief commentary.

Klein, R. W. "Ezra and Nehemiah in Recent Studies." In *Magnalia Dei: The Mighty Acts of God. In Memoriam G. Ernest Wright*. Ed. F. M. Cross, W. E. Lemke, and P. D. Miller. Garden City, N.Y.: Doubleday, 1976. Pp. 361–76. Survey of modern research.

Myers, J. M. *Ezra, Nehemiah*. AB 14. Garden City, N.Y.: Doubleday, 1965. A commentary.

Talmon, S. "Ezra and Nehemiah (Books and Men)." *IDBSup* 317–28. A survey article.

Williamson, H. G. M. *Ezra, Nehemiah*. WBC 16. Waco, Tex.: Word, 1985. A commentary.

Sources Dealing with the Portrayal of Ezra or Nehemiah in Other Particular Documents

Bergren, T. A. *Fifth Ezra: The Text, Origin, and Early History*. SBLSCS 25. Atlanta: Scholars Press, 1990. Detailed analysis of the origin of 5 Ezra.

Himmelfarb, M. *Tours of Hell: An Apocalyptic Form in Jewish and Christian Literature*. Philadelphia: Fortress, 1985. A thoroughgoing study of the history and characteristics of the genre.

James, M. R. "Ego Salathiel qui et Ezras." *JTS* 18 (1917) 167–69. First study to address the issue of "two Ezras."

———. "Salathiel qui et Esdras." *JTS* 19 (1918) 347–49. Continues the preceding study.

Klijn, A. F. J., ed. *Der lateinische Text der Apokalypse des Esra*. TU 131. Berlin: Akademie, 1983. Pp. 20–22. A survey of further materials concerning "two Ezras."

Lazarus-Yafeh, H. *Intertwined Worlds: Medieval Islam and Bible Criticism*. Princeton, N.J.: Princeton University Press, 1992. Chapter 3 is a fascinating study of the *Nachleben* of Ezra in Islam.

Norelli, E. "Due 'testimonia' attribuiti a Esdra." *Annali di Storia dell' Esegesi* 1 (1984) 231–82. Detailed study of the testimonia of Justin and Hippolytus on Ezra.

Schürer, E. *The History of the Jewish People in the Age of Jesus Christ*. Rev. ed. 3 vols. Ed. G. Vermes, F. Millar, and M. Goodman. Edinburgh: T. & T. Clark, 1986. Vol. 3. Material on 1 Esdras, 4 Ezra, etc.

Stone, M. E., ed. *The Armenian Version of 4 Ezra*. Missoula, Mont.: Scholars Press, 1979. Pp. 35–39. These pages survey Armenian materials concerning "two Ezras."

CUMULATIVE BIBLIOGRAPHY

Aberbach, M. "Ezekiel." *EncJud* 6.1095–96.

Abrams, D. "The Boundaries of Divine Ontology: The Inclusion and Exclusion of Metatron from the Godhead." *HTR* 87 (1994) 291–321.

Abramsky, S., and I. Ta-Shemaʿ. "Ezekiel." *The Encyclopaedia Hebraica*. Ed. Y. Klausner et al. Jerusalem and Tel Aviv: HE — The Society of Encyclopaedias Publishing, 1949–81. 19.744–48. In Hebrew.

Adler, W. *Time Immemorial: Archaic History and Its Sources in Christian Chronography from Julius Africanus to George Syncellus*. Washington, D.C.: Dumbarton Oaks Research Library and Collection, 1989.

Agus, R. E. *The Binding of Isaac and Messiah*. Albany: State University of New York Press, 1988.

Albeck, C. *Das Buch der Jubiläen und die Halacha*. Sieben und vierzigster Bericht der Hochschule für die Wissenschaft des Judentums in Berlin. Berlin-Schöneberg: Siegfried Scholem, 1930.

———, ed. *Midrash Bereshit Rabbati ex Libro R. Mosis Haddarsan*. Jerusalem: Mekize Nirdamim, 1940. Reprint, Jerusalem: Mossad Harav Kook, 1967.

Alexander, P. S. "Comparing Merkavah Mysticism and Gnosticism: An Essay in Method." *JJS* 36 (1984) 1–18.

———. "Enoch-Idris in Early Islamic Tradition." In *Studies in Muslim-Jewish Relations*. Vol. 3. Harwood Academic Publishers / Oxford Centre for Hebrew and Jewish Studies. Forthcoming.

———. "The Fall into Knowledge: The Garden of Eden/Paradise in Gnostic Literature." In *A Walk in the Garden: Biblical, Iconographical, and Literary Images of Eden*. Ed. P. Morris and D. Sawyer. Sheffield: JSOT Press, 1992. Pp. 91–103.

———. "The Historical Setting of the Hebrew Book of Enoch." *JJS* 28 (1977) 156–80.

———. "The Targumim and Early Exegesis of 'Sons of God' in Genesis 6." *JJS* 23 (1972) 60–71.

Alexandre, M. *Le Commencement du Livre Genèse I–V: La version grecque de la Septante et sa réception*. Paris: Beauchesne, 1988.

Allegro, J. *Qumrân Cave 4*. DJD 5. Oxford: Clarendon, 1968.

Alter, R. *The Art of Biblical Narrative*. New York: Basic Books, 1981.

Amzalak, M. B. *Da Amizade ou Livro de Henoch*. Lisbon, 1928.

367

Anderson, G. A. "Celibacy or Consummation in the Garden: Reflections on Early Jewish and Christian Interpretations of the Garden of Eden." *HTR* 82 (1989) 121–48.

———. "The Penitence Narrative in the *Life of Adam and Eve.*" *HUCA* 63 (1993) 1–38.

Anderson, G. A., and M. E. Stone, eds. *A Synopsis of the Books of Adam and Eve.* SBLEJL 5. Atlanta: Scholars Press, 1994.

Aptowitzer, V. "Asenath, the Wife of Joseph: A Haggadic Literary-Historical Study." *HUCA* 1 (1924) 239–306.

———. "Malkizedek: Zu den Sagen der Agada." *MGWJ* 70 (1926) 93–113.

Argyle, A. W. "Joseph the Patriarch in Patristic Teaching." *ExpTim* 67 (1955–56) 199–201.

———. "O. Cullmann's Theory Concerning κωλύειν." *ExpTim* 67 (1955) 17.

Armstrong, A. H. "Gnosis and Greek Philosophy." In *Gnosis: Festschrift für Hans Jonas.* Ed. B. Aland. Göttingen: Vandenhoeck & Ruprecht, 1978. Pp. 87–124.

Astour, M. "Melchizedek." *ABD* 4.684–86.

Attridge, H. W. *The Epistle to the Hebrews.* Hermeneia. Philadelphia: Fortress, 1989.

———. *The Interpretation of Biblical History in the "Antiquitates Judaicae" of Flavius Josephus.* Missoula, Mont.: Scholars Press, 1976.

———. "Josephus and His Works." In *Jewish Writings of the Second Temple Period.* Ed. M. E. Stone. CRINT. Assen: Van Gorcum; Philadelphia: Fortress, 1984. Pp. 185–232.

Attridge, H. W., and J. Strugnell, eds. "Prayer of Enosh." In *Qumran Cave 4. VIII: Parabiblical Texts, Part 1.* Ed. J. C. VanderKam and J. T. Milik. DJD 13. Oxford: Clarendon, 1994. Pp. 353–56.

Avigad, N. "Baruch the Scribe and Jerahmeel the King's Son." *IEJ* 28:1–2 (1978) 52–56.

Avishur, Y. "Judeo-Arabic Folksongs Sung by Iraqi Jewry on Pilgrimages to Saints' Graves (Ziyyara)." In *Studies on the History and Culture of Iraqi Jewry.* Ed. Y. Avishur. Vol. 2. Or-Yehuda: Institute for Research on Iraqi Jewry, 1982. Pp. 151–92. In Hebrew.

Baarda, T. "The Shechem Episode in the Testament of Levi." In *Sacred History and Sacred Texts.* Ed. J. N. Bremmer and F. García Martínez. Kampen: Kok Pharos, 1992. Pp. 11–73.

Baird, W. "Abraham in the New Testament: Tradition and the New Identity." *Int* 42 (1988) 367–79.

Baker, A. "Justin's Agraphon in the *Dialogue with Trypho.*" *JBL* 87 (1968) 77–87.

Bandstra, A. J. *The Law and the Elements of the World.* Kampen: Kok, 1964.

Barc, B. "Samaël — Saklas — Yaldabaôth: Recherche sur l'origine d'un mythe gnostique." In *Colloque International sur les Textes de Nag Hammadi, Québec, 22–25 Août 1978.* Ed. B. Barc. Bibliothèque Copte de Nag Hammadi, Etudes 1. Quebec: Université Laval; Louvain: Peeters, 1981. Pp. 123–50.

Bardy, G. "Melchisédech dans la tradition patristique." *RB* 35 (1926) 496–509; 36 (1927) 25–45.

Barker, M. *The Lost Prophet: The Book of Enoch and Its Influence on Christianity.* London: SPCK, 1988.

Barr, J. *The Garden of Eden and the Hope of Immortality.* Minneapolis: Fortress, 1993.

Barthélemy, D., and J. T. Milik. *Qumran Cave 1.* DJD 1. Oxford: Clarendon, 1955.

Bassler, J. M. "Philo on Joseph: The Basic Coherence of *De Iosepho* and *De Somniis* ii." *JSJ* 16 (1985) 240–55.

Bauckham, R. J. "The Martyrdom of Enoch and Elijah: Jewish or Christian?" *JBL* 95 (1976) 447–58.

―――. "A Quotation from *4Q Second Ezekiel* in *Apocalypse of Peter.*" *RevQ* 15 (1992) 438–45.

Baumgarten, J. M. "The Laws of Orlah and First Fruits in Light of *Jubilees*, the Qumran Writings, and the *Targum Ps.-Jonathan.*" *JJS* 38 (1987) 195–202.

Baumgarten, J. M., and J. T. Milik. *Qumran Cave 4.XIII: The Damascus Document (4Q266–273).* DJD 18. Oxford: Clarendon, 1996.

Beasley-Murray, G. R. *Baptism in the New Testament.* Grand Rapids, Mich.: Eerdmans, 1962.

Beckwith, R. *The Old Testament Canon of the New Testament Church.* London: SPCK, 1985.

Beer, B. *Leben Abrahams nach Auffassung der jüdischen Sage.* Leipzig: Leiner, 1859.

Bellinzoni, A. J. *The Sayings of Jesus in the Writings of Justin Martyr.* SNT 17. Leiden: Brill, 1967.

―――. "The Source of the Agraphon in Justin Martyr's *Dialogue with Trypho* 47:5." *VC* 17 (1963) 65–70.

Beltz, W. "Melchisedek — Eine gnostische Initiationsliturgie." *ZRGG* 33 (1981) 155–58.

―――. "Samaritanertum und Gnosis." In *Gnosis und Neues Testament: Studien aus Religionswissenschaft und Theologie.* Ed. K.-W. Tröger. Berlin: Evangelische Verlagsanstalt, 1973. Pp. 89–95.

Ben-Hayyim, Z., ed. and trans. *Tibat Marqe: A Collection of Samaritan Midrashim.* Jerusalem: Israel Academy of Sciences and Humanities, 1988.

Benisch, A., ed. and trans. *The Travels of Rabbi Petachia of Ratisbon.* London: Trubner, 1856.

Ben Yaacob, A. "Ezekiel." *EncJud* 6.1096–97.

Ben-Ya'akov, A. *Holy Tombs in Babylonia.* Jerusalem: Mossad Harav Kook, 1973. In Hebrew.

Berger, K. "Abraham in den paulinischen Hauptbriefen." *TRE* 1.372–82 (also *MTZ* 17 [1966] 47–89).

―――. *Das Buch der Jubiläen.* JSHRZ 2, 3. Gütersloh: Mohn, 1981.

―――. *Die Gesetzesauslegung Jesu: Ihr historischer Hintergrund im Judentum und im Alten Testament.* WMANT 40. Neukirchen-Vluyn: Neukirchener Verlag, 1972.

―――. "Henoch." *RAC* 14.473–545.

Bergren, T. A. *Fifth Ezra: The Text, Origin, and Early History.* SBLSCS 25. Atlanta: Scholars Press, 1990.

———. "Nehemiah in 2 Maccabees 1:10–2:18." *JSJ* 28/3 (1997) 249–70.

Bernstein, M. J. "4Q252: From Rewritten Bible to Biblical Commentary." *JJS* 45 (1994) 1–17.

Betz, H.-D. *Galatians.* Hermeneia. Philadelphia: Fortress, 1979.

———, ed. *The Greek Magical Papyri in Translation.* Chicago: University of Chicago Press, 1986.

Beyer, K. *Die aramäischen Texte vom Toten Meer.* Göttingen: Vandenhoeck & Ruprecht, 1984.

———. *Die aramäischen Texte vom Toten Meer: Ergänzungsband.* Göttingen: Vandenhoeck & Ruprecht, 1994.

Bezold, C., ed. and trans. *Die Schatzhöhle.* Leipzig: J. C. Hinrichs, 1883.

Biblia Patristica. Vols. 1–4. Paris: Editions du Centre National de la Recherche Scientifique, 1975–87. *Biblia Patristica Supplément.* Paris, 1982.

Bidez, J., and F. Cumont. *Les mages hellénisés: Zoroastre, Ostanès et Hystaspe d'après la tradition grecque.* 2 vols. Paris: "Les belles Lettres," 1973.

Bietenhard, H. *Die himmlische Welt im Urchristentum und Spätjudentum.* Tübingen: Mohr-Siebeck, 1951.

Bilde, P. *Flavius Josephus between Jerusalem and Rome.* JSPSup 2. Sheffield: JSOT Press, 1988.

Billerbeck, P. "Abrahams Leben und Bedeutung nach Auffassung der älteren Haggada." *Nathanael* 15 (1899) 43–57, 118–28, 137–57, 161–79; 16 (1900) 33–57, 65–80.

Black, M. *Apocalypsis Henochi Graece.* PVTG 3. Leiden: Brill, 1970.

———. *The Book of Enoch or 1 Enoch.* SVTP 7. Leiden: Brill, 1985.

Blinzler, J. "Lexikalisches zu dem Terminus 'ta stoicheia tou kosmou' bei Paulus." In *Studiorum Paulinorum Congressus Internationalis Catholicus 1961.* AnBib 18. Rome: Pontifico Instituto Biblico, 1963. 2.427–43.

Bogaert, P.-M. *Apocalypse de Baruch: Introduction, traduction du syriaque et commentaire.* SC 144–45. Paris: Cerf, 1969.

———. "De Baruch à Jérémie: Les deux rédactions conservées du livre de Jérémie." In *Le livre de Jérémie: Le prophète et son milieu, les oracles et leur transmission.* Ed. P.-M. Bogaert. BETL 54. Leuven: Leuven University Press, 1981. Pp. 168–73.

———. "Le nom de Baruch dans la littérature pseudépigraphique: L'apocalypse syriaque et le livre deutérocanonique." In *La littérature juive entre Tenach et Mischna: Quelques problèmes.* Ed. W. C. Van Unnik. RechBib 9. Leiden: Brill, 1974. Pp. 61–72.

———. "Le personnage de Baruch et l'histoire du livre de Jérémie: Aux origines du livre de Baruch." *BIOSCS* 7 (1974) 19–21.

———. "Le personnage de Baruch et l'histoire du livre de Jérémie: Aux origines du Livre deutérocanonique de Baruch." In *Studia Evangelica.* Ed. E. A. Livingstone. Vol. 7. TU 126. Berlin: Akademie, 1982. Pp. 73–81.

———, ed. *Abraham dans la Bible et dans la tradition juive.* Brussels: Institutum Iudaicum, 1977.

——, ed. *Le livre de Jérémie: Le prophète et son milieu, les oracles et leur transmission.* BETL 54. Leuven: Leuven University Press, 1981.

Böhlig, A., and F. Wisse, eds. and trans. *Nag Hammadi Codices III,2 and IV,2: The Gospel of the Egyptians.* NHS 4. Leiden: Brill, 1975.

Bonner, C. *The Homily on the Passion by Melito Bishop of Sardis and Some Fragments of the Apocryphal Ezekiel.* SD 12. Philadelphia: University of Pennsylvania Press, 1940.

Bonner, C., and H. C. Youtie. *The Last Chapters of Enoch in Greek.* SD 8. London: Christophers, 1937.

The Book of Ben Sira: Text, Concordance, and an Analysis of the Vocabulary. The Historical Dictionary of the Hebrew Language. Jerusalem: The Academy of the Hebrew Language and the Shrine of the Book, 1973.

The Book of the Angel Raziel. Amsterdam, 1804.

The Book of the Cave of Treasures. Trans. E. A. Wallis Budge. London: Religious Tract Society, 1927.

Bousset, W. *The Antichrist Legend.* London: Hutchinson, 1896.

Bowker, J. *The Targums and Rabbinic Literature: An Introduction to Jewish Interpretations of Scripture.* London: Cambridge University Press, 1969.

Bowley, J. E. "The Compositions of Abraham." In *Tracing the Threads: Studies in the Vitality of Jewish Pseudepigrapha.* Ed. J. C. Reeves. SBLEJL 6. Atlanta: Scholars Press, 1994. Pp. 215–38.

——. "Traditions of Abraham in Greek Historical Writings." Ph.D. diss., Hebrew Union College–Jewish Institute of Religion, 1992.

Boyancé, P. "Dieu cosmique et dualisme: Les archontes et Platon." In *Le Origini dello Gnosticismo, Colloquio di Messina 13–18 Aprile 1966; Testi e discussioni publicati a cura di Ugo Bianchi.* Supplements to Numen XII. Leiden: Brill, 1967. Pp. 340–86.

Braun, M. *History and Romance in Graeco-Oriental Literature.* Oxford: Blackwell, 1938.

Bregman, M. "The Parable of the Lame and the Blind: Epiphanius' Quotation from an Apocryphon of Ezekiel." *JTS* 42 (1991) 125–38.

Brock, S. P. "Abraham and the Ravens: A Syriac Counterpart to *Jubilees* 11–12 and its Implications." *JSJ* 9 (1978) 135–52.

——. *Testamentum Iobi.* PVTG 2. Leiden: Brill, 1967.

Brongers, H. A. *De Jozefsgeschiedenis bij Joden, Christenen en Mohammedanen.* Wageningen: Veenman, 1962.

Brooke, G. J. "Ezekiel in Some Qumran and New Testament Texts." In *The Madrid Qumran Congress: Proceedings of the International Congress on the Dead Sea Scrolls, Madrid, 18–21 March 1991.* Ed. J. Trebolle Barrera and L. Vegas Montaner. STDJ 11, 2. Leiden: Brill; Madrid: Editorial Complutense, 1992. Pp. 317–37.

——. "4QTestament of Levi[d] and the Messianic Servant High Priest." In *From Jesus to John: Essays on Jesus and New Testament Christology in Honour of Marinus de Jonge.* Ed. M. C. de Boer. JSNTSup 84. Sheffield: JSOT, 1993. Pp. 83–100.

——. "The Genre of 4Q252: From Poetry to Pesher." *Dead Sea Discoveries* 1 (1994) 161–79.

———. Review of *Enosh and His Generation: Pre-Israelite Hero and History in Post-biblical Interpretation*, by S. D. Fraade. *JSS* 31 (1986) 257–61.

———. "The Thematic Content of 4Q252." *JQR* 85 (1994) 33–59.

Brooke, G. J., ed. *Qumran Cave 4.XVII: Parabiblical Texts, pt. 3.* DJD 22. Oxford: Clarendon, 1996.

Broshi, M., ed. *The Damascus Document Reconsidered.* Jerusalem: Israel Exploration Society, 1992.

Bruce, F. F. *Galatians.* NIGTC. Grand Rapids, Mich.: Eerdmans, 1982.

Buber, S., ed. *Midrasch Tanchuma: Ein agadischer Kommentar zum Pentateuch von Rabbi Tanchuma ben Rabbi Abba.* Vilna: Romm, 1885.

Buchholz, D. D. *Your Eyes Will Be Opened: A Study of the Greek (Ethiopic) Apocalypse of Peter.* SBLDS 97. Atlanta: Scholars, 1988.

Budd, L. J. "Mark Twain on Joseph the Patriarch." *American Quarterly* 16 (1964) 577–86.

Budge, E. A. W., ed. *The Book of Governors: The Historia Monastica of Thomas, Bishop of Marga.* London: K. Paul, Trench, Trübner, 1893.

Bullard, R. A. *The Hypostasis of the Archons.* Patristische Texte und Studien 10. Berlin: de Gruyter, 1970.

Burchard, C. *Gesammelte Studien zu Joseph und Aseneth.* SVTP 13. Leiden: Brill, 1996)

———. "Joseph et Aseneth." In *Concordance grecque des pseudépigraphes d'Ancien Testament.* Ed. A.-M. Denis. Louvain-la-Neuve: Université Catholique de Louvain, Institut Orientaliste, 1987. Pp. 851–59.

———. "Joseph und Aseneth." *Dielheimer Blätter zum Alten Testament* 14 (1979) 2–53; 16 (1982) 37–39.

———. *Joseph und Aseneth.* JSHRZ 2, 4. Gütersloh: Mohn, 1983.

———. "Der jüdische Asenethroman und seine Nachwirkung: Von Egeria zu Anna Katharina Emmerick oder von Moses aus Aggel zu Karl Kerényi." *ANRW* 20, 1. Pp. 543–667.

Burke, D. G. *The Poetry of Baruch: A Reconstruction and Analysis of Baruch 3:9–5:9.* SBLSCS 10. Chico, Calif.: Scholars Press, 1982.

Burton, E. *A Critical and Exegetical Commentary on the Epistle to the Galatians.* ICC. New York: Scribners, 1920.

Caquot, A. "Jubilés." In *Ecrits intertestamentaires.* Paris: Gallimard, 1978. Pp. 629–810.

Carroll, R. P. "Arguing about Jeremiah: Recent Studies and the Nature of a Prophetic Book." In *Congress Volume: Leuven 1989.* Ed. J. A. Emerton. VTSup 43. Leiden: Brill, 1991. Pp. 222–35.

———. *Jeremiah.* OTL. London: SCM, 1986.

Charles, R. H. *The Book of Enoch.* 2d ed. Oxford: Clarendon, 1912.

———. *The Book of Jubilees or the Little Genesis.* London: A. & C. Black, 1902.

———. *The Greek Versions of the "Testaments of the Twelve Patriarchs."* Oxford: Clarendon, 1908.

———, ed. *Apocrypha and Pseudepigrapha of the Old Testament.* 2 vols. Oxford: Clarendon, 1913.

Charlesworth, J. H., ed. *The Old Testament Pseudepigrapha.* 2 vols. Garden City, N.Y.: Doubleday, 1983–85.

Chwolson, D. *Die Ssabier und der Ssabismus.* 2 vols. St. Petersburg, 1856.

Clarke, E. G. *The Wisdom of Solomon.* CBC. Cambridge: Cambridge University Press, 1973.

Clarke, E. G., et al., eds. *"Targum Pseudo-Jonathan" of the Pentateuch: Text and Concordance.* Hoboken, N.J.: Ktav, 1984.

Coats, G. W. *From Canaan to Egypt: Structural and Theological Context for the Joseph Story.* CBQMS 4. Washington, D.C.: Catholic Biblical Association of America, 1976.

———. "The Joseph Story and Ancient Wisdom: A Reappraisal." *CBQ* 35 (1973) 285–97.

Coggins, R. J., and M. A. Knibb. *The First and Second Books of Esdras.* CBC. Cambridge: Cambridge University Press, 1979.

Cohen, H. H. *The Drunkenness of Noah.* Tuscaloosa: University of Alabama Press, 1974.

Cohen, S. J. D. *Josephus in Galilee and Rome.* Leiden: Brill, 1979.

Collins, J. J. "The Jewish Apocalypses." *Semeia* 14 (1979) 21–59.

———. "The Sage in the Apocalyptic and Pseudepigraphic Literature." In *The Sage in Israel and the Ancient Near East.* Ed. J. G. Gammie and L. Perdue. Winona Lake, Ind.: Eisenbrauns, 1990. Pp. 343–54.

———. "A Symbol of Otherness: Circumcision and Salvation in the First Century." In *To See Ourselves As Others See Us: Christians, Jews, "Others" in Late Antiquity.* Ed. J. Neusner and E. S. Frerichs. Chico, Calif.: Scholars Press, 1985. Pp. 164–86.

Copenhaver, B. P. *Hermetica: The Greek Corpus Hermeticum and the Latin Asclepius in a New English Translation, with Notes and Introduction.* Cambridge: Cambridge University Press, 1992.

Coxe, A. C., trans. *The Apostolic Fathers with Justin Martyr and Irenaeus: American Edition Chronologically Arranged, with Brief Notes and Preface.* Vol. 1. London: T. & T. Clark, 1885. Reprint, Grand Rapids, Mich.: Eerdmans, 1989.

Crahay, R. "Elements d'une mythopée gnostique dans le Grèce classique." In *Le Origini dello Gnosticismo, Colloquio di Messina 13–18 Aprile 1966; Testi e discussioni publicati a cura di Ugo Bianchi.* Supplements to Numen XII. Leiden: Brill, 1967. Pp. 323–38.

Crone, P., and M. Cook. *Hagarism: The Making of the Islamic World.* Cambridge: Cambridge University Press, 1977.

Cullmann, O. *Baptism in the New Testament.* SBT 1. London: SCM, 1950.

Cyril of Alexandria. *In sancti patris nostri Cyrilli archiepiscopi Alexandrini in d. Joannis evangelium.* Ed. P. E. Pusey. 3 vols. Oxford, 1892. Reprint, Brussels: Impression Anastaltique Culture et Civilisation, 1965.

Dan, J. *Gershom Scholem and the Mystical Dimension of Jewish History.* New York: New York University Press, 1987.

Daniélou, J. "Abraham dans la tradition chrétienne." In *Abraham, Père des croyants.* Ed. Cardinal Tisserant. Cahiers Sioniens 5. Paris: Cerf, 1952. Pp. 68–87.

Dassmann, E. "Hesekiel." *RAC* 14, cols. 1132–91.

Davenport, G. L. *The Eschatology of the Book of Jubilees.* SPB 20. Leiden: Brill, 1971.

Davies, P., and B. Chilton. "The Aqedah: A Revised Tradition History." *CBQ* 40 (1978) 514–46.

Davis, P. G. "Divine Agents, Mediators, and New Testament Christology." *JTS* 45 (1994) 480–503.

———. "The Mythic Enoch: New Light on New Testament Christology." *SR* 13 (1984) 335–41.

Dedering, S., ed. *Apocalypse of Baruch.* Pt. 4, fascicle 3. Peshitta Institute. Leiden: Brill, 1973.

Dehandschutter, B. "L'Apocryphe d'Ezechiel: Source de l'Exégèse sur l'ame." *OLP* 10 (1979) 227–35.

de Jonge, M. "Hippolytus' 'Benedictions of Isaac, Jacob and Moses' and the *Testaments of the Twelve Patriarchs.*" In de Jonge, *Jewish Eschatology.* Pp. 204–19.

———. *Jewish Eschatology, Early Christian Christology, and the "Testaments of the Twelve Patriarchs": Collected Essays.* Ed. H. J. de Jonge. NovTSup 63. Leiden: Brill, 1981.

———. "The *Testament of Levi* and 'Aramaic Levi.'" *RevQ* 13 (1988) 367–85 (= de Jonge, *Jewish Eschatology,* 244–62).

———. *The "Testaments of the Twelve Patriarchs": A Study of Their Text, Composition, and Origin.* Assen: Van Gorcum, 1953.

———. "Two Messiahs in the *Testaments of the Twelve Patriarchs?*" In de Jonge, *Jewish Eschatology.* Pp. 191–203.

de Jonge, M., et al., eds. *The "Testaments of the Twelve Patriarchs": A Critical Edition of the Greek Text.* PVTG 1, 2. Leiden: Brill, 1978.

Delcor, M. "Melchizedek from Genesis to the Qumran Texts and the Epistle to the Hebrews." *JSJ* 2 (1971) 115–33.

Delling, G. "Einwirkungen der Sprache der Septuaginta in 'Joseph and Aseneth.'" *JSJ* 9 (1978) 29–56.

———. *Jüdische Lehre und Frömmigkeit in den Paraleipomena Jeremiae.* BZAW 100. Berlin: Töpelmann, 1967.

Démann, P. "La signification d'Abraham dans la perspective du Nouveau Testament." In *Abraham, Père des croyants.* Ed. Cardinal Tisserant. Cahiers Sioniens 5. Paris: Cerf, 1952. Pp. 44–67.

de Meynard, C. B., and P. de Courteille. *Maçoudi, Les Prairies d'Or: texte et traduction,* vols. I–IX. Paris: L'Imprimerie Impériale / L'Imprimerie Nationale, 1863–77.

De Menasce, P.-J. "Traditions juives sur Abraham." In *Abraham, Père des croyants.* Ed. Cardinal Tisserant. Cahiers Sioniens 5. Paris: Cerf, 1952. Pp. 96–103.

Denis, A.-M. *Concordance grecque des pseudépigraphes d'Ancien Testament: Concordance, corpus des textes, indices.* Louvain-la-Neuve: Université Catholique de Louvain, 1987.

———. *Fragmenta pseudepigraphorum quae supersunt graeca.* PVTG 3. Leiden: Brill, 1970.

————. *Introduction aux pseudépigraphes grecs d'Ancien Testament.* SVTP 1. Leiden: Brill, 1970.

Derpmann, M. *Die Josephgeschichte: Auffassung und Darstellung im Mittelalter.* Beihefte zum "Mittellateinischen Jahrbuch" 13. Ratingen-Kastellaun-Düsseldorf: Henn, 1974.

Didyme L'Aveugle. *Sur la Genèse.* Ed. and trans. P. Nautin. 2 vols. SC 233, 244. Paris: Cerf, 1976–78.

Diez Macho, A., ed. *Neophyti I.* 6 vols. Madrid and Barcelona: Consejo Superior de Investigaciones Científicas, 1968–79.

Dimant, D. "The Apocalyptic Interpretation of Ezekiel at Qumran." In *Messiah and Christos: Studies in the Jewish Origins of Christianity.* Ed. I. Gruenwald, S. Shaked, and G. G. Stroumsa. Tübingen: J. C. B. Mohr (Paul Siebeck), 1992. Pp. 31–52.

————. " 'The Fallen Angels' in the Dead Sea Scrolls and in the Apocryphal and Pseudepigraphic Books Related to Them." Ph.D. diss., Hebrew University (Jerusalem), 1974.

————. "*1 Enoch* 6–11: A Methodological Perspective." In *SBL Seminar Papers 1978.* Missoula, Mont.: Scholars Press, 1978. Pp. 323–39.

————. "New Light from Qumran on the Jewish Pseudepigrapha — 4Q390." In *The Madrid Qumran Congress: Proceedings of the International Congress on the Dead Sea Scrolls, Madrid, 18–21 March 1991.* Ed. J. Trebolle Barrera and L. Vegas Montaner. STDJ 11, 2. Leiden: Brill; Madrid: Editorial Complutense, 1992. Pp. 405–47, with plates.

————. "The Pesher on the Periods (4Q180) and 4Q181." *Israel Oriental Studies* 9 (1979) 77–102.

Dindorf, W., ed. *Georgius Syncellus et Nicephorus.* Corpus scriptorum historiae Byzantinae 6. Bonn: Weber, 1828.

Dols, M. W. "The Black Death in the Middle East." Ph.D. diss., Princeton University, 1971.

Donner, E. "Die literarische Gestalt der alttestamentlichen Josephgeschichte." In *Sitzungsberichte der Heidelberger Akademie der Wissenschaften, Phil.-Hist. Klasse.* 1976, 2. Heidelberg: Winter-Universitätsverlag, 1976.

Doran, R. *Temple Propaganda: The Purpose and Character of 2 Maccabees.* CBQMS 12. Washington, D.C.: Catholic Biblical Association of America, 1981.

Drusius, J. *Henoch: Sive de patriarcha Henoch, eiusque raptu et libro quo Judas Apostolus testimonium profert.* 1615.

Duhm, B. *Das Buch Jeremia.* Kürzer Hand-Kommentar zum Alten Testament 11. Tübingen: J. C. B. Mohr, 1901.

Eckart, K.-G. "Die Kuh des apokryphen Ezechiel." In *Antwort aus der Geschichte.* Ed. W. Sommer and H. Ruppell. Berlin: Christlicher Zeitschriftenverlag, 1969. Pp. 44–48.

Ehrhard, A. *Überlieferung und Bestand der hagiographischen und homiletischen Literatur der grieschen Kirche: Von den Anfängen bis zum Ende des 16. Jahrhunderts.* Vol. 1. TU 50:1. Leipzig: Hinrichs, 1937.

Eisenberg, J. "Ḥizḳil." *EI²* 3.535.

Eisenman, R. H., and M. Wise. *The Dead Sea Scrolls Uncovered.* Shaftesbury: Element, 1992.

Eisenstein, J. D. *Ozar Midrashim.* 2 vols. New York: Eisenstein, 1915.

Elsas, C. *Neuplatonische und gnostische Weltablehnung in der Schule Plotins.* Berlin and New York: de Gruyter, 1975.

Emmerson, R. K. *Antichrist in the Middle Ages.* Manchester: Manchester University Press, 1981.

Endres, J. C. *Biblical Interpretation in the Book of Jubilees.* CBQMS 18. Washington, D.C.: Catholic Biblical Association of America, 1987.

Ephraem Syrus. *Des heiligen Ephraem des Syrers Hymnen de Nativitate (Epiphania).* Ed. E. Beck. 2 vols. CSCO 186, 187. Louvain: Peeters, 1959.

——. *Sancti Ephraem Syri in Genesim et in Exodum commentarii.* Ed. R.-M. Tonneau. 2 vols. CSCO 152, 153. Louvain: Peeters, 1957.

——. *Sermones I.* CSCO 305. Louvain: Université Catholique de Louvain, 1970.

Epiphanius of Salamis, *Ancoratus und Panarion.* Ed. K. Holl. 3 vols. GCS 25, 31, 37. Leipzig: Hinrichs, 1915, 1922, 1933.

Epstein, I., ed. *The Soncino Talmud.* 18 vols. London: Soncino, 1938.

Eusebius Pamphili. *Evangelicae praeparationis.* Ed. and trans. E. H. Gifford. Four volumes in five. Oxford: E Typographeo Academico, 1903.

——. *Die praeparatio evangelica.* Ed. K. Mras. 2 vols. GCS 43. Berlin: Akademie, 1954–56.

Evans, J. M. *Paradise Lost and the Genesis Traditions.* Oxford: Clarendon, 1968.

Evelyn-White, H. G. *The Monasteries of the Wadi'n Natrun.* New York: Metropolitan Museum of Art, 1926–33. Reprint, New York: Arno, 1973.

Fabricius, J. A. *Codex pseudepigraphicus veteris testamenti.* 2d ed. 2 vols. Hamburg: Felginer, 1722–41.

The Facsimile Edition of the Nag Hammadi Codices. 10 vols. Published under the auspices of the Department of Antiquities of the Arab Republic of Egypt and UNESCO. Leiden: Brill, 1973–77.

Faur, J. "The Biblical Idea of Idolatry." *JQR* 69 (1978) 1–15.

Faur, J., and L. I. Rabinowitz. "Idolatry." *EncJud* 8.1227–37.

Feldman, L. H. "Abraham the Greek Philosopher in Josephus." *Transactions of the American Philological Association* 99 (1968) 143–56.

——. "Josephus." *ABD* 3.981–98.

——. "Josephus as a Biblical Interpreter: The 'Aqedah.'" *JQR* 75 (1985) 212–52.

——. "Josephus' Portrait of Joseph." *RB* 99 (1992) 379–417, 504–28.

——. "Josephus' Portrait of Noah and Its Parallels in Philo, Pseudo-Philo's *Biblical Antiquities,* and Rabbinic Midrashim." *PAAJR* 55 (1988) 4–57.

——. "The Sources of Josephus' *Antiquities,* Book 19." *Latomus* 21 (1962) 320–33.

Feltes, H. *Die Gattung des Habakukkommentars von Qumran (1QpHab): Eine Studie zum frühen jüdischen Midrasch.* FB 58. Würzburg: Echter, 1986.

Finkelstein, L. "Some Examples of the Maccabean Halakha." *JBL* 49 (1930) 21–25.

Firestone, R. *Journeys in Holy Lands: The Evolution of the Abraham-Ishmael Legends in Islamic Exegesis.* Albany: State University of New York Press, 1990.

Fishbane, M. *Biblical Interpretation in Ancient Israel.* Oxford: Clarendon, 1985.

———. "From Scribalism to Rabbinism: Perspectives on the Emergence of Classical Judaism." In *The Sage in Israel and the Ancient Near East.* Ed. J. G. Gammie and L. Perdue. Winona Lake, Ind.: Eisenbrauns, 1990. Pp. 439–56.

———. "Use, Authority and Interpretation of Mikra at Qumran." In *Miqra.* Ed. M. J. Mulder. CRINT. Assen: Van Gorcum; Philadelphia: Fortress, 1989. Pp. 339–77.

Fitzmyer, J. A. "The Aramaic 'Elect of God' Text from Qumran Cave 4." In *Essays on the Semitic Background of the New Testament.* SBLSBS 5. Missoula, Mont.: Scholars Press, 1974. Pp. 158–60.

———. "Further Light on Melchizedek from Qumran Cave 11." *JBL* 86 (1967) 25–41.

———. *The Genesis Apocryphon of Qumran Cave 1.* 2d ed. BibOr 18a. Rome: Biblical Institute Press, 1971.

Fossum, J. E. *The Name of God and the Angel of the Lord: Samaritan and Jewish Concepts of Intermediation and the Origin of Gnosticism.* WUNT 36. Tübingen: Mohr-Siebeck, 1985.

Fraade, S. D. *Enosh and His Generation: Pre-Israelite Hero and History in Postbiblical Interpretation.* SBLMS 30. Chico, Calif.: Scholars Press, 1984.

———. "Enosh and His Generation: Scriptural Translation and Interpretation in Late Antiquity." Ph.D. diss., University of Pennsylvania, 1980.

———. *From Tradition to Commentary: Torah and Its Interpretation in the "Midrash Sifre" to Deuteronomy.* Albany: State University of New York Press, 1991.

Fraxman, T. W. *Genesis and the "Jewish Antiquities" of Flavius Josephus.* BibOr 35. Rome: Biblical Institute Press, 1979.

French, P. J. *John Dee: The World of an Elizabethan Magus.* London: Routledge and Kegan Paul, 1972.

Friedländer, M. "La secte de Melchisédec et l'epître aux Hébreux." *REJ* 5 (1882) 1–26, 188–98; 6 (1883) 187–99.

———, trans. *Pirkê de Rabbi Eliezer.* Reprint, New York: Hermon, 1965.

Friedmann, M., ed. *Pesikta Rabbati: Midrasch für den Fest-cyclus und die ausgezeichneten Sabbathe.* Vienna, 1880.

Frost, S. B. *Old Testament Apocalyptic.* London: Epworth, 1952.

Galling, K. *Studien zur Geschichte Israels im persischen Zeitalter.* Tübingen: Mohr (Siebeck) 1964.

Garbini, G. *Storia e ideologia nell'Israele antico.* Brescia: Paideia, 1986.

García Martínez, F. *Qumran and Apocalyptic.* STDJ 9. Leiden: Brill, 1992.

Gardet, L. "al-Ḳiyāma." EI^2 5.235–38.

Geiger, A. *Judaism and Islam.* Tel Aviv: Zohar, 1969.

Geller, B. "Joseph in the Tannaitic Midrashim." In *Studies on the Testament of Joseph*. Ed. G. W. E. Nickelsburg. SBLSCS 5. Missoula, Mont.: Scholars Press, 1975. Pp. 139–46.

Gianotto, C. *Melchisedek e la sua tipologia*. Supplementi alla Rivista Biblica 12. Brescia: Paideia Editrice, 1984.

Gibb, H. A. R., et al., eds. *The Encyclopaedia of Islam*. New ed. Leiden: Brill; London: Luzac, 1960–.

Ginzberg, L. "Adam, Book of." In *The Jewish Encyclopedia*. New York and London: Funk and Wagnalls, 1901. 1.179–80.

———. *Die Haggada bei den Kirchenvätern und in der apokryphischen Litteratur*. Berlin: S. Calvary, 1900.

———. *The Legends of the Jews*. 7 vols. Philadelphia: Jewish Publication Society of America, 1909–38.

Glessmer, U. "Antike und moderne Auslegungen des Sintflutberichtes Gen 6–8 und der Qumran-Pesher 4Q252." In *Mitteilungen und Beiträge 6: Forschungsstelle Judentum theologische Fakultät Leipzig*. Leipzig: Thomas, 1993. Pp. 3–79.

Goitein, S. D. "On the Way to Visit Ezekiel's Tomb." In *Studies on the History of Iraqi Jewry and Their Culture*. Ed. S. Moreh. Vol. 1. Or-Yehuda: Institute for Research on Iraqi Jewry, 1981. Pp. 13–18. In Hebrew.

Goldschmidt, L. *Sefer hajaschar, das Heldenbuch: Sagen, Berichte und Erzählungen aus der israelitischen Urzeit*. Berlin: Harz, 1923.

Goldstein, J. A. *2 Maccabees*. AB 41A. New York: Doubleday, 1984.

Goldziher, I. "Dhū 'l-Kifl." *EI*[1] 2.962–63.

Goodenough, E. R. *By Light, Light*. New Haven: Yale University Press, 1935.

———. *Jewish Symbols in the Greco-Roman Period*. 12 vols. New York: Bollingen, 1965.

Grabbe, L. L. "Josephus and the Reconstruction of the Judean Restoration." *JBL* 106 (1987) 231–46.

Grabowski, V. *Die Geschichte Josefs von Mar Narses nach einer syrischen Handschrift der Königl. Bibliothek in Berlin herausgegeben, übersetzt und kritisch bearbeitet*. Pt. 1. Berlin: Itzkowski, 1889.

Graupner, A. "Jeremia 45 als 'Schlusswort' des Jeremiabuches." In *Altes Testament und christliche Verkündigung: Festschrift für Antnius H. J. Gunneweg zum 65. Geburtstag*. Ed. M. Oeming and A. Graupner. Stuttgart: Kohlhammer, 1987. Pp. 287–308.

Gray, J. *I & II Kings*. 2d ed. London: SCM, 1970.

Green, T. M. *City of the Moon God: Religious Traditions of Harran*. Leiden: Brill, 1992.

Greenfield, J. C., and E. Qimron. "The Genesis Apocryphon, Col. XII." In *Studies in Qumran Aramaic*. Ed. T. Muraoka. Louvain: Peeters, 1992. Pp. 70–77.

Greenfield, J. C., and M. E. Stone. "The Aramaic and Greek Fragments of a Levi Document." In H. W. Hollander and M. de Jonge, *"The Testaments of the Twelve Patriarchs": A Commentary*. SVTP 8. Leiden: Brill, 1985. Appendix 3.

———. "The First Manuscript of the *Aramaic Levi Document* from Qumran (4QLevi[a] aram)." *Mus* 107 (1994) 257–81.

———. "Remarks on the *Aramaic Testament of Levi* from the Geniza." *RB* 86 (1979) 214–30.

Grelot, P. "Hénoch et ses écritures." *RB* 82 (1975) 481–500.

———. "La légende d'Henoch dans les apocryphes et dans la Bible: Origine et signification." *RSR* 46 (1958) 5–26, 181–210.

———. "Le Livre des Jubilés et le Testament de Lévi." *Mélanges Dominique Barthélemy: Etudes bibliques offerts à son 60e anniversaire.* Ed. P. Cassetti, O. Keel, and A. Schenker. OBO 38. Fribourg: Editions Universitaires; Göttingen, Vandenhoeck & Ruprecht, 1981. Pp. 109–33.

Grintz, Y. M. "Baruch ben Neriah." *Encyclopaedia Hebraica.* 9.502. In Hebrew.

Gruenwald, I. "The Messianic Image of Melchizedek." *Mahanaim* 124 (1970) 88–98. In Hebrew.

Grünbaum, M. "Zu 'Jussuf und Suleicha'" and "Zu Schlechta-Wssehrd's Ausgabe des 'Jussuf und Suleicha.'" In *Gesammelte Aufsätze zur Sprach- und Sagenkunde.* Ed. F. Perles. Berlin: Calvary, 1901. Pp. 515–51, 552–93.

Guillaumont, A. "Une Citation de l'Apocryphe d'Ezechiel dans l'exégèse ou sujet de l'ame." In *Essays on the Nag Hammadi Texts.* Ed. M. Krause. Leiden: Brill, 1975. Pp. 35–40.

Gündüz, S. *The Knowledge of Life: The Origins and Early History of the Mandaeans and Their Relation to the Sabians of the Qur'an and to the Harranians.* Oxford: Oxford University Press, 1994.

Gutmann, J. "Joseph Legends in the Vienna Genesis." *Proceedings of the Fifth World Congress of Jewish Studies* 4 (1973) 181–84.

Haas, C. "Job's Perseverance in the *Testament of Job.*" In *Studies on the Testament of Job.* Ed. M. A. Knibb and P. W. van der Horst. SNTSMS 66. Cambridge: Cambridge University Press, 1989. Pp. 117–54.

Habicht, D. *2. Makkabäerbuch.* JSHRZ 1, 3. Gütersloh: Mohn, 1976.

Hagner, D. A. *The Use of the Old and New Testaments in Clement of Rome.* SNT 34. Leiden: Brill, 1973.

Halford, M. E. B. "The Apocryphal *Vita Adae et Evae:* Some Comments on the Manuscript Tradition." *Neuphilologische Mitteilungen* 82 (1981) 417–27.

Halperin, D. *Faces of the Chariot: Early Jewish Responses to Ezekiel's Vision.* Texte und Studien zum antiken Judentum 16. Tübingen: J. C. B. Mohr, 1988.

———. "Heavenly Ascension in Ancient Judaism: The Nature of the Experience." *SBLSP 1987.* Ed. K. H. Richards. Atlanta: Scholars Press, 1987. Pp. 218–32.

Hamburger, K. *Thomas Manns biblisches Werk: Der Joseph-Roman, Die Moses-Erzählung, "Das Gesetz."* Munich: Nymphenburger, 1981.

Hammond, G. *The Making of the English Bible.* Manchester: Carcanet, 1988.

Hansen, G. W. *Abraham in Galatians: Epistolary and Rhetorical Contexts.* JSNTSup 29. Sheffield: Sheffield Academic Press, 1989.

Hanson, P. D. *The Dawn of Apocalyptic.* Rev. ed. Philadelphia: Fortress, 1979.

Harl, M. *La Bible d'Alexandrie—La Genèse.* Paris: Cerf, 1986.

Harlow, D. C. *The Greek Apocalypse of Baruch ("3 Baruch") in Hellenistic Judaism and Early Christianity.* SVTP 12. Leiden: Brill, 1996.

Harrington, D. J. "Abraham Traditions in the *Testament of Abraham* and in the 'Rewritten Bible' of the Intertestamental Period." In *Studies on the Testament of Abraham.* Ed. G. W. E. Nickelsburg. SBLSCS 6. Missoula, Mont.: Scholars Press, 1976. Pp. 165–72.

―――. "Joseph in the *Testament of Joseph,* Pseudo-Philo, and Philo." In *Studies on the Testament of Joseph.* Ed. G. W. E. Nickelsburg. SBLSCS 5. Missoula, Mont.: Scholars Press, 1975. Pp. 127–31.

―――. "The Wisdom of the Scribe according to Ben Sira." In *Ideal Figures in Ancient Judaism.* Ed. G. W. E. Nickelsburg and J. J. Collins. SBLSCS 12. Chico, Calif.: Scholars Press, 1980. Pp. 181–89.

Harris, J. R. *The Rest of the Words of Baruch.* London: Clay, 1889.

―――. *Testimonies I.* Cambridge: Cambridge University Press, 1916.

Hartom, A. S. *Pentateuch, Prophets, Hagiographa: Bible Exegesis according to M. D. Kasuto's Method.* Tel Aviv: Yavneh, 1972. In Hebrew.

Harvey, W. W., ed. *Irenaeus, libros quinque adversus haereses.* Cambridge: Academy, 1857. Reprint, Ridgewood, N.J.: Gregg, 1965.

Hay, D. M. "Politics and Exegesis in Philo's *Treatise on Dreams.*" *SBLSP* 26 (1987) 429–38.

Hayek, M. *Le Mystère d'Ismaël.* Paris: Maison Mame, 1964.

Heidel, A. *The Gilgamesh Epic and Old Testament Parallels.* Chicago: University of Chicago Press, 1963.

Heller, D. "Ezra the Scribe in Islamic Legend." In *Zion.* Jerusalem: The Society of History and Ethnography in Eretz-Israel & Darom Publishers, 1933. Pp. 214–17. In Hebrew.

Herford, R. T. *Talmud and Apocrypha.* New York: Ktav, 1971.

Hess, R. S. "Enoch." *ABD* 2.508.

Hilgert, E. "The Dual Image of Joseph in Hebrew and Early Jewish Literature." *Papers of the Chicago Society of Biblical Research* 30 (1985) 5–21.

Himmelfarb, M. *Ascent to Heaven in Jewish and Christian Apocalypses.* New York: Oxford University Press, 1993.

―――. *Tours of Hell: An Apocalyptic Form in Jewish and Christian Literature.* Philadelphia: Fortress, 1985.

Hippolytus. *Refutatio omnium haeresium.* Ed. P. Wendland. GCS 26:3. Hildesheim and New York: Olms, 1977.

Höffken, P. "Warum schwieg Jesus Sirach über Esra?" *ZAW* 87 (1975) 184–201.

Holl, K., ed. *Epiphanius, Ancoratus und Panarion.* 3 vols. GCS 25, 31, 37. Leipzig: Hinrichs, 1915, 1922, 1933.

Holladay, C. R. *Fragments from Hellenistic Jewish Authors.* Vol. 1, *Historians.* Vol. 2, *Poets.* SBLTT 20, 30. Pseudepigrapha Series 10, 12. Chico, Calif.: Scholars Press, 1983, 1989.

―――. "Pseudo-Eupolemus (Anonymous)." In *Fragments from Hellenistic Jewish Authors.* Vol. 1, *Historians.* Pp. 157–87.

Hollander, H. W. "El 'hombre bueno' en los pasajes éticos del Testamento de Benjamín." *Estudios Franciscanos* 80 (1979) 209–21.

———. "The Influence of the *Testaments of the Twelve Patriarchs* in the Early Church: Joseph as Model in Prochorus' *Acts of John.*" *OLP* 9 (1978) 75–81.

———. *Joseph as an Ethical Model in the "Testaments of the Twelve Patriarchs."* SVTP 6. Leiden: Brill, 1981.

Hollander, H. W., and M. de Jonge. *"The Testaments of the Twelve Patriarchs": A Commentary.* SVTP 8. Leiden: Brill, 1985.

Horst, F. "Die Notiz vom Anfang des Jahwehkultes in Genesis 4,26." In *Libertas Christiana: Friedrich Delekat zum 65. Geburtstag.* Ed. E. Wolf and W. Matthias. Munich: C. Kaiser, 1957. Pp. 68–74.

Horton, F. L., Jr. *The Melchizedek Tradition: A Critical Examination of the Sources to the Fifth Century A.D. and in the Epistle to the Hebrews.* SNTSMS 30. Cambridge: Cambridge University Press, 1976.

Houtsma, M. T., et al., eds. *The Encyclopaedia of Islam.* 1st ed. Leiden: Brill; London: Luzac, 1913–31.

Hultgård, A. *L'eschatologie des Testaments des Douze Patriarches.* 2 vols. Acta Universitatis Upsaliensis, Historia Religionum 6–7. Uppsala: Almqvist & Wiksell, 1977, 1981.

———. "The Ideal 'Levite,' the Davidic Messiah, and the Saviour Priest in the *Testaments of the Twelve Patriarchs.*" In *Ideal Figures in Ancient Judaism: Profiles and Paradigms.* Ed. J. J. Collins and G. W. E. Nickelsburg. SBLSCS 12. Chico, Calif.: Scholars Press, 1980. Pp. 93–110.

Hurtado, L. W. *One God, One Lord: Early Christian Devotion and Ancient Jewish Monotheism.* Philadelphia: Fortress, 1988.

Hussan, P., and P. Nautin. *Origène: Homilies sur Jérémie.* SC 238. Paris: Cerf, 1977.

Hyman, H. *Toledot tanna'im we'amora'im.* Rev. ed. 3 vols. Tel Aviv: Dvir, 1979. In Hebrew.

Idel, M. "Enoch Is Metatron." In *Proceedings of the First International Conference on the History of Jewish Mysticism: Early Jewish Mysticism.* Jerusalem Studies in Jewish Thought 6.1–2. Jerusalem: Hebrew University of Jerusalem, 1987. Pp. 151–70. In Hebrew.

In der Smitten, W. T. *Esra: Quellen, Überlieferung und Geschichte.* SSN 15. Assen: Van Gorcum, 1973.

Isaac, E. "The Ethiopic *History of Joseph:* Translation with Introduction and Notes." *JSP* 6 (1990) 3–125.

Jagic, V. "Slavische Beiträge zu den biblischen Apocryphen, I, Die altkirchenslavischen Texte des Adamsbuche." *Denkschr. kais. Akademie der Wissenschaften, philos.-hist. Classe* (Vienna) 42 (1893) 1–104.

James, M. R. "The Apocryphal Ezekiel." *JTS* 15 (1914) 236–43.

———. "Ego Salathiel qui et Ezras." *JTS* 18 (1917) 167–69.

———. Introduction to *The Fourth Book of Ezra.* Ed. R. L. Bensly. TextsS 3, 2. Cambridge: Cambridge University Press, 1895.

———. *The Lost Apocrypha of the Old Testament: Their Titles and Fragments.* London: SPCK, 1920.

———. "Salathiel qui et Esdras." *JTS* 19 (1918) 347–49.

————, ed. *Apocrypha Anecdota.* TextsS 2, 3. Cambridge: Cambridge University Press, 1893.

————. *Apocrypha Anecdota II.* TextsS 5, 1. Cambridge: Cambridge University Press, 1897.

Jansen, H. L. *Die Henochgestalt: Eine vergleichende religionsgeschichtliche Untersuchung.* Skrifter utgitt av det Norske Videnskaps-Akademi i Oslo, II, Historisk-Filosofisk Klasse, 1939.1. Oslo: I Kommisjon Hos Jacob Dybwad, 1939.

Jansen, J. G. *Studies in the Text of Jeremiah.* HSM 6. Cambridge: Harvard University Press, 1973.

Jastrow, M. *A Dictionary of the Targumim, the Talmud Babli and Yerushalmi, and the Midrashic Literature.* New York: Pardes, 1943.

Jaubert, A. *La notion d'alliance dans le judaïsme aux abords de l'ère chrétienne.* Patristica Sorbonensia 6. Paris: du Seuil, 1963.

————, ed. *Clement de Rome: Epître aux Corinthiens.* SC 167. Paris: Cerf, 1971.

Jellinek, A., ed. *Bet Ha-Midrasch.* 3d ed. 6 vols. Jerusalem: Wahrmann, 1967.

Jeremias, J. *Die Kindertaufe in den ersten vier Jahrhunderten.* Göttingen: Vandenhoeck & Ruprecht, 1958.

————. *Unknown Sayings of Jesus.* 2d ed. London: SPCK, 1964.

Josephus. *Complete Works.* Ed. and trans. H. St. J. Thackeray et al. 9 vols. LCL. London: Heinemann; Cambridge: Harvard University Press, 1926–65.

Kahle, P. E. *Bala'izah: Coptic Texts from Deir El-Bala'izeh in Upper Egypt.* London: Oxford University Press, 1954.

Kampen, J. *The Hasideans and the Origin of Pharisaism: A Study of 1 and 2 Maccabees.* SBLSCS 24. Atlanta: Scholars, 1988.

Käsemann, E. "The Faith of Abraham in Romans 4." In *Perspectives on Paul.* Philadelphia: Fortress, 1971. Pp. 79–101.

Katz, P. *Philo's Bible.* Cambridge: Cambridge University Press, 1950.

Kellermann, U. *Nehemia: Quellen, Überlieferung, und Geschichte.* BZAW 102. Berlin: Töpelmann, 1967.

Kenyon, F. G. *The Chester Beatty Biblical Papyri: Descriptions and Texts of Twelve Manuscripts on Papyrus of the Greek Bible.* Fascicle 8: *Enoch and Melito.* London: E. Walker, 1941.

Kessler, M. "Jeremiah Chapters 26–45 Reconsidered." *JNES* 27 (1968) 81–88.

Khadduri, M. *War and Peace in the Law of Islam.* Baltimore: Johns Hopkins University Press, 1955.

Kikawada, I. M. "Noah and the Ark." *ABD* 4.1123–31.

King, J. R. "The Joseph Story and Divine Politics: A Comparative Study of a Biographic Formula from the Ancient Near East." *JBL* 106 (1987) 577–94.

Kirschbaum, E., ed. *Lexikon der christlichen Ikonographie.* 8 vols. Rome: Herder, 1968–76.

Kister, M. "Barnabas 12:1; 4:3 and 4Q Second Ezekiel." *RB* 97 (1990) 63–67.

————. "Observations on Aspects of Exegesis, Tradition, and Theology in Midrash, Pseudepigrapha, and Other Jewish Writings." In *Tracing the Threads: Studies in the Vitality of Jewish Pseudepigrapha.* Ed. J. C. Reeves. SBLEJL 6. Atlanta: Scholars Press, 1994. Pp. 1–34.

————. "Some Aspects of Qumranic Halakhah." In *The Madrid Qumran Congress: Proceedings of the International Congress on the Dead Sea Scrolls, Madrid, 18–21 March 1991.* Ed. J. Trebolle Barrera and L. Vegas Montaner. STDJ 11, 2. Leiden: Brill; Madrid: Editorial Complutense, 1992. Pp. 571–88.

Kister, M., and E. Qimron. "Observations on 4QSecond Ezekiel." *RevQ* 15 (1992) 595–602.

Klauser, T. "Abraham." *RAC* 1.18–27.

Klausner Y., et al., eds. *The Encyclopaedia Hebraica.* Jerusalem and Tel Aviv: HE—The Society of Encyclopaedias Publishing, 1949–81. In Hebrew.

Klein, M. L., ed. *The Fragment-Targums of the Pentateuch according to Their Extant Sources.* 2 vols. Rome: Biblical Institute Press, 1980.

Klein, R. W. "Ezra," "Nehemiah." *HBC* 372–78, 379–86.

————. "Ezra and Nehemiah in Recent Studies." In *Magnalia Dei: The Mighty Acts of God. In Memoriam G. Ernest Wright.* Ed. F. M. Cross, W. E. Lemke, and P. D. Miller. Garden City, N.Y.: Doubleday, 1976. Pp. 361–76.

Klijn, A. F. J. *Seth in Jewish, Christian, and Gnostic Literature.* NovTSup 46. Leiden: Brill, 1977.

————, ed. *Der lateinische Text der Apokalypse des Esra.* TU 131. Berlin: Akademie, 1983.

Klostermann, E., ed. *Origenes Werke: Zehnter Band-Origenes Matthäuserklärung: 1 Die griechische erhaltenen Tomoi.* GCS 40. Leipzig: Hinrichs, 1935.

————, ed. *Origenes Werke: Elfter Band-Origenes Matthäuserklärung: 2 Die lateinische Übersetzung der Commentariorum Series.* GCS 38. Leipzig: Hinrichs, 1933.

Knibb, M. A. *The Ethiopic Book of Enoch.* 2 vols. Oxford: Clarendon, 1978.

Knox, W. L. "Abraham and the Quest for God." *HTR* 28 (1935) 55–60.

Kobelski, P. J. *Melchizedek and Melchiresa'.* CBQMS 10. Washington, D.C.: Catholic Biblical Association of America, 1981.

Korteweg, T. "The Meaning of Naphtali's Visions." In *Studies on the "Testaments of the Twelve Patriarchs": Text and Interpretation.* Ed. M. de Jonge. SVTP 3. Leiden: Brill, 1975. Pp. 261–90.

Kraft, R. A. "Christian Transmission of Greek Jewish Scriptures: A Methodological Probe." In *Paganisme, judaisme, christianisme: Influences et affrontements dans le monde antique: Mélanges offerts à Marcel Simon.* Ed. A. Benoit et al. Paris: Boccard, 1978. Pp. 207–26.

————. *The Didache and Barnabas.* Vol. 3 of *The Apostolic Fathers.* Ed. R. M. Grant. New York: Thomas Nelson & Sons, 1965.

————. "'Ezra' Materials in Judaism and Christianity." *ANRW* II.19.1. Ed. W. Haase. Berlin: de Gruyter, 1979. Pp. 119–36.

————. "Philo on Seth." In Layton, ed., *Rediscovery* 2.457–58.

————. "The Pseudepigrapha in Christianity." In *Tracing the Threads: Studies in the Vitality of Jewish Pseudepigrapha.* Ed. J. C. Reeves. SBLEJL 6. Atlanta: Scholars Press, 1994. Pp. 55–86.

Kraft, R. A., and A.-E. Purintun, eds. and trans. *Paraleipomena Jeremiou.* SBLTT 1, Pseudepigrapha Series 1. Missoula, Mont.: Society of Biblical Literature, 1972.

Krämer, H. J. *Der Ursprung der Geistmetaphysik.* Amsterdam: B. R. Grüner, 1964. 2d ed., 1967.

Krause, M., and P. Labib, eds. and trans. *Die drei Versionen des Apocryphon des Johannes im koptischen Museum zu Alt-Kairo.* Abhandlungen des deutschen archäologischen Instituts Kairo, koptische Reihe 1. Wiesbaden: O. Harrassowitz, 1962.

Kronholm, T. *Motifs from Genesis 1–11 in the Genuine Hymns of Ephrem the Syrian with Particular Reference to the Influence of Jewish Exegetical Tradition.* ConBOT 11. Lund: Gleerup, 1978.

Kugel, J. L. *In Potiphar's House: The Interpretive Life of Biblical Texts.* San Francisco: Harper, 1990.

———. "Levi's Elevation to the Priesthood in Second Temple Writings." *HTR* 86 (1993) 1–64.

———. "The Story of Dinah in the *Testament of Levi.*" *HTR* 85 (1992) 1–34.

———. "Two Introductions to Midrash." *Prooftexts* 3 (1983) 131–55.

Kugler, R. A. *From Patriarch to Priest: The Levi-Priestly Tradition from Aramaic Levi to "Testament of Levi."* SBLEJL 9. Atlanta: Scholars Press, 1996.

Kvanvig, H. S. *Roots of Apocalyptic: The Mesopotamian Background of the Enoch Figure and of the Son of Man.* WMANT 61. Neukirchen-Vluyn: Neukirchener Verlag, 1988.

Lafargue, M. "The Jewish Orpheus." *SBLSP 1978.* Ed. P. K. Achtemeier. Missoula, Mont.: Scholars Press, 1978. 2.137–44.

Lambert, W. G. "Enmeduranki and Related Matters." *JCS* 21 (1967) 126–38.

Lambert, W. G., and A. Millard. *Atra-hasis.* Oxford: Oxford University Press, 1969.

Lamy, T. J., ed. *Sancti Ephraem Syri, Hymni et Sermones.* 4 vols. Mechliniae: Dessain, 1882–1902.

Larcher, C. *Le Livre de la Sagesse ou la Sagesse de Salomon.* Ebib, n.s., 3. Paris: Gabalda, 1984.

Lauterbach, J., ed. and trans. *Mekilta de-Rabbi Ishmael.* 3 vols. Philadelphia: Jewish Publication Society, 1933–35.

Layton, B., ed. *The Rediscovery of Gnosticism: Proceedings of the International Conference on Gnosticism at Yale, March 28–31, 1978.* Vol. 2: *Sethian Gnosticism.* Supplements to Numen 41. Leiden: Brill, 1981.

———, trans. "The Hypostasis of the Archons." In *Nag Hammadi Codex II,2–7, Together with XIII,2*, Brit. Lib. Or. 4926(1) and P. Oxy. 1, 654, 655.* Vol. 1: *"Gospel according to Thomas," "Gospel according to Philip," "Hypostasis of the Archons," and Indexes.* Ed. B. Layton. NHS 21. Leiden: Brill, 1989.

Lazarus-Yafeh, H. *Intertwined Worlds: Medieval Islam and Bible Criticism.* Princeton, N.J.: Princeton University Press, 1992.

Lebeau, J. *Salvator Mundi, L' 'exemple' de Joseph dans le théâtre allemand au XVIe siècle.* 2 vols. Nieuwkoop: De Graaf, 1977.

Lebram, J. C. H. *Legitimiteit en charisma: Over de herleving van de contemporaine geschiedschrijving in het jodendom tijdens de 2e eeuw v. Chr.* Leiden: Brill, 1980.

Le Déaut, R. "Le titre de *summus sacerdos* donné a Melchisédech est-il d'origine juive?" *RSR* 50 (1962) 222–29.

Lee, T. R. *Studies in the Form of Sirach 44–50.* SBLDS 75. Atlanta: Scholars Press, 1986.

Leslau, W. *Falasha Anthology.* Yale Judaica Series 6. New Haven: Yale University Press, 1951.

Lévi, I. "L'apocalypse de Zorobabel." *REJ* 68 (1914) 129–60.

Levison, J. *Portraits of Adam in Early Judaism: From Sirach to 2 Baruch.* JSOTSup 1. Sheffield: JSOT Press, 1988.

Lewis, J. P. *A Study of the Interpretation of Noah and the Flood in Jewish and Christian Literature.* Leiden: Brill, 1968.

Licht, J. "The Plant Eternal and the People of Divine Deliverance." In *Essays on the Dead Sea Scrolls in Memory of E. L. Sukenik.* Ed. C. Rabin and Y. Yadin. Jerusalem: Heikal ha-sefer, 1961. Pp. 49–75. In Hebrew.

Liebes, Y. "The Angels of the Shofar and Yeshua Sar ha-Panim." In *Proceedings of the First International Conference on the History of Jewish Mysticism: Early Jewish Mysticism.* Jerusalem Studies in Jewish Thought 6.1–2. Jerusalem: Hebrew University of Jerusalem, 1987. Pp. 171–96. In Hebrew.

Lieu, S. N. C. *Manichaeism.* Manchester: Manchester University Press, 1985.

Lim, T. H. "The Chronology of the Flood Story in a Qumran Text (4Q252)." *JJS* 43 (1992) 288–98.

Lindars, B. "Enoch and Christology." *ExpTim* 92 (1980–81) 295–99.

Lipscomb, W. L. *The Armenian Apocryphal Adam Literature.* University of Pennsylvania Armenian Texts and Studies 8. Atlanta: Scholars Press, 1990.

Loewenstamm, S. E. "The Death of Moses." In *Studies on the Testament of Abraham.* Ed. G. W. E. Nickelsburg. SBLSCS 6. Missoula, Mont.: Scholars Press, 1976. Pp. 185–217.

Lohse, E. *Colossians and Philemon.* Hermeneia. Philadelphia: Fortress, 1971.

Lowenthal, E. I. *The Joseph Narrative in Genesis.* New York: Ktav, 1973.

Lührmann, D. *Galatians.* Continental Commentaries. Minneapolis: Fortress, 1992.

———. "Noah und Lot (Lk 17,26–29)." In *Die Redaktion der Logienquelle.* WMANT 33. Neukirchen-Vluyn: Neukirchener Verlag, 1969. Pp. 75–83.

Lundbom, J. R. "Baruch, Seraiah, and Expanded Colophons in the Book of Jeremiah." *JSOT* 36 (1986) 89–114.

Macdonald, J. "Joseph in the Qur'an and Muslim Commentary: A Comparative Study." *The Muslim World* 46 (1956) 113–31, 207–24.

Mach, M. *Entwicklungstudien des jüdischen Engelglaubens in vorrabbinischer Zeit.* Texte und Studien zum antiken Judentum 34. Tübingen: Mohr-Siebeck, 1992.

MacRae, G. W. "Seth in Gnostic Texts and Traditions." *SBLSP 1977.* Ed. P. K. Achtemeier. Missoula, Mont.: Scholars Press, 1977. Pp. 17–24.

————, trans. "The Apocalypse of Adam." In *Nag Hammadi Codices V,2–5 and VI with Papyrus Berolinensis 8502,1 and 4.* Ed. D. M. Parrott. NHS 11. Leiden: Brill, 1979.

Mahé, J.-P. "Le livre d'Adam géorgien." In *Studies in Gnosticism and Hellenistic Religions.* Ed. R. van den Broek and M. J. Vermaseren. Leiden: Brill, 1981. Pp. 227–60.

Margalioth, M. *Sepher ha-Razim.* Jerusalem: American Academy of Jewish Research, 1966.

Margulies, M., ed. *Midrash Wayyikra Rabbah.* 5 vols. Jerusalem, 1953–60. Reprint, five volumes in three, Jerusalem: Wahrmann, 1972. In Hebrew.

Marmorstein, B. "Die Gestalt Josefs in der Agada und die Evangelien-geschichte." *ΑΓΓΕΛΟΣ: Archiv für neutestamentliche Zeitgeschichte und Kulturkunde* 4 (1932) 51–55.

Martin-Achard, R. *Actualité d'Abraham.* Neuchâtel, Switzerland: Delachaux & Niestle, 1969.

Massignon, L. "Inventaire de la littérature hermétique arabe." In *La révélation d'Hermès Trismégiste.* Ed. R. P. Festugière. 2d ed. 4 vols. Paris: Gabalda, 1950. 1.384–400.

Masson, D. *Le Coran et la révélation Judéo-Chrétienne.* Paris: Adrien-Maisonneuve, 1958.

Mathews, E. [and J. Amar]. *St. Ephrem the Syrian, Selected Prose Works.* Washington, D.C.: Catholic University of America Press, 1994.

Matter, E. A. "The 'Revelatio Esdrae' in Latin and English Traditions." *RBén* 42 (1982) 376–92.

Mayer, G. "Aspekte des Abrahambildes in der hellenistisch-jüdischen Literatur." *EvT* 32 (1972) 118–27.

Meinhold, A. "Die Gattung der Josephgeschichte und des Estherbuches: Diasporanovelle." *ZAW* 87 (1975) 306–24; 88 (1976) 72–93.

Meyer, W. "Die Geschichte des Kreuzholzes vor Christus." *Abhandlungen der philosophisch-philologischen Klasse der königlich bayerischen Akademie der Wissenschaften* (Munich) 14 (1879) 187–250.

————. "Vita Adae et Evae." In *Abhandlungen der königlich bayerischen Akademie der Wissenschaften, Philosophisch-philologische Klasse.* Munich, 1878. Pp. 185–250.

Midrash rabba 'al hamissa hummese tora wehamesh megillot. 2 vols. Vilna: Romm, 1884–87. In Hebrew.

Midrash tanhuma 'al hamissa hummese tora. Jerusalem: Lewin-Epstein, 1973–74. In Hebrew.

Milgrom, J. *The Binding of Isaac.* Berkeley, Calif.: Bibal, 1988.

Milik, J. T. *The Books of Enoch: Aramaic Fragments of Qumran Cave 4.* Oxford: Clarendon, 1976.

————. "4Q Visions de 'Amram et une citation d'Origène." *RB* 79 (1972) 77–97.

————. "Le testament de Lévi en araméen: Fragment de la grotte 4 de Qumrân." *RB* 62 (1955) 398–406.

————. "Turfan et Qumran, livre des Géants juif et manichéen." In *Tradition und Glaube: Das frühe Christentum in seiner Umwelt.* Ed. J. Jeremias,

H.-W. Kuhn, and H. Stegemann. Göttingen: Vandenhoeck & Ruprecht, 1971. Pp. 117–27.

————, ed. *Qumran Cave I*. DJD 1. Oxford: Clarendon, 1955.

Mir, M. "The Qur'anic Story of Joseph: Plot, Themes, and Characters." *The Muslim World* 76 (1986) 1–15.

Molenberg, C. "A Study of the Roles of Shemihaza and Asael in *1 Enoch* 6–11." *JJS* 35 (1984) 136–46.

Moore, C. A. "Toward Dating the Book of Baruch." *CBQ* 36 (1974) 312–20.

Mopsik, C. *Le livre hébreu d'Hénoch*. Paris: Verdier, 1989.

Morray-Jones, C. "Transformational Mysticism in the Apocalyptic-Merkabah Tradition." *JJS* 43 (1992) 1–31.

Moubarac, Y. *Abraham dans le Coran*. Paris: J. Vrin, 1958.

Mowinckel, S. *Zur Komposition des Buches Jeremia*. Kristiania: Dybwad, 1914.

Mozley, J. H. "The Vitae Adae." *JTS* 30 (1929) 121–49.

Mueller, J. R. *The Five Fragments of the Apocryphon of Ezekiel: A Critical Study*. JSPSup 5. Sheffield: Sheffield Academic Press, 1994.

————. "Riding Piggyback in Antiquity: The Motif of the Lame Man and the Blind Man in Ancient Literature." Paper presented at the Annual Meeting of the Society of Biblical Literature, Atlanta, November 1986.

Muilenburg, J. "Baruch the Scribe." In *Proclamation and Presence*. Ed. J. I. Durham and J. R. Porter. Richmond: John Knox, 1970. Pp. 232–38.

Munk, M. "Esra der Schriftgelehrte nach Talmud und Midrasch." Diss., Würzburg, 1930.

Muntner, Z. *Introduction to the Book of Asaf the Physician*. Jerusalem: Geniza, 1961.

Murdoch, B. "An Early Irish Adam and Eve: *Saltair na Rann* and the Traditions of the Fall." *Mediaeval Studies* 35 (1973) 146–77.

Murphy, F. J. *Pseudo-Philo: Rewriting the Bible*. New York: Oxford University Press, 1993.

————. *The Structure and Meaning of Second Baruch*. Atlanta: Scholars Press, 1985.

Murtonen, A. "The Figure of Metatron." *VT* 3 (1953) 409–11.

Myers, J. M. *Ezra, Nehemiah*. AB 14. Garden City, N.Y.: Doubleday, 1965.

————. *I and II Esdras*. AB 42. Garden City, N.Y.: Doubleday, 1974.

Nabholz-Oberlin, M. *Der Josephroman in der deutschen Literatur von Grimmelshausen bis Thomas Mann*. Marburg: Bauer, 1950.

Näf, H. *Syrische Josef-Gedichte: Mit Übersetzung des Gedichts von Narsai und Proben aus Balai und Jaqob von Sarug*. Zürich: Schwarzenbach, 1923.

Nagel, M. "La Vie grecque d'Adam et d'Eve." Ph.D. diss., Strassbourg, 1974.

Nagel, T. "Die Qiṣaṣ al-Anbiyā: Ein Beitrag zur arabischen Literaturgeschichte." Thesis, Bonn, 1967.

Neusner, J. "Note on Barukh ben Neriah and Zoroaster." *Numen* 12:1 (1965) 66–69.

————. "Sage, Priest, Messiah: Three Types of Judaism in the Age of Jesus." In *Judaism in the Beginning of Christianity*. Philadelphia: Fortress, 1984. Pp. 35–44.

————, trans. *Genesis Rabbah: The Judaic Commentary on the Book of Genesis, a New American Translation.* 3 vols. BJS 101. Atlanta: Scholars Press, 1985.

Neuss, W. *Das Buch Ezechiel in Theologie und Kunst.* Münster: Aschendorf, 1912.

Nickelsburg, G. W. E. "Apocalyptic and Myth in *1 Enoch* 6–11." *JBL* 96 (1977) 383–405.

————. "The Bible Rewritten and Expanded." In *Jewish Writings of the Second Temple Period.* Ed. M. E. Stone. CRINT. Assen: Van Gorcum; Philadelphia: Fortress, 1984. Pp. 97–104.

————. "*1 Enoch* and Qumran Origins: The State of the Question and Some Prospects for Answers." *SBLSP 1986.* Atlanta: Scholars Press, 1986. Pp. 341–60.

————. *Jewish Literature between the Bible and the Mishnah.* Philadelphia: Fortress, 1981.

————. "Narrative Traditions in the *Paraleipomena of Jeremiah* and *2 Baruch.*" *CBQ* 35 (1973) 60–68.

————. *Resurrection, Immortality, and Eternal Life in Intertestamental Judaism.* HTS 26. Cambridge: Harvard University Press, 1972.

————. "Revealed Wisdom as a Criterion for Inclusion and Exclusion: From Jewish Sectarianism to Early Christianity." In *To See Ourselves As Others See Us: Christians, Jews, "Others" in Late Antiquity.* Ed. J. Neusner and E. S. Frerichs. Chico, Calif.: Scholars Press, 1985. Pp. 73–81.

————. "Some Related Traditions in the *Apocalypse of Adam,* the *Books of Adam and Eve,* and *1 Enoch.*" In Layton, ed., *Rediscovery* 2.514–39.

————, ed. *Studies on the Testament of Abraham.* SBLSCS 6. Missoula, Mont.: Scholars Press, 1976.

————. *Studies on the Testament of Joseph.* SBLSCS 5. Missoula, Mont.: Scholars Press, 1975.

Niehoff, M. *The Figure of Joseph in Post-biblical Jewish Literature.* AGJU 16. Leiden: Brill, 1992.

Nohrnberg, J. *Fairie Queen: The Analogy of the Fairie Queen.* Princeton, N.J.: Princeton University Press, 1976.

Norelli, E. "Due 'testimonia' attribuiti a Esdra." *Annali di Storia dell' Esegesi* 1 (1984) 231–82.

North, R. "Ezra." *ABD* 2.726–28.

Novak, D. *The Image of the Non-Jew in Judaism: An Historical and Constructive Study of the Noahide Laws.* Toronto: Mellen, 1983.

Obermann, J. "Islamic Origins: A Study in Background and Foundation." In *The Arab Heritage.* Ed. N. A. Faris. Princeton, N.J.: Princeton University Press, 1944. Pp. 58–119.

Odeberg, H., ed. and trans. *"3 Enoch"; or the Hebrew Book of Enoch.* Cambridge: Cambridge University Press, 1928. Reprint with a prolegomenon by J. C. Greenfield, New York: Ktav, 1973.

Olyan, S. M. "Ben Sira's Relationship to the Priesthood." *HTR* 80 (1987) 261–86.

Pagels, E. *Adam, Eve, and the Serpent.* New York: Random Books, 1988.

The Palestinian Targum to the Pentateuch: Codex Vatican [Tg. Neofiti]. Facsimile ed. Jerusalem: Makor, 1970.

Parrott, D. M. "Evidence for Religious Syncretism in Gnostic Texts from Nag Hammadi." In *Religious Syncretism: Essays in Conversation with Geo Widengren.* Ed. B. A. Pearson. Missoula, Mont.: Scholars Press, 1975. Pp. 175–80.

———. "Introduction." In *Nag Hammadi Codices III,3–4 and V,1 with Papyrus Berolinensis 8502,3 and Oxyrhynchus Papyrus 1081: Eugnostos and the Sophia of Jesus Christ.* Ed. D. M. Parrott. NHS 27. Leiden: Brill, 1991.

———, trans. "Eugnostos the Blessed." In *Nag Hammadi Codices III,3–4 and V,1 with Papyrus Berolinensis 8502,3 and Oxyrhynchus Papyrus 1081.*

Pearson, B. A. "The Figure of Melchizedek in Gnostic Literature." In Pearson, *Gnosticism, Judaism, and Egyptian Christianity.* Pp. 108–23.

———. "The Figure of Norea in Gnostic Literature." In *Proceedings of the International Colloquium on Gnosticism, Stockholm, August 20–25, 1973.* Ed. G. Widengren. Kungl. Vitterhets Historie och Antikvitets Akademiens Handlingar, Filologisk–filosofiska serien 17. Stockholm: Almqvist & Wiksell, 1977. Pp. 143–52. Reprint in Pearson, *Gnosticism, Judaism, and Egyptian Christianity.* Pp. 84–94.

———. "The Figure of Seth in Gnostic Literature." In Layton, ed., *Rediscovery.* 2.472–504. Reprint in Pearson, *Gnosticism, Judaism, and Egyptian Christianity.* Pp. 52–83.

———. "Gnosticism as Platonism: With Special Reference to *Marsanes.*" *HTR* 77 (1984) 55–73. Reprint in Pearson, *Gnosticism, Judaism and Egyptian Christianity.* Pp. 148–64.

———. *Gnosticism, Judaism, and Egyptian Christianity.* SAC 5. Minneapolis: Fortress, 1990.

———. "Introduction." In *Nag Hammadi Codices IX and X.* Ed. B. A. Pearson. NHS 15. Leiden: Brill, 1981.

———. "Is Gnosticism a Religion?" In *The Notion of "Religion" in Comparative Research: Selected Proceedings of the XVI IAHR Congress.* Ed. U. Bianchi. Roma: "L'Erma" di Bretschneider, 1994. Pp. 105–14.

———. "Jewish Haggadic Traditions in the *Testimony of Truth* from Nag Hammadi (CG IX,3)." In *Ex Orbe Religionum: Studia Geo Widengren.* Ed. J. Bergman et al. Supplements to Numen 21. Leiden: Brill, 1972.

———. *Nag Hammadi Codices IX and X.* NHS 15. Leiden: Brill, 1981.

———. "The Pierpont Morgan Fragments of a Coptic Enoch Apocryphon." In *Studies in the Testament of Abraham.* Ed. G. W. E. Nickelsburg. SBLSCS 6. Missoula, Mont.: Scholars Press, 1976. Pp. 227–84.

———. "Revisiting Norea." In *Images of the Feminine in Gnosticism.* Ed. K. L. King. Studies in Christianity and Antiquity. Philadelphia: Fortress, 1988. Pp. 265–75.

———. "The Tractate *Marsanes* (NHC X) and the Platonic Tradition." In *Gnosis: Festschrift für Hans Jonas.* Ed. B. Aland. Göttingen: Vandenhoeck & Ruprecht, 1978. Pp. 373–84.

———, trans. "Marsanes." In *Nag Hammadi Codices IX and X.* Ed. B. A. Pearson. NHS 15. Leiden: Brill, 1981.

Pearson, B. A., and S. Giverson, trans. "Melchizedek" and "The Thought of Norea." In *Nag Hammadi Codices IX and X*. Ed. B. A. Pearson. NHS 15. Leiden: Brill, 1981.

Perkins, P. "Apocalyptic Schematization in the *Apocalypse of Adam* and the *Gospel of the Egyptians*." *SBLSP 1972*. Missoula, Mont.: Scholars Press, 1972. Pp. 591–95.

Perrot, C., and P.-M. Bogaert, eds. *Pseudo-Philon: Les antiquités bibliques.* Vol. 2: *Introductione littéraire, commentaire et index.* Paris: Cerf, 1976.

Peshitta Institute, Leiden. *Vetus Testamentum Syriace: Iuxta simplicem syrorus versionem.* Pt. 1, fascicle 1. Leiden: Brill, 1977.

Petuchowski, J. J. "The Controversial Figure of Melchizedek." *HUCA* 28 (1957) 127–36.

Philo. *Complete Works.* Ed. and trans. F. H. Colson, R. Marcus, and C. H. Whitaker. 10 vols. and 2 supp. vols. LCL. London: Heinemann; Cambridge: Harvard University Press, 1929–62.

Philonenko, M. "Une allusion de l'Asclépius au livre d'Henoch." In *Christianity, Judaism, and Other Greco-Roman Cults.* Ed. J. Neusner. 4 vols. Leiden: Brill, 1975. 2.161–63.

———. *Joseph et Aséneth: Introduction, texte critique et notes.* SPB 13. Leiden: Brill, 1968.

———. "Paradoxes Stoïciens dans le Testament de Lévi." In *Sagesse et Religion: Colloque de Strasbourg.* Ed. E. Jacob. Paris: Presses Universitaires de France, 1979. Pp. 99–104.

Picard, J.-C. "Observations sur l'Apocalypse grecque de Baruch I: Cadre historique fictif et efficacité symbolique." *Sem* 20 (1970) 77–103.

———, ed. *Apocalypsis Baruchi Graece.* PVTG 2. Leiden: Brill, 1967.

Pichard, A. *De livre d'Hénoch sur l'amitié.* Paris: Dondey-Dupré, 1838.

Pohlmann, K.-F. *3. Esra-Buch.* JSHRZ 1, 5. Gütersloh: Mohn, 1980.

Prawer, J. *The History of the Jews in the Latin Kingdom of Jerusalem.* Oxford: Clarendon, 1988.

Priebatsch, H. *Die Josephgeschichte in der Weltliteratur: Eine legendgeschichtliche Studie.* Breslau: Marcus, 1937.

Prigent, P., and R. A. Kraft. *Epître de Barnabé.* SC 172. Paris: Cerf, 1971.

Puech, E. "Fragments d'un apocryphe de Lévi et le personnage eschatologique: 4QTest Lévi[c-d] (?) et 4QAJa." In *The Madrid Qumran Congress: Proceedings of the International Congress on the Dead Sea Scrolls, Madrid, 18–21 March 1991.* Ed. J. Trebolle Barrera and L. Vegas Montaner. STDJ 11, 2. Leiden: Brill; Madrid: Editorial Complutense, 1992. Pp. 449–501.

———. "Le Testament de Qahat en araméen de la grotte 4 (*4QTQah*)." *RevQ* 16 (1991) 23–54.

Purvis, J. D. "Joseph in the Samaritan Traditions." In *Studies on the Testament of Joseph.* Ed. G. W. E. Nickelsburg. SBLSCS 5. Missoula, Mont.: Scholars Press, 1975. Pp. 147–53.

Qimron, E., and J. Strugnell. *Qumran Cave 4. V: Miqsat Ma'ase ha-Torah.* DJD 10. Oxford: Clarendon, 1994.

Quinn, E. C. *The Quest of Seth for the Oil of Life.* Chicago: University of Chicago Press, 1962.

Rahlfs, A., ed. *Septuaginta: Vetus Testamentum Graece iuxta LXX interpretes.* 2 vols. Stuttgart: Württembergische Bibelanstalt, 1935.

Reese, G. " Die Geschichte Israels in der Auffassung des frühen Judentums." Ph.D. thesis, Heidelberg, 1967.

Reeves, J. C. *Jewish Lore in Manichaean Cosmogony.* HUCM 14. Cincinnati: Hebrew Union College Press, 1992.

Rendsburg, G. A. "Literary Structures in the Qur'anic and Biblical Stories of Joseph." *The Muslim World* 78 (1988) 118–20.

Resch, A. *Agrapha: Aussercanonische Schriftfragmente.* 2d ed. TU 30/3–4. Leipzig: Hinrichs, 1906.

Riaud, J. "La figure de Jérémiae dans les Paralipomena Jeremia." In *Mélanges bibliques et orientaux en l'honneur de M. Henri Cazelles.* Ed. A. Caquot and M. Delcor. AOAT 212. Kevelaer: Butzon & Bercker; Neukirchen-Vluyn: Neukirchener Verlag, 1981. Pp. 373–85.

Richard, E. "The Polemical Character of the Joseph Episode in Acts 7." *JBL* 98 (1979) 255–67.

Ringgren, H. "Die Versuchung Josefs (Gen 39)." In *Die Väter Israels. Beiträge zur Theologie der Patriarchenüberlieferungen im Alten Testament.* Ed. M. Görg and A. R. Müller. Stuttgart: Katholisches Bibelwerk, 1989. Pp. 267–70.

Robinson, J. M. "The *Three Steles of Seth* and the Gnostics of Plotinus." In *Proceedings of the International Colloquium on Gnosticism, August 20–25, 1973.* Stockholm: Almqvist and Wiksell, 1977. Pp. 132–42.

———, ed. *The Coptic Gnostic Library: Edited with English Translation, Introduction, and Notes.* Published under the auspices of the Institute for Antiquity and Christianity. NHS 4, 11, 13, 15, 21, and 28. Leiden: Brill, 1975–.

Robinson, J. M., and M. W. Meyer, eds. *The Nag Hammadi Library in English.* San Francisco: Harper and Row, 1981.

Rönsch, H. *Das Buch der Jubiläen.* Leipzig: Fues, 1874.

Rosenthal, F., trans. *The History of al-Tabari.* Albany: State University of New York Press, 1989.

Rosner, B. S. "A Possible Quotation of *Test. Reuben* 5:5 in 1 Corinthians 6:18 A." *JTS*, n.s., 43 (1992) 123–27.

Roth, C., et al., eds. *Encyclopaedia Judaica.* Jerusalem: Keter, 1971–72.

Rowland, C. C. *The Open Heaven: A Study of Apocalyptic in Judaism and Early Christianity.* London: SPCK, 1982.

———. "The Visions of God in Apocalyptic Literature." *JSJ* 10 (1979) 137–54.

Rowley, H. H. "Melchizedek and Zadok (Gen 14 and Ps 110)." In *Festschrift Alfred Bertholet.* Ed. W. Baumgartner et al. Tübingen: Mohr-Siebeck, 1950. Pp. 461–72.

Rudolph, W. *Chronikbücher.* HAT 1, 21. Tübingen: Mohr (Siebeck), 1955.

Ruppert, L. "Zur neueren Diskussion um die Josefsgeschichte der Genesis." *BZ* 33 (1989) 92–97.

Russell, D. S. *The Method and Message of Jewish Apocalyptic.* London: SCM, 1964.

Ruwet, J. "Les 'agrapha' dans le oeuvres de Clement d'Alexandrie." *Bib* 30 (1949) 133–60.

———. "Clement d'Alexandrie, canon des escritures et apocryphe." *Bib* 29 (1948) 77–99, 240–68.

Sandmel, S. "Genesis 4:26b." *HUCA* 32 (1961) 19–29.

———. *Philo's Place in Judaism: A Study of Conceptions of Abraham in Jewish Literature.* Cincinnati: Hebrew Union College Press, 1956. Reprint, New York: Ktav, 1971.

Sarna, N., et al. "Abraham." *EncJud* 1.111–25.

Satran, D. *Biblical Prophets in Byzantine Palestine: Reassessing the Lives of the Prophets.* SVTP 11. Leiden: Brill, 1995.

Sawyer, J. F. A. "Cain and Hephaestus: Possible Relics of Metalworking Traditions in Genesis 4." *AbrN* 24 (1986) 155–66.

Sayler, G. B. *Have the Promises Failed? A Literary Analysis of 2 Baruch.* SBLDS 72. Chico, Calif.: Scholars Press, 1984.

Schaeder, H. H. *Esra der Schreiber.* BHT 5. Tübingen: Mohr, 1930.

Schäfer, P. "Adam in jüdischen Überlieferung." In *Vom alten zum neuen Adam: Urzeitmythos und Heilsgeschichte.* Ed. W. Strolz. Freiburg: Herder, 1986. Pp. 69–93.

———. "Der Götzendienst des Enosch: Zur Bildung und Entwicklung aggadischer Traditionen im nachbiblischen Judentum." In *Studien zur Geschichte und Theologie des rabbinischen Judentums.* AGJU 15. Leiden: Brill, 1978. Pp. 134–52.

———. *Rivalität zwischen Engeln und Menschen: Untersuchungen zur rabbinischen Engelvorstellung.* SJ 8. Berlin and New York: de Gruyter, 1975.

———. *Synopse zur Hekhalot-Literatur.* Tübingen: Mohr-Siebeck, 1981.

Schäfer, P., and K. Hermann. *Übersetzung der Hekhalot-Literatur I.* Tübingen: Mohr-Siebeck, 1995.

Schalit, A. *Yosef ben Mattatyahu (Flavius Josephus), Qadmoniot ha-Yehudim.* 2d ed. Jerusalem: Mosad Bialik, 1967. In Hebrew.

Schenke, H.-M. "Bemerkungen zur Apocalypse des Allogenes (NHC XI,3)." In *Coptic Studies: Acts of the Third International Congress of Coptic Studies, Warsaw, 20–25 August 1984.* Ed. W. Godlewski. Centre d'Archaeologie Mediterranéenne de l'Academie Polonaise des Sciences. Warsaw: PWN, 1990. Pp. 417–24.

———. "Die jüdische Melchisedek-Gestalt als Thema der Gnosis." In *Altes Testament-Frühjudentum-Gnosis: Neue Studien zu "Gnosis und Bibel."* Ed. K.-W. Tröger. Berlin: Evangelische Verlagsanstalt, 1980. Pp. 111–36.

———. "The Phenomenon and Significance of Gnostic Sethianism." In Layton, ed., *Rediscovery* 2.588–616.

———. "Das sethianische System nach Nag-hammadi-Handschriften." In *Studia Coptica.* Ed. P. Nagel. Berliner byzantinische Arbeiten 45. Berlin: Akademie, 1974. Pp. 165–73.

Schermann, T., ed. *Prophetarum vitae fabulosae: Indices apostolorum discipulorumque domini Dorotheo, Epiphanio, Hippolyto aliisque vindicata.* Leipzig: Teubner, 1907.

Schiffman, L. H. *Reclaiming the Dead Sea Scrolls*. Philadelphia: Jewish Publication Society, 1994.

———. *Sectarian Law in the Dead Sea Scrolls*. BJS 33. Chico, Calif.: Scholars Press, 1983.

Schlosser, J. "Les Jours de Noé et de Lot." *RB* 80 (1973) 13–36.

Schmid, H. "Melchisedek und Abraham, Zadok und David." *Kairos* 7 (1965) 148–51.

Schmidt, C. *Plotins Stellung zum Gnosticismus und kirchlichen Christentum*. TU 20. Leipzig: Hinrichs, 1901.

———, ed. *The Books of Jeu and the Untitled Text in the Bruce Codex*. Trans. V. MacDermot. NHS 13. Leiden: Brill, 1978.

———. *Pistis Sophia*. Trans. V. MacDermot. NHS 9. Leiden: Brill, 1978.

Schmitz, O. "Abraham im Spätjudentum und Urchristentum." In *Aus Schrift und Geschichte: Theologische Abhandlungen A. Schlatter dargebracht*. Ed. K. Bornhäuser. Stuttgart: Calwer, 1922. Pp. 99–123.

Schneemelcher, W. "Esra." *RAC* 6.595–612.

Schneemelcher, W., and R. McL. Wilson, eds. *New Testament Apocrypha*. 2 vols. Rev. ed. Louisville, Ky.: Westminster/John Knox, 1991–92.

Scholem, G. *Jewish Gnosticism, Merkabah Mysticism, and Talmudic Tradition*. 2d ed. New York: Jewish Theological Seminary, 1965.

———. "Metatron." *EncJud* 11.1443–46.

Schreiner, J., trans. *Baruch*. Die neue echter Bibel Altes Testament 14. Würzburg: Echter, 1986.

Schulte, H. "Baruch und Ebedmelech — Persönliche Heilsorakel im Jeremiabuche." *BZ* 32:2 (1988) 257–65.

Schürer, E. *The History of the Jewish People in the Age of Jesus Christ*. Rev. ed. 3 vols. Ed. G. Vermes, F. Millar, and M. Goodman. Edinburgh: T. & T. Clark, 1986.

Schussman, A. *Stories of the Prophets in Muslim Tradition, Mainly on the Basis of "Ḳiṣaṣ al-Anbiyā" by Muhammad b. 'Abd Allāh al-Kisā'ī*. Jerusalem: The School for Advanced Studies Press at the Hebrew University, 1981. In Hebrew.

Schwarzbaum, H. *Biblical and Extra-biblical Legends in Islamic Folk-Literature*. Beiträge zur Sprach- und Kulturgeschichte des Orients 30. Waldorf-Hessen: Orientalkunde Dr. H. Vorndran, 1982.

Schweizer, E. "Die Elemente der Welt." In *Beiträge zur Theologie des Neuen Testaments*. Zurich: Zwingli, 1970. Pp. 147–63.

———. "Slaves of the Elements and Worshippers of Angels: Gal 4:3, 9 and Col 2:8, 18, 20." *JBL* 107 (1988) 455–68.

Scopello, M. "Les citations d'Homère dans le traité de l'Exégèse de l'ame." In *Gnosis and Gnosticism*. Ed. M. Krause. NHS 8. Leiden: Brill, 1977. Pp. 3–12.

———. *L'exégèse de l'ame (Nag Hammadi, II,6): Introduction, traduction, commentaire*. NHS 25. Leiden: Brill, 1985.

———. "Les 'Testimonia' dans le traité de 'L'exégèse de l'ame' (Nag Hammadi, II, 6)." *RHR* 191 (1977) 159–71.

Sed-Rajna, G. *Ancient Jewish Art*. Paris: Flammarion, 1975.

Segal, A. F. "Heavenly Ascent in Hellenistic Judaism, Early Christianity, and Their Environment." *ANRW* II.23.2 (1980) 1333–94.

Seitz, C. R. "The Prophet Moses and the Canonical Shape of Jeremiah." *ZAW* 101 (1989) 3–27.

Sevrin, J.-M. *Le dossier baptismal séthien: Etudes sur la sacramentaire gnostique.* BCNH, "Etudes" 2. Quebec: Université Laval, 1986.

———. "La rédaction de l'Exégèse de l'ame (Nag Hammadi II, 6)." *Mus* 92 (1979) 237–71.

Seymour, J. D. "The 'Book of Adam and Eve' in Ireland." *Proceedings of the Royal Irish Academy* 36 (1922) 121–33.

Shiloah, A. "The Musical Tradition of Iraqi Jewry." In *Studies on the History and Culture of Iraqi Jewry.* Vol. 3. Or-Yehuda: Institute for Research on Iraqi Jewry, 1983. Pp. 122–29. In Hebrew.

Sidersky, D. *Les origines des légendes musulmanes dans le Coran et dans les vies des prophétes.* Paris: P. Geuthner, 1933.

Sieber, J. H. "An Introduction to the Tractate Zostrianos." *NovT* 15 (1972) 233–40.

———. "Introduction" to *Zostrianos* (NHC VIII,1): *Nag Hammadi Codex VIII.* Ed. J. H. Sieber. NHS 31. Leiden: Brill, 1991. Pp. 19–25.

Siker, J. S. "Abraham in Graeco-Roman Paganism." *JSJ* 18 (1987) 188–208.

———. *Disinheriting the Jews: Abraham in Early Christian Controversy.* Louisville: Westminster, 1991.

———. "From Gentile Inclusion to Jewish Exclusion: Abraham in Early Christian Controversy with Jews." *BTB* 19 (1989) 30–36.

Silberman, L. H. "Unriddling the Riddle: A Study in the Structure and Language of the Habakkuk Pesher." *RevQ* 3 (1961–62) 323–35.

Simon, M. "Melchisédek dans la polémique entre juifs et chrétiens et dans la légende." In *Recherches d'histoire judéo-chrétienne.* Etudes juives 6. Paris: Mouton, 1962. Pp. 101–26.

Skehan, P. W., and A. A. DiLella. *The Wisdom of Ben Sira.* AB 39. New York: Doubleday, 1987.

Smend, R. *Die Weisheit des Jesus Sirach.* Berlin: Reimer, 1906.

Smith, E. W., Jr. "Joseph Material in Joseph and Asenath and Josephus Relating to the *Testament of Joseph.*" In *Studies on the Testament of Joseph.* Ed. G. W. E. Nickelsburg. SBLSCS 5. Missoula, Mont.: Scholars Press, 1975. Pp. 133–37.

Smith, M. "Ezra." In *Ex Orbe Religionum I.* Leiden: Brill, 1972. Pp. 141–43.

———. *Palestinian Parties and Politics That Shaped the Old Testament.* New York: Columbia University Press, 1971.

———. "Pseudo-Ezekiel." In *Qumran Cave 4. XIV: Parabiblical Texts, Part 2.* Ed. M. Broshi et al. DJD 19. Oxford: Clarendon, 1995. Pp. 153–93.

Snaith, J. G. *Ecclesiasticus or the Wisdom of Jesus Son of Sirach.* CBC. Cambridge: Cambridge University Press, 1974.

Soards, M. L. "The Early Christian Interpretation of Abraham and the Place of James within That Context." *IBS* 9 (1987) 18–26.

Sokoloff, M., ed. *The Geniza Fragments of Bereshit Rabba.* Jerusalem: Israel Academy for Sciences and Humanities, 1982. In Hebrew.

Sparks, H. F. D., ed. *The Apocryphal Old Testament*. Oxford: Clarendon, 1984.

Sperber, A., ed. *The Bible in Aramaic*. 4 vols. Leiden: Brill, 1959–73.

Speyer, H. *Die biblischen Erzählungen im Qoran*. 2d ed. Hildesheim: Olms, 1961.

Sprödowsky, H. *Die Hellenisierung der Geschichte von Joseph in Ägypten bei Flavius Josephus*. Greifswald: Dallmeyer, 1937.

Stählin, O., ed. *Clemens Alexandrinus: Protrepticus und Paedagogus*. GCS 17, 52.1. Leipzig: Hinrichs, 1909, 1972.

Standhartinger, A. *Das Frauenbild im Judentum der hellenistischen Zeit: Ein Beitrag anhand von "Joseph und Aseneth."* AGJU 26. Leiden: Brill, 1995.

Steiner, R. "The Heading of the *Book of the Words of Noah* on a Fragment of the Genesis Apocryphon: New Light on a 'Lost' Work." *Dead Sea Discoveries* 2 (1995) 66–71.

Stern, M. S. "Muhammad and Joseph: A Study of Koranic Narrative." *JNES* 44 (1985) 193–204.

Stone, M. E. *Armenian Apocrypha Relating to Adam and Eve*. SVTP 14. Leiden: Brill, 1996.

———. *Armenian Apocrypha Relating to the Patriarchs and Prophets*. Jerusalem: Israel Academy of Sciences and Humanities, 1982.

———. "Enoch, Aramaic Levi, and Sectarian Origins." *JSJ* 19 (1988) 159–70. Reprinted in *Selected Studies*. Pp. 247–58.

———. "The Fall of Satan and Adam's Penance: Three Notes on the Books of Adam and Eve." *JTS* 44 (1993) 142–56.

———. *Fourth Ezra*. Hermeneia. Minneapolis: Fortress, 1990.

———. *A History of the Literature of Adam and Eve*. SBLEJL 3. Atlanta: Scholars Press, 1992.

———. "Ideal Figures and Social Context: Priest and Sage in the Early Second Temple Age." In *Ancient Israelite Religion: Essays in Honor of Frank Moore Cross*. Ed. P. D. Miller, Jr., P. D. Hanson, and S. D. McBride. Philadelphia: Fortress, 1987. Pp. 575–86.

———. "Jewish Tradition, the Pseudepigrapha, and the Christian West." In *The Aramaic Bible: Targums in Their Historical Context*. Ed. D. Beattie and M. McNamara. JSOTSup 166. Sheffield: JSOT Press, 1994. Pp. 438–41.

———. "The Metamorphosis of Ezra: Jewish Apocalypse and Medieval Vision." *JTS*, n.s., 33 (1982) 1–18.

———. *The Penitence of Adam*. 2 vols. CSCO 429–30. Louvain: Peeters, 1981.

———. "Report on Seth Traditions in the Armenian Adam Books." In Layton, ed., *Rediscovery* 2.459–71.

———. *Selected Studies in Pseudepigrapha and Apocrypha*. SVTP 9. Leiden: Brill, 1991.

———, ed. *The Armenian Version of 4 Ezra*. Missoula, Mont.: Scholars Press, 1979.

Stone, M. E., and J. C. Greenfield. "The Prayer of Levi." *JBL* 112 (1993) 247–66.

Stone, M. E., D. Satran, and B. G. Wright, eds. *The Apocryphal Ezekiel*. Forthcoming.

Stork, H. *Die sogenannten Melchisedekianer, mit Untersuchung ihrer Quellen auf Gedankengehalt und dogmengeschichtliche Entwicklung.* Forschungen zur Geschichte des neutestamentliche Kanons und der altkirchlichen Literatur 8:2. Leipzig: A. Deichertsche Verlagsbuchhandlung D. Werner Scholl, 1928.

Stoyanov, Y. "The Enochic Traditions in the *Secret Supper.*" Unpublished paper.

―――. *The Hidden Tradition in Europe.* London: Arkana, 1994.

Stroumsa, G. A. G. *Another Seed: Studies in Gnostic Mythology.* NHS 24. Leiden: Brill, 1984.

Strugnell, J., and D. Dimant. "4Q Second Ezekiel." *RevQ* 13 (1988) 45–58.

―――. "The Merkabah Vision in Second Ezekiel (4Q385 4)." *RevQ* 14 (1990) 331–48.

Strugnell, J., and E. Qimron, eds. *Qumran Cave 4. V: Miqsat Ma'ase Ha-Torah.* DJD 10. Oxford: Clarendon, 1994.

Stuckenbruck, L. T., ed. *The Book of Giants from Qumran.* TSAJ 63. Tübingen: Mohr-Siebeck, 1997.

Stulman, L. *The Other Text of Jeremiah: A Reconstruction of the Hebrew Text Underlying the Greek Version of the Prose Sections of Jeremiah with English Translation.* Lanham, Md.: University Press of America, 1985.

Suter, D. W. *Tradition and Composition in the Parables of Enoch.* SBLDS 47. Missoula, Mont.: Scholars Press, 1977.

Tal, A., ed. *The Samaritan Targum of the Pentateuch: A Critical Edition.* 3 vols. Tel-Aviv: University of Tel-Aviv Press, 1980–83.

Talmon, S. "The 'Dead Sea Scrolls' or 'The Community of the Renewed Covenant'?" In *The Echoes of Many Texts: Reflections on Jewish and Christian Traditions — Essays in Honor of Lou H. Silberman.* Ed. W. G. Dever and J. E. Wright. BJS. Atlanta: Scholars Press, forthcoming.

―――. "Ezra and Nehemiah (Books and Men)." *IDBSup* 317–28.

―――. "The Internal Diversification of Judaism in the Early Second Temple Period." In *Jewish Civilization in the Hellenistic-Roman Period.* Ed. S. Talmon. Philadelphia: Trinity Press International, 1991. Pp. 16–43.

Tardieu, M. "Les livres mis sous le nom de Seth et les Séthiens de l'hérésiologie." In *Gnosis and Gnosticism: Papers Read at the Seventh International Conference of Patristic Studies, Oxford, September 8th–13th, 1975.* Ed. M. Krause. NHS 8. Leiden: Brill, 1977. Pp. 204–10.

―――. "Les trois stèles de Seth." *RSPT* 57 (1973) 545–75.

Taylor, M. A. "Jeremiah 45: The Problem of Placement." *JSOT* 37 (1987) 79–98.

Tennant, F. R. *The Sources of the Doctrines of the Fall and Original Sin.* Cambridge: Cambridge University Press, 1903. Reprint, New York: Schocken, 1968.

Teugels, G. "De kuise Jozef: De receptie van een bijbels model." *NedThT* 45 (1991) 193–203.

Thackeray, H. St. J., R. Marcus, and L. H. Feldman, trans. *Josephus.* LCL. 9 vols. Cambridge, Mass.: Harvard University Press, 1926–1965.

Theodor, J., and C. Albeck, eds. *Midrash Bereshit Rabba: Critical Edition with Notes and Commentary.* 3 vols. Berlin, 1903–36. Reprinted with corrections, Jerusalem: Wahrmann, 1965.

Tiller, P. A. *A Commentary on the Animal Apocalypse of "1 Enoch."* SBLEJL 4. Atlanta: Scholars Press, 1993.

Tischendorf, C. *Apocalypses Apocryphae Mosis, Esdrae, Pauli, Iohannis.* Leipzig: Mendelssohn, 1866.

Tishby, I. *The Wisdom of the Zohar.* 3 vols. Littman Library of Jewish Civilization. Oxford: Oxford University Press, 1989. 2.625–32, 643–45.

Tisserant, Cardinal, ed. *Abraham, père des croyants.* Cahiers Sioniens 5. Paris: Cerf, 1952.

Tobin, T. H. "Logos." *ABD* 4.348–56.

———. "Tradition and Interpretation in Philo's Portrait of the Patriarch Joseph." *SBLSP* 25 (1986) 271–77.

Tonneau, R.-M., ed. *Sancti Ephraem Syri in Genesim et in Exodum Commentarii.* CSCO 152–53. Louvain: Durbecq, 1955–65.

Torrey, C. C. *The Apocryphal Literature.* London: Archon, 1963.

———. *The Jewish Foundation of Islam.* New York: Ktav, 1967.

Tov, E. "The Relations between the Greek Versions of Baruch and Daniel." In *Armenian and Biblical Studies.* Ed. M. E. Stone. Jerusalem: St. James, 1976. Pp. 27–34.

———. *The Septuagint Translation of Jeremiah and Baruch: A Discussion of an Early Revision of Jeremiah 29–52 and Baruch 1:1–3:8.* HSM 8. Missoula, Mont.: Scholars Press, 1976.

———. "Some Aspects of the Textual and Literary History of the Book of Jeremiah." In *Le livre de Jérémie: Le prophète et son milieu, les oracles et leur transmission.* Ed. P.-M. Bogaert. BETL 54. Leuven: Leuven University Press, 1981. Pp. 145–67.

———, ed. and trans. *The Book of Baruch.* SBLTT 8. Missoula, Mont.: Scholars Press, 1975.

Treu, K. " 'Apocryphe relatif à Jacob et Joseph' (van Haelst no. 571) und der Sitz im Leben von Apocrypha-Papyri." In *Text and Testimony: Essays on New Testament and Apocryphal Literature in Honour of A. F. J. Klijn.* Ed. T. Baarda et al. Kampen: Kok, 1988. Pp. 255–61.

Tritton, A. S. "al-Ba'th." *EI²* 1.1092–93.

Tromp, J. *The "Assumption of Moses": A Critical Edition with Commentary.* SVTP 10. Leiden: Brill, 1993.

———. "Taxo, the Messenger of the Lord." *JSJ* 21 (1990) 200–209.

Turner, J. D. "The Gnostic Threefold Path to Enlightenment: The Ascent of Mind and the Descent of Wisdom." *NovT* 22 (1980) 324–51.

———. "Gnosticism and Platonism: The Platonizing Sethian Texts from Nag Hammadi in Their Relation to Later Platonic Literature." In *Neoplatonism and Gnosticism.* Ed. R. T. Wallis. Albany: State University of New York Press, 1992. Pp. 424–59.

———. "Sethian Gnosticism: A Literary History." In *Nag Hammadi, Gnosticism, and Early Christianity.* Ed. C. W. Hedrick and R. Hodgson. Peabody, Mass.: Hendrickson, 1986. Pp. 55–86.

———, trans. "Trimorphic Protennoia." In *Nag Hammadi Codices XI, XII, and XIII.* Ed. C. W. Hedrick. NHS 28. Leiden: Brill, 1990.

Turner, J. D., and O. Wintermute. "Text, Translation, and Notes." In *Nag Hammadi Codices XI, XII, and XIII.* Ed. C. W. Hedrick. NHS 28. Leiden: Brill, 1990.

———, trans. "Allogenes." In *Nag Hammadi Codices XI, XII, and XIII.* Ed. C. W. Hedrick. NHS 28. Leiden: Brill, 1990.

Tyan, E. "Djihād." *EI²* 2.538–40.

Ulrich, E. "Ezra and Qoheleth Manuscripts from Qumran (4QEzra, 4QQoh^{A,B})." In *Priests, Prophets, and Scribes.* Ed. E. Ulrich et al. JSOTSup 149. Sheffield: Sheffield Academic Press, 1992. Pp. 139–57.

———. "An Index of the Passages in the Biblical Manuscripts from the Judean Desert." *Dead Sea Discoveries* 1 (1994) 113–29; 2 (1995) 86–107.

Urbach, E. E. "Gog and Magog." *Encyclopaedia Hebraica* 10.297–99. In Hebrew.

Vaillant, A. *Le livre des Secrets d'Hénoch: Texte slave et traduction française.* Paris: Institut d'études slaves, 1952.

Vajda, G. "Dhū 'l-Kifl." *EI²* 2.242.

———. "Idris." *EI²* 3.1030–31.

———. "Melchisédec dans la mythologie ismaélienne." *Journal Asiatique* 234 (1943–45) 173–83.

VanderKam, J. C. "The Birth of Noah." In *Intertestamental Essays in Honour of Jósef Tadeusz Milik.* Ed. Z. J. Kapera. Qumranica Mogilanensia 6. Krakow: Enigma, 1992. Pp. 213–31.

———. *The Book of Jubilees.* 2 vols. CSCO 510–11. Louvain: Peeters, 1989.

———. *Enoch: A Man for All Generations.* Studies on Personalities of the Old Testament. Columbia: University of South Carolina Press, 1996.

———. *Enoch and the Growth of an Apocalyptic Tradition.* CBQMS 16. Washington, D.C.: Catholic Biblical Association of America, 1984.

———. "*Jubilees* and the Priestly Messiah of Qumran." *RevQ* 16 (1991) 353–65.

———. "The Righteousness of Noah." In *Ideal Figures in Ancient Judaism.* Ed. J. J. Collins and G. W. E. Nickelsburg. Chico, Calif.: Scholars Press, 1980. Pp. 13–32.

———. "Studies in the Apocalypse of Weeks (*1 Enoch* 93:1–10; 91:11–17)." *CBQ* 46 (1984) 511–23.

———. *Textual and Historical Studies in the Book of Jubilees.* HSM 14. Missoula, Mont.: Scholars Press, 1977.

VanderKam, J. C., and J. T. Milik. "The First Jubilees Manuscript from Qumran Cave 4: A Preliminary Publication." *JBL* 110 (1991) 243–70.

———. "A Preliminary Publication of a Jubilees Manuscript from Qumran Cave 4: 4QJubᵃ (4Q219)." *Bib* 73 (1992) 62–83.

———, eds. *Qumran Cave 4. VIII: Parabiblical Texts, Part 1.* DJD 13. Oxford: Clarendon, 1994.

van der Merwe, B. J. "Joseph as Successor of Jacob." In *Studia Biblica et Semitica, Theodoro Christiano Vriezen dedicata.* Wageningen: Veenman, 1966. Pp. 221–32.

van der Woude, A. S. "Melchisedek als himmlische Erlösergestalt in den neuge-fundenen eschatologischen Midraschim aus Qumran Höhle XI." *OTS* 14 (1965) 354–73.

van Seters, J. *Abraham in History and Tradition*. New Haven: Yale University Press, 1975.

Veldman, I. M., and H. J. de Jonge. "The Sons of Jacob: The Twelve Patri-archs in Sixteenth-Century Netherlandish Prints and Popular Literature." In *Simiolus: Netherlands Quarterly for the History of Art* 15 (1985) 176–96.

Vermes, G. *Scripture and Tradition in Judaism*. 2d ed. Leiden: Brill, 1973.

———, ed. *The Dead Sea Scrolls in English*. 4th rev. ed. London: Penguin, 1995.

Violet, B., and H. Gressmann. *Die Apokalypsen des Esra und des Baruch in deutscher Gestalt*. GCS 32. Leipzig: Hinrichs, 1924.

Völker, W. "Das Abraham-Bild bei Philo, Origenes, und Ambrosius." *TSK* 103 (1931) 199–207.

von Gall, A., ed. *Der hebräische Pentateuch der Samaritaner*. Giessen: Töpel-mann, 1914–18.

von Mutius, H.-G. "Gen. 4,26, Philo von Byblos und die jüdische Haggada." *Biblische Notizen* 13 (1980) 46–48.

von Rad, G. "The Joseph Narrative and Ancient Wisdom." In *The Problem of the Hexateuch and Other Essays*. Edinburgh: Oliver and Boyd, 1965. Pp. 292–300.

———. "Josephsgeschichte und ältere Chokma." In *Gesammelte Studien zum Alten Testament*. 2 vols. Munich: Kaiser, 1958–73. 1.272–80.

———. *Wisdom in Israel*. New York: Abingdon, 1978.

Wacholder, B. Z. *Eupolemus*. Cincinnati: Hebrew Union College–Jewish Insti-tute of Religion, 1974.

———. "Pseudo-Eupolemus' Two Greek Fragments on the Life of Abraham." *HUCA* 34 (1963) 83–113.

Wacholder, B. Z., and M. G. Abegg, eds. *A Preliminary Edition of the Unpub-lished Dead Sea Scrolls: The Hebrew and Aramaic Texts from Cave Four, Fascicle Two*. Washington, D.C.: Biblical Archaeology Society, 1992.

Waldman, M. R. "New Approaches to 'Biblical' Materials in the Qur'an." *The Muslim World* 75 (1985) 1–16.

Wallis, R. T. "Plotinus and the Gnostics: The Nag Hammadi Texts." Unpub-lished paper.

Walter, N. *Fragmente jüdisch-hellenistischer Exegeten: Aristoboulos, Demetrios, Aristeas*. JSHRZ 3, 2. Gütersloh: Mohn, 1975.

———. *Pseudepigraphische jüdisch-hellenistische Dichtung*. JSHRZ 4, 3. Gü-tersloh: Mohn, 1983.

Wanamaker, C. A. *The Epistles to the Thessalonians*. NIGTC. Grand Rapids, Mich.: Eerdmans, 1990.

Wanke, G. *Untersuchungen zur sogenannten Baruchschrift*. BZAW 122. Berlin: de Gruyter, 1971.

Ward, R. B. "Abraham Traditions in Early Christianity." In *Septuagint and Cognate Studies* 2. Ed. R. A. Kraft. Missoula, Mont.: Scholars Press, 1972. Pp. 165–79. (Also in *Studies on the Testament of Abraham*. Ed.

G. W. E. Nickelsburg. SBLSCS 6. Missoula, Mont.: Scholars Press, 1976. Pp. 173–84.)

———. "The Works of Abraham: James 2:14–26." *HTR* 61 (1968) 283–90.

Wensinck, A. J. "Idris." *EI*¹ 3.449–50.

———. "Yādjūdj wa-Mādjūdj." *EI*¹ 8.1142.

Wertheimer, A. *Batei Midrashot.* 2d ed. 2 vols. Jerusalem: Mosad haRav Kook, 1950–53. Reprint, Jerusalem: Ktav veSepher, 1968. In Hebrew.

Whybray, R. N. "The Joseph Story and Pentateuchal Criticism." *VT* 18 (1968) 522–28.

Wieser, F. E. *Die Abrahamvorstellungen im Neuen Testament.* Bern: Lang, 1987.

Wilckens, U. "Die Rechtfertigung Abrahams nach Römer 4." In *Studien zur Theologie der alttestamentlichen Überlieferungen.* Ed. R. Rendtorff and K. Koch. Neukirchen: Neukirchener Verlag, 1961. Pp. 111–27.

Wilken, R. "The Christianizing of Abraham: The Interpretation of Abraham in Early Christianity." *CTM* 43 (1972) 723–31.

Williams, F., trans. *The Panarion of Epiphanius of Salamis.* Bk. 1, secs. 1–46. NHMS 35. Leiden: Brill, 1987.

———. *The Panarion of Epiphanius of Salamis, Books II & III.* NHMS 36. Leiden: Brill, 1994.

Williams, N. P. *The Ideas of the Fall and of Original Sin.* London: Longmans, Green and Co., 1927.

Williamson, H. G. M. *Ezra, Nehemiah.* WBC 16. Waco, Tex.: Word, 1985.

Williamson, R. *Philo and the Epistle to the Hebrews.* ALGHJ 4. Leiden: Brill, 1970.

Wilson, R. R. *Prophecy and Society in Ancient Israel.* Philadelphia: Fortress, 1980.

Winston, D. *The Wisdom of Solomon.* AB 43. Garden City, N.Y.: Doubleday, 1979.

Wire, A. "Introduction" to *Allogenes: Nag Hammadi Codices XI, XII, and XIII.* Ed. C. W. Hedrick. NHS 28. Leiden: Brill, 1990.

Wise, M., M. Abegg, Jr., and E. Cook. *The Dead Sea Scrolls: A New Translation.* San Francisco: HarperSanFrancisco, 1996.

Wisse, F., and M. Waldstein, eds. *The Apocryphon of John: Synopsis of Nag Hammadi Codices II, 1; III, 1 and IV, 1, with BG 8502, 2.* NHMS 33. Leiden: Brill, 1995.

Woude, A. S. van der "Melchisedek als himmlische Erlösergestalt in den neugefundenen eschatologischen Midraschim aus Qumran Höhle XI." *OTS* 14 (1965) 354–73.

Wright, B. G. "*1 Clement* 50:4 and Clement of Alexandria, *Prot.* 8.81.4: Citations of an Ezekiel Apocryphon?" Paper presented at the Annual Meeting of the Society of Biblical Literature, Chicago, November 1994.

———. "A Fragment of Apocryphal Ezekiel Contained in *First Clement.*" Paper presented at the Annual Meeting of the Society of Biblical Literature, Atlanta, November 1986.

———. "Qumran Pseudepigrapha in Early Christianity: Is *1 Clement* 50:4 a Citation of 4QPseudo-Ezekiel (4Q385)?" Paper presented at the Orion Center for the Study of the Dead Sea Scrolls and Associated Literature Conference, "Pseudepigraphic Perspectives," January 1997.

Wright, J. E. "Baruch, the Ideal Sage." In *"Go to the Land I Will Show You": Studies in Honor of Dwight W. Young.* Ed. J. E. Coleson and V. H. Matthews. Winona Lake, Ind.: Eisenbrauns, 1996. Pp. 193–210.

———. *The Cosmography of the Greek Apocalypse of Baruch and Its Affinities.* Ann Arbor, Mich.: University Microfilms, 1992.

———. "The Social Setting of the Syriac Apocalypse of Baruch." *JSP,* forthcoming.

Wuttke, G. *Melchisedech der Priesterkönig von Salem: Eine Studie zur Geschichte der Exegese.* Giessen: Alfred Töpelmann, 1927.

Yates, F. A. *Giordano Bruno and the Hermetic Tradition.* London: Routledge and Kegan Paul, 1964.

Yohannan, J. D. *Joseph and Potiphar's Wife in World Literature: An Anthology of the Story of the Chaste Youth and the Lustful Stepmother.* New York: New Directions, 1968.

Zandee, J. "Iosephus contra Apionem: An Apocryphal Story of Joseph in Coptic." *VC* 15 (1961) 193–213.

Ziegler, J., ed. *Sapientia Jesu Filii Sirach.* Vol. 12, pt. 2. Septuaginta: Vetus Testamentum Graecum. Göttingen: Vandenhoeck & Ruprecht, 1965.

Zimmerli, W. *Ezekiel 1.* Trans. R. E. Clements. Hermeneia. Philadelphia: Fortress, 1979.

INDEX OF ANCIENT SOURCES

PHILO AND JOSEPHUS

NEW TESTAMENT

RABBINIC AND COGNATE LITERATURE

INDEX OF NAMES AND TERMS